W9-ARJ-589

The Structure of Freedom

The Structure of Freedom

by Christian Bay

STANFORD UNIVERSITY PRESS

STANFORD, CALIFORNIA

Til mine foreldre,

JENS OG RUTH BAY,

som har lært meg alt det viktigste

Stanford University Press
Stanford, California
© 1958 and 1970 by the Board of Trustees of the
Leland Stanford Junior University
Preface to the 1965 (Atheneum) Printing © 1965 by Christian Bay
Printed in the United States of America
Cloth ISBN 0-8047-0539-9
Paper ISBN 0-8047-0540-2
First published 1958
Last figure below indicates year of this printing:
79 78 77 76 75 74 73 72 71 70

Preface to the 1970 Printing

It is gratifying to learn that this book is still in demand, and I accept with pleasure the opportunity to write a brief preface to the new printing. A new edition it is not; only a few printing errors that went undetected in the second printing have been corrected.

In the 1965 Preface I recorded a number of relevant respects in which my views had changed in the years following the initial publication of this book in 1958. "Six years older and conceivably six years wiser," I wrote, "I will try to replace some defective parts in the structure of an argument on liberty which on the whole I still consider valid and useful."

After another five years it is a bit unsettling to discover that the 1965 Preface continues to express my present views. At least largely and in substance it does, although I would have changed a few words here and there (for example, I like the word "liberal" less now and prefer, especially when applied to my own stance, words like "humanist" and "radical"). No substantive gains in wisdom in five years?

I still like to distinguish "politics" proper from "pseudopolitics"; I still believe in the crucial importance of new research and theory-building regarding human nature and needs, as an integral part of political inquiry; and, with this proviso, I still consider myself a behavioralist (that is also true, I believe, of a large proportion of the generation that has brought about, in David Easton's not quite appropriate phrase, "the post-behavioral revolution"; see his "The New Revolution in Political Science," *American Political Science Review*, LXIII [1969], 1051–61). I still believe in the vital importance of bridging the gulf that existed between mainly normative political inquiry, too often scholastic or entirely speculative in approach, and mainly empirical inquiry, only fact-oriented and mainly sociological in approach.

But the field has been moving, so much so that by comparison I may seem to have been standing still. The gulf that existed is gone in some areas, and is nowhere as wide and intimidating as it used to be. Political theory is in the ascendancy, and Leo Strauss and those he has influenced are no longer the most influential or even the most visible political philosophers. Indeed, the very terms "normative theory" and "empirical theory" have become a bit disreputable, as indicating a division of labor that makes no sense. Put in Harold D. Lasswell's terms, the separation of "political theory" from "political philosophy" has few spirited defenders today, even though it continues to make sense for many purposes—also to this writer—to distinguish as carefully as possible between empirical and normative propositions.

Issues of human nature and needs are exceedingly complex with respect to distinguishing propositions that can and cannot, in fact or in principle, be put to empirical test. Yet these are areas of research that can no longer be kept out of systematic political inquiry. And not the least important good news, these last five years, is the real upsurge of interest in the normative and the personality and motivation aspects of political research. Even the better voting studies are taking in increasingly "messy" psychological indicators; more important, in the writings of younger political scientists there is a decreasing tolerance for the conventional behavioralist proneness to reduce political behavior to attitudes (passive) and voting (active). Political activists themselves, many younger colleagues have been cutting down to size the importance of voting and voting research in the practice and study of political behavior.

Among the prime movers in this direction are those who have sponsored or supported or taken an interest in the Caucus for a New Political Science. It is perhaps a hopeful sign of the times that essentially similar groupings have been formed within virtually all the social science professions. While there has been no general stampede to have the young turks elected and anointed as leaders of the traditional professional organizations, the impact of the new breed in the literature and on the teaching of political science in many departments has been considerable already, and shows every sign of still being on the increase.

Many factors no doubt should help account for this healthy trend. Most important, I suspect, have been the increasingly glaring contradictions between the humane and democratic pretensions and the brutal and oppressive realities of the American polity, with respect to its wars of aggression abroad as well as the deepening despair among the underprivileged at home. The utter irrelevancy of perhaps the bulk of traditional behavioral political science to the most pressing problems of public policy of our time has become a scandal to be stomached only by people exceedingly well trained and socialized in the ways of value-blind and need-exempt positivism. Many more among the young political scientists are now apparently becoming educated as well as trained, and learn or find out about war and peace, ecology, mental health, etc., as well as systems theory, voting behavior, comparative political parties, and Guttman scales.

Consequently, political science departments are becoming more exciting places, in which generations discourse and also do battle as never before; and in which politics as well as pseudopolitics is being practiced as well as taught, on a wide scale, with students often as influential in both kinds of dialogue as their professors. This is all to the good. I have come to believe that the most serious problems of an age of rapidly accelerating technological and social developments can be coped with only by a new breed of citizen capable of fresh perspectives as well as having effective access to accumulated knowledge and experience. In other words, I believe that a continuing political dialogue, in which different generations (including students and professors) take part as essentially equals, has become a real prerequisite for achieving the qualities of responsible citizenship that may yet save our civilization, if we and our children are lucky.

Is it worth saving? I, for one, believe that our freedoms and human rights, for all their underdeveloped states as yet, are supremely worth saving, roughly according to the priorities proposed in this volume. If so, then the same goes for all those institutions that in fact serve these freedoms and rights—and for those institutions only. Which institutions do and which don't are in principle researchable questions. Research and action dictated by these concerns are of course what the problem of National Defense should have been about, and perhaps could have been, had not the vested interests of powerful, overprivileged minorities succeeded, in this as in other countries, in brainwashing large majorities into believing that they live in a democracy and into confusing "defense" with "military ascendancy."

The effective defense of our freedoms and their supporting institutions may conceivably require military equipment, among other resources. But surely a prior requirement is a kind of rationality that insists on first asking exactly what it is that must be defended; and subsequently, in the spirit of scientific inquiry and unencumbered by special pleading, seeks to determine the most likely effective means within the resources now or later available. It may well be found, for example, that the progressive pollution of our environment has created defense problems already far more pressing than even the more alarmist and ethnocentrically lopsided interpretations of, say, Chinese or Soviet behavior can make credible. To speculate a bit further, it may be found that crucial to our defense is a kind of citizenship that makes us insist on vindicating our freedoms in our daily lives and on defending them for all; and that makes us insist on democratic practices to the fullest extent possible in our living and working environments (like universities, or factories, or offices, or schools, or neighborhoods). For what is to be defended surely is not the pretenses of democracy achieved, or the alleged intentions of long-dead Founding Fathers, but the achievements that have been reached in the protection of and respect for human lives, with rights and liberties. While the structures of privilege and power remain as lopsided as they are in this country today, to say nothing of the situation within humanity as a whole, our rights and liberties remain not only precarious but, for some, virtually nonexistent; here, surely, Defense is most badly needed.

My interest in problems of freedom and of advancing and defending freedoms has persisted, and has led me to do subsequent work on the related subjects of citizenship, human needs and wants, civil disobedience, education, and student political activism. Some of my recent papers in these and neighboring areas will be published later this year by Odyssey Press in New York, under the title *Politics for Man*, edited by Susan B. Hendershott.

CHRISTIAN BAY

Oslo, March 25, 1970

Preface to the 1965 Printing

My distinguished friend Dr. Alexander Meiklejohn told me after reading this book that he expects me to keep rewriting it all my life. He did not solely have the book's many weaknesses in mind; his remark also reflected the observation that the subject of liberty is an inexhaustive one as well as an engrossing one to every serious student. He should know.

And he was right. Unlike every other reader of this book, I'm sure, I haven't been able to put it down. There has been no opportunity as yet to attempt a complete restatement of my position on the politics of freedom, however; and a patchwork repair job would not do for this occasion. Save for the correction of a few minor errors, therefore, this edition is unchanged.

My position on liberty and on the uses of social science for libertarian aims is fundamentally the same as it was six years ago. Some of my views on related issues have changed, however, and are perhaps still in the process of further development. It is good to be given the opportunity now to make explicit at what points of substance I today differ with positions adopted in the book. Six years older and conceivably six years wiser, I will try to replace some defective parts in the structure of an argument on liberty which on the whole I still consider valid and useful.

Useful for what? A good portion of this new Preface will examine critically some of the main currents in contemporary political research; in this way I hope to articulate what I take to be some neglected problems and perspectives of inquiry to which the present volume addresses itself. Though in some respects well qualified, if hardly impartial, I shall not attempt a review of my own book, and aside from a passing reference or two there will be no review of the reviews, either. Within the short space available I'd rather speak to the purposes the book is intended to serve, in the context of somewhat modified views on the general objectives of political inquiry.

Let me begin with the term "politics." It so happens that on the issue of how to define this crucial term I do differ significantly with the position adopted in the book. My new perspective on this issue has ramifications for the problem of how to relate value commitments to political inquiry; in a sense it triggers off (or is itself one manifestation of) the whole argument that will be the main theme in this essay: that the prevailing trends in political behavior research, and to a considerably lesser extent research in comparative politics as well, have restricted the role that political inquiry could perform in the service of human needs. (It will be noted in passing that the most vocal among the contemporary critics of the New Science of Politics, neo-Aristotelian by persuasion, have failed to produce any viable alternative approach.)

"Politics refers to all the processes by which public values are promoted and distributed by means of power and authority." This is the definition adopted in the present volume (p. 21), substantially following David Easton. It is a normatively neutral definition, quite properly; it refers to processes that may or may not spring from acceptable motivations or intentions.

The drawback to this way of defining politics, which has many followers, appears to me now to be the virtual absence of a reference to the relatedness of politics to human needs and problems. In the development of political inquiry as a behavioral science there has been an understandable tendency, as we shall see, to fasten on basic concepts that are operationally useful; with modern research techniques, processes of promotion of values by means of power and influence can be measured, so that purely sociological hypotheses can be put to the test and some behavioral knowledge accumulated. This is true also when what is promoted are schemes for distributing public values, or values "oriented toward the assumed needs or desires or interests of large numbers of people" (p. 13). But the usual approach in the modern behavioral study of politics is to be concerned with desires and *perceived* interests only. To my mind the more crucial reference of political activity in the real world is to the *needs* and to the *real* interests (however they may be conceptualized and studied) of human beings.

To put it more concretely: The mass of behavioral research in political science today deals with voting and with opinions and attitudes on social, political, and economic issues. This literature has filled debilitating gaps in previous knowledge, and we need more studies of voting and of political preferences. But we should not mistake the political horizon we encounter in this research for the whole realm of the political. There is too much that gets lost when attention is focused on what we can readily measure by the standard kinds of sociological techniques—individual meanings of political commitments, for one example.

One sign that all is not well with the current state of political research is the prevailing tendency not to try to relate behavioral data meaningfully to normative theories of democracy or of the good society, whether traditional or new. For example, a prominent team of researchers a decade ago concluded a painstaking analysis of voting behavior with an astonishingly superficial attempt at bringing their data to bear on democratic theory. The American system of democracy, concluded Bernard R. Berelson, Paul F. Lazarsfeld, and William N. McPhee, "does meet certain requirements for a going political organization" and, indeed, "it often works with distinction." But these authors apparently saw no need to enlighten their readers on the nature of their criteria for "distinction," or on what works well and what works less well in the American system, according to their normative criteria of democracy—for good reasons, as these criteria were left unanalyzed. And yet we are told that, of the book's two themes, the "confrontation of democratic theory with democratic practice is the second implied theme that runs throughout the book." And this is the final statement in the book: "Twentieth-century political theory—both analytic and normative —will arise only from hard and long observation of the actual world of politics, closely identified with the deeper problems of practical politics." (*Voting*. Chicago: University of Chicago Press, 1954, pp. 312 and 323.)

Assuredly not—or at any rate not *only*. With a more adequate conception of politics it will become clear, I believe, that what these and many other authors of books on political behavior are looking at is only a limited range of data, which badly needs to be supplemented by more intensive psychological inquiry, and also by a much larger canvas of political theory that includes a place for concepts such as needs, growth, and the common good, to name a few only.

I shall attempt to contribute toward a more adequate definition of politics in a moment, but it will be well first to give one or two more examples of normative imprudence among leading political sociologists. Berelson *et al.* are by no means unrepresentative; some go much further toward ruling out any need for careful articulation of the normative commitments to which their empirical research is related. One highly respected writer has cheerfully claimed that democracy "is the good society itself in operation"; "the give-and-take of a free society's internal struggles" is the best man can hope for on this earth—so good that political ideology is becoming a superfluous commodity, at least in the West, according to S. M. Lipset (*Political Man*. Garden City: Doubleday, 1960, pp. 403 and 415).

For a less extreme example of the same tendency, consider the most recent book by one of the nation's ablest and most versatile political scientists, whose recent death is a great loss. In V. O. Key, Jr.'s *Public Opinion and American Democracy* (New York: Knopf, 1961), we are given an admirably organized survey of current knowledge on the state of American public opinion and on its bearing on governmental decision processes. Yet once again there is hardly a hint of the bearing this knowledge is supposed to have, or could have, on the relevant normative issues of democracy. Only toward the very end there are a few stray remarks on such issues, including the point that political deviants "play a critical role in the preservation of the vitality of a democratic order as they urge alterations and modifications better to achieve the aspirations of men. Hence the fundamental significance of freedom of speech and agitation." There is no attempt to clarify such concepts as "vitality of a democratic order" or "the aspirations of men," or any other aims beyond keeping democracy, in some nebulous sense, going.

For present purposes these examples must suffice. Determined to utilize the available arsenals of sociological techniques, this line of research has stressed the phenomena that can be weighed and counted to the exclusion of more diffuse and elusive aspects of politics. In their desire to be scientific, these investigators have shied away from normative inquiry to such an extent that they unblushingly relate their fine empirical work to the crudest notions of and assumptions about democracy—either as an end in itself or as a means to even vaguer conceptions of human wants.

Now, it is proper to define "politics" in a normatively neutral manner, as I have said. But we are bound to be led astray if we work with a concept of politics which permits us to consider activities of and around voting and related attitudes as all there is to it. For politics in its more adequate concept must in my opinion be considered an essential dimension of social life, and even of individual man as a social being; and this dimension not only bears on but *is* the individual's relatedness (in whatever role) to perceptions of the welfare of his whole nation, or other largest reference group. And this relatedness, in turn, is in the nature of a recognized or unrecognized common interest in the solution of social problems (or in alleviating them, or in seeking to forestall the development of more distressing human problems).

Social problems are discrepancies between aspirations and realities, or anticipated discrepancies, in so far as the aspirations are shared, and in so far as the discrepancies conceivably can be remedied by governmental or other social action. It may be a matter of deficiencies in security; the problem may be to defend better what we have; what is required may be to think more clearly about what must be defended, to do better research on the nature of the hazards and on the costs of alternate means of defense and to take more effective action on policy decisions arrived at. Or the problem may be a matter of realizing potentialities for improvements; it may be a question of making progress toward a better state of affairs—perhaps more freedom, or more well-being—in some limited respect or more generally; what is required may be clearer thinking about how we ought to live, better research on how we do live and on how we could live, and more effective social and political action.

There is no room here for greater detail or more precision; let us conclude that "politics," whatever else its reference, must also refer to the process of grappling with social problems. I cannot offer any really satisfactory definition as yet; perhaps in another six years a more adequate conception will be at hand. Let me suggest the following working definition, which must do for the present essay: *"Politics" refers to all activity addressing itself toward the solution or alleviation of perceived social problems.*

This formulation leaves open what kinds of problems political actors may perceive, or give priority to. It makes no explicit reference to power, influence, or authority; it leaves open what the categories should be for observing the means employed. It requires the intent of acting toward an objective larger than just a personal or a business corporation's economic stake in a particular policy. According to this definition, activities on behalf of, say, Standard Oil become *political* only to the extent that the actor convinces himself that the policies he promotes would benefit the nation or large communities in it, and not just Standard Oil. I reserve *"pseudopolitical"* as the term to refer to private interest-oriented activities that interact with political activities and utilize the political institutions without any intention, or perceived (imagined) intention, of serving any larger social interest or the public interest.

Only if we in some such fashion attempt to distinguish the political from the pseudopolitical can we, in my judgment, hope to achieve a more adequate political theory and research, inconvenient and initially difficult as the distinction may be from the point of view of sociological research at this time.

While normatively neutral, the type of definition of "politics" that I have just proposed does suggest that the student of politics should concern himself more adequately with values than he does now. For behavior-oriented political scientists, "values" have come to refer to preferences that respondents happen to hold, and they are analysed as just another set of facts. In much of this literature it is not determined or even speculated on whether the preferences of respondents have been embedded in a whole framework of commitment to the public good, or are related to business or class interests, or perhaps have no psychological anchorage whatever; indeed, most survey research instruments are in a position to tap only fragmentary responses anyway.

In real life it makes all the difference in the world, of course, whether political opinions are carefully thought out or not; are based on personal anxieties or ambitions, on group loyalties, or on sympathy for others; are strongly felt or superficially held (or simply expressed to get an interviewer off one's neck); and so on. Moreover, it makes a great deal of difference whether or not people think politically as distinct from pseudopolitically, in the sense specified.

It would seem to follow that the political scientist had better try to discover the totality of salient views that political actors hold, if he is to understand the dynamics of their voting behavior and other political behavior. Aside from Harold Lasswell, who has been ahead of his time in several fields of political inquiry, psychologists have been the first to understand this necessity. Among psychologists M. Brewster Smith has been the most influential innovator in this area, and the volume entitled *Opinions and Personality,* which he wrote with Jerome Bruner and Robert White (New York: John Wiley, 1956) is after less than a decade widely considered a classic in this new field. In recent years the first few political scientists have ventured into the intensive study of personalities and political views; notably Robert E. Lane (*Political Ideology.* New York: The Free Press, 1962) and A. F. Davies (*Private Politics.* Mimeo. University of Melbourne, 1962).

Another welcome development is that the study of comparative politics has become broadened to include political cultures as well; leading students of comparative cultures insist on observing political behavior in the framework of the total systems of values, in so far as possible. (There will be more comment on this literature below).

Yet in my opinion the role of values in political inquiry should be expanded even further. The political scientist should feel responsible for articulating his own values, and for structuring as explicitly as possible the totality of his own political commitment. This is not to say that he should be politically active; perhaps so, but that is a choice he must make as a citizen, not as a professional. As a political scientist he merely owes it to himself and to his audience to make it as clear as he can where he stands with respect to those fundamental issues of politics that are relevant to each of his inquiries. If politics once is conceptualized as the activity that addresses itself to the solution of social problems, and if it is desired that political science should have an impact on politics, it not only follows that intelligent political inquiry must evaluate the normative as well as the factual basis of political institutions, opinions, and behavior. It also would seem to follow that the political scientist must be in a position to examine critically the value assumptions of political actors not merely on an *ad hoc* basis, but on the basis of carefully structured positions of his own on the larger issues of politics.

Every social problem, from the trivial ones to those that bear crucially on human well-being, consists in a discrepancy between what exists and what should be, I have said; and both sides of this relationship are equally in need of careful study. The study of what exists has become the specialty of most modern students of political behavior, and good strides have been made. The trouble is that few behavioralists have taken any interest whatever in the serious study of the "ought-side" of politics. The prevailing view appears to be that the scientist, even the political scientist, not only needs not but should not take a public stand except to report on and to witness to the validity of established facts. (For a recent statement to this effect by an eminent student of political behavior, see Heinz Eulau. *The Behavioral Persuasion in Politics.* New York: Random House, 1963, especially the Epilogue). The unfortunate result is that political *philosophy* (in the now widely accepted sense in which Lasswell distinguishes this discipline from that of political *science*) lately by default has become the almost exclusive domain of a neo-Aristotelian breed of political scientists which has no use at all for such facts as the behavioralists produce!

Not only a bridge but a multilane freeway covering the gulf between factual knowledge and normative study is a necessity, in my opinion, if the rigors of rational inquiry are ever to make a dent in precisely the realm of human behavior in which the spirit of scientific inquiry is least in evidence till now and is most badly needed—the political.

The present volume was above all else intended as a contribution to building such a bridge. It tackles a very broad problem: The general discrepancies between the qualities of liberty that we now enjoy and the qualities that would appear attainable, so far as logical and factual inquiry can ascertain. Such inquiry necessitates a number of normative decisions of priority between freedoms and between types of freedom demands. Many more such decisions would be proper, at least on a tentative basis, if the problem to be studied had been a narrower one—say, the issue of racial discrimination in the rental of houses, or the issue of conscientious objection against military service. But it was hoped that the *general* liberal position advanced in this book would provide a sufficiently viable framework of basic norms to give a common ground to liberal students of more specific political or legal *de lege ferenda* issues. For example, *if* the least free are to be given priority in the advancement of freedom, then it would seem that the interest of the Negro in escaping the ghetto with his family must as a rule take precedence over the desire of some landlords not to rent to Negro tenants. *If* physical violence is the worst evil that our political institutions exist to prevent, or reduce, then conscientious objection would seem an obvious individual right—at least until it can be demonstrated, first, that many will want to exercise it regardless of cost in terms of the fairly mild dysincentives that under the U. S. Constitution are and could be established; *and,* secondly, that the irreducible number of insistent objectors, if tolerated, would be large enough to make a significant difference in America's military posture; *and,* thirdly, that this difference would substantially increase the danger of war.

In both examples issues of empirical as well as normative inquiry are involved, even though the former example would seem to permit only one solution, too obvious to require inquiry (as a rule), if one starts out with the present basic liberal commitment. Other issues of competing freedom demands—say, between proponents and opponents of public aid to parochial schools—raise far more complex empirical as well as normative issues. If political scientists are to promote more rational political processes in their professional capacity, they must be ready to study dispassionately the scope and importance of the rival freedoms involved, in this as in other public controversies, and recommend whatever solutions, if any, that in terms of their own carefully developed value positions appear to support the claim of the side for whom the more basic elements of welfare are at stake.

It is time, I submit, that the notion of a value-free political science be abandoned altogether. Every social problem, the proper subject matter of political inquiry, implies one value commitment or another from the moment it is perceived as such; and the clarification of any`social problem involves, unless we are deceiving ourselves (for example, by the use of pseudoscientific terms suitable to concealing the value elements involved), a further sharpening of the normative as well as the factual premises from which we wish our inquiry to proceed.

What is important in the scientific study of politics is not to avoid a framework of normative choice—which remains implicitly there if we fail to explicate it—but to separate the operations of factual research from the operations of normative analysis and choice. On this point it is necessary to take issue with the neo-Aristotelians in our midst, who claim that "the political can better be seen by minds that do not draw [the distinction between facts and values] too sharply." (Cf. Walter Berns. "The Behavioral Sciences and the Study of Political Things: The Case of Christians Bay's 'The Structure of Freedom'," in the *American Political Science Review,* Vol. LV (Sept. 1961), p. 550). On the contrary, it is only if we keep quite clear the difference between statements that can be shown to be (probably) true or false, and statements expressing a value commitment, that we can hope to develop a body of political knowledge that can be communicated among scientists of different political convictions, or who are concerned with different political problems; a knowledge tuned to problems and thus to values, but with clear contours of empirical knowledge which can be utilized for quite different normative purposes as well.

My position on the bearing of political commitment on political research is as sharply at variance with purist logical positivism as it is with anti-positivist neo-Aristotelianism. This is well illustrated by the fact that critics from both extremes have charged that the commitment to freedom advanced in this volume is vacuous. Walter Berns the neo-Aristotelian, being of a mind to "not draw [the fact-value] distinction too sharply," attributes to my refusal to claim objective validity for my commitment to freedom the implication that freedom cannot exist. Felix Oppenheim the logical positivist, on the other hand, claims that my commitment to freedom as the supreme value is empty on the ground that I use some terms to which he attributes value implications—such as, for example, "degree of harmony between basic motives and overt behavior" in my definition of psychological freedom. (Cf. Felix E. Oppenheim. *Dimensions of Freedom*. New York: St. Martin's Press, 1961, p. 168). Granted, I value such harmony, as does every clinical psychologist and psychiatrist; but this preference of mine in no way interferes with the task of developing progressively sharper criteria for determining degrees to which such harmony is present or absent.

During the six years since the book was published I have moved a step or two away from Oppenheim's and toward Berns's position, in that I now am willing to affirm a belief in the probability that certain elements of a humanitarian or liberal commitment may eventually be shown to possess a certain kind of objective validity, in the sense that human nature may be shown to make us gravitate toward these tendencies to the extent that we learn to cope with our anxieties. (Cf. my "A Social Theory of Intellectual Development," in Nevitt Sanford (ed.) *The American College.* New York: John Wiley and Sons, 1961, especially pp. 1000-1005). Perhaps there are some rights that can be considered *natural* after all; not because Aristotle made this claim, but because socio-psychological research may be in the process of establishing a basis for such a claim by way of increasing our knowledge of universal human propensities. The current doctrine of natural law in political science is deficient, asserts James C. Davies, "not in its reasonableness, or even validity, but rather in its relative non-empiricism. It has not been subjected to empirical test and therefore remains more a faith than a tested theory" (*Human Nature in Politics*. New York: John Wiley, 1963, p. 53). Nor is it a testable theory, in most of its formulations so far.

In the meantime I hope that more political scientists, and students of behavior as well as of institutions, will spend less time on debating the merits of parochial approaches, and more time on learning to communicate beyond them. The present state of affairs in political science makes no sense at all, with neo-Aristotelian philosophers disdainful of empirical inquiry on one side of the gulf, confronted with logical positivist behavioralists who shy away from any and all normative commitments on the other side. To make matters worse, communications across the chasm at times suggest the existence of two enemy camps, not two kinds of scholars with complementary contributions to make toward a common objective (cf. especially Leo Strauss. *What is Political Philosophy?* Glencoe: The Free Press, 1959; Strauss's "Epilogue" in Herbert J. Storing (ed.) *Essays on the Scientific Study of Politics*. New York: Holt, Rinehart and Winston, Inc., 1962; and the review article on the latter volume by John H. Schaar and Sheldon S. Wolin, with rejoinders, in the *American Political Science Review,* Vol. LVII (1963) pp. 125-160).

The best hope for a development toward a politically more useful political science, in my opinion, rests with an increasingly close interaction between students of politics and students of psychology. There are dangers, of course, in making this an exclusive liaison, with temptations to jump from the demonstration of aggressive instincts to assumptions about how war comes about, for example; it is essential that intervening variables are supplied from the coffers of sociology, anthropology, and economics. There is safety in numbers—of variables, of disciplines, and of critics who can move across traditional borders. And yet we get into trouble if numbers in the context of measurement and statistics become all-important. The narrowness of most political behavior literature stems not at all from a disinclination to learn from neighboring disciplines, but from an interest only in the readily quantifiable goods and methodological equipment that they have had to offer. As we have seen, political scientists have eagerly gone to work with tools such as attitude scales, procedures for small group analysis, and indices of social and economical stratification; they have been slow to get involved (excepting an occasional bold pioneer such as Lasswell) with problems of, say, political identity or political motivation.

The stress on sociological variables and scale data in political behavior research has led to a tendency for the lowest common denominator of citizenship—or, more strictly, for the most apolitical or pseudopolitical orientations—to become taken for granted as the mainsprings of our democratic way of political life. Most people vote for reasons of status anxiety, perceived economic interest, or prejudices magnified in election campaigns, we are told; but somehow democracy survives, in some fashion, and individuals adjust to a system in which it appears to be left to chance who will worry about the public interest. Perhaps majorities do tend to be apolitical; but much could be gained by study of those minorities that are not, and also by more study of human and social needs and their relationship to various conceptions of the public interest. Perhaps we might then not only discover how individuals can adjust to ongoing systems and ensure their continued stability, but also develop some knowledge on how social institutions can become better adapted to the service of basic and possibly permanent human needs.

In one area of inquiry it does seem that political scientists are now moving toward a better proportioned interdisciplinary perspective. That is, as already mentioned, in comparative politics, and to some extent also in the study of foreign political systems. In the latter field I consider Lucian W. Pye's study of "Burma's search for identity" in this respect an example of what can and should be achieved (*Politics, Personality, and Nation Building*. New Haven: Yale University Press, 1962). Important landmarks in the new broad-gauged study of comparative politics are Gabriel A. Almond and James S. Coleman (eds.) *The Politics of Developing Areas* (1960), and Almond and Sidney Verba, *The Civic Culture* (1963), both from Princeton University Press.

Yet in this literature, too, there is room for improvement. The theoretical framework and the careful development and integrated study of a broad range of psychological, social and cultural variables are most impressive, but the latter are all cast in the role of independent variables. There appears to be two preponderant aims: To understand the political process in its totality, and to understand how it bears on the prospects for democratic institutions. A third objective is missing; one which to my way of thinking should take precedence over the second one: To understand how the totality of human welfare is affected by the same political processes, or by feasible modifications in them. *The Civic Culture,* the most recent of the three books just referred to, in the last chapter posits "democratic stability" as the dependent variable, or the overriding goal that political processes should serve, and we are given a summary review of findings pertaining to how particular independent variables, some of them conceptualized or given careful study for the first time in this volume, are likely to bear on the prospects for democratic stability. Yet the latter concept is hardly discussed at all.

The result, probably unintended, is a conservative and at times almost an ethnocentric bias. Now, it may be argued that the present British and American democracies clearly do belong to the most successful experiments so far in political government, and I grant that a conservative acceptance of these particular patterns of political culture might be arrived at by the wisest of men. But it does make a difference how political commitments are arrived at, or at least how they are articulated. Ideally, in my opinion, the commitments of political scientists should reflect a fair amount of careful study and reflection on what are the needs of man that political institutions ought to serve. Perhaps many past and present political scientists have been too cautious or have felt that they knew too little psychology to attempt to develop or explicate their own political commitments in this manner; and anyway, it was not long ago widely and comfortably believed that their own commitments should not be related to their scientific work. But the modern students of comparative political culture are in the avantgarde; they plainly state their commitment to democratic stability; they display all the skills and insights needed for analysing behavioral and institutional variables and sub-variables bearing on democratic stability; and yet, paradoxically, they have felt no urge to go beyond such pat formulations of purpose and ask questions, for example, such as these: What particular aspects of a political order, or what institutions within it, ought to be stable, in what order of priority? What categories of citizens have a particular stake in stability, whether partial or total, and whether democratic or not? What are the costs of stability, in general or, say, in Britain or in the United States, or in parts of either country? How is democratic stability related to liberty? To social justice?

But the work of these investigators has helped substantially to create what is now surely a wide open field for political studies that can more directly and more effectively than hitherto serve the political development of mankind. We now have the theoretical and conceptual equipment, much of which was lacking as late as a decade ago, for beginning to approach empirically, within specified contexts and with more precise definitions, some of the great issues formulated already by Plato and Aristotle: How can men learn to live with each other so as to bring out the best in their nature? What is responsible citizenship? How can justice be made to prevail? What are the limits to political obligation? How much individual freedom is compatible with social justice? And so on.

Students of political behavior have established an increasingly tenacious body of knowledge on the bearing of various situational and background determinants on political opinions and attitudes; and great strides have been made toward understanding how governmen⸱al and other political institutions (including, of course, the courts of law) actually work. Of necessity, perhaps, the study of personalities in politics lags behind; it is perhaps the most difficult area in which to produce cumulative knowledge. More by accident, or if you will by necessity in the particular intelle⸱⸱ual climate that has prevailed until recently, the study of political norms and of the implications of commitments has also lagged behind. It is perhaps in this area the real bottleneck has been. Only when the implications and consequences of alternative ideas and policy proposals can be anticipated and evaluated over the long run, as they would affect the welfare and development of various people, will we have a political science capable of improving the dialogue and the political decision processes. Stability is an important achievement of politics, and many countries badly need more of it than they have achieved so far. But it surely is not the only objective of government; a more advanced political science will consider and study a variety of hypothetical improvements in our social order which, if feasible, conceivably could improve the quality of social and individual life.

It may well be asked if this volume and also this new Preface may not rest on overly optimistic assumptions concerning the qualities and potentialities of human nature. In an important sense the basic premise that individual freedom ought to be maximized assumes that, by and large, men are or could become able to live peacefully together under conditions of lessened restraint.

No proof is available for this premise, of course. Neither could its negation be proved. History as well as the contemporary scene are replete with examples of beastliness in men, and also of saintliness, not to mention simple kindness and nobility of spirit. A study of the frequencies of each category of deviance from the "average" would establish no new knowledge on the general goodness or badness of human nature, I submit; at most we could discover some of the extremes, in either direction, toward which human behavior can be pushed, by constellations of external and internal factors.

The difficulty with understanding human nature is at least twofold: it can be studied only by way of indirection—by eventual generalization from unending series of studies of individual behavior in different cultures and under different exigencies. We are in ignorance, so far, about the nature of the attributes we all may have in common as men, for one thing because they are so well camouflaged and so thoroughly transformed by culture and personality.

The other and in some ways more pernicious aspect of our ignorance about human nature stems from the powerful incentives in many quarters toward stereotyping our beliefs about human nature. Every man of power and every conservative (whether in socio-economic or in religious matters) has certain important incentives toward portraying our human nature as weak or bad. In the first place, our human nature is one of the best scapegoats for explaining away shortcomings of public policies and damages to individuals that may result from them or from more permanent aspects of the social order, or from privileges enjoyed by some sections within it. In the second place, a bleak view of human nature would in effect rule out any hope of radical improvements by way of social change; it would predispose even many of those who are underprivileged to being grateful that things are not worse, and rally them to the defense of their nation against subversives at home and supposed enemies abroad.

My position is to grant our lack of firm knowledge about human nature, and then tentatively seek to explain anti-social behavior as outcomes of circumstances and events that can be studied, without jumping prematurely from inconclusive evidence to assumptions about human universals. Even if we were to find that far more people behaved anti-socially than altruistically, if placed in experimental situations of real choice, I would ask what is the matter with their particular culture(s) or backgrounds, rather than attempt on that basis to generalize about human nature. A constructive research approach toward grasping some of the positive potentialities of human nature would be to study individuals who behave strikingly more altruistically than their neighbors, so as to seek to establish what factors in *their* backgrounds and personalities may account for this kind of deviance. Equally important, of course, is research into circumstances surrounding destructive behavior. The point is that we must look for other explanations for a long time before resorting to a convenient residual explanation such as "instinct" or "human nature."

My bias, then, is tentatively to "blame" society, or at times chance constellations of circumstances, for the anti-social behavior that we see; and to assume that the more widespread such behavior appears to be, the more likely that it is the outcome of structural dislocations or inequities in the social order, which for many reasons have been inadequately studied. This is by no means a unique bias among social scientists, whose business it is, after all, to study the social origin of human events; many of us may have an unconscious vested interest in presenting social rather than psychological, biological or genetic diagnoses; perhaps our behavior may be of a piece with the chiropractor's proneness to diagnose bodily pains as attributable to trouble in the spine. (Kenneth Boulding suggests this possibility in a review article, "Philosophy, Behavioral Science, and the Nature of Man," in *World Politics,* Vol. XII (1960) pp. 272-79, especially 277-78). Nevertheless, I suspect that a conservative climate of thought has imperceptibly conditioned many social scientists to refrain from asking politically radical questions. For example, questions like this: If it is true that most people vote according to the horizon of their pocketbooks, could it be that competitive pressures in our social order deny them the opportunity to develop into public-spirited citizens? Perhaps all people, as it has been said about the French, in more than the literal sense carry their hearts on the left side and their wallets on the right; if so, under what social and cultural conditions can the dictates of our hearts become the stronger?—While complex, such problems are by no means out of reach for empirical explorations.

The magnitude of the problem of building attitudes and behavior oriented toward conceptions of the public good is suggested not only by the fondness of conservatives of many kinds for denigrating human nature and depicting life on this earth as a merciless struggle. It is brought home more forcefully still if we consider that every social order, once established, will produce its conservatives as surely as it will produce inequality; and that the cards will be stacked in their favor, in that they will enjoy more than their share of economic and political resources, which particularly in ~ur time can be converted into means of persuasion as well.

Yet a deterministic defeatism in the face of so many imponderables has as little to recommend itself as a conservatively inspired defeatism about human nature. After all, conservative orders have been overthrown in the past, and others have proved flexible enough to permit great though gradual strides toward freedom or social justice or affluence for large proportions of people. Perhaps *this* is where invariant attributes of human nature may come in; perhaps there always will be people who worry about social justice, and more so the more unjust a society becomes—or, by way of enlightenment and better living conditions, the more discerning the standards become for judging what is just and unjust.

Whatever the explanations may be, and they are sure to be complex, this volume was written in the belief that the science of politics exists as a means, not as an end in itself. The end, as I like to formulate it nowadays, is a more effective politics, or a more effective promotion of institutions under which all men can live according to their needs. Let me recapitulate: "Politics," I have defined, refers to all activity addressing itself toward the solution or alleviation of perceived social problems. Problems are discrepancies between what is and what ought to be. It is for political scientists to be in the forefront among those who seek to articulate and appraise proposals on what ought to be; it is for us to carry on a dialogue on the normative aspects of such proposals, and to do continuing research, in cooperation with other social scientists and psychologists, on their empirical aspects. The integration of all these aspects of what ought to be, and the continuing study of their logical, normative, and empirical implications pose enormous and, to my way of thinking, immensely challenging tasks. Tasks to be added to the continuing ones, already in good hands, of exploring what exists and what has existed in the past.

Clearly, there is much work to be done on the agenda of political science. The quality of the politics of the future and the odds for human survival will to some extent hinge, I believe, on the seriousness and the vision and skills with which political scientists proceed with their study of how our social and human problems can become more effectively resolved. The most massive of these problems, I still believe, is the problem of liberty, as I conceive of it; for it is in this volume stated broadly enough to include peace and justice as necessary aspects. The opportunity to live a natural life span is the most fundamental of all freedoms; and the first priority goal for which political institutions exist, according to my view, is to maximize freedom for all, with priority for those who at a given time are least free.

Stanford, February 6, 1964   CHRISTIAN BAY

Preface to the First Printing, 1958

The rather favorable view I take of human nature has been confirmed many a time during my work on this book. Friends, acquaintances, and even strangers have gone out of their way to help, time and time again. And I have avidly seized and made use of many of the suggestions I have received.

Perhaps the best way to acknowledge some of my debts is to sketch out a brief biography of the line of thought and study that eventually became this book. Personally speaking, it all started with my luck in drawing gentle and wise parents who kept encouraging me to ask questions and seek answers for myself. Politically speaking, it all became urgent with the monstrosity of a Second World War, and with the indignity of having German occupants tell us in Norway that we belonged to the Master Race and therefore would be better off than the Czechs or the Poles. Professionally speaking, it all became possible by a succession of fortunate circumstances.

One of these was the extracurricular wartime seminars led by Arne Naess, Professor of Philosophy at the University of Oslo. From under his wing came the group of young social scientists, students at the time, who established the Institute for Social Research in Oslo after the war. This Institute was in the enviable position of being privately financed—mainly by Mr. Sigurd Rinde in the first decade—and yet independent enough to allow its staff complete freedom in developing their own research interests and projects, with no holds barred. A unique interdisciplinary milieu developed, combining an emphasis on general theory and methodology with a strong concern for social and political problems. During the earliest stages of this inquiry, I received much advice and support from Vilhelm Aubert, Harald Ofstad, Erik Rinde, and Herman Tennessen, to name just a few.

The Institute would not have done so well without the Fulbright program, which brought us a succession of stimulating, competent, and liberal American scholars. David Krech was the first of these to spend a full year with us; he set me going on the freedom problem (being himself at the time a "refugee" from the loyalty-oath–ridden Berkeley campus), and he also set the important precedent of having each Fulbright Fellow at our Institute help select his successor. The Krech dynasty has included such eminent men and women as Herbert H. Hyman, Daniel Katz, Eugene

Jacobson, and Else Frenkel-Brunswik, to mention only those who gave me much help on my own project.

Back in 1946 I was granted a Rockefeller Fellowship to study political science and sociology in the United States, and I had my first acquaintance with this country's eminent institutions of higher learning at the University of Chicago and at Harvard. Returning to this country in 1953, I went to California, where I did most of the actual writing on this book—first in the excellent library on the Berkeley campus of the University of California, and subsequently at the Center for Advanced Study in the Behavioral Sciences at Stanford. In Berkeley my good friends Grant McConnell and Duncan MacRae, Jr., read large portions of my manuscript as I wrote it, and offered valuable criticism. Also, sections of my manuscript were read and commented on by Haskell Fain, Julian Friedman, Norman Jacobson, David Krech, Warren Mullins, David Rynin, Nevitt Sanford, Joseph Tussman, and Richard B. Wilson.

Else Frenkel-Brunswik, whose recent death is a very tragic loss, had been a warm friend ever since her first visit to Oslo and also took a keen interest in my project. Her wisdom, her humanitarian faith, and her tremendous erudition account for much of what I like best in this book. She followed and stimulated the progress of my manuscript in Berkeley, and my own progress as a person as well. In addition, it was her recommendation that gave me the unique opportunity of spending a year as Fellow of the brand-new Behavioral Sciences Center.

This institution, under the able leadership of Ralph W. Tyler, is truly a Shangri-La for intellectuals, with the single drawback that it does not offer tenure to its Fellows. Not only does it provide economic support without asking any specific service in return, but it also assembles a very stimulating group of first-rate minds, and yet leaves it to each Fellow to choose his own privacy/participation ratio. A friendly, efficient staff, including a fine library service, also helped make this year at the Center the most productive year I ever had. Let me also mention two young ladies who did a beautiful typing job for me—Mrs. Barbara Baxter and Mrs. Emma Christine.

It makes me blush to think of how many co-Fellows at the Center took the time and trouble to read sections of my manuscript and give me advice: Robert E. Agger, Franz Alexander, Arthur J. Brodbeck, Richard Christie, John Gillin, Herbert C. Kelman, Clyde Kluckhohn, Harold D. Lasswell, Charles E. Lindblom, Frank A. Pinner, Arnold A. Rogow, Louis Schneider, Morris Stein, and Wayne Untereiner.

The first draft of this manuscript was finished shortly after my return to Oslo, with the spirited assistance of Mrs. Thordis Saxlund, who stayed up nights to finish the typing before the target date. Among other Norwegian friends who have offered constructive criticism, I must give thanks to Arild Haaland, Arne Naess, and Stein Rokkan, and in particular to Jens Arup Seip, who did a truly impressive job of a critical analysis of nearly the whole first draft.

It would take a second volume, almost, should I account for all the good turns I have received during my work on this book. I am very grateful to Nancy Bay, who has been of help in innumerable ways. Ella Graubart Arensberg has helped me improve many sentences. Dagmar Horna, now Mrs. Gerald Perman, gave me a tremendous spiritual support across a continent. James Wresinski, my Research Assistant in the Department of Political Science at Michigan State University, where I enjoyed teaching for half a year in 1957, gave me much thoughtful advice. Milton Rokeach, eminent psychologist at Michigan State, gave me detailed comments after reading my chapter on Psychological Freedom. Fredric Sonenberg, my Reader in the Department of Speech on the Berkeley campus, helped me get started on the Index. Barbara Hartman did a fine job of compiling and typing the Bibliography.

To J. Christopher Herold and John Kotselas, my editors, I am deeply grateful for all that they have done toward making the publication of this book possible, and for the grace, consideration, and efficiency with which they have removed all hurdles. Only when Mr. Kotselas had finished editing my manuscript did I realize how much I had left unclear, awkward, and redundant; in the spirit of my own intentions, he was able to hand back to me a much better manuscript than he had received.

I am grateful to the Department of Law of the University of Oslo for supporting me during most of the time I have been working on this book, including the two years I spent in California with leave of absence; the University Fellowship (*adjunktstipend*) offered by that University provides a golden opportunity for those who are chosen. Also, I am very grateful to the Norwegian Research Council for Science and the Humanities, which has provided a generous grant toward the publication of this book.

CHRISTIAN BAY

Berkeley, June 15, 1958

Contents

PART TWO: REALITIES OF BEHAVIOR

CONCLUSION

INTRODUCTION

1

Human Freedom in Today's World

$\mathcal{T}$he rise and development of mass democracies have failed to solve some of the pressing problems of individual freedom. The average man's sphere of freedom has been much extended, but in some respects the expression of his individuality has probably become more narrowly controlled and confined. Ever since the splitting of the atom in 1945 thoughtful persons have seen a new urgency in a rapid development of the sciences of man in society. It was widely hoped that better insights into human nature and the laws of social behavior would somehow contribute toward wiser decisions, not only about how to use the frightful powers unleashed by the advances in the physical sciences, but also about how to use more creatively the power inherent in human beings.

The advances both in democracy and in the behavioral sciences carry great promise for the future of human freedom and dignity, but they also bring new hazards into human existence. In contemporary democracies along with the popular vote has come a new concern among men of power for what is going on in the minds of the voters. One outcome of new levels of competence in the behavioral sciences is that it has become easier to invade the privacy of large numbers of people, and to manipulate their minds and activities. The demand for the services of behavioral scientists has been in connection with leading or manipulating people. How to forestall race riots, how to make better soldiers, how to promote magazines, how to reduce the number of divorces, how to increase immunity to communist propaganda—these are a few random examples of the kinds of problems that behavioral scientists are asked and paid to work on. Much of this work is to be commended, but perhaps not all of it, depending on the values of the observer. Yet, even if all such projects had served worthwhile objectives, the amount of manipulation of minds and emotions going on today should be of concern to those who care for the growth of genuine individuality in men and women.

It is about time, I submit, that behavioral scientists pay more attention to the opposite side of the manipulation problem: How can increased insights into human behavior be employed in the service of sheltering the growth of individuality and freedom in the modern society? With this book I hope to make a contribution toward understanding the nature of this task.

All scientific activity, as indeed all human activity, is related to values, explicitly or implicitly. No man in his right mind would seriously occupy himself with a problem unless its clarification or solution were of some value to him. The chief value may, of course, be in the joy of expanding knowledge, but even then the chances are that the selection of the problems to be studied is influenced by an interest in promoting other values as well, directly or indirectly. The task of the social scientist, with respect to values, is basically twofold. First, he brings together available empirical and logical insights in order to clarify implications of (and in this way influence) our choice of end values. Secondly, he tries to clarify factual relationships among possible combinations of available means and desirable ends.

The choice of goal values is ultimately a matter of personal faith. In the field of ethics, specifically devoted to the study of values, one goes about laying down canons for value choice. It is up to each person, however, to accept or reject the particular canon suggested by any particular writer in ethics.[1] Yet two particular canons, at least, seem to have a wide acceptance, in so far as such questions are raised at all. One is the canon of logical consistency. Most of us do not wish to be self-contradictory, not even in our system of goal values, in so far as this can be avoided.[2] Secondly, there is the canon of insight. We generally want to be as aware as possible of the practical implications of our important values, so that we can know how to promote them and how to avoid counteracting them.[3]

In the social sciences, on the other hand, a system of ultimate values is usually taken for granted by the student, who searches for factual relationships between cause and effect, or within chains of mutual dependence. In this way he gains insight into the relationships between ends and means.

Among the social sciences, political science has, however, been relatively slow to develop empirical knowledge applicable to problems of ends and means.[4] Political philosophers have for many centuries been concerned

---

[1] Some philosophers deny this, claiming that ethical judgments can be proved true or false by empirical test. The rejection of an ethical judgment fully supported by proof, if such a thing were possible, would, of course, amount to a rejection of logic or science as well.

[2] "In our civilization people want to be rational and objective in their beliefs. We have faith in science and are, in principle, prepared to change our beliefs according to its results." Myrdal, *An American Dilemma: The Negro Problem and Modern Democracy,* pp. 1027 ff.

[3] "The value of insight seems never to be questioned. No writer makes out any case for self-deception. Not infrequently insight is exalted to the highest place among the virtues, or therapeutically is regarded as a panacea for all mental ills." Allport, *Personality: A Psychological Interpretation,* p. 221.

[4] Consider the following three statements and the year in which each was made.

1895: "Even today political science has not yet entered upon its truly scientific period." Mosca: *The Ruling Class,* p. 6.

1929: "Nobody takes political science very seriously, for nobody is convinced that it is a science or that it has any important bearing on politics." Lippmann, *Preface to Morals,* p. 260.

1953: "Without a conscious understanding of the role of·theory and its possibility, I shall argue, political research must remain fragmentary and heterogeneous, unable to fulfill the promise in its designation as a political *science.*" Easton, *The Political System: An Inquiry Into the State of Political Science,* p. 5.

principally with thought about how a society ought to be governed and have neglected the empirical study of how existing societies actually are governed. Constitutional lawyers have divided their time between interpreting current laws and proposing better ones. Only in our time have we seen a growing interest among political scientists in determining how laws actually operate and in assessing their psychological and social effects. Only in our time also have we seen empirically supported attempts toward studying laws along with other social institutions as contributing strands toward explaining how man, the social animal, behaves.

With all this recent progress, there is a weakness of a different kind in contemporary empirical political science. Modern students of political behavior have been so eager to break with a past dominated by value discussions that they have tended to neglect the value aspects of their own problems. One result of this is the tendency, even among the most scholarly of these writers, to fall back upon rather loose generalities about "the requirements of the democratic process" when they are looking for standards by which to judge the merits of particular institutions or behavior patterns. Indeed, most definitions of democracy are loose, having reference to a particular process for deciding issues and for choosing representatives and the government. Here is one fairly typical example from among many:

If democracy means anything, it means government by the people. . . . "Government by the people" means that the major policies of the government should be determined by the people or by their representatives, freely elected at reasonably frequent intervals, and that the administration should be conducted by those who are accountable to the people or their representatives.[5]

Either the concept is vague enough to mean all things to all men, or it gets specific enough in some authors to make it evident that there is no universal or even very wide agreement on what specific kind of governmental process is desirable above all others.[6]

There is something basically wrong in referring to a process—and especially a vaguely defined and often poorly understood process—as a crucial political value. The democratic process, whatever that means, is valuable, I shall argue, only in so far as it leads to the maximization of substantive values.

What substantive values should be maximized as much as possible by means of the political process? The English utilitarians had their ready answer: the greatest happiness of the greatest number. The trouble with this formula, as I shall attempt to show, is that it is too poorly defined to provide criteria for progress and retrogression. But I share the basic utilitarian notion that the way to advance in politics, wherever possible, is to formulate a goal and then to inquire empirically into the comparative utility of alternate approaches to this goal.

[5] Pennock, *Liberal Democracy: Its Merits and Prospects,* p. 98.
[6] Various statements on "democracy" are listed in Appendix I, of Naess, Christophersen, and Kvalo, *Democracy, Ideology, and Objectivity: Studies in the Semantics and Cognitive Analysis of Ideological Controversy.*

In this book I wish to inquire into what the consequences will be of as-signing to "a maximum freedom of expression for all" the same all-per-vasive value-status as the utilitarians gave to "the greatest happiness of the greatest number." Let me for the moment without any substantiation as-sume that freedom of expression is the supreme political value. (Later I shall discuss alternate value formulations and attempt to explain my position.) I am now also in effect assuming that it is worthwhile to study the condi-tions for freedom maximization. Moreover, I am implying that I consider the democratic process, or any particular kind of democratic or other po-litical process, valuable chiefly to the extent that it is in fact promoting the freedom of all individuals.

It is immediately evident that I must take great pains to clarify what I mean by "freedom." I shall touch on that aspect at the end of this chapter but shall develop it more substantially in Chapter 3. In the first two chap-ters the word "freedom" will be used somewhat loosely, and it will embrace all the meanings that men may conventionally put into the word.

It is also clear that my objective requires an empirical inquiry into the compatibility of different freedom values and of different freedom demands. The question of compatibility between freedom values is the question of to what extent, if any, one freedom value may tend to cancel out another, for the same individual. For example, to what extent can I become liberated from institutional pressures without developing isolation-anxiety and a compulsive need to join some Messianic group. The question of compati-bility between freedom demands, on the other hand, is the question of to what extent a particular freedom of one individual tends to interfere with another individual's opportunity to enjoy the same freedom, or another freedom. For example, does one man's demand for free speech at times, say, when exercised from a sound truck, interfere with another man's right to listen or not to listen? Different freedom values may but need not be involved in conflicts between different freedom demands.

Both of these inquiries belong in Chapter 3, as integral parts of the effort to state my value position in detail. The question of relationships between freedom values can only be discussed after a relatively careful presentation of my freedom concepts in Chapter 3. But it is already possible at this stage to make some preliminary generalizations about criteria for handling con-flicts between freedom demands.

It is convenient to think of freedom demands as "human rights" and in this way relate the issue before us to a perennial issue in writings on democ-racy: What is the proper balance between majority rule and minority rights? Perhaps the present concept of "human right" can contribute toward an acceptable answer to this problem. As I have just implied, I use this term to refer to a demand for a specified sphere of freedom around every individual. A human right has been "realized" to the extent that this demand is in fact generally honored.[7] Human rights in this sense are not

---

[7] A "right," analogously, means a demand for a specific sphere of freedom around one or more specific individuals. Cf. Plamenatz, who includes additional criteria in an otherwise similar definition: "A right is a power which a creature ought to possess, either because its exercise by him is itself good or else because it is a means to what is good, and in the exercise of which all rational beings ought to protect him." *Consent, Freedom and Political Obligation*, p. 89. Cf. also below, pp. 75–76.

God-given or inalienable. In a democratic society there is usually a law or constitutional clause enforcing every human right, or there is a demand for such a law or constitutional clause. For this reason the term "civil right" is often used in the same sense.

The problem of freedom maximization, to the extent that it can be conceived as a problem of maximal realization of freedom demands, is best approached by making a distinction between human rights and social privileges.[8] A human right is a freedom demand that can, in principle, be vindicated for all human beings. The right of free speech is such a human right.[9] Other examples are the right to work, the right to health services, the right to leisure. A social privilege, on the other hand, is a right that by its very nature must be limited to some. A privilege is not necessarily something bad. Social privileges—for example, the private ownership of factories—tend to extend the freedom of the few at the expense of the freedom of the many. However, if this kind of an economic system is believed to be particularly effective in delivering goods that men need, it may conceivably contribute in other respects to extend the freedom of everybody. Such a possibility should not be rejected offhand. But since there are always two sides to questions of social privilege, it is reasonable to hold that they should be regulated by majority rule.

When it comes to human rights, however, majority rule should not apply. If an exercise of a particular freedom by an individual does not interfere with someone else's freedom, he should not be denied his right no matter how small the minority of which he is a member. This position, to which I shall later refer as the *human rights approach,* is a value orientation that differs sharply from that of Bentham and the orthodox utilitarians. It is my faith, as it was theirs, that society exists for the benefit of all. But Bentham's method for assigning priorities between freedom demands was a simple addition of pleasures and subtraction of pains to achieve the highest sum of happiness. My method is instead to assign top priority to the removal of the heaviest constraints on freedom first, throughout society, before one should worry about the less serious constraints. A society is as free as its underdogs are.

In other words, in my value position the extension of the more basic human rights to the last few individuals takes precedence over the extension of less basic rights to much larger numbers of individuals. Although Bentham, too, believed in the equality of all individuals, his notion of equality was essentially a computation device. For me, a society is free only to the extent that its least privileged and its least tolerated members are free. Needless to say, the distinction between more basic and less basic rights or freedoms raises enormously complicated questions, as I shall indicate briefly in the following section. Most of what I have to say in this matter, however, will be said in appropriate contexts in Chapter 3.[10]

---

[8] Both "human rights" and "social privileges" are "rights" as defined in the previous footnote. They are normally "rights" also in Plamenatz's sense, from the point of view of those who claim them.

[9] A possible qualification to this general rule has already been suggested in the discussion of the compatibility of freedom demands on p. 6. See also below, pp. 126–36.

[10] See below, pp. 92–94, 101–3, and 105–7.

THE CHOICE OF VALUES AND THE PROBLEM OF CONSENSUAL VALIDATION

The word "value" may have at least two meanings: it may refer to what men want, or it may refer to what men ought to want.[11]

The social scientist who strictly limits himself to the role of an observer of human behavior can only report what it appears that men actually do want, or in fact believe they ought to want. Statements about what men ought to want would amount to a projection of the observer's own values, so that they become standards by which he evaluates other people's behavior.

Social scientists inevitably both observe and evaluate. What is really important is that they try to keep these two functions as separate as is humanly possible. One essential precaution, if this is to be attempted, is for the scientist to state his value choices as explicitly and as fully as possible.[12] Another precaution is to devise methods of observation that make his data liable to be observed and confirmed by other people with different values or value priorities.

Now, if it can be assumed that the canons of logical consistency and of insight are fairly generally accepted, a new kind of *consensual validation of value judgments* becomes possible. If we know what men ultimately want more than anything else, it becomes possible with the help of social science and common sense to say something about what men ought to do in order to accomplish their most important goals. One task of applied science is to study causal relationships, to gain knowledge about available means toward consensually desired ends.

There are various difficulties which considerably limit this hopeful outlook, however. To derive means from ends is often a very complex task, especially if psychological as well as logical considerations are brought to bear on it. On the other hand, in some respects there is a brightening outlook for a wider consensus on the choice of ends, as I shall try to show in a few moments.

The first difficulty is in the very categories of "ends" and "means." John Dewey observed many years ago:

Means and ends are two names for the same reality. The terms denote not a division in reality but a distinction in judgment. . . . Only as the end is converted into means is it definitely conceived, or intellectually defined, to say nothing of being executable. Just as end it is vague, cloudy, impressionistic. We do not *know* what we are really after until a *course* of action is mentally worked out. Aladdin with his lamp could dispense with translating ends into means, but nobody else can.[13]

This difficulty is not a crucial one, however, if we are prepared to deal with the dichotomy purely as a tool for analyzing concrete courses of action.

11 The study of culture in large measure deals with "values" in apparently a third sense: with what men feel or believe they ought to want. However, this feeling or belief constitutes an actual want in its own right, even if at times it may be canceled out in the individual's behavior by more powerful immediate wants.

12 "There is no other device for excluding biases in social sciences than to face the valuations and to introduce them as explicitly stated, specific and sufficiently concretized value premises." Myrdal: *An American Dilemma*, p. 1043 and pp. 1027–64.

13 *Human Nature and Conduct: An Introduction to Social Psychology*, pp. 36–37.

C. L. Stevenson, for example, distinguishes between intrinsic and extrinsic values, or values desired (or desirable) for their own sake and values desired (or desirable) as means to something else.[14] While he grants that most values are both extrinsic and intrinsic at the same time, or both ends and means to further ends, he suggests that each concrete course of action can be evaluated in terms of its *focal aims,* or the end predominating the actor's conscious attention at a given time, in a given behavioral context.[15] In this work the terms "ends" and "means" or "goal values" and "instrumental values" are always used in the same way that Stevenson employs "focal aims" and (by implication) "focal means." In other words, they are terms applied to the analysis of concrete chains of events; they do not raise questions of value ultimates. Even the crucial goal formulation of "a maximal freedom of expression for all" is nothing more than my dominant long-term focal aim, since I am assuming that freedom in turn allows and promotes other values, such as health and growth, enlightenment, human dignity, and the like.

If it is agreed now that it can make sense to discuss ends and means, if we are cautious, another hurdle arises when we take a closer look at our two canons for value choice: logical consistency and maximal insight. In certain realms of decision making, for example in *some* economic choice situations, they probably are in fact determining concrete behavior. But in most realms of behavior, even in economic behavior, these anemic norms of narrow rationality can easily be pushed aside by more vigorous and vastly more complex individual motivations. We all develop vested interests in some of our habitual perceptions, cognitions, and behavior patterns.

It is true by definition, of course, that if a man has only one really important goal value, which can be made explicit, then all other values become subordinate, and it is possible to make many valid statements about how he ought to behave to realize this one value. But this simple kind of man does not exist. For a living man there always is a point in the pursuit of any one value when the most efficient or utilitarian approach is abandoned because these particular means would jeopardize other values too much.[16]

A further complication, which is a commonplace in contemporary psychology, is the phenomenon of ambivalence in value preferences. It is well known that a person may want simultaneously a set of opposite and mutually contradictory values. Also he may both want and not want the same value at the same time. This does not mean that the canon of consistency in value choice is deliberately rejected, but the complexities in human nature make it inapplicable to our behavior as a whole. The canon is still applicable, however, as a general *norm* for those phases of behavior that con-

---

[14] *Ethics and Language,* p. 174.

[15] *Ibid.,* pp. 179, 203, 229–30. John Dewey speaks of "ends-in-view" in the same sense. See his "Theory of Valuation" in *International Encyclopedia of Unified Science,* II, No. 4 (1939), 66.

[16] In addition, the partial achievement of a goal may reduce our desire for its complete achievement. "Most of us are marginalists. Generally we experience diminishing marginal utility the more we attain any one goal; or in the language of contemporary psychology, goal attainment reduces the drive value of the stimulus." Dahl, *A Preface to Democratic Theory,* p. 51.

sist in the conscious effort to invest energies and resources in the service of specific goals.

A special kind of internal value conflict is so common in human behavior that some writers have appeared to make it their point of departure in defining the concept of value. Clyde Kluckhohn, notably, offers this definition:

A value is a conception, explicit or implicit, distinctive of an individual or characteristic of a group, of the desirable which influences the selection from available modes, means, and ends of actions.[17]

On this basis, he draws a sharp distinction between what the individual or group in fact desires and what is held desirable, not by the observer but by the individual or group in question. A man may hold chastity desirable, and yet when the occasion arises desire a woman. In Kluckhohn's terms, chastity would be described as a value for this man, while sexual intercourse would be a nonvalued or disvalued impulse, or cathexis. He observes further:

The reason that cathexis and value seldom coincide completely is that a cathexis is ordinarily a short-term and narrow response, whereas value implies a broader and long-term view. A cathexis is an impulse; a value or values restrain or canalize impulses in terms of wider and more perduring goals.[18]

To me it seems more convenient to work with a simple value concept, one that embraces fundamental long-term goals and norms as well as more shallow or short-term preferences. Along with Harold D. Lasswell and Myres S. McDougal, I shall use the term "value" to designate all *preferred events,*[19] regardless of the nature, duration, and mutual compatibility of the various preferences. But the type of internal value conflict that Kluckhohn describes must be noted and taken into account in any attempt toward a comprehensive observation and understanding of human value behavior.

All human behavior can be seen as value behavior, when "value" is used in this broad sense. All men are motivated in their behavior by needs or imagined needs or impulses or preferences, or by norms about "right" behavior. But values differ in the importance assigned to them, whether by the observer, by the individuals themselves, or by their group or culture.

---

[17] Kluckhohn, "Values and Value-Orientations in the Theory of Action: An Exploration in Definition and Classification," in Parsons and Shils (eds.), *Toward a General Theory of Action,* p. 395. It is not Dr. Kluckhohn's intention to offer a persuasive definition of "value," he has been kind enough to inform me. Nor does he wish to imply a generalized preference for gratifications of superego needs over those of the id. His argument in the paper nevertheless lends itself to such an interpretation, and it is a convenient one for my illustrative purposes.

[18] "More abstractly, we may say that the desired which is disvalued (i.e., cathected but not desirable) is that which is incompatible with the personality as a system or with the society or culture as systems." *Ibid.,* p. 399. See also Dewey, "Theory of Valuation," in *International Encyclopedia of Unified Science,* II, No. 4 (1939), 31–33. Dewey pegs the distinction between "desired" and "desirable" exclusively on the difference between (1) spontaneous impulse and (2) desires influenced by meditation about conditions and consequences.

[19] Lasswell and McDougal, *Law, Science and Policy,* working paper 1954, Part II, p. 1. I am very grateful to Dr. Lasswell for his generosity in having permitted me to read major portions of this manuscript. Cf. also Lasswell and Kaplan, *Power and Society: A Framework for Political Inquiry,* p. 16.

Let us now inquire whether there is any prospect for a wide consensual validation of some broad criteria for the choice of goal values or goal value priorities. Keep in mind that I am discussing focal aims, not ultimate values.

One possible approach might be read into Kluckhohn's conceptual scheme. On the basis of empirical study, you decide which values are more enduring than others in the behavior of one or more individuals. Or you choose an only slightly different emphasis and try to find out which goals and norms tend to be used as standards for judging in moral terms the individual's own behavior and that of others. The observer may rank his own values by the same criteria and apply them in his judgment of the behavior of other people.

A somewhat different value orientation[20] will be adopted in this book. My basic criterion for the ranking of values, as an evaluator of behavior, will be *the assumed psychological importance of the value in question,* for the individual's health and growth toward the full attainment of his individuality. Before I explain this statement, let me emphasize the strict empirical limits that are set on the application of this criterion by the fact that men are living together and by the previously adopted position that all men have the same minimum claims to human rights.

What I am proposing may perhaps be expressed in psychoanalytic terms. While the previous criterion for value ranking would give the decisive say to the superego, I suggest in effect that the claims of the id may be equally important. In other words, I wish to rank values according to their importance for the balanced ego, or for the welfare and growth of the total personality. In social terms, my value orientation proceeds from the notion that men must have the same basic rights and from the knowledge that this limits the amount of freedom that can be given to each. Within these limits, however, I value psychologically more important gratifications more highly than those that are psychologically less important.

The psychological importance of alternative gratifications for man's health and growth is in principle an empirical problem, although an immensely complex one. In fact, at the present stage in the behavioral sciences not even a satisfactory formulation of this problem has been achieved. But trends both in depth psychology and in anthropology are pointing toward an early and important expansion of our knowledge of the various psychological needs of man.

Erich Fromm's work has contributed prominently to this trend in depth psychology. He claims that it is for psychology and neighboring disciplines to discover the principles of a "universal ethics" that is tuned to the universal needs of man.[21] The most advanced expression of this view I have

20 I follow Kluckhohn's definition of this term, even if I use "value" in a broader sense: "It is convenient to use the term *value-orientation* for those value notions which are (a) general, (b) organized, and (c) include definitely existential judgments. A value-orientation is a set of linked propositions embracing both value and existential elements." See Kluckhohn, in Parsons and Shils, *Toward a General Theory of Action,* p. 409.

21 Fromm, *Escape from Freedom,* and especially *Man for Himself.* See also his *The Sane Society.* Fromm also speaks of "socially immanent" ethics, referring to "those norms in any culture which contain prohibitions and commands that are necessary only for the functioning and survival of that particular society." He observes that, in different degrees, "the historically

found in a book by A. H. Maslow, who argues in favor of a conceptual scheme of "higher" versus "lower" needs. Superficially, this may seem like a return to very old and long since abandoned ideas; perhaps it would be preferable to talk of "complex" versus "simple" needs. What is important in Maslow's presentation is that he proposes a number of promising hypotheses on the relationships between "higher" need-gratification and both mental and physical health. One important outcome of advances in depth psychology, says Maslow, is that "we can now see not only what man is, but what he may become. That is to say, we can see not only surface, not only the actualities, but the potentialities as well." He claims to have demonstrated "the possibility that a *scientist* could study and describe normality in the sense of excellence, perfection, ideal health, the fulfillment of human possibilities."[22] What this line of inquiry promises is not an objectively valid system of ethics,[23] but a deductive system based on a very few and widely accepted value premises: that maximal health and maximal development of intercompatible human potentialities are supremely desirable.

The corresponding trend in anthropology is expressed in an increasing concern with studying cross-cultural universalities in human behavior patterns and values. One advanced exploration of uniformities and variations in the value orientations of different cultures, emphasizing the methodological problems involved, has been made by Florence Kluckhohn. She starts out from three basic premises:

There is a limited number of common human problems for which all peoples at all times must find some solution. . . . While there is variability in solutions of all the problems it is neither fruitless nor random. . . . All variants of all solutions are in varying degrees present in all societies at all times.

She proceeds to propose typologies for comparing dominant (and variant) value orientations in various cultures, focusing on five universal problems of human existence.[24]

A more general expression of the same orientation in modern anthropology is found in a paper by David Bidney, who is critical of previous trends toward value relativism or "pluralism" among his colleagues:

But if anthropology is to attain the stage of making significant generalizations concerning the conditions of the cultural process and the values of civilization, then comparative studies of cultures and their values must be made with a view

---

conditioned social necessities clash with the universal existential necessities of the individual"; and he concludes: "The contradiction between immanent social ethics and universal ethics will tend to disappear to the same extent to which society becomes truly human, that is, takes care of the full human development of all its members." See *Man for Himself*, pp. 241–44. No kind of ethics, of course, can permit complete satisfaction of all unique individual needs.

[22] Maslow, *Motivation and Personality,* pp. 342 and 346. Cf. also Maslow, "A Theory of Human Motivation," in Harriman (ed.); *Twentieth Century Psychology*, pp. 22–48. Also see below, pp. 327–28.

[23] See below, pp. 13–14.

[24] These five problems are: What is the character of innate human nature? What is the relation of man to nature? What is the temporal focus of human life? What is the modality of human activity? What is the modality of man's relationship to other men? See Florence R. Kluckhohn, "Dominant and Variant Value Orientation," working paper 1955. For an earlier version, see "Dominant and Substitute Profiles of Cultural Orientations," *Social Forces*, XXVIII, No. 4 (1950), 376–93.

to demonstrating universal principles of cultural dynamics and concrete, rational norms capable of universal realization. Hitherto the task of suggesting and pre-scribing normative ideals and goals has been left, for the most part, to utopian philosophers and to cynical sociologists who equated social ideals with myths. I suggest that it is high time that anthropology comes of age and that anthropolo-gists show their respect for human reason and science by co-operating with other social scientists and scholars with a view to envisaging practical, progressive, ra-tional ideals worthy of winning a measure of universal recognition in the fu-ture.[25]

In a more recent summary of the problem of "universal behaviors" Clyde Kluckhohn concludes: "The underlying 'genotype' of all cultures is the same; the 'phenotypic' manifestations vary greatly."[26]

These lines of inquiry in recent psychology and anthropology seem to offer some hope for expanding our knowledge about universal needs, be-yond what we have known for a long time about biological necessities. To the extent that this knowledge is expanded, it becomes *possible to make categorical statements in these terms about the comparative psychological importance of different institutional values.* At the same time we are gain-ing some fundamental standards differentiating between more basic and less basic human rights or freedoms.

Let it be stressed that I do not envisage a development toward a com-plete system of "objective" values to govern human lives. For one thing, a crucial distinction must be made between public and private values: Public values are oriented toward the assumed needs or desires or interests of large numbers of people. Private values set the goals for purely indi-vidually oriented behavior without reference to the goals of other individ-uals.[27]

The individual's private values, both end and means values, are and will always be at least in part a matter of his own choice, provided he claims his sovereignty and his claim is institutionally protected; but this claim to sov-ereignty is justifiable and indeed possible (on a social scale) only in govern-ing his private sphere of life. In social and political interaction some com-

[25] "The Concept of Value in Modern Anthropology," in Kroeber (ed.), *Anthropology Today: An Encyclopedic Inventory,* p. 698. A similar, if more calmly expressed orientation is found in Clyde Kluckhohn, "Universal Categories of Culture," and in Hallowell, "Culture, Personality and Society," both in *ibid.,* pp. 507–23 and 597–620. See also Linton, "The Prob-lem of Universal Values," in Spencer (ed.), *Method and Perspective in Anthropology: Papers in Honor of Wilson D. Wallis,* pp. 145–68.

[26] "Culture and Behavior," in Lindzey (ed.), *Handbook of Social Psychology,* II, 955. See also below, p. 328.

[27] The categories of private vs. public values are not logically exhaustive as they are de-fined. In between comes a category of values oriented toward the assumed needs, desires, or interests of *small* numbers of people—for example, the persons with whom the individual identifies the most strongly. Note that the distinction between public and private values is not the same as a distinction between *cultural* and *personal* values, meaning culturally determined versus personality-determined values. Private value positions, like the desire for cigarettes, may well be cultural; and public value positions, like a belief in pacifism or in a maximum freedom of expression, may well in large measure be personality-determined. The cultural-personal dimension refers to the origin or determinants of values; the public-private dimension refers to the scope of values, or the range of persons for whose benefit each value is desired. Needless to say, each of the four types of values can motivate "selfish" or "unselfish" and "re-sponsible" or "irresponsible" behavior.

mon institutionalized norms are necessary, as we shall see in Chapters 5 and 6. But even with respect to public values it is usually sufficient to comply in overt behavior; it is generally not necessary to give one's full allegiance to the consensual or conventional behavior standards.[28]

The trend toward objectivity in fundamental values may be a slow one, but it offers much promise provided it is kept within its proper confines. And what confines are proper will be concluded from a consideration of the basic functions of consensus. Let me for a moment anticipate an important point that will be more fully treated in Chapter 5. Social institutions are necessary and useful in so far as they promote cooperation among men and reduce violent conflicts. A consensus on fundamental norms is desirable to a parallel extent—that is, to the extent that it promotes human cooperation in the service of important needs and provides standards for resolving conflicts when conflicting needs are involved. Beyond the requirements of this function—and one of the objectives of this book is to analyze these requirements in order to draw a limit around them—any pressure toward consensus on behaviorally important values is undesirable, because we are now in the realm of individual rather than social components of needs.

In the beginning of this chapter the reader was asked to assume with me that a maximal freedom of expression is the supreme political value. First of all, let it be stressed that I do not claim objective validity for this value position. It is and must remain in large measure a matter of personal faith. Let it be noted, however, that I have called it the supreme *political* value. This means that I am relating this value to social rather than to individual aspects of human needs; and I am saying that a maximal freedom of expression is a political goal more conducive than other goals are to the realization of the social prerequisites for increasing satisfaction of the most important human needs.

It is decidedly premature at this stage of the behavioral sciences to expect a full proof or rejection of the contention that a maximal freedom of expression is supremely desirable on this ground. All I can do is to advance some tentative supporting considerations and beyond that, for the time being, fall back on a declaration of faith. There are two reasons why a couple of further remarks in substantiation of my basic value choice should be advanced. First, I have been claiming as a probability that what is now a personal faith to some extent may "materialize" into consensually validated political standards, in so far as some recent trends in psychology and anthropology will prove fruitful. Secondly, may I add that I wish to communicate also with people whose political goal formulations in many respects differ from mine.

---

[28] It is generally not sociologically necessary (for social cohesion or harmony) to demand more than overt compliance from would-be deviates, I am asserting; and I am recommending that, for this reason, nothing more ought to be politically required. Cf. below, pp. 276–80.

By a *norm* I understand an individual's expectation about behavior, whether justified or not, or his desire for a certain kind of behavior, whether shared with others or not, and whether accommodated or not. The expectation or the desire may refer to his own behavior or to that of other persons. Norms may or may not become institutionalized. Cf. below, pp. 262–63 and note 78.

No matter what values men hold, the freedom to pursue these values is important for them. To this extent they have a stake in a maximal freedom of expression, at least for themselves. And if a specific group is in no position to dominate the rest, it has a stake in a maximal freedom of expression for all, even if its goals in other respects may run counter to this one. I conclude that my inquiry is of relevance to some goal values, at least, of probably every individual and group in modern society.[29]

A fundamental value position cannot be proved, but it can be set forth in persuasive terms as an alternate line of approach toward consensual validation.[30] I believe in the fullest development of all human potentialities and faculties, in so far as they are nondestructive and not mutually incompatible. As a general rule, I believe that this development is furthered by a maximal freedom of expression for all individuals.

This position does not imply either a rejection or an affirmation of the materialist position that man's material needs in some sense "determine" his spiritual needs. I believe that a good standard of material living is a prerequisite for the fullest attainment of freedom of expression, but I do not think it guarantees a high level of freedom or even that it is necessarily a strong influence toward freedom. I do not affirm that free speech is more important than food in the stomach. On the contrary, if people starve, it is nonsense to expect them to care for free speech except, at most, as a means to articulating their demand for food. Starvation can confine the freedom of expression more effectively than can political tyranny.

"FREEDOM" AND OTHER VALUES

"Freedom," my crucial value concern in this book, means expression of individuality, or self-expression. This concept will be developed more fully in Chapter 3, with specification of its component sub-concepts. Let me at this stage be content with some vagueness, and choose as my empirical point of departure this observation: A person is free to the extent that he has the *capacity,* the *opportunity,* and the *incentive* to give expression to what is in him and to develop his potentialities.

No society can give full freedom to all individuals or, indeed, even to one individual. The price of social cooperation in the service of joint needs is acceptance of restraints; even a mere physical coexistence in the same society requires some restraints. Moreover, there are conflicts within every individual, too. He must keep some goals and impulses in check if he wants to promote or express others. I have already referred to the observation that men are apt to have short-term desires as well as long-term ideas of what is desirable. No person in any society can achieve maturity without experienc-

---

[29] Furthermore, a discussion of the strategy implications to be derived from one goal orientation is from a methodological point of view relevant to strategy problems connected with quite different goal orientations. This point is well stated in a forthcoming volume by Lasswell and McDougal: *Law, Science and Policy.*

[30] Albert Einstein has said that "It is the privilege of man's moral genius . . . to advance ethical axioms which are so comprehensive and so well founded that men will accept them as grounded in the vast mass of their individual emotional experiences. Ethical axioms are found and tested not very differently from the axioms of science. *Die Wahrheit liegt in der Bewährung.* Truth is what stands the test of experience." Quoted from Feigl and Brodbeck (eds.), *Readings in the Philosophy of Science,* p. 780.

ing conflicts of this and other kinds and thus sensing at times the necessity of restraining some of his impulses and drives.

The study of freedom maximization is clearly a very complex line of inquiry. It is in part an empirical investigation and in part a series of evaluations involving a number of more or less subjective decisions.[31] I am starting out, of course, with a valuation: that a maximal freedom of expression is supremely desirable; or, at the very least, that it is worth inquiring into the implications of this value orientation. The next type of question is empirical. To what extent do different exercises of freedom tend to cancel each other out within each individual? And to what extent do the possible freedom demands from different individuals tend to create conflicts? To the extent that seeds of conflict are discovered, a return to problems of evaluation is called for. By what criteria should conflicts between freedom values be solved? Or, more modestly, to what extent is it possible to establish such criteria plausibly enough to make it possible to hope for a wide consensus?

These problems will be the main concern of Part One. In Part Two I shall assemble empirical theory and research bearing on the extent to which each of the freedom values can be promoted by social techniques. In the concluding chapter I shall try to apply my findings about freedom values and their relationships in a discussion of freedom-promoting policies.

I wish to start out with taking for granted the restraints of our physical universe, as mediated by advances in modern technology. I shall be concerned with modern man in Western civilization. What types of restraints are operating on him to hamper his goals, narrow his vision, interfere with his ability and opportunity to formulate and execute an enduringly satisfying plan for his own life? Within my area of concern there appear to be three principal types of obstacles to the full development of human beings.

The first type of obstacle may be called *defensiveness*.[32] A variety of unfortunate circumstances in a person's social relationships from infancy on, and perhaps particularly in his defenseless early years, may contribute to neuroses of various kinds. Common to all neuroses is a deficiency in the orientation to one's self and to one's social surroundings. There is always too much anxiety to face some of the facts of life, outside oneself and above all inside oneself. This inability to cope with anxiety amounts to a strictly limited consciousness; the individual will energetically try to avoid perceiving the full play of his basic motives or needs. The result is an enduring deficiency in communication and, consequently, an enduring disharmony between his fundamental motives and his conscious self and overt behavior. It is plain that this state of affairs interferes with the free expression of a man's full individuality. This incapacity inside the person is in this book said to limit his *psychological freedom*.

A second type of obstacle to a full freedom of expression refers to the more obvious categories of *external rewards and punishments*. When a person strongly wants to do something (or remain passive) and is forcibly

---

[31] By "less subjective" decisions I mean decisions supported by a wide consensus.

[32] This term is used in a broad sense in this book. See below, p. 83.

restrained (pushed), we speak of "coercion." The same word is used also if he is still able to do what he wants but has to suffer as a consequence a severe punishment or the loss of a very important reward. It is also convenient to consider less severe or "noncoercive" punishments under this heading, which refers to restraints on what I call *social freedom.* Obstacles to social freedom presuppose the preexistence of a motive to do or not do something and consist typically in the interference of a negative-sanction probability that may or may not lead the person to comply with the norm or expectation to which the sanction is attached. At some point of severity of the sanction, and of strength of the original motive, I shall speak of *coercive* restraints on social freedom.

The third type of restraint on freedom that I wish to consider differs from the other two in that it does not interfere with the spontaneous functioning of the individual. These restraints hamper his potential behavior, not his actual behavior. They put limitations on what I call the individual's *potential freedom,* or his freedom from *manipulation.*

Karl Marx claimed that religion is an opiate for the people. It is not necessary either to agree or disagree with this assertion in order to realize that it points at the feasibility of an important social technique: for men of great power it is always possible to manipulate large numbers of people's beliefs in a direction that makes them more faithful subjects. Marx and his successors posed a new vision of society themselves, and they did not hesitate to try to countermanipulate people in order to promote this new ideal.

With the advent of mass communications this technique of manipulating people's beliefs has assumed greater and greater importance. Large-scale capitalist economies depend on the power of advertising. It instills in the people wants that they would otherwise presumably not have, and it greatly affects priorities among wants. And more and more the techniques of advertising are entering also the political arena, until we have reached the stage where the success or failure of candidates for important political office to a large extent depends on the amount of capital they can put into their advertising campaigns.[33]

To what extent do modern voters express choices that are really "their own"? This is one example of the type of question that I wish to consider in the discussion of potential freedom. It must first be asked to what extent man can become "autonomous."[34] We all live under social institutions and are dependent on them. Is it possible to distinguish between social institutions that are necessary for the welfare of each and all individuals and, on the other hand, institutions operating essentially for the benefit of a few? If this is possible, then one approach toward maximization of potential freedom is to find ways to increase man's ability for detachment and indepen-

---

[33] In *The Golden Kazoo* (Dell, 1956), a utopian novel about the American.Presidential election of 1960, John G. Schneider draws an amusing but sobering picture of U.S. politics completely in the hands of the big advertising firms. See also Part II, "Persuading Us as Citizens," in Vance Packard, *The Hidden Persuaders* (1957).

[34] "The 'autonomous' are those who on the whole are capable of conforming to the behavioral norms of their society . . . but are free to choose whether to conform or not." Riesman, with Glazer and Denney, *The Lonely Crowd: A Study of the Changing American Character* (Anchor Books), p. 278.

dence when confronted with institutions of the second type. Also, this involves increasing man's ability to resist deliberate manipulation by other men. In our culture, the latter type of restraint may be fully as important as institutional restraints.[35]

Let me now consider how the values of free expression can be related to the well-known scheme of eight values proposed by Harold Lasswell.[36] He does not claim that all humanly "preferred events" can be subsumed under these headings, but it will be generally agreed, I believe, that the net he spreads is a very wide one. Here is the list:

Power	Well-being
Respect	Wealth
Affection	Enlightenment
Rectitude	Skill

I believe that most people try to achieve some measure of all of these values, and they all figure in my own value scheme, too. I am not in this book concerned with finding out how each of these values rates, however, whether among my own preferences or among those of other people. Neither do I intend to inquire into the extent to which a wide sharing of values is feasible in each of these eight lines.

A belief in the supremacy of freedom of expression implies a concern that people so far as possible should have access to the values they actually or potentially want, and the word "potentially" refers to estimates of what they would want with progressing psychological freedom *and* autonomy.

If I had chosen to study the problem of "value maximization" in general, instead of the problem of freedom maximization, the inquiry would to a certain extent run parallel with the present one, but I should soon be faced with even much more complex problems of analysis. It is a great advantage, it seems to me, to be able to seek a common unit of analysis in terms of individual expression (actual or potential) of value demands. And, above all, it seems sensible also from a social engineering point of view to give top priority to the value of maximal freedom of expression, since this value, to the extent that it is achieved, automatically provides information about what other values are wanted, in what proportions, by what individuals. And freedom of expression assures each individual the opportunity to realize his different values, according to the relative importance each of them has to him.

It is surely not by chance that "freedom" is left out in Lasswell's scheme of values. It is a value concept of a different order—one that cuts across the eight values listed, not only as a means value, but as an intrinsic value as well. Men obviously want many different things in life—love, new experiences, travel, long life, and so on. A peculiar characteristic of the freedom value seems to be that it tends to enter other values as a necessary ingredient. At least in our civilization other values tend to be appreciated only

---

[35] Cf. below, pp. 331–34.
[36] See Lasswell, *Power and Personality*, p. 17; and Lasswell and Kaplan, *Power and Society*, pp. 55–56.

to the extent to which they can be enjoyed in freedom. Love tends to lose its attraction where it is enforced; a new experience is attractive only if one is free to stop and go back to the familiar. Even a long life may not appear worthwhile if it has to be a life in bondage. Freedom, indeed, seems to be a common element or an integral part of almost all other substantive values, for most people in our culture. Freedom is the soil required for the full growth of other values.

There is also another kind of value, for which all people seem to strive, that is not included among the eight. This is the value of *security*, which I would term a derivative value: *"Security" refers to the actual or perceived probability of the extension over time of the enjoyment of other values.*[37] Lasswell and Kaplan offer the following definition: *"Security* is high value expectancy, position, and potential; realistic expectancy of maintaining influence."[38] It will be seen that this concept is somewhat narrower than mine, in two respects: I am not assuming a "high" value expectancy, position, and potential, but only an expectancy or potential on a par with the present position, whether high or low. Furthermore, I am not focusing my security concept on the maintaining of influence; my use of the term implies that men conceivably may be or feel secure even in situations where they have no say at all, but are utterly dependent on other people. The typical situation of the infant is the first example that comes to mind.

Security is an important concept in this book, and it will be developed at some length in Chapter 3. I shall differentiate between component subconcepts: In the first place, there is the difference between objective and subjective security, or between being and feeling secure. But it is also important for various purposes to distinguish between two kinds of subjective security, which for lack of better terms I shall call "basic" and "surface" security, meaning the relative absence, respectively, of anxiety and of fear.

One crucial value that is included in Lasswell's list, but perhaps should not have been, is *power*. "Power" may, in the same way as "security," be used to refer to a derivative value, one that cuts across the other seven in the list. Indeed, my preference is to relate the two concepts quite closely, taking "power" to refer to the individual's degree of control over his security. More precisely, the "power" of an individual shall here refer to *the probable difference his own effort will make in his access to or advancement of values (including access to more power) in desired amounts and kinds.* A man is powerful to the extent that his own effort, whether by command, persuasion, or any other means, can affect the behavior of other people, or the course of impersonal events, toward maximizing the security of the values he shares or wishes to promote. One man's power may, but need not, mean restrictions on another man's freedom, depending on the

---

[37] "To speak of security is to emphasize that one is or expects to be free *over time*. But since this emphasis is already implicit in our definition of freedom, it is correct to say that security is merely an aspect or mode of freedom." Dahl and Lindblom, *Politics, Economics, and Welfare*, p. 49. Bentham, too, at times used a similar security concept, asserting that it "implies extension in point of time, with respect to all the benefits to which it is applied." See below, p. 42.

[38] *Power and Society*, p. 61.

way in which the power is exercised and on the initial commitments and inclinations of the other person.[39]

The power concept is of peculiar importance in this book because it is
closely related to the concept of politics. My book is in part (especially Part
One) a study in political ideals. Moreover, I shall argue that the freedom
of *political* speech is a freedom of crucial importance in the defense and promotion of the whole range of freedoms of expression.

Some writers have come close to identifying the study of political science
with the study of power or political power. Lasswell and Kaplan, for example, consider political science as a policy science concerned with the study
of influence and power as instruments of value distribution and integration.[40] Talcott Parsons conceives of political science as "the discipline concerned with political power and its use and control."[41] And David Easton
states that "political science is the study of the authoritative allocation of
values as it is influenced by the distribution and use of power."[42] The last
formulation seems a happy one, and I concur in this conception of political
science. I would, however, prefer to say "public values" instead of just
values."[43]

There are many good arguments for defining political science as the
science of power. Most important is the argument that all power phenomena, whether in the family, the community, or the state, should be
studied in the same context because they are alike in important respects.
Lasswell was the first behavioral scientist to point out effectively the advantage of studying the quest for governmental power in terms of personality dynamics,[44] and this important liaison between depth psychology and
the study of political science in a narrower sense is surely here to stay.

And yet, these considerations do not require anything more than a close
integration between the two fields, expressed in academic training and in
cooperative research. A strong tradition and some good reasons exist for
distinguishing between political science and the study of power. Many
problems of power need be of concern to few students of politics—for example, power relations among siblings, or spouses, or neighborhood retail merchants. On the other side, political science is also a study of values and goals
over and beyond the competition for power. Ludwig Freund has defined
politics as "those activities which aim at the satisfaction of public wants
(needs) and desires."[45] This definition may be too wide, since it would seem
to include such activities as the Sunday sermon, the human interest story in

---

[39] For a further discussion of concepts of "power," see below, pp. 248–60.

[40] *Power and Society*, p. xii. The function of the "policy sciences," it is said in the same
context, is "to provide intelligence pertinent to the integration of values realized by and embodied in interpersonal relations." See also Lerner and Lasswell (eds.), *The Policy Sciences:
Recent Developments in Scope and Method*, especially pp. 3–5.

[41] *The Social System*, p. 551.

[42] *The Political System: An Inquiry into the State of Political Science*, p. 146.

[43] Cf. above, p. 13, and note 27.

[44] See *Psychopathology and Politics*, and *World Politics and Personal Insecurity*.

[45] "A public *want* is a necessity, the satisfaction of which is demanded or consciously
striven for by the group. A public *desire* is the longing or striving on the part of the group, or
an important section thereof, for an object or a situation the realization of which would not
constitute a vital necessity." Freund, "Power and the Democratic Process: A Definition of
Politics," *Social Research*, XV (1948), 242–43.

the newspapers, and perhaps even the provision of pornography and prosti-tutes. And yet, Freund's definition also covers some pertinent grounds that elude those who define politics exclusively in power terms, such as the ques-tion of the aims of foreign and domestic policy beyond the attainment and maintenance of power. It seems to me, then, that there are three essential components in an adequate concept of politics or political science: power, public values, and authority. David Easton's concept of political science is the only one among those cited that includes reference to all three elements. If I may paraphrase his definition: *Politics refers to all the processes by which public values are promoted and distributed by means of power and authority.*

"Power" has just been defined, and the concept will be discussed at some length in Chapter 5. "Public values" has been defined as values oriented toward the assumed needs, desires, or interests of large numbers of people.[46] "Authority," finally, will be defined as the quality by virtue of which di-rectives are obeyed, independently of external sanctions.[47]

All power is not political, then; an apolitical example is the power of the robber in a holdup situation. All public values are not political, at least not in all situations; for example, the value of opening free public access to woods and beaches of large private estates is a public value to the extent that one or more individuals even tacitly favor such an arrangement, but it becomes a political value only if and when a demand to this effect, with public policy implications, is formulated. Authority relationships, again, are not always political; the authority of a father over his son, of the teacher over his student, or of the scientist over the layman is ordinarily not political. Indeed, in democratic theory it is assumed that authority relationships like these ought not to be extended to political matters; this is not to deny that they may, and at times quite properly, have political effects.

My conception of politics deviates, it is clear, from the traditions that have identified political science with the "science of the state"—whether the unity of territory or the monopoly of legitimate force has been considered the crucial attribute of the state in this context.[48] In my terminology every phenomenon is "political" to the extent that it has or is given relevance to the struggle for power and authority on behalf of public policies. Alfred de Grazia distinguishes between "politics, the politically relevant, and the po-litically conditioned."[49] I prefer to call political all phenomena that are studied as parts of the political process or as related to it. But in the study

[46] See above, p. 13.

[47] See below, p. 27 and note 107. This concept is different, be it noted, from Easton's definition of the same term: "A policy is authoritative when the people to whom it is intended to apply or who are affected by it consider that they must or ought to obey it." *The Political System*, p. 132. By his usage, unlike mine, authority may consist in a threat of brute force.

[48] Examples of such definitions: " 'Politics' connotes that organization of energies for the achievement of collective action which is concerned with social relationships within a given territory." (Niemeyer, *Law without Force: The Function of Politics in International Law*, p. 133.) " 'Politics' or 'political' includes the events that happen around the decision-making centers of government." (De Grazia, *The Elements of Political Science*, p. 13.) "Political sci-ence is a subject whose main and self-confessed object is knowledge of the actual government of political communities and, in the first place, of states." (Eisenmann, "On the Matter and Method of the Political Sciences," in *Contemporary Political Science: A Survey of Methods, Research and Teaching*, p. 103.)

[49] *The Elements of Political Science*, p. 13.

of political behavior one should distinguish between purposive and non-purposive political behavior and between effective and noneffective political behavior. "Purposive political behavior" refers to all behavior that is intended to influence public policies or the policies of groups that in turn intend to influence public policies. "Effective political behavior" refers to all behavior that does *in fact* exert such an influence, whether intended or not. By these two sets of categories all human behavior can be characterized in terms of one of these four logically possible combinations (though in practical life there are, of course, many borderline and composite cases) : purposive and effective political behavior; purposive and noneffective political behavior; effective though nonpurposive political behavior; and nonpolitical behavior. The political scientist, I submit, should be concerned with all but the last of these four kinds of behavior. His task is to study human behavior to the extent that it has political implications, or at the very least to study these implications.

It is of no important consequence to decide to what extent this inquiry falls inside the scope of political science, thus conceived. The problem I pose is primarily a political one, in the sense that I am seeking insight into the nature and implications of the freedom of expression and ultimately am trying to find out how it can be maximized by political means. In this process I shall have to draw on the insights and methods of the sciences of human behavior, in order to try to elucidate the underlying processes. This necessity emerges from the nature of the problem, however, and is indeed common to all comprehensive inquiries where problems of man and society are involved.

Controversies over the nature of "freedom" have been rampant since the dawn of philosophy. In much of this discussion, however, the object has been to discover whether man is a "free agent" in some ultimate sense—for example, in the sense that his decisions are not wholly determined by external causes or by general laws. The controversies have shifted ground as the definitions of "freedom" or of "free will" have shifted.[50] As a general rule, it has been found convenient to call the believers in some kind of a free will "indeterminists" and to call their opponents, who reject the various notions of a free will, "determinists."

For purposes of political theory, even when the task is to discuss "freedom," it is unnecessary to take a stand on the free-will issue. What matters in politics is not to discover whether man is or is not free in an ultimate sense where it is of no demonstrable factual consequence which answer is affirmed. For purposes of political analysis a freedom concept with clear

---

[50] An exhaustive critical study of the principal formulations of these problems has been done by Harald Ofstad, whose volume is forthcoming at the Oslo University Press. For a preliminary mimeographed edition, see Ofstad, *An Inquiry into the Freedom of Decision: An Analytical Approach to a Classical Problem,* Vols. I–IV. The breadth of his scope is indicated in the following chapter headings: Freedom as Absence of Compulsion, Freedom as Indeterminacy, Freedom as Self-Expression, Freedom as Rationality or Virtue, Freedom as Power. Unlike almost all previous writers in this field, Ofstad asserts and proceeds to demonstrate that "a thorough understanding of beliefs about man's freedom presupposes . . . interdisciplinarian research." *Ibid.,* I, 3.

behavioral implications is needed, a concept of *empirical* rather than *transcendental* freedom. When speaking of "freedom" as a policy goal, one needs some definite reference, either to an ascertainable *feeling* of freedom, or to an equally ascertainable objective state of affairs encouraging or permitting individual expression. Or one may wish to refer to both of these, or to other aspects of freedom as well. The aspects must be perceptible, however, at least to observers of the individuals whose freedom is being studied, if not also to the individuals themselves.[51]

Whatever the empirical reference, and my own choice will be made explicit in Chapter 3, the point I wish to make here is very simple: political theory is properly concerned with behavioral rather than transcendental problems. In proposing freedom in some experiential sense as the crucial policy goal, I am deliberately avoiding the question whether our human nature leaves us any scope to exert freedom in some transcendental or ultimate sense.

Only in one sense does it appear proper for a social scientist to have a bias in favor of a determinist position on the free-will problem. As a basic working hypothesis in psychological and social inquiry, it is expedient to assume that human behavior is explicable in terms of cause-effect relationships or at least in terms of probabilities of predictable relationships between events. The opposite assumption would, in effect, block any further inquiry. It may be said that the progress of all sciences generally has followed in the wake of bold hypotheses about relationships not yet explicable in empirical terms. All scientific theorizing, if it is to serve as a basis for useful, reliable knowledge, must not only assume the operation of general probability laws of causation or interrelation, but also give reference to crucial ways of testing their more specific derivations.

As a general working hypothesis, then, I assume that all kinds of human behavior that concern me in this book are potentially explicable in terms of predictable and demonstrable interrelationships. But I refrain from trying to answer the fundamental question whether this is really the case, as well as the related question whether or in what sense man may be said to have a free will.

It will be convenient in the following chapters to discuss "security" as if it were a value entirely independent of "freedom." This is and always has been the convention, for good reasons. While the logical interconnection between these two concepts is close, at least in my conceptual scheme, I grant that psychologically and socially it makes good sense to contrast the values of freedom and security. On the perceptual level, a sense of security and a sense of freedom are distinct psychological phenomena. It is at least arguable that the one can occur without the other, even if the present book will try to demonstrate a close interconnection, also psychologically, between the two. Exactly the same points can and will be made regarding freedom

---

[51] It would, of course, be impossible to study aspects of freedom that were perceptible to individuals but could not be communicated to others. Turning to the logical opposite, it makes sense to Rousseau and Bosanquet to speak of a kind of freedom that is perceptible to observers but not to the individuals in question; this assumption is implied in the notion of forcing men to be free. My concept of potential freedom rests on the same assumption.

and security as objective or social phenomena. The important point to be stressed here is that I wish to demonstrate and discuss these interconnections instead of taking them for granted by definition. This is the chief reason why in Chapters 2 and 3 "freedom" will be contrasted with "security."

To assert that "security" is desirable, moreover, is not necessarily to assert that "freedom," too, is desirable, for the former term may be used to refer to the stability over time of any substantive values. The only constant minimum of meaning that I shall always attribute to such an assertion is that some amount of stability is desirable. For reasons to be developed later,[52] no serious psychologist or social scientist can fail to assert that a certain minimum of stability or security is desirable or indeed necessary, for all individuals and for all societies, in so far as the continued life or health of these people is held desirable.

My concern in Part One will be with the clarification of the freedom values, including the security values. Chapter 2 will discuss the uses of freedom and security concepts in two important traditions in political philosophy. I shall try to show how my conception of "freedom" draws on the insights of empiricists as well as idealists. A systematic exposition of the freedom values will be attempted in Chapter 3.

[52] See below, pp. 162–69 and 265–67.

Part One

THE FREEDOM VALUES

2

Empiricist and Idealist Contributions

to the Study of Freedom

The English utilitarians combined a passion for political reform with a persuasive philosophy that grew out of empiricist antecedents. I shall consider, in this section, some empiricist views on "freedom" and "security," as a preliminary to stating and evaluating the relevant tenets of utilitarianism. The utilitarian views that I shall discuss are those of William Godwin, Jeremy Bentham, James Mill, and John Stuart Mill. Among their predecessors, I shall refer briefly to contributions of Thomas Hobbes, John Locke, and David Hume.

All these philosophers were empiricists in the sense that they insisted on relying on their own power of observation rather than on the observations of Aristotle or the Bible. With the partial exception of Locke, they recognized no a priori imperatives, no a priori virtues or duties—or so they thought. These men were among the earliest proponents of the empirical approach in social and political theory. This approach later proved victorious in several social sciences, notably in economics, psychology, and sociology, and it has also made deep inroads in political theory.[1]

The somewhat overconfident positivism of most empiricists has been challenged successfully by Burke and by many others since. There are few social scientists today who seriously believe that all social and political problems can be successfully or definitely solved even if all our resources of observation and research techniques and reason are invested. Many problems may be beyond our reach—either because they are unsolvable or because we have not advanced far enough yet in general or in some special knowledge.

Modern political scientists have a greater sense of the complexities of

---

[1] In present-day terminology, one may define "empirical political theory" as follows: "A body of propositions generalizing the experience from numerous controlled observations of political phenomena, being continually subject to further confirmation or disconfirmation, on all levels of abstraction." In our day many large-scale research projects on political behavior are being carried out, and their conclusions are of increasing concern to political theorists.

political society and political behavior, which recommends a cautious em-pirical approach and a measure of skepticism about conclusions, since no scientifically derived answers are final in the sense that they cannot be modified by further research.[2] We realize also the important role in politics of value positions or preferences about which men permanently may differ. Finally, we realize that human beings are rational only to a limited extent and that they have honest differences in their conceptions of the truth, even in areas of relative simplicity and even about the best means to promote shared values.

Thomas Hobbes (1588–1679)

"Liberty, or Freedome," according to Hobbes, "signifieth (properly) the absence of Opposition; (by Opposition, I mean externall Impediments of motion;) . . . A FREE-MAN, is he, that in those things, which by his strength and wit he is able to do, is not hindered to doe what he has a will to."[3] This conception of freedom as an absence of an "externall im-pediment of motion" is essentially shared by all the empiricist philosophers. And it is certainly a plausible and legitimate way of using the term. If one could count the usages of the word in modern everyday life, this conception would probably, in its various nuances, prove the most widespread of all.

According to this conception a man cannot be considered unfree unless he is coerced against his own will. In this sense of freedom, Hobbes as-sumes that a subject in his authoritarian dictatorship is much more free than a man in the state of nature. The latter, though theoretically perfectly free to act as he pleases, is in practice living in a state of perpetual fear and unfreedom, constantly hampered and threatened by his fellow men, who are equally "free."

Hobbes seems to have envisaged a considerable amount of economic free-dom in the sense of laissez-faire in his authoritarian state. He considered a relatively free flow of goods as much less dangerous than a comparable free flow of ideas. When enumerating a number of "Diseases of a Common-wealth" he puts in the second place "the poyson of seditious doctrines; whereof one is, *That every private man is Judge of Good and Evil actions.*"[4] He pictured every political criticism as the first step toward sedition and civil war, and he advocated stern suppression of any such tendencies.

The obligation to obey Hobbes's sovereign is conditional only on the lat-ter's ability to provide protection for his subjects, both against civil disorder and against foreign invasion. If he fails in this, automatically the social order on which sovereignty is based ceases to exist. Society reverts to the state of nature with free-for-all fighting once more, unless a new Leviathan appears who is strong enough to maintain order.

[2] This attitude was shared and indeed first developed in Hume's theory of knowledge, but it was conspicuously absent in most utilitarian writings, especially in those of Bentham, James Mill, and William Godwin.

[3] *Leviathan* (Everyman's Library), p. 110; cf. p. 66.

[4] *Ibid.,* p. 172. Compare from another context: ". . . in a multitude of men there are many who, supposing themselves wiser than others, endeavour to innovate, and divers in-novators innovate divers ways; which is a mere distraction and civil war." Even a parliamentary system (and Hobbes favors the preservation of the existing political system, whatever it is) would indeed be functioning in an authoritarian manner to the extent that this orientation prevails. See Hobbes, *Philosophical Elements of a True Citizen,* in his *English Works,* II, p. 67.

One of the few basic concepts that Hobbes leaves vaguely defined is "security," and this was the value that he placed above all others. He favored an authoritarian dictatorship because he believed that the most security for individual lives could be found at the opposite pole from anarchy. For the same reason, he favored the preservation of whatever political system is actually insuring peace and order at the time. In civil society, according to Hobbes, "all the duties of rulers are contained in this one sentence, *the safety of the people is the supreme law*."[5] The security that Hobbes valued above anything else was not limited to bare physical survival: "But by safety here, is not meant a bare Preservation, but also all other contentments of life, which every man by Lawful Industry, without danger, or hurt to the Commonwealth, shall acquire to himselfe."[6]

This conception of security serves the function of embracing everything that Hobbes considered valuable—much as the present writer tends to use "freedom" in a corresponding way. But an attempt will be made in this study to analyze some specific meanings of freedom, while Hobbes, who was otherwise so concise and careful with his terms, was content to take the meaning of "security" for granted.

John Locke (1632–1704)

Locke's *Second Treatise of Government*[7] was in a sense an answer to the *Leviathan,* but it was a weak reply in that Locke never achieved a level of clearness about fundamentals or a degree of consistency even remotely comparable to what Hobbes achieved. Nevertheless, this brief essay has had a tremendous influence in the practical promotion of human freedom, especially in the Anglo-Saxon world. This is above all due to Locke's persuasive vindication of what he called natural rights.

The function of the theories of natural law and of social contract, in Locke's version, is to explain the existence, since time immemorial, of inviolable human rights. Or, more accurately, to vindicate such rights by giving them the sanctity of eternal law and timeless tradition and ultimately of God Himself. Before looking into the basic values embodied in these natural rights, let us for a moment consider how he derives them from his construction of the state of nature: "The natural liberty of man is to be free from any superior power on earth, and not to be under the will of legislative authority of man, but to have only the law of Nature for his rule."[8] There are three principal inconveniences in the state of nature that men want to remedy by instituting a civil society: the lack of a written and generally accepted law; the lack of a generally recognized and impartial judge to apply the law; and the absence of an authorized police power to enforce it.[9]

The social contract is the remedy, and it has no *raison d'être* beyond being a remedy for these specific wants. It cannot legitimately take away

[5] *Ibid.*, p. 166.
[6] *Leviathan*, p. 178. Cf. *Philosophical Elements*, p. 167 and below, pp. 65–66.
[7] The title of the essay that is usually referred to as the Second Treatise is "An Essay Concerning the True, Original Extent and End of Civil Government." It is printed in John Locke, *Two Treatises of Civil Government* (Everyman's Library).
[8] *Ibid.*, p. 127.
[9] *Ibid.*, p. 180.

anything from individuals beyond what is required for this purpose. In other words, no party to the social contract can ever be assumed to have given up his natural liberty except in exchange for a maximum amount of civil liberty. Locke derived his vindication of human rights by deduction from his conception of the nature of political society, as it was instituted by the social contract under the laws of nature. His very definition of political power, as opposed to both paternal and despotic power, embodies this vindication: "Political power is that power which every man having in the state of Nature has given up into the hands of the society, and therein to the governors whom the society hath set over itself, with this express or tacit trust, that it shall be employed for their good and the preservation of their property."[10] He indicates, however, that he uses "property" in an unusually broad sense, as he speaks of "the mutual preservation of their lives, liberties and estates, which I call by the general name—property."[11]

Elements of both security and freedom are immersed in this concept. Yet it is scarcely by chance that Locke chose the word "property" as the common denominator for his range of basic political values. He certainly had a strong sense for the sanctity of property in the conventional sense, and so had the Whig audience for whom he wrote. At times it seems that the right to property in his scheme of values takes precedence over the right to life itself.[12]

Freedom, as Locke understands this concept, is inseparable from security. He rejects Sir Robert Filmer's definition, "A liberty for every one to do what he lists, to live as he pleases, and not to be tied by any laws," and instead states that "freedom of men under government is to have a standing rule to live by, common to every one in that society, and made by the legislative power erected in it. . . . This freedom from absolute, arbitrary power is so necessary to, and closely joined with, a man's preservation, that he cannot part with it but by what forfeits his preservation and life together."[13] The purpose of legislation is to promote freedom by promoting stability and security under the law.[14] Locke's conception of the relationship between freedom and security comes rather close to the view advanced in this book to the effect that security is the time dimension of freedom.[15] At any rate, in his very definition of freedom he stresses the intimate interconnection between these two values.

[10] *Ibid.*, pp. 205–6.

[11] *Ibid.*, p. 180.

[12] A conqueror, Locke states on p. 209, *ibid.*, has an absolute right over the lives of those who, by an unjust war, have forfeited them, but he has no right to take their possessions. "The right, then, of conquest extends only to the lives of those who joined in the war, but not to their estates" (p. 211). Also, on the same page, "I may kill a thief that sets on me in the highway, yet I may not (which seems less) take away his money and let him go; this would be robbery on my side."

[13] *Ibid.*, p. 128. This is also a further development of the argument for declaring invalid any social contract that would abolish or drastically reduce the freedom of individuals.

[14] "The end of the law is not to abolish or restrain, but to preserve and enlarge freedom. For in all the states of created beings, capable of laws, where there is no law there is no freedom. For liberty is to be free from restraint and violence from others, which cannot be where there is no law." *Two Treatises of Civil Government,* p. 143.

[15] See above, p. 19.

Locke was a proponent of "freedom" in a second sense also, however, a sense that on the surface might seem less compatible with the security value. That is the assertion of the (propertied) people's right to make revolution against an oppressive government.[16] On closer scrutiny this kind of freedom, too, serves to buttress the kind of security under the law that Locke is advocating. He argues that a right to revolution will never be utilized except as the very last resort in an intolerable situation. He assumes, therefore, that the practical effect of asserting such a right, rather than fomenting lawlessness on the part of the people, will be to encourage any government to respect the people's freedom and rights under the law.

With regard more specifically to freedom of speech, Locke does not make a frontal approach to this problem in his treatises on government, although he clearly implies the desire for a wide latitude. He emphasizes, in one context, the need for mature debate as a prerequisite for intelligent voting.[17] He speaks most clearly on this subject in the *Letters on Toleration,* even if the context is theological. Locke favored what were for his time rather wide limits for freedom of expression. He excepted, however, Catholics and atheists, scoring the former for having an alien loyalty and the latter for having no loyalty to any authority or indeed to any moral standard. But for Protestant Christians who were loyal to their country he favored a wide freedom of speech on political matters, even to the extent, as we have seen, of arguing for a right to advocate a revolution.[18]

David Hume (1711–76)

Hume is the first of the philosophers discussed here who includes both freedom and security as basic political values and tries to strike a balance between the two. Unlike Locke, he tends to see these values primarily as opposites:

> In all governments, there is a perpetual intestine struggle, open or secret, between *authority* and *liberty*; and neither of them can ever absolutely prevail in the contest. A great sacrifice of liberty must necessarily be made in every government. . . . It must be owned that liberty is the perfection of civil society; but still authority must be acknowledged essential to its very existence; and in those contests which so often take place between the one and the other, the latter may, on that account, challenge the preference. Unless perhaps one may say (and it may be said with some reason) that a circumstance which is essential to the existence of civil society must always support itself, and needs be guarded with less jealousy, than one that contributes only to its perfection, which the indolence of men is so apt to neglect, or their ignorance to overlook.[19]

In *A Treatise on Human Nature* the young Hume had been inclined toward a libertarian position in this most basic dilemma in the conflict between liberty and authority, the dilemma that we today may call the question of conditional or unconditional loyalty to the nation's government.

---

[16] *Two Treatises of Civil Government,* pp. 195–96.
[17] *Ibid.,* pp. 229–30.
[18] *Works, V,* see esp. p. 49.
[19] *Theory of Politics,* pp. 156 ff.

He had followed Locke in asserting a people's right to defend itself, by revolution if necessary, against abuse of governmental power. Indeed, he is quite vehement on this point, claiming that those "who would seem to respect our free government, and yet deny the right to resistance, have renounced all pretensions to common sense, and do not merit a serious answer."[20] Resistance in cases of tyrannical oppression is perfectly justified, he claims, because tyranny is in conflict with all good reasons of utility behind the establishment and the continual support of political government. "Whenever the civil magistrate carries his oppression so far as to render his authority perfectly intolerable, we are no longer bound to submit to it. The cause ceases; the effect must cease also."[21] And he is not opposed to militant measures if necessary to bring the downfall of a tyranny: "In all our notions of morals, we never entertain such an absurdity as that of passive obedience, but make allowances for resistance in the more flagrant cases of tyranny and oppression."[22]

In the *Essays* we find no statements of this kind, but quite a few that indicate a more authoritarian position on the basic liberty-security dilemma. At this stage his conceptions of political loyalty are more reminiscent of Hobbes than of Locke: "A small degree of experience and observation suffices to teach us that society cannot possibly be maintained without the authority of magistrates, and that this authority must soon fall into contempt where exact obedience is not paid to it."[23] Like Hobbes, he is now more afraid of anarchy than of tyranny, and majority rule would in his opinion amount to the same as as anarchy, at least if it were to be established suddenly: "In reality, there is not a more terrible event than a total dissolution of government, which gives liberty to the multitude, and makes the determination or choice of a new establishment depend upon a number which nearly approaches to that of the body of the people."[24]

Conceptions of human nature are usually good indicators of attitudes toward freedom vs. authority. If you have a poor opinion of the average human being or of his ability to master a difficult existence (Hobbes), it is natural to favor many external restraints on his behavior. If you are optimistic about human nature, on the other hand, it is natural to believe in a wide freedom of expression. Hume took a moderate position on this issue: "The qualities of the mind are *selfishness* and *limited generosity*. . . . The selfishness of men is animated by the few possessions we have, in proportion to our wants; and it is to restrain this selfishness, that men have been obliged to separate themselves from the community, and to distinguish betwixt their own goods and those of others."[25] These considerations appear so obvious to Hume that he leaves his habitual skepticism behind and calls

---

20 *A Treatise on Human Nature* (Everyman's Library), II, 262–63.
21 *Ibid.*, p. 250.
22 *Ibid.*, p. 252.
23 *Theory of Politics*, pp. 208–9.
24 *Ibid.*, p. 200.
25 *A Treatise on Human Nature*, II, 199–200. Immediately preceding the last paragraph, he says: "Increase to a sufficient degree the benevolence of men, *or the bounty of nature,* and you render justice useless, by supplying its place with much nobler virtues, and more valuable blessings." My italics.

it "a proposition, which, I think, may be regarded as certain, *that it is only from the selfishness and confined generosity of man, along with the scanty provision nature has made for his wants, that justice derives its origin.*"[26] Our notions of justice and injustice, or right and wrong, have two foundations, "that of *interest,* when men observe that it is impossible to live in society without restraining themselves by certain rules; and that of *morality,* when this interest is once observed, and men receive a pleasure from the view of such actions as tend to the peace of society, and an uneasiness from such as are contrary to it."[27] Standards of morality and of justice are what Hume calls "artifacts"; they are neither divinely ordained, nor an integral part of original human nature, nor revealed by pure reason. They are an outcome of the practical experience of mankind, and the sole consideration in the slow test of time is the utility each moral rule can demonstrate toward promoting human welfare. Hume may be called a precursor to Darwin in the sphere of ethics. In effect, he proclaimed a doctrine of the survival of the fittest among human conventions—fittest not in terms of good teeth but in terms of maximum social utility.

William Godwin (1756–1836)

William Godwin was the most radical political theorist among the utilitarians. Though he was eight years younger than Bentham, his brief period of influence came before Bentham's fame had reached his own country. Godwin's principal political work, *Political Justice,* which was published in 1793, presented a spirited vindication of an unlimited freedom of expression.[28]

Godwin's conception of freedom is in the empiricist tradition. He does not define the concept explicitly and contributes no important new insights about the nature of freedom. But among the empiricists he was the most extreme advocate of this value, and it may be instructive to follow some aspects of his main argument.

Godwin shared with Hobbes and other English empiricists the conviction that government is instituted for the benefit of the people and that the exercise of governmental power can be justified only to the extent that it can be proved beneficial for the people—more beneficial, that is, than no government, less government, or a different kind of government. That is about as far as the agreement goes between Hobbes and Godwin. Their conceptions of human nature and of the nature of society were extremely different.

The maximum freedom of individual minds from the shackles of authority is Godwin's basic value premise. It is on this assumption that the core of his empirical argument rests. His most important empirical premises are these: (1) Human nature is subject to change, and it is perfectible: "Man considered in himself is merely a being capable of impression,

26 *Ibid.,* p. 200.
27 *Ibid.,* p. 234.
28 William Godwin. *An Enquiry Concerning Political Justice and Its Influence on General Virtue and Happiness.* When not otherwise stated, my references will be to the first edition, as it was reissued in a slightly abbreviated form by Raymond A. Preston and published by Knopf.

a recipient of perceptions. What is there in this abstract character that precludes him from advancement? We have a faint discovery in individuals at present of what our nature is capable; why should individuals be fit for so much, and the species for nothing?"[29] (2) Organized force exerted by governments is constantly aiding error to block the spread of truth and is therefore keeping the minds of men in bondage. Government, Godwin says, "is nothing more than a scheme for enforcing by brute violence the sense of one man or set of men upon another."[30] The further we advance in our search for the truth, "the more simple and self-evident will it appear, and it will be found impossible to account for its having been so long concealed than from the pernicious influence of positive institution."[31] (3) The gradual reduction of governmental authority and power will automatically make the citizens more free and thus more just and reasonable. "Simplify the social system in the manner which every motive but those of usurpation and ambition powerfully recommends and the whole species will become reasonable and virtuous.[32] [Again,] free men in whatever country will be firm, vigorous and spirited in proportion to their freedom."[33]

The society Godwin envisages is almost diametrically opposed to that of Hobbes. Hobbes, in his aversion for anarchy, proposed an all-powerful state giving no institutional restraints against the emergence of the most ruthless despotism. Godwin's position is that "anarchy is a horrible calamity, but it is less horrible than despotism."[34] So much less horrible is anarchy to him that the political community he hoped would be established would have no substantial institutional guarantees against disintegration toward anarchy. Yet it must be pointed out, in fairness to Godwin, that he was a consistent gradualist who wanted the reforms to come only when the people were ready for them. It is easy to ridicule his lyrical vision of the future dissolution of government,[35] but it is by no means obviously unrealistic to maintain, as he did, that men may progressively become more socially responsible, and gradually somewhat less in need of judges and jails, as they become more enlightened.

Though one cannot, in the light of modern psychology and psychiatry, accept his conception of man as primarily a rational being, I submit that Godwin had an admirable insight, for his time, into the relationship be-

---

[29] *Ibid.,* I, 248–49. On p. 11, in the same volume: "Perfectibility is one of the most unequivocal characteristics of the human species."

[30] *Ibid.,* p. 126.

[31] *Ibid.,* II, 27. On p. 11 in vol. 1 he assumes "that of all the modes of operating upon mind government is the most considerable."

[32] *Ibid.,* p. 70.

[33] *Ibid.,* I, 30. Godwin concludes, in another context (*ibid.,* p. 126): "That government therefore is the best which in no one instance interferes with the exercise of private judgment without absolute necessity."

[34] He continues: "Where anarchy has slain its hundreds, despotism has sacrificed millions upon millions, with this only effect, to perpetuate the ignorance, the vices and the misery of mankind. Anarchy is a short lived mischief, while despotism is all but immortal." Quoted from the second edition of *Political Justice,* II, 175.

[35] "With what delight must every well-informed friend of mankind look forward to the auspicious period, the dissolution of political government, of that brute engine which has been the only perennial cause of the vices of mankind." *Political Justice,* Preston's version of the first edition, II, 71.

tween social structure and personality type. In a true democracy, he declares, "Each man would thus be inspired with a consciousness of his own importance, and the slavish feelings that shrink up the soul in the presence of an imagined superior would be unknown."[36] By contrast, in a monarchy you have not only an autocrat but an authoritarian society:

There must be the ministers of ministers and a long bead roll of subordination descending by tedious and complicated steps. Each of these lives on the smile of the minister, as he lives on the smile of the sovereign. Each of these has his petty interests to manage and his empire to employ under the guise of servility. Each imitates the vices of his superior and exacts from others the adulation he is obliged to pay.[37]

Like Locke before him and John Stuart Mill after him, Godwin maintains that the benevolent autocrat creates even more harm than the outright despot, in the long run: all the mischief of an authoritarian society is "more strongly fastened upon us under a good monarch than under a bad one. In the latter case it only restrains our efforts by violence; in the former it seduces our understandings."[38] And in his most general statement on power and personality he anticipated a famous maxim of Lord Acton's: "Where powers beyond the capacity of human nature are intrusted, vices the disgrace of human nature will be engendered."[39]

How far is it possible to agree with Godwin?

I accept his belief that a near-perfect freedom of expression should be the most important goal of a democratic society, with the reservation that considerations of security against violence—a crucial aspect of the same value—must be given equally high priority.

I accept his premise of human perfectibility, with the important reservations that I do not know just how far human beings can advance in social consciousness and responsibility and that I do not believe the advance can proceed by leaps and bounds.

I accept a watered-down version of his second empirical premise that governments tend to discourage, if they can, the spread of "dangerous" ideas. But I emphatically reject Godwin's implication that governments are the only, or even necessarily the most effective, agents of suppression.

For this reason, I reject his third premise outright. Contrary to Godwin's belief, a gradual abolition of government would immediately increase the leeway for private power hierarchies. And this means, be it noted, an increase primarily in institutionally irresponsible power, at the expense of a power hierarchy that can be made subject to some measure of control from

---

[36] *Ibid.*, I, 101.

[37] *Ibid.*, p. 219. This is an admirable statement of the manipulative orientation, to be discussed in psychological and sociological terms below. See especially pp. 191–92 and 329–34. To what extent men of power in an authoritarian society tend to be defensive authoritarians is a different problem; see especially pp. 191–92 and 307–12.

[38] *Ibid.*, p. 238. Cf. Locke, *Two Treatises of Civil Government* (Everyman's Library), p. 202, and John Stuart Mill, *Representative Government* (Everyman's Library), p. 378.

[39] *Political Justice*, I, 251.

below, by way of elections and parliaments.[40] Godwin's perception of society was entirely political; the only power structure he saw was that of the political government.

Jeremy Bentham (1748–1832), James Mill (1773–1836), and John Stuart Mill (1806–73)

Each of the four empiricists referred to above contributed to the cause of freedom extension, though in very different ways. Hobbes and Hume contributed chiefly on a philosophical level, in developing concepts, distinctions, and hypotheses that remain at the basis of whatever we have today of a science of politics. Locke, too, contributed toward a more adequate formulation of the problem of freedom, but it is the practical impact of his vindication of human rights that makes him so important in the history of the growth of freedom. Godwin was the least important of these four, although his zeal for freedom was the greatest. I believe his vindication of a maximal freedom of expression has not been given the attention it deserves. A progressively more enlightened age may well make his premises appear less naïve and some of his conclusions less absurd.

It remained for the Benthamites, also called philosophical radicals or utilitarian liberals, to develop a whole system of philosophy that would transform the promotion of human welfare into a science of politics and legislation. Their explicit goal was not a maximal freedom for all, it is true, but the greatest happiness of the greatest number. There are indeed some very important differences in value priorities between their philosophy and the view expounded here. But the similarities are also great, and it is worth while to consider critically, not only the conceptions of freedom defended by the Benthamites, but also some of the fundamentals of the utilitarian approach to politics. I hope to make clear in the process how much I am indebted to them.

Jeremy Bentham, James Mill, and John Stuart Mill were the most important utilitarian liberals. Bentham and the older Mill worked intimately together throughout the last decades of their lives and apparently agreed on most issues. I shall refer to these two as the orthodox utilitarians. After their death John Stuart Mill, though never consciously abandoning the utilitarian cause, nevertheless developed many views that deviated from Bentham's and the elder Mill's.

The philosophical premises that were adopted wholeheartedly by Bentham, James Mill, and many of their followers, though not without crucial reservations by the younger Mill, may be listed as follows:[41]

1. Happiness is the only fundamental and intrinsic value. Happiness is equivalent to the sum of pleasure minus the sum of pain.

[40] Among nongovernmental pressure centers and sources of power certain types of associations, such as trade unions, are as susceptible to some degree of control from below as a political government—and possibly more so.

[41] Plamenatz lists substantially the same doctrines as indicated in the following nos. 1, 3, and 5, and then adds as a fourth tenet a negative formulation· roughly equivalent to a combination of my Nos. 2 and 5: "Men's obligations to the government of the country in which they live, and that government's duties to them, have nothing to do with the way in which the government first acquired power or now maintains it, except to the extent to which these origins and methods affect its ability to carry out these duties." *The English Utilitarians*, p. 2.

2. The only legitimate standard with which to evaluate social institutions, and things and events in general, is their probable or demonstrable utility in promoting happiness.

3. All men are equal, in the sense that an equal amount of happiness for any two people is equally valuable.

4. Men's only duty to themselves is to promote their own happiness. In Bentham's words, "Private ethics teaches how each man may dispose himself to pursue the course most conducive to his own happiness." The corresponding virtue is called "prudence."[42]

5. Men's only duty to their fellow men and to society is to promote the general happiness: "Ethics at large may be defined, the art of directing men's actions to the production of the greatest possible quantity of happiness, on the part of those whose interest is in view." The corresponding virtues are called "probity" and "beneficence."[43]

6. All values, positive and negative, can be reduced to common units of pleasure and pain, and are thus in principle subject to comparative measurement. This enables the legislator or the scientist to make objectively correct choices between alternative policies, by calculating, on the basis of all available knowledge, the amounts of happiness and unhappiness likely to be produced by each policy alternative.[44]

I have now stated five basic value premises and one methodological premise concerning the nature of values. The latter assumption has implications about human nature as well. The orthodox utilitarian view of human nature is more directly indicated, however, in the following four assumptions:

7. The human mind consists of sensations that are tied together by associations. Sensations are desired or detested according to the extent to which they are associated with pleasure or pain. To the extent that the legislator or the moral authority can provide an incentive system that associates the pleasure of one individual with the pleasure of all, it is possible to make human nature more agreeable to and productive of social harmony. This optimistic psychological view was elaborated in James Mill's *Analysis of the Phenomena of the Human Mind* (1829).

8. Men are predominantly selfish. "In the general tenor of life, in every human breast, self-regarding interest is predominant over all other interests put together."[45] But the pleasures individuals seek are not *necessarily* in conflict; for example, among the pleasures enumerated in the *Introduction to Morals and Legislation* are benevolence, as well as malevolence.

[42] "An Introduction to the Principles of Morals and Legislation," in Bentham, *Works,* I, 143, 148.

[43] *Ibid.*, pp. 142, 148. "Probity" means "forbearing to diminish" the happiness of others; "beneficence" means "studying to increase it."

[44] The reputation of utilitarians for being "mere calculating machines" (Cf. John Stuart Mill, *Autobiography,* p. 109) does not seem altogether far-fetched in view of a statement like this: "The utility of all these arts and sciences . . . is exactly in proportion to the pleasure they yield. Every other species of pre-eminence which may be attempted to be established among them is altogether fanciful. Prejudice apart, the game of push-pin is of equal value with the arts and sciences of music and poetry. If the game of push-pin furnish more pleasure, it is more valuable than either." Bentham seems in general to lean toward push-pin, as it can be enjoyed by more people, and, unlike poetry, always is harmless. *Works,* II, 253–54.

[45] From the Preface to the "Constitutional Code" (1827), in Bentham, *Works,* IX, 5.

9. Men are individualists, in the sense that their goals tend to be private rather than public, separate rather than shared. Each man is the master of his own goals. This conception of society as essentially a sum of free-floating individuals has been called atomism, and it was more or less explicitly adhered to by all the English empiricists reviewed in this chapter, with the possible exception of John Stuart Mill.[46] It is crucial in the thought of Bentham and James Mill, because their imposing structure of policy recommendations rested explicitly on this view of human nature.

10. Finally, the Benthamites made the assumption that man is essentially a rational being. Bentham and James Mill apparently were just as confident as Godwin was that men will go about the rational pursuit of intelligently premeditated goals, to the extent that they become sufficiently well educated.

Among these ten most important tenets in the utilitarian credo, particularly the first three must have been instrumental in creating the strong appeal this ideology had among intellectuals—Utility was seen as the shining key to the coming Kingdom of Happiness on this earth. None of these thoughts was new, but the way they were combined, and the confidence and radicalism with which they were applied, was something new and exciting. The new vistas of a more sensible and a better world, built on easily comprehensible principles, were bound to give rise to a real intellectual movement, once they were made accessible to readers of moderate literacy—above all by the simple and forceful expositions of James Mill.

From these assumptions Bentham and his followers derived a number of plausible practical conclusions. First of all, it is up to the legislator to establish a social incentive system of maximum utility toward promoting general happiness. In Halévy's phrase, the utilitarians considered legislation "the science of intimidation."[47] In criminal law, they agreed, sanctions of punishment are much more important than rewards, but in other fields of law the utilitarians were just as eager to encourage good behavior by positive incentives as they were to discourage bad behavior by "intimidation."

Secondly, they advocated universal education, as a means of enabling the greater number to protect their interest against the "sinister interest" of the more powerful few. Since happiness was the only goal, Bentham was during most of his life not much concerned with problems of intellectual advancement by education for the people as a whole.[48] But after his friendship with Mill Bentham realized that democracy, or a representative government based on a fairly wide suffrage, was a necessary means of reducing political exploitation and, furthermore, that universal education was a necessary means of making democracy work.

---

[46] *Cf.* below, p. 40.

[47] Cf. Halévy, *The Growth of Philosophical Radicalism*, p. 487.

[48] In the "Panopticon," when discussing the inspection-house principle in application to schools, Bentham argues that the school boys ought to be under inspection twenty-four hours a day. In this context he makes a statement, which has often been quoted, about the goal of education: "Would *happiness* be most likely to be increased or diminished by this kind of discipline?—Call them soldiers, call them monks, call them machines: so that they were but happy ones, I should not care." *Works,* IV, 64.

I am now anticipating the third and perhaps the most important part of the political program of the utilitarians: the advocacy of reforms toward making parliament a more representative assembly, both by reapportionment of seats in favor of the populous areas at the expense of the rotten boroughs and by gradual extension of the suffrage. Bentham died just after the third reading of the Reform Bill in 1832, which was the first great victory for utilitarian principles, even if the parliamentary victory of course was the immediate work of the Whigs.

Let me briefly state here the main points at which John Stuart Mill slipped out of the old utilitarian scheme—perhaps without a full awareness of the extent to which he deviated. While ostensibly affirming that happiness is the only intrinsic value, Mill conceded to the critics of utilitarianism that some pleasures are inherently superior to others.[49] Secondly, he came out for the freedom of the individual as an intrinsic value. Regardless of its consequences for individual happiness, Mill placed a high value on a maximum freedom to develop and express individual tastes and beliefs without interference.[50]

By these two concessions Mill actually denied five of the six fundamental utilitarian assumptions concerning values—all except the equality assumption. All five imply that happiness is the only value. If some pleasures are superior to others, it is no longer possible to calculate the merits of social policies simply on the basis of mere amounts of pleasure and pain expected to follow in their wake. Questions of deliberate choice by other criteria as well creep in, much as Mill tries to lock the door.[51] And if there are other ultimate values in addition to mere pleasure or mere happiness, the whole felicity-calculus is left hanging in the air, and it becomes a new and more complicated problem how to define men's duties to themselves and each other or men's "true interests."

These heresies are placed in a wider context in his *Logic*—a context affecting also the four premises about human nature in orthodox utilitarianism. In fact, Mill takes issue with the Benthamites' very method of scientific reasoning.[52] In his own words, he objected that they used the geometrical or abstract deductive instead of the physical or concrete deductive model in their reasoning about social and political phenomena. In substance, his objection was that they took only part of the complex empirical reality into account as anchorage for chains of reasoning assuming a simple, one-way causality. Mill insisted that social scientists must be more cautious in their empiricism. In the first place, their theory must be geared to a high level of

[49] Mill, "Utilitarianism," in *Utilitarianism, Liberty, and Representative Government* (Everyman's Library), pp. 9–14. His argument is essentially the Socratic one; see Plato's *Republic* (Modern Library), pp. 344 ff.

[50] Mill, "On Liberty," in *Utilitarianism*, chap. iii.

[51] "It would be absurd that while, in estimating all other things, quality is considered as well as quantity, the estimation of pleasures should be supposed to depend on quantity alone." He fails to acknowledge that the element of quality creates an entirely new problem in the measurement of happiness. See "Utilitarianism," *ibid.*, p. 10.

[52] Mill relates in his autobiography that it was Macaulay's attack on his father's essay on Government that first led him to question the logic of utilitarian thought. Cf. *Autobiography*, p. 158.

complexity in their assumptions and hypotheses about social phenomena and their causation. In the second place, their hypotheses must constantly be subjected to the process of verification by new observation, and their underlying assumptions and over-all theory must be adjusted accordingly.[53]

As to the more specific assumptions about human nature, the younger Mill appears to have been a bit inconsistent. In one place, he qualifies the belief in universal selfishness as follows: "Any succession of persons, or the majority of any body of persons, will be governed in the bulk of their conduct by their personal interests."[54] Yet in another context he claims that "mankind is capable of a far greater amount of public spirit than the present age is accustomed to suppose possible"; in a communist society, it is at least in theory possible to train large numbers of people "to feel the public interest their own."[55] This amounts to a denial that either selfishness or the predominance of private over public goals is an essential element of human nature. From these two premises, the elder Mill had concluded that the interests of rulers always must be conflicting with the public interest, unless the rulers are representative of and dependent upon the people. John Stuart Mill retorts that the behavior of rulers, as of people in general, quite apart from possible surges of benevolence "is largely influenced by the habitual sentiments and feelings, the general modes of thinking and acting, which prevail throughout the community of which they are members."[56]

Here goes not only the "atomism" of the Benthamites, but also their faith in the rationality of man. Mill disclaims any dominating rationality even in monarchs, who are presumably among the well-educated men. Mill in effect, in a statement such as this, rejects Hartley's and his father's simple associationism and asserts that society is a part of the individual just as much as individuals are a part of society. He makes this even clearer in another context: "The social state is at once so natural, so necessary, and so habitual to man, that, except in some unusual circumstances or by an effort of voluntary abstraction, he never conceives of himself otherwise than as a member of a body."[57]

However, this is not the whole truth about John Stuart Mill the psychologist. With characteristic inconsistency, he comes out just as squarely, in other contexts, for a radically atomistic view of human society:

The laws of the phenomena of society are, and can be, nothing but the laws of the actions and passions of human beings united together in the social state. Men, however, in a state of society, are still men; their actions and passions are obedient to the laws of individual human nature . . . Human beings in society have no properties but those which are derived from, and may be resolved into, the laws of the nature of individual man.[58]

A statement such as this exposes the younger Mill to the same kind of criticism that Plamenatz directs against his father: "What, indeed, could

[53] *System of Logic, Ratiocinative and Inductive*, II, 469–507.
[54] *Ibid.*, p. 483.
[55] *Principles of Political Economy*, I, 264–65.
[56] *System of Logic*, II, 484.
[57] "Utilitarianism," *Utilitarianism*, p. 38.
[58] *System of Logic*, II, 469.

be less scientific than to construct the notion of man, in abstraction from society, and then to explain society in terms of his desires?"[59]

Having tried to relate the basic schemes of values and empirical assumptions of the three utilitarian liberals, I now turn to the more specific question of their attitudes to "freedom" and "security."

Common to Bentham and James Mill was a strict adherence to the greatest happiness formula, which reduced all other values, including freedom and security, to an instrumental status. For the younger Mill also happiness was avowedly the main if not the only intrinsic value. The main question to ask, therefore, is whether the three utilitarian liberals considered security and freedom valuable as conducive to general happiness.

Bentham was in his early and middle life not averse to benevolent despotism, provided the despot was sufficiently intelligent to be willing to institute some of Bentham's reforms. He was then inclined to enhance security as more important than political freedom in the broad sense. As Dumont interprets his master, no doubt faithfully:

He thinks that the best constitution for a people is the one to which it is accustomed. He thinks that happiness is the only *end*, the only thing with an intrinsic value, and that political liberty is only a *relative* good, one of the means of arriving at this end. He thinks that a people which has good laws can arrive at a high degree of happiness even without having any political power, and, on the contrary, that it may have the widest political powers and yet necessarily be unhappy, if it has bad laws.[60]

About the instrumental value of free speech, at least for the educated, Bentham seems to have had a high appreciation all along. In his "Principles of Penal Law," which was written in the 1780s, he comes out strongly in favor of a free press:

The liberty of the press has its inconveniences, but the evil which may result from it is not to be compared with the evil of censorship. . . . Every interesting and new truth must have many enemies, because it is interesting and new. Is it to be presumed that the censor will belong to the infinitely small number who rise above established prejudices?[61]

Bentham's view of the relationship between "freedom" and "security" is on the surface quite simple in each context where he discusses it. But he is not consistent. In some contexts he nearly equates the two terms. In others he considers them opposites.

"As to this word *liberty*," he writes in one context,

it is a word, the import of which is of so loose a texture, that, in studied discourses on political subjects, I am not (I must confess) very fond of employing it, or of seeing it employed: *security* is a word, in which, in most cases, I find an ad-

[59] Plamenatz, *The English Utilitarians,* p. 152.

[60] Quoted in Halévy, *The Growth of Philosophical Radicalism,* p. 143, from Dumont's Introduction to the *Traités de Législation.*

[61] *Works,* I, 538. Cf. pp. 574–75.

vantageous substitute for it: *security* against misdeeds by individuals at large: *security* against misdeeds by public functionaries: *security* against misdeeds by foreign adversaries—as the case may be.[62]

In his "Principles of the Civil Code," written in the 1780s, Bentham lists four distinct objectives of the civil law: the achievement of subsistence, abundance, equality, and security. Among these values, security must be the principal objective, because it "implies extension in point of time, with respect to all the benefits to which it is applied"—including subsistence, abundance, and equality. He continues:

It may appear surprising, that liberty is not placed among the principal objects of the law. But in order that we may have clear notions, it is necessary to consider it as a branch of security: personal liberty is security against a certain species of injury which affects the person; whilst, as to political liberty, it is another branch of security—security against the injustice of the members of the government. What relates to this object, belongs not to the civil, but to the constitutional code.[63]

On the very next page, however, Bentham indicates that there may be some rivalry between the values of liberty and security: "Liberty, which is one branch of security, ought to yield to general security, since it is not possible to make any laws but at the expense of liberty."[64] His intention here is not to state a sweeping preference for security over liberty, but to state what he in this context considers a truism: that laws always infringe on liberty but must at times be adopted nevertheless.

This is not the whole truth, however. When dealing with the concepts of "right" and "obligation," Bentham is aware of a greater complexity than his uses of "liberty" and "security" indicate. He states that a right *may* consist in just the absence of an obligation to do or refrain from doing something. But he also affirms that there are more complex rights, which consist in obligations imposed on other men, to do or refrain from doing something.[65] The natural conclusion would seem to be, though Bentham does not draw it in these terms, that the amount of freedom in a society may have a positive as well as a negative correlation with the amount of security, depending on what rights are considered the most important. It is true, as he points out, that legislation in the interest of security limits the scope of my freedom; but in another sense it may at the same time increase my freedom, by extending the limitations on what other people can do to me. If he had made the last point, which ought to follow from his discussion of rights and obligations, it might have had repercussions on his laissez-faire attitude toward industrial and economic problems.

For all his indifference to democracy or autocracy in his early life, it is important to note that Bentham in his very first book, the *Fragment on Government* (1776), defended the right and even the duty to make revolu-

---

[62] In the third letter to Count Toreno, on the proposed Spanish penal code, dated 1821. *Ibid.*, VIII, 509–10.

[63] *Ibid.*, I, 302.

[64] *Ibid.*, p. 303.

[65] *Ibid.*, IX, 19. On the concepts of "positive" and "negative" freedom, see below, pp. 57–58.

tion, from a strictly utilitarian point of view: "It is *then,* we may say, and not till then, allowable to, if not incumbent on, every man, as well on the score of *duty* as of *interest,* to enter into measures of resistance; when, according to the best calculation he is able to make, *the probable mischiefs of resistance* (speaking with respect to the community in general) *appear less to him than the probable mischiefs of submission.*" He stresses that he knows of no clear-cut common sign saying when the time is ripe; for each man the decisive factor must be "his own internal persuasion of a balance of *utility* on the side of resistance."[66]

Bentham, in other words, favors a loyalty to principles, not men, or a loyalty to the people as a whole, to the public interest, instead of a loyalty to the government. He states this position more unequivocally than did either Locke or Hume.[67] Let it be enough comment in this context to say that there is one crucial weakness in Bentham's position, with which I otherwise am in sympathy: he fails to point out even a general direction for the search of objective criteria for determining just when a government has violated its trust to such an extent that it deserves to be overthrown by unconstitutional means if necessary. Bentham's rejection of the idea of inherent human rights is logically as sound as Hume's; yet it is a question whether some functional equivalent may not be necessary to solve the problem of making loyalty to universal values compatible with national as well as international security.[68]

James Mill, who in all important respects shared Bentham's conclusions but was quite capable of arguing for himself, was also quite explicit on the right to make revolution. In the beginning of his essay on the "Liberty of the Press," he takes the following bold and unusual stand: *"Exhortations to obstruct the operations of government in detail should, exhortations to resist all the powers of government at once should not, be considered offences."*[69] The freedom of the people to revolt, as a measure of last resort, must be kept open. Indeed, Mill sees it as one of the important objectives of a free press to be in a position to stimulate a general consensus in favor of overthrowing the government by force, if this becomes necessary. Short of such extreme situations, however, he finds that every society requires a measure of security that takes precedence over the freedom to advocate insubordination with respect to any particular law.

In meeting an argument that possibly might have sounded plausible to Bentham himself in his younger days—the view that the liberty of the press may be less necessary when a really good representative government has been attained—James Mill says that, quite on the contrary, "it is doubtful whether a power in the people of choosing their own rulers without the liberty of the press would be an advantage."[70] In his view there are three

[66] *Ibid.,* I, 287–88.

[67] See above, pp. 31–32.

[68] Cf. below, pp. 371–73.

[69] "Liberty of the Press," in Jeremy Bentham, James Mill, and John Stuart Mill, *Essays,* ed. by Philip Wheelwright, p. 255.

[70] *Ibid.,* p. 263.

functions, all essential to the process of representative government, that can be served only by a free press: (1) to provide the voters with information to form the basis for intelligent choice; (2) to make the conduct of the rulers known to the people (really a part of the first objective); and (3) to bring current public opinion to the attention of the government. He concludes: "To impose any restraint upon the liberty of the press is undoubtedly to make a choice. If the restraint is imposed by the government, it is the government that chooses the directors of the public mind. If any government chooses the directors of the public mind, that government is despotic."[71]

Mill's optimism about the attainment of truth as a consequence of free discussion is reminiscent of Godwin's *Political Justice,* which appeared in 1793, when Mill was twenty years old. "When various conclusions are, with their evidence, presented with equal care and with equal skill, there is a moral certainty, though some few may be misguided, that the greater number will judge aright, and that the greatest force of evidence, wherever it is, will produce the greatest impression."[72] I cannot share his "moral certainty," but on a strict interpretation of his premises, which severely limit the scope of his hypothesis, it is probably sound. I certainly accept as pertinent and true his observation that "to attach advantage to the delivering of one set of opinions, disadvantages to the delivering of another, is to make a choice."[73] Whether it follows that such a choice should never be made, considering that the facts of a complex social structure may have loaded the dice already, perhaps without any conscious or deliberate human choice, is another question.[74]

Another conclusion to which I subscribe is the importance of a strict definition of any limitations that, in the interest of security and law-abidingness, may be imposed on the freedom of the press. "To all those who profit by the abuses of government . . . it is of great importance to leave as undefined as possible the sort of exhortation that ought to be forbidden." This is in effect the same insight that made the authors of the United States Constitution define the concept of treason very explicitly and narrowly— little suspecting the later rise of substitute or "front" concepts such as subversion, disloyalty, and un-Americanism.[75]

Now, just where does Mill try to draw the sharp line between legitimate and illegitimate attacks on concrete governmental operations or specific laws? In spite of his good intentions, his criteria do not provide any clearcut solution. He does make it clear that "all censures must be permitted equally, just and unjust,"[76] but his main criterion is that only the "direct" advocacy of obstruction against specific laws should be punished, and not the "implicit and constructive" argument of obstruction.[77] Another criterion is that he would have punished, on the same principles as in private

---

[71] *Ibid.*, pp. 266–67.
[72] *Ibid.*, p. 268.
[73] *Ibid.*, p. 278.
[74] See below, pp. 348–53.
[75] "Liberty of the Press," p. 259. Cf. Madison, *The Federalist* (Modern Library), pp. 280–81.
[76] "Liberty of the Press," p. 267.
[77] *Ibid.*, pp. 259–63.

libel, those who impute to public officials acts that they are not guilty of, and do so "by mere forgery and without appearance of ground." Again, this is a sensible distinction, but hardly an exact one.[78] It is widely put into practice, but it is left to the courts of law to sharpen it, or to adjust it according to the sentiments of the time, in each country.

Both Bentham and James Mill, though in theory they subordinated the values of security and freedom to the ultimate goal of general happiness, nevertheless showed a real concern for these two values and, for their time, a particularly radical concern for the freedom of speech as an indispensable tool for the good government.

With a fair degree of inconsistency, John Stuart Mill joined in the defense of the greatest happiness principle. He argued more eloquently for free speech than perhaps anyone else has done, and yet his main emphasis was on its utility rather than on its intrinsic merit, and on its utility for happiness rather than for other ultimate values.[79] The second chapter in his essay *On Liberty*, which is by far the longest chapter, is entirely devoted to proving the utility of free speech for the advancement of "the mental well-being of mankind (on which all their other well-being depends)." The summary of his argument, in his own words, is worth repeating here:

First, if any opinion is compelled to silence, that opinion may, for aught we can certainly know, be true. To deny this is to assume our own infallibility. Secondly, though the silenced opinion be an error, it may, and very commonly does, contain a portion of the truth. . . . Thirdly, even if the received opinion be not only true, but the whole truth; unless it is suffered to be, and actually is, vigorously and earnestly contested, it will, by most of those who receive it, be held in a manner of a prejudice, with little comprehension or feeling of its rational grounds. And not only this, but fourthly, the meaning of the doctrine itself will be in danger of being lost, or enfeebled, and deprived of its vital effect on the character and conduct; the dogma becoming a mere formal profession, inefficacious for good, but cumbering the ground, and preventing the growth of any real and heart-felt conviction, from reason or personal experience.[80]

In the next chapter, however, Mill crashes out of the utilitarian greatest happiness scheme and comes very close to affirming freedom and individual spontaneity as intrinsic values on a par with happiness itself. He quotes with approval Wilhelm von Humboldt's statement that "the end of man, or that which is prescribed by the eternal or immutable dictates of reason, and not suggested by vague and transient desires, is the highest and most harmonious development of his powers to a complete and consistent whole."[81] Mill pleads for recognition of the values of individuality, diversity, even eccentricity. He might have added—had he lived today—con-

[78] *Ibid.*, p. 274.
[79] It should be pointed out that it is in the nature of rational argument to defend values in terms of their utility in promoting more basic values (or in terms of consistency in not counteracting other values); to the extent that a value is considered intrinsically good and not instrumentally good, it may be communicated by appeals to emotions, but there are strictly speaking no rational grounds on which to defend it. Cf. above, p. 15.
[80] "On Liberty," in *Utilitarianism*, pp. 148–49.
[81] *Ibid.*, p. 154.

troversy, nonconformity. For lack of a wider freedom of individual development, he believes that most people even in his relatively free England "are but starved specimens of what nature can and will produce."[82] He stresses that men differ in their sense of pleasure and in their conditions for growth and concludes that, "unless there is a corresponding diversity in their modes of life, they neither obtain their fair share of happiness, nor grow up to the mental, moral, and aesthetic stature of which their nature is capable."[83] In this statement Mill certainly makes it explicit that he believes in a second scheme of ultimate values besides happiness.

Like his father, Stuart Mill also made a notable attempt to draw the line between the proper spheres of freedom and social regulations: "As soon as any part of a person's conduct affects prejudicially the interests of others, society has jurisdiction over it, and the question whether the general welfare will or will not be promoted by interfering with it, becomes open to discussion. But there is no room for entertaining any such question when a person's conduct affects the interests of no persons besides himself."[84] We are free to avoid the company of persons whose private habits and values we loathe, but any sanctions beyond this sort of a natural reaction are unjustified. We can exercise our own individuality in this way but not deliberately oppress the individuality of someone else. Purposive sanctions are legitimate only against people whose behavior is harmful to others.

This distinction has some practical value in that it tends to cut the ground from under most justifications of religious and "patronizing" intolerance. By any reasonable interpretation it guarantees, if accepted, at least a certain minimum of privacy, self-determination, and dignity to the individual. In a language Mill would not approve of, it would guarantee some basic human rights. Yet for the purpose of drawing a neat and clear line between legitimate and illegitimate interference with individual freedom, the son's criterion is no better adapted than the father's. It is instructive in this respect to note a couple of the applications Mill derives from his guiding principle: In industry any social pressure against fellow workers who speed up production, or "rate busters" as they are called today, is unjustified. Any scheme for legal prohibition against the use of alcohol is a monstrosity. Without discussing the merit of Mill's attitude to these two policy questions, so often contested during the last hundred years, I wish to point out that his conclusions are not obviously the right ones, and, what is more crucial in the present context, they do not by necessity follow from his own general distinction between rightful and wrongful interference with individual freedom. The trouble with his guiding principle is that it is not of much help in practical decision-making. With respect to many if not most kinds of human behavior, it is a matter of individual judgment whether the interests of others are sufficiently affected to warrant interference, whether by law or by social sanctions, in the public inter-

82 *Ibid.*, p. 157.
83 *Ibid.*, p. 168.
84 *Ibid.*, p. 177.

est. And yet, my own approach borrows considerably from this principle of Mill's.[85]

One of John Stuart Mill's main purposes in his essay on liberty was to warn against the twin dangers of a social and a political tyranny by the majority. Although he warmly supported the trend toward a more democratic society, he did not expect unmixed blessings to follow in its wake. He perceived a very real danger of a democratic tyranny, a danger that his father had been inclined to dismiss as a contradiction in terms.[86] A tyranny of the majority, warns John Stuart Mill, may be exerted both by repressive laws and by intolerant attitudes and behavior.

This new insight into the social facts of life made him inclined toward a new kind of identification of security with liberty, on a psychological level, where such a conceptual merger has much to recommend itself. Unlike the assumed inverse relationship on the social level, which made Bentham and James Mill, generally also John Stuart Mill, convinced that laissez faire promoted economic freedom in every sense,[87] the new interrelationship that John Stuart Mill implied amounted to a positive identification of freedom with security within the individual personality.

Mill's concern for security as an important value, one of the basic preconditions for general happiness, is evidenced in a statement such as this: "The moral rules which forbid mankind to hurt one another (in which we must never forget to include wrongful interference with each other's freedom) are more vital to human well-being than any maxims, however important, which only point out the best mode of managing some department of human affairs."[88] This statement in effect equates the individual's freedom to develop and express his personality with his security from intolerant interference by others, whether by public policy or by private meddling. The close interrelationship between security and freedom on this level is one of the important themes in the essay on liberty.

Perhaps Godwin approached this insight from his own angle, but he had the important weakness of being quite unaware of any nongovernmental sources of lack of freedom and insecurity. Among the empiricists whose thought I have reviewed, only John Stuart Mill came close to an empirically useful conception of social freedom. He was also the only one in this philosophical tradition to take one or two steps toward a concept of psychological freedom as well.

IDEALIST CONCEPTIONS OF FREEDOM: THE REALIZATION OF THE "SELF"

External restraints on expression make up only one of the facets of the freedom problem: these are only one type of phenomena interfering with man's ability to express what he actually or potentially is capable of ex-

---

[85] Cf. below, pp. 126–27.

[86] "The community cannot have an interest opposite to its interest. To affirm this would be a contradiction in terms. The community within itself, and with respect to itself, can have no sinister interest." James Mill, "Government," in Burtt (ed.), *English Philosophers*, p. 861.

[87] This belief was perhaps not inconsistent with a belief in legislative "intimidation" in other spheres; a choice was involved, which the Benthamites resolved in favor of freedom in economics and in favor of security in most other spheres.

[88] "Utilitarianism," in *Utilitarianism*, p. 74.

pressing of his individuality. Not the absence of coercion, but the presence of self-expression is the crux of the phenomenon I wish to call "freedom." I wish to consider the *capacity,* the *opportunity,* and the *incentive* to express the actual and potential self.[89]

The empiricists all were concerned with the opportunity only; this was for them the whole freedom problem. They differed in their views of what kinds of restraints were most damaging to man's opportunity for self-expression. To take the two extreme views, Hobbes saw a society without effective government as the most oppressive, whereas Godwin anticipated greater freedom with less government. None of the seven philosophers discussed above questioned the basic premise that the problem of freedom is entirely a problem of the relationship *between* human beings.

I turn now to another philosophical tradition, in which the problem of freedom has been considered primarily a problem of the state of affairs *inside* the individual. Unlike the empiricists who were concerned with freedom as social opportunity of expression, it may be said that the idealists were concerned primarily with freedom as individual capacity for self-expression.

My discussion of idealist views shall be confined to a consideration of the concepts and views on freedom and security advanced by Jean Jacques Rousseau, Thomas Hill Green, and Bernard Bosanquet. It would lead much too far to venture into the towering mansions of the thought of Kant and Hegel and their German successors. For present purposes it may be assumed that the essential idealist contributions toward a more comprehensive freedom concept are adequately covered within the modest scope of my limited excursion into idealist thought.

There are two principal reasons why idealist philosophers are often difficult to understand: most of them tend to thrive on high altitudes of abstraction, and many of their important concepts and propositions seem to be without a clear behavioral reference. These characteristics are very apparent in idealist literature on the nature of freedom or the free society. But one must not overlook the possibility that the greater ambiguities and obscurities in their propositions on "freedom," as compared to those of the empiricists, in part may be the outcome of a greater sensitiveness to the complexity of the phenomenon under discussion. Indeed, there is no doubt that the idealists tended to have a more adequate conception of the human self, the subject of the freedom attribute.

It is easy to understand why empiricists such as Hobbes and Bentham tended to conceive of man as primarily selfish: narrow selfishness has been an obvious element in most human conflicts. Compassionate qualities have not by themselves caused social problems; social and political writers had therefore not been as much concerned with these qualities. The empiricists in general, while conceding, and in Godwin's case stressing, such impulses as sympathy and benevolence in man, nevertheless tended toward an atomistic view of society. Each individual self was seen as an independent unit, and the needs of society were deduced from assumptions about the needs of

[89] Cf. above, pp. 15 ff., and below, pp. 83–101.

individuals. The idealists, on the other hand, frequently committed the opposite mistake of constructing the notion of society, or the state, in abstraction from the individuals composing it and then explaining individual man and his duties in deduction from the requirements of this abstraction. For Hegel, "law, morality, the State, and they alone, are the positive reality and satisfaction of freedom. The caprice of the individual is not freedom. . . . Only the will that obeys the law is free, for it obeys the law and, being in itself, is free."[90]

Preposterous from a common sense point of view as the Hegelian premise may appear—that the state in effect is more "real" than the individual—it may be taken as an indicator that something important was missing in the individualistic self concept of the empiricists. The latter did tend to overlook the important process of *identification* as a process affecting the very constitution of the self. For the full-time chauvinist it may not be so misleading to say that to him the state means everything and that the interests of the state determine his own interests. For the average person, if I may deflate and yet utilize the grandiose insights of Hegel the patriot, it may be assumed that the interests of his most immediate family and friends are integrated into his own self, to the point where the needs of certain other people literally become his own needs.

Ironically, the more recent influence of Sigmund Freud seems in some ways to have served to strengthen the Hobbesian stereotype of man as a primarily selfish individual. This great explorer of the human unconscious was anything but naïve about the social nature of the individual self, but he created the impression that the id is in some sense, and not only chronologically, prior to the superego in the development of the infant's and child's personality. He also tended to dramatize the continuing struggle between the individual's id and society's agent inside him, the superego. The mediating function of the ego serves to resolve this conflict, in Freud's theory, but the impression remains that "originally" and "basically" there is a violent conflict, and not much spontaneous harmony, between the individual and his social surroundings. I argue in this book that the needs and impulses of the superego are just as original and basic in the individual as are the needs and impulses of the id; man is a social as much as he is a biological phenomenon.[91]

On this particular score of enlightenment about the social components of human nature it may be said that the Greeks were well ahead of Bentham. While Bentham sought legislation to direct private selfishness toward the common good, Aristotle saw it as a special business of the legislator to create a "benevolent disposition," for example toward private property.[92] In Plato's *Republic* the whole argument stresses the affinity between the nature of man and the nature of the society in which he lives; "the same principles which exist in the State exist also in the individual."[93]

The idealists inherited some obscure concepts and some pseudoproblems

[90] *Reason in History: A General Introduction to the Philosophy of History,* trans. by Hartman, pp. 50, 53. The opposite fallacy of the utilitarians is referred to above, pp. 40–41.
[91] Cf. Chapter 4, especially p. 171 and note 66.
[92] *Politics,* trans. by Benjamin Jowett (Modern Library), p. 88.
[93] *The Republic,* trans. by Benjamin Jowett (Modern Library), p. 160.

from the Greeks, but along with them also a number of useful insights. The insight of particular concern to me here is a conception of the self that permits us to study "freedom" as a phenomenon inside the individual, not only as a type of relationship between individuals. Plato speaks of the man who is the "master of himself" and of him who is "the slave of self," depending on whether the "better" or the "worse" principle in the human soul is in control.[94] The idealists are true to the Platonic tradition when they speak of "self-realization" as the most important end in human life.[95]

Jean Jacques Rousseau (1712-78)

Rousseau in his *Discourse on the Origin of Inequality* sharply challenges two views that he attributes to Hobbes: that man is naturally wicked and that the state of nature must lead to infinite warfare. It may be said that he misinterprets Hobbes on the first score, but he certainly also adds something of vital importance to the naïve atomistic conception of individual human nature that Hobbes had entertained.

There is one principle that moderates the striving for self-preservation in human beings, says Rousseau, and that is *compassion,* "which is a disposition suitable to creatures so weak and subject to so many evils as we certainly are: by so much the more universal and useful to mankind, as it comes before any kind of reflection; and at the same time so natural, that the very brutes themselves sometimes give evident proofs of it."[96] The process of compassionate *identification* is to Rousseau the source of all goodness.[97] And it is a "natural" goodness: the more society and culture develop, the more the individual learns not to feel compassion for his fellow men.[98]

The tenor of Rousseau's discourse on the origin of inequality was to deplore the advent of civilization. He idealized precivilized human nature and contended against Hobbes that there was bound to be less warfare among savages before the institution of property was invented. There were no good reasons for killing each other, and the natural human compassion was an effective inhibition against unnecessary cruelty. And there were no civilized notions of "shame" in running away, should somebody want to pick a fight.

The origin of civilization is attributed to one colossal fraud: the invention of the idea of property. "The first man who, having enclosed a piece of ground, bethought himself of saying, 'This is mine,' and found people simple enough to believe him, was the real founder of civil society."[99] After

[94] *Ibid.,* pp. 144–45.
[95] For example, see Bradley, *Ethical Studies (Selected Essays),* pp. 9 ff., and below, pp. 54–57.
[96] "Discourse on the Origin of Inequality," in *The Social Contract and Discourses,* trans. by G. D. H. Cole (Everyman's Library), pp. 224. This discourse, usually known as the "Second Discourse," was first published in 1754.
[97] *Ibid.,* pp. 222–26.
[98] "Nothing but such general evils as threaten the whole community can disturb the sleep of the philosopher, or tear him from his bed. A murder may with impunity be committed under his window; he has only to put his hands to his ears and argue a little with himself, to prevent nature, which is shocked within him, from identifying itself with the unfortunate sufferer. Uncivilized man has not this admirable talent; and for want of reason and wisdom, is always foolishly ready to obey the first promptings of humanity." *Ibid.,* p. 226.
[99] *Ibid.,* p. 234.

the gradual destruction of equality in this fashion, Rousseau continues, it came to pass that the rich men found themselves easily outnumbered and overpowered by the poor, who might gang up on them. This was the origin of the need for government: "The rich man, thus urged by necessity, conceived at length the profoundest plan that ever entered the mind of man: this was to employ in his favor the forces of those who attacked him, to make allies of his adversaries, to inspire them with different maxims, and to give them other institutions as favourable to himself as the law of nature was unfavourable."[100]

In *The Social Contract,* which has been called the "sublimation of the *Discourse,*"[101] Rousseau comes closer to accepting civilized government as a necessity for the needs of man, not only for the needs of rich men. In common with Hobbes and Locke, he now affirms the need for a governmental order to prevent free-for-all fighting among men. But Rousseau goes further: he sees in political government a "motive power" serving to provide direction and coordination for individual lives toward the "common good."[102]

There is no occasion here for a lengthy discussion of the complex nature of Rousseau's social contract. To him this contract, with the establishment of political government under its terms, was an instrument toward the attainment of man's complete "civil liberty"—a liberty qualitatively superior to any that could reign even in a peaceful state of nature. Rousseau admits, it is true, that the social contract deprives man of his "natural liberty and an unlimited right to everything he gets and succeeds in getting"—in exchange for much, however: "What he gains is civil liberty and the proprietorship of all he possesses. . . . We might, over and above all this, add, to what man acquires in the civil state, moral liberty, which alone makes him truly master of himself; for the mere impulse of appetite is slavery, while obedience to a law which we prescribe to ourselves is liberty."[103]

"To renounce liberty," says Rousseau, "is to renounce being a man, to surrender the rights of humanity and even its duties."[104] So far from renouncing liberty by accepting the social contract, this very instrument serves to increase the freedom of all men: "Instead of a renunciation, they have made an advantageous exchange: instead of an uncertain and precarious way of living they have got one that is better and more secure; instead of natural independence they have got liberty; instead of the power to harm others security for themselves, and instead of their strength, which others might overcome, a right which social union makes invincible."[105]

This last passage would have been acceptable both to Hobbes and to Locke. One important point of departure from these predecessors is in Rousseau's introduction of the concept of "general will." This concept is difficult to comprehend fully, and apparently it is used with some inconsist-

---

[100] *Ibid.,* p. 250. This is a cogent statement of the basic theory of political manipulation. See below, Chapter 6.

[101] Talmon, *The Rise of Totalitarian Democracy,* p. 39.

[102] "The Social Contract," in *The Social Contract and Discourses,* pp. 13–16.

[103] *Ibid.,* p. 19.

[104] *Ibid.,* p. 9.

[105] *Ibid.,* p. 31.

ency by Rousseau himself. What is important to note at this point is that he stuffs his freedom concept with this somewhat obscure notion of a "general will," and consequently he arrives at a usage of "freedom" that is very different from the usages in the empiricist tradition:

In order then that the social compact may not be an empty formula, it tacitly includes the undertaking, which alone can give force to the rest, that whoever refuses to obey the general will shall be compelled to do so by the whole body. This means nothing less than that he will be *forced to be free*; for this is the condition which, by giving each citizen to his country, secures him against all personal dependence.[106]

To many minds, including those of the English empiricists, "freedom" and "coercion" have been irreconcilable opposites. And yet, Rousseau's idea of "coercion toward freedom" has had a considerable following, and it is perhaps not altogether absurd.[107] At this point I am content to point out that Rousseau is prepared to support a lot of coercion against individuals in order to bolster their "freedom"—in his own special sense. Anything goes, if a government representing the "general will" finds that the best interests of the state are at stake:

The social treaty has for its end the preservation of the contracting parties. He who wills the end wills the means also, and the means must involve some risks, and even some losses. He who wishes to preserve his life at others' expense should also, when it is necessary, be ready to give it up for their sake. Furthermore, the citizen is no longer the judge of the dangers to which the law desires him to expose himself; and when the prince says to him: "It is expedient for the State that you should die," he ought to die, because it is only on that condition that he has been living in security up to the present, and because his life is no longer a mere bounty of nature, but a gift made conditionally by the State.[108]

What makes this doctrine particularly hazardous for the preservation of individual freedom in the empiricist sense is the difficulties involved in pinning down what the "general will" is and who expresses it or is authorized to do so. In theory, each individual will is a part of it, but only in a special, rather obscure sense; the "general will" is by no means the same as the "will of all."[109] This vagueness makes it correspondingly easy for a nonrepresentative government to claim that it expresses the general will,

---

106 *Ibid.*, p. 18. My italics.

107 Cf. below, pp. 104–5.

108 "The Social Contract," in *The Social Contract and Discourses*, p. 32. Note, however, the following passages from his "Discourse on Political Economy," pp. 303–4: "Is the welfare of a single citizen any less the common cause than that of the whole state? . . . if we are to understand . . . that it is lawful for the government to sacrifice an innocent man for the multitude, I look upon it as one of the most execrable rules tyranny ever invented . . . and a direct contradiction of the fundamental laws of society." It is hard to reconcile this view with the passage cited in the text. One is free to assume either an inconsistency, or a premise of "guilt" in some obscure sense in the passage in the text.

109 "There is often a great deal of difference between the will of all and the general will; the latter considers only the common interest, while the former takes private interest into account, and is no more than a sum of particular wills: but take away from these same wills the pluses and minuses that cancel one another, and the general will remains as the sum of the differences." "The Social Contract," in *The Social Contract and Discourses*, p. 26. This is as close as Rousseau gets toward a definition of this crucial concept. See also *ibid.*, pp. 289–90, and below, pp. 62–63.

without effective refutation, to the extent that Rousseau's ideas are influential.[110]

The first dictatorships to advance this claim were those emerging from the French Revolution—first the Jacobin regime, and then Napoleon. Rousseau may be called the ideological father of the French Revolution, just as Locke was the most important source of the ideas that precipitated the American Revolution. Yet, while Locke's ideas were useful also in preserving the accomplished revolution in the New World, Rousseau's ideas proved just as useful for the subverters of the new democratic order in France. While the empiricist philosophers have provided the basic rationale for the growth of liberal democracy, Rousseau may be called the most important originator of another important tradition, which has been termed "totalitarian democracy" and is entrenched in a large part of the world today. It has been suggested that the basic philosophical difference separating these two hostile traditions may consist in contrasting definitions of "freedom": "Both schools affirm the supreme value of liberty. But whereas one finds the essence of freedom in spontaneity and the absence of coercion, the other believes it to be realized only in the attainment of an absolute collective purpose."[111]

This description no doubt is well taken with reference to many aspects of the applied philosophies, or ideologies, descending from Locke and Bentham on the one side and from Rousseau and Hegel on the other. In the "cold war" struggle of our time, democratic proponents of the Western side tend to stress the inviolability of human rights as the earmark of a good society, while their communist opponents tend to emphasize the long-term interest of the collectivity or society as a whole. Yet, when it comes to theory, a communist is likely to insist that the collective purpose he wishes to promote is the creation of a society offering a fuller freedom of expression to all its inhabitants.[112]

Some further reservations are due if one wishes to compare the original thought of our idealist and empiricist philosophers in these terms. In the first place, we have seen that the empiricists tended to apply a negative

---

[110] "The very idea of an assumed preordained will, which has not yet become the actual will of the nation; the view that the nation is still therefore in its infancy, a 'young nation,' in the nomenclature of the *Social Contract,* gives those who claim to know and to represent the real and ultimate will of the nation—the party of the vanguard—a blank cheque to act on behalf of the people, without reference to the people's actual will." Talmon, *The Rise of Totalitarian Democracy,* p. 48.

[111] *Ibid.,* p. 2.

[112] Lenin proclaims, as William Godwin had asserted before him: "While the state exists there is no freedom. When there is freedom, there will be no state." Lenin, *The State and Revolution,* p. 79. The withering away of the state as the beginning of a fuller freedom for the individual had earlier been predicted in Engels, *Anti-Dühring.* For a recent discussion in the same tradition, see the pamphlet by Hilton, *Communism and Liberty.* Hilton ridicules the empiricist notion, so "dear to the bourgeoisie," that liberty is merely the absence of restraints; to him, as to the idealists, freedom means positive rights and powers. See also Haldane, "A Comparative Study of Freedom," in Anshen (ed.), *Freedom: Its Meaning,* p. 449: "Liberty (the communists claim) is such a precious thing that it must be rationed." And the *Communist Manifesto* declares: "In place of the old bourgeois society, with its classes and class antagonisms, we shall have an association in which the free development of each is the condition for the free development of all."

definition of freedom: they conceptualized "freedom" as the absence of external restraints hampering individual pursuits. Only John Stuart Mill, among those reviewed here, in effect advocated a more positive view of "freedom" as well, as a vehicle of spontaneous expression and intellectual growth.[113] And in fairness to the idealist side, it should be said that many idealists do not attribute to the state or to a "collective purpose" an importance that goes beyond the purpose of securing the welfare of all individuals. Even Rousseau, who is often held suspect on this count, does make it fairly clear that the social contract in his opinion is nothing else than an instrument for securing the welfare and "freedom" of all individuals. And various later idealists such as Green and Bosanquet, who are influenced by Rousseau and by Kant and Hegel, support the authority of the state because they believe, with Rousseau, that man's potentialities for growth can be realized only within the confines of a healthy and secure sociopolitical organism.

Thomas Hill Green (1836–82)

Thomas Hill Green was a somewhat atypical idealist in at least two respects: he was liberal in his politics, and he also recognized important limitations in the rights of the state over its citizens. These two attitudes are perhaps logically interdependent. Green's view of "freedom" as essentially the opportunity to strive for self-perfection, and his view of the state as essentially the provider of this opportunity for all are indicated in the following passage:

The value then of the institutions of civil life lies in their operation as giving reality to these capacities of will and reason,[114] and enabling them to be really exercised. In their general effect, apart from particular aberrations, they render it possible for a man to be freely determined by the idea of a possible perfection of himself, instead of being driven this way and that by external forces, and thus they give reality to the capacity called will: and they enable him to realise his reason, i.e., his idea of self-perfection, by acting as a member of a social organisation in which each contributes to the better-being of all the rest.[115]

The modern state, says Green in another context,

in that full sense in which Hegel uses the term (as including all the agencies for the common good of a law-abiding people), does contribute to the realisation of freedom, if by freedom we understand the autonomy of the will or its determination by rational objects, objects which help to satisfy the demands of reason, the effort after self-perfection.[116]

The last quotation is taken from Green's lecture "On the Different Senses of 'Freedom' as Applied to Will and to the Moral Progress of Man."

---

[113] Perhaps Locke, too, should be added; in his *Essay Concerning Human Understanding* (Everyman's Library edition), p. 136, he defines freedom in terms of "a power to act or not to act." Cf. below, p. 57, note 132, for Bosanquet's dismissal of the distinction between "positive" and "negative" definitions of freedom.

[114] "Will is the capacity in a man of being determined by the idea of a possible satisfaction of himself." "Practical reason is the capacity in a man of conceiving the perfection of his nature as an object to be attained by action." *Lectures on the Principles of Political Obligation*, p. 31. See also p. 20.

[115] *Ibid.*, pp. 32–33.

[116] *Ibid.*, p. 7.

Much of his discussion here is concerned with the freedom of will, or freedom in an ultimate sense with which we are not concerned in this book. His references, however, to rational objects as a source of motivation, and to the motive of self-perfection, are psychologically meaningful. Green is even more clearly referring to "freedom" in a psychological sense when he asserts, in another context in the same lecture, that "the feeling of oppression, which always goes along with the consciousness of unfulfilled possibilities, will always give meaning to the representation of the effort after any kind of self-improvement as a demand for 'freedom.' "[117]

Some of Green's clearest statements of his conception of "freedom" in an empirical sense are given in a lecture on the topic of "Liberal Legislation and the Freedom of Contract." The substance of his argument here is a rejection of the notion held by the utilitarian economists and later the Manchester liberals, to the effect that all interference with economic private enterprise meant an automatic reduction in "freedom." Green holds that in many cases a specific type of interference with the freedom of contract— say, a law to insure the safety and health of industrial workers—may serve to increase "freedom in the higher sense," by which he means "the general power of men to make the best of themselves."[118]

When we speak of freedom as something to be so highly prized, we mean a positive capacity of doing or enjoying something worth doing or enjoying, and that, too, something that we do or enjoy in common with others. We mean by it a power which each man exercises through the help or security given him by his fellow-men, and which he in turn helps to secure for them.[119]

Freedom of contract, freedom in all the forms of doing what one will with one's own, is valuable only as a means to an end. That end is what I call freedom in the positive sense; in other words, the liberation of the powers of all men equally for contributions to the common good.[120]

Unlike Rousseau and also Bosanquet, as we shall see, Green clearly does not see it as one of the purposes of the state to have the citizens "forced to be free." He objects to Rousseau's concept of a general will, both on account of its ambiguity, which paves the way "for the sophistries of modern political management, for manipulating electoral bodies" (etc.); and on account of Rousseau's failure to define his basic values in objective terms: "What really needs to be enacted by the state in order to secure the conditions under which the good life is possible, is lost sight of in the quest for majorities."[121] And in another context Green states emphatically that "of course there can be no freedom among men who act not willingly but under compulsion."[122]

Yet Green insists, in the continuation of the same statement, that the removal of compulsion is not sufficient to insure freedom in the positive sense. Although the context here is the freedom-of-contract issue, the same

[117] *Ibid.*, p. 18.
[118] *Works*, Vol. III: *Miscellanies and Memoir*, p. 383.
[119] *Ibid.*, p. 371.
[120] *Ibid.*, p. 372. See also *Lectures*, pp. 209–10.
[121] *Ibid.*, p. 83.
[122] *Works*, III, 371.

logic applied to the general theory of the state would seem incompatible with viewing coercion as an instrument for liberating its victims.[123] Green defined "freedom" positively: "The liberation of the powers of all men equally for contributions to the common good." He would surely recognize the necessity of some coercion in any society, but only to inhibit powers to do harm, not to increase the freedom of those who are being coerced.

Bernard Bosanquet (1848–1923)

Bernard Bosanquet, who was one of Green's students, went further than his teacher in rejecting the utilitarian "negative" conception of freedom as the absence of external restraints on individual action. In effect, he vindicates Rousseau's philosophy of a "general will" as the sole vehicle of both social and individual freedom. In his *Philosophical Theory of the State,* Bosanquet makes it his principal objective to show "how man ... demands to be governed; and how a government ... is essential ... to his becoming what he has it in him to be."[124]

Bosanquet never makes a clear distinction between "society" and "state." In fact, he tends to use these terms almost as synonyms,[125] and thus he becomes the victim of the ambiguities that usually follow if one tries to stretch the meaning of terms with a common usage; they have a way of slipping back to their habitual sense when the author is not looking. For example, Bosanquet says: "Each individual mind, if we consider it as a whole, is an expression or reflection of society as a whole from a point of view which is distinctive and unique."[126] This statement appears quite sound as far as it at first seems to go. However, if one were to substitute "state" for "society" it at once becomes highly questionable. This is in effect what Bosanquet does, and it leads him to accept Rousseau's assertion that men in general must be forced to be free. In Bosanquet's words, "if the social person is taken as the reality, it follows, as Rousseau points out, that force against the physical individual may become a condition of freedom."[127]

"Liberty," Bosanquet says, "is the being ourselves, and the fullest condition of being ourselves is that in which we are ourselves most completely."[128] As men are social beings, and no society can function except in the political framework of the state, legislation is essential to insure a measure of stability both in society and inside each individual and thus to provide opportunities for rational choice. "The quality of freedom does not depend

[123] In his *Lectures,* Green fails to discuss the idea of forcing men to be free, though he discusses many other ideas from Rousseau extensively. Cf. note 122 for a reference to his *Works.*

[124] *The Philosophical Theory of the State,* p. 73.

[125] "The State, as thus conceived, is not merely the political fabric. The term State accents indeed the political aspect of the whole, and is opposed to the notion of an anarchical society. But it includes the entire hierarchy of institutions by which life is determined, from the family to the trade, and from the trade to the Church and the University. It includes all of them, not as the mere collection of the growths of the country, but as the structure which gives life and meaning to the political whole, while receiving from it mutual adjustment, and therefore expansion and a more liberal air. The State, it might be said, is thus conceived as the operative criticism of all institutions—the modification and adjustment by which they are capable of playing a rational part in the object of human will." *Ibid.,* p. 139.

[126] *Ibid.,* p. 161.

[127] *Ibid.,* p. 90.

[128] *Ibid.,* p. 135.

on the great or small amount of social compulsion and fixed enactment, but on two characteristics which belong to life as a whole; and these are: —First, its comprehensiveness, and secondly, its rationality."[129] By comprehensiveness, Bosanquet means opportunity for choice, which implies opportunity for self-expression; the wider the avenues of choice, presumably the greater the chance that the individual can behave in conformity with his own basic needs or drives. Rationality, as understood by Bosanquet in this context, refers to the justification of the social compulsion that is applied; if it is beneficial to society as a whole, it is rational, and serves indirectly to augment the individual's freedom even while he is being coerced.[130]

It is at this point in Bosanquet's reasoning that I wish to object, along with L. T. Hobhouse, one of Bosanquet's severest critics: You add insult to injury if you tell the victim of coercion that he is being forced to be free.[131] Yet it must be admitted that this construction is not entirely illogical or implausible, once one starts out with Bosanquet's definition of "freedom" as "the being ourselves." Rightly or wrongly, many educators and also many politicians, not to mention prison administrators, believe in considerable amounts of coercion to foster individual growth and responsibility. If they are wrong, and quite possibly they are, it must be proved empirically, for it is not logically demonstrable. Furthermore, I have already granted that the idealist conception of "freedom"—and Bosanquet's is a typical example—has considerable merit from a psychological point of view.

But this conception of freedom is not inclusive enough. "Freedom" also means, or should mean, the right to be let alone, and even to be allowed to make one's own mistakes while others mind their own business. This is the empiricist usage, as we have seen. If the "positive" definition of freedom, in terms of opportunities for individual growth and self-expression, is legitimate and necessary, so is the "negative" definition, too, that equates freedom with the absence of external restraints on the individual.

Or, in different words—for Bosanquet is right when he points out that both conceptions of freedom are equally "positive" or "negative"[132]—one justifiable definition of freedom refers to the scope of self-expression made possible by the absence of obstacles *inside* the individual. Another, equally justifiable definition refers to the scope of self-expression made possible by the absence of obstacles external to the individual.[133] Both concepts are

[129] Bosanquet, "Liberty and Legislation," in *Civilization of Christendom*, pp. 367–68.

[130] Although Bosanquet does not say this in the essay from which I have just quoted, this is a clear inference when compared to his reasoning in *The Philosophical Theory of the State*.

[131] See Hobhouse, *The Metaphysical Theory of the State*, esp. p. 40.

[132] "The higher sense of liberty, like the lower, involves freedom *from* some things as well as freedom *to* others. And that which we are freed from is, in this case, not the constraint of those whom we commonly regard as others, but the constraint of what we commonly regard as part of ourselves." *The Philosophical Theory of the State*, pp. 127–28. The "higher sense" of liberty of course refers to Bosanquet's idealist usage, as opposed to the "lower," or utilitarian, usage. Bosanquet at this point refers to the famous Socratic discussion of the concepts of being master or slave of oneself. See Plato, *The Republic*, pp. 144–45.

[133] Harold J. Laski states in the preface to the second or 1929 edition of his *Grammar of Politics* that he, during the four years since the book was first published, had changed his mind with respect to the nature of liberty: "In 1925 I thought that liberty could most usefully be

essential, I submit, in a meaningful study of man's predicament in modern society.

TOWARD A THIRD FREEDOM CONCEPT

The freedom concepts developed by empiricists and idealists—I shall label them "social freedom" and "psychological freedom"—are both essential in the study of the individual's self-expression at a given time, with a given "self." Between them they are not adequate, however, in the analysis of the potentialities of the individual self and its expression. A third concept is needed, and I shall try to show that Rousseau came close to supplying it.

First, let me state my main points of disagreement with the liberal utilitarians. I contend, first of all, that "a maximal freedom of expression for all" is a goal formulation with three important advantages compared to the Benthamite goal of "the greatest happiness of the greatest number": (1) My goal lends itself to some precision,[134] based on reasonably acceptable criteria, I believe, and is thus better equipped to become a useful guide for policies. (2) It is a goal likely to be shared by large numbers of people in our culture, but not by all—which is one indication that it has cognitive and not only emotive content. (3) The acceptance of this goal, unlike the greatest happiness principle, will have *some* definite consequences for behavior—which is one indication of a consensual common core of meaning.

It is one of the purposes of this book as a whole to attempt to substantiate these claims. On the relative disadvantages of Bentham's goal formulation as an alternate policy guide, let me suggest only these points: (1) "Happiness" is an elusive concept, with less consensual clarification possibilities than "freedom." (2) "Happiness" nevertheless is limited in its reference to states of mind; these, however, may be produced, if happiness is the only value, at the expense of such widely shared goals as "truth" or "growth." (3) To determine what makes other people happy can be exceedingly difficult, even for individuals that we know well; it is probably somewhat easier for individuals to decide for themselves, if they are sufficiently free. (4) Even if happiness could be measured, it would be much more complicated to calculate with "the greatest number" than it is to study the troubles of the marginal cases.

"Equality" was to the Benthamites an instrument for making neat calculations about human happiness, rather than a conceptual part of their greatest happiness goal. They tended to take it for granted that the greatest possible sum of happiness was to be achieved in an unequal society, with a large and prosperous middle class. "Artificial" interference with free trade and free enterprise might increase the amount of equality, but, in their

---

regarded as more than a negative thing. I am now convinced that this was a mistake, and that the old view of it as an absence of restraint can alone safeguard the personality of the citizen." Laski's later conception of freedom is set forth in his *Liberty in the Modern State* (Penguin Books), pp. 49, 91–93, 159. In substance, my position is close to what appears to be the younger Laski's view. In terminology, as I have pointed out, it is misleading to call one of these conceptions negative, any more than the other. If Laski had considered the idea that there may be psychological as well as social restraints operating on the individual, he might have avoided both the dilemma and the "conversion."

[134] See below, pp. 136–52.

opinion, the economic disturbances involved by such measures would be sure to reduce the sum of happiness. Therefore, they were against such policies.

In this book, "equality" is by definition a part of the goal of free expression: expression is not maximally free if some people are deprived of it, or have less of it than others. While the utilitarians were interested in maximizing the sum of happiness, my concern is with maximizing the freedom of the marginal man, or the least privileged individual. I am taking what has been called a human rights approach:[135] the top priority goal for democratic politics is seen as that of safeguarding a sphere of freedom for each individual. In summary: while the utilitarians wanted to promote happiness without equality, I wish to extend freedom by expanding human rights. My goal, then, is equality in expanded freedom for all individuals, to be approached by giving priority to those who initially are the least privileged.

Now for the utility principle. As an abstract and general principle of political policy-making, it has my blessing. Considerations of utility or rationality in promoting shared values appear essential both for advancing these values effectively and for providing shared behavior standards to insure social cooperation. But there are important logical and empirical objections to the way the Benthamites tended to apply this principle.

If an important social goal is clearly defined and also widely accepted, there is a strong argument for pursuing the policy that, considering the best available evidence, promises the maximum utility toward promoting that value. One weakness in utilitarian thought, as we have seen, was that their greatest happiness goal is a rather elusive concept. Yet there is another reservation of at least equal importance. In our world, with human nature and social institutions as complex as they are, there is rarely if ever before us just one goal of importance at a time. Therefore, any choice of policies designed to promote the attainment of one value is almost certain to affect other values as well. There are, consequently, other norms that also affect the choice of means to a given end, and these, as well as the norm of maximum utility for attaining the end, must be considered. For example, as anthropologists often point out, traditional ways of doing things, however ineffective in accomplishing the ostensible goals, may serve other purposes at the same time. They may serve the interest of group cohesion, perhaps, or provide relatively harmless outlets for aggression.[136]

If the empirical understanding is broad enough and clear enough to take all relevant and important values into account, the principle of utility is hardly a controversial one. Perhaps one may even, like Bentham, call it a self-evident principle—at least in the sense that it is implied in much of our language about ends and means. If we say that we want, above all, to try to achieve a certain goal, we are generally implying an intention to apply the most effective means we know—within the limits of choice left

---

[135] See above, pp. 4–7, and below, pp. 371–78.

[136] A classical analysis of probable constructive functions of a pattern of cultural superstitions is found in Clyde Kluckhohn, *Navaho Witchcraft.* The problem of complexities in individual goals is discussed above, pp. 9–14. On the general problem of functional analysis of social institutions, see pp. 240–48.

open by other relevant norms—that we may either believe in or take for granted. At any rate, the principle of empirically oriented utility is in fact involved in all rational planning, and indeed in all purposive behavior, at least as one element.

The four utilitarian assumptions about human nature remain to be disposed of. Again, I shall be very brief, perhaps unjustly so.

Bentham and James Mill, we remember, believed in an associationist theory of psychology, which conceived of the problem of making man fit for a better society as a rather simple attitude-engineering problem, by way of education and legislation. At the same time they believed in an overriding human selfishness, in a preponderance of private over public goals, and in a prevalent rationality of man—at least among educated men.

I have noted that John Stuart Mill at times wrote like a modern social psychologist, to the effect that society with its customs and prejudices is part of man just as man is part of society. At other times he insisted that man in society must be studied entirely in terms of individual psychology. With respect to the question of human selfishness, he sometimes accepted the orthodox premise in a watered-down version, to the effect that *most* people necessarily are selfish, and at other times he asserted that proper education and environments could make men altruistic.

In our time, the evidence of modern social science is incontestably that human nature and human goals are shaped both by individual biology and by social and cultural environments, past and present. Furthermore, there is a consensus among modern clinical psychologists that the earliest social experiences of the child are among the most potent of all influences in shaping the individual's enduring personality. Consequently, education for a better society, even if the objectives can be specified and agreed on, becomes a much more complex problem than that of implanting the proper attitudes by way of creating the right associations. The functions a set of attitudes have for a given type of individual (in a given type of situation) must be taken into consideration.[137]

It will be argued in this book that an educational system propagating tolerant and humanitarian attitudes by no means is sufficient and possibly not even among the most effective means toward developing tolerant and humanitarian individuals. It may turn out to be more effective, in the long run, to encourage child-rearing attitudes that provide more individuals in the next generation with a maximum degree of security and protection of psychological freedom, from as early in life as possible. The propagation of humanitarian attitudes probably does no harm and may do much good, but it is possible that humanitarian attitudes are more effectively encouraged by social reforms that give a fuller life or hope for a fuller life to those who had reasons to be dissatisfied.[138]

It may be said that the Benthamite conception of the rationality of human nature is an eighteenth-century illusion that few people share today. We are able to reject outright the notion that man is able to make life

[137] Cf. pp. 191–92.
[138] Cf. Chapter 4, especially pp. 228–39.

entirely or even mainly an intelligent pursuit of successive, deliberately chosen goals, because we know today that human consciousness is just the surface of human nature. Perhaps it may be possible to talk about a rationality of the organism as a whole; perhaps the human personality may be assumed always to move irresistibly toward the best available satisfaction of its vital needs.[139] If so, however, this is a process in which consciousness participates only to a limited extent.

Since society and culture are reflected and integrated in each personality, individual goals are necessarily conditioned, though not wholly determined, by the structure of incentives in the surrounding community and society. An individualistic society may encourage people to seek gratification in pursuing mostly private goals, while a more collectivistic society may condition most people to make public goals their own to a larger extent, not just in rhetoric but in psychological fact.

The traditional problem of selfishness or unselfishness is surely to a considerable extent a pseudoproblem. In a broad sense, selfishness is necessary and desirable, in so far as the physical survival and social well-being of each individual normally must be his own concern more constantly than anyone else's. I see no reason to lament this state of affairs. In a narrow sense, selfishness seems both undesirable and unnecessary, if one defines it as callousness to the interests of other people. The social problem involved is not one of making people more unselfish, but of encouraging a sense of identification with other human beings, and a perceptive desire to avoid hurting people unnecessarily. As we shall see, this is a problem of social organization, of child up-bringing, and of education. It is above all, perhaps, a problem of creating the optimal conditions for individual basic security and psychological freedom.[140]

It is easy to overstate the case against the Benthamites, on impeccable grounds of logic and common sense. As enthusiasts for humanitarianism and reform, they have been a particularly easy prey for cynics and skeptics and for all philosophers whose teachings amount to a warning that man should stay in his place and not dream about perfectibility.[141] For people who never stick their own necks out to promote humanitarian values, it is particularly easy to discover naïveté and inconsistencies on the part of those who do. The more passivity and indifference you exhibit toward the world's troubles, the easier it is to escape all charges of this kind. But the utilitarians were obstinate "do-gooders," and they did a lot of good. They did much

[139] Cf. Krech and Crutchfield, *Theory and Problems of Social Psychology*, especially p. 168.

[140] See Chapter 4.

[141] It is unfortunate that Christians today often choose as their principal charge against the communists that the latter promise "a complete redemption of man in history." Such a goal may be unrealistic, but does not strike me as wicked or immoral in any sense. In a recent pamphlet issued for the World Council of Churches, five principal points of conflict "between Christianity and the atheistic Marxist Communism of our day" are listed. The first point is the communist promise just cited, and the next two are related to it, and equally unobjectionable from a humanistic point of view. Only the last two points (last in importance?) deal with ruthlessness and coercion under communist dictatorship. Cf. *The Responsible Society*, An Ecumenical Inquiry Published by the Study Department of the World Council of Churches, p. 22.

to insure a gradual development of democratic institutions in England and the British Commonwealth, to say nothing of the many reforms they inspired in many branches of legislation. The values they did so much to promote are essentially the same values that are affirmed by humanitarian democrats the world over today.

The human perfectibility of Godwin's imagination was related to problems of social organization only, and the same was true about most utilitarian thought about progress. The good man was there, encapsuled, waiting to be set free either by less government (Godwin) or by better legislation (Bentham).

In idealist literature man is more complex and malleable. The problem of man's liberation, especially in Rousseau, is not limited to the realization of his present self, if he is to reach his full stature. Rousseau implies an idea of freedom as the expression of man's potential self, a "better self" that in some obscure way is already in existence in each individual *because* he is a member of a society with a *general will*.

At times Rousseau comes close to describing a majority vote, or particularly a unanimous vote, as a sure symptom of the verdict of the general will.[142] But in other contexts he states quite clearly that there is no one-to-one correspondence, and even less, of course, an identity, between the will of the majority and the general will.[143] The general will may in all contexts in Rousseau be interpreted, I believe, as the shadow of perfection, social and political—a dimly perceived collective potentiality that is in some sense already embedded in each individual self.

Whatever is the right interpretation of the "general will," and there is much room for controversy about this, the point I wish to stress is beyond reasonable doubt: the requirements of the general will toward a more perfect society include the need for improvements in human nature. And, what is equally important, Rousseau believes that such improvements can be accomplished by political means:

If it is good (for a republican government) to know how to deal with men as they are, it is much better to make them what there is need that they should be. The most absolute authority is that which penetrates into a man's inmost being, and concerns itself no less with his will than with his actions. . . . If you would have the general will accomplished, bring all the particular wills into conformity with it; in other words, as virtue is nothing more than this conformity of the particular wills with the general will, establish the reign of virtue.[144]

And the reign of virtue equals for Rousseau the reign of freedom.[145]

---

[142] Cf. *The Social Contract and Discourses,* especially pp. 104, 106, 320, and also p. 291: "The voice of the people is in fact the voice of God."

[143] *Ibid.,* pp. 26, 30. In one passage Rousseau defines a republican government as "not merely an aristocracy or a democracy, but generally any government directed by the general will, which is the law. . . . In such a case even a monarchy is a Republic." *Ibid.,* p. 36, footnote.

[144] "Discourse on Political Economy," in *The Social Contract and Discourses,* pp. 297–98.

[145] "Rousseau . . . tended to conceive of the fundamental freedom, or of the fundamental right, as such a creative act as issues in the establishment of unconditional duties and in nothing else: freedom is essentially self-legislation. The ultimate outcome of this attempt

In the *Social Contract* there is a passage in which Rousseau states that the general will "is found by counting votes." He advises the minority voter that his being in the minority proves that he was mistaken: if his will had carried the day, he would have achieved the opposite of what was his will. Let us note Rousseau's usage of "freedom" in this context. By voting against the general will, I am also voting against "my will," meaning something like my potential "rational" or "virtuous" or "fundamental" will; "in that case I should not have been free."[146]

Passages like these—and others could be cited—suggest that Rousseau here operates with a freedom concept that presupposes basic changes in human nature as a prerequisite for being free. This is freedom in the sense of the individual's potential achievement of a perfect harmony with his society and its general will.

This points toward a conception of "freedom" in the sense of realizing what the individual potentially is capable of becoming, beyond whatever he has "in himself" in embryo or in substance at each time. I shall use the term "potential freedom," and attempt to clarify a concept along this line in the next chapter.

Rousseau himself nowhere tries to distinguish explicitly between the realization of man's actual and of his potential self; he is probably not even aware of the possibility of making this distinction.

My conception[147] of a potential freedom will in a sense place the related conception in Rousseau upside down. While he conceived of freedom in this sense as maximized by the manipulation of particular wills toward conformity with the general will, this book starts from the observation that much manipulation of wills is in fact going on and that the potential freedom of the individual is maximized to the extent that resistance to political manipulation, at least of certain kinds, is maximized. I share with Rousseau the general belief that human nature can change, but I differ with him both on the value question of how it ought to change and on the psychological question of how it can change.

The measure of desirable change is in my judgment not a greater convergence toward a better and more uniform pattern of citizenship, but a development toward the greatest individuality and divergency compatible with citizenship. For Rousseau, "all institutions that set man in contradiction to himself are worthless"; he wants a full-time citizenship in unani-

---

was the substitution of freedom for virtue or the view that it is not virtue which makes man free but freedom which makes man virtuous." This is hardly a valid distinction in Rousseau, considering his own habit of using "freedom" in several meanings and of blurring the distinctions between them; this latter habit is noted on the same page 281 in Strauss, *Natural Right and History*. Perhaps this issue in Rousseau can be resolved as follows: Virtue makes man free in the sense of moral freedom, but it is the civil freedom enjoyed in a well-governed society that can make men virtuous.

[146] *The Social Contract and Discourses*, p. 106.

[147] A "conception" is something more than a "concept." Any definition provides a concept, which is neither true nor false, only useful or useless. A conception implies a concept as well as an assumption that this concept refers to something definite in the real world; a conception is an articulated image. This assumption can be true or false. Therefore, when I refer to my "conception" of potential freedom, I assert that the term refers to something empirically ascertainable and susceptible to research.

mous consensus around the dictates of the general will. To me, contradictions and divided loyalties are essential characteristics of a society offering its individuals a reasonable amount of potential freedom. In the words of Clark Kerr, to which I fully subscribe:

The ultimate justification of a democratic society lies in the development of . . . the independent individual, the unique person. We must insist upon the right *not* to be unified; upon the right *not* to be integrated; upon the right to an independent viewpoint that is *not* totally furnished by any single organization, state or lesser; on the right to be conscientious objectors within the state, the union, and the corporation. In a word, we must insist upon the right to privacy.[148]

The psychological premise on which I differ from Rousseau is in my assumption that changes in human nature toward greater individuation and diversity are both more feasible and more rewarding than changes toward a unified rationalist ideal of better citizenship. Rousseau's notion of forcing men to be free and virtuous is not absurd, and it is as a matter of fact put into some limited practice in certain institutions in our own society, such as in most of our elementary schools, for example.[149] It is my belief, in principle subject to empirical research, that a more effective way toward making adult human beings productive individuals *and* good citizens is to try to maximize both their psychological and their social freedom—their freedom from internal defensiveness and their freedom from external coercion. And a third remedy that I advocate, in extreme opposition to Rousseau, is the maximization of man's potential freedom, too, in the sense of increasing the ability of most men to resist many kinds of manipulation.

---

[148] Kerr, "What Became of the Independent Spirit?" *Fortune* (July, 1953), p. 136.
[149] Cf. above, p. 57.

3

Basic Values for a Society
Aspiring toward Freedom

It is time now to attempt a systematic statement of the freedom values that I support. I shall try to state in some detail what it entails, in my judgment, to accept as the supreme value commitment "a maximum freedom of expression for all." My conception of freedom (or synonymously, freedom of expression) consists of three components or subconcepts. They relate, roughly speaking, to the capacity, the opportunity, and the incentive to free expression.

"Security" will be discussed as a crucial aspect of freedom, because my concern with freedom is in a social-process context. I wish to see maximized freedom through time—a continual expansion of freedom. I shall start out in this chapter with a discussion of "security" concepts. In this case, too, I shall define three subconcepts. They relate, roughly speaking, to the negation of objective danger, of fear, and of anxiety.

After defining the security values and then the freedom values, I shall study the interrelationships between the freedom and security values. This inquiry will try to bring out the inherent conflicts that may occur in a value position favoring freedom maximization for all, and I shall take a position on priorities between possible competing freedom and security values.

This chapter will be partly analytical, partly empirical, and partly normative. It will be analytical when I seek logically necessary or possible implications of crucial value statements; empirical when I study the compatibility or conflict between two goal values or the pursuit of them; and normative both in the initial choice of values and in the choice of priorities when value conflicts are found. I shall do my best to make it clear in each context which statements are analytical, which empirical, and which evaluative.

DEFINITIONS OF SECURITY

Thomas Hobbes defined "security" as "the foresight of . . . preservation, and of a more contented life thereby; that is to say of getting . . . out from that miserable condition of Warre."[1] Security against physical violence is clearly the basic concern of Hobbes, but it is equally clear that this is not all he has in mind. "But by *safety* must be understood, not the sole preservation of life in what condition soever, but in order to its happiness."[2] For one thing, he hoped the Leviathan would protect property as well as person and the opportunity to make an honest living.

My own preliminary definition of security is quite close to Hobbes's conception: "security" refers to the actual or perceived probability over time of the enjoyment of other values.[3] I conceive of security as a derivative value, a value referring entirely to other values, but Hobbes does the same. Hobbes tended to stress security against physical violence as the most important aspect of security. My orientation is much the same in this respect: the probability of freedom is to me the most important aspect of security, and physical violence is to me the supreme negation of freedom and the supreme evil.[4]

Like Hobbes, I hold that a civilized society must provide security also against other hazards than physical violence; security for certain property rights, social services, and privacy rights are to me essential components of freedom. Like Hobbes, again, I have so far refrained from trying to make explicit just where to draw the limits around my security concept; I have so far not tried to distinguish between threats and inconveniences.

Unlike Hobbes, I wish to include psychological considerations in my formulation and discussion of security definitions. I wish to distinguish between the objective fact of danger and the subjective perception of danger. And among types of subjective insecurity, I wish to distinguish between basic insecurity and surface insecurity.[5]

The most convenient way to conceptualize these three components of "security" is to tie each subconcept to the negation of an actual or imagined type of threat. The *absence* of objective danger, subjective fear, or subjective anxiety will be the foci of my three definitions.

Perhaps it might be asked whether it would not be preferable to define "security" in positive rather than in negative terms—as "security to" rather than "security from." It appears that there is no real dilemma involved here, by the same reasoning as Bosanquet applied with respect to "freedom": security *from* danger, fear, or anxiety is at the same time security *to* continue the normal pursuits without hindrance.[6]

---

[1] *Leviathan*, p. 87.

[2] *Philosophical Elements*, p. 167; cf. *Leviathan*, p. 178.

[3] See above, p. 19.

[4] See below, pp. 74–77 and 115–16.

[5] An alternate terminology that I find even less satisfactory is a distinction between unconscious and conscious subjective insecurity; consciousness is a simple-sounding but immensely complex criterion, to be avoided as reference in basic definitions. The discussion in Chapter 4 should support this judgment.

[6] Conversely, as Kurt Riezler has observed: "Man's fear is fear *of* something or *for* something: *of* illness, loss of money, dishonor; *for* his health, family, social status." See "The Social Psychology of Fear," *American Journal of Sociology*, XLIX (1944), 489. Cf. above, p. 57, note 132.

Subjective Security: Basic and Surface Security

"Security" means (a) the relative absence of anxiety. "Security" means (b) *the relative absence of fear.* The empirical usefulness of these two definitions evidently hinges on the extent to which it is possible to provide a clear and empirically specific distinction between "anxiety" and "fear." Before embarking on this task, perhaps one or two cautionary remarks are in order.

In the first place, the phenomena I am about to define are complex and not easily accessible to exact observation; consequently, my aspiration with respect to the exactness of the criteria conveyed by the definitions should be somewhat modest. Theorizing concerning dynamic processes in the human personality must be more tentative, at this stage, than in fields that are more open to direct observation and experiment. Our only hope of successive clarifications and increasing preciseness in this field lies in our ability to collect increasingly specific evidence about the explanatory and predictive usefulness of each tentative theory as a whole.[7]

Secondly, it should be stressed that the immediate task is to make the concepts of "anxiety" and "fear" as clear as possible with a minimum of reference to the dynamic context and origin of these phenomena. In this context, my concern is merely to clarify the definitions I use; my reference is to the manifestations of the phenomena, not to their genesis.[8] And yet, the real significance of distinguishing between "anxiety" and "fear" can be made clear only in Chapter 4, when I come to the discussion of causes and consequences of insecurity. It is not possible to steer completely clear of references to the dynamic processes in this section, but I shall do my best.

There is a vast literature on the psychological phenomena referred to as "anxiety" and "fear." It is therefore not surprising that the precise delimitations of these concepts have been the subject of much controversy. Nor is it surprising, in view of the complexities just referred to, that many authors have been either vague or inconsistent, or both, in their usage of the two terms, particularly "anxiety."[9] These considerations may perhaps serve as a partial excuse for the degree of vagueness and the probable inconsistencies in my own usage of the two terms.

Since I cannot hope to improve on the understanding of psychological processes as produced by specialists in psychology and psychiatry, it may be asked why I venture into this particular problem field at all. The answer

---

[7] Cf. below, pp. 155–57.

[8] I want, in other words, phenotypical rather than genotypical definitions. Again, cf. pp. 155–57.

[9] Some authors have preferred, at least in some contexts, to use the two words interchangeably, in the belief either that a clear distinction cannot be made (Sandor Rado), or that it would not be useful for their purposes (O. Hobarth Mowrer). See Rado, "Emergency Behavior," in Hoch and Zubin (eds.), *Anxiety*, pp. 150–51, and Mowrer, *Learning Theory and Personality Dynamics*, pp. 15–16, note 1. Note that Mowrer lumps the two concepts together only in his discussion of experiments on learning; in his discussion of personality dynamics he finds it necessary to distinguish between the two. *Ibid.*, especially Chapter 19, "The Problem of Anxiety."

is quite simple: it appears necessary for a full understanding of "freedom" to inquire into the processes bearing on individual capacity for self-expression. "Anxiety" and "fear," however defined plausibly, bear intimately on "psychological freedom" as well as on "security." Thus, it seems essential for an adequate conceptualization of "freedom" to understand what is involved in these two variants of psychological insecurity.[10]

A wide range of criteria for distinguishing between fear and anxiety has been suggested by a good number of authors. And more often than not, the same author has listed several criteria referring to factors that conceivably may vary independently of each other. For my purposes it seems preferable to peg the distinction to one criterion only; this kind of a concept avoids taking empirical interrelationships for granted. And I choose the realistic accuracy of the perception of danger as the crucial criterion: *"Anxiety" is a state of apprehension or uneasiness expressing a sensation of a danger that is not perceived, diffusely perceived, or imaginary. "Fear" is a state of apprehension or uneasiness in response to a realistically perceived, specific danger.*

It should be stressed right away that the realism of individual perceptions must be judged from the person's own situation and previous experience. A specific danger may appear very real and on good grounds, even if an observer tends to scoff at it and is "vindicated" in that it does not materialize.[11]

Secondly, it should be stressed that my concepts are analytical: in real life concrete fear reactions may be composed of both elements, in varying proportions. To make clear what I mean, I shall in this chapter at times speak of "concrete fear" and reserve the term "fear" for analytical usage.[12] Let me now survey some of the more important fear and anxiety concepts in the literature, in order to draw comparisons, extract insights, and give some impression of the language problems in this field.

It is natural to begin with the pioneer explorer in the realms of the unconscious. Sigmund Freud, unlike many other great minds, remained an explorer all his life, revising and at times rejecting earlier conclusions. His theories of anxiety underwent significant change, but the revisions concerned the dynamic explanation of anxiety rather than the conception of

---

[10] Many psychiatrists, including the great Harry Stack Sullivan, have performed most constructive amateur explorations into social and political theory. See, for example, Chisholm, "The Psychiatry of Enduring Peace and Social Progress," *Psychiatry,* IX (1946), 3–20; Sullivan, "Tensions Interpersonal and International: A Psychiatrist's View," in Cantril (ed.), *Tensions That Cause Wars*; and for a sociologist's criticism, Schneider, "Some Psychiatric Views on 'Freedom' and the Theory of Social Systems," *Psychiatry,* XII (1949), 251–64.

[11] By the same reasoning it may in retrospect be considered prudent and realistic for a man to have paid-up membership in a funeral association even if it turns out in the end that he disappears on the ocean.

[12] In other chapters, the context will make it clear whether "fear" is used in the analytical or in the more concrete sense. "Anxiety" does not raise the same problem. In a concrete state of anxiety, elements of fear may be involved to a minor extent, but can be disregarded. If they cannot, then it is more natural to speak of a concrete fear, or of concrete fears. Another way to handle this purely verbal problem is to say that "fear" may be used in a generic as well as in a specific sense: "it is common to speak of fearing death, hunger, injury, poverty, or unemployment, meaning to fear their possible future occurrence, so that fear is the more generic term and can be held to refer to what is more strictly anxiety." Cf. Symonds, *The Dynamics of Human Adjustment,* p. 137, note 1.

its manifestation. It is therefore permissible in this context to stick to his early definitions, which are the most explicit ones and which he appears never to have abandoned in his later writings.

Anxiety (or, in German, "Angst," which is a somewhat stronger word and may be closer to "anguish" or "dread"), according to Freud, "needs no description; everyone has personally experienced this sensation, or to speak more correctly this affective condition, at some time or other."[13] He distinguishes, however, between "objective anxiety" and "neurotic anxiety." In this book Freud's objective or object-directed "anxiety" is called "fear." As examples of neurotic anxiety, he mentions phobias, some forms of hysteria, and a general "free-floating anxiety, as we call it, ready to attach itself to any thought that is at all appropriate, affecting judgments, inducing expectations, lying in wait for any opportunity to find a justification for itself."[14] These are phenomena that are either unrelated to perceptions of an external danger or not fully accounted for by such stimuli. Tensions of this kind are expressions of anxiety, in my terms, and for the moment I leave out the question whether they are always connected with "neurosis."

In the same lecture, Freud does make a distinction between "anxiety" and "fear": "In my opinion, *anxiety* relates to the condition and ignores the object, whereas in the word *fear* attention is directed to the object."[15] This distinction applies primarily, as is evident, to the realm of what he calls "object-directed anxiety" and I call "fear," but also to the more usual and complex situations where both "anxiety" and "fear" are involved (or, in Freud's terms, both "objective" and "neurotic" anxiety). There is one important difference in descriptive terminology between Freud and some contemporary psychoanalysts. To Freud, "anxiety" and "fear" are two aspects of the same affective condition, whereas, in some of the neo-Freudian literature, they are theoretically separate phenomena although in practice often closely integrated in the same affective condition.

Karen Horney, in particular, has written prolifically on this subject and has been somewhat inconsistent in her terminology. In one of her books she offers a specific distinction based on three criteria; in a more recent work she has a chapter on "Fears,"[16] describing phenomena that are really "states of anxiety" according to the same three criteria:

Anxiety is an emotional response to danger, as is fear. What characterizes anxiety in contradistinction to fear is, first, a quality of diffuseness and uncertainty. . . . Second, what is menaced by a danger provoking anxiety is . . . something belonging to the essence or the core of the personality. As there is wide variation in what different individuals feel to be their vital values, there is also variation in what they feel to be a vital menace. . . . Third, as Freud emphasizes rightly,

---

[13] *A General Introduction to Psychoanalysis,* trans. by Joan Riviere, p. 341.

[14] *Ibid.,* p. 345. See also *New Introductory Lectures on Psychoanalysis,* trans. by W. J. H. Sprott, pp. 107–9.

[15] *A General Introduction to Psychoanalysis,* p. 343. This context appears to be the only one where Freud defines the manifestation of "anxiety" as opposed to "fear." He has, of course, written extensively on the dynamic explanation of anxiety and has revised his views in the process. His principal discussions of anxiety are found in the lecture just quoted, in the *New Introductory Lectures,* and in his *The Problem of Anxiety.*

[16] *Our Inner Conflicts: A Constructive Theory of Neurosis,* Chapter 9.

anxiety in contradistinction to fear is characterized by a feeling of helplessness toward the danger. The helplessness may be conditioned by external factors, as in the case of an earthquake, or by internal factors such as weakness, cowardice, lack of initiative. Thus the same situation may provoke either fear or anxiety depending on the individual's capacity or willingness to tackle the danger.[17]

My criterion is related to the first of these three criteria only. And note that in my conception, unlike Horney's, anxiety is not necessarily a response to a real external danger or to a definite perception of an imagined danger; the "quality of diffuseness and uncertainty" may be extreme. Yet in a broader sense there is perhaps always a danger present, in the sense that it would cause us pain to have to face the subconscious roots of our anxiety. Secondly, while all important states of anxiety are menacing the foundations of a personality's security system, there are also more trivial species of anxiety, expressed, for example, in a slight uneasiness over some unrecognized and not very important event.

The last of Horney's criteria appears to be the most dubious one of the three, at least for the purpose of making an empirically useful distinction. As a consequence of the usually less specific quality of the perception of danger, it is true that it is harder to find remedies for anxiety than for fear, and this is a factor making a feeling of helplessness more likely in one case than in the other. Yet a very concrete and specifically perceived danger may produce an equally realistic feeling of helplessness—for instance, during an earthquake or at the receiving end of "strategic bombing." If the distinction between anxiety and fear is to be psychologically meaningful, the definitions should not allow differences in the objective situation to predetermine the diagnosis of the response.[18]

In another context, Horney comes much closer to the definitions proposed here: "Fear is a reaction that is proportionate to the danger one has to face, whereas anxiety is a disproportionate reaction to danger, or even a reaction to an imaginary danger."[19] She points out that the cultural setting determines what reaction is proportionate; I shall make the same point with respect to "realistic" in our definition.

A closely related formulation is offered by Erik H. Erikson: "Fears are states of apprehension which focus on isolated and recognizable dangers so that they may be judiciously appraised and realistically countered. Anxieties are diffuse states of tension . . . which magnify and even cause the illusion of an outer danger, without pointing to any avenue of defense or mastery."[20]

---

[17] *New Ways in Psychoanalysis*, pp. 194–95.

[18] Horney illustrates the difference with respect to the last criterion in the following example: when hearing noises during the night as if burglars were breaking in, a mother became frightened and went into her eldest daughter's room. Unlike the mother, who was too frightened, the daughter had the courage to chase the burglars away. Horney concludes that the mother experienced *anxiety*; the daughter, *fear*. To me, they both appear to have responded with fear to a specific danger, even if the daughter was less afraid or less paralyzed by her fear. Horney's description would have appeared justified only if the mother had been unable to connect her anxiety with any realistic hypothesis on what might have caused the noise. *New Ways in Psychoanalysis*, p. 195.

[19] *The Neurotic Personality of Our Time*, p. 42.

[20] *Childhood and Society*, pp. 362–63.

It should be noted that Erikson avoids the implication that the state of apprehension is caused or preceded by a danger or an illusion of danger. In my definitions, I have taken the same precaution regarding "anxiety," while retaining in the definition of "fear" the assumption that it is "in response to" a perceived danger. In the conceptual scheme offered here, one of the crucial criteria of "anxiety," as opposed to "fear," is that only the latter state of apprehension is accounted for by stimuli indicating a danger; if the fear seems exaggerated, it is assumed that it has been reinforced by preconditioned anxiety. A final difference in preference is that my definitions of fear and anxiety do not state a difference in possibilities of individual defense. Yet it seems empirically obvious that a defense against something diffuse tends to be more complicated than measures against a specifically perceived danger.

Some writers stress the seriousness of the perceived danger as the crucial criterion of anxiety as opposed to fear. The most pronounced advocate of this conceptual approach is Kurt Goldstein, a specialist in the treatment and study of patients with brain lesions: "The phenomenon of anxiety belongs to the catastrophic condition. That is, anxiety corresponds on the subjective side to a condition in which the organism's existence is in danger. Anxiety is the subjective experience of that danger to existence."[21] And in another context: "As manifold as states of anxiety may be, with regard to intensity and kind, they all have one common denominator: the experience of danger, of peril for one's self."[22]

A process of mounting fear, according to Goldstein, turns into anxiety from the point when not only an individual goal but the person himself feels threatened.[23] All experiences of catastrophe, whether specific or diffuse, are subsumed under anxiety in his terminology, and this "anxiety" is always catastrophic: "What is it then that leads to fear? Nothing but the experience of the possibility of the onset of anxiety. What we fear is the impending anxiety. . . . The person in fear infers, from certain indications, that an object is apt to bring him into a situation of anxiety."[24] Perhaps the principal objection to Goldstein's terminology should be leveled against his limitation of "anxiety" to situations perceived as catastrophic. Common sense tells us that many states of apprehension of a milder degree are widely referred to as "anxiety" and have, in fact, much in common with the more extreme degrees of terror assumed in his concept of anxiety.

A survey of theories of anxiety was presented by Rollo May a few years ago.[25] His own set of definitions are of interest in this context chiefly because they represent a middle way between Freud and Goldstein:

Anxiety is the apprehension cued off by a threat to some value which the individual holds essential to his existence as a personality. . . . An individual ex-

[21] *Human Nature in the Light of Psychopathology,* p. 91.
[22] *The Organism: A Holistic Approach to Biology Derived from Pathological Data in Man,* p. 291.
[23] "Actually, it may be true that a state of fear, if increasing in degree, may ultimately turn into a state of anxiety." *Ibid.,* pp. 292–93.
[24] *Ibid.,* pp. 296–97.
[25] *The Meaning of Anxiety.*

periences various fears on the basis of a security pattern he has developed; *but in anxiety it is this security pattern itself which is threatened.*[26]

Within the realm of anxiety, May introduces a distinction closely resembling Freud's:

Normal anxiety is, like any anxiety, a reaction to threats to values the individual holds essential to his existence as a personality; but normal anxiety is that reaction which (1) is not disproportionate to the objective threat, (2) does not involve repression or other mechanisms of intrapsychic conflict, and as a corollary to the second point, (3) does not require neurotic defense mechanisms for its management, but can be confronted constructively on the level of conscious awareness *or* can be relieved if the objective situation is altered.

Neurotic anxiety is defined as the logical opposite, with disproportionate reaction, involving repression, and accompanied by neurotic symptoms and defense mechanisms.[27]

It will be seen that my own analytical concept of "fear" takes in May's "normal anxiety" as well, while my "anxiety" conforms roughly with his "neurotic anxiety"[28]—roughly speaking, that is, since my definitions are pegged to the "realism" or "proportion" between danger and apprehension and disregard his two other criteria, which have a dynamic rather than a manifest reference.

What does "realistic" mean? "Fear" is in this book defined as a response to a *realistically* perceived, specific danger; does this indicate that the danger must be a real one, not just a figment of the imagination? Yes and no. It must have the *appearance* of a real danger, not just idiosyncratically to the individual in question, but also to other individuals who would have the opportunity of perceiving the danger from the same angle. If a masked gunman in a dark alley demands my money, I experience fear; my fear is genuine to begin with, even if it turns out that some friend is playing a practical joke on me. If, however, the shock I experience is strong enough to produce, in cooperation with my latent anxieties, a constant fear of new holdups, or even hallucinations of meeting robbers again, my perception of danger is no longer realistic. It is grossly exaggerated, and most of my trouble from then on must be attributed to anxiety rather than fear.

The test of a "realistic" perception in this context, then, is not objective, but "intersubjective." If most people in a given milieu perceive a given stimulus or a given future prospect as a danger, then each individual who draws on the community's experience is "realistic" in shaping his perceptions of danger accordingly.[29] For example, the danger of being killed in a battle and the danger of being relegated to hell afterwards may both be

---

[26] *Ibid.*, p. 191. For a more popular discussion, see May, *Man's Search for Himself*, p. 40.

[27] *The Meaning of Anxiety*, pp. 194, 197.

[28] May acknowledges that a terminology such as suggested in this book, and not his own, is more in harmony with general usage in scientific literature. *Ibid.*, p. 197, note 9.

[29] As Karen Horney points out, "the decision as to whether the reaction is proportionate depends on the average knowledge existing in the particular culture." *The Neurotic Personality of Our Time*, p. 44. What does "knowledge" mean? The reference should be, I suggest, to the structure of fairly stable beliefs, and not include beliefs implanted in a transitory wave of collective hysteria (see below, p. 74).

sources of pure fear in the individual soldier, regardless of the observer's possible disbelief in the reality of the latter danger. It is probable for other reasons that both of these fears are accompanied by anxieties, but the perceptions of both dangers may be equally "realistic" in the sense employed here.

It must be remembered, however, that anxiety, like other emotional states, influences our perceptions. *"Perception is functionally selective,"* states a modern textbook in social psychology. It elaborates: "The objects that are *accentuated are usually those objects which serve some immediate purpose of the perceiving individual."*[30] In consequence, what is perceived as a clear and present danger may be so perceived *because* the individual suffers from anxiety and seeks an external explanation and possible relief.[31] In the dusk in a forest a stone may be perceived as a dangerous bear. If there is a fair likeness and likelihood, the illusion perhaps aided by movements in trees and bushes caused by wind and rain, it may be that a genuine fear arises, unconditioned by any previous anxiety. Yet the chances are, if an individual is running away from a stone, that an inner anxiety is the primary cause and that the perception of the external danger is shaped by that anxiety, with the stone serving as a mere prop. Erikson gives an example of an anxiety-enhanced state of fear, which illustrates the need for clinical analysis of concrete fears whenever the reaction to danger appears much stronger than what seems realistic:

If, in an economic depression, a man is afraid that he may lose his money, his fear may be justified. But if the idea of having to live on an income only ten times, instead of twenty-five times, as large as that of his average fellow-citizen causes him to lose his nerve and to commit suicide, then we must consult our clinical formula, which may help us find out, for example, that wealth was the cornerstone of his identity and that the economic depression coincided with the man's climacteric. The fear of losing his money, then, became associated with the anxiety aroused by having to live a role not characterized by unlimited resources, and this at the time when fear of losing his sexual potency had mobilized an infantile anxiety once connected with ideas of being inactivated and castrated. In the adult, then, impairment of judgment by infantile rage is the result of a state of irrational tension brought about by a short circuit between rational adult fears and associated infantile anxieties.[32]

It must be stressed that cultural patterns are important factors in determining (a) individual security systems and dangers to which these are exposed and (b) individual perceptions of dangers to which the whole

[30] Krech and Crutchfield, *Theory and Problems of Social Psychology*, pp. 87–88.

[31] Anxiety may be extremely painful. "There is a kind of fear that is not fear of something definite for something definite. It can be described as fear of everything for everything or of nothing for nothing. In extreme cases this indefinite fear can be more 'total' and worse than the fear of death. Men may commit suicide to escape its extreme misery." Riezler, "The Social Psychology of Fear," *American Journal of Sociology*, XLIX (1944), 490–91. The invention or the gross exaggeration of an external danger may give some relief from anxiety in that it is easier to face an external threat than a threat to one's mental equilibrium, and easier to face a specific danger that allows countermeasures than a diffuse, all-pervasive, and undefinable sense of danger.

[32] *Childhood and Society*, p. 363.

society is exposed. The last point is explained by the extent to which the individual's social and political attitudes are shaped by the information and propaganda to which he is exposed. A whole society may share realistic fears, and/or drift into something analogous to individual anxiety. For example, while a *fear* of war or of Soviet power may appear realistic, it may perhaps also be said that large segments of the American people in recent times have suffered from a diffuse *anxiety* about what deviltry a handful of American communists may have been up to. A state of anxiety, if it is widely shared at a given time, may be impressed on the individual by his surroundings and thus apparently form an exception to the rule that anxiety, unlike fear, originates inside the individual personality. Or, as I should prefer to put it: a society may develop something resembling individual anxiety neuroses, and the cognitive projections of a collective neurosis may be a source of concrete fears also for individuals who are not predisposed toward anxiety.[33] The differences in individual predispositions toward anxiety are likely to show up even in contexts approaching collective hysteria: those who are heavily predisposed toward anxiety can probably be relied on, statistically speaking, to respond with a greater concrete fear also of communists, for example, compared to the basically more secure individuals.

Objective Security

"*Security*" *means (c) the relative absence of danger.* In other words, *an individual (or a society) is more secure the lower the probability that he (or the society) will suffer damages or harm to vital interests.*

My frame of reference, it will be seen, is here transferred from the individual's perceptual world to the common objective world. An individual's security in this objective sense is, of course, influenced by his subjective ability to combat or evade the danger, once it is perceived, but the rise of an objective danger is not necessarily influenced or even perceived by the exposed individual. The same goes for a society, which may drift toward annihilation without anyone necessarily being aware of it. A danger facing a society is always a danger facing individuals—few or many (some of them may yet be unborn).

It will be seen right away that a high correlation is likely between the amount of dangers to which the individuals are exposed in a given society and the amount of specific fears that these dangers are likely to provoke. Yet the correlation cannot be assumed to be complete. In the first place, various kinds of objective dangers may not be experienced as such by the individuals concerned. This may be true, for example, in many cases of individuals drifting toward dope addiction or alcoholism. In the second place, specific fears may be strengthened by anxiety, and there is no obvious connection between levels of anxiety and amounts of objective danger lurking in a given society. The conceptual difficulty so far as the present definition of security is concerned is to determine more precisely what is to

---

[33] In the strictly analytical sense of "fear," a so-called collective neurosis can give rise to fear in the individual, as opposed to anxiety, only to the extent that he is not personality-wise predisposed to anxiety.

be understood by "danger." This problem is of significance also for the two previous definitions, of course.

It is necessary, first of all, to distinguish between specific and diffuse dangers. There may be many kinds of diffuse dangers, but probably the most important kind, and the kind I shall be concerned with in this book, is the danger of *anomie* or the disintegration of authoritative norms and institutions. However, let me first make a few remarks about types of *specific* objective dangers and the problems of value priorities they occasion. The diffuse but equally objective danger of anomie will be discussed immediately afterwards.

Let me list a few specific threats that are definitely serious enough to constitute "dangers"—threats directed toward somebody's life or health, toward basic freedoms of movement or speech, toward the opportunity to earn a living and support a family. Even if threats of this order may not provoke fear in all cases, there will be an almost universal agreement with the view that a free society so far as possible should endeavor to protect its members from such dangers; they are definitely to be considered first-order dangers.

With respect to other kinds of specific threats, the agreement may be less universal—for example, moderately severe threats to somebody's reputation or prestige, living standard, privacy, choice of consumption items, or leisure activities. Both in more general and more specific formulations, the problem of how much protection the individual should have against threats like these is unlikely to find a unanimous solution in our culture.

And yet it is crucial to the purpose of this book to determine tentatively the scope of society's legitimate concern with individual security against second-order dangers. This is clearly a part of the general problem of determining priorities of freedom. In this section, only a few preliminary remarks toward conceptual clarification of this part of the priority problem are in order. First, let me consider the general problem of dangers facing individuals, and afterwards the more specific, and in our times so urgent, problem of dangers facing entire societies or nations.

With respect to weighing the relative value of different aspects of individual security against various types of threats, I believe that the best way in which to phrase this problem is to apply the term "human rights." In this vein, the problem becomes one of determining the maximum scope of rights, meaning in effect the maximum amount of freedom and security that it is, in fact, possible for each state to guarantee for all its members at a given time. This problem is partly an empirical one, concerned with the nature of man and the nature of society; partly a logical one, concerned with clarification of definitions and of relationships between them; and partly a problem of ordering value priorities.

A "human right" means a demand that the individual be protected against certain types of private or public coercion, or against coercive interference depending on certain types of individual behavior.[34] Habeas

[34] Cf. above, pp. 6–7.

corpus and the prohibition of torture are examples of the former *procedural* type of human rights; free speech and free assembly are examples of the latter *substantive* type.

When in this book I speak of specific types of individual claims on society as "human rights," it follows only, strictly speaking, that *I* consider that the state or the community is obliged to enforce protection of these claims, if it is committed to the promotion of freedom. To the extent that such claims are in fact enforced, I shall speak of "effective human rights" or at times "effective legal rights." To the extent that I believe a demand for enforcement is generally shared, I shall speak of "generally accepted human rights."

My position differs from John Locke's and from the beautiful opening passage in the American Declaration of Independence, in that I am not assuming that human rights, by implication effective human rights, are inalienable from the Creator's hand. My position is that it is the task of politics, law, and education to try to *make* certain human rights inalienable, in an empirical rather than a metaphysical sense.

The security of a whole nation is, of course, another aspect of individual security, too, in the sense that genuine objective dangers confronting the nation are at the same time confronting all or some of the citizens as well. I do not know what a "national danger" means unless it means a danger to which individuals in the nation are exposed. How can it be determined what types of threats against the state[35] are important enough to constitute real dangers? This question raises almost infinitely complex problems, and all I can do at this stage is to indicate the direction toward an operational clarification of the interest of "national security." As it will be seen later in this chapter, this particular problem of security raises more important conflicts with the goal of free expression than the previously defined security values.

In the first place, a threat of military attack from another nation or combination of nations may represent a serious objective danger to the state provided (1) the potential opponents are stronger or approximately equally strong militarily, economically, and psychologically; (2) their leaders entertain the belief that they are stronger; or (3) their leaders, even without such a belief, may be foolhardy enough or clumsy enough to allow a war to begin.

In the second place, a threat of forcible overthrow of the government may represent a serious danger to the state provided (1) the movement desiring revolution is strong enough to hope to bring it about at a convenient moment, or (2) the revolutionists have allies abroad who are in a position to aid them by going to war against their country or by strengthening them sufficiently in other, less drastic ways.

In the third place, an oppressive, corrupt, or inefficient government can provoke the development of another danger affecting national security—a

---

[35] For many purposes it is important to distinguish a "state" sharply from a "nation." But on the present general level of analysis of types of security this distinction is not a crucial one. A threat against the state is perhaps primarily a threat against its political regime, which in a democratic country presumably is a group with which large sections of the people identify.

widespread disaffection among citizens. This factor in turn may or may not increase the growth of revolutionary movements. Whether or not it does, it is likely to increase the momentum of the first and second types of danger in weakening the psychological (and indirectly also the economic and military) power to resist a potential attack.

The main point to stress with respect to dangers affecting national security is that they are unavoidable in the modern world. The problem is not to eliminate them but to try to reduce them by rational means. This problem in turn branches off into two, only one of which will be a major concern in this book.

The first of these problems is the difficulty in achieving rational, purposive behavior on the part of political leaders who try to increase the national security.[36] The trouble is that so many political problems are deeply interwoven, so many conflicting political goals are pursued at once, both personal goals and public goals. Even the very perceptions of dangers are influenced by personal anxieties, as we have seen, by private interests, and by innumerable interpretations of the public interest. For example, a secretary of defense may suffer from a certain degree of paranoia; his family may own stock in an aircraft industry specializing in one type of bomber; or he may be worried about a recession if a decrease of tension and fear should lead to a political demand for reduction in armaments spending. Extraneous personal influences may operate on the best and most honest minds. They can never be entirely eliminated, but their bad effects (in terms of their failure to achieve optimal efficiency in assessing and protecting the national security) may be counteracted if there is a wide freedom of speech, so that intelligent opinions can be formed and expressed by a considerable number of concerned observers, whose biases may serve to even out the bias prevailing among the actual policy-makers.

The problem of achieving rationality in the search for optimal national security is in part a problem of defining the goal clearly, in isolation from other goals, and of deciding what means are adapted to promote this one goal with a maximum efficiency. I have touched on some of the difficulties involved in this task, but a discussion at length would be beyond the scope of this book.

The second part of the national security problem is of much greater concern to me: the problem of weighing the goal of national security against other goals. I shall discuss this problem in several contexts below in the section on the general relationships between security and freedom.

Let me now consider security against anomic dangers, the diffuse dangers that arise when institutional patterns either fluctuate or become too complex to provide effective standards for human motivation and behavior.

This third type of objective insecurity may be fully as disastrous as specific first-order dangers against human lives. This is evident in the title of the study in which the concept of "anomie" was first applied in empirical

---

[36] Some of the complexities involved in the choice of objectives are reviewed in Chapter 1, pp. 8–15. Cf. also below, p. 118, note 157.

research by a sociologist—Emile Durkheim's *Suicide* (1897). The empirical fruitfulness of this concept was demonstrated in that pioneering study.[37]

In his first major work, *The Division of Labor in Society* (1893), Durkheim discusses what he calls "the anomic division of labor." He refers to the isolation of functions that may follow increasing specialization in many fields, in science as well as in industry.[38] The concept of anomie is not carefully defined in this work, however; it is equated with "lack of organic solidarity" or lack of adequate "regulation determining the mutual relations of functions."[39] The social consequences of anomie are described in a very general manner. One suspects that Durkheim discovered the importance of this concept in the process of writing this book, and was led to attempt its empirical isolation in the *Suicide*. "Anomie" is a concept of basic importance throughout Durkheim's work, as is his "collective conscience."[40] These two may be considered approximate opposites in his conceptual scheme, in the sense that anomie is held to increase automatically whenever the collective conscience is weakened. Durkheim concludes the *Division of Labor in Society* with a note on the importance of a more definite moral code for producing relief from anomie.[41] In *The Elementary Forms of Religious Life* (1915), the last of his major works, he seeks to establish the basic function of religious systems in building social solidarity around a "collective conscience." He sees religion, in other words, as originating in society's need to prevent the growth of anomie.

In *Suicide* Durkheim presented empirical data strongly supporting his inference that a state of anomie is one of the causes of many suicides. He showed that the number of suicides tends to increase, not only in times of economic decline and crises, but also in times of abrupt economic growth. Human satisfaction depends, he explained, not upon the amount of gratification alone, but on the relationship between aspirations and gratifications. Times of depression lead many to despair and some to suicide because gratifications decline; periods of sudden expansion lead many to despair and some to suicide because "there is no restraint upon aspirations. . . . The less limited one feels, the more intolerable all limitation appears."[42]

"If therefore industrial or financial crises increase suicides," Durkheim concluded, "this is not because they cause poverty, since crises of prosperity have the same result; it is because they are crises, that is, disturbances of the collective order."[43] Anomic suicide, he defined, is the kind of suicide that "results from man's activity lacking regulation and his consequent suffer-

---

[37] *Suicide: A Study in Sociology*, trans. by Spaulding and Simpson. In his combination of theoretical sophistication and scrupulous use of statistical-empirical methods, Durkheim was far ahead of his time; as late as in 1954 his *Suicide* was called "still an unrivaled model" for successful integration of theory and research in social science. Jahoda, *Studies in the Scope and Method of 'The Authoritarian Personality'*, p. 19.

[38] *The Division of Labor in Society*, trans. by Simpson, pp. 353–73.

[39] *Ibid.*, pp. 365, 368.

[40] The French word *conscience* has often been translated as "consciousness" instead of "conscience." Cf. *ibid.*, p. ix.

[41] In this way, the specialization following from the division of labor is somewhat remedied, too, in that a common purpose produces awareness of connections between functions. See *ibid.*, pp. 408–9 and 372–73.

[42] *Suicide*, pp. 252–54.

[43] *Ibid.*, p. 241.

ings."[44] If the state of anomie in many cases leads to suicide, it is clear that in many other cases it must lead to serious mental disturbances with a less drastic outcome.

While it has been clear to social scientists since Durkheim that the danger of anomie represents an objective danger to many individuals in modern societies,[45] there appears to be no general awareness in the public about this problem except in so far as many political and religious movements warn against spiritual or economic chaos and offer their own formulas for relief. Among social scientists, on the other hand, an increased awareness of this problem is to be expected in the future and also some basic disagreements about the proper remedies.

Among recent writers, Sebastian de Grazia is apparently the only one who has taken an even more serious view of the danger of anomie than Durkheim did. He concludes that man needs above all a "sense of community," something that comes close to Durkheim's "collective conscience" but that specifically includes both political and religious beliefs. And the economic system based on competitiveness must be abolished, says De Grazia, in order to provide the human relations where man may "cease to act the wolf of man. The world's peoples will be loath to accept America's leadership so long as they see it as the promise of glittering objects in the clutch of competition. There can be no single world-embracing political community until the idea of competition as the guiding principle for the relation of man to man is ruled out."[46]

De Grazia distinguishes between *simple* and *acute* anomie. "Simple anomie is . . . the result of a clash between belief-systems or, more precisely, a conflict between the directives of belief-systems"; its psychological result is an "intermittent apprehension."[47] If a belief-system disintegrates, however, "the result is acute anomie, not the mere apprehension but the actual attack of anxiety."[48] De Grazia compares passages from Tocqueville's impressions of America more than a century ago with Durkheim's description of anomie, and he concludes that the state of simple anomie was and is a problem in the United States.[49] The state of acute anomie arises for individuals who feel "alone in an unmanageable, hostile environment"—for

---

[44] *Ibid.*, p. 258.

[45] When discussing specific dangers, I found it convenient and also conventional to distinguish between dangers facing individuals one by one and dangers facing a whole society or nation. A similar arrangement of my discussion might have been made with respect to the diffuse threat of anomie, but in this context there appears to be no particular advantage in that procedure. What I have to say about anomic dangers applies to individuals and to larger groups in much the same way, and it is not usual to separate the two kinds of concern about this type of danger.

[46] *The Political Community: A Study of Anomie*, p. 187.

[47] *Ibid.*, pp. 71, 72.

[48] *Ibid.*, p. 74. De Grazia defines an "ideology" or a "belief-system" as follows: "All systems of belief describe (1) certain activities which the rulers are obliged to perform for the benefit of members of the community, (2) certain activities and attitudes which the members owe the rulers, and (3) a time and place for these activities. . . . In this book, the actions which members of the communities owe the rulers have been designated 'directives.' In brief generalization for all ideologies, they are three: filial love, faith, and conformity to directives." *Ibid.*, p. 80.

[49] *Ibid.*, pp. 90–109.

example, among the hopelessly unemployed during times of depression. De Grazia quotes from a study of attitudes among the unemployed the following description as characteristic of acute anomie: "fear of the cruel tomorrow, the feeling of being hunted to earth, of being hemmed in, and absolutely helpless."[50]

De Grazia's concept of "simple anomie" corresponds to Durkheim's "anomie." The new concept of "acute anomie" is left rather unclear, however. For one thing, it is not clear whether it is an entirely psychological concept or not. De Grazia's description of attitudes among unemployed people seems to have no necessary reference to a disintegration of belief-systems; it is plausible in describing the despair of people who have been hit by any kind of catastrophe for which there is no remedy. Under such circumstances the individual may conceivably feel the same despair and anxiety whether he has a faith or not and whether his faith be that of a Catholic or a communist.

One may question, indeed, De Grazia's assumption that a cultural belief-system can disintegrate, except in a conflict with another, victorious belief-system. Such a conflict, while it lasts, gives rise to what he calls "simple anomie." *For an individual,* it is true, all belief-systems may disintegrate and be replaced by gray apathy, and this psychological reaction is probably what De Grazia wishes to call "acute anomie." I shall not follow him here, as it seems more convenient to reserve the concept of anomie for describing a certain diffuse *objective* danger, or a social rather than a psychological variable. De Grazia's description of the psychological consequences of "simple" versus "acute" anomie also has to be rejected; I submit that what he terms "simple anomie" may lead also to acute anxiety, not only to a mere apprehension.

Despite an unhappy terminology and conceptual scheme, however, there is much to be said for De Grazia's description of the psychological consequences of feeling that one belongs or does not belong to the community. His application of the psychological concept of separation-anxiety[51] to the political community seems particularly useful: "Give the child the security of home about him; give the man the orderliness of the world and its denizens. . . . To be freed of separation-anxiety is the citizen's bliss."[52] This way of placing political institutions in their psychological context for the individual adds new depths to our understanding of the impact of many social catastrophes, whether we relate them to the concept of anomie or not. Consider the reality of unemployment once again: "Possession of a job insures the holder of his status in the community; he has the income and respect which fend off separation-anxiety."[53] Let me add that it insures the individual's feeling of having an identity and his

[50] *Ibid.,* p. 123. Quoted from Zawadski and Lazarsfeld, "The Psychological Consequences of Unemployment," *Journal of Social Psychology,* VI (1935), 238.

[51] It is reasonable to assume that De Grazia uses "anxiety" in roughly the same sense as I do. See above, pp. 68–74.

[52] *The Political Community,* p. 98.

[53] *Ibid.,* p. 122.

self-esteem as well, and so we understand some of the depths of anxiety to which unemployment may plunge a man.

My principal objection to De Grazia's thought is to a large extent a matter of basic values. It is true that we may observe in man a need to believe, even a need to be a "true believer" in Eric Hoffer's sense.[54] Yet, rather than accept as innate in human nature a need to submit blindly to whatever faith a man may be born into, I wish to study empirically the conditions under which man may be enabled to tolerate more chaos in the belief-systems around him.[55] In other words, the intensity and all-pervasiveness of the "need to belong" may vary greatly, according to psychological and social circumstances.[56] I wish to inquire empirically into this problem: how much can the level of potential freedom be enhanced in modern societies without seriously increasing the amount of anomic suffering?[57]

The most promising recent attempt at revising the concept of anomie is found in two essays by Robert K. Merton.[58] Unlike Durkheim and De Grazia, he starts out with a basic distinction between ends and means in cultural belief-systems: "The first consists of culturally defined goals, purposes and interests, held out as legitimate objectives for all or for diversely located members of the society. . . . They are the things 'worth striving for.' . . . A second element of the cultural structure defines, regulates and controls the acceptable modes of reaching out for these goals."[59] This latter element is what I call "norms" as cultural facts and "institutions" as social facts.[60]

"An effective equilibrium between these two phases of the social structure is maintained so long as satisfactions accrue to individuals conforming to both cultural constraints, *viz.*, satisfactions from the achievement of goals and satisfactions emerging directly from the institutionally canalized modes of striving to attain them."[61] This equilibrium will tend to break down, however, to the extent that the norms of behavior fail to be perceived as effective in bringing goal satisfaction and to the extent that alternate procedures are perceived as much more effective. Tensions arise, in that case, between institutional demands and the demands of rationality or

---

[54] *The True Believer: Thoughts on the Nature of Mass Movements.*

[55] Cf. the following passage from a review of De Grazia's book: "It is probably true that for some people the anxieties of childhood set the pattern for the anxieties of adulthood. But it is obviously a dispeptic and sophomoric reading of current psychological thought to argue that no man ever matures, or *ever can mature,* to the point of becoming a self-reliant person who has no deep-seated need for a strong father-figure." Krech, *Journal of Abnormal and Social Psychology,* XLIV, No. 3 (1949), 433.

[56] "A rising mass movement attracts and holds a following not by its doctrine and promises but by the refuge it offers from the anxieties, barrenness, and meaninglessness of an individual existence. . . . [Hitler] knew that the chief passion of the frustrated is 'to belong,' and that there cannot be too much cementing and binding to satisfy this passion." Hoffer, *The True Believer,* pp. 39–40.

[57] Cf. below, pp. 181–88 and 274–80.

[58] "Social Structure and Anomie," *Social Theory and Social Structure,* pp. 131–94.

[59] *Ibid.,* pp. 132–33.

[60] Cf. below, pp. 262–64 and note 78.

[61] *Social Theory and Social Structure,* p. 134.

efficiency. "The technically most effective procedure, whether culturally legitimate or not, becomes typically preferred to institutionally prescribed conduct. As this process of attenuation continues, the society becomes unstable and there develops what Durkheim called 'anomie' (or normlessness)."[62]

Before describing various patterns of individual adaptation to this discrepancy between the demands of institutions and of rationality, Merton makes the point that nonconformist behavior may be just as "psychologically normal" as conformist behavior. With reference to anomic societies or situations, it is indeed a mere tautology to say that people will not all conform—whether the specific reference is to traditional institutions or to generally accepted new standards of efficiency. Merton's point of substance, or his "central hypothesis," is actually quite simple: he suggests that it is fruitful to study the state of anomie as a contributor to nonconformist behavior.[63] This is an assumption in the present study as well. And it is an additional assumption here that a certain measure of anomie is essential to insure social change and thus a possibility for human progress. No reforms are possible without deviators who sow the seeds of change.[64]

Merton suggests the following typology of individual responses to an institutional structure that has sufficient anomic strains to allow for alternatives to conformity and rebellion: *Conformity* means the acceptance of both the culture goals and the institutionalized means. *Innovation* means the promotion of conventional goals by unconventional means. *Ritualism* means sticking to the traditional ways regardless of their inefficiency in promoting the desired goals. *Retreatism* means the passive rejection of both goals and norms, and *rebellion* means the rejection of both along with the substitution of a new, action-oriented belief-system.[65]

It will generally be agreed that, except for "retreatism" and *possibly* "ritualism," all these responses to social institutions may be valuable at times.

---

[62] *Ibid.*, p. 135. Durkheim suggested the synonym "deregulation." See *Suicide*, p. 253. Cf. the following note.

[63] "It is, indeed, my central hypothesis that aberrant behavior may be regarded sociologically as a symptom of dissociation between culturally prescribed aspirations and socially structured avenues for realizing these aspirations." *Ibid.*, p. 134. Merton's synonym of "normlessness" for "anomie" is actually not a happy one, for the concept of nonconformity presupposes some degree of prevalence of a certain norm, or norm-system. "Norm-ambiguity" would be a less misleading approximate synonym; it is possible though not necessary to interpret "normlessness" (and also Durkheim's "deregulation") as equivalent with the absence of *unchallenged* norms. "Norm-ambiguity" indicates norm conflicts of a kind that typically finds the individual not taking sides but caught in the middle.

[64] Durkheim apparently was aware that too little anomie may be a danger, too, though he would hardly have approved of saying it in this way. He spoke of *fatalistic suicide* as the opposite of anomic suicide: "It is the suicide deriving from excessive regulation, that of persons with futures pitilessly blocked and passions violently choked by oppressive discipline." He thought this type of suicide to be relatively rare. Cf. *Suicide*, p. 276, note 25. As a problem of freedom, however, this extreme opposite of anomie is much the more urgent danger in the modern world.

[65] "It is a primary assumption of our typology that these responses occur with different frequency within various sub-groups in our society precisely because members of these groups or strata are differentially subject to cultural stimulation and social restraints." *Social Theory and Social Structure*, p. 140, note 12. In his most recent essay on anomie, Merton has elaborated on and broadened his application of these categories of individual response to his social situation. Cf. *ibid.*, pp. 176–94.

Both "innovation" and "rebellion" in Merton's sense are essential ingredients to prevent the social structure from petrifying. The danger threshold of anomie is reached, I suggest, when the amount of deviating behavior reaches the level where individual and social planning or purposive behavior is seriously impaired. It must remain possible for a state, for a social organization, and for the individual to carry out specific policies in support of specific goals.[66]

DEFINITIONS OF FREEDOM

Freedom means to me self-expression, or the individual's capacity, opportunity, and incentive to express whatever he is or can be motivated to express.

Corresponding roughly to the "capacity," "opportunity," and "incentive," I shall define three component freedom concepts, or aspects of freedom. Psychological freedom will be defined in positive terms, while the definitions of social and potential freedom, like my security concepts, will be formulated in the negative.

Psychological Freedom

"Freedom" (a) means degree of harmony between basic motives and overt behavior. The shorthand term "defensiveness" will frequently be used to designate deficiencies in psychological freedom.[67] Before explaining and interpreting the definition as it stands, let me say a few words about how I arrived at it.

My point of departure is the idea of "freedom" in the idealist tradition in philosophy, as represented by Green and Bosanquet. Green spoke of "freedom in the higher sense" as "the general power of men to make the best of themselves," as "a positive capacity of doing or enjoying something worth doing or enjoying." And Bosanquet's definition is in the same vein: "Liberty is the being ourselves, and the fullest condition of being ourselves is that in which we are ourselves most completely."[68] The idealists did not make it very clear what they meant by self-realization, but it is hardly fair to expose them to severe criticism on this count, if we remember that the growing science of psychology at the time of their writing did not have much help to offer. They may be taken to task for their general habit of neglecting to define many other important concepts as clearly as possible, but they deserve credit for an intuitive anticipation of some important insights of modern psychology.[69]

---

[66] So far, this is admittedly a rather vague criterion statement; for a few somewhat more precise elaborations, see below, pp. 118–21 and 275–80.

[67] "Defensiveness" is sometimes, though not by psychologists, used to designate a conscious or even deliberate cautiousness. In this book its reference is limited to "neurotic" attitudes that involve "repression"; cf. below, pp. 183–85. Psychoanalysts speak of "ego defensiveness" in roughly the same sense.

[68] Cf. above, pp. 55–57.

[69] Intuition plays an important role in all scientific work, of course, even in the most exact sciences. And in psychology, particularly in the field of personality, intuition is more all-pervasive than in most fields. While the idealists on the whole made their assertions the outcome of pure speculation, however, most personality psychologists have tried to sift their intuitions and conclusions against clinical experience and, so far as possible, against experimental observations. See below, Chapter 4.

The most forceful modern exposition of "freedom" in a psychological sense is given by Erich Fromm, and the resemblance between his concept of "positive freedom" and the idealist concept is surprisingly close, considering the differences in general orientation: *"Positive freedom consists in the spontaneous activity of the total, integrated personality."*[70] Or: "Positive freedom . . . is identical with the full realization of the individual's potentialities, together with his ability to live actively and spontaneously."[71]

In the book from which I have quoted, Fromm's main objective is to show why "freedom" in the utilitarian sense (absence of external restraints) is psychologically self-defeating unless the social and cultural context gives nourishment to the growth of "positive" freedom.[72] Or, in the terms I shall use, he attempted to demonstrate that social freedom may become a burden or a threat to the individual, unless he is enabled to develop a minimum of psychological freedom as well.

Fromm by no means deprecates the value of social freedom, however, and in this respect he departs radically from the idealist tradition.[73] The essential difference may perhaps be stated in terms of contrasting conceptions of human nature. Both Bosanquet and Fromm observe in man a need to be governed. But Bosanquet sees this need as a permanent one, forever embedded in human nature, while Fromm is inclined to view it as a transient need, conditioned by the impact of a given society and culture on human nature. Bosanquet's conclusion is that man must submit himself and accept the all-pervasive authority of the state; Fromm concludes that man must be made psychologically free in order to escape the psychological need for a meek submission under the state.[74]

Fromm's view, and the view of all psychologists today, is that man demands society because he is a social being and needs the company and affection of others and a certain amount of order and stability in his society. But the psychological need to be governed arises, according to Fromm, from anxiety caused by the lack of a psychological belongingness or basic security in man. He warns that the rise of individualism and social freedom in modern times may intensify men's demand to be governed, unless the individual learns how to avoid a psychological isolation from his fellow men. Men will try to escape from freedom if freedom means a loosening of most emotionally important ties to their fellows and to their community.

One who is inclined to share this belief is, nevertheless, bound to admit that the dilemma said to confront modern man is not stated in very rigorous

---

[70] *Escape from Freedom*, p. 258.

[71] *Ibid.*, p. 270. See also Fromm, *Man for Himself: An Inquiry into the Social Psychology of Ethics.* Another formulation akin to idealist conceptions of freedom is found in the subtitle and in the introduction to one of Karen Horney's recent books, where she says that "the ideal is the liberation and cultivation of the forces which lead to self-realization." See *Neurosis and Human Growth: The Struggle Toward Self-Realization,* p. 16.

[72] "It is the purpose of this book to analyze those dynamic factors in the character structure of modern man which made him want to give up freedom in Fascist countries and which so widely prevail in millions of our own people." *Escape from Freedom,* p. 6.

[73] The notion of forcing men to be free is the extreme expression of the general idealist tendency to view the growth of the state as the instrument of expanding individual "freedom" vicariously. Green, as we have seen, was much less inclined to identify with the state than were Rousseau and Bosanquet.

[74] Compare a somewhat parallel point above on p. 81.

terms by Fromm. The largest element of vagueness stems from his conception of "positive freedom" as indicated by "spontaneous activity of the total, integrated personality." It must also be admitted, however, that it is not easy to formulate definitions and hypotheses in rigorous terms about phenomena largely inaccessible to direct observation. The accumulation of knowledge about the total personality is a slow process of theorizing by inference from imperfect research covering limited areas. The very concepts we use are largely hypothetical constructs: their clarification can advance only as their usefulness is tested indirectly in patient, theoretically comprehensive research.[75] An operationally satisfactory definition of "psychological freedom" is impossible at the present stage of our knowledge, therefore, but it nonetheless appears possible to come a little bit closer to this goal than Fromm has brought us.

In the first place, let us see if the definition I have chosen from *Escape from Freedom* can be simplified. It may be suspected that a capacity for spontaneity is in itself an indication of, perhaps *the* crucial criterion for a well-integrated personality. This is borne out if we consider Fromm's definition of spontaneity:

Spontaneous activity is not compulsive activity, to which the individual is driven by his isolation and powerlessness; it is not the activity of the automaton, which is the uncritical adoption of patterns suggested from the outside. Spontaneous activity is free activity of the self and implies . . . the acceptance of the total personality and the elimination of the split between "reason" and "nature"; for only if man does not repress essential parts of his self, only if he has become transparent to himself, and only if the different spheres of life have reached a fundamental integration, is spontaneous activity possible.[76]

According to Fromm, in other words, to be psychologically free means having a fundamentally integrated personality. Capacity for spontaneity indicates the presence of such integration.

The task of making empirical sense out of the concept of "fundamental personality integration" is still ahead, however, and it is no simple task. Integration is not simply the absence of internal tensions caused by conflicting motives. The degree of fundamental integration may be high even if powerful contradictory motivations are at work on a conscious or near-conscious level; conflicting goals and conflicting motives are ever-present in most human lives.

In every human personality, and particularly in the child, there is an intermittent struggle going on between biologically rooted impulses or drives and the social or socially conditioned impulses or drives or inhibitions, which are usually called "conscience." Or, in the terms of the Freudian tradition, a struggle between the "id" and the "superego." It takes time before a more or less precarious modus vivendi is established, in the form of a set of more or less well-structured habitual attitudes about "right" and "wrong." These become internalized in the decision-making agency in each person, and this "agency" or function has by the Freudians and others

---

[75] Cf. below, the introduction to Chapter 4.
[76] *Escape from Freedom*, pp. 258–59.

been termed the "ego."[77] At times, however, the truce is more apparent than real: the conscience, instead of compromising with and channeling some basic drives (often the sex drive), strives to suppress them by denying their existence. At times the drive may be transformed by "sublimation"— that is, find indirect, symbolic outlets that are satisfactory to the total personality, including the conscience. More often, it is "repressed" and keeps hammering on the conscience, creating guilt feelings and ensuing anxiety that generates the need for more repression—and so on, in a vicious circle.[78]

The fundamentally integrated personality is the personality in which a successful solution has been found in the conflict between biological drive and social conscience, so that a minimum of self-deception by repression or other defense mechanisms has been necessary. Psychological freedom, then, is achieved to the extent that the total behavior integrates and allows expression for the basic drives, so that these are channeled instead of blocked by the conscience. And now I come to my definition, as already stated: *Freedom (a) means degree of harmony between basic motives and overt behavior*. If this formulation makes sense from the point of view of Freudian theory, it still remains to be shown that it is not entirely inaccessible to the application of operational research criteria.

It is evident that overt behavior is subject to empirical study, but what about basic motives? Fortunately, steady progress has been made over the last decades, in finding ways to study both basic motives and conflicts between motives and behavior. In the present context it must suffice to say that the so-called nondirective and projective techniques in psychological research have given increasingly plausible and reliable clues about the force and contents of unconscious motives. In addition, there are the various clinical techniques of the psychoanalysts, whose interpretations are somewhat more controversial. They tend to involve various assumptions about which men may differ, and they tend to be imprecise and thus not easily subject to statistical comparison techniques. More recently, however, it has been found possible to develop empirical techniques adapted to quantitative research in processes of depth motivation.

In the most notable pioneer project in this direction,[79] the authors were able to demonstrate the existence of two opposite personality types, one of which is psychologically relatively free, in my sense, and the other relatively unfree. The unfree type is called the authoritarian personality and is characterized, above all, by the inability of the individual to give expression to some of his own basic motives, which are blocked from consciousness

---

[77] It should be stressed that many people operate a so-called "double standard," having discrepant conceptions about "right" and "wrong" in general and in application to themselves. In such cases the latter sense of "right" and "wrong" is the relevant one in the present context: the ego is formed when *its* personal adjustment habits between drives and conscience are stabilized. This gradual adjustment operates on both conscious and subconscious levels; even the "conscience" is not necessarily any more conscious than the drives are.

[78] "Repression" has been defined as follows: "The process of excluding repugnant mental contents from access to consciousness," English, *A Student's Dictionary of Psychological Terms*, listed in Murphy, *Personality: A Biosocial Approach to Origins and Structure*, p. 996. See also Freud, *The Problem of Anxiety*, p .19, and Horney, *New Ways in Psychoanalysis*, p. 25. This process is discussed below, pp. 183–85.

[79] Adorno et al., *The Authoritarian Personality*.

by the operation of various self-deceptive defense mechanisms. Typical expressions of this unfreedom are various attitude-syndromes character-ized by strong ethnocentrism, "black-white thinking," and strong support to conventions about good manners. Less unity was found in the attitude syndromes of democratic personalities, or those who in my terms are psychologically more free; except in so far as they were "low scorers" on scales designed to measure the prevalence of authoritarian syndromes.[80]

That study, which has been followed by many others, demonstrates that a definition of "psychological freedom" along the lines suggested here is not devoid of empirical sense.

It is possible to distinguish analytically between actual and potential correspondence between basic motives and overt behavior and to peg the definition of psychological freedom to either alternative. This distinction is important enough in Harald Ofstad's study of the free-will issues to be the basis for two different chapters.[81] In this book such a distinction is not equally justified, and it would involve great difficulties to try to apply it in research. My concept of psychological freedom, consequently, shall refer both to the actual correspondence between overt behavior and basic motives and to the individual's capacity or power to bring about such a correspond-ence. As the latter criterion is the more inclusive one, however, it must also be the crucial one in the definition.[82]

For purposes of determining how psychological freedom can be max-imized, it probably makes no difference whether we focus on the process or the potential as our goal. And the empirical difficulties of applying such a distinction are considerable in a research area in which direct observation is so narrowly confined. "Basic motives" can at best be identified by the use of projective tests and other nondirective techniques, and the degree of integration of these motives in the individual's behavior can only be judged at specific times, often in "artificial" experimental situations. This makes it exceedingly difficult to distinguish between the capacity and the process of integration in forecasts about the individual's behavior in other situ-ations.

Is psychological freedom desirable? If so, is it desirable to an unlimited extent? This is clearly not a question subject to a scientifically proven answer; elements of faith or attitude enter into it. All the behavioral scientist can hope to demonstrate is that a high degree of psychological freedom is attainable under given circumstances. He can also work toward

---

[80] Authoritarianism is probably only one among several types of deficiencies in psycho-logical freedom; but this is the type of defensiveness we know the most about today. Cf. below, pp. 188–228.

[81] Cf. Ofstad, *The Freedom of Decision,* chap. 4, "Freedom as Self-Expression," and chap. 6, "Freedom as Power."

[82] One may have the power or ability to express certain motives without ever doing so. Certain relatively basic motives might, if expressed in overt behavior, be self-defeating, or lead to serious reductions in social freedom. The test of psychological freedom is under these cir-cumstances in the capacity, not in the overt act. Awareness of such motives is sometimes but perhaps not always an indication of a psychological capacity to act on them. Cf. below, p. 88.

accumulating knowledge on how such circumstances and, consequently, psychological freedom can be promoted. This is the essential task of Chapter 4.

I see no inherent limitation in the desirability of maximizing psychological freedom. If there are limits, they must be determined by conflicts with other freedom values or in the clash of competing freedom demands. This problem will be discussed in later sections of this chapter.

This is not to say, however, that the overt actions of a person ideally should be expressive of every single motive existing below the surface of his consciousness. Such an ideal would be a self-defeating one, since the expression of certain types of motives nearly automatically would lead to actions that would thwart the expression of many other and possibly more basic motives. Antisocial impulses should be recognized and tolerated in the self, but they should not necessarily be permitted to lead to antisocial acts. Homosexual drives, to take another example, are accepted and faced as part of himself by the psychologically free person, if they are significantly strong, but they are not necessarily expressed in overt action in inappropriate situations.[83] The ideal of psychological freedom requires minimally only the awareness of and the capacity to express the more basic motives: their actual expression may depend on the perceived appropriateness of social circumstances.

"Know thyself" and "be thyself," then, express in a nutshell the two basic components of the ideal of psychological freedom. I suspect, if I may venture an extremely tentative empirical generalization bearing on the problem of definition just discussed, that the mere appearance of antisocial or profoundly inappropriate-if-expressed basic motives will be less frequent, in a given personality, the higher his level of psychological freedom.

Social Freedom

"Freedom" (b) means the relative absence of perceived external restraints on individual behavior. In essence, this definition is equivalent to the formulations of Hobbes and Locke,[84] which were never departed from, in any important respect, in the empiricist-utilitarian tradition. A principal point at issue between these philosophers was whether a powerful, active state was desirable to protect the individual against restraints instituted by his neighbors or whether a circumscribed, passive state should be preferred, to keep down the scope of restraints imposed by law and government.

What the empiricists tended to overlook is that the individual as a social being demands restraints, if this word is taken in a wide sense, as much as he demands freedom, if not much more. Life in groups and in society implies and necessitates many kinds of restraints on the individual, but they are not all perceived as restraints. Some are internalized and are consequently either taken for granted as part of the situation in which the individual acts or are incorporated in his personality as a part of his superego

---

[83] Homosexuality is quite compatible with a high degree of psychological freedom, even if it presumably in many instances develops under circumstances that affect psychological freedom adversely.

[84] Cf. above, pp. 28 and 30, and note 14.

or ego.[85] Others are adhered to with pleasure; they push in the direction the individual wished to go anyway. Others again are complied with as matters of necessity or as lesser evils; or they are not complied with, resulting in some kind of damage for the individual.

Let us note that "restraint" is used in a broad and objective sense, referring to all the potential obstacles that limit the possibilities of individual choice or put penalties on alternatives. Anything that pushes or punishes the individual is a restraint, but so is also anything that hypothetically and probably *would* push or punish him, should he be inclined to a certain kind of behavior at a given time and place.

Restraints are necessary in any society, and they are not emerging at random. This book proceeds on the general assumption that social facts, including social restraints, have functions. To explain institutional regularities and predict their further development one must develop hypotheses about the kinds of needs they serve, individual and social.

When social restraints on individual behavior are studied in terms of their probable functions in social interaction, I shall prefer to call them "sanctions." A *sanction,* then, is any type of restraint on individual behavior that is viewed as an inducement toward or away from a certain kind of behavior.[86] The inducement can consist in the possibility of either rewards or punishments and usually implies both, depending on which side of the coin is looked at. Every kind of sanction, whether light or heavy, is assumed to serve at least one function, either for one or more individuals and/or for one or more social institutions in a social system.[87]

In this context no dynamic discussion of sanctions will be attempted; I am here only interested in a clarification of the concept of social freedom, and in making some tentative suggestions about the extent to which social freedom should be considered desirable.[88]

"Restraint" is not the only very broad term in my definition of social freedom. "External" hardly is much of a delimitation, since it includes everything that is external to the individual personality. A body defect, for example, is considered an external restraint, especially, but not only, if it interferes with the individual's ability to enjoy normal social relationships. In fact, even the physical limitations on what a healthy body can do are external restraints on the personality.[89] Yet, my focus of interest is on interpersonal restraints.

[85] I am speaking of internalization in a wider sense than is usual in psychological literature; internalization in a narrower, more strictly psychological sense would refer to the incorporation in superego or ego only. Cf. below, pp. 252–53.

[86] This is in substance a widely used definition. Margaret Mead, for example, defines sanctions as "mechanisms by which conformity is obtained, by which desired behavior is induced and undesired behavior prevented." *Cooperation and Competition among Primitive Peoples,* p. 493.

[87] The concept of function is defined, and some general problems of functional analysis of institutions are discussed below, cf. pp. 240–48. The concept of sanction is discussed again on pp. 263–64. "Institution" is defined on p. 262.

[88] A study of the dynamics of social freedom will be attempted in Chapter 5.

[89] I am here following Talcott Parsons: "The actor is an ego or a self, not an organism, and . . . his organism is part of the 'external world' from the point of view of the subjective categories of the theory of action." *The Structure of Social Action,* p. 49, note 3.

"Behavior," again, is no limitation on the concept of social freedom. This term, too, is understood in its very broadest sense, covering attitudes and actions; opinions, emotions, perceptions, cognitions, and motivations; verbal and nonverbal expression; actual and intended activity and passivity.

The one saving circumstance that allows me to delimit this freedom concept is the qualification that the restraints must be *perceived as restraints*. If a government follows Rousseau's advice and is able to succeed in redirecting the wills of the people, it does to this extent not interfere with their social freedom. If a minority is penalized for trying to oppose this manipulation of minds, then this minority is deprived of social freedom. But the majority whose opinions have changed as a result of skillful manipulation are as free as before in this sense; what they have suffered is a reduction in potential freedom.[90]

Let me take one more example to clarify the difference between social and potential freedom. A law prohibiting interracial marriages in a given state curbs the social freedom of a given individual only to the extent that he is aware of the possibility of such a marriage, for himself or for others. Only to the extent that such an idea is completely outside his psychological field—as a biological possibility or as a social arrangement that anybody could want—would it follow from my definition that such a law does not interfere with this particular individual's social freedom.[91]

The *intention* of the restraining agent is irrelevant for determining whether or not an individual is being subjected to restraint. A good husband, for example, may either intentionally or unintentionally impose considerable restraints on his wife, and the same goes the other way.

Even if a given obstacle may not suffice to change the individual's attitudes or overt behavior, it is still limiting his social freedom to the extent that it has been brought to his awareness or half-awareness as a restraint and thus has influenced his motivational behavior. Only if the relevance or seriousness of a possible threat or obstacle to a given individual or to his plans is totally unperceived by him, may it properly be said that his social freedom is wholly unaffected by the event.

If external circumstances become completely internalized, they cease to interfere with the individual's social freedom as defined here. In heroic moments a man may identify so completely with his cause or country that even a mission involving death as a certain consequence does not interfere with his social freedom; a call to action may in fact liberate him from the intolerable restraints of enforced passivity "in times that try men's souls."[92]

Problems of social freedom are intimately connected with problems of power. In this context a few remarks must be made on the surface relationship between these two concepts.

"Power" has preliminarily been defined as an individual's degree of

---

[90] Cf. below, pp. 95–100.

[91] It surely interferes with the social freedom of other people, however, as it is hardly conceivable that such a law would be called for unless there was a widespread awareness that interracial marriage is biologically and socially possible.

[92] Needless to say, the enemy, or whatever poses the prospect of death, is necessarily a restraint, in threatening to take away all his social freedom forever.

control over his security. The power of an individual refers to the probable difference his own effort will make in his access to or advancement of values (including more power) in desired amounts and kinds.[93]

It is useful to distinguish between *independent* and *dependent* power: independent power means autonomous control over values, while dependent power means a kind of control that depends on carrying out obligations in deference to a superior power center. This power center may be one or more individuals (for example, an organization) or an institution, meaning a sanctioned pattern of expected behavior. Very often power is exercised in part independently and in part dependently. A bureaucrat, for example, is independent within a certain sphere, the sphere of his own discretion, while he is dependent on rules and regulations and on the orders of his superiors in many other spheres of his exercise of power.

Power is conceived as a *potential,* to be distinguished from the *process* of *exercising power.* We speak of a *power subject* with reference to the source of independent power; a *power agent* is a holder of dependent power; and a *power object* is an individual over whom power is exercised.

Probably all human beings living in society at all times are both subjects, agents, and objects of power, in proportions differing among individuals and varying from one situation to another for each individual. Nobody is or ever was all-powerful; even a despot needs some cooperation in order to control certain values. And nobody is or ever was completely without power; even a slave is not entirely without at least a subtle bargaining power, unless he is about to be put to death. Every power agent is at the same time a subject and an object of power.

Power as a potential does not necessarily limit anybody's freedom. Even the exercise of power—actual, predicted or expected—does not *necessarily* interfere with anybody's freedom; it depends on the means by which power is exercised. These can for present purposes be sketchily listed as: physical force or threats of force; other value deprivations (or indulgences) or threats (promises) of such; fraud; and persuasion.[94]

The ends of power exercise, or the ends-in-view, may be deliberate or nondeliberate. This is the distinction between rational and institutional exercise of power, corresponding to the distinction between rational and institutional behavior.[95]

It is the means and not the ends of power exercise that determine the extent to which social freedom is interfered with. The intention of the power subject or power agent is irrelevant; it does not necessarily make any difference whether he is acting deliberately or merely by habit of convention, or even in the mistaken belief that he is just helping the power object. What does matter is the means he employs. Threats of physical force or other value deprivations, down to mere withdrawal of approval—

---

[93] Cf. above, p. 19. "Influence" is in this study synonymous with "power."

[94] "Manipulation" is a term that overlaps with both "fraud" and "persuasion." Cf. below, pp. 98 and 259. This typology is similar to Russell's: "An individual may be influenced: A. By direct physical power over his body, e.g., when he is imprisoned or killed; B. By rewards and punishments as inducements, e.g., in giving or withholding employment; C. By influence on opinion, i.e., propaganda in its broadest sense." *Power: A New Social Analysis,* p. 36.

[95] "Rational" is here used in a broad sense. Cf. below, pp. 314 and 313–20.

all serve to reduce the social freedom of the power object, to the extent that he perceives the sanctions and considers them at all significant as threats. Promises of indulgence conditional on performance can usually be seen as threats of deprivations conditional on nonperformance, and thus as a rule fall in the same category of interfering with social freedom by way of negative sanctions.[96]

If, on the other hand, fraud is employed, it is not the social but the potential freedom of the power object that is affected. And to the extent that pure persuasion is utilized, free of elements of fraud, power can be exercised without anybody's loss of freedom in any sense. In both the latter cases there are no perceived external restraints on individual behavior occasioned by the exercise of power.

Let us now consider whether and to what extent social freedom is desirable. Clearly, it follows from my general position favoring a maximal freedom of expression in the fullest sense that social freedom is desirable, generally speaking. On the other hand, it is quite clear also that many limitations on social freedom are desirable, for the simple reason that life in society necessitates many kinds of restraints. To a certain extent, one man's freedom means another man's restraints, which is almost the same as saying that one man's power often means another man's oppression.

Is it possible to draw a line between desirable and undesirable restraints on social freedom? This is basically an empirical problem, once the value premise of freedom maximization is given. But it involves some further value assumptions as well: one must take at least some general position on the hierarchy of importance of freedom demands. In other words, one has to formulate some criteria on the relative importance for human freedom as a whole of different types of human rights. Once it has been decided which rights are more basic, it becomes an empirical question, though perhaps a complex one, to decide what privileges and what less basic rights have to be curbed in order to extend the more basic rights to all and, first of all, to those who are the most deprived to begin with.

An almost universal consensus can be expected in support of the proposition that murder is a worse deprivation for the victim than is a not fatal blow. It will be less universally but still widely agreed that physical assault is a worse interference with freedom and dignity than is verbal scolding, on the whole. Beyond this it is hard to achieve consensus on more specific hierarchies of values in the realm of social freedom (which is the same as hierarchies of negative values in the realm of damages to social freedom).

My general position is intentionally simple in the hope of qualifying it for a wide support: I consider *coercion* the supreme political evil. I desire for the individual and for society, first of all, the maximization of freedom from coercion, and consequently I consider all other freedom values second-priority goals.

The utility of this formula evidently hinges on what is understood by "coercion." It is well-nigh impossible, I believe, to find a very specific definition that is at the same time generally acceptable. But this is perhaps not

96 Cf. below, p. 93.

a crucial obstacle: it may well be desirable to use a coercion concept with somewhat flexible limits toward the border area of the neighboring concept of noncoercive restraint, provided there is general agreement on what constitutes the more central areas of coercion. A natural and desirable consequence of social and cultural growth may be that the reference of "coercion" gradually is extended to include new and somewhat subtler kinds of sanctions, parallel to the gradual reduction in occurrences of the more brutal and direct ones.

Lasswell and Kaplan define coercion simply as "a high degree of constraint and/or inducement."[97] Loosely delimited as this concept is, it nevertheless at first seems to depart from common sense and thus from the probability of consensus in one respect: inducements (rewards) are not ordinarily thought of as coercive. Yet, I believe it is in the interest of clear thinking to admit that they can be, if strong enough. If a man in dire poverty is offered a very large sum of money to perform some deed on the shady side of the law, and this appears to him his only chance ever to get into the money, he may yield to the temptation against his principles. The high degree of inducement has for him created a new perspective of the future, and from that moment on the necessity of either performing the deed or letting go of the new perspective may be psychologically equivalent to a high degree of constraint.[98]

Following the general approach of Lasswell and Kaplan, *coercion* in this study means *(a) the application of actual physical violence,* or *(b) the application of sanctions sufficiently strong to make the individual abandon a course of action or inaction dictated by his own strong and enduring motives and wishes.* A man who conforms willingly, abandoning his earlier desires, is no longer coerced. The more repugnant the induced course of action is to the power object, the more it presumably takes of pressure to make him comply, and still more it would take to make him conform willingly. Among two men whose initial wishes endure, a timid man is more easily coerced toward compliance than is a courageous man. Institutions can be just as coercive on the individual as the exercise of power in the service of deliberate plans.

Degrees of coercion are determined according to the power of the coercive sanctions toward making the individual abandon important intentions in order to comply. Judged on a social scale, coercive pressures are more severe the more of the average man's individuality they are able to suppress. Judged in the individual case, coercion is more severe the stronger the motives and wishes that the power object abandons in order to comply. Actual physical violence is considered coercive regardless of whether the victim succumbs and complies—and coercive to the highest degree.

Coercion can take place without being intended; the perennial overprotecting mother is a case in point. On the other hand, intentions of even the most flagrant coercion are not always successful. It depends on whether or not the victim succumbs to the pressures.

The means of power are insufficient as criteria for determining whether

97 *Power and Society,* p. 97.
98 The example has been suggested by Harold D. Lasswell in conversation.

coercion is accomplished; the decisive criterion is the outcome. Yet, one particular means, the actual application of physical violence, is for my purposes considered coercive even if the victim does not comply or does not even try to comply. Physical violence is usually a potent means of making potential victims take heed, and it always interferes with the actual victim's own strong motives and wishes. With the possible exception of confirmed masochists, we may assume that every human being strongly desires physical integrity and inviolability.

Now let me return to the value question. My position is that coercion is the supreme political evil, or the supreme evil that results from power processes and that can be reduced by political means. A maximal amount of freedom from coercion is supremely desirable. Coercion can be justified only if it serves to reduce the occurrence of worse kinds of coercion. And the worst kind of coercion is the actual application of substantial physical violence; degrees of violence are determined medically in the consequences for the victim's health, physical and mental.[99] Degrees of violent *intent* are, of course, judged by the intended or expected consequences of the act of violence.

The total abolition of coercion is an ideal that can possibly never be fully vindicated in practice, but it can be approached in practice and is not unattainable in principle. It is not inconceivable that psychologically free individuals can be made to endure willingly all the restraints that an enlightened, self-restraining government and public opinion may impose. A society within which all children go to school motivated by a spontaneous quest for knowledge, in which there are no criminals to lock up, and in which reasonable taxes are paid willingly—such a conception strains the imagination but does not surpass it.[100]

Let me assert, therefore, not only that a maximal freedom of expression for all should be the supreme goal of a civilized society, but also this: among all freedom goals, the goal of maximizing everyone's freedom from coercion should take first priority.[101]

Beyond this, I shall not assert that external restraints on individual behavior in general are undesirable or, for that matter, desirable. The extent to which social restraints are required in social life, for purposes such as social solidarity, division of labor, prevention of anomie, mental health, and cultural growth, will become clearer in Chapters 5 and 6, where determinants of social and potential freedom will be discussed in the context of a theory of social systems.

[99] Poisoning usually involves fraud but is also a specimen of physical violence, to be judged by its outcome, just as other kinds of violence. Confinement or imprisonment is considered physical violence only if and to the extent that it damages the individual's health, physical or mental.

[100] Cf. below, pp. 278–80 and 311–12.

[101] My human rights approach means that the liberation of the more coerced individuals takes precedence over the liberation of those who are less coerced, even if the latter are more numerous. Kenneth Boulding sees a possibility for consensus on a more moderate version of this value position: "It should be possible to agree that coerciveness *in itself* is an evil, and that any development in society toward less coercive forms of social organization that have survival value is desirable." *The Organizational Revolution*, p. 217.

Potential Freedom

"Freedom" (c) *means the relative absence of unperceived external restraints on individual behavior.*

I observed earlier that Plato and Aristotle in some ways understood better than Bentham did the extent to which human nature, including minds and motives, is subject to change by legislative and other institutional means. Plato, for example, attributes to Socrates the view that the rulers of the state, "in their dealings either with enemies or with their own citizens, may be allowed to lie for the public good."[102] The maxim of Karl Marx that religion is the opiate of the people is only an extreme statement of a very old discovery. J. B. Bury, writing on the later Roman Republic and the early Empire, says: "Most of the leading men were unbelievers in the official religion of the State, but they considered it valuable for the purpose of keeping the uneducated populace in order."[103] Machiavelli in his turn observes that ecclesiastical principalities can endure without much ability or fortune on the part of their princes. Their rule is

sustained by ancient religious customs, which are so powerful and of such quality, that they keep their princes in power in whatever manner they proceed and live. These princes alone have states without defending them, have subjects without governing them, and their states, not being defended, are not taken from them; their subjects not being governed do not resent it, and neither think nor are capable of alienating themselves from them. Only these principalities, therefore, are secure and happy.[104]

Rousseau was clear and forceful on this point. In his *Discourse on the Origin of Inequality,* he explains the origin of political society in the invention by rich men of "the profoundest plan that ever entered the mind of man: this was to employ in his favour the forces of those who attacked him, to make allies of his adversaries, to inspire them with different maxims, and to give them other institutions as favourable to himself as the law of nature was unfavourable." And in his *Discourse on Political Economy* he offers the following advice: "that government which confines itself to mere obedience will find difficulty in getting itself obeyed. It is good to know how to deal with men as they are, but it is much better to make them what there is need that they should be."[105] The tradition of "totalitarian democracy,"[106] of which Soviet communism is the foremost example today, has followed Rousseau's advice: the way toward a more secure and a "better" social order is evidently seen as leading through thoroughly organized efforts to make men "what there is need that they should be."

In liberal democracy, on the other hand, in so far as a highly developed individuality and thus a wide diversity among men is hoped for, the problem of political manipulation must be approached from the opposite angle: How can we insure conditions under which men can develop into

[102] *The Republic,* pp. 86–87.
[103] *A History of Freedom of Thought,* p. 39.
[104] "The Prince" in *The Prince and The Discourses* (Modern Library), pp. 41–42.
[105] *The Social Contract and Discourses,* pp. 250 and 297. Cf. above, p. 62.
[106] In Talmon's phrase.

what they have it *in themselves* to become? How can the growth of individuality be sheltered against institutional and reformist pressures—against being pushed into whatever harness is adapted toward the improvement and perfection, in some sense, or preservation, of social and political institutions?

Tocqueville, who was an aristocrat in the best sense of the word, was keenly aware of this problem and was for this reason apprehensive about the extreme majoritarianism in the United States, as·this country looked to him more than a century ago:

The authority of a king is physical and controls the actions of men without subduing their will. But the majority possesses a power that is physical and moral at the same time, which acts upon the will as much as upon the actions and represses not only all contest, but all controversy. I know of no country in which there is so little independence of mind and real freedom as in America.[107]

Speaking of the contemporary American scene, Phillips Bradley declares:

The "tyranny" we have to fear today, especially as to our legislatures, is not the defeat of majority demands, however transitory. It is rather the distortion of majority concern—the promotion of the general welfare—by the organized and concentrated minorities pursuing special interests.[108]

The literature focusing on potential freedom is as scant as the literature on social freedom is plentiful. Even the very concept of potential freedom, or any approximate equivalent, has to my knowledge never been given much attention. The problem has been perceived by many writers, some of whom have just been cited. But none of them has attempted to place this problem in the systematic context of a study of freedom, whether philosophically or empirically. Philosophers throughout history and behavioral scientists in recent times have been much concerned with problems of how people in societies ought to live and how they can be influenced toward living that way. How to help people resist the manipulation of their benefactors, or would-be benefactors, is a relatively new problem of freedom, however. Its significance, at least, has not been as apparent until recent times.[109]

The concept of potential freedom is a difficult one to delimit. Human behavior is restrained by innumerable circumstances, and the great majority of these are not perceived as restraints. Factors in childhood backgrounds, conventions, biological and social needs, interpersonal relations, aspirations and expectations for the future—all these aspects of life can be said to imply numerous restraints on the individual, restraints that as a rule either are taken for granted as part of the self or the situation or are unperceived parts of the unconscious ego, id, or superego.

Such a broad concept is not of much use as it stands. A goal of maximizing potential freedom in this sense would be difficult to conceptualize.

---

[107] *Democracy in America* (Vintage), I, 273. Cf. below, p. 100.

[108] "A Historical Essay," Appendix II in Tocqueville, *Democracy in America*, II, 454.

[109] Cf. above, pp. 3–4. It must be said that Thoreau recognized the practical significance of the problem when he wrote: "If I knew for a certainty that a man was coming to my house with the conscious design of doing me good, I should run for my life."

It might well turn out to be a nonsensical goal, somewhat like a goal of maximizing everybody's power over everybody else or of maximizing everybody's prestige and fame.

When discussing social freedom, a much narrower concept, I found it convenient to limit the scope of my concern to the freedom from coercion and to refrain from asserting in general that it is desirable to maximize individual freedom from perceived restraints that are no longer coercive. When it comes to potential freedom, some corresponding kind of a limitation is even more evidently necessary.

My value position with respect to potential freedom can be stated in general terms as follows: *I wish to see maximized the ability and potential incentive of every man to resist manipulation, whether institutional or deliberate, in so far as the manipulation serves other interests at the expense of his own.*

"Interest" is to be understood in an objective sense. It is assumed to be in a man's interest: (1) to achieve a maximum of health, physical and mental, and a maximum of psychological freedom; (2) to develop his talents and potentialities toward maturity and achievement; (3) to gain an adequate access to other values according to freely expressed preferences; (4) to have security that circumstances will continue to favor his freedom, growth, and value position; and (5) to gain access to information bearing on alternatives of behavior including value choices, that are or can become open to him. Manipulation serving other interests *at the expense of* his own means manipulation that interferes with one or more of these five basic interests of man without demonstrably serving one or more of them. I shall call this phenomenon *special interest manipulation,* assuming that all manipulation going on is in *somebody's* special interest if it is not in the interest of the objects of manipulation.[110]

I consider it as part of the total goal of a maximal freedom of expression, in other words, that man should become as *autonomous* as possible, roughly in David Riesman's sense:

The "autonomous" are those who on the whole are capable of conforming to the behavioral norms of their society . . . but are free to choose whether to conform or not. . . . The person here defined as autonomous may or may not conform outwardly, but whatever his choice, he pays less of a price, and he *has* a choice: he can meet both the culture's definitions of adequacy and those which (to a still culturally determined degree) slightly transcend the norm for the adjusted.[111]

Many social institutions operate as essential supports for freedom and security in civilized societies. Large sections of criminal law tend to serve this end as their main function. Many other institutions derive their main

---

[110] If manipulation is in the general interest, it is also in the interest of the object of manipulation. Provided, of course, that he would agree and provided, also, that humanitarian but personally detached observers, relying on the best available psychological knowledge, would not disagree. As an objective condition, I would add: provided his psychological freedom is not reduced. Cf. below, pp. 106–7. Note that I assume in this context the existence of some hierarchy of basic human needs. Cf. above, pp. 11–14, and below, p. 327.

[111] *The Lonely Crowd: A Study of the Changing American Character* (Anchor Books), pp. 278–79.

independent support[112] from limited groups in society, and it can frequently be demonstrated that such institutions benefit these groups more than others. The young Rousseau believed that all political institutions, at any rate in the first political societies, fell into this category.[118] For my own part, I might suggest the institution of racial segregation as a relatively clear example of this second kind. Let me for brevity's sake talk about *nonspecially supported* as opposed to *specially supported* institutions. Both may in fact be generally supported, but only in the latter case do certain necessarily limited interest groups have a special stake as power subjects in supporting them.

It may be objected that criminal laws according to this logic should be considered specially supported institutions, since governmental agencies have a special stake in supporting them. However, governments in their role of upholding the laws are not in principle acting as power subjects. They are, particularly in democracies, supposed to act on behalf of the people, the parliament, and the laws themselves. Secondly, democratic governments are not in principle limited interest groups. Their interest is supposedly diffusely defined as equivalent with the nation's interest, as they see it, and the composition of the governing group is in principle flexible, offering openings to those who can gain sufficient amounts of public support. Criminal laws in democratic countries are emphatically to a considerable extent nonspecially supported institutions. Only certain kinds of laws, say "class laws" such as those prohibiting strikes, may be considered specially rather than nonspecially supported institutions, marking the preponderance of a limited class interest in the legislature. In some nondemocratic countries the impact of specially supported institutions in defining and dealing with crime is likely to be much more pronounced. The ruling group in such countries is sometimes more of a limited special interest group, and revisions of criminal law can be made in support of their special interests.

"Manipulation" in this book means the process of regulating the supply of information in the interest of encouraging or discouraging certain types of behavior. All education is manipulative to a certain extent, at least in its earlier stages, but advanced education may approach the ideal type of neutrality, in the sense that the teacher may strive to present all facts and opinions pertaining to certain problems without partiality.

It does not follow from my value position that education *ought to* approach the ideal type of impartiality, however, even at the advanced stage. On the contrary, note that I am not posing a reduction in the amounts of manipulation as a part of my freedom goal. Manipulation produces restraints only to the extent that it is effective. It is the ability to resist manipulation I wish to see increased, and this ability can best be developed in institutions in which not impartiality but controversy is fostered. Genuine controversy implies manipulation of the same audience from opposite

---

[112] By independent support is meant the support of men as power subjects, not as power agents. See above, p. 91.
[118] Cf. above, pp. 50–51.

sides at the same time, and on this general level of analysis I know of no better type of incentive toward autonomous or independent thinking than direct exposure to lively controversy. On this score I swear to the wisdom of Socrates.

If I assert that cross-pressures of manipulation in the educational process can stimulate the growth of potential freedom, I am also saying, of course, that education itself can promote freedom in this sense. But I wish to say more than this: education is essential to accomplish this purpose. Man's ability and potential incentive to resist manipulation hinges on his access to knowledge. The merits of manipulative persuasion can be judged only by placing its contents in a context of a relatively systematically organized knowledge, or in relation to knowledge about facts and opinions that are relevant to but not manipulatively related to the purposes for which persuasion is being employed.

The process of manipulation can be either *institutional* or *deliberate*, or both at the same time, in varying proportions. As a power subject, a manipulator is deliberately pursuing purposes of his own, though his goals may be public or private, and in either of these cases they may be narrowly selfish or include a concern for the interests of others. As a power agent, a manipulator may be pursuing the deliberate purposes of his superior, or he may act in support of institutional expectations, without conscious considerations about the impact of each institution on values in which he believes. It is probable that consciousness takes a relatively larger part than unconsciousness in deliberate manipulation, while institutional manipulation is carried on unconsciously to a greater extent.

Note that it is man's ability or potential incentive to resist manipulation that I wish to see maximized. As Riesman's discussion of autonomy makes clear, there is no value in nonconformity as such.[114] In fact, every society demands a lot of conformity, and every individual needs the kind of relationships to groups that implies conformity and submission to some manipulation, both institutional and deliberate.

The ability to resist manipulation is ideally put to use whenever the individual is pushed toward behavior detrimental to his own interests. To the extent that he enjoys psychological freedom, he knows what his own goals are, and to the extent that he has potential freedom, he knows his situation and prospects, including the various action alternatives that in fact are open to him. To the same extent he knows when it is in his interest to resist manipulation.

But ability is not enough. There must also be some incentive to act unconventionally when the time comes, regardless of inconvenience or other consequences. If, for example, a war scare is contrived in a given country, potential freedom is not demonstrated by moments of individual insight into the phoniness of the propaganda avalanche. It requires also an incentive for the individual to achieve detachment and to protect his detach-

114 *The Lonely Crowd*, Part III. General pleas for nonconformity, says William H. Whyte, Jr., "have an occasional therapeutic value, but as an abstraction, nonconformity is an empty goal, and rebellion against prevailing opinion merely because it is prevailing should no more be praised than acquiescence to it." Cf. *The Organization Man*, p. 11.

ment—by actually resisting the manipulation in one way or another, even if it may be more convenient to glide along with most other people. Manipulation may be resisted either by independent thinking, by a stubborn memory, by seeking access to unorthodox information, or by a general distrust of certain leaders, to give a few examples only. These are examples of resistance within the personality. Resistance within the social system would, of course, require overt expression of attitudes and insights acquired by these means. For example, when Tocqueville in the 1830s deplores the extent of uniformity of opinion in the United States, he is in effect referring to deficiencies in potential freedom: "I found very few men who displayed that manly candor and masculine independence of opinion which frequently distinguished the Americans in former times, and which constitutes the leading feature in distinguished characters wherever they may be found. It seems at first sight as if all the minds of the Americans were formed upon one model, so accurately do they follow the same route."[115] People who are without incentive to develop independence of opinion and to express it with candor are potentially unfree. If they have the incentive but are inhibited by the anticipation of sanctions, they are socially unfree. If they lack the capacity of caring for goals and issues beyond the requirements of ego defense, they are psychologically unfree.

Note on Terminology

The terms "psychological," "social," and "potential" freedom are far from ideal, and it is hoped that better terms will be found eventually.

Psychological factors are important in the development of freedom on all three levels. The perception of external restraints is certainly a psychological process and so is the internalization of external restraints. Yet the dependent variable to be studied under the label "psychological freedom" is essentially an intrapersonal relationship and thus is in the special domain of psychology.

"Social freedom" is perhaps the worst of the three terms. Not only are all levels of freedom in general exposed to social restraints, but in special cases what I call "social freedom" may be nonsocial in the sense that the external restraints are purely physical. Yet my concern is with social restraints on freedom in this sense; for most purposes it is further limited to a concern with coercive social restraints.

"Potential freedom" is a term with merit only in so far as it indicates that the individual is not actually unfree in the common-sense usage of "free." His state of social freedom is unstable, however, in the sense that he would, with more information, have been liable to act contrary to institutions or to the designs of manipulators and thereby be likely to encounter sanctions reducing his actual freedom (though not necessarily to a coercive extent). It is a far from ideal term, nevertheless, in the sense that "poten-

---

[115] It is true that Tocqueville also and perhaps more consciously has deficiencies in social freedom in mind, since he in what follows says that he "sometimes" meets people who dissent in private but are not willing to do so in public. These people, apparently a minority, are found to comply with conformity pressures without internalizing them. Cf. *Democracy in America*, I, 277.

tial" is a concept applicable to all levels of freedom. A person suffering from a neurosis might have potentials for a high degree of psychological freedom, capable of actualization by way of psychoanalysis. And a prisoner on the eve of his release might be said to enjoy "potential freedom" in a different sense.[116] I shall, however, consistently avoid using "potential freedom" in any sense at variance with my principal definition. For most purposes on this level of analysis my focus shall be limited to freedom from special interest manipulation.[117]

Imperfect as the present terminology is, it is hoped that the difference between the three levels of analysis by now is fairly clear and that it from here on will be beyond doubt which kind of freedom or freedom value is referred to in each context.

GENERAL RELATIONSHIPS BETWEEN SECURITY AND FREEDOM

In this section I shall consider in a general way the interrelationships between the different aspects of "security" and "freedom" as defined in the foregoing. The object of my inquiry at this stage is essentially to discover to what extent various goal values of security and freedom tend to be compatible, and to what extent incompatible, from the individual's point of view. To what extent is it logically necessary, or empirically obvious, that my demands for security must be modified in the interest of my freedom, or vice versa? To what extent must my security or freedom as a private citizen be modified in order to safeguard my security or freedom as a citizen?

At this stage the *contents* of expression need not be considered. I shall analyze the universe of values from the individual's point of view. Even when I discuss national security versus individual social freedom, it will be a matter of considering the *individual's* interest comprehensively. Whatever the individual wishes to express, his freedom to do so is equally valuable, on this level of analysis.

Levels of Security

For a full estimate of a man's security at a given time, information is needed on his amounts of basic security, surface security, and objective security—or, in negative terms, his degree of avoidance of anxiety, fear, and objective danger.

From the individual's point of view, anxiety tends on the whole to be more painful and more irremediable than fear. The anxious person tends to become threat-oriented rather than goal-oriented, to inflate existing concrete fears and to create new ones.[118] Anxiety may in extreme cases lead to suicide, while a state of fear *not* reinforced by anxiety even in extreme cases leads to resistance or flight or, at the very worst, preparedness to accept inevitable death.

---

[116] Cf. also the distinction above on p. 87.

[117] Cf. above, pp. 97–98.

[118] The basically insecure person is likely to develop a *general threat-orientation*—a general tendency to perceive obstacles "not in relation to the goal of his on-going motive pattern but in relation to a new goal made necessary because he interprets the obstacle as a personal threat of some kind." Newcomb, *Social Psychology,* p. 352.

Objective first-order dangers to the individual, or to the entire society, are not always perceived as such. Nevertheless, from a political point of view the most important security objective must be the reduction of specific dangers threatening the destruction of human beings or the destruction of what is the most dear to them—such as their health, freedom, and dignity. Certain diffuse types of dangers should perhaps be considered on a par with the specific ones, however. It has been pointed out that anomie may lead to destruction of human lives, notably in suicide. The danger called anomie, in other words, may be fully as disastrous for individuals as a specific, first-order danger.

All the same, it seems clear that the first-priority objective of the state, in the realm of the security of the individual, must be to protect him against specific first-order dangers. Not only does it seem probable that people are killed more often by specific blows than by anomic anxiety, though one can perhaps not be wholly certain about it, but the crucial consideration is that concrete dangers threatening life and limb as a rule are relatively suitable for attempts at immediate remedies by governmental action. Anxiety, or anomie as one of its objective causes, may perhaps also be reducible by political means, but at best only over time as a healthier society is being constructed.

When considering first-order specific dangers, how do we assign priorities between objective security demands? The utilitarian position emphasizes the number of people being threatened as the most important consideration. However, it follows from the human rights approach adopted in this book that we must first ask how serious is each type of danger. Even among first-order dangers some types are more serious than others; some dangers are threatening more basic human rights than others. The most important consideration, therefore, is that the more basic rights must be protected before the less basic rights, even if it is a choice between one individual's more basic rights and a whole society's less basic rights.

Who determines what human rights are more basic than others? We all do. The result is considerable controversy, around a core of apparent consensus. Everyone, I believe, will agree that the right to stay alive and healthy, or the right of everyone to protection against avoidable dangers to life and limb, is the most basic of all human rights, if he believes in human rights at all. The desired extent of this protection for everyone is somewhat more controversial. Does it include the right to be fed in case of need or the right to the best available medical treatment? Again, the rank order of other rights may be controversial—such as between the right to emigrate, to fair pay, or to free speech.

Human lives are in principle equally valuable. From this premise it follows that a threat to an entire nation presents a security problem of a higher urgency than a threat to any individual—*provided,* however, that the national danger with an equal (or higher) degree of probability is directed against human lives. Most governments have felt justified in calling young men to arms and in demanding that they risk their lives in order to protect the whole nation against the enemy's destructive power. The pacifists have refused to accept this justification, arguing not only that it is wrong to kill any human being for whatever purpose, but also that the actual killing even in a defensive war deters only a hypothetical threat against the nation or the lives of its citizens. Let the enemy occupy our territory, the pacifist says; if we do not resist with arms, he will have no incentive to make use of his own arms.[119]

My position on this question of value priorities is not far from the pacifist view, even if I do not share the optimism of many pacifists with respect to expected consequences of unilateral disarmament. While agreeing in the most obvious value judgment that the destruction of many lives is an even worse calamity than the destruction of few lives, I submit that the readiness to destroy lives in war can only be justified on near-conclusive evidence that failure to resist would mean, not just the impoverishment or weakening of the nation, but the actual destruction of considerable numbers of lives.

The achievement of objective security, then, is a political goal of high urgency, at least with respect to avoidance of first-order dangers threatening any or all individuals. Basic subjective security is also an important value, but it is one that can be promoted only slowly and subtly, by increasing the general level of mental health and *perhaps* by checking anomic tendencies.

When we come to surface security, or avoidance of fear, however, I submit that this is no value in itself. Having defined fear as a response to a realistically perceived, specific danger, I hold that fear on the whole is beneficial rather than harmful, in that it alerts the individual against objective dangers. Concrete fears become harmful only when pure fear is reinforced by anxiety, thus reducing the individual's ability to take rational countermeasures and over time perhaps constricting his general outlook from an expansive goal-orientation to a defensive threat-orientation.[120] Pure fear may be painful, but no more painful than the realization of the danger against which it warns. If by political means the important objective dangers can be reduced, an increase in surface security will be likely to follow—that is, concrete fears will be subdued with the information about reduced dangers, except in so far as the concrete fears are nurtured by anxiety.

Levels of Freedom

Coercive acts against individuals, according to my scheme of values, can be justified only on the concrete show of evidence that each type of coercive act serves to protect or extend some considerably more important freedoms than it destroys—whether the freedoms of the same individuals, of others, or of all individuals. As a political goal, social freedom from coercion has in general a higher priority, in my judgment, than psychological or potential freedom.[121] Open coercion is the most blatant type of violation of freedom, particularly if it is exerted by means of physical

---

[119] See, for example, Russell, *Which Way to Peace?* (1936), chap. 8, "Pacifism as a National Policy." Perhaps I should add that Russell apparently has changed some of these views later on.

[120] See above, p. 101, note 118.

[121] Cf. above, pp. 92–94.

violence. Compared to the goal of freedom from coercion, then, freedom from defensiveness and freedom from manipulation assume the status of second priority goals.

The rule I propose in the area of social freedom is that some types of deliberate coercion may be justified, but only if this serves to reduce the amount or effectiveness of other and definitely worse types of coercion, whether purposive or institutional. For example, dangerous highway robbers are imprisoned by common consent, since the freedom to travel about safely is considered more valuable than the freedom to assault strangers for profit.[122]

Coercion to extend freedom in any sense other than "reduced coercion" may be justified only exceptionally, and the principal exception I have in mind concerns children and very young people. The process of child upbringing and education is to some extent a coercive process—perhaps (I am not certain) necessarily so. The goal of this process is, or ought to be, the growth of individual freedom, both on the psychological and on the potential level. In other words, education ought to foster, in my opinion, both a wholesome personality integration and an informed, open mind that is able to consider the merits of new ideas.

However, once the young people have come of age, at the very latest, all coercion for such purposes ought to stop. All adults should have a strictly enforced right to escape all coercion aimed at "improving" them—according to the standards of other people.[123] This right of the individual to act from his own lights is, indeed, a basic precondition for his chances to collect and integrate new experience of his own and in this way develop his own mind; so far as possible, it should be extended to children as well.[124]

What about Rousseau's notion of forcing men to be free? From a

[122] Perhaps it may be objected that by jailing a highway robber we are depriving one individual of more basic rights in order to protect the less basic rights of the vast majority. My answer is that the right not to be physically molested without provocation should be considered more basic than the right to freedom of movement after the molesting of other persons. I further conclude that capital punishment is never justified, and that jailing so far as possible should be replaced by psychological or psychiatric treatment. Vilhelm Aubert, in summing up a recent inquiry into the sociology and psychology of crime and punishment, concludes: "All in all, it is improbable that a substitution of punishment by [psychological] treatment will lead to a considerable increase in the amount of delinquency as a result of less effective deterrence . . . Regardless of fear of legal sanctions most people will try to maintain an image of themselves as mentally healthy and socially adjusted." Cf. Aubert: *Om straffens sosiale funksjon (On the Social Function of Punishment)*, pp. 224–25. Cf. below, pp. 278–79.

[123] An exception, again, must be made for mentally deficient persons who cannot protect their own welfare. I do not agree, however, with the doctrine of "individual prevention" in criminology, which seeks to justify imprisonment on the grounds that it may improve the convict's character. Detention *may* be justifiable only in terms of society's interest in not letting loose people who are actually menacing the freedom and security of others.

[124] From one point of view it is even more important to avoid coercing a child than an adult: the child is in the process of integrating the more basic and the more enduring components of his personality. Karen Horney offers the following hypothesis to explain why "healthy" and "neurotic" people differ in their ability to know when to trust other people: "Perhaps the differences are to be accounted for by the fact that the healthy person made the bulk of his unfortunate experiences at an age when he could integrate them, while the neurotic person made them at an age when he could not master them, and as a consequence of his helplessness reacted to them with anxiety." *The Neurotic Personality of Our Time*, p. 95.

psychological point of view, coercion to extend freedom is by no means an absurd notion.[125] The human personality is complex and may be driven toward mutually incompatible goals simultaneously, without apparent awareness of their relative importance. At times, an individual may be driven by a mere whim toward self-destruction, which would mean an end to all freedom. Or he may walk into an imminent and serious danger of which he is unaware, due to carelessness or lack of knowledge. Even John Stuart Mill states, as Bosanquet is happy to report, that it is no curtailment of freedom to prevent a man from crossing an untrustworthy bridge.[126] At such times a temporary interference with an individual's immediate freedom may, as a matter of empirical fact, serve to increase his freedom in the long run—so much so that the individual concerned in retrospect is almost sure to be grateful for the force that was applied against him.

If this factual possibility is granted, then the next question is, under what circumstances can the extension of freedom by coercion be justified? At this point my disagreement with the position of Rousseau and Bosanquet is wide. I do not necessarily reject their philosophical belief to the effect that most political coercion of individuals as applied by the well-ordered state serves, when considered in its entirety, to extend individual freedom in some ultimate sense. This view may for all I know be true or false, or partly true and partly false, depending on definitions and metaphysical beliefs. It may even be possible to translate this problem into terms sufficiently operational to approach an empirical answer to it, but that is not my concern in this book. I believe that the standards for judging the importance of the freedoms concerned must in general be acceptable either to the individual who is being coerced or to the majority of those who can imagine being in his place, to the extent of being able to judge his interest in the controversy fairly.

There are two main difficulties in my position. One is in my commitment to "security" as well as "freedom," which conceivably may justify coercion for the sake of "security," even if I have ruled out most justifications in terms of psychological and potential freedom. This problem will be considered later in this chapter.

The second difficulty, to be dealt with right away, is that social freedom is not the same as the absence of coercion. Social freedom is a wider concept, referring in general to the "relative absence of perceived external restraints." In other words, many additional pressures that tend to reduce social freedom would have to be considered in a full discussion of the value priorities in this field. What about economic or political pressures that can be resisted, though under penalties of sanctions? Are they justifiable in the promotion of psychological or potential freedom?

This is a question that is hard to answer in a general and yet clear-cut way. Pressures that can be and are resisted, however unjustified or unfair

---

125 Cf. above, pp. 52–54 and 56–57.
126 Bosanquet, *The Philosophical Theory of the State,* pp. 64–65, and Mill, "On Liberty," in *Utilitarianism,* p. 204.

their penalties may seem in concrete situations, nevertheless do represent a less serious threat to social freedom than the pressures of successful coercion. And these pressures exhibit all degrees of sanctions from mild and momentary losses of prestige or affection to serious and lasting economic damage. It is implausible, therefore, to generalize in few words about their justification in conflict-of-interest situations.

If mild prestige pressures can furnish incentives toward a wider tolerance of controversy in a given society, and thus increase the potential freedom level, I see no objections to them. If such pressures would involve economic ruin for the people involved, I should be more doubtful about them, and certainly leave the decision up to those concerned. If prestige pressures can induce parents or teachers to behave so as to encourage the growth of psychological freedom in children, all is well and good. Whether teachers who seem to foster the growth of authoritarianism or sado-masochism in children ought to be fired is a question, on the other hand, that is difficult to answer in a wholesale manner.

One additional point that may seem paradoxical at first must also be considered. An increase in potential freedom may well result in an automatic decrease in social freedom. Social freedom means the relative absence of *perceived* external restraints. The slave who is told that he ought to be free, the illiterate serf who is educated to think for himself, or the indoctrinated subject of a totalitarian state who becomes aware that he is never told more than one side of the truth at best—all these new awarenesses in subject persons serve to increase the amount of felt oppression and thus actually reduce the amounts of social freedom.

In cases such as these, however, the value of increased potential freedom, in my opinion, is positive regardless of, or even because of, the consequences to which I have referred. Stated in general terms, any increase in potential freedom, brought about by noncoercive means, is valuable in itself, regardless of its consequences for social freedom.[127] And any decrease in social freedom is valuable, provided it is due *solely* to increased awareness of continued coercive pressures. Free expression in a full sense requires ability to perceive unnecessary oppression as unnecessary, an opportunity to do something about it, and an incentive to act on such perceptions and opportunities. In terms of rational action to reduce oppression, potential freedom is indeed logically prior to social and psychological freedom, in that coercion must be recognized as such before anything purposively can be done to reduce it.

The same does not necessarily hold in relation to psychological freedom, however. A sudden increase in awareness of oppression may conceivably produce psychological neuroses that stifle the individual's free expression more than external instruments of oppression could ever do. In a family situation, a sudden discovery that a beloved father or mother is a crook or a tyrant (or not the real parent) may result in a devastating trauma; something parallel may conceivably occur in political society. For example, Erich Fromm's description of the modern prematurely independent indi-

---

[127] Priority problems do arise in relation to "security," however. See below, pp. 123–25.

vidual's "fear of freedom" may be considered a statement of a problem in psychological freedom arising from a relatively sudden increase in *potential* as well as social freedom.

It seems evident, therefore, that priority problems between the values of psychological and potential freedom can and do arise. However, in Western democracies it should be assumed that every increase in empirically reliable knowledge about social relationships in the end will serve to extend rather than to reduce "freedom" in the total sense and therefore is desirable. The problem in our culture, it seems to me, is not so much a psychological vulnerability to new social knowledge as it is a psychological inability to register and make use of available knowledge, to the extent that it is at odds with our preconceived notions about our own best interest. In other cultures the problem of potential versus psychological freedom may conceivably create more real dilemmas, at least as problems of transition.[128]

My next task is to consider the various freedoms and security values that I have defined in relation to each other—in an effort to state general points on compatibility or conflict and on priority in cases of conflict. My frame of reference will still be the individual's situation, although the individual will be considered both as a private person and as a member of his society.

Basic Security and Psychological Freedom

Anxiety is one aspect of, and perhaps the primary cause or effect of, the failure to achieve the fundamental personality integration that makes a harmony between basic motives and overt expression possible. Hostility, or a sense of weakness, is repressed,[129] because the person is basically insecure and afraid to acknowledge these aspects of himself. The child's hostility against his parents may give rise to guilt feelings, and the accompanying anxiety may be alleviated, though never completely done away with, by repression of the hostility impulses. The resulting vacuum in consciousness is quickly filled with the antidote of glorifying the parents,

---

[128] In 1945 some American anthropologists urged their government to retain and respect the authority of the emperor in defeated Japan, as a means of preventing a serious breakdown in Japanese institutions. Japanese society, they pointed out, has always rested on hierarchical rather than democratic assumptions, and a void at the sacred apex of the hierarchy—sacrosanct since time immemorial—might lead to anomie and anarchy. Their advice was heeded. See Benedict, *The Chrysanthemum and the Sword: Patterns of Japanese Culture,* pp. 31, 128–29, 150, 196, 297, 309.

A similar point has been made by Eric Hoffer to explain the inconvenient "awakening of Asia" outside Japan: "The Western colonial powers offered individual freedom. They tried to shake the Oriental out of his lethargy, rid him of his ossified traditionalism, and infect him with a craving for self-advancement. The result was not emancipation but isolation and exposure. An immature individual was torn from the warmth and security of a corporate existence and left orphaned and empty in a cold world. It was this shock of abandonment and exposure that brought about the awakening in Asia." See "The Awakening of Asia," in *The Reporter,* X, No. 13 (1954), p. 16.

[129] Not to be confused with "controlled," of course, or hidden from the observation of others; repression hides it from one's *own* consciousness. For a discussion of the process of repression, or, as Harry Stack Sullivan prefers to call it, "dissociation," see below, pp. 183–85.

as if to make hostility a logical absurdity. Thus the overt behavior, verbal and nonverbal, becomes discrepant from the basic motivations.

The intolerance of weakness in an individual's self-image arises in a similar fashion. As all awareness of hostility is channeled away from relationships to persons who are symbols of authority and strength, the individual comes to identify with the authoritative and the strong and directs both his hostility and his contempt toward persons who are symbols of weakness and submission. This sort of personality, which is called authoritarian,[130] is characterized by an image of himself as strong and masterful. Yet the elements of weakness are still there, in every person, and when they cannot be faced they are repressed and result in anxiety. This anxiety makes the whole self-image ambivalent;[131] dominance and submissiveness attitudes are frequently present in the same individuals, therefore, and even in their relationships to the same other people.

These are some of the phenomena bearing equally on psychological freedom and on basic security. Wherever these two values overlap, I shall prefer to discuss the phenomena in terms of psychological freedom, since "freedom" is my main concern in this study. "Security" is my concern only to the extent that it is an aspect of "freedom."

It should be noted, however, that anxiety is not necessarily a destructive phenomenon. On the contrary, some measure of anxiety may be a crucial incentive in human creativity and growth. According to Sören Kierkegaard, "the possibility of freedom announces itself in anxiety. . . . He therefore who has learned rightly to be in anxiety has learned the most important thing."[132]

The crucial question to ask about anxiety in relation to psychological freedom is not, it would seem, how can we minimize human anxiety as far as possible? Rather, we should ask, how can we maximize man's ability to cope with his anxiety? This problem is an important theme in the next chapter.

Anxiety is an evil only to the extent that the individual is unable to cope with his anxiety and keeps trying to flee from it by the continual use of self-deceptive mechanisms, which prevent the harmonious integration of motives and behavior.

Or, to put it in opposite terms, basic subjective security is not necessarily

---

[130] Some authoritarian personalities go to the other extreme and see themselves as entirely weak and dependent, but vicariously they participate in strength. They seek refuge in close identification with some other person or group or deity to whom great or even supernatural strength and courage are attributed. The concept of authoritarianism is discussed below, pp. 189–94.

[131] This is a self-reinforcing process. Reluctance to face weakness in oneself (or aggression, hostility, selfishness, etc.) generates repression. Repression generates new anxiety. This diffuse anxiety introduces elements of ambivalence in the self-image. The ambivalence leads to additional anxiety and to the need for further defensive "armaments" in the shape of further distortion and further repression.

[132] *The Concept of Dread,* trans. by Lowrie, pp. 66 and 139. In the present study I depart consistently from Lowrie's use of "dread" as a translation of Kierkegaard's "Angst." "Anxiety" is the accustomed translation of Freud's "Angst." There is an overwhelming convention in favor of "anxiety" in the translation of Freud's works, and it should be extended to Kierkegaard's, too; the Dane talked about many of the same phenomena and anticipated some of Freud's most important insights.

to be valued unreservedly. This might mean evaluating docility and smug-ness highly. In so far as it is to be valued highly, however, there is a close empirical relationship, or perhaps a conceptual near-identity, between basic security and psychological freedom. From now on, therefore, I shall dis-regard basic subjective security as an independent value concern; this also serves to simplify my consideration of value priorities in the sections to follow.[133]

Psychological Freedom and Objective Security

In this section psychological freedom will first be discussed in relation to specific kinds of insecurity and then in relation to anomie.

There are two main groups of specific dangers, those directed at one or a few individuals and those directed at entire societies or nations. Analytically there is no clear borderline, of course, but in our world ques-tions of national security are more unstructured, in the sense that there is no effective international agency to protect the security of nations. For the protection of individual human rights, the state operates an elaborate system of legislation, courts, police, etc.[134]

The protection of the basic human rights means protection equally of the objective security and of the social freedom of the individual. The problem of value priorities between individual psychological freedom and objective individual security is, therefore, the same problem as that of priorities between psychological and social freedom. It may be repeated that the protection of the most basic human rights should have the un-questioned priority in this conflict.

New complexities arise when we consider psychological freedom in relation to national security. In comparing national and individual security, I raised the question whether a government is ever justified in sending its young men to kill or to die in battle, barring conclusive evidence that the enemy will kill larger numbers if there is no resistance.[135] This is primarily a question of social freedom versus national security, but it has a bearing on the psychological freedom-value as well. For the psychologi-cally free individual is able to express his own basic motives in his behavior, and he is correspondingly less easily commanded by his government. He may or may not obey a call to arms, depending on his own sense of the justice of this war and of his obligations to obey laws and decrees, his deep-lying reluctance to kill or die, or his fear of the penalties facing the objector.

It may at first seem, then, that the growth of psychological freedom might over time serve to reduce the national security. In a world crisis, after all, the power of a nation depends on its government's ability to count

---

[133] The choice between assigning an empirical or a logical (or tautological) nature to the affinity between two concepts is a crucial one in most contexts, but not in the present one, as either type of affinity (and the choice would depend on the outcome of a much more thorough analysis), if demonstrated, will permit the shortcut I desire: to refer to psychological freedom alone with respect to value considerations bearing on basic security as well, and take the latter inference for granted.

[134] "A human right is a freedom demand that can, in principle, be vindicated for all human beings." See above, p. 7.

[135] Cf. above, pp. 102–3, and below, pp. 117–18.

on the willing service for the national cause of all its citizens. This view is a bit too simple, however. It rests on the assumption that the government *always* knows best and that its policies always are sufficiently in the national interest to *deserve* unhesitating obedience. One of the fundamental assumptions in a democratic system, however, is that a government policy may be wrong and that it consequently is necessary to criticize governments and to change them at times. In general, a democratic government may be entitled to obedience, but there are limits to its justifiable demands on citizens. If it orders citizens to kill or to die, it comes close to the limits that even Hobbes put down around the authority of his Leviathan.[136] Even in a proclaimed national emergency the individual's right not to kill or die for a cause he considers unjust should be respected by the government.

There is another angle to this issue, which will be clearer after a few words about the nature of loyalty. Bentham was credited, in an earlier context, with having in effect insisted that loyalty to principles is more important than loyalty to men or loyalty to specific government policies.[137] William Godwin, his contemporary, expressed this position even more forcefully: "I have a paramount obligation to the cause of justice and the benefit of the human race. If the nation undertake what is unjust, fidelity in that undertaking is a crime. If it undertake what is just, it is my duty to promote its success not because I am one of its citizens, but because such is the command of justice."[138] Bentham's and Godwin's views on loyalty are ethical statements, or statements about right and wrong, and I share this ethical position. There are reasons today to believe that this position is one toward which more people's views will demonstrably tend to gravitate as the average level of psychological freedom increases.

Whether critical attitudes toward governmental authority in general are believed to be beneficial or harmful for the common interest in preserving a nation, there are increasing amounts of evidence that "authoritarian personalities" tend to be less critical of the powers that be than non-authoritarians. Reductions in neurotic predispositions toward authoritarianism in a changing society mean increasing proportions of individuals who have a high degree of psychological freedom and who are less predisposed toward automatic obedience to orders from whatever authority.[139] In Erich Fromm's terms, increased psychological freedom carries with it an increased affinity for a *humanistic* as opposed to an *authoritarian* ethics. The authoritarian personality will tend to develop an *authoritarian conscience,* says Fromm, which he defines: "An authoritarian conscience is the voice of an internalized external authority, the parents, the state, or whoever the authorities in a given culture happen to be. . . . The prescriptions of authoritarian conscience are not determined by one's own *value judgments* but exclusively by the fact that its commands and tabus are

---

[136] "A Covenant not to defend my selfe from force, with force, is alwayes voyd." *Leviathan,* p. 72, cf. pp. 80 and 114–15.
[137] Cf. above, p. 43.
[138] *Political Justice,* II, 109.
[139] Cf. below, Chapter 4, especially pp. 189–90.

pronounced by authorities."[140] The opposite is the *humanistic conscience* of the person enjoying a high degree of psychological freedom: "It is our own voice, present in every human being and independent of external sanctions or rewards. . . . Humanistic conscience is the expression of man's self-interest and integrity."[141]

Loyalty, too, may be more humanistic or more authoritarian. *"Loyalty" means an enduring identification with something—*be it a nation, a cause, a person, an idea, a symbol. "Identification" takes place when a person comes to consider the needs or interests he attributes to something or somebody or some group as *his own* needs or interests, or as *more important* than the needs or interests he perceives as his own.[142] Loyalty, in other words, exists as an enduring orientation of an individual toward something separable from himself but at present incorporated in the person's need structure. A person who is loyal to some cause experiences to this extent immediate gratification when his cause fares well and immediate depriva- tion when it suffers setbacks; the cause, as perceived by him, is a part of his self.[143]

A humanistic loyalty, I submit, *is a loyalty expressive of the individual's basic motives.* It is a loyalty freely given by individuals who are relatively free also in our psychological sense. *An authoritarian loyalty is a loyalty that is imposed on the individual from without* and, although internalized, *is not harmoniously integrated with his basic motive pattern.* An authori- tarian loyalty is a mark of psychological unfreedom.[144]

Let me now return to the problem of objective national security versus individual psychological freedom. The intervening discussion of "loyalty" makes me a little better prepared to tackle this complex problem of value priorities.

It appears very doubtful whether even the authoritarian type of loyalty can be created and increased by such artifices as, for example, enforced loyalty oaths as a condition for public employment. The external appear- ance of loyalty can clearly be induced in this manner, but the value of mere appearances as a protection of national security may be negative rather than positive, in that they may induce a government to entertain unrealistic ideas about the amount of genuine, enduring support for its policies.

It must be granted, nevertheless, that a widespread psychological un- freedom would tend to increase the apparent success of various coerci-

---

[140] *Man for Himself,* pp. 143–45 and also pp. 8–13. It may be added, perhaps, that on the surface the precepts of authority become integrated in the individual's "own" value judg- ments.

[141] *Ibid.,* pp. 158–59.

[142] *Ibid.,* pp. 174–77.

[143] Cf. below, Chapter 4, pp. 173–74.

[144] A similar distinction between two kinds of loyalty seems implied in the following passage: "The deeper loyalty, therefore, is not that which slavishly follows the social code— 'My country, right or wrong'—but that which responds to it in the spirit and the obligation of the common cause for which, however imperfectly, it stands. The individual who slavishly follows the code of nation or class or religion or other group is unconscious of or unfitted for a greater social obligation. Within him society has, paradoxically, no deep roots. He is bound to the code by the superficial and uncreative bonds of imitation and compliance: he reflects but does not express society." MacIver and Page, *Society: An Introductory Analysis,* p. 208.

measures that may be instituted in connection with so-called governmental loyalty programs. Authoritarian personalities can relatively easily be brought to internalize authoritarian loyalties, so that they in their overt behavior are ready to support whatever the governmental policies may be at a given time or whatever some particular leader may wish them to support. Superficially, therefore, it might seem that this sort of loyalty would benefit the nation's objective security. In other words, it might seem that there is a basic value conflict between "national security" and "psychological freedom."

This would be true, though, only on the assumption that national unity is desirable even around policies that may lead to disaster. If one makes the rather obvious point that it is in the long-term interest of national security that a people is ready to support only policies that are genuinely conducive to security, it follows that a public capable of detached, independent criticism is vastly preferable to a noncritical public that is ready to cheer for any governmental policy.[145]

The advantage of a widespread humanistic loyalty pattern is that such a loyalty distinguishes—to the extent that the public is sufficiently informed—between policies in harmony and policies in disharmony with individual values. If the individual in a genuine sense is the judge of policies and decides for himself which to support, it would seem likely that peaceful policies would receive a lot more support than aggressive policies. At any rate, a humanistic loyalty has to be *earned* in that a government wishing support has to take genuine public preferences into account, to a much larger extent than a government angling for support of an authoritarian type.

Do I assume that every person's basic motives are humanistically inclined? Yes, in a very broad sense of the term I do. I assume that man is a social being, seeking community with other men. It is true that competition for scarce necessities of life or social institutions stressing competitiveness can throw men into a state of mutual enmity. But loyalty to antihumanistic principles in general, apart from the perceived necessity of protection against other men, is invariably, I believe, a symptom of deficiencies in *somebody's* psychological freedom. A high degree of psychological freedom insures the access to consciousness of man's basic sympathies for other men, or, more strictly speaking, it largely consists in this access to consciousness. This access can be blocked by ego deficiencies that make the individual take refuge, say, in self-aggrandizing, punitive attitudes or in self-sacrificing, authoritarian loyalties. It can also be blocked by strong conformity pressures in the social structure or political system or by hardships in the struggle for the necessities of life. The growth of humanistic loyalties presupposes, in other words, a society or group offering the individual a certain minimum of social freedom and objective security,

[145] Psychologically free persons are able to identify with persons whose policy views they take exception to. Indeed, it is a characteristic of psychological freedom to be able to identify without sacrificing one's personal integrity, and it is part of personal integrity to live by one's own values.

including national security. These are also minimum requirements for maintaining the small child's spontaneity and psychological freedom in the adult individual.

An additional advantage of a preponderance of humanistic loyalties from the point of view of a long-term national security lies in the fact that these loyalties tend to be more stable than authoritarian loyalties. A loyalty imposed by an external authority may be equally "strong" at the moment in terms of motivation, but its object may be replaced relatively easily, both logically and psychologically.[146]

If these observations are valid, it follows (a) that a high degree of psychological freedom is conducive to the development of humanistic as opposed to authoritarian loyalties and (b) that humanistic loyalties, which are individually motivated in a more fundamental sense, are greater assets than are authoritarian loyalties from a long-term national security point of view. In a national emergency situation, a widespread readiness to obey the commands of those in power may in extreme cases be a condition for survival. But extreme emergencies are likely to be the outcome of insufficient application of intelligence in foresight and policy-making. A high level of participation in policy appraisals and planning within a humanistically motivated citizenship presumably assures a richer supply of independent intelligence in serving the national security interest.

A high level of national security, on the other hand, either has no effect on the level of psychological freedom or it has a positive effect on it. It has no direct effect if one assumes that the level of psychological freedom is determined once and for all in early childhood. It may have an indirect, positive effect even on this assumption if a sense of security makes parents less tense and punitive. On the alternate assumption, that levels of psychological freedom can be influenced by social circumstances after the end of childhood, one can safely expect conformity pressures to be more severe the greater the sense of danger and insecurity in a nation. If conformity pressures affect the individual's personality integration at all, they serve to hamper rather than help the flow of communication between his consciousness and his basic motives.

As a general rule, then, there is no value conflict between psychological freedom and national security. If there is any functional interrelationship between the two variables, it is a positive one, in which an increase in the one value promotes an increase in the other value as well, at least in the long run.

Superficially it might seem that the growth of psychological freedom would increase the threat of anomie. If people become more critical toward institutions, will not the institutions lose some of their power? Certainly any democratic society is likely to appear chaotic to extreme authoritarian personalities, who develop an urge to "escape from freedom." Because they have basically insecure personalities, they need much security, stability, and

146 Cf. below, pp. 122–23 and note 169.

unambiguity in the external world, in order to reduce their anxiety. Consequently, they may take refuge in a political or religious authoritarian creed and movement.

There will always be conflicting norms in a democratic society. In other words, there will always be some degree of anomie, varying in the different communities and groups of which the society is composed. The same social and political situation may appear chaotic to some individuals and oppressively structured to others, depending on the ability of each person to tolerate ambiguity in his environments.

Out of these considerations come two important empirical problems, to be considered in the following chapters. How is it possible to influence personality development so as to increase the ability to tolerate anomie and other kinds of environmental ambiguity? This, as we shall see, is equivalent to asking how the growth of psychological freedom can be promoted.[147]

Secondly, given a certain average amount of psychological freedom, how much anomie can a society develop without seriously impairing constructive social interaction? One part of this question, as we shall see, asks in effect, what are the *sociologically* necessary limitations to the freedom of expression, if organized political society is to be maintained?[148]

If it can be said that increasing psychological freedom reduces the danger of anomie, or increases the level of security against anomic dangers, it does not follow that increasing security against anomie in turn would serve to increase the level of psychological freedom. Indeed, a very low level of anomie means a very high degree of regimentation and conformity pressures. If this state of affairs influences the state of psychological freedom in the citizenry, it influences it adversely, not favorably, as I have observed already.

It should be kept in mind, however, that anomie is considered an evil or a danger only in rather extreme doses. Security against anomie is considered a value only in small amounts—the minimum required for keeping social interaction going and mental health unimpaired. Within this narrowly limited range, increasing security against anomie surely improves the prospects for psychological freedom as well.

It may be concluded, therefore, that there is no value conflict between psychological freedom and security against anomie, to the extent that each is considered a value. Increases in psychological freedom are in this book considered valuable without any upper limit, while reductions in anomie are considered valuable only up to a point just beyond the danger threshold. The growth of psychological freedom is also the development of resistances against psychological damage resulting from the impact of anomie. A similar absence of conflict was found between psychological freedom and national security against specific dangers; efforts to increase individual capacities for freedom are likely to benefit national security as well, at least in the long run.

Only when it comes to *individual* security against *specific* dangers, in

---

[147] Cf. below, Chapter 4, pp. 200–205 and 217–39.
[148] Cf. below, pp. 275–80.

relation to psychological freedom, are value conflicts and priority problems likely to arise, for the analyst and for the freedom-oriented policy-maker. As we shall see in the following subsection, this is essentially the problem of priority between psychological freedom and social freedom, as individual security and social freedom are very nearly the same thing.

Social Freedom and Objective Security

Here again is a threefold problem. "Objective security" is a concept encompassing both the security of the individual and of the nation against specific dangers and the security of both against the more diffuse danger of anomie.

The perceived security of the individual's human rights is a value largely identical with his social freedom, at least in the most important areas of each value context. In Montesquieu's most famous definition of liberty, this identity is made complete: "The political liberty of the subject is a tranquility of mind arising from the opinion each person has of his safety."[149] In this book "social freedom" has been defined as the relative absence of perceived external pressures on the individual, and "objective security" has been defined as the relative absence of dangers—whether perceived or unperceived.

My human rights approach involves the following generalized value judgment: The protection of each individual's more basic human rights has priority over the less basic human rights even of large numbers of individuals. And the most basic human right is physical inviolability, which can be forfeited only by individuals who present a manifest and immediate threat to the physical inviolability of others. In my discussion of the concept of "social freedom," a distinction was made between coercive and noncoercive pressures. "Coercion" was defined as the use of actual physical violence or of sanctions strong enough to make the individual abandon a strongly desired course of action.[150]

The two values of "physical inviolability" and "freedom from coercion" are so widely overlapping that a value conflict between the two is inconceivable, from the individual's point of view. "Freedom from coercion" includes a perceptual variable, it is true, that is missing in the objective concept of security against physical violence. Also, coercion may refer not only to physical violence and threats of physical violence, but to other sanctions as well, provided they are strong enough to force the individual to abandon important plans or wishes. Finally, a person may choose to incur the risk of physical violence, while it would be a contradiction in terms to choose to be coerced.[151] At most one can choose to pretend he is being coerced. In spite of these differences, however, these two crucial values—the most basic ones in my entire value scheme—may still be considered closely enough related to justify a joint discussion of them in relation to other values. Whether you speak in terms of reducing the scope of severe

[149] *The Spirit of the Laws,* trans. by Nugent, I, 151.
[150] See above, p. 93.
[151] Except in the limiting case of exposing oneself directly to physical blows.

coercion, or in terms of enlarging the scope of security against physical violence, the policies would be the same, and the basic hierarchy of human rights to be vindicated would be the same.

From here on, I shall only occasionally refer to "individual security against physical violence" as an objective. I shall take account of the same points of substance when speaking of "freedom from coercion." This latter formulation represents the supreme value in my position and determines my conception of the most basic human rights.

With respect to the less basic human rights a wide overlap between social freedom and perceived objective security is sure to exist. Every freedom from specific kinds of external pressures may also be discussed in terms of security against such pressures. Throughout this book I shall prefer to discuss the relevant topics in terms of social freedom, not in terms of individual security.

A definite conflict between the values of social freedom and objective security does arise with respect to dangers facing the entire nation. Even here it would be quite possible to talk about conflicting freedom demands or conflicting security demands. "The national security" may plausibly be defined as equivalent or nearly equivalent with "the national freedom": coercion applied against a nation means coercion against some or all of its inhabitants, just as dangers facing a nation are dangers facing some or all of its people. And if the sacrifice of individual interests is demanded, this sacrifice may be called either a sacrifice of their freedom or of their personal security. Nevertheless, as it is usual to discuss this problem as one of national security versus individual freedom, it is convenient to follow this usage. But we must keep in mind that the dilemma basically involves a weighing of the individual's private freedom against his civil freedom, or his general sphere of freedom as a member of a human-rights-protecting nation.

Harold Lasswell's book *National Security and Individual Freedom* is a notable attempt to tackle this priority problem in both a general and a practical way. Lasswell phrases the dilemma as follows:

Every program put forward on behalf of national security needs scrutiny in terms of four questions: 1. Is there a threat to the principle of civilian supremacy in our system of government? 2. Does the policy involve a threat to freedom of information? 3. Is there danger to the civil liberties of the individual? 4. Does the policy violate the principle of a free as against a controlled economy?" . . . If the answer to any question is in the affirmative, the problem is to determine whether the potential loss of freedom can be avoided or reduced without endangering national security beyond the margin of reasonable risk.[152]

Excepting the fourth of Lasswell's freedom values, concerning the economy,[153] his basic value position with respect to "freedom" is essentially

---

[152] *National Security and Individual Freedom*, p. 57.

[153] In my opinion, there is considerable doubt about what Lasswell apparently takes for granted: that a "free economy" compared to a "controlled economy" establishes a wider range of genuine choice for the capitalist, the worker, and the consumer. His apparent certainty

the same as the one adopted in this book. His first point, the principle of civilian supremacy, is essential to, and indeed logically inseparable from, the democratic doctrine of free elections as a basis for political power. This concrete aspect of democratic theory nonetheless falls outside the scope of my study. Concerning his second and third points, freedom of information refers to both social and potential freedom, and the individual's civil liberties concern equally his social freedom and his security.

"The distinctive meaning of national security," says Lasswell, "is *freedom from foreign dictation*. National security policy implies a state of readiness to use force if necessary to maintain national independence."[154] He fails to ask, however, whether it is at all possible in our age to maintain national independence by means of a perpetually superior military force. Also, he fails to allow for the fact that national independence or freedom from foreign dictation are matters of degree rather than absolutes.[155]

In this book "national security" is defined in the same terms as individual security. The most vital interests of the individuals in a nation are the protection of life and limb and the maintenance of freedom from other kinds of coercion. The most vital concern of national security, therefore, is the prevention of war or comparable amounts of destruction brought on by terroristic oppression. And the second most vital concern is the avoidance of situations where the society is subjected to large-scale coercion, either by foreign domination or by native dictatorship.

Security is, by my definition, a matter of degree. No nation can achieve absolute security against war; even if it conquered the world, there could never be an absolute security against revolt or civil war. The objectives of national security policies must, therefore, be stated in terms of degrees— except for the objective of preventing open war. The other objectives of security on a national scale consist in increasing the national government's independence of decisions made unilaterally abroad and in maximizing the protection of human rights by extending domestic institutional safeguards.

My ambitions in this book fall far short of recommending specific national security policies. What I wish to contribute in this area is limited to a few general theoretical considerations derived from my value position and from my empirically broad approach to the problem of maximizing freedom.

The most basic human rights, I have suggested, should have priority. Whichever other human rights are considered important, certainly the right to life and limb is the most basic one. Consequently, to call young men to arms, to command them to kill and expose them to being killed, is a policy that can be justified only on evidence that this is necessary to forestall far more extensive dangers to human lives. Whether this kind of evidence is on hand in the present cold war situation is a question of crucial

---

might be due to the fact that the world's richest country, in which he lives, traditionally has had a relatively "free economy." The economic system explains in part America's wealth, but the country's largeness, natural resources, and past shelteredness, perhaps also its democratic traditions, are probably essential parts of the explanation.

[154] *National Security and Individual Freedom*, p. 51.
[155] *Ibid.*, p. 1.

importance, which urgently needs detached inquiries, or inquiries going beyond the preconceived assumptions of national policy-makers.[156]

Even if my position of primacy for the most basic human rights were accepted by all governments, that would not end the danger of war, however. In times of tensions between nations, it is very difficult to achieve a sober appraisal of the dangers ahead, especially perhaps for those who have the additional responsibility of political power.[157] All we can do is to strive for the increase of rationality in the protection of the national security. The chances for maximizing the rationality of important political judgments in times of crises appear inextricably connected with the amount of free criticism tolerated by the government and by public opinion. Here again, then, is a level of analysis on which increased freedom in one sense appears to contribute to increased security as well.

Yet, this is not the whole story. It is clear that not all kinds of criticism, to say nothing of nonverbal expression, will contribute to increased rationality of political decision-making in times of acute insecurity. Some argue, for example, that the more extreme kinds of anti-Semitic expression ought to be suppressed, because, as it is rightly argued, these types of expression do not contribute to rational self-government.[158] Those of us who accept this factual observation but reject the policy conclusion, since we consider freedom of expression a higher value than democracy, are left with a dilemma. Certain kinds of expression may endanger the nation's security and thus place in jeopardy its future ability to protect free expression. The only course to be recommended, given the present value position, is (1) a general policy that expression should be free in all realms and in all situations and (2) the application of the criterion that specific limitations on free expression are justifiable only on detached and convincing evidence that basic human rights would be seriously endangered without them.[159]

Complete social freedom is inconceivable in any society. The amount of insecurity in a totally lawless state of nature, I agree with Hobbes, would probably turn men into beasts. The optimum amount of social freedom that can theoretically be achieved in a given society, under ideally secure external circumstances, is determined, I submit, by the optimum of anomie that a people can live with. In other words, there is a basic actual or

---

[156] It would seem particularly questionable, from my value position, whether the use of the new weapons of mass destruction, such as the atom or hydrogen bomb, or chemical or bacterial warfare, can be justified under any conceivable circumstances.

[157] First, because they frequently become excessively *threat-oriented,* since they are responsible for the nation's security. Cf. above, p. 101, note 118. Second, because they tend to work too hard and become too tense to allow themselves a relaxed use of their full rational faculties. (President Eisenhower may be one salutary exception to this rule.) On the value of idleness versus the alleged virtues of hard work, cf. Russell, *In Praise of Idleness and Other Essays,* chap. 1.

[158] Cf. Wilson, *Freedom of Speech and Public Opinion,* typewritten Ph.D. thesis, University of California, Berkeley, 1952. Also see below, pp. 142–43 and 150.

[159] In the section "Conflicting Freedom Demands," below in this chapter, I shall return to this issue. And in the following section, "A Crucial Freedom: Freedom of Political Speech," a distinction will be proposed between freedom of political speech and other freedoms of expression, in the belief that the former freedom is a crucial one. Some limitations on even this crucial freedom are considered on pp. 144–52.

potential conflict between freedom and security on this level. The amount of institutional unity required for effective social interaction and for a reasonable amount of peace of mind is an empirical question.[160]

If this priority problem is rephrased as a choice between increased social efficiency and increased individual privacy, it appears plausible to state that the need for social efficiency may vary according to a society's resources, security, social standard, etc., and to conclude that it should allow as much privacy as it can afford to all inhabitants. The difficulty is that the various efficiency needs will always be backed by strong organizational demands, while the demand for privacy is much less likely to be pressed by efficient organizations. Partly for this reason, and partly because I consider free expression the highest value, I wish to shift the weight to the other foot and instead recommend that a modern democracy should be as efficient as it can without infringing on basic human rights.[161]

These considerations move the problem a little way, but they do not solve it. I am saying, in effect, that a basic sphere of individual freedom must have priority over the goal of social efficiency. Yet it is evident that the problem of anomie does not arise unless freedom of expression—or at least the choice between different inhibitions—already is very wide. At a stage where so much freedom has been achieved, my basic human rights approach may be of little use. Beyond a vindication of the right not to suffer physical violence, there are probably diminished consensus possibilities on which rights are more basic than others.

Nor is it relevant to my present purpose to observe that in times of war many kinds of freedom of expression tend to be reduced. In times of acute national danger the threat of anomie is also sharply diminished:[162] the specific external danger is shared and everybody's "duties" are clearly spelled out. The problem of anomie may grow into serious proportions on a national scale only in a relatively free country and in the *absence* of one acute specific danger that unifies the whole population in defense.

It may well be asked how this observation can be reconciled with De Grazia's and Merton's observations of anomie in present-day United States. Is not the population strongly concerned about and united in defiance of Soviet Russia and Soviet-supported communism? There are several reasons why this sense of danger fails to check the growth of anomie, I believe. Except for sudden crises, such as the outbreak of the Korean War, the communist danger becomes customary to the point where it does not interfere with most people's sleep at all. The communist menace is used for partisan purposes, and most people cease to believe in its imminence. Another reason is that communism is not the only danger. Many people, at least privately, may be even more afraid of a new war that may wipe out communists, democrats, and capitalists alike. Some people, again,

---

[160] Cf. below, pp. 232–34 and 278–80.

[161] This position is, in effect, if I have interpreted his guarded language correctly, the same as Hume's that is quoted above, p. 31.

[162] One kind of evidence is the sharp reduction in suicides during wartime (before defeat for one side appears certain). See the two right columns in the table reproduced on p. 457 in Bunzel, "Suicide," in the *Encyclopedia of the Social Sciences*, Vol. XIV.

have been concerned about other dangers, such as McCarthyism, a possible economic depression, etc. The great majority of modern Americans, however, appear not to have any appreciable political worries at all.[163]

Anomie consists in conflicts among norms. There are political norm conflicts in America, which with a more widespread concern for public issues might give occasion to serious anomic strains. Vastly more important, however, is surely, as De Grazia and Merton have emphasized, the basic norm conflict of a competitive business civilization: the conflict between the morality-norms of the good neighbor and the efficiency-norms of the "hardheaded" businessman.

Every democratic society has to live with conflicting norms and institutions. The degree of anomie becomes a menace only when (a) the predictability of behavior becomes affected to the point where planning and concerted action become precarious or (b) the rootlessness and anxiety of individuals become strong enough to develop in them an urge to escape from freedom. A society may become so anomic that some social freedom must be sacrificed to establish the authority of essential institutions. However, even in such a situation efforts to reduce the degree of anomie below the danger threshold should so far as possible avoid interference with social freedom. In accordance with the danger criteria just related, I suggest two alternate lines of approach:

When institutional pressures are insufficient to channel behavior into predictable patterns, positive incentives rather than negative sanctions should be utilized as much as possible as both a short- and long-term policy. For example, in combating juvenile delinquency it is better to provide harmless opportunities for adventure than to punish delinquency. It is more fruitful, in the long run, for an employer to praise good work by his employees than to criticize their bad work. In general, legislation and appropriation policies can do much to insure predictable (and "good") behavior patterns without limiting social freedom in any way, or at least without extending coercion.[164] In other words, I believe it is possible to extend the role of the democratic state (and of other democratic organizations) considerably without increasing the amount of coercion. Whether this is true or not is an empirical question.[165]

In the very long run, secondly, the harmful psychological consequences of anomie can be reduced by the encouragement of psychological freedom. If the homes, nurseries, and schools can furnish the soil for the growth of more basically secure individuals, their tolerance of ambiguities in the social world is likely to extend to the point where they are able to live

---

[163] This is strongly suggested by the evidence presented in Chapter 3 ("Is there a national anxiety neurosis?") of Stouffer, *Communism, Conformity, and Civil Liberties: A Cross-Section of the Nation Speaks Its Mind.*

[164] One good example may be taken from Scandinavia: In the early thirties it was frequently argued that increasing the level of general sex education would hasten the population decline then taking place in those countries. The sex reformers had their way, however, and information about contraceptives is now very widely available, which means that the number of unwanted childbirths has surely been considerably reduced. Yet the population is now on the increase again in Denmark, Sweden, and Norway, probably due to such factors as better housing, family exemptions in taxation, and child subsidies.

[165] Cf. below, p. 292.

constructive lives even in an ideologically complex and discordant democracy.[166]

Potential Freedom and Objective Security

Potential freedom means, according to my definition, the relative absence
of unperceived restraints on individual behavior. My value position favors
maximizing the individual's ability and incentive to resist manipulative
restraints serving other interests at the expense of his own.[167] The immediate task is to inquire whether any conflict of values may arise between
the objectives of potential freedom and objective security and, if so, whether
something can be said about general criteria for solving the problem of
priorities. Again, I shall first consider the problem in relation to individual
human rights, then in relation to national security against specific threats,
and finally in relation to anomie.

An increase in potential freedom for the individual is likely to increase
his security as well. The removal of "ideological blinders" makes him less
disposed to prejudge new events and more prepared to assess them realistically. An individual's protection against objective dangers must be
assumed to be better—other things being equal—the more realistically he
is able to perceive them. For example one who has been taught and is sure
that all Presbyterians are honest and all Catholics or Jews or atheists are
dishonest is more likely to get hurt in life than another who is prepared
to find both relatively honest and relatively dishonest people in most large
categories of people.

An increase in potential freedom in society as a whole might on the
face of it seem to reduce individual security, as it possibly might lead to
increased controversy and struggle. However, verbal controversy does not
ordinarily provoke violence against individuals unless both of these conditions are present: (1) a high level of psychological insecurity, leading to
a strong fear of heresies; (2) the unwillingness or inability of law enforcement agencies to protect individuals at the minority end of important
controversies.

Once a people with democratic traditions has come to tolerate many
opinions, and the basic right to physical inviolability is fairly well protected,
it may be assumed that further increases in potential freedom will serve
to increase rather than diminish individual security. The more potential
freedom in a society, the fewer people will go around with the conviction
that they and *only* they know the Truth, the whole Truth, and nothing but
the Truth. The relaxation of indoctrination pressures serves to stimulate
the empirical approach to life in general and to political problems in particular. People become better prepared to look for elements of merit even
in the assertions of extremely unorthodox minorities. In this kind of an
atmosphere, individual human rights are apt to be more secure than in

[166] In stating that this ability is valuable, I am not implying that *extreme* ideological
anomie would be desirable even if people could live with it. Such an assertion would probably
be nonsensical. Cf. above, pp. 96–97, and below, p. 320.
[167] See above, p. 97.

an atmosphere of Truth versus Heresy or Patriotism versus Treason (in the realm of opinions).

When it comes to considerations of national security, my reasoning and conclusions are very similar to those in an earlier context where I discussed psychological freedom in relation to security.[168] Increased potential freedom means increased awareness of facts that may favor either side of important issues and a consequent reduction in the public's readiness to black-white thinking, fanaticism, and unquestioning support of whatever the government's policies may be. In other words, there is less automatic, authoritarian loyalty to be expected, the higher the level of potential freedom.

Psychological freedom involves, as we have seen, a capacity to judge issues in relation to and in harmony with the individual's own basic motives. Correspondingly, it may be said that potential freedom, to the extent that it is developed, provides the individual with the basic external requirements for making his judgments realistic or instrumental in promoting his own values—namely, an increased awareness of facts and ideas that are an objective part of the empirical and normative situation in which he acts. While a high psychological freedom means smooth functioning of the personality as an "intellectual organism" serving basic needs, a high potential freedom means floodlighting the world in which the individual lives, making him aware of his resources, trends that affect his interests, alternative goals and means he might strive for, alternative dangers he might wish to avoid.

In the short run, and if one assumes a nation's specific security policy to be above criticism, a high level of potential freedom may appear detrimental to security because it produces somewhat skeptical citizens rather than obedient subjects. But a decline in authoritarian loyalty is actually likely to promote rather than diminish national security, for these reasons: (1) If a small de facto ruling circle can count on a wide and unconditional acceptance of their foreign policy, this policy may or may not be well-considered and rational. It is less likely to be well-considered, on the whole, than a foreign policy generally supported only after careful criticism by large numbers of citizens (who were able and willing to accept or reject it on its merits). In other words, I assume that the addition of the pooled and freely operating intelligence of private citizens is a valuable corrective to governmental intelligence in the framing of policies, even from a narrowly security-oriented point of view. A pattern of automatic, authoritarian loyalties severely limits this pooling of intelligence. (2) Authoritarian loyalty is less dependable in the long run than humanistic loyalty because it is superficial in terms of each personality's basic needs, and, consequently, one authority may easily be switched for another in times of stress.[169]

---

[168] See above, pp. 109–13.

[169] Eric Hoffer speaks of the "interchangeability of mass movements" and refers to sources describing disciplined communists as potential nazi converts and vice versa. See *The True Believer*, p. 17.

Policies that are enlightened enough to inspire a spontaneous, humanistic loyalty can for this reason count on much more stable and dependable support.

One still has to ask, however, can the level of potential freedom never become too high from a national security point of view? If there are no organized pressures on opinion processes, is it possible for a society to rally around defensive measures against aggression? William Godwin thought that it was. Even if his country were invaded, he wanted no conscription because he was sure that almost all men would volunteer to fight for a just cause. "It would be a glorious spectacle to see the champions of the cause of truth declaring that they desired none but willing supporters. It is not conceivable that so magnanimous a principle should not contribute more to the advantage than to the injury of their cause."[170]

There is a good deal to be said for Godwin's view. When the smaller European countries were invaded by Hitler's armies, the complete absence of previous provocations from their side created a strong sense of national unity around a cause that was felt to be entirely just. In my own country, Norway, even confirmed pacifists in many cases took up arms. If a new war should come, however, the long history of mutual provocations that we have witnessed in the cold war will hardly make this spontaneous growth of humanistic loyalties possible. If we assume, for a moment, that the population of Europe would not be destroyed by nuclear weapons, and that most of Europe would be occupied by the Russians, it seems likely that collaboration with the occupant would take place on a much larger scale than in the last war. Indoctrinated loyalty patterns are less stable, even if they favor "free world solidarity," than the spontaneous loyalties inspired by an entirely just cause.

And yet, it is impossible to go along with Godwin all the way, even for one who follows him further than most people would. Some amount of force is required to uphold any state's security; it may at times be justified, even from my value position, to order men into battle. And it may be added here that some amount of nationalist indoctrination may be defensible too, to the extent that it inspires a sense of identification with one's fellow countrymen. Because modern technology has made the world shrink and has made continued international anarchy extremely dangerous, however, I submit that an internationalist indoctrination toward sympathy for all peoples is more desirable today than a nationalist indoctrination, even from a national security point of view.[171] The main point of theory in this context is, however, that *some* amount of manipulation of attitudes may be desirable for promoting national security. In other words, though the level of potential freedom should be high, it could become too high, from a national security point of view.

[170] *Political Justice*, II, 137.

[171] It follows that a type of nationalist identification that is compatible with internationalist identification is vastly preferable to a type that is not. It may be said that *people-oriented* nationalism is preferable to *power-oriented* nationalism (the former inspires humanistic loyalty, the latter authoritarian loyalty). See Bay, Gullvag, Ofstad, Tennessen: *Nationalism*, I, 20, 25.

How can it be determined what level is "too high"?

It must be stressed that the level of potential freedom is in this problem formulation related entirely to nationalist and internationalist pressures whose function is to protect national and international security. Pressures serving to bolster a religion, a type of family, or an economic system can never be justified on security grounds unless there is convincing empirical evidence that changes in this field would result in widespread destruction of lives or of basic human rights.

When it comes to institutional pressures in favor of national or international unity (and I am not here speaking of coercive pressures, which limit social freedom), it should further be stipulated that they, to be justified on national security grounds, must be oriented toward generally accepted freedom values, not specific policies or men. If most media of communication had a bias in favor of national and international solidarity, stressing themes such as equality and freedom and the need to protect human rights anywhere, this would be a limitation on potential freedom of opinion that would be desirable, on the balance, because it favors national and international security without seriously impairing freedom. On the other hand, the merit of a similarly uniform bias in favor of a specific organization such as the United Nations would be much more questionable, to say nothing of such a bias in favor of a military alliance such as NATO or against any specific state.

From a national and international security point of view, to conclude, the level of potential freedom can become too high only in the absence of all institutional incentives to identify with fellow citizens or fellow human beings, or all incentives to support basic values involving the recognition of and defense of every man's and woman's right to some measure of freedom and security and dignity. All other limitations on potential freedom are detrimental to national and international security, I believe, in limiting (for purposes whose necessity for national security has not been empirically established) the scope of human intelligence and perceptiveness. The only possible reservation that remains to be considered is in the relationship between potential freedom and anomie. It is conceivable that a high level of potential freedom may be conducive to an anomic breakdown of social interaction patterns.

I have just recognized one type of desirable limitation on potential freedom. This limitation is at the same time, if put into practice, likely to serve as a limited deterrent to anomie. It would be a deterrent, because, to the extent that people share a few basic humanistic values, they are not entirely without a sense of direction or a shared sense of right and wrong. Yet the deterrent would be limited because agreement on some basic values is no bar to wide conflicts about how they are promoted, and conflicting groups and institutions may serve other goals at the same time.

A more effective deterrent to anomie could be approached from this side only if the limitations on potential freedom were broadened to include the achievement of consensus on goals that are specific enough to give some definite criteria for evaluating means as well. I have suggested that the goal of a maximum freedom of expression for all is potentially more fruitful in this respect than the goal formulation of the utilitarians: "the greatest happiness of the greatest number."

In this sense, then, and in this sense only, do I consider "indoctrination to freedom" justified and valuable. It is useful in promoting both security and freedom, I believe, to encourage a consistent bias in favor of protection of basic rights, including a wide freedom of expression, throughout the mass media of communication, including the schools. It must be stressed, however, that this statement concerns a limited interference with potential freedom and not with social freedom. I favor encouragement of certain general attitudes favorable to freedom by persuasion, but I never favor coercion as an instrument to sway attitudes even in this direction (at least not in the world of adults).

Summary

In this section I have tried to bring out some general interrelationships between the values of "freedom" and "security" as defined earlier in the chapter and to say something about value priorities wherever I found evidence of conflict. In general, my position may be summarized as follows: Freedom from coercion is the most important of all freedom values, and it should be vindicated as completely as is possible without exposing the society or nation to an immediate danger of a far more serious coercion than the preventive measures bring about. The most important objective of a democracy is a progressive widening of the social freedom of all individuals, instituted by the widening and strengthening of human rights—first the basic right of inviolability from the most blatant and insufferable kinds of coercion, such as physical violence, and then gradually the less basic rights of security against the less extreme and subtler coercive pressures.

There is only one general exception to the rule that reduction of coercion is the supreme freedom value, in my position. Increasing potential freedom is desirable even at the expense of a reduction in social freedom for the same people, if this reduction consists merely in the perception of coercive pressures that previously went unperceived (and therefore were not coercive or only potentially so). Information and propaganda bringing home to power objects the fact that they are manipulated is on the whole desirable, even if they as an immediate consequence feel much abused and coerced. Insight, I assume, is in general functional rather than dysfunctional from the point of view of expanding freedom of expression in the total sense.

As a second priority set of goals, a democratic society should strive to enlarge freedom in the full sense as employed here—a widening also of psychological freedom and of potential freedom. On the whole, these different aspects of freedom may be promoted as parallel goals. Conflicts may occur, but it is difficult to say anything in general about priorities further down, once I have assigned supremacy to freedom from coercion.[172]

"Subjective security" has disappeared as a value independent of "freedom": the absence of repression-producing anxiety is nearly the same as psychological freedom, and the absence of fear, in the analytical sense as

[172] It would also be of a limited interest, even if it were possible to make further generalizations, since the level of analysis in this section does not take the rivalry between individuals and between groups into account, and does not include reference to the contents of expression.

distinguished from anxiety, is not to be desired as a value in itself. There remains "objective security" against specific and diffuse dangers. Here again, the security of the individual person, or his realistic perception of this security, is closely overlapping with his social freedom from coercive pressures. Only national security against specific dangers and security against anomie present real priority problems for a society aspiring to "freedom," in being occasionally incompatible with a maximal social or potential freedom.

The problem of taking precautions at the point where the growth of freedom leads to critical anomic strains is of a great theoretical interest, as it is in inquiries of this kind one must seek elucidation of the ultimate limits to human freedom in society. Value conflicts may arise between security against anomie and either social or potential freedom; only the goal of a maximum psychological freedom cannot increase the danger of anomie. In Chapters 5 and 6, where "social freedom" and "potential freedom," respectively, are discussed in more systematic relation to empirical theory and research, the limiting factor of security against anomie will be considered again.

The only conflict of practical urgency between "freedom" and "security" arises between "social freedom" and "national (and international) security." My basic value position is that demands of national security may take precedence over individual basic rights to freedom from coercion only if this coercion will in fact avert substantially worse kinds of coercion. Deliberate coercion should never go any further than this objective danger requires.

CONFLICTING FREEDOM DEMANDS

In the previous section I have discussed compatibilities, conflicts, and priorities between freedom values. My frame of reference was the individual's point of view, as an individual and as a social and political being. This discussion could be carried on without considering questions of contents of expression, for the problems necessitating limitations on the kinds of expression to be tolerated emerge only when relationships between individuals are brought into the picture.

The problem of priorities between conflicting freedom demands is more complex; for one thing, the question of contents of expression now assumes a crucial significance. From one individual's point of view, whatever serves to increase his freedom in one sense also increases his freedom in the total sense, except to the limited extent that there are incompatibilities between the three levels of freedom or between freedom and security. But the picture changes when even one other individual is considered. An increase in A's freedom may well mean a decrease in B's, depending on what types of behavior or what kinds of expression are involved. For example, an increase in A's freedom to advertise his merchandise by the use of sound trucks may well mean a reduction in B's freedom to enjoy privacy. An increase in A's freedom to dispose of his property may mean a decrease in B's freedom from want. An increase in A's salary may be possible only if B's is reduced.

It will be convenient to use the plural term "freedoms" or "freedoms of expression" in many cases when I am referring to content categories of "freedom"—such as freedom of speech, freedom of movement, political freedom, freedom to seek publicity, freedom to seek privacy.

Among the English empiricists whose thought was reviewed in Chapter 2, only John Stuart Mill proposed a general formula for distinguishing between conduct that should not and conduct that should be subject to regulation, whether by public or private sanctions:[173] "As soon as any part of a person's conduct affects prejudicially the interests of others, society has jurisdiction over it."[174] This distinction between self-affecting and others-affecting conduct may perhaps be considered a wider application of Locke's distinction between matters inside and outside the civil magistrate's jurisdiction, which in turn is related to Christ's distinction between what belongs to God and what belongs to Caesar.

One trouble with Mill's distinction is that it is not of much use as a guide for concrete policy-making. Practically all behavior is both self-affecting and others-affecting, though in varying proportions, and so far as I know nobody has tried to formulate criteria for just when the one element is to be considered strong enough and the other insignificant enough to justify an unconditional exemption of this sort of conduct from social control. Yet is it not devoid of meaning to subscribe to his principle to this extent: Conduct that is (almost) entirely self-affecting should be (almost) entirely free from regulation, and deliberate efforts should be invested in liberating it from institutional regulation not in the individual's or the common interest. This norm is in harmony with my general position on coercion as the supreme evil among values affected by political action. Indeed, it may in part be considered as one application of my most general norm for laying down priorities between freedom values: coercion can be justified only when it clearly serves to reduce coercion.

There is a second reason why Mill's general distinction must be considered insufficient. In order to preserve and enlarge the scope of freedom of expression in general, it is vitally important that one crucial kind of freedom is protected above all others—freedom of speech on political issues. By Mill's standard, this freedom would fall in the category that is subject to *more* social control than other freedoms.

Almost a century has elapsed since the first appearance of *On Liberty*. No comparable general argument for freedom has appeared during this time. So far as I know, only Bertrand Russell has proposed a comparably ambitious *general* criterion for priorities between freedoms of expression or conduct. Writing early in the First World War, Russell starts out from two basic criteria for progress toward what he considers the good society: "1. The growth and vitality of individuals and communities is to be promoted as far as possible. 2. The growth of one individual or one community is to be as little as possible at the expense of another."[175] The second criterion really follows from the first. And the first criterion comes close to my own

---

[173] His father proposed a formula for distinguishing between unconditionally and conditionally free speech; see above, p. 43, and below, p. 144.
[174] "On Liberty," *Utilitarianism*, p. 177.
[175] *Why Men Fight: A Method of Abolishing the International Duel*, pp. 248–49.

position in favor of a maximal freedom of expression as a supreme value. It should be remembered that "freedom" in this study is used in a sense comprehensive enough to include "self-realization" in a psychological sense and also "realization of the potential self." My "freedom" includes reference to the capacity, the opportunity, and the incentive for growth and vitality, although my value emphasis (unlike Mill's and Russell's) is on freedom itself rather than on its use.

To aid in the application of his criteria, Russell suggests the following distinction between two types of human goals or human behavior:

Men's impulses and desires may be divided into those that are creative and those that are possessive. Some of our activities are directed to creating what would otherwise not exist, others are directed toward acquiring or retaining what exists already. . . . The best life is that in which creative impulses play the largest part and possessive impulses, the smallest. The best institutions are those which produce the greatest possible creativeness and the least possessiveness compatible with self-preservation. . . . The supreme principle, both in politics and in private life, should be to promote all that is creative, and so to diminish the impulses and desires that center round possession.[176]

At this point Walter Lippmann has objected to Russell's position in the name of liberty: "Like every authoritarian who has preceded him, [Russell] is interested in the unfettered development of only that which seems good to him. Those who think that 'enlightened selfishness' produces social harmony will tolerate more of the possessive impulses, and will be inclined to put certain of Mr. Russell's creative impulses under lock and key."[177] What Lippmann appears to overlook is that the point at issue is in part an empirical one. It must be admitted, however, that Russell's position would have been less vulnerable if he had emphasized much more this empirical aspect, which he does recognize: "The creative impulses in different men are essentially harmonious, since what one man creates cannot be a hindrance to what another wishes to create. It is the possessive impulses that involve conflict."[178] This is an observation of fact, not a statement of value. If a believer in freedom to be consistent must refuse to face facts about self-defeating consequences of a complete lack of regulation, then Russell's belief in freedom is not consistent. However, I doubt that consistency in this sense is much of a virtue or much of a goal to strive for. It seems a much more appealing task to try to determine the empirical conditions under which the freedom of all people in a society can be maximized, while realizing that a complete freedom is as impossible as a complete security or a complete knowledge.

Perhaps one particular statement in Russell's discussion has been misunderstood by Lippmann: the assertion that an expansion of the creative impulses or a reduction of the possessive impulses makes for a better life.

---

[176] *Ibid.*, pp. 256, 258.

[177] *Liberty and the News*, pp. 34–35. It should be mentioned that Lippmann surely does not intend to include Russell under the label "authoritarian," for he places him beside Milton and Mill as a great, though inconsistent libertarian. ("Of living men, Mr. Bertrand Russell is perhaps the most outstanding advocate of liberty." *Ibid.*, p. 26.)

[178] *Why Men Fight*, p. 259.

This is, of course, a tenable position. But if it appears to Lippmann that this is the premise from which Russell concludes that society should encourage one kind of behavior and discourage the other, then it would seem quite reasonable to accuse Russell of arguing for tolerance only for the kinds of behavior of which he happens to approve. It seems to me, however, that it is more plausible to interpret Russell's conclusion as being based entirely on his value premise of the desirability of human vitality and growth and on the empirical premise that possessive behavior is more likely to put men at odds with one another than is creative behavior. Logically it is certainly possible to arrive at his conclusion from these premises.

I have no important disagreement with Russell on his value criteria, but his empirical belief that creative behavior, as he defines it, tends to produce social harmony is questionable, and he himself eventually modified this belief considerably. Writing twenty-odd years later, on the eve of the Second World War, Russell finds two sources of conflict in men's desires—their desire to possess and their desire to exert power. The exertion of power, I take it, may be stimulated in part by "creative" and in part by "possessive" impulses. This dichotomy is discarded, however, and Russell seeks new ways to solve the problem of how to establish priorities between freedoms of expression. He now says: "Every man desires freedom for his own impulses, but men's impulses conflict, and therefore not all can be satisfied."[179] This is a formulation reminiscent of Hobbes, and it is so patently an empirical approach that is no longer vulnerable to the kind of objection that Lippmann leveled against Russell's earlier argument.

The problem of how to regulate possessive behavior creates no difficulties on the theoretical level. The conflict can be solved, in theory, "by decreeing equality of distribution, as has been done by the institution of monogamy." Indeed, this conflict can be solved by *any* stable distribution pattern that is generally accepted as "fair" or is not considered as sufficiently "unfair" to provoke violence. The problem of regulating power behavior in the interest of freedom maximization for all is a much more difficult one. After observing that it is possible for power impulses to find outlets compatible with social freedom,[180] Russell concludes in very general terms that the providing of such outlets "is a problem partly of individual psychology, partly of education, and partly of opportunity. . . . If freedom is to be secure, it is essential both that useful careers shall be open to energetic men, and that harmful careers shall be closed to them. It is important also that education should develop useful forms of technical skill, and that the circumstances of childhood and youth should not be such as to generate ferocity."[181]

The chief merit of Russell's later approach, it seems to me, is in his recognition of the complexity of the problem of allocating freedoms of expression and in his pointing out that the problem must be approached from

---

[179] "Freedom and Government," in Anshen (ed.), *Freedom: Its Meaning*, p. 259.

[180] In Russell's language, unlike mine, "social freedom" is contrasted to "physical freedom," or the mastery over the physical world. "Modern scientific technique has increased physical freedom, but has necessitated new limitations of social freedom." *Ibid.*, p. 251.

[181] *Ibid.*, p. 259.

the angles of several social sciences simultaneously. Yet his proposals on the problem of freedom maximization are rather vague, even considering the brief space within which the more recent of the two discussions was confined.

It must be admitted, however, that the proposals that I have to offer do not represent a great improvement in specificity. There are at least three possible ways, it seems to me—apart from those suggested by Mill and Russell—toward laying down general priority rules for maximizing freedom of expression for all.

One approach would distinguish between "free" and "unfree" expression in my psychological sense—also in my potential sense—and claim that expressions and behavior that are relatively "free" on both of these levels should have priority over those that are relatively "unfree" on either of the two levels. In other words, a necessary minimum of coercion could be justified in order to insure the prevalence of expressions that are relatively "free" in a full sense over expressions that are relatively "unfree" on one or two levels.

Another approach would draw a distinction between verbal and nonverbal behavior and claim that freedom of speech should always take precedence over freedom of action other than speech. A plausible extension of this principle might add that freedom to discuss general principles should take precedence over freedom to incite to action.

A third approach would be based on the general norm that coercion can be justified only if it by a fair margin and by generally acceptable criteria serves to reduce coercion. The problem of priorities between freedoms of expression could then be rephrased as a problem of regulating social coercion in the interest of keeping it at a minimum.

Let me now try to appraise the merits and limitations of each of these three possible approaches. There is no reason why we could not try to integrate all three lines of approach. It is practical to discuss them one by one, however, and I shall proceed in the same order as they have been suggested.

Perhaps the impression may emerge from my whole conception of "freedom" that some kinds of expression are considered more deserving than others, in that they are more in harmony with the individual's actual or potential "true self." In defining psychological freedom as harmony between basic motives and overt behavior, I may be open to the interpretation that the expressions of the psychologically unfree do not need or deserve the same amount of social freedom as the expressions of the psychologically free persons because the former expressions are already, after all, unfree in a psychological sense. Correspondingly, it might be concluded from my definition of potential freedom that the expression of opinions resulting from pure indoctrination deserves less social freedom than the expression of opinions arrived at after a more detached investigation and reflection.

There is something to be said for considering the expressions of the psychologically and potentially more free persons as more valuable, on the whole, than those of their opposites. On the average, more realistically useful insights come from people who are both relaxed and well-informed. On the other hand, many of the most creative and brilliant men of all times have been either anxiety-ridden or fanatics. Perhaps the individuals with the most fertile brains or the most sensitive hearts tend to be driven into psychological crises or underdog fanaticism, respectively, by the very fact that they are more perceptive or more generous to begin with.

Let us consider another argument for discrimination against "unfree" opinions. It is true that all kinds of expression do not contribute equally to the process of self-government. If the promotion of a more genuine and effective self-government is seen as the basic political goal—a position held by many political scientists—then it is quite logical to argue that speech of demonstrably unfree personalities should be barred from public dissemination.[182] If, however, freedom of expression itself is seen as the most basic value, then it is obvious that suppression cannot be justified by extraneous considerations.

The position taken here is that a society as much as possible should guarantee to all its inhabitants a maximal degree of freedom of expression, on the basis of equality. If democratic institutions, as I assume, tend to encourage a wider freedom than does an autocratic system, then I am for democracy. Otherwise I am not. Freedom of expression is seen as the most important goal of democratic societies, not just as an instrumentality to make democracy work. It is seen as an important complex of human rights, to which all persons should be entitled to equal access.

It is unnecessary, once this position is reaffirmed, to go into the many dangerous consequences likely to ensue when a democratic government starts out on the road to discriminate between "free" and "unfree" opinions. Even such an apparently (to some people) moderate and reasonable scheme as that of requiring a public labeling of some opinions as "psychotic" or "dictated," or some psychological equivalent, would raise so many questions about the criteria chosen and about the selection and detachment of the judges that, at best, one kind of restraint would be replaced by another one, which is likely to be much more coercive because it is endorsed by a public instead of a private authority.[183]

I believe in the desirability of an equal freedom of expression, then, for "neurotics" and "normals" and for fanatics and skeptics. In other words, I reject entirely the first of the three suggested lines of approach toward establishing general priorities between freedoms of expression.

A second possibility, I have said, is to lay down a general rule that all speech is sacred, in the sense that nobody should be restrained from expressing all that is on his mind so long as he confines himself to mere words and does not force anyone to listen to him. Then coercion should properly

---

182 This is the position taken in Wilson, *Freedom of Speech and Public Opinion.*

183 The House Un-American Activities Committee unanimously approved, on April 28, 1948, a "Subversive Activities Control Act, 1948," in which section 11 would have provided: No organization on the Attorney General's list of "Communist fronts" has the right to circulate any literature through the mails unless it bears this label: "Disseminated by . . . , a Communist organization." New York *Herald Tribune*, April 29, 1948. This bill did not become law, though it had many supporters at the time.

be applied only against people who forcibly interfere with the freedom of others to speak or to listen as they please. Depending on one's degree of acceptance of this approach, one might justify coercion only to counteract physical force or else extend this justification until it authorizes counter-measures also against economic pressures aiming at interference with speech.

At a first glance, this approach might seem to solve many problems. Speech is rarely coercive in itself, it is often assumed, and a society that extended tolerance to all kinds of speech might seem to be conducive to the growth of freedom on all my three levels. And from an intellectual's point of view, the sacredness of verbal expression—his own cultivated skill—would seem a very attractive principle. Yet there are at least two difficulties involved in this principle. It is empirically not so readily applicable as it might seem at first. And there is some doubt about the extent to which this principle would actually serve to extend freedom from coercion.

Let us first consider the practicality of this approach. Is it so certain that speech is rarely coercive? All threats of sanctions have to be communicated in one way or another, and words are probably the most frequent vehicle. Should a man be free to say that somebody ought to kill anyone who talks or behaves as Mr. X is doing? The answer is not obvious.

The effect of libelous speech may be harmful to the victim, and every country's legislators and judges apply some of their most intricate efforts to determining the fine distinctions between libels and legally permissible insults. It is not an easy line to draw. And more recently, the issue of "group libel" has added new complexities to the law in several countries.[184]

Then there is the well-known issue in American law of the right of a person to shout "fire" in a crowded theater just for the fun of it. Everybody seems to agree that no one has a right to do so, but there is disagreement about the proper reasoning for reaching this result.[185]

For my part, I believe the sum of these considerations should amount to an admission that verbal and nonverbal behavior may be equally coercive and equally harmful—or beneficial—to human freedom and security. Coercion has here been defined as (a) the application of actual physical violence or (b) the application of sanctions sufficiently strong to make the individual abandon a course of action or inaction dictated by his own strong and enduring motives.[186] The worst kind of coercion, I have said, is the actual application of substantial physical violence.

Only one argument could be submitted, it would seem, in favor of a preference for the freedom of speech in clashes between speech and non-verbal expression: speech can never involve actual physical violence. In certain settings, therefore, such as the political arena, individuals and organizations relying on persuasion by speech should on the whole be protected against those who forcibly would stifle speech.

This argument may be considered an application of the general norm

---

[184] See Riesman, "Democracy and Defamation: Control of Group Libel," *Columbia Law Review*, XLII (1942), 728–80; cf. *ibid.*, pp. 1085–1123 and 1282–1318. Also see below pp. 147–52.

[185] Cf. below, p. 147.

[186] Cf. above, pp. 93.

that coercion can be justified only in the service of reduced coercion. Let us therefore proceed to consider the more basic norm relating directly to the use and abuse of coercion.

This principle may be formulated as follows: *Coercion,* over sane, adult human beings, *can be justified only if it in fact serves to reduce coercion or prevent increased coercion.* The reductions accomplished or the increases forestalled, must be substantial and by some margin unquestionably outweigh the deliberately applied coercion.

This problem of "weighing" actual and hypothetical states of coercion is not a simple, quantitative problem, however. True, I consider all individuals entitled to equal protection against unnecessary coercion, but the various *kinds* of coercion are by no means equal or quantatively comparable.

My human rights approach implies that the principal freedom goal is not the reduction of the "sum" of coercion, that is, the reduction of the number of persons who suffer coercion, according to specified criteria. More important is the goal of entirely abolishing the worst kinds of coercion, even if only a few individuals are affected. My basic norm on coercion justifies its use, in other words, not in order to reduce some "sum total" of coercion, but only to forestall and reduce the worst kinds of coercion. The coercion of an individual is never justified, according to my position, except to prevent worse *kinds* of coercion over himself or others.

The chief difficulty in this approach toward the maximization of freedom is the lack of consensus about the priorities between human rights—apart from a general acceptance, I believe, of the right to stay alive and not suffer physical violence, as the most basic of all human rights.[187] There is by no means a general agreement about which freedoms or rights are more important among, for instance, the following: the right to work, the right to a living wage, the right to vote, the right to medical care, the freedom to travel, the right to plan parenthood, freedom of association, freedom of speech, freedom to advertise, and the right to leisure and privacy.

In a few types of situations, then, there is likely to be a full consensus about which freedom of expression is more important. For example, a saying goes, "your freedom of action ends where my nose begins." If we wish first of all to insure physical inviolability to all individuals—and it is assumed here that we all do—then it is empirically necessary to impose certain restraints on the freedom to swing one's fists about.

However, another example is more representative of the many real dilemmas created by the lack of consensus about the priorities between freedoms or rights. If we wish to protect all individuals against unemployment, or against drastic reductions in living standards, it may be empirically necessary to impose certain restraints on the employer's freedom to dispose

---

[187] It may be objected that a great many authors have claimed priority for some other freedom. For one example among many, consider Milton's famous phrase: "Give me the liberty to know, to utter, and to argue freely according to conscience, above all other liberties." *Areopagitica and Other Prose Works* (Everyman's Library), p. 35. Such statements mean what they say, but are invariably advanced within a specific frame of reference. I feel sure that Milton and all other advocates of freedom would agree that the right to stay alive, and to be physically unmolested, is *at least* as important, in general, as the access to knowledge and argument.

of his property. Now, which freedom is more important? Clearly, this is in large measure a question of one's politics. And yet, if what is at stake for the employee is his own and his family's health, and for the employer some loss of expendable wealth, my basic norm leads to the conclusion that the employer should yield.[188] Few people will challenge either the general norm or its application under these conditions, but perceptions of what is involved in conflict situations of this kind will vary, and further value considerations and beliefs about consequences may be brought in. Such questions have a way of becoming too complex for the achievement of a rational consensus, partly also because vested interests may have incentives toward confusing issues. They become issues tossed about on the arena of partisan politics.

The political process has been called a struggle to determine who gets what, when, how. Clearly, it may be seen as a struggle between competing freedom demands, and it may be said that each party's political program, if it says anything at all, says something about what the priorities should be between human rights. Few political parties are frankly advocating the advancement of one group or class at the expense of all others; they are almost all advocating a universalistic program, though with value priorities conforming to demands of specific parts of the population.[189] Conservatives tend to argue that freedom of initiative and freedom to make decisions about private property are among the most important of all freedoms. The parties on the left argue that the right to work, fair pay, and leisure are of prior importance. The ensuing dilemmas are the meat of practical politics—local, national, and world politics.

The problem of freedom allocation is solved daily, always tentatively, depending on which side is able to enforce how many of its own security and freedom demands. In modern democracies, as well as in dictatorships, it has become customary for the state to intervene in many of the specific power struggles—for example in certain important industrial collective bargaining processes. Either, as in the United States, it purports to intervene only to assure nonviolence or "fair play" or to protect "the public interest." Or, as in Scandinavia under socialist governments, the state intervenes frankly to influence also the results of the contests, according to preconceived notions of social justice tempered by considerations of gradualness and practicality.

Trends in the support given to competing parties with different views on priorities between freedom demands may give a rough impression about the public's sense of justice from time to time. However, these trends are by no means reliable indications of genuine shifts in opinion. Election re-

---

[188] It is not always easy, though, to judge just how expendable a given amount of wealth may be in psychological terms; cf. Erikson's example, cited above on p. 73. The extent to which such factors should be taken into account in the political solution of economic conflicts is, of course, debatable.

[189] "In principle all polities are devoted to the welfare, well-being, or happiness of their members. This moral purpose of polity has been recognized from the beginning of political thought. It appears in every act of policy-making, when the proponents of a new measure are obliged not only to prove its workability and its profit to those special interests on which it immediately impinges and who perhaps instigated it, but also to reconcile it with all other interests." Perry, *Realms of Value: A Critique of Human Civilization*, p. 211.

sults are to some extent determined by demagogic skills and by the average levels of potential and psychological freedom or the ability of the electorate to resist demagogues. And political issues during elections are frequently so tangled and complex that it is not easy to say on what particular issues, if any, the victors were given a mandate.

Social science research techniques today offer some hope for achieving more clarity in interpreting election results and more real knowledge about the shifting climates of opinion with respect to priorities between conflicting freedom demands.[190] But we must realize that no amount of knowledge can take away the probability that people always have disagreed and always will disagree widely on the principles for determining priorities between specific human rights.

An admission of the complexity inherent in social reality is, of course, no argument against proposing a relatively simple system of norm-integration as a basis for policies. Where people act from a large number of competing specific norms, anyone who wants to influence people ought to start out on a very general level and try to win support for his own specific norms only if he can first achieve support for a basic system of norm-integration.

My basic approach has been set forth as posing a maximum of freedom from coercion as the supreme value, based on equality between people and precedence for the more basic human rights such as the right to physical inviolability. This is in itself surely a plausible and in substance a widely shared value position. Many might prefer a different formulation, but few people in democratic societies would reject the values given priority in this approach.

It must be admitted that this approach does not lead us very far toward determining priorities between specific freedoms of expression, because people differ widely in their conceptions of freedom and of a free society. I believe, nevertheless, that the present approach is a more useful one than the other lines of approach reviewed in this section. I believe my general position on coercion as the supreme political evil is widely accepted, on the whole, though by implication in generally shared democratic values rather than explicitly.[191] If so, it can provide a stable framework or reference system for the democratic political struggle: each democratic party is brought to accept the priority of the same most basic human rights, and the struggle turns on what should be the next priority rights to be vindicated. Barring sudden catastrophic setbacks, this approach to politics holds

---

[190] Cf. the following studies of voting behavior in American presidential elections: Lazarsfeld, Berelson, and Gaudet, *The People's Choice: How the Voter Makes Up His Mind in a Presidential Campaign*; Campbell and Kahn, *The People Elect a President*; Berelson, Lazarsfeld, and McPhee, *Voting: A Study of Opinion Formation in a Presidential Campaign*; Campbell, Gurin and Miller, *The Voter Decides*; and by the same authors, "Political Issues and the Vote: November, 1952," *American Political Science Review,* XLVII, No. 2 (1953), 359–85; Eugene Burdick and Arthur J. Brodbeck (eds.), *American Voting Behavior* (1957).

[191] There is at least one exception to be noted: many otherwise humanistically oriented people apparently accept capital punishment as suitable for certain categories of criminals. Cf. below, pp. 137 and 276.

promise of an ever widening scope of generally accepted and also effective human rights.

And for every individual or for every political party, my approach provides a convenient frame of reference for arguing that some specific new freedoms ought to be made into enforced rights before others. For example, a socialist can argue that the right to work is a more basic right than most others, because enforced idleness or a strong fear of unemployment for a worker tends to paralyze both his psychological and his social freedom. Or the capitalist can argue that full private disposal over private factories is essential both for the free functioning of the man with superior capabilities and for creating incentives for developing new such talent. So long as such arguments can continue inside a mutual commitment to protect the growth of man's individuality—every man's and woman's equally— the chances are that many political issues can be simplified and clarified to a point where majority decisions become less fictitious than they frequently are in today's democracies.

In other words, my approach fails to lead very far toward an answer to the problem of allocating specific freedoms of expression, with a view to maximizing the sum total for all, but it does provide a point of departure for democratic politics and a frame of reference for the citizen who wishes to exert political influence for the extension of the freedom values or human rights that he cherishes the most.

A CRUCIAL FREEDOM: FREEDOM OF POLITICAL SPEECH

Failing to achieve a general answer to the problem of deducing specific freedom demand priorities from the goal of freedom maximization, I shall in this section argue that freedom of political speech is an instrumentally crucial freedom and that the long-run protection of other freedoms in large measure depends on the protection and enlargement of this particular freedom. One principal objective of this discussion is to show that the goal of a maximum freedom of expression for all is a goal lending itself to some practically useful specification.

In assigning to freedom of speech on political issues a crucial significance, I am not offering a specification in a logical sense of the word.[192] It is on empirical grounds that I consider the more limited objective equivalent with a specification of the more general goal: I shall argue that free speech on political issues is instrumentally crucial in the defense and expansion of the whole range of actual and potential human rights.

If I can deliver a convincing argument to this effect, I shall have demonstrated that the goal of a maximum freedom of expression for all is capable of providing at least indirectly some guidance for policy-making—assuming, of course, that the political means toward expanding free speech on politics are ascertained more easily than the political means toward ex-

---

[192] The assignment of priority to freedom from coercion, on the other hand, is a specification, logically speaking, even if its practical usefulness for policy guidance is more limited. Freedom from coercion is valuable in itself; it is an important part of the freedom value. Freedom of political speech is only for instrumental reasons given a higher value, under certain conditions, than various other freedoms.

panding free expression in the total sense. A similar demonstration of potentialities for policy guidance has not, to my knowledge, been made with respect to Bentham's goal of the greatest happiness for the greatest number, unless one is satisfied with such essentially rationalist, unrealistic performances as James Mill's essay on *Government*.[193]

In attaching an instrumentally crucial value to a maximal freedom of political speech, I am not contradicting what limited priorities I have established between general freedom of expression demands. Coercion is still the supreme evil. A more severe kind of coercion to restrain nonpolitical expression is worse, according to my position, than a milder kind of coercion to stifle the expression of political opinions. For an example, put in positive terms, the abolishment of capital punishment for criminals is, in my judgment, a goal of a greater urgency than, for example, extending the political freedom of teachers or other public servants.[194]

Freedom of political speech should take precedence over other freedoms only when there are no substantial differences in degrees of coercion to be remedied. Within this limitation a freedom-oriented government should focus its policies around the primary necessity of safeguarding and extending the freedom of political speech before other freedoms, whenever it is a question of either–or.

What is "political speech"? It means verbal expression dealing with or bearing on political phenomena. I use "political" in a broad sense.[195] How far is it realistically possible to extend freedom of political speech for all? My approach to this question is analogous to my approach to the general freedom of expression: the stifling of political speech is justified and required to the extent that it demonstrably is necessary to reduce the total amount of equal or worse kinds of coercion.

By itself, speech is perhaps never coercive, but it always takes place in some context, and the context may give it a severely coercive impact. Political speech may well be a vehicle for communicating threats of coercive sanctions. Speech may also be used to build up attitudes that are likely to result in coercive behavior. Even an ostensibly tolerant and peaceful speech may be calculated to provoke violence and coercion.[196]

My preference for safeguarding a wide freedom of political speech over comparable other freedoms[197] does not rest on any belief that the gagging of political expression is more painful for the individual concerned than the gagging of other kinds of expression. A suppression of even the

---

[193] In Burtt, ed., *English Philosophers from Bacon to Mill.*

[194] The conclusion that capital punishment is a supreme evil that should be remedied by political means follows from my value position. This deduction could *perhaps* be challenged if there had been some convincing evidence that capital punishment as an institution substantially contributes toward reducing the number of murders and manslaughters. Cf. below, p. 276.

[195] Cf. above, pp. 20–24.

[196] "The ways in which mob violence may be worked up are subtle and various. Rarely will a speaker directly urge a crowd to lay hands on a victim or class of victims. An effective and safer way is to incite mob action while pretending to deplore it after the classic example of Antony, and this was not lost on Terminiello." Justice Jackson's dissenting opinion in *Terminiello v. Chicago,* 337 U.S. 1, 35 (1949).

[197] Comparable, that is, with respect to the severity of coercion involved in restraining each of the freedoms.

most inconsequential private gossip, if it were possible, might conceivably be as oppressive to the itching tongue or cause as much restraint on the individual as a suppression of political opinions. I believe that freedom of political speech is of crucial importance among comparable other freedoms because this freedom is instrumental to the vindication of all other freedoms.

It is true that there is no a priori necessity for assuming that the general level of freedom in a democracy tends to be wider, the wider the freedom of political speech. Also, such a thesis is too general to be subjected easily to empirical proof. It is probable, however, that considerable evidence from recent history could be marshaled to strengthen the assumption. But my belief in an instrumental relationship is based on a simple series of conclusions from certain widely accepted factual assumptions. In a democracy, political decisions are influenced by a continual contest between differing opinions as put forward by various parties and pressure groups. Even decisions of the courts are certainly not unaffected by the shifting climates of public opinion. Many of the political decisions that are made and remade over and over again are in effect dealing with priorities between conflicting demands for free expression. As long as there is a wide freedom of political speech, there is some possibility that all groups will get a hearing for their freedom demands and vindicate at least a few of them. If there is little freedom of political speech, on the other hand, the total freedom of expression for all groups outside the ruling circle will be as precarious as are their means of defending it in an open forum.

I wish to argue that the tradition of Arthur F. Bentley and David B. Truman in political theory tends to support and illuminate this thesis. The chief merit of their approach is in their attempt to consider all pressures according to their actual potency in the political process—whether they have a legal or an extralegal status, are emanating from organized or unorganized groups, consist in actual or potential measures. Particularly useful for my immediate purpose is Truman's concept of *potential group*:

Any mutual interest, however, any shared attitude, is a potential group. A disturbance in established relationships and expectations anywhere in the society may produce new patterns of interaction aimed at restricting or eliminating the disturbance. Sometimes it may be this possibility of organization that alone gives the potential group a minimum of influence in the political process—the possibility that severe disturbances will be created if these submerged, potential interests should organize necessitates some recognition of the existence of these interests and gives them at least a minimum of influence.[198]

The relationship of this observation to the importance of free speech on politics is in the necessity of free political expression for the recognition of the shared attitudes that potentially unite men into protest organizations. To the extent that free speech on politics is suppressed, freedom of ex-

---

[198] *The Governmental Process: Political Interests and Public Opinion*, pp. 511–12. The analysis of politics in terms of competing group pressures (from both organized and unorganized groups) was pioneered in Bentley, *The Process of Government: A Study of Social Pressures*.

pression relating to art, science, religion, and other spheres is also insecure. To the extent that free speech on politics is vindicated, any attempted political limitation on an artist's freedom, or the freedom of a religious group, is likely to provoke a lively protest. This likelihood for immediate political countermeasures, where potential opponents are free to try to arouse a widespread concern to support the potential protest is in any society the strongest of all guarantees against infringements on all freedoms of expression.

It is true that a constitutional Bill of Rights and corresponding provisions are important in providing both a yardstick for assessing infringements and additional motivations for resisting invasions of specific freedoms. Crucial among the rights, however, is the right to speak out when it is felt that any freedom is violated. Without a wide freedom of political speech, no other human right, even if it enjoys constitutional sanction, can be vindicated by peaceful means. Because there are potential opposition groups in all societies,[199] this approach is well suited for studying the relative merits of democratic and dictatorial systems of government.

It may be argued in the same terms that freedom of political speech is as important for national security as it is for general freedom of expression. Unless frustrated elements are allowed to express their frustrations, there is no knowing when the amounts of frustration may reach the revolutionary boiling point. On the other hand, it is conceivable that a narrow freedom of political speech may result in a relatively slow growth of potential groups toward awareness of the strength of their demands. In whatever way this question is to be answered in general, my concern is with societies where a good amount of freedom of political speech has become traditional. In such societies, any drastic curtailment of accustomed freedoms is likely to arouse a widespread opposition, at least in times of peace.

The chief policy recommendation I wish to draw from the present brief considerations is implied in this tentative hypothesis: It is probable that general freedom of expression is protected and extended in a society to the extent that policy-making is directed toward protecting and extending the effective freedom of all camps and individuals to express attitudes and opinions on political issues.

Some readers may consider the full realization of a genuine democracy or self-government the supreme political goal. They may reject the supremacy of the freedom of expression over all other values and the validity of the reasoning that led me to conclude that freedom of political speech must be vindicated before all other freedoms. For the benefit of these readers, I wish to point out that it is also possible to reach my conclusion from the premise that the perfection of the process of self-government is

[199] Both Bentley and Truman are primarily concerned with democratic governments but are not excluding a wider application of their theorizing. Cf. Bentley, *The Process of Government*, pp. 314–15. Bertrand Russell reasons from the same premise about governments in general when he asserts that "the tendency of every government toward tyranny cannot be kept in check unless governments have some fear of rebellion. Governments would be worse than they are if Hobbes's submissive attitude were universally adopted by subjects." *A History of Western Philosophy*, p. 578.

the supreme political good. I wish to review briefly this other line of argument, in the hope of extending thereby the relevance of the policy applications that may be drawn from my position.

Let me begin by stating my disagreement with those who place the perfection of self-government over all other values. In the first place, I consider even the best form of government an instrument to promote individual human goals and, above all, to extend the freedom of men and women to grow and develop their capabilities. Secondly, I believe that it is a fiction to assume that even a fair degree of self-government has been achieved so far in any sizeable or even any small state. Government requires organizations, and organizations are governed by leaders and bureaucracies, which may at best be subject to some form of public control. And in the third place, this fiction invariably tends to be tied up with other fictions in the manner of legalistic thinking.

Alexander Meiklejohn is a foremost representative in the United States of what may be called the self-government approach to the vindication of free speech. He is a distinguished educator, not a lawyer, but has chosen, after the fashion of lawyers, to base what is essentially an argument of political philosophy on an unorthodox interpretation of the American Constitution. This is indeed the principal weakness in his important little book, and it gives his opponents a much too easy chance to refute his argument.[200]

Meiklejohn argues for a certain interpretation of the First Amendment to the United States Constitution. Substantially, his argument deals with perennial issues of political philosophy, and may be stated as follows: Democracy, or self-government, offers the best hope for wisdom in government. With the free interplay of opinions, human intelligence is given free vent, and the government can select its policies from a wide choice of insights and policy proposals. The perfection of this process is the purpose of free speech on political issues. "What is essential is not that everyone shall speak, but that everything worth saying shall be said. . . . The principle of the freedom of speech springs from the necessities of the program of self-government. It is not a Law of Nature or of Reason in the abstract. It is a deduction from the basic American agreement that public issues shall be decided by universal suffrage."[201]

Meiklejohn supports his argument for free speech on politics by the analogy of the parliamentary privilege. Since the revolution of 1688, the members of the English Parliament have vindicated their ancient demand for a complete freedom of speech in both houses. And the United States Constitution declares in its article 1, section 6, about the members of Congress, "for any speech or debate in either House, they shall not be questioned in any other place."

Nobody disputes today the contention that a complete freedom of speech on political issues for the elected representatives as such is a prerequisite for their ability to carry out their political functions properly. However,

---

[200] *Free Speech and Its Relation to Self-Government.* See also a review of the book by Chafee, in the *Harvard Law Review*, LXII (1948–49), 891–901, especially p. 894.
[201] *Free Speech*, pp. 25, 26–27.

if this is a valid contention as applied to the legislature, it must also be a valid contention as applied to the electorate. The electorate, after all, may be seen as another branch of a democratic government. It has, at any rate, its own peculiar and essential political functions to perform: to determine the choice of representatives, on the basis of adequate information about the policies each candidate intends to pursue and about the views the various candidates take on the various policy proposals. In some states the electorate votes directly on policy issues. In all democratic states the voters are expected to shape a "public opinion" and to express it periodically in elections. The fact that the elections provide the mandate for the legislative and executive power, and indirectly even for the judiciary power, indicates that the ultimate source of legitimate political authority is vested in the electorate. Meiklejohn himself says: "In the last resort, it is not our representatives who govern us. We govern ourselves, using them. . . . The freedom which we grant our representatives is merely a derivative of the prior freedom which belongs to us as voters."[202]

Applying this line of reasoning to a burning issue in recent American politics, Joseph Tussman has coined the phrase *contempt of the electorate*:

The heart of the matter is that the demand of Congressional committees for the answers to its questions about the political activities of members of the electorate poses a clash of "contempts." On the one hand refusal to answer is said to deprive Congress of needed information. On the other hand the demand for an answer to such questions invades the protective privacy or privilege of the electorate, entailing, as it does, sanctions in one way or another. . . . Stated in this form the question almost answers itself. I doubt if even the hardiest Senator or Representative would seriously claim that the political power of the electorate must defer and give way to his own.

In other words, the citizen is within his rights if he refuses to answer questions about his political views and activities before a congressional committee: "He is not in contempt of Congress. Congress is in contempt of the electorate. It is interfering with its free functioning. It is exposing to censure and reprisal. It is intimidating its master. And it needs to be called to heel."[203]

This contention has so far not been vindicated in the courts of the United States. Tussman is critical of the present Supreme Court majority for construing these issues as issues between the government and the individual, instead of seeing them as issues between two government agencies, Congress and the electorate. It seems to me that his argument is a strong one, once it is agreed that the electorate has political functions at least as important as those of the legislature, the executive, and the judiciary.

As a *de lege ferenda* legal argument from the postulates of democratic constitutional theory, I subscribe to Meiklejohn's and Tussman's reasoning. As an argument of political philosophy, I should have subscribed to it, had I been able to accept the basic value premise: that the perfection of the process of self-government is the ultimate political objective. My con-

---

[202] *Ibid.*, p. 37.
[203] "Contempt of the Electorate," an unpublished paper, Berkeley, California, 1953.

tention, it will be remembered, is that the supreme practical political objective is to vindicate the freedom of political speech on political issues. So is Meiklejohn's, and so is Tussman's. And we all agree, it would seem, that this special freedom has primarily an instrumental value, and in this capacity only should be given priority over other freedoms of expression. Where Meiklejohn and Tussman consider this freedom a crucial prerequisite for the perfection of self-government, however, I see it as a crucial prerequisite for the protection and enlargement of all other freedoms of expression.

This difference is more than a quibble. Once you say that the value of any freedom is derived from the value of some extraneous political function, you also say, it seems to me, that it may be justified to curb that freedom to the extent that these extraneous objectives might require. It is perfectly logical from there on to argue as follows: Since the improvement of self-government is the ultimate goal, and it can be demonstrated that many kinds of political speech serve to impair rather than to advance the democratic process, it is legitimate to suppress free speech to that extent. For instance, there is evidence that many neurotic individuals take pleasure in extreme hate-propaganda against Jews and other minorities and that this sort of speech impedes rather than contributes to rational self-government. Ergo, the anti-Semitic lunatic fringe ought to be deprived of their freedom of political speech.[204]

I shall not dwell on the many dangers of arbitrary judgment and of the use of flimsy evidence that this sort of theorizing might in the end serve to justify. It follows from my own bias that any argument for suppressing any kind of political speech is suspect. But I am particularly worried about an approach that seeks to justify suppression of speech as a means to an end that is only vaguely defined. And "self-government" is an end that in my opinion can never be clearly defined because a serious attempt at precision would lead one to realize that it is an unrealistic end, both sociologically and psychologically. By any reasonable and fairly precise interpretation that I can conceive of, "self-government" is a political goal that cannot be approximated, let alone provide specific criteria for a gradual approximation.[205]

[204] This argument is advanced in Wilson, *Freedom of Speech and Public Opinion,* pp. 156, 177: "The only public purpose upon which speech limitations can be justified is that of maintaining and improving self-government. But, it must be remembered that self-government is compounded of *both* the practice of interest-group combat and the theory of reasoned consideration of the public good. Only speech which proves a serious threat to the delicate balance which must be maintained between these two factors can legitimately be restricted under this theory. . . . Thus, while self-government is impossible without freedom of expression, it is equally impossible if the expression of numerous ethnocentric opinions remains unchecked."

[205] Wilson describes the concept in these terms: "Self-government, practically conceived, is thus a combination of two contradictory elements. It consists of an *ideal*—the translation of majority will into majority rule by a rational process of allowing each citizen an equal voice in the deliberate process. It also consists of a strongly institutionalized *practice* whereby public policy is a function of the dynamics of intergroup struggle. In this sense self-government is essentially a process of compromise rather than reasoned deliberation about the requirements of the public interest. For the foreseeable future, both of these elements, compromise and

I prefer to turn the argument around and consider democratic institutions as means to the end of a maximally free expression. Freedom of political speech is also a means to the end of a full freedom of expression. However, it is at the same time an integral part of the end. It can and should be maximized as far as possible, without empirically unnecessary limitations on the contents of expression, because free speech on politics is valuable in itself, as is any other freedom of expression.

Should freedom of speech on political issues be extended also to alleged and real enemies of political freedom? Should a democracy prohibit, not only the use of force and violence in politics, but also the advocacy of principles recommending such coercive measures? To what extent is political freedom compatible with political suppression?

In the election campaigns of many modern democracies it is a standard phenomenon to see contesting politicians and parties predict dire consequences in the event that the opposing side should win. And many politicians no doubt bring themselves and each other to believe sincerely that the other party would lead the country toward economic ruin, war, or dictatorship. Quite obviously no theory of free speech in the Western tradition can seek to justify suppression of speech on the basis of such opinions and attitudes, however strongly held. This is the rationale, as I would justify this tradition: Whatever party A's beliefs about the horrible amounts of coercion that would follow if party B should win the election, it is normally not possible to demonstrate a high empirical probability that all of the following predictions will come true: (1) B will win the election; (2) B will in fact take the dictatorial measures which are allegedly feared; and (3) counterpropaganda has no possibility of preventing B's victory or of restraining B's policies after the probable victory.

In the unlikely event that all three sets of predictions in advance could be proved valid to the satisfaction of detached observers (observers who are not committed to either side and are competent to judge empirical evidence in a critical manner), it might at first seem that a theoretical element of justification for curbing party B's activity would emerge. However, even in this marginal case, this one element of justification would be canceled out by another empirical consideration. Party B would in this case have a very wide support and attempts to check its activities would be almost certain to be met with many kinds of resistance. It would be virtually impossible to prove in advance that suppression would not provoke more violence and coercion, in the long run, than the popular party would bring about deliberately after ascending to power through peaceful competition.

It will be recalled that a people's right, not merely to advocate but to carry out revolution, at least as a means of last resort, was supported by most of the English empiricists. Locke, Hume, Bentham, and especially

---

reason, will probably remain as integral parts of our concept of democratic government. And in fashioning a theory of free speech both elements must be taken into account. Respect for the part played by the one must be tempered by consideration for the part played by the other."
Ibid., pp. 150–51.

James Mill—all were quite explicit on this point. James Mill took this position in his essay on the freedom of the press: "Exhortations to obstruct the operations of government in detail should, exhortations to resist all the powers of government should not, be considered offences."[206] For my part —and since my premises are different, there is probably no disagreement involved—I reject the right to revolution in a society practicing a high level of free speech on political issues. By "revolution" I understand the use of large-scale armed violence to change the government or form of government. And by "a high level of free speech on political issues" I understand, in this context, an opportunity for all political movements, including revolutionary movements, to communicate their views in fair competition. I do recognize the right to revolution, however—and here I am sharing the premises and the conclusion of the empiricists—for any movement that is in fact denied the right to try to gain its objectives by the peaceful propagation of its doctrine.

To come back to the specific topic of freedom of political speech, I am led to subscribe to Mill's view that exhortations to resist all the powers of government should be within the sphere of free speech. The press should be a channel for the airing of any existing amounts of discontent, as well as of content with things as they are, and provide signals for an enlightened government that wishes to pursue such policies as would progressively reduce the "general obstructionists" to a harmless lunatic fringe.

The second part of James Mill's position raises the problem of the right to advocate specific unlawful acts. This problem cannot be answered, in my judgment, before a few words are said about what aspects of human behavior may properly be regulated by means of legislation. The latter subject is, of course, a huge one in any democratic country's constitutional law. The *raison d'être* of a constitution in the first place is to be sought not only in its function of establishing a certain form of government, but also, in most states, in its function of laying down certain substantive limits for legislative and governmental action. In each country's constitutional tradition, the courts have over the years tried to specify ever more concretely the precise borderline between substantively constitutional and unconstitutional law or executive action.

There is no such thing as a clear-cut borderline in the law of any country, and the differences from state to state may be considerable.[207] I shall not try to summarize a consensus between the courts in various democratic countries on what are the proper substantive limits on governmental powers. My few remarks on the topic will be of a philosophical, not of a juristic nature. My task in this chapter is to outline a philosophy of free expression, not to outline the scope of free expression in the various systems of constitutional law.

Constitutions should, I believe, in part be seen as political defense systems for whatever amounts of human rights have been vindicated in

---

[206] Cf. above, p. 43.

[207] In Britain, where there is no judicial review, it is up to the legislative power to restrain itself and stay inside the limits of its constitutional tradition.

each state and as instruments for the attainment of whatever additional rights are desired and in fact possible. The rights listed in a constitutional Bill of Rights may be extended by legislation, but it should never be possible or legitimate to narrow them down. They mark the degree of achievement or intended achievement in a society aspiring toward freedom.

On the most general level, I wish to argue that legislation enacted in a democratic manner is entitled to obedience *provided* it does not narrow down whatever scope of individual human rights[208] had previously been vindicated, institutionalized, and constitutionally sanctioned. Legislation that narrows down the scope of human rights by introducing new coercive pressures is justifiable only if it sets out to reduce other restraints that are generally considered more coercive. Individuals who decide that this justification is not present, on the basis of some efforts of open-minded inquiry, should be entitled to urge noncompliance with this particular law—not resistance by violence, but passive resistance. In this manner only the citizenry, or private pressure groups, can provide an added incentive for the legislature to keep coercive legislation down to whatever minimum has so far been achieved in each country's democratic tradition.

Let me amplify by way of examples. Legislation against murder or theft or blackmail is clearly above controversy. There is an overwhelming consensus favoring the protection of this scope of personal freedom and security for everybody as against antisocial privileges. The rate of punishment, or even the desirability of applying any punishment at all, is of course debatable. But the straight advocacy of violations of the basic criminal law should at times be prohibited, particularly if the occasion makes it likely that such advocacy is an important chain in the causation of an ensuing crime or an ensuing preparation to commit a crime. No clear line can be drawn. Among the circumstances influencing culpability should be included such factors as, for example, the prestige of the speaker among those he addresses, his inferred intentions, his inferred awareness of probable consequences of his speech, and the actual consequences.

The only general points I wish to make are, first, that an incitement to commit a specific crime may be liable to punishment for complicity in that crime, whether it was actually carried out or was checked while in preparation. But, secondly, if a previously legal and not antisocial type of behavior is declared a crime in a new law, then the suppression of advocacy of noncompliance can no more be justified than the law itself can be justified.

For an example of the second situation, if an American state legislature or the federal Congress declares membership in a certain organization a crime, then the scope of the previously enjoyed freedom of association has clearly been narrowed down, and there is no demonstrable compensation

---

[208] My distinction between "human rights" and "social privileges" should be kept in mind; a "human right" is a claim to a freedom from restraints that is in principle extendable to all citizens; a "social privilege" is a claim to a freedom that must by its own nature be limited to a minority. Examples of the former type of claims are a possible right to work, to health care, or to free speech. Examples of the latter type are a possible right to employ other peopole, to own and run a factory, or a claim to pay lower or stationary taxes to an expanding government.

in a resulting reduction in other and worse coercive pressures. The advocacy of noncompliance with such a law—for example, an advocacy that the suppressed organization is morally entitled to continue its activity secretly, in violation of such a law—should, in my opinion, not be punished, even in the event that the courts should fail to perform their proper constitutional function of throwing aside such a law.[209]

Returning to James Mill's distinction, I wish to qualify his assertion that incitement to obstruct specific governmental actions or laws should be punishable. I wish to say *may* be, provided the action or law in question is not an instrument for the abolition of or reduction in a previously vindicated right.

Mill added a second criterion with respect to advocacy for the obstruction of specific laws: only "direct" advocacy of obstruction should be punished, not "implicit and constructive" argument.[210] It is perhaps a better way to state essentially the same criterion as follows. *The advocacy of a general principle, however antisocial, should always be free of punishment. The advocacy of a specific act may be liable to punishment if the act is a crime under a law within the proper substantive sphere of legislation.*[211]

It must be pointed out, however, that this criterion is not much more clear-cut than Mill's, for it cannot be applied literally. The grammar of the sentences cannot be the only consideration. What is concealed as a general argument may in intention and in effect be a specific advocacy. The nature of the audience and of the temper of the moment must certainly be taken into account. What takes the form of advocacy of general principles may under certain circumstances be equivalent with a specific incitement, with foreseeable, immediate effects. If the audience is composed of teen-agers, for example, or is emotionally excited, what might otherwise be an advocacy

---

[209] Consequently, I feel that the late Albert Einstein was entirely within his rights when he urged teachers not to cooperate with the House Committee on Un-American Activities when they are asked questions about their political associations or beliefs. And no responsible officials demanded at the time that this incitement be prosecuted. *New York Times,* June 12, 1953.

[210] Cf. above, p. 44.

[211] Roger Baldwin, the prominent American civil libertarian, once argued as follows: "You can, in Hyde Park, London, advocate the assassination of kings and be protected by the king's own guards, but you may not advocate the assassination of the king; you may not advocate the direct incitement to commit the specific act, but may advocate the political philosophy of assassination, which is the same as the law in the United States." This statement was made before a Special Committee of the House of Representatives in Washington, charged with investigating communist propaganda, pursuant to H. Res. 220, in the 71st session of the U.S. Congress (1930). I am not sure that Baldwin is right in asserting that such *is* the law of the United States, or even of Britain, but I agree in his attitude that this ought to be the law in a democratic country; somewhere in this border area, I believe, are the empirical limits on the maximization of freedom of political speech, in a traditionally democratic country.

Justice Roberts, speaking for a unanimous U.S. Supreme Court, has stated the position of American law as follows: "When clear and present danger of riot, disorder, interference with traffic upon the streets, or other immediate threat to public safety, peace, or order, appears, the power of the State to prevent or punish is obvious." *Cantwell v. Connecticut,* 310 U.S. 296, 308 (1940).

Justice Jackson, in his dissenting opinion in *Terminiello v. Chicago,* argues that the Court in deciding this case departed from the previous position as formulated by Justice Roberts, 337 U.S. 1, 27–28 (1949). But cf. *Feiner v. New York,* 340 U.S. 315, 321 (1951), and below, pp. 150–52.

of a doctrine may in effect and intention become a call to immediate action.[212]

I have discovered one desirable limit to the freedom of political speech, while despairing of the possibility of making it a clear-cut and ready tool for a quick and easy classification. Even the best of laws for the protection of political discussion need a constant remodeling in the courts, once we recognize the need for placing the specific advocacy of substantial crimes beyond the pale of free expression.

This is not the only desirable limitation, however. For one thing, it is possible to cause much physical violence or coercion by the use of words that cannot be described as advocacy. "The most stringent protection of free speech," said Oliver Wendell Holmes, Jr., "would not protect a man in falsely shouting fire in a theater, and causing a panic."[213] Meiklejohn would place such utterances beyond the realm of "public speech," since the man who shouts fire and knows there is no fire is only pretending to speak in the public interest.[214] However, it may clearly be a political utterance in my sense if the cry resounds in a meeting arranged by a political party. Since a restriction on speech barring this kind of utterance clearly is much less coercive than the possible results of this sort of calculated speech, a false cry of "fire," if it could result in serious damage to individuals, should in my judgment be prohibited on a par with direct acts of physical violence.

Another more complex group of limitations on the desirable freedom of political speech is found in the area of libel and slander. My general justification for supporting the prohibition of certain kinds of speech in this area is in the fact that libel and slander can effectively reduce the freedom of the victims and that this effect may amount to a worse coercion than the coercion involved in barring people from making libelous verbal assaults in the first place.

The defamation of a man's reputation may paralyze his psychological freedom and expose him to social pressures that severely restrict, or are perceived as severely restricting, his former freedom of action. On the other hand, if libel laws are too strict, the potential libeler may experience a real restriction on his freedom of speech, in being legally restrained from speaking the truth as he perceives it, and potential listeners may be deprived of important and relevant information.

New complexities are added when we consider the question of group

---

212 "Every idea is an incitement. It offers itself for belief and if believed it is acted upon unless some other belief outweighs it or some failure of energy stifles the movement at its birth. The only difference between the expression of an opinion and an incitement in the narrower sense is the speaker's enthusiasm for the result." Most "incitements," argued Holmes, are within the constitutional boundaries of free speech. "Only the emergency that makes it immediately dangerous to leave the correction of evil counsels to time warrants making any exception to the sweeping command: 'Congress shall make no law . . . abridging the freedom of speech.'" See Holmes's dissenting opinions in *Gitlow v. New York*, 268 U.S. 673 (1925), and in *Abrams v. United States*, 250 U.S. 631 (1919).

213 Holmes, speaking for the Supreme Court, in *Schenck v. United States*, 249 U.S. 52 (1919).

214 *Free Speech*, pp. 41–42. Cf. Chafee, *Free Speech in the United States*, pp. 129–30.

libel, or defamation of groups—such groups, for example, as Negroes, Jews, Jehovah's Witnesses, Republicans, Communists, lawyers, or the bankers in Middletown. It is clearly a legitimate and necessary part of the democratic process to exchange views, both kind and rancid, about many social groups. However, many kinds of epithets may contribute to real hardships suffered by underprivileged groups, such as the Negroes or Jehovah's Witnesses, in the United States.

It would lead us much too far to consider how the legislatures and courts have, in fact, handled the problem of political libel and defamation in democratic countries. Comparative studies have tended to bring out wide variations both in laws and in social attitudes, from the strict libel laws and attitudes in Britain to the system of leniency toward Nazi libel campaigns in Weimar Germany. In the United States a middle ground has been taken, though with considerable variations from state to state.[215] The important point I wish to make is that the application of libel laws is a necessary instrumentality to maximize the total freedom of political speech in any country. The substantive maximization of this freedom does by no means *a priori* imply a maximization of the leniency of libel law enforcement.

It is an exceedingly intricate empirical question whether this maximization can be achieved by one type of libel legislation or another. This question urgently needs extensive inquiry, for we are far from a plausible answer, even on a rather general level, and yet this terra incognita is a stumbling block in democratic theory and democratic practice alike.[216]

The necessity for a pragmatic approach in a field of inadequate knowledge may justify either a relatively strict or a relatively lenient libel law, depending on the conditions and experience in each country. In my judgment, the one important consideration is that the *purpose* of the libel law should be a legitimate one. And the only legitimate purpose is to achieve a maximum substantive freedom of expression for all, including the marginal people and groups.

Let me try to develop this general position at least one step toward more specificity, without getting into extensive discussions of positive law.

With respect to libels against individuals, it is clear that name-calling may impose considerable restrictions on the victim's freedom or security, and the same is true of implicit and explicit accusations. The reasonable test of culpability is, in principle, a weighing of the potential sanctions the victim would experience as against the restraints implied by enforcing silence on the potential libeler.

[215] See Riesman, "Democracy and Defamation," *Columbia Law Review,* XLII (1942), 728–80, 1085–1123, and 1282–1318; Wilson, *Freedom of Speech and Public Opinion;* Chafee, *Free Speech in the United States.*

[216] Wilson seeks to demonstrate, on the basis of a comparison between developments in Weimar Germany and England (between the two wars), that a "vigorous application of legal sanctions" against political libel and defamation campaigns is necessary to save the democratic process from breaking down under the pressures of psychotic hate campaigns. *Freedom of Speech,* especially chap. 2. However, his description of German and English experience furnishes no proof that a difference in laws and court behavior might have prevented the rise of fascism in Germany, nor that this particular aspect of British law was essential in preventing the rise of fascism in Britain.

This weighing of freedoms is no easy task in concrete cases, of course, and the courts must invariably play a large part in shaping the libel laws even in civil law countries.[217] And the law must change in a changing political climate. For example, to call an American a "communist" was at first not considered libelous, but some years ago the New York courts caught on to the fact that nowadays this label is apt to carry along quite considerable social sanctions and decided that a false accusation of this nature is a libel.[218]

With respect to group libels, the law should have exactly the same purpose: to prevent the arbitrary imposition of restraints and intimidations. It seems natural to conclude that accusations against majorities should never be considered libels, since it is hard to see how any individual hardships could follow. It is the weak and underprivileged minorities that need protection against group defamation. For example, in the midst of prevailing anti-Semitism, the Jews may need the barricade of a legal right to have scurrilous anti-Semitic attacks punished, in order to protect what remains of their freedom and human rights. However, if there is only a moderate amount of anti-Semitism about, such a legal barricade may not be required, and it should be dispensed with whenever the Jews in general rather than a specific individual is involved in the accusation. To the extent that a community is enlightened, hate-mongering against substantial groups is rarely sufficiently catching to result in serious freedom limitations to the individual member of the group.

In the struggle between political parties, a minority party may be more in need of protection against group defamation than the majority party. However, it goes without saying that minority views cannot be given a premium. No minority can claim the freedom to use invectives against majority parties while insisting that they as a minority need protection against corresponding invectives coming the other way. This is rarely if ever a practical problem, however; the practical problem is to guarantee an equal scope of free speech to minorities. Minority parties are sometimes extremists in one way or another, and invectives *against* them may appear level-headed and restrained when viewed with the prevailing bias of the orthodox; while *their* invectives from the same point of view may appear excessively scurrilous or even criminal.

This amounts to another argument in favor of particular caution in group libel legislation and enforcement when political parties are involved. Freedom of political speech is a crucial freedom, and it should be restrained

---

[217] Among the relevant considerations in judging the victim's interests are estimates of the damage he is suffering, his ability to sustain the damage, his dependence on a good professional reputation, etc. And on the other side, the actual and perceived veracity of the accusation, the possibility of previous provocations, the perceived relevance of the libelous remarks to the promotion of the accuser's own legitimate interests, etc.

[218] References to changing state court decisions are found in Riesman, "Democracy and Defamation," *Columbia Law Review*, XLII (1942), pp. 1300–1308, especially pp. 1304–5.

American courts have frequently been caught in a dilemma when confronted with the name-calling of anti-Semites: If they deem the label "Jew" a libelous one, this might seem an acquiescence in anti-Semitism. If they refuse to consider it a libel, they disregard the real damage that may be suffered and encourage the anti-Semites to continue their name-calling. "The sound resolution," says Riesman, "would seem to be the unhypocritical recognition of the prejudice in the award of damages to the plaintiff, while condemning in the opinion both the defendant and the prejudice he exploits." *Ibid.*, p. 1296.

only when necessary to provide others with an equal amount of freedom of political speech (or when necessary to protect a more basic and general human right, such as physical inviolability). Furthermore, it should never be limited when the same objective can be reached by other means.

To accuse a person of being a crook may very severely limit that person's freedom if the accusation is generally believed. In England such an accusation against a politician is a serious matter, perhaps justifying punishment in many cases. In the United States, where such accusations are more likely to be discounted, since people are more used to invectives in the "great game of politics," it is more doubtful whether punishment is justified.

To accuse a political party as a whole of being crooked, or traitorous, or unpatriotic may also result in imposing restraints on its leaders and members. But to limit the right to make such accusations may impose far more serious restraints on the vital freedom of political criticism. In general, it seems to me, the defamation of large groups should be punishable only in extreme cases, and the defamation of political parties never, unless the attacks actually amount to incitements to violence, in defiance of regular criminal law.

One alternative to my value position, as applied in stating the proper purposes of group libel legislation, is to assert that the law in this area should promote "self-government" or "the democratic cause."[219] In substance, this difference in purpose formulations may not amount to important differences in judging concrete cases, since the problems are invariably too complex anyway to permit clear-cut deductions from general purposes to concrete judgments. I do believe, however, that the goal of freedom maximization, or at least the goal of maximizing freedom of political speech, is somewhat more specific than the other goals and, unlike the latter, is potentially capable of further specification. In other words, I believe in better practical guidance of judgments also in libel cases as new strides are made in the clarification of the goal of "freedom." I do not believe there are corresponding prospects for clarification in concepts such as "democracy" or "self-government."

Secondly, and more important, once you consider a value other than "freedom" the ultimate goal, you are, in principle, supporting the suppression of freedom whenever necessary to advance that extraneous value. To paraphrase a well-known saying about "truth": it makes a lot of difference whether you place freedom in the first place or in the second place.

There is still another alternative purpose formulation applied to libel laws that is far more insidious, however. That is the purpose of preventing violence. In itself this is, of course, an admirable purpose, whose legitimacy has been attested to quite extensively in this chapter. What is important to stress, however, is that the suppression of political speech should be the last and not the first means of preventing physical violence. In a democratic

---

[219] Wilson, *Freedom of Speech*, pp. 150–51, and Riesman, "Democracy and Defamation," *Columbia Law Review*, XLII (1942), p. 731. Cf. above, pp. 139–43, and note 205.

country we have a police force to insure the public safety. And if political speech provokes violence, the task of the police should emphatically be to restrain those who would deny to others the right to speak or to listen and not to restrain those who speak (provided they force nobody to listen).

This issue was brought sharply into focus in an important American Supreme Court decision a few years ago. A radical student had been arrested for making an inflammatory street corner speech; among other things, he had urged the Negroes to rise up in arms and fight for equal rights. The listeners were split on the issues he presented, and there was some danger of fist fights breaking out. The immediate cause of the arrest, however, was a threat from one listener to a police official that he would take direct action against the speaker unless the police stepped in. The student was later convicted and carried his fight to the Supreme Court, where the conviction was upheld. Chief Justice Fred Vinson, speaking for the court, said: "It is one thing to say that the police cannot be used as an instrument for the suppression of unpopular views, and another to say that, when as here the speaker passes the bounds of argument or persuasion and undertakes incitement to riot, they are powerless to prevent a breach of the peace."[220]

A breach of the peace was in fact threatened, not so much by the speaker, however, as by those who would make use of their fists, and particularly by the man who threatened to assault the speaker. Freedom of political speech is tenuous, indeed, if its legal limitations are to be determined by the amount of tolerance or the readiness to vigilantism in each audience. Justice Black in his dissenting opinion objected that "today's holding means that as a practical matter, minority speakers can be silenced in any city . . . while previous restraints cannot be imposed on an unpopular speaker, the police have discretion to silence him as soon as the customary hostility to his views develops."[221] Justice Douglas, concurring in Justice Black's dissent, added that the record shows "an unsympathetic audience and the threat of one man to haul the speaker from the stage. It is against that kind of threat that speakers need police protection. If they do not receive it and instead the police throw their weight on the side of those who would break up the meetings, the police become the new censors of speech."[222]

Nevertheless, such a power "reasonably to regulate free speech . . . has been slowly creeping into our constitutional law," as Justice Douglas complains in a dissent in a later case.[223] Whatever the future course of American law, it seems to me desirable that the police power should be used to enforce a maximum tolerance of free political speech and never to silence speakers just because intolerant individuals threaten to do so unlawfully.

Admittedly, it is no easy task to determine just when the speaker, under the given circumstances, in effect and intention, is provoking unlawful

---

[220] *Feiner v. New York*, 340 U.S. 321 (1951); cf. Justice Jackson's dissenting opinion in *Terminiello v. Chicago*, 337 U.S. 1, 13–37, especially 31–37 (1949), and above, p. 146, note 211.

[221] *Feiner v. New York*, pp. 328–29.

[222] *Ibid.*, p. 331.

[223] *Poulos v. New Hampshire*, 345 U.S. 425 (1952).

violence that the police are powerless to prevent. The general assumption should be, I believe, that the police have the duty to protect the speaker who provokes primarily his opponents, however maliciously. The speaker who in effect incites his supporters to direct physical aggression, on the other hand, is passing beyond the boundaries of his justifiable demand for free political speech.

We have seen that there are certain justifiable limitations to the freedom of political speech. Under certain circumstances, it may be legitimate to punish incitements to unlawful acts, malicious provocation of panics, and libels against persons or groups, even in the context of political speech. These, in my judgment, are the only qualifications to the doctrine I advocate—that a crucial practical objective of a democracy should be to maximize freedom of political speech. And it will be seen that these qualifications are no real exceptions to the general principle, if I have succeeded in making it clear that they are merely rules of regulation in the interest of a maximum freedom for all.

As to the severity or laxity of libel legislation, I am not prepared to state that one or the other alternative, or some middle road, is preferable. This is in part an empirical question in need of inquiry within each society or culture. The only reasonably definite conclusion I have reached is that the law bearing on group libels between political parties should be lenient, as, indeed, it appears to be in most democratic countries.

A value position has been adopted and spelled out in Part Two favoring a maximization of the freedom of expression. Three definitions of freedom have been chosen, and certain priorities among freedom values and among freedom demands have been proposed.

The task in Part Three will be to survey contemporary behavioral theory and research data with a bearing on a crucial empirical problem: Which kinds of factors do in fact influence the growth or decline of the freedom of expression in modern societies?

The freedom values will now be discussed as dependent variables. Since my conception of freedom is composed of three subconcepts, this discussion will be divided in three chapters. First comes an inquiry into the probable determinants of psychological freedom, in Chapter 4. Chapters 5 and 6 will be given to corresponding searches for influences bearing on social and potential freedom.

Part Two

REALITIES OF BEHAVIOR

———————————

4

Determinants of Psychological Freedom

INTRODUCTION: DYNAMIC THEORY AND RESEARCH

$\mathcal{I}$n previous contexts my discussions of psychological freedom[1] have on the whole been of a phenotypical nature. I wished to isolate as clearly as possible a certain type of indirectly observable phenomena, which could offer some hope of utility in empirical study, at least as a beginning toward further clarification. It must be said, however, that the phenotypical approach does not lead us very far in the study of human behavior. Problems of motivation are not as simple as assumed by classical economists, for example, who conceived of the "economic man" as a rational creature in deliberate pursuit of fixed, preconceived goals.[2] If there is such a thing as a consistent pursuit of values underlying human behavior, sufficiently enduring to be called "rational" and sufficiently universal to be attributed to "human nature," then it must be a rationality of the whole organism, quite unlike the mind-directed rationality attributed to the economic man.[3]

It follows that any fruitful substantive discussion of psychological freedom must proceed within the framework of a genotypical and developmental theory. Nevertheless, the discussion cannot be divorced from the phenotypical or manifest phenomena. The emerging dilemma is how to be empirical without being superficial. How can we discover the important facets of motivation without the use of constructs whose ties to observable phenomena become too tenuous for consensual validation, among the various faiths or schools within the scientific community?

This problem is a persistent one among psychologists. The experimentalists in perception and learning theory claim that only their own strict procedures produce new insights whose validity can be established by retesting. Depth psychologists, on the other hand, claim that only they are tackling important problems and that their approach is as rigorous as the

---

[1] See above, p. 83.

[2] See, for a recent discussion, Edwards, "The Theory of Decision Making," *Psychological Bulletin*, LI, No. 4 (1954), 380–82.

[3] See above, p. 61, for reference to a psychological theory of human behavior as a "rational" striving for tension reduction, toward an equilibrium of the organism.

nature of their problems permits.[4] There is certainly something to be said for the claims of each side in this controversy and even more to be said for the criticisms directed against the more sweeping claims one can meet in each camp.[5] It is fortunate indeed that current trends point toward less warfare and more cooperation between experimentalists and depth theorists.

Since the Second World War, and especially since the publication of *The Authoritarian Personality* in 1950, there has been a great increase in the amount of research and thinking devoted to empirical use of psychoanalytic constructs. It has been increasingly realized that speculative models with reference also to unconscious processes are a matter of necessity in a comprehensive psychological theory and that important elements in such a theory can be tested only indirectly, and at times only through many links of inference. Increasing insights into the complex dynamics of human motivation have been made possible by the advent of psychoanalysis, and the book just referred to is both a principal achievement and a point of direction for much subsequent research in this area. One of its authors has claimed in a recent paper: "We may go as far as to say that it is the very shift from the level of external, overt manifestation to the level of motivational dynamics which opens the way to a science of personality. This shift is altogether the merit of psychoanalysis."[6]

Robert K. Merton's interest in the advancement of "theories of the middle range" in sociology[7] is paralleled in psychology by the approach to which reference has just been made. Another recent discussion of the same general problem suggests that it may be "useful to distinguish between the *terminal hypothesis* designed to meet the requirements of rigorous experimental tests and the *intermediate hypothesis* formulated for the sole purpose of guiding observation. The former must be couched in operational terms; the latter, although it strives for clarity and precision, need not be stated in testable or even communicable form. . . . In the last analysis, the intermediate hypothesis, like the conceptual framework from which it derives, is valuable only insofar as it leads ultimately to testable hypotheses of crucial significance for science."[8]

This observation suggests that not only human behavior, but also theorizing about human behavior, is a dynamic process exhibiting different characteristics at different stages of development. "It is probably correct," says Leon Festinger, "that if a theory becomes too precise too early it can have tendencies to become sterile. It is also probably correct to say that if

[4] According to Urie Bronfenbrenner, "It is perhaps possible to say—with only moderate exaggeration—that the study of human behavior in America shows a bimodal distribution with undisciplined speculation at one mode and rigorous sterility at the other." "Toward an Integrated Theory of Personality," in Blake and Ramsey (eds.), *Perception: An Approach to Personality*, p. 209.

[5] For an amusing take-off on some kinds of psychoanalytic theorizing, study the new theory of de-umbilification, mammary envy, and digital gratification, as advanced in Borgatta, "Sidesteps Toward a Non-Special Theory," *Psychological Review*, LXI, No. 5 (1954), 343–52.

[6] Frenkel-Brunswik, *Psychoanalysis and the Unity of Science*, p. 293.

[7] Merton, *Social Theory and Social Structure: Toward the Codification of Theory and Research*, pp. 5–10.

[8] Bronfenbrenner, in Blake and Ramsey (eds.), *Perception*, p. 210.

a theory stays too vague and ambiguous for too long it can be harmful in that nothing can be done to disprove or change it."[9] My aim in this chapter is to build a tentative theory of psychological freedom, handling intervening depth variables, but seeking ultimate anchorage in observable phenomena, both on the independent and the dependent side of the variable pattern. For a long time, I believe, personality theory will depend on this sort of a marriage between intermediate theory and terminal hypotheses about tangible relationships.

It must be admitted, however, that the depth theory is the stronger partner in this marriage for the time being because of the limited amounts of significant research data available. This scarcity is a reflection of the complexity and relative inaccessibility to observation of the variables involved in human motivation. A great deal of research has been done on intercorrelations between personality characteristics or behavior tendencies; most of the research on the composition of the authoritarian syndrome, to be discussed later in this chapter, falls in that category. But my concern is with factors contributing to the growth or stifling of psychological freedom, not with mapping the broad patterns of intercorrelations between degrees of freedom and other characteristics. This chapter is, therefore, essentially a theory of the development of psychological freedom, with references included to some research data that have a bearing on this theory.

SOME BASIC ASSUMPTIONS

It is a good principle in theory-building, sometimes referred to as Occam's Razor, to avoid making more assumptions than necessary to seek an explanation of the processes you wish to understand. A second good rule is to avoid the pitfall of assuming that a name by itself contributes to knowledge. In psychology it was once fashionable to assume the existence of an "instinct" every time human behavior seemed to deviate with some regularity from the observer's conception of rationality as applied to the subject's situation. And such assumptions were often treated as if they were explanatory findings.[10]

Strictly speaking, only overt human behavior can be observed. But processes signified by terms such as "motive" and "need" can be inferred, and the use of such terms is justified to the extent that they add to our ability to explain and predict human behavior developmentally.[11] The barrenness of instinct theory in this respect lies in the static nature of this conception; the adding of a number of constants never helps in the solu-

[9] "Informal Social Communication," in Festinger, Back, Schachter, Kelley, and Thibaut, *Theory and Experiment in Social Communication,* p. 3.

[10] See, for example, McDougall, *An Introduction to Social Psychology,* chaps. 1–4. Freud, too, for all his unprecedented thoroughness in the study of human motivation, at times fell back on "instinct" as an explanatory device. The most questionable example is perhaps his "death instinct," which, he assumed, "can never be absent in any vital process" and "whose aim it [is] to abolish life once more and to re-establish the inorganic state of things." *New Introductory Lectures,* pp. 146–47, and *Beyond the Pleasure Principle,* especially pp. 47–49.

[11] These two terms in this book are used as synonyms. Most writers in psychology use either the one or the other, thus indicating indirectly that they may be considered roughly equivalent. "Drive" is a third term that may be considered synonymous with "need" and "motive."

tion of equations. Maybe there are instincts, in some sense; I do not wish to deny such a possibility, but to avoid using the concept "instinct" for purposes of dynamic theorizing. The crucial requirement of the theoretical assumptions to be chosen, then, is that they provide a useful tentative framework as anchorage for testable hypotheses. The latter, to the extent that they can be confirmed in research, should be the building blocks of a plausible, integrated system of theoretical explanation and prediction.

There is no doubt, it seems to me, that the psychoanalytic approach offers the most promising over-all scheme for theorizing about the growth of human freedom, from the complete dependency and spontaneity of the infant up to the modest autonomy the fortunate adult may achieve and the confined spontaneity he may retain. I have no need for all of Freud's assumptions, nor for all the theory of any one of his successors or critics. But it will be seen throughout this chapter that I am building freely on his foundations. At the risk of stating the obvious or trivial, let me be explicit on three basic assumptions that we owe principally to Freud and two of his successors.

First of all, there is the assumption of the vital importance of infancy and childhood experience in the formation of the adult personality.[12] This is not to say that the adult is completely predestined by the child. As Freud acknowledged, and as many of the neo-Freudians have stressed, experiences later on in life, if sufficiently strategic and significant, may repair early damage or tear to pieces early harmony.

Secondly, there is the assumption, stressed especially by Erich Fromm, that certain kinds of childhood experience can create a disposition toward "authoritarianism" in the adult. In my conceptual scheme this is one principal type of deficiency in psychological freedom.[13] Fromm advanced this thesis for the first time in his contribution to Max Horkheimer's *Autorität und Familie* in 1936, and it has proved most useful for later research.[14]

Thirdly, there is the assumption, most consistently stressed by Harry Stack Sullivan, to the effect that personality growth and mental health are functions of the growth and health of man's interpersonal relationships. "The field of psychiatry is the field of interpersonal relations, under any and all circumstances in which these relations exist. . . . A *personality* can never be isolated from the complex of interpersonal relations in which the person lives and has its being."[15] Whereas Freud stresses the importance of the infant's and child's relations with his parents, one of Sullivan's achievements is to bring the crucial role of all important social relationships into focus, and to offer the following definition of personality: "Personality is the relatively enduring pattern of recurrent interpersonal situations which characterize a human life."[16]

[12] Some data giving inferential evidence in support of this assumption will be discussed later on in this chapter. See below, pp. 217–28.

[13] Cf. below, pp. 189–94, especially p. 192.

[14] See Fromm, "Sozialpsychologischer Teil" ("Theoretische Entwürfe über Autorität und Familie") in Max Horkheimer (ed.), *Studien über Autorität und Familie*, pp. 77–135. Fromm uses here the term "Der autoritär-masochistische Charakter."

[15] *Conceptions of Modern Psychiatry*, p. 10.

[16] *The Interpersonal Theory of Psychiatry*, pp. 110–11.

This is in some respects an improvement on Gordon W. Allport's classic definition of personality as "the dynamic organization within the individual of those psycho-physical systems that determine his unique adjustments to his environments."[17] For one thing, Sullivan omits a number of unnecessary assumptions ("psycho-physical systems," "determine," "unique"). Also, instead of referring to "adjustments," a word with one-way connotations, Sullivan speaks of "interpersonal situations," which suggests a constant give-and-take, and he moves this aspect to the center of the definition.[18]

While it appears useless to postulate innate instincts, the concepts of "need" and "motive" are dynamic and may be given explanatory and predictive functions in various models for understanding human behavior. Take the homeostasis model, for example, in which an over-all tendency toward equilibrium is postulated: "Instabilities in the psychological field produce 'tensions' whose effects on perception, cognition, and action are such as to tend to change the field in the direction of a more stable structure."[19] Note that this proposition makes no reference to processes underlying the tensions. It is in harmony with the principle referred to at the beginning of this section: never make unnecessary assumptions. Tensions are phenomena that can be observed and perhaps measured. Underlying needs or motives can only be inferred, and every inference requires a new assumption.

For my purposes it seems most convenient, and probably necessary, to use the concept of "need" or "motive," and to refer to "need-satisfaction" or "motive-satisfaction" as processes underlying "tension-reduction." With these additional elements, I achieve a better model for differentiating between various tensions that between them may have vastly different functions in individual personality development. The significance and effect of a disequilibrium in the organism may depend not only on the degree of tension observed, but also on the nature of the underlying need, which may be inferred. I want to work with a model that is differentiated enough to take account of this complication in the human organism.

THE INFANT'S QUEST FOR SECURITY AND POWER

For some years it has been unfashionable to try to make exhaustive lists of human needs.[20] I do not intend to go against this trend, which is probably a healthy one. I shall concentrate on a few assumed needs and processes that I believe are crucial in the development or maintenance of psychological freedom.

In the previous chapter I attempted a preliminary analysis of psychological aspects of both "freedom" and "security." My concept of psychological freedom was compared to my concept of basic subjective security, and I concluded that the two concepts are widely overlapping. I took the

---

[17] *Personality: A Psychological Interpretation*, p. 48.

[18] There are a vast number of definitions of personality in the literature. Allport alone lists forty-nine alternate approaches before settling for his own definition as the fiftieth.

[19] Krech and Crutchfield, *Social Psychology*, p. 40.

[20] The last major attempt is found in Murray, *Explorations in Personality*, chap. 2.

position that anxiety is not necessarily an evil, unless there is enough of it to bring about repression and thus delimit psychological freedom. While a mild sense of anxiety can stimulate the organism to constructive behavior, a state of more severe anxiety can lead the individual to flight from a realistic self-perception and to a severe loss in psychological freedom: he is led to suppress all awareness of some of his important impulses and motives.[21] In the next section I shall consider the functions of anxiety more fully. First of all, however, something must be said about the setting of the stage on which anxiety at first will intrude: I shall make a sketch of the infant's personality, with special reference to his quest for security.

In infancy there are apparently no conflicts between motives and overt behavior. The infant may not "know" what he wants, but he is completely frank about his needs and wishes. He does not "know" how to cover himself up and pursue indirect strategies, but neither has he yet learned to be ashamed of any of his needs.[22] The newborn infant behaves with complete spontaneity; his psychological freedom is maximal.[23] At the same time, his social freedom is minimal, for he is wholly exposed to coercion. As his mind develops, his potential freedom, too, is minimal at first; the child can be manipulated more easily, on the average, than the adult.[24]

The infant's high degree of psychological freedom is not accompanied by a complete freedom from anxiety, however. Some writers, indeed, have assumed that the very process of birth is a traumatic experience that is bound to leave behind heavy residues of anxiety. Otto Rank is the most pronounced exponent of this view. To him, the shock of the birth is the prototype of stress that lends a traumatic character also to life's later separation experiences.[25]

Sigmund Freud takes issue with Rank, to whom he attributes the claim of having solved the fundamental problem of neurosis.[26] Freud insists that the danger attending birth can have no psychic content, since "we cannot imagine as existing in the foetus anything which in the least approaches any sort of knowledge of the possibility of death as an outcome."[27] This is hardly a convincing argument, since apprehensions later in life do not necessarily correspond to perceptions of specific dangers. And Freud goes on to grant that the foetus may be aware of "a gross disturbance in the economy of its narcissistic libido."

A middle road between Rank and Freud has been taken by Phyllis Greenacre. She suggests that a predisposition to anxiety may be the outcome of the birth experience, which should also be seen in the context of prenatal and immediate postnatal experience. She operates with a concept of "preanxiety," and she assumes that preanxiety operates at the reflex level

---

[21] See above, pp. 107–9. See also below, especially pp. 164–69 and 183–85.

[22] "Small children are notoriously a-moral. They have no internal inhibitions against their pleasure-seeking impulses." Freud, *New Introductory Lectures*. p. 89.

[23] It was found in Chapter 3 that Fromm's concept of spontaneity may be considered a less precise version of my concept of psychological freedom. See above, pp. 84–86.

[24] This is reflected in everyday language: people who are easily manipulated are frequently called "suckers."

[25] See *The Trauma of Birth*, and also *Will Therapy and Truth and Reality*, pp. 72–73.

[26] *The Problem of Anxiety*, p. 97.

[27] *Ibid.*, p. 73.

and lacks psychic content. "Variations in the birth process may similarly increase the (organic) anxiety response and heighten the anxiety potential, causing a more severe reaction to later (psychological) dangers."[28]

A similar view of infantile anxiety seems implied in Harry Stack Sullivan's conceptual scheme. His concept of *"prehension,"* as he relates it to *"perception,"* may furnish a parallel example to illustrate Greenacre's *"preanxiety"* as a concept related to *"anxiety"*: "To prehend is to have potential information or misinformation about something; to perceive is to have information or misinformation in or readily accessible to awareness."[29] Note that the word "potential" here is used in a rather special sense, referring to something that is registered or incorporated at some level but that is not at all or not readily accessible to awareness. This concept becomes clearer by reference to Sullivan's conception of three modes of experience, the *prototaxic,* the *parataxic,* and the *syntaxic.* His associate Patrick Mullahy interprets this scheme as follows:

Prototaxic symbolization lacks formal distinctions. . . . The infant vaguely feels or "prehends" earlier and later states [of satisfaction-dissatisfaction, or security-insecurity] without realizing any serial connection. Furthermore, prototaxic symbolization occurs without reference to an ego, to "I" or "me," because the infant has no, or only a rudimentary, self. . . .

Parataxic symbolization succeeds the first, the prototaxic. As the infant develops, he learns to make some distinction between himself and the rest of the world. . . . With the development of the parataxic mode of symbol activity, the original undifferentiated wholeness, oneness, of experience is broken. But the "parts," the diverse aspects, the various kinds of experience are not related or connected in any logical fashion. . . . Inferences cannot be made. Experience is undergone as momentary, unconnected organismic states. . . . Parataxic symbols are evoked mainly through visual and auditory channels. . . . The autistic is a verbal manifestation of the parataxic. . . . Consensual validation is lacking. . . . Consensually validated symbols carry a meaning which has been acquired from group activities, interpersonal activities, social experience. [This latter type of symbol activity is the syntaxic mode of experience.] It involves an appeal to principles which are accepted as true by the hearer.[30]

Only the two latter modes of experience—parataxic and syntaxic—can be observed, and one important observation is that adults as well as children mix up their syntaxic symbol activity with many parataxic elements. In plainer English, we all tend to resort to autistic or magical thought processes at times, perhaps particularly when other people do not collaborate with us in the way we would like them to. The prototaxic mode of experience, on the other hand, can only be inferred, and perhaps roughly in the sense that Greenacre infers preanxiety. Sullivan grants that he has

[28] "The Predisposition to Anxiety," *Psychoanalytical Quarterly,* X (1941), 66–94, 610–38, especially pp. 86–87, 93–94. See also Blum, *Psychoanalytic Theories of Personality,* pp. 1–2, 5–6. For a fuller evaluation of research on the birth trauma theory, see Wile and Davis, "The Relation of Birth to Behavior," in Kluckhohn and Murray (eds.), *Personality in Nature, Society, and Culture,* pp. 297–314.

[29] *Conceptions of Modern Psychiatry,* pp. 78–79, note 29.

[30] Mullahy, "A Theory of Interpersonal Relations and the Evolution of Personality," in Sullivan, *Conceptions of Modern Psychiatry,* pp. 252–56 and footnote. Cf. Sullivan, *Interpersonal Theory,* pp. 28–29.

no "higher source of information" about what an infant of six months experiences.[31] He, and all of us, have to make our inferences by projections from what we know about later phases of child development and construct plausible conceptual tools for such projections. In this endeavor a good intuition is certainly required no less than a good hand with logic.

I know of no writer who has approached this subject of infantile anxiety with more perceptivity than Harry Stack Sullivan. And perhaps it is a good idea to avoid the term "preanxiety," as he does, since "anxiety" itself, also in adult life, can manifest itself prototaxically—or, in other words, can fail to manifest itself in any but the vaguest and most all-pervasive, indefinable fashion.

I cannot tell you what anxiety feels like to an infant but I can make an inference which I believe has very high probability of accuracy—that there is no difference between anxiety and fear so far as the vague mental state of the infant is concerned.[32] . . . I have reason to suppose, then, that a fearlike state can be induced in an infant under two circumstances: one is by rather violent disturbance of his zones of contact with circumambient reality; and the other is by certain types of emotional disturbance within the mothering one. From the latter grows the whole exceedingly important structure of anxiety, and performances that can be understood only by reference to the conception of anxiety.[33]

The growth of this "exceedingly important structure" will be considered in the next subsection. In this context, let us consider what it is that the infant needs and postpone the further discussion of what happens when he does not get it. I have observed that the infant is at first maximally free in the psychological sense of spontaneity (approximately), and yet we have found that anxiety begins early in life. What is it that the child is after and "worries" about? Once again Harry Stack Sullivan seems to offer the best approach, and what he says may be applied to infancy and adulthood equally:

The most general basis on which interpersonal phenomena, interpersonal acts, may be classified is one which separates the sought and stakes into the group which we call satisfactions and those which we call security or the maintenance of security. Satisfactions in this specialized sense are all those end stakes which are rather closely connected with the bodily organization of man. . . . On the other hand, the pursuit of security pertains rather more closely to man's cultural equipment than to his bodily organization.[34]

With the former group of the infant's needs—satisfactions—I shall not be concerned; they may for my purposes be considered biologically given. And I shall feel free to make a more conventional use of the word "satisfaction" than Sullivan does; I shall speak of "need-satisfaction" and, synonymously, "motive-satisfaction." What is really important in Sullivan's approach, for present purposes, is his insistence that the quest for security

[31] *Interpersonal Theory*, p. 118.

[32] The fact that Sullivan makes his own original distinction between these two concepts makes no difference in this context. See below, pp. 165 and 185–86.

[33] *Interpersonal Theory*, pp. 8–9.

[34] *Conceptions of Modern Psychiatry*, pp. 12–13.

always must be seen in its interpersonal setting and his use of the distinction between bodily satisfactions and interpersonal security as the base line
for distinguishing between fear and anxiety.

In my first reference to "security" in this book, the term was preliminarily defined as follows: " 'Security' refers to the actual or perceived
probability of the extension over time of the enjoyment of other values."[35]
Subjectively, the perceived probability is what matters; how much it matters
depends on the importance of the substantive values involved. For the
infant the possibility of life itself hinges on the services of at least one other
person, whom Sullivan conveniently calls "the mothering one." So utterly
dependent is the infant that only the perceived certainty of having his
wants provided for can make him feel secure. And the only means to
convey this sense of certainty is by way of the emotional guarantees of
motherly love, which give rise to "empathy" between mother and child.[36]

My theorem is this: *The observed activity of the infant arising from the tension
of needs induces tension in the mothering one which tension is experienced as
tenderness and as an impulsion to activities toward the relief of the infant's needs.*
. . . The manifest activity by the mothering one toward the relief of the infant's
needs will presently be experienced by the infant as the undergoing of tender behavior; and these needs, the relaxation of which requires cooperation of another,
thereon take on the character of a general *need for tenderness.*[37]

Now, there are good reasons for believing that the functions of love
and tenderness for the infant go beyond the production of a sense of certainty that his bodily needs will be attended to also in the future. Among
grown-ups, love and affection certainly are values independent of or sur-
passing the sexual or nutritional satisfactions they may assure. In the beginning of infancy, however, purely social needs may or may not exist
in addition to the need for interpersonally assured certainty of future need-
satisfactions. The value of Sullivan's conception of tenderness is that it
makes the infant's quest for security a sufficient explanation of the function of motherly love.

Also, this approach provides a new angle in assessing the importance
of *power* for the infant. Power is essentially an individual's degree of
control over his security.[38] Subjectively, the perceived control, or the sense
of control, is what matters. "To gain satisfactions and, particularly, security,
is to have power in interpersonal relations. So far as one cannot do so, that
is to be power-less, helpless," says Mullahy.[39] Motherly love gives to the
infant a feeling of power, in a vague or prototaxic way, as we may infer.
Crying causes activity, smiling meets response. "For Sullivan, power refers

[35] See above, p. 19.

[36] "*Empathy* is the term that we use to refer to the peculiar emotional linkage that subtends
the relationship of the infant with other significant people—the mother or the nurse. Long
before there are signs of any understanding of emotional expression, there is evidence of this
emotional contagion, or communion." Sullivan, *Modern Psychiatry,* p. 17.

[37] Sullivan, *Interpersonal Theory,* pp. 39–40.

[38] See above, pp. 19–20. See also below, pp. 248–60.

[39] In Sullivan, *Conceptions of Modern Psychiatry,* p. 244. Also: "In fact, power refers
to any activity where there is accomplishment, satisfaction of needs, mutual attainment of goals
not distorted by unfortunate—that is, thwarting—experience." *Ibid.,* p. 243.

to the expansive biological striving of the infant and states characterized by the feeling of ability, applying, in a very wide sense, to all kinds of human activity."[40] Again, Sullivan's approach has the double merit of making the infant's need for power perfectly explicable in terms of a need for certainty of future biological need-satisfactions and at the same time leaving open the possibility of a much more complex pattern of a fuller explanation.

The extreme state of dependence of the infant gives a maximal urgency to his need for interpersonal security and to his need for power when he begins to become aware of its use. A number of studies have demonstrated empirically the tendency of motherless children to develop more slowly than other children.[41] And there are some reasons for believing that severe frustrations of infantile security needs are likely to show up as character deficiencies in the child and also in the adult individual, deficiencies that reduce the prospects for psychological freedom. A consideration of such evidence must wait until the section "Authoritarianism and Psychological Freedom" in this chapter. At this point it must suffice to quote the following two theory formulations, the first one an interpretation of Sullivan's position by Mullahy and the second one a statement by Harold Lasswell:

A "power drive," in the narrow sense, results from the thwarting of the expansive biological striving [which Sullivan refers to as the "power motive"], and the feeling of the lack of ability. In other words, a "power drive" is learned, resulting from the early frustration of the need to be, and to feel, capable, to have ability, to have power. A "power drive" develops as a compensation when there is a deep, gnawing, inner sense of powerlessness, because of early frustration of the expanding, developing latent potentialities of the organism. . . . So important and fundamental is the power motive that the degree to which it is satisfied and fulfilled mainly determines the growth and characteristics of personality.[42]

Our key hypothesis about the power seeker is that he pursues power as a means of compensation against deprivation. *Power is expected to overcome low estimates of the self.*[43]

Let me now turn to the general problem of anxiety and attempt a brief general statement of a functional theory of anxiety. This is in my judgment one of the most crucial and also most difficult problems in personality theory. A clarification of this problem must be attempted before I return to my discussion of personality development, this time at the somewhat later stage where the development of a self begins.

A FUNCTIONAL THEORY OF ANXIETY

According to Sullivan, we have no way of knowing just when the process of anxiety first appears in the infant. Other writers tend to believe

---

[40] *Ibid.*, p. 242.

[41] Many studies are referred to in Bowlby, *Maternal Care and Mental Health,* especially pp. 15–45.

[42] Mullahy, in Sullivan, *Conceptions of Modern Psychiatry,* pp. 242–43.

[43] Lasswell, *Power and Personality,* p. 39. This statement does not apply to the infant's situation, although it is assumed that the low estimates of the self normally derive from infancy and childhood experience. In Chapter 5, I shall come back to these hypotheses, and try to appraise their merit. Cf. below, pp. 297–301.

that anxiety begins at birth, if not earlier. "That the infant, even the new-born infant, undergoes anxiety, is beyond doubt. His expressive movements indicate this, and most observers agree upon this fact," says Kurt Goldstein.[44] Whether one wishes to doubt this or not, the only prudent course is to concede that anxiety may begin as early in life as life itself outside the womb and conceivably even earlier.

The same cannot be true about fear, however, as this term has been defined here. It is quite clear that the newborn infant is incapable of responding to a "realistically perceived, specific danger." "At birth the infant's perceptive and discriminatory capacities are not sufficiently developed to permit him adequately to identify and localize danger. . . . Some neurological maturation is presupposed before the infant can respond to threatening stimuli with undifferentiated emotion (anxiety), and greater maturation is necessary before the infant can differentiate between various stimuli, objectivate the danger, and respond to it as fear."[45] The state of fear requires a more differentiated organism than does a state of anxiety. The problem is how to explain the continuation of anxiety responses in human beings once they have developed perceptual and cognitive capacities that might be believed sufficient for a fairly realistic appraisal of danger situations.

From a common sense point of view, it would seem that the response of fear is a good deal more functional for adjustment and survival than is anxiety. Freud and many other writers have stressed the adaptive value of fear; in the previous chapter I concluded that the fear reaction is not an undesirable state of insecurity, assuming that an objective danger exists.[46] A basic assumption of this book is that there must be *some* constructive functions in all enduring behavior patterns. My initial belief, therefore, is that the phenomenon of anxiety may be explicable in functional terms. And I am prepared if necessary to enter a complex level of analysis to discover such constructive functions, rather than be satisfied with a diagnosis of mere maladaptive pathology.

Perhaps the best clues are to be found in Harry Stack Sullivan's interpersonal approach to psychiatric problems. While I prefer not to tie the concept of anxiety by definition to the interpersonal aspects of life, as he does, it seems a fruitful empirical approach to look for an explanation of the phenomenon in an interpersonal setting. Sullivan groups all human needs or "sought end states" under two headings: satisfactions and security. The former are related to biological drives, and their actual or potential frustration causes pain or fear. The need for security, on the other hand, is a social need, and its frustration occasions anxiety.

Even if I stick to my simple definition of anxiety as an unrealistic sense of danger, there is much to be said for believing that it is normally a socially induced phenomenon. A reservation should be made for the infant, though,

[44] *The Organism*, p. 277.

[45] May, *The Meaning of Anxiety*, p. 201. There are three types of response to danger, according to May: "(1) The *startle pattern*, a pre-emotional, innate reflexive reaction; (2) *anxiety*, the undifferentiated emotional response; (3) *fear*, a differentiated emotional reaction."

[46] See above, p. 103. Freud, of course, speaks of "objective anxiety" rather than of "fear." See above, p. 69.

who does not yet have the nerve equipment and experience to concretize threats. Once an individual has gained this ability, however, it appears plausible to hypothesize that his failure to use it must be either a constructive adaptation to difficulties in his present social situation or a maladaptation due to difficulties experienced in earlier social situations.

The physical universe is on the whole a fairly reliable or predictable setting in which to live. You can tell the difference between edible and nonedible objects, on the whole. You thatch a roof, and the rain does not come through. The fertility of the fields depends of course on the weather, and aboriginal peoples may resort to magic to supplement their daily food-growing labor. In modern societies the important uncertainties do not relate to physical and biological factors as much as to social factors. There are, of course, the uncertainties of disease and death. But even these may be moderately predictable; or, to be more precise, it is fairly predictable just what one can do to minimize these unavoidable types of danger.

In relation to many facets of our social surroundings, no approximately comparable degree of predictability exists. It is true that the behavioral sciences tend to increase our knowledge about, and also some people's control over, other people's behavior, but this is confined mainly to external or at least nonprivate aspects of behavior and to statistical averages. It is possible to predict the probable voting behavior of many socioeconomic groups without making a sample survey. It is much harder to predict whether Mr. Jones is going to remain a true and loyal friend of Mr. Smith all his life, come what may.

The young child has learned to seek satisfaction of all his needs by social means; and has learned to blame a person instead of circumstances when things go wrong. "The child personifies the surrounding world but pays the price for his imagination with his anxieties. The baby does not believe in chance nor has it any knowledge of physics; it is convinced that the table which hurts it when it bumps itself against it is activated by malice as much as are the shoes that pinch it because they are too narrow."[47]

It is to be expected that later deprivation fears in childhood as well as in adulthood maintain overtones of association with this basic orientation from infancy: The only real and lasting protection from danger is in tenderness and love; the only real source of deprivation is in the malice or hostility of significant other persons. Thus, the constant receipt of tenderness from significant other people becomes the most crucial of all concerns, and the pivot of everyday experience. Following frustrations, the need for tenderness is multiplied, even if objectively the other person had not caused them.

An even more significant aspect of this association with the infancy situation is this: In typical cases, deprivations of all kinds are blamed on the person whose tenderness failed to give sufficient protection, and hostility is released against the love object. Either the hostility is expressed, and may, except in the good mother-child relationship, objectively reduce the other person's ability to respond with the tenderness that is now needed

---

[47] Schmideberg, "Anxiety States," *Psychoanalytic Review*, XXVII (1940), 442.

even more than before; or else the hostility is repressed, resulting in a basic ambivalence that keeps a gnawing sense of insecurity in this important social relationship. This ambivalence in turn increases the person's susceptibilities to further frustration and further repression, and thus a vicious circle of increasing anxiety ensues.[48]

Now, a vicious circle is by definition not a constructive process. I have yet to explain what good the development of anxiety can do to human beings. While the infant's anxiety is an adaptive mechanism, in drawing the mother's attention to his needs, it remains obscure what contribution to survival or well-being anxiety makes in the child or grown-up, after the development of fear reactions. For fear is the "rational" or utilitarian reaction, as I have defined it.

Two writers, it seems to me, have contributed more substantially than anyone else to a general functional explanation of anxiety.[49] One is Sören Kierkegaard, and the other is Harry Stack Sullivan. Kierkegaard, in my opinion, has most persuasively connected anxiety with the growth of the mature mind; Sullivan has brought out the significance and the more concrete modes of this connection in everyday life.

"One may liken anxiety to dizziness," says Kierkegaard: "He whose eye chances to look down into the yawning abyss becomes dizzy. But the reason for it is just as much his eyes as it is the precipice. For suppose he had not looked down. . . . Thus anxiety is the dizziness of freedom which occurs when the spirit would posit the synthesis, and freedom then gazes down into its own possibility, grasping at finiteness to sustain itself."[50] I believe that Kierkegaard's intention with the last sentence is to describe the terror of uncertainties facing the individual who ceases to take himself for granted and to take his course of life for granted. As he says in another context, "To exist as an individual is the most terrible thing of all";[51] in other words, the growth of the independent mind is inextricably interrelated with anxiety. This is an anticipation of Otto Rank's view of the process of individuation as a succession of intellectual birth traumas marked by separation anxieties, and perhaps also of Erich Fromm's thesis that the lack of belongingness of our age of individualism creates strains that make many men search for an "escape from freedom."

Perhaps the following passage from Kierkegaard renders the most important single aspect of his contribution to a functional theory of anxiety: "He who is educated by possibility remains with anxiety, does not allow himself to be deceived by its countless counterfeits, he recalls the past pre-

---

[48] A not-quite-so-vicious circle may, of course, ensue also from the open expression of hostility, with consequent reduction in tenderness and again more hostility. Things that are not repressed may be talked about, however, and the conflict may be solved; also, such conflicts do not push down as deeply in the subconscious.

[49] Other writers, especially Freud, have contributed more, of course, toward the understanding of anxiety neuroses and their treatment. "Functional" in the rest of this chapter always means "constructively functional" as opposed to "dysfunctional." For a discussion of the term, including alternate usages, see below, pp. 240–48.

[50] *The Concept of Dread*, p. 55. "Anxiety" is substituted for "dread" in the quotations from Kierkegaard. Cf. above, p. 108, note 132.

[51] "Fear and Trembling," in *Fear and Trembling and The Sickness Unto Death* (Anchor), p. 85.

cisely; then at last the attacks of anxiety, though they are fearful, are not such that he flees from them. For him anxiety becomes a serviceable spirit which against its will leads him whither he would go."[52]

What does he mean by being "educated by possibility"? "Possibility means *I can*," and he states that "anxiety is the reality of freedom as the possibility anterior to possibility."[53] In other words, the price for realizing that *I* can as compared to *we* can, or the price for accepting the necessity and potency of individual choice, is the torment of anxiety. But the mind that is "educated by possibility" accepts the anxiety instead of trying to flee from it; as Freud and his followers have pointed out much later, such an individual does not deceive himself by counterfeiting a spotless self-image but "recalls the past precisely." Most important of all, "anxiety becomes a serviceable spirit which against its will leads him whither he would go." This is the most general answer to my problem of function: anxiety provides an enduring incentive for human beings to develop their resources and achieve the mental stature they are potentially capable of achieving.

Anxiety teaches one subject more than others—man's attentiveness to his social relationships. But it is a stern teacher. All too frequently the anxiety becomes unbearable and results in neurosis, by way of mechanisms that delimit both self-attentiveness and attentiveness to others. Sometimes the neurosis stiffens into a psychosis, in which the barriers become almost insurmountable. Anxiety that can be accepted, on the other hand, stimulates the growth of a healthy personality; in fact, it may increase mental health, much as exercise of the body may increase physical health. "One achieves mental health to the extent that one becomes aware of one's interpersonal relations," says Sullivan.[54] And the road toward perfection of this awareness leads through countless experiences of anxiety, from infancy to old age.

Just how does anxiety teach? Severe anxiety, says Sullivan, does not teach at all. "The effect of severe anxiety reminds one in some ways of a blow on the head, in that it simply wipes out what is immediately proximal to its occurrence."[55] In small doses, however, anxiety is the salt of social life:

Less severe anxiety does permit gradual realization of the situation in which it occurs, and there is unquestionably, even from very early in life, some learning of an inhibitory nature; that is, the transfer of attributes of "my body" to the "not-me" aspects of the universe. But regardless of all these refinements, the first greatly educative influence in living is doubtless anxiety, unqualified. . . . Vastly more important, in fact perhaps astoundingly important in its relation to our coming to be human beings acceptable to the particular society which we inhabit, is the next process of learning, which is learning on the basis of the *anxiety gradient*—that is, learning to discriminate increasing from diminishing anxiety. . . . The all-or-nothing character of anxiety and euphoria has disappeared very early in life—in fact, I doubt that it ever existed—and an immense

[52] *The Concept of Dread*, p. 142.

[53] *Ibid.*, pp. 44, 38.

[54] *Modern Psychiatry*, p. 207.

[55] *Interpersonal Theory*, p. 152.

amount of what is human behavior in any society is learned simply on the basis of this gradient from anxiety to euphoria.[56]

In the beginning, the learning process is exclusively related to the mothering one; perhaps both the cry and the smile are used "purposively" to reduce anxiety and increase euphoria long before the dawn of the infant's consciousness of his separate individuality. Gradually, other social relationships also begin to assume importance for the child. His incentive to leave the autistic stage and seek "consensual validation" both in the use of language and in other behavior must again be sought in the anxiety gradient. This learning process does not relate to infantile needs only. As the child begins to become aware of his own individuality, he is developing his own *self,* and the needs of this self assign new functions to anxiety as an educator. Let me now turn to a consideration of the growth of the self.

THE SELF AND THE EGO

The self is a crucial conception in a theory of psychological freedom. My first and very rough definition of "freedom" has equated this concept with "self-expression."[57] Idealist philosophers and neo-Freudian psychologists alike have stressed the futility of formal freedom (or, in my language, social freedom) if people pay for it with loss of purpose or anxiety neurosis. Unless people have the psychological capacity for self-expression, a free society can become a menace that they will want to escape.

In the following discussion of the growth of the self I shall leave aside all the more specific problems of the stages in the child's development. For my purposes it does not matter, for example, just when in his young life the infant begins to differentiate between "me" and "not-me." Theorizing about child development will be resorted to only to seek explanation for deficiencies in the adult self.[58] The adult self is a part or aspect of the adult personality. A human life at any one time is a biological as well as a social entity; these two entities are clearly interdependent, however. Even if my concern is with social man rather than biological man, I shall find it impossible to analyze social behavior without continual reference to biological needs and the processes they give rise to within each personality.

What kind of self is characteristic of a personality enjoying psychological freedom, in my sense? It will be seen at once that the conceptual problem of delimiting the self must be dealt with before we can estimate what kinds of selves are either conducive to, or symptoms of, a high ability to express basic motives in overt behavior. It will also be found, in Chapter 6, that the conceptual delineation of the self is a prerequisite for a theory of potential freedom, or individual autonomy in relation to one's surrounding institutions.[59] It is a difficult but an urgent task, if we want to

---

[56] *Ibid.,* p. 153. Sullivan defines "euphoria" as "a state of utter well-being," characterized by the complete absence of anxiety and other tensions. *Ibid.,* p. 34.

[57] See above, p. 15.

[58] Note that the word "adult" in this study is used, unless otherwise indicated, in a chronological sense, designating a biological and not necessarily a psychological coming of age.

[59] See below, "Perceptions of the Self and Potential Freedom," pp. 357–59.

arrive at an empirical theory of psychological freedom, to find ways to delimit the "self" in specific terms. We also need a dynamic understanding of the role of the self in the motivational process.

The self is the individual's awareness of acceptable aspects of his personality; it is part of the individual's consciousness. Let me choose this preliminary definition, which will be revised in the next section:[60] *The self is the image of one's own qualities, or evaluated characteristics.*

But man's total personality can be compared to an iceberg, in the sense that only a small part of it is visible, even to himself. In other respects it may be compared to a battleground, if we follow Freud's dramatic descriptions of the everlasting and ruthless contest between the id, the superego, and the ego. There is something to be said for the criticism that Freud tended to reify these concepts, in discussing them as if they referred to real layers in the unconscious.[61] "It appears more convenient to distinguish different functions of the mind than to divide it into air-tight compartments," says Franz Alexander,[62] and I agree, even if the reference to "airtight compartments" is rather exaggerated and certainly does not represent Freud's view.

I shall follow Alexander's conception of the basic functions of the id, superego, ego, and ego ideal. To those, however, who are allergic to these words, and many social scientists feel that they have been thrown around too freely in view of their tenuous anchoring in indirect evidence, the following substitutes may be suggested. For "id," read "impulse"; for "superego," read "conscience"; for "ego ideal," read "the kind of person one would like to be." It is harder to find a substitute for the term "ego," but "ego" is also less objected to than are "id" and "superego." Perhaps the closest one can get, in everyday language, is "the kind of person I really am"—provided, however, that sufficient humility is put into this conception, so that one realizes that our acquaintance with our own personalities is in some respects quite superficial.[63] My fondness for the terms "ego" and "ego ideal" is hardly surprising in view of their brevity. My preference in this context for "id" and "superego" over "impulse" and "conscience" stems from my dependence on psychoanalytically oriented theoretical assumptions, which are easier to keep in mind when key words have fewer distracting connotations from everyday language.

Alexander's functional approach makes it unnecessary either to accept

---

[60] See below, pp. 172–79.

[61] One example among many: "I hope you will by now feel that in postulating the existence of a super-ego I have been describing a genuine structural entity, and have not been merely personifying an abstraction, such as conscience." In another context he does warn against imagining "sharp dividing lines (between ego, superego, and id) such are artificially drawn in the field of political geography." But his alternative analogy is "areas of color shading off into one another that are to be found in modern pictures." *New Introductory Lectures*, pp. 92, 110.

[62] *Fundamentals of Psychoanalysis*, p. 83.

[63] Some authors equate the ego with the self, the latter term being broadened to include subconscious processes. For example, see Bronfenbrenner, "Toward an Integrated Theory of Personality," in Blake and Ramsey (eds.), *Perception*, p. 253.

or to challenge Freud's view that the ego is a part of the id.[64] I am no longer interested in what the ego is, only in what it does. And here I shall be brief and systematic, and shall not be concerned with the distribution of credits between Freud himself and his successors.

The id may be considered a shorthand expression for the demands and wishes of the organism in their original, unorganized stage. It is true that Alexander questions whether, even at birth, one can speak of a completely unorganized mass of instinctual urges.[65] Yet, when we are speaking of functions, it is easy to abstract and assign to the term "id" this process of a constant eruption of spontaneous, not-yet-socialized wishes.

The superego, on the other hand, represents socialization, including social discipline. Each individual is a social being, and the infant perhaps particularly so, since he could least of all survive in social isolation. He needs not only the services of other persons, but also their tender attention, almost from the very beginning. In turn, the infant very early responds to other people. The first smile is soon seen on the face of the baby that is well cared for. From earliest childhood on, the individual is taught to check some of his id-impulses, and others are held permissible or are encouraged. This channeling function is not the whole function of the superego, however. The superego is a source of impulses of its own, whose origin is to be sought not in the biological needs of the organism but in the person's social responsiveness, and later in his need for social acceptance and self-esteem. The point to emphasize is that the needs or motives attributable to the superego are just as *basic* in the human personality, even in that of the child, as are the id-occasioned needs or motives. Man's social needs are not derived from his individual needs; both are equally deeply embedded in him.[66]

The ego function is analogous to that of the driver in an automobile or, in Freud's words, the rider on a horse. "The horse provides the locomotive energy, and the rider has the prerogative of determining the goal and of guiding the movement of his powerful mount toward it."[67] The analogy to the superego is brought in if we picture our horseman on a crowded street; and the drama of the conflict is portrayed if we assume that the horse after a long stay in the stable is aching to run at a high speed.

---

[64] *New Introductory Lectures*, p. 107. See also Freud, *The Ego and the Id*, pp. 29 and 19–33.

[65] "The notion of the id, as originally defined, is problematical. Strictly speaking, a completely unorganized, inherited mass of instinctual urges is not found even at birth. The organism has even then a considerable amount of reflex coordination." *Fundamentals of Psychoanalysis*, p. 83.

[66] In Alexander's words, as the conscience becomes more and more "intimately absorbed in the personality," it becomes "second nature." "Thus it becomes possible for the claims of conscience to act directly upon the life of the instinct, without having to involve consciousness in this inhibitory function." *The Psychoanalysis of the Total Personality*, p. 18. For an understanding of my concept of psychological freedom, it is important to keep in mind this basic quality of superego needs. See above, pp. 49 and 88, and below, p. 228.

I believe Freud is mistaken when he says, "It has long been our contention that 'dread of society (soziale Angst)' is the essence of what is called conscience." *Group Psychology and the Analysis of the Ego*, p. 10. See also *The Future of an Illusion*, pp. 9, 19.

[67] Freud, *New Introductory Lectures*, p. 108.

The ego, then, is the mediator between organism and environment; it has or is the decision-making function. It organizes motives and behavior. For the ego, it may be said that the individual organism, too, is part of the environment, and that the task is to decide on and execute a synthesis between the two kinds of demands, the individual's original wishes and the socially derived motives. Alexander suggests that there are three ego functions: "external and internal perception, integration, and executive action."[68] These correspond to the basic functions of the administrator of a social organization; in Lasswell's and McDougal's terms, these are the intelligence function, the recommending function (approximately), and the applying function.[69] "The ego is that part of the organism which assumes the task of harmoniously gratifying our needs and desires," says Alexander, and he proposes that "a healthy ego can best be compared to a democratic state which recognizes private needs of all kinds, gives them a hearing, and meets the conflicting interests by mediation and compromise."[70]

Two points need stressing before I consider the important concept of the ego properly introduced. The government of the democratic state is not necessarily wise and neither necessarily is the ego, even a healthy ego. Its foresight may be poor, and certainly it is as a rule much inferior to the hindsight of the conscious self. Also, the ego may be "unjust," if we continue the analogy with the democratic state. Some egos tend to favor the demands of the id, others those of the superego, while again others tend to be inconsistent. I still speak of a healthy ego, so long as it is not (a) incapable of solving the conflict, (b) able to solve it only precariously, with a high degree of ambivalence, or (c) completely dominated by the id or the superego. The problem of the ailing or failing ego is the problem of neurosis (or psychosis), to which I shall return.[71]

The second important point is that the ego is to a large extent composed of unconscious and preconscious functions. This is well brought out in a discussion by Solomon Asch of the relationship between the ego "and its conscious representative, the self. . . . The self, being a phenomenal representation, does not include all that belongs to the ego and at times apprehends the ego wrongly. The ego is prior to the self and far wider than it. The self is not the mirror image of the ego; there is between them the same kind of relation as between the physical object and its psychological representation. There can be grave differences between the person as he is, as science would describe him, and as he would view himself."[72]

TYPES OF IDENTIFICATION AND THE ROLE OF SELF-ESTEEM

As a preliminary approximation, the "self" has been defined as the image of one's own qualities, or evaluated characteristics. For reasons of

---

[68] *Fundamentals of Psychoanalysis*, p. 87.

[69] *Law, Science, and Policy.*

[70] *Fundamentals of Psychoanalysis*, p. 194. When speaking of the ego as a "part of the organism," incidentally, Alexander comes close to opening himself to the same kind of criticism to which he has subjected Freud; cf. above, p. 170.

[71] See below, "Mental Health, Maturity, and Psychological Freedom," pp. 179–88.

[72] *Social Psychology*, pp. 276, 278.

linguistic convenience I shall at times speak of "self-image" or "self-aware-ness" as synonymous with "self."

In terms of the internal dynamics of the individual personality, the boundaries of the self are drawn by the process of repression or dissociation. The self is the individual's awareness of acceptable characteristics of his own personality. As we have seen in the last section, many events and insights are so anxiety-provoking that they become barred from conscious-ness. Psychotherapy consists partly in trying to reduce the anxiety evoked by such events and insights and partly in trying to increase the individual's capacity to tolerate or face the anxiety that remains, so as to reduce the amount of repression. One task of the therapist, in other words, is to extend the patient's self: he learns to register and be aware of a higher proportion of his painful or humiliating experiences and the unflattering self-insights they may occasion.

The problem of mental health and neurosis is for the next section. The only important point that must be anticipated here is this: on the intra-individual level, the widest possible extension of the self is to be desired, because it is equivalent to the minimum amounts of repression and neurosis. The self-image of the mentally healthy individual, in other words, is a fairly realistic picture of his own personality, consisting of both praise-worthy and blameworthy features.

The present task is to try to draw the boundaries of the self on the extra-individual level. Sullivan says that "the self may be said to be made up of reflected appraisals."[73] But the appraisals of some people evidently are more crucial than those of many others. Lasswell and McDougal equate the self with "the conscious pattern of significant demands, expectations and identifications."[74] Again, the crucial question is one of determining which demands, expectations, and identifications are significant. In another context the same authors assert that "the identifications are the boundaries of the self system, comprehending the components in terms of which values and expectations are assessed."[75] The question before us, then, is whether it is possible to define "identification" in a way that can make these bound-aries either clear or sharp.

There are, it seems to me, two main lines of approach in trying to carve out a useful identification concept. One alternative is the operational approach, which can be taken only at the price of some degree of be-havioristic superficiality. The other alternative is the dynamic or depth approach, which makes a number of unproved theoretical assumptions necessary. This dilemma is, of course, only one aspect of the general issue between empiricism and the depth approach in psychology.[76]

It should be noted in passing that William James many years ago took a middle road between operationalism and depth psychology in his dis-cussion of the "consciousness of self": *"In its widest possible sense,* how-ever, *a man's Self is the sum total of all that he* CAN *call his,* not only his

[73] *Modern Psychiatry,* p. 22; cf. also p. 265.
[74] *Law, Science and Policy,* working paper, Part II, p. 102.
[75] *Ibid.,* Part IV, p. 6.
[76] See above, pp. 155–57.

body and his psychic powers, but his clothes and his house, his wife and children, his ancestors and friends, his reputation and works, his lands and horses, and yacht and bank-account. All these things give him the same emotions. If they wax and prosper, he feels triumphant; if they dwindle and die away, he feels cast down."[77]

James discriminates between this "wide self" and the narrower "selves" of which the former may be considered composed. Thus, he divides the constituents of the wide self into these components: the material self (body, family, property); the social self; the spiritual self ("psychic faculties"); and the pure ego (the integrative principle). And he continues the process of division—here, for example, of the social self: "Properly speaking, *a man has as many social selves as there are individuals who recognize him* and carry an image of him in their mind. To wound any one of these images is to wound him."[78] There is an apparently direct line from this approach to Sullivan's conception of the self as the outcome of reflected appraisals.

Instead of defining "identification" operationally in terms of vicarious satisfactions in the success of other people, I wish to try a preliminary depth definition in terms of expansion of or abandonment of the self. *A person identifies with someone or something to the extent that he incorporates this object into his own self or incorporates his self into this object.* This is a preliminary and perhaps somewhat cryptic formulation, which will be improved upon as I proceed. The first real difficulty, it would seem, is how to conceptualize this incorporation process. One plausible and helpful distinction has been suggested by Freud: "Identification is a very important kind of relationship with another person, probably the most primitive, and is not to be confused with object-choice. One can express the difference between them in this way: when a boy identifies himself with his father, he wants to *be like* his father; when he makes him the object of his choice, he wants to *have* him, to possess him; in the first case the ego is altered on the model of his father, in the second case that is not necessary."[79]

In the conceptual scheme of James, a man's bank account is as much part of his self as is his wife. It would seem an important improvement, however, to try to distinguish as sharply as we can between property attitudes and identification attitudes, as Freud does. The former type of attitude involves acquisition, while the latter involves giving something or even sacrificing. Acquiring things, or controlling people, requires no restructuring of the ego, as Freud observes. Neither deeply affects the underlying currents of id and superego, on which the self is floating. Identification with other people, on the other hand, means that images of these people's needs and norms are incorporated in the ego ideal or the superego (or at times take over the superego functions), necessitating a new balance to be established by the ego.

Not all identification attitudes are equally important, however, and at

[77] *The Principles of Psychology*, I, 291.
[78] *Ibid.*, pp. 292–305.
[79] *New Introductory Lectures*, pp. 90–91.

some point on a scale of diminishing importance it is convenient to speak of a mere "favorable attitude" instead of "identification." An individual has many "social selves," as James observed, but not all of them should be considered components of the *self,* as I prefer to use the latter term. A man may be a son, a husband, a father, a teacher, a member of a political party, a member of an orchestra, a friend of Mr. B, an acquaintance of Mr. C, and a great admirer of President Eisenhower. In each of these capacities different attitudes give rise to different demands and expectations on the total self. Which of these attitudes should be deemed important enough to be considered identifications? Or, to ask the same question in a different way, which of these roles in an individual's life are constituents of his self and which of them are only to be considered external orientations?

The answer is not purely a question of verbal preferences. It must be psychologically plausible, and it should preferably be in terms that lend themselves to empirically meaningful interpretations (it is too much to hope for empirically concise terms at this point). The closest I have been able to get toward an answer satisfying these two criteria is to conceive of the individual's *self-esteem* as a kind of seismograph for determining the relative importance of the various roles and attachments in his life.

Thus, the self has preliminarily been defined as the image of one's own qualities. This image consists primarily of an appraisal of one's own record and competence in all one's important roles or social relationships. What I am saying now is that each role is important to the extent that the individual's self-esteem is enhanced when he feels he is performing the role well or diminished when he feels he is doing poorly in it. When the self-esteem is affected, the role is either part of the self or the self has gone into the role.[80] Or, in identification terms, A's attitude toward B becomes an identification to the extent that A's self-esteem hinges on his constant readiness to exert himself in favor of B's needs and demands.

"Self-esteem" must not be confused with a simple calculation of how one's self adds up, if all "good" qualities are summed up and all "bad" qualities subtracted.[81] A person's self-esteem is in a psychological sense prior to the self-image; it is a concept referring to the person's fundamental feeling of his own worth. It is the fundament on which the self-image is built. If this fundament is firm, the self is capable of facing many unflattering truths. If the fundament is shaky, the self is likely to compensate by refusing to acknowledge weaknesses or other undesirable qualities.

A person's self-esteem may be considered the cathexis of the self or the love of the self. It is developed, as are other aspects of the self, from "reflected appraisals." But the relative importance of the most intimate relationships is probably much greater in the development of self-esteem than in the formation of the more cognitive aspects of the self or self-image.

---

[80] See below, pp. 176–78, for a discussion of the two alternatives.

[81] For an example of an otherwise interesting study where "high self-esteem" is confused with just this kind of calculation of a "positive self-image," see Perlmutter, "Relations between the Self-Image, the Image of the Foreigner, and the Desire to Live Abroad," *Journal of Psychology,* XXVIII (1954), 131–37. Also see below, pp. 214–17.

The child who is deeply reassured of the love of his parents, the adult who is securely enjoying the devotion of his spouse or of intimate friends—such people are likely to have a high self-esteem, no matter what many other people may think of them.

And conversely, it may be assumed that persons with a high self-esteem to this extent are able to give their full love to other people. Sullivan observes: "As one respects oneself so one can respect others. That is one of the peculiarities of human personality that can always be depended on. If there is a valid and real attitude toward the self, that attitude will manifest as valid and real toward others. It is not as ye judge so shall ye be judged, but as you judge yourself so shall you judge others; strange but true so far as I know, and with no exception."[82] Similarly, as you love and esteem yourself (or yourself in the role of pursuing your ego ideal), so you are able to love and esteem other people.

The concept of self-esteem will be considered further in the section "Authoritarianism and Psychological Freedom" in this chapter. It was introduced here because it helps me make a crucial distinction between two types of identification: the identifications accompanied by high self-esteem and those accompanied by low self-esteem.

The process of identification serves to extend the self only in so far as the individual has a securely positive self-esteem. Only to that extent does the welfare of certain other people genuinely concern the individual, in the sense that his own well-being is felt to depend immediately on theirs. Only a person enjoying the basic security of a high self-esteem has the surplus from which he can draw a real concern for other people, a concern that equals but never overshadows his concern for his own dignity or maintained self-esteem.

The individual low in self-esteem will have a different type of incentive to identify with other people. He is in a sense fleeing from his self, in search of a new and more satisfactory identity. Let us take Eric Hoffer's "true believer" as our prototype. He is constantly prepared to sacrifice himself for some cause, because his self apart from that cause is worthless. Only a "self-extinguishing" identification with a movement gives him a sense of purpose and personal worth.

The point that belongs in this context is by now clear: *depending primarily on the degree of self-esteem, the process of identification may either enlarge or diminish the individual self.*

By now I am equipped for a second attempt toward defining the identification process. It is convenient to define two analytical types of identification, while assuming that the complexities of life invariably exhibit composite patterns, with elements of both types in different proportions. One type confines the self; the other enlarges it.

Self-sacrificing identification takes place to the extent that an individual comes to consider the general needs of other persons more important than his own. His own needs are substituted by the perceived needs of others,

[82] *Modern Psychiatry*, p. 15.

and beyond biological essentials he is concerned with only vicarious satisfactions.

Self-expansive identification takes place to the extent that an individual
comes to consider the general needs of other persons *his own*. His individual self incorporates the perceived needs of those persons as equivalent
with his own.[83]

Identification, generically considered, takes place to the extent that the
individual comes to consider the general needs of one or more other persons
either his own or more important than those perceived as his own. One
may ask: in the latter case, how can any needs be more important to me
than my own? Must we not say that all needs that are important to me
are my own, and more so the more important they are? The answer is that
the self-sacrificer does make the distinction; he is *in general* motivated to
belittle needs he considers "his own," in comparison to the needs he attributes to certain other persons or groups. If he does not make a distinction between "his own" needs and the needs of his objects of identification
—it is for most self-sacrificers, probably, quite a sharp dichotomy—then it
is a self-expanding and not a self-sacrificing kind of identification. Essentially the same distinction was made by Erich Fromm twenty years ago:

Psychologically rather different realities are hiding under Freud's description of
"identification," and a less formalistic conceptual scheme would have to differentiate between at least three main types of identification: an acquiring type,
i.e., an identification in which I take the other person into my own and by this
acquisition strengthen my own ego; an impoverishing type, in which I project
myself into some other person and become a part of him, and, lastly, a (conscious
or unconscious) feeling of identity, with the conviction that I and the other person are alike and exchangeable.[84]

It seems to me that the last type is subsumable under the first of the three,
since this kind of identification may be seen as an expansion of the self.

There are those who wish to reserve the term "identification" for the
self-sacrificing type only, in order to avoid a confusion between two very
different psychological processes. Nevitt Sanford argues that there has
been a tendency among psychoanalysts to use the term in a loose and
shallow manner in deference to common sense usage and in an effort to
show that Freudian concepts are adequate also for describing much surface
behavior. In harmony with one psychoanalytic usage, Sanford considers
identification a *mechanism of defense.* Properly speaking, in his terms, an
analyst who is functioning well does not identify with his patient, even if
he to some extent must put himself emotionally in the patient's place and
be fond of him, though without for a moment losing his task-orientation.
"When a patient may properly be said to identify with the analyst, on the
other hand, we deal with a process that is unconscious and unrealistic, with

[83] "Two people who love each other well will react to each other's needs and their own
indiscriminately. Indeed, the other's need *is* his own need." Maslow, *Motivation and Personality,* p. 149. The same holds, in differing degrees, for all who identify self-expansively
with other individuals or groups.

[84] "Sozialpsychologischer Teil," in Horkheimer (ed.), *Studien über Autorität und Familie,* p. 83. (Translated by this writer.)

a patient who is unsure of himself and, at the moment at least, unconcerned about other people; in desperation he adopts a piece of poor economy as a means of escape from a critical situation."[85] I do not wish to dispute the merits of a narrow identification concept in psychoanalytic theory and therapy, but in a general behavioral theory I wish to make the best of both worlds by using a broad concept close to common usage and at the same time keeping in mind that self-sacrificing identifications as a rule may be considered defense mechanisms set in motion by deficiencies in the ego.

O. H. Mowrer uses the term broadly and makes a distinction between developmental and defensive identification. Sanford, incidentally, objects that both of these processes are developmental and neither is identification.[86] Developmental identification, in Mowrer's terms, is the process whereby the infant becomes stimulated to try to do what his mother does, thus making him learn "to talk, to walk, and to perform other rudimentary *ego functions.*" Defensive identification, on the other hand, is what happens when the child internalizes the parental norms to the point of punishing himself for impulses of which the parents would disapprove. This is the beginning of his conscience or superego.[87]

In my terms, both of Mowrer's types of identification should be considered self-expansive, as a rule, since he incorporates the needs and wishes of other people into his self. However, if the ego development is neglected, and life becomes a tug of war between "bad" impulses and parental superego, then a self-sacrificing type of identification with parents may ensue. The child's attitude to one or both parents may in this case become not unlike the patient's attitude to the analyst after transference; his identification with and complete dependency on his parents become a defense mechanism. He wishes to sacrifice everything for the welfare and glory of his parents, for he is, in the extreme case, totally without ego control and thus without the minimum independence required as a basis for self-esteem.

Among adults extreme cases of self-expansive identification are found in some good marriages and in some friendship relations. It is a matter of unconditional solidarity without any loss of personal identity and integrity. Extreme cases of self-sacrificing identification are found in the sado-masochistic or "symbiotic" marriage situation described by Fromm,[88] in some mothers who "live for their children only," and in Hoffer's "true believer." These identifications are clingings to some substitute for a worthwhile self.

To what extent is man's self-esteem stable, and to what extent does it fluctuate? This is in part a problem of psychological freedom. It may be assumed that the self-esteem tends to be stable to the extent that the general

[85] "The Dynamics of Identification," *Psychological Review*, LXII, No. 2 (1955), 108, 106–18. The concept of "defense mechanism" is discussed below, p. 183.

[86] *Ibid.*, p. 106.

[87] *Psychotherapy: Theory and Research*, pp. 71–72.

[88] *Escape from Freedom*, p. 159: "Symbiosis, in this psychological sense, means the union of one individual self with another self (or any other power outside of the own self) in such a way as to make each lose the integrity of the own self and to make them completely dependent on each other."

pattern of personality integration has achieved stability. In other words, when basic needs and overt behavior are in fundamental harmony, there would appear to be no internally derived threat to the self-esteem.

Partly, it is also a problem of interpersonal relations. Sudden drops (or increases) in important other people's affection and deference certainly can affect the self-esteem. But the better it has been anchored in a well-integrated personality, the less can it be threatened by a change in other people's behavior.

A low degree of psychological freedom produces two types of instability of self-esteem. The individual may become very easily affected by day-to-day appraisals of other people, so that he may bristle with self-esteem one day and feel terribly inferior the next day. Often, however, a defense mechanism intervenes to remove the strain that extreme fluctuations of this kind would induce and *ambivalence* toward the self is introduced. This is the second type of instability.

In the ambivalence situation, an apparently good self-esteem is achieved by way of removing unflattering insights about oneself from consciousness. But the anxiety is still there, and in turn it stimulates further self-distortions or delusions and further insecurity.

It is time now to turn to the problem of mental health and neurosis in relation to psychological freedom. The crucial problem of understanding the conditions for stability in man's self-esteem cannot be answered without a discussion of neurotic processes. Also, it is important for the clarification of my psychological freedom concept to explain how it differs from concepts such as "maturity" and "mental health."

MENTAL HEALTH, MATURITY, AND PSYCHOLOGICAL FREEDOM

Occasional references to "neurosis" and (mental) "health" have been made in this chapter and in previous ones. I have so far avoided any commitment on the relationship between psychological freedom and mental health, because the problem is too important and too complex to be settled in a few side remarks. Since psychological freedom has been defined in terms of intrapersonal harmony between important needs and overt behavior, however, it may well be asked whether this conception should not be considered a synonym for "mental health." Also, it may be asked whether "maturity" should be considered a synonym for maximal psychological freedom.

There are good reasons, however, for holding the concept of psychological freedom apart from both of these related concepts. The reason for this preference differs in the two cases. As we shall see, "maturity" is a term with excellent connotations but hardly any consensually validated cognitive content. "Mental health" also is a term that in the past has been subjected to many different uses, but present trends appear to indicate an increasing censensus toward a widely acceptable descriptive meaning of this term.

There are two opposite poles in the ways "maturity" has been defined.

One extreme has been to equate maturity with maximal social adjustment, while the other extreme has tended to equate it with maximal individuality and independence vis-à-vis institutions. A caricature of the former approach is attributed to Harry Stack Sullivan, who had a wry sense of humor: "And now, when you have ceased to care for adventure, when you have forgotten romance, when the only things worth while to you are prestige and income, then you have grown up, then you have become an adult."[89]

This caricature is not very far-fetched, however. It is widely observed and agreed that some trends in contemporary education, social work, and psychotherapy are oriented toward helping individuals adjust to their milieus at almost any price, even at the price of suppressing all individuality in the process. Admittedly, it is most important to help individuals get along with their fellows, especially if they have no practical choice between different kinds of milieus. But to make social adjustment the only goal, and to equate it with "maturity," as is often done, would seem to stimulate both individual and, in the long run, social stagnation.[90]

For an opposite type of maturity concept, with no reference to the demands of the social environments, take the following: "We can characterize the mature personality as one who has succeeded in integrating a relatively steady internal environment that is capable of remaining comparatively independent of the immediately present external environment."[91] This is a good definition, both in being cognitively meaningful and in making capacity for independence the criterion, not the capacity for slavish adaptation. But this definition, it seems to me, may be more fruitfully related to "psychological freedom," as the discussion in the remainder of this section will indicate.

Many textbook writers tend to describe as signs of maturity the kind of personality qualities they like; perhaps these also tend to be qualities they have themselves, or want to believe they have. Gordon Allport, for example, lists these criteria of maturity: ability to "lose oneself" in work or contemplation, in recreation, or in loyalty to others (in other words, ability to concentrate energies, attention, and emotion); self-insight, accompanied by a good sense of humor; and the possession of some unifying philosophy of life.[92] Without having known Dr. Allport personally, I am almost sure that he possesses these qualities to a high degree. And I agree with him that this is a good way to approach the concept of maturity.

"Maturity," as this word has been used, is perhaps best suited as a label for each writer's subjective conception of the ideal, or productive, or "good" personality. "Immaturity," then, is a word for relatively strong deviation from such an ideal.

---

[89] Quoted in Arnold, *The Folklore of Capitalism*, p. 163.

[90] For two examples of this conception of maturity, see Klein, *Society—Democracy—and the Group*, pp. 91–94, and Strecker, *Their Mothers' Sons*, p. 211. This attitude may be seen as an illustration of David Riesman's thesis about the emergence of the other-directed character type in American society. Riesman believes that social adjustment without individual value commitments is devoid of genuine satisfaction: members of this kind of crowd remain lonely.

[91] Lasswell and McDougal, *Law, Science and Policy*, working paper, Part II.

[92] Allport, *Personality*, pp. 213–14.

"Mental health" and "neurosis" are a different pair of terms, which can be given fairly clear and convenient cognitive meanings. And the most useful employment of these terms, it seems to me, is in relation to the individual's ability to tolerate a realistic self, meaning a realistic image of his own qualities and experiences.

It should be pointed out that "neurosis" as usually conceived is not the logical opposite of mental health. As Abraham H. Maslow says, "It would now be universally agreed upon that the classical neurosis as a whole as well as single neurotic symptoms are characteristically coping mechanisms. If a neurotic symptom does have a function, does do a job for the person, then we must assume that the person is better off for having this symptom."[93] It is the psychosis rather than the neurosis that comes close to being a logical opposite of good mental health. A psychosis has been defined as "a relatively severe mental disease, i.e., one in which there is a loss or disorder in mental processes."[94]

The neurotic individual is struggling to regain his mental health. The psychotic has practically given up the struggle and has little or no help to offer the psychiatrist in his own cure.[95] The mentally healthy person may have avoided the struggle. It is not to be taken for granted, however, that the avoidance of this kind of struggle is always desirable.

Before I elaborate on this last point, let me say that the psychotics do not present any theoretical problems in the study of psychological freedom, in that they are, as long as the psychosis lasts, completely the victims of their condition. They have barred themselves from insight into important aspects of reality, including some of their own important wishes and needs. The neurotic, too, is deficient in self-insight, but in one sense that is true of all people. "Know thyself" is, strictly speaking, an ideal that can never be attained in full. But while the completely nonneurotic person, if there is such a being, has no internal barriers against self-exploration, the neurotic is able to pry into certain areas of himself only, while other areas are bolted with various "defense mechanisms"—a term that will be explained shortly.

It is possible to avoid anxiety, and it is possible to avoid neurosis by not looking down "into the abyss," as Kierkegaard said. An example is the case of Phyllis reported by Rollo May, who avoided facing the problems of life by accepting a life in bondage under her strong-willed mother.[96] As this case illustrates, the avoidance of neurosis is not always a desirable goal, if one cares for the growth of freedom. Avoidance of insight and responsi-

[93] Maslow, "The Expressive Component of Behavior," in Brand (ed.), *The Study of Personality: A Book of Readings*, p. 371.

[94] Quoted from English, *A Student's Dictionary of Psychological Terms*, in Murphy, *Personality*, p. 995. Alexander says: "In a psychosis . . . the difference between conscious and unconscious disappears to a large degree and the unconscious dominates the whole personality, whereas in a neurosis the principal achievement of the later ego-development, the acceptance of reality, remains more or less intact, and the unconscious tendencies penetrate the ego only in isolated symptoms, which are like foreign bodies embedded in normal tissue." *Fundamentals of Psychoanalysis*, p. 20.

[95] For the neurotic, who is in a state of disequilibrium, says Alexander, "two courses are open for the attainment of a real equilibrium. One leads to psychosis; the other to health." *Psychoanalysis of the Total Personality*, p. 47.

[96] *The Meaning of Anxiety*, pp. 305–9.

bility may prevent the growth of anxiety and neurosis, but at the price of preventing the growth of individuality as well.

The scope of this dilemma becomes a huge one, however, when we consider the impact of society on the individual. Social institutions require conformity to certain kinds of behavior patterns and strongly encourage conformity to the corresponding thought and evaluation patterns as well. Resistance to social pressures easily gives rise to anxieties about one's own values and about oneself, especially if resistance is followed by a measure of social rejection. The safe course of conduct in order to reduce this kind of anxiety is to become a strict conformist—again at the price of giving up the chance of developing individual potentialities. Erich Fromm has described the mechanisms leading to "automaton conformity," and David Riesman has pointed out how the "other-directed" character is heavily predisposed for just this kind of anxiety reduction.

Fromm raises the further question, however, of whether societies may not differ greatly in the extent to which their institutions tend to do violence to individual growth potentials. He poses the problem of how to conceive of a society whose institutional patterns are compatible with meaningful and heterogeneous individual lives: "The sane society is that which corresponds to the needs of man; not necessarily to what he *feels* to be his needs—because even the most pathological aims can be felt subjectively as that which the person wants most—but to what his needs are objectively, as they can be ascertained by the study of man."[97]

After describing the modern "automaton conformist," Fromm concludes that "he suffers from a defect of spontaneity and individuality that may seem incurable." But he gets along, as do millions of his fellows: "For most of them, the culture provides patterns which enable them *to live with a defect without becoming ill*. It is as if each culture provided the remedy against the outbreak of manifest neurotic symptoms which would result from the defect produced by it."[98]

The background of these considerations causes me to endorse Fromm's "defense of the neurotic," if one may call it that: "The neurotic person can be characterized as somebody who was not ready to surrender completely in the battle for his self . . . from the standpoint of human values, he is less crippled than the kind of normal person who has lost his individuality altogether."[99] Among others who have stressed this point, that the neurotic may be "right" and society "wrong," the most forceful writers have been Robert Lindner and Lawrence K. Frank.[100]

The fact remains, however, that the neurotic suffers and is in distress. More specifically, a neurosis is an unstable blocking of self-awareness at one or more important points. The reason for this blocking, which may

---

[97] "The Psychology of Normalcy," *Dissent*, I (1954), 143. In *The Sane Society*, Fromm makes an extensive inquiry into this problem. Cf. also his *Escape from Freedom*, p. 138.

[98] *The Sane Society*, p. 16. On "automaton conformity," see also *Escape from Freedom*, pp. 185–206.

[99] *Escape from Freedom*, p. 139.

[100] See Frank, *Society as the Patient: Essays on Culture and Personality*; Lindner, *Prescription for Rebellion*. This problem is further developed below, pp. 186–88.

take the form of one or more of a number of "defense mechanisms," must be sought in the nature of anxiety.

A person "has a neurosis," or "is neurotic," to the extent that he engages in behavior which serves to reduce anxiety directly (symptomatically) but does not alter the realities *which produce the anxiety*. . . . A neurotic symptom, so-called, is any habit which resolves anxiety but does not lessen the ultimate, realistic problem which the anxiety represents.[101]

A neurosis, if I may paraphrase this definition, is a relatively enduring pseudosolution to a problem of anxiety: it provides a surface reassurance by pushing the threatening insights away from consciousness. Yet, the realities that gave rise to the sense of threat are still there, and the anxiety-provoking insights are lurking in subconsciousness or preconsciousness.

In psychoanalytic theory and therapy it is usual to distinguish between a good number of defense mechanisms, each characterized in part by the hypothesized constellations between ego, id, and superego, and in part by the individual's characteristic response to situations in the external world. For my purposes it would lead too far to go into a discussion of these different types of defense mechanisms. I shall limit myself to a consideration of the most important of them all—namely, the mechanism of *repression*.[102]

The central importance of this mechanism appears universally agreed upon, and it is not surprising that in Gardner Murphy's glossary of psychological terms these two terms are given closely similar definitions: A defense mechanism is "an adjustment which enables a person to avoid facing a painful fact or an unpleasant situation." Repression is "the process of excluding repugnant mental contents from access to consciousness."[103] It is possible to consider repression as a common denominator of most neuroses, and to consider all other defense mechanisms as either reinforcements of repression or as partial solutions of the repression conflict.[104]

The fundamental logic of repression is quite simple. The ego, as we have seen, is the moderator between the cross-pressures coming from the id and the superego. In the healthy individual, compromises are reached according to certain stable patterns, which permit a presumably maximal expression of id-impulses in so far as they are compatible with a maximal measure of social responsibility. Some healthy individuals lean a little over to the id-side and are known as "impulsive" people; others lean more toward the opposite side and are known as "conscientious" people. Whichever side appears to have the upper hand, the point is that in mentally healthy people there is a dependable truce. Since the truce is stable, the ego and even the conscious self can tolerate facing all the pressures from the id

[101] Mowrer, *Learning Theory and Personality Dynamics*, pp. 535, 537.

[102] For discussions of the various defense mechanisms, see, for example, Anna Freud, *The Ego and the Mechanisms of Defense*; Fenichel, *The Psychoanalytic Theory of Neurosis*, chap. 9; Symonds, *The Dynamics of Human Adjustment*, chap. 7; and Murphy, *Personality*, chap. 23. *Student's Dictionary of Psychological Terms.*

[103] Murphy, *Personality*, pp. 982, 996. Both definitions are quoted from English, *A*

[104] Alexander, "Development of the Fundamental Concepts of Psychoanalysis," in Alexander and Ross, *Dynamic Psychiatry*, p. 12. See also his *Fundamentals of Psychoanalysis*, pp. 96–100.

and the superego. In other words, none of these pressures creates unbearable amounts of anxiety.

Complete mental health may be equated with the complete absence of anxiety, or complete stability in the relationship between id and superego, with the ego firmly in control and everything open for inspection by the self. Fortunately, complete mental health is never achieved; it would mean a complete stagnation of mental processes.

Less fortunately, neuroses are quite frequently achieved because the hazards of human existence all too frequently give rise to unbearable amounts of anxiety. A neurosis is, as we have seen, a means of alleviating extreme anxiety, and the fundamental mechanism employed is repression, which is equivalent to barring from consciousness. This mechanism is introduced very early in life, when the hazards of human existence are the greatest, considering the infant's or child's lack of experience and power. He depends on social relationships for his very existence, and, as we have seen, handling people presents vastly more complicated problems than handling nonsocial environments. The only kind of reassurance that can form a solid basis for anxiety reduction in the infant and child is a constant, unconditional, and generous flow of love and tenderness from the parents, especially the mother or mother substitute.[105] But even in near-perfect home surroundings there will be times when the child is frustrated in his wishes and reacts with aggressiveness against his parents. These aggressive impulses are normally the first impulses to be repressed.

Why are they repressed? Because parents tend to be human beings, who at some point in the child's development will react against his bursts of aggression. And parental punitive reactions almost invariably will appear more threatening to the child than anticipated or even realized by the parent. In effect, even very lenient punishment will give rise to some sense of threat of loss of the parent's love. At this point the child will either repress his aggressive feelings and become "good," or he will continue to be "bad." In both cases he will suffer from guilt feelings. The "good" child will suffer anxieties lest his aggressive impulses reemerge, as does happen. But he refuses to admit them to consciousness, and the guilt feelings stay with him in his unconscious. The "bad" child will give vent to some of his aggression, but at the price of both guilt feelings and anxieties about future repercussions for himself. He will tend to repress his need for dependence. The "good" child's self-image tends to be highly but very precariously favorable in terms of the virtues the parents value in children. His anxiety reduction depends on his confidence that he deserves the love of his parents. The "bad" child's self-image will tend to stress toughness and independence, since he represses his strong dependency needs. Needless to say, the "good" and the "bad" children I have presented are cardboard illustrations of oversimplified types; all children are both "good" and "bad" in this sense, in innumerable combinations. Also, of course, there are innumerable types of parents; some cause much repression in (some of)

[105] See above, pp. 163–64.

their children, others much less. All I have wished to do is to illustrate how the mechanism of repression first comes into use.

Later this mechanism is on hand to help the child or the adult "forget" anxiety-provoking past experiences, present predicaments, or future prospects—if he cannot face them. And one crucial factor in determining what kinds of threats the adult can face is his past history of facing or repressing other threats that appear similar to him. The obvious neurotic is, for example, the man who is afraid of walking on the street or is terrified by horses. In such cases, the task of psychoanalysis is to ferret out traumatic experiences from his early life in order to help him face the corresponding anxieties that once overwhelmed him and put him "on the run."

The word "repression" is not used in Sullivan's books; he speaks instead of "dissociation." At times he gives the impression that this latter term is a much broader one: "For the expression of all things in the personality other than those which were approved and disapproved by the parent and other significant persons, the self refuses awareness, so to speak. It does not accord awareness, it does not notice; and these impulses, desires, and needs come to exist disassociated from the self, or *dissociated*."[106] Everything, however, that we fail to make a note about in our awareness is dissociated in this sense, regardless of whether our "selective inattention"[107] is a matter of pure economy (excluding the irrelevant), or is a matter of repression (excluding the threatening insights).

In other contexts, though, Sullivan tends to use "dissociated" in about the same sense as the Freudian "repressed": "In dissociation, the trick is that one shall carry on within awareness processes which make it practically impossible, while one is awake, to encounter uncanny emotions."[108] Moreover, it is quite clear that "dissociation" is used in roughly the same sense as "repression" when it is made the crucial criterion of mental health: "We may say, however, as a generality, that healthy development of personality is inversely proportionate to the amount, to the number, of tendencies which have come to exist in dissociation. Put in another way, if there is nothing dissociated, then whether one be a genius or an imbecile, it is quite certain that he will be mentally healthy.[109]

In Sullivan's theory, health or neurosis is entirely a matter of the interpersonal relations characteristic of a given individual. It is a matter of accepting full consciousness of all significant relationships with other people. "Anxiety" is in Sullivan's theory entirely a matter of *interpersonal* insecurity. Thus, he arrives at the following dictum: "One achieves mental health to the extent that one becomes aware of one's interpersonal relations."[110] Conversely: "If the term, mental disorder, is to be meaningful,

---

[106] *Modern Psychiatry*, pp. 21–22.

[107] Sullivan, *Interpersonal Theory*, p. 319.

[108] *Ibid.*, pp. 317–18. See also *Modern Psychiatry*, p. 46. Patrick Mullahy points out the inconsistency in Sullivan's usage, and settles for this latter interpretation: "Dissociated dynamisms not only exist outside awareness but ordinarily are not accessible to the self, unlike experiences neglected by selective inattention." *Ibid.*, p. 264.

[109] *Modern Psychiatry*, p. 47.

[110] *Ibid.*, p. 207.

it must cover like a tent the whole field of inadequate or inappropriate performance in interpersonal relations."[111]

Only one line of cautionary remarks should be added to Sullivan's definitions of mental health versus disorder. It may be highly arguable, in many cases, just what kind of performance is adequate and appropriate in given social relationships. Sullivan certainly has not intended to make social convention the king under all circumstances. His ideal was surely not the extremely other-directed character in Riesman's sense, nor was it Fromm's automaton conformist.

Standards for judging the social appropriateness of behavior are and must remain controversial in many fields, and especially in the political arena. Our hope for increasing consensus on such standards rests, I believe, and as Fromm and Maslow have stressed, on a gradual increase in scientific knowledge about human needs and potentialities and about social patterns capable of facilitating the growth of individuality and freedom.[112] At the present state of society and knowledge it is often necessary to offer maladjusted and unhappy people psychiatric help, regardless of whether we at times may feel that these people are really "right" or "healthy" and *society* is "wrong" or "neurotic."

Both families and societies differ greatly in the amounts and types of strain to which they subject different types of individuals. One type of childhood background or community milieu may have made Mr. A an extreme neurotic, while Mr. B with a similar background and social situation may have no symptoms of neurosis. Mr. A's defenses must have been weaker in crucial respects or at crucial times than Mr. B's. Not only do individuals differ in capacity to adjust to a particular type of family or community situation, but societies also differ in their handling of particular individual types. Thus, an individual who in our society might be hospitalized as a schizophrenic, might well, if he were a Pokomám Indian, have been an admired and wealthy curer of magical illnesses.[113]

If it remains true that neurotics tend to suffer and to want help, even in cases where an observer may insist that they are "right" and society "wrong," we must nevertheless keep in mind that mental health is not the only worthy objective of psychotherapy. Especially, of course, if mental health is equated with a good, pain-reducing adjustment to whatever institutions one lives with.[114] As a matter of practical convenience, many psychoanalysts have narrowed their focus to this objective only and have

---

[111] *Interpersonal Theory*, p. 313. Sullivan consistently speaks of "mental disorder" instead of "neurosis."

[112] Cf. above, pp. 11–14.

[113] See Billig, Gillin, and Davidson, "Aspects of Personality and Culture in a Guatemalan Community: Ethnological and Rorschach Approaches," Part II, *Journal of Personality*, XVI, No. 3 (1948), 367. The general problem of social structure and psychological freedom is discussed below, pp. 228–39.

[114] Reinhard Bendix, a sociologist who has participated in many psychiatric staff meetings at a California hospital, notes the dilemma posed by the fact that psychotherapy sometimes has adverse effects on the patient's creative ability. A discussion of this problem applied to a concrete case, he says, "often ends with the assertion that a person's creative ability which is adversely affected by his therapy was probably not worth preserving." See Bendix, "Compliant Behavior and Individual Personality," *American Journal of Sociology*, LVIII, No. 3 (1952), 295, note 12.

in effect become the advocates of the status quo. In extreme cases, psychoanalysts may make a god of society as it is, a god to be accommodated slavishly by the patient.

From the point of view of my freedom values, this type of limitation in the objectives of psychotherapy does violence both to the larger needs of the patient and to those of society. The "adjusted-at-any-price" individual becomes stymied in the development of his individuality,[115] and the society in its turn becomes deprived of the contributions toward change and progress that individuals who are "perfectly adjusted" are unable to offer.

While it is true that a neurosis always implies some shortcomings in psychological freedom, then, it does not follow that cures will always increase the patient's capacities for free expression. The patient often merely learns to substitute socially acceptable (or desirable) defense mechanisms for socially unacceptable ones. This sort of "cure" may be successful in giving the patient a sense of relief; he may meet with diminishing disapproval and sanctions from other persons and from himself alike. But it does not necessarily increase his self-awareness. A cure in a real and full sense restores the patient's communication with his own basic motives. It reduces his anxieties to the point where he can accept a realistic image of himself. By this test, an increase in mental health is certain to imply an increase in psychological freedom as well.

And here we come to the point where one can state fairly explicitly the difference between the goals of mental health and psychological freedom. Mental health is measured by the individual's capacity to maintain anxiety-reducing social relationships. Psychological freedom is measured by his capacity to accept and act upon a realistic image of his self and of other people.

A neurosis or mental disorder is an impairment of both health and freedom. We have seen that a neurosis is a pseudosolution to the problem of anxiety, in that it provides a surface reassurance by pushing the threatening insights away from consciousness. Ideally the cure of a neurosis leads the patient both to a satisfactory mental health and to a full psychological freedom. In practical terms, these two goals are likely to be approached simultaneously a part of the way, but at some point the psychiatrist chooses, perhaps without being aware of it, between the goals of health and of freedom as matters of primary and secondary emphasis, respectively.

A primary emphasis on maximizing a patient's mental health—and this appears to be the most usual top priority concern—means that the patient learns enough about himself to be able to accept previously intolerable

[115] The sociologist R. M. MacIver has stated this point in discussing the concept of "maladjustment": "It is futile to attribute maladjustment to those who merely follow different norms from those of their fellows. . . . It is only when the individual manifests symptoms of personal or inner disequilibrium—not when his personality is unified in a behavior discordant with that of his fellows, but when it is distracted by the failure to live his life in accordance with norms valid for himself—that psychological maladjustment can be predicated in any unambiguous sense." "Maladjustment," *The Encyclopedia of the Social Sciences.*

I believe that "maladjustment" is more plausibly used in the sense that MacIver is attacking. But I share his substantive position, which in my terms would state that psychotherapy should let the goal of psychological freedom take precedence over the social adjustment goal, whenever this course is compatible with the individual's long-range welfare.

aspects of his relationships to important other people. A married woman, for example, learns to understand or comes to believe that her own repressed desire for sexual adventure was the basis of her constant worries over her husband's possible infidelity. Her hatred abates, her accusations cease, her marital relationship becomes tolerable or good, and she is to this extent cured and "mentally healthy." Her acute anxiety about her own self-esteem (as reflected in her husband's and her own faithful love), which may have derived from the guilt feelings connected with her repressed sexual desires, has now been reduced by her ability to face what was previously repressed. In effect, she finds a plausible reason for her anxieties, which no longer jeopardize her marriage.

Now, a primary emphasis on maximizing a patient's psychological freedom would imply a parallel course a good part of the way. The married woman in my example would have to come to grips with her repressions, in the sense of first learning to tolerate a self-image that includes certain frivolous characteristics of which her "better self" emphatically disapproves. However, it is not enough, in this case, to remove the barriers between herself and her husband and become "happy" or "adjusted." To approach psychological freedom also she must continue her self-explorations and unravel her repressions all the way to the point where she has become aware of all her own important characteristics. The test is no longer her adjustment to her husband and to other important people. Even at the possible price of some disharmony in some of these relationships, the goal of psychological freedom means a maximum understanding of and inter-action with herself—a realistic awareness of what her basic needs and potentialities are and the ability and enduring effort to develop this self in the direction of an equally realistic ego ideal.[116]

A high psychological freedom implies at least a good measure of mental health, since anxiety in considerable amount tends to result in repression and neurosis. A high degree of mental health, on the other hand, does not necessarily imply a highly developed psychological freedom, since it may be contingent on a fairly sheltered place in the social structure. It is possible to appear blissfully free from neurotic traits just because one is free from the challenge of coping with anxiety-provoking problems. Mental health means avoidance of anxieties that one cannot face or capacity to face anxieties that one cannot avoid. Psychological freedom means acceptance of and capacity to cope with all the anxieties to which man in modern society may be exposed.

DEFENSIVE SYNDROMES AND PSYCHOLOGICAL FREEDOM

The elements in a developmental theory of psychological freedom have been assembled. Beginning with the infant's quest for security and power, I have considered the role of anxiety in the development of the self, the

---

[116] "Realistic" does have a slightly different meaning in the two cases, by necessity. A realistic self-image is an approximately true picture of the self that exists. A realistic ego ideal is a set of enduring goals that the self in fact can approximate to the extent that its potential qualities are nurtured, brought out, and applied. It is a difference between *actually* and *potentially* realistic.

relation of the self to other personality components, and the way it is affected by interpersonal relations. Lastly I have also discussed the problem of mental health and neurosis in relation to psychological freedom. The remaining task in this chapter is to survey some of the more important research data bearing on the theory of psychological freedom and to reinterpret and suggest further development and applications of the theory on this basis.

Most experimental and survey research bearing on psychological freedom has evolved around the theory of the *authoritarian personality,* and the most important concern in the remainder of this chapter will be to make explicit what these research data imply about man's psychological capacity for free expression. First, the concept of authoritarianism will be defined, and we shall see how it is related to the concept of psychological freedom. Then will follow a discussion of the "authoritarian syndrome," meaning the most important correlates and symptoms of authoritarianism. An opposite and yet in some respects similar syndrome of *antiauthoritarian* attitudes will then be discussed, as well as a deviating type of authoritarian personality, the authoritarian rebel. Finally, I shall try to bring together a variety of data on the genesis of authoritarian as well as antiauthoritarian syndromes and other defensive tendencies. Data on the genesis of deficiencies in freedom are of course at the same time data on the development and maintenance of freedom or the psychological capacity for freedom.

The Concept of Authoritarianism

The concept of authority is as old as political science and theology. The psychological concept of authoritarianism is of comparatively recent origin, however. So far as I know, Erich Fromm was the first to make use of it roughly in the sense that has since become conventional. More than twenty years ago he asserted that a general submissive orientation is characteristic of "the authoritarian-masochistic character": "The feature common to all authoritarian thinking is the conviction that life is determined by forces outside of man's own self, his interest, his wishes."[117] In *Escape from Freedom* he speaks of authoritarianism in this sense as one of three main "mechanisms of escape" from freedom:[118] "The more distinct forms of this mechanism are to be found in the striving for submission and domination, or, as we would rather put it, in the masochistic and sadistic strivings as they exist in varying degrees in normal and neurotic persons respectively."[119] These tendencies are described at some length and both are explained as "the outcomes of one basic need, springing from the inability to bear the isolation and weakness of one's own self."[120]

In *The Authoritarian Personality* (often to be referred to here as "the California study") the original task was to study susceptibility to anti-

---

[117] Fromm, *Escape from Freedom,* p. 171. The same statement, practically verbatim, was made by Fromm in Horkheimer (ed.), *Autorität und Familie,* p. 120.

[118] The other two being "destructiveness" and "automaton conformity." *Escape from Freedom,* pp. 136–206.

[119] *Ibid.,* pp. 141–42.

[120] *Ibid.,* p. 158.

democratic, especially fascist, propaganda, and there is no thorough discussion of the concept of authoritarianism. Adorno's brief discussion of the "authoritarian syndrome" merely reiterates Fromm's (and Maslow's) earlier descriptions,[121] illustrated by questionnaire quotes. His most concise point is that the authoritarian type "is governed by the superego and has continually to contend with strong and highly ambivalent id tendencies. He is driven by the fear of being weak."[122] Furthermore, "authoritarianism" is also used in a wider sense in the same work—for example, in the title itself—as equivalent with all the "high scoring" syndromes. Richard Christie is right in suggesting that in their predominant usage of the word, the authors of the California study have given authoritarianism "a highly operational definition. Individuals scoring relatively high on the California F scale have been designated as authoritarian, those scoring lower have been viewed as nonauthoritarian."[123]

For his own purposes of evaluation, Christie lists four criteria of authoritarianism, which he believes are implied both in *The Authoritarian Personality* and in most other research prior to his writing. Authoritarian individuals tend to be: punitive and condescending toward inferiors, unreceptive to scientific investigation, less sensitive to interpersonal relationships, and prone to attribute their own ideology to others.[124] This is a synthetic list, in the sense that it is culled and abstracted from concepts used in large numbers of research studies about tendencies termed "authoritarian." Neither of these characteristics seems entirely plausible as it stands if we want to extract *one* central criterion of authoritarianism; and for my purposes of analysis one crucial criterion is wanted. The first one on Christie's list comes the closest, but I prefer to turn it around and make a submissive and masochistic attitude toward superiors the most crucial criterion of authoritarianism. If we want an at once relatively simple and plausible analytical concept, it should in my opinion be focused on a type of orientation toward authorities.

For my analytical purposes I suggest the following definition: *"Authoritarianism" in this study means a defensive predisposition*[125] *to conform uncritically to standards and commands supported by some or by all perceived authorities.* My present task is to clarify this concept and relate it to my definition of psychological freedom. In the next subsection I shall consider a more complex, synthetic authoritarianism concept, to be referred to as the "authoritarian syndrome."

We should not consider all kinds of conformity to the wishes of men of power as indications of authoritarianism. Frequently, individuals may

[121] See below, pp. 194–95.

[122] Adorno, Frenkel-Brunswik, Levinson, and Sanford, *The Authoritarian Personality*, pp. 759–62 and 753.

[123] Christie and Jahoda (eds.), *Studies in the Scope and Method of "The Authoritarian Personality*," p. 125.

[124] *Ibid.*, p. 140. "Ideology" strikes me as an unhappy word here; it seems above all to be impulses and especially repressed impulses that the authoritarian tends to project to others.

[125] A "predisposition" means a personality-derived tendency, or operationally a tendency that persists uninterruptedly in all different situations.

wish to conform because they happen to agree for their own reasons with the purposes of the powers that be, or they wish to avoid the inconveniences connected with indicating their dissent. Authoritarians are people who are invariably ready to agree with the authorities *because* they need the approval, or imagined approval, of authorities as a relief from personal anxiety. They are adaptive enough to be able to follow the directives of authorities because they identify with them in a self-sacrificing manner and have no enduring convictions of their own. This sketch, of course, represents an ideal or extreme type, rather than real people. Perhaps the best way to distinguish between authoritarian and nonauthoritarian conformity to the demands of authorities is to consider the functions of the conformity attitude for the individual.

Irving Sarnoff and Daniel Katz have suggested that attitudes such as anti-Negro prejudice, for example, emerge as the outcome of an interplay between three kinds of motivational processes. First, there is the need for reality testing, or rationality, or for a cognitive map, or for making sense of the surrounding world. On the basis of facts available to a particular individual, it may be logically plausible to conclude that Negroes are inferiors. Secondly, there is the need for social acceptance, for the balance of rewards over punishments that tends to follow from voicing the "correct beliefs." If you grow up among poor whites in Mississippi, it would not be wise to be considered a "Nigger lover." Finally, there are the requirements of ego defense, or holding anxiety in check. If you have learned to repress all hostility against authorities and strong people, then you need scapegoats, and Negroes tend to be relatively suitable for this purpose.[126]

Let me choose another example more directly related to authoritarianism, for it is clear that this scheme of analysis can be fruitfully applied to all types of attitudes. Take a young social scientist who conforms to the views of an older, more experienced, prestigious, and powerful colleague. Again, three types of motives may interplay, or one of them may be dominant.

First, the younger man's views may be the outcome of a serious effort to make sense of his field of inquiry; the senior scholar's work may have aided him considerably in this effort. He may be aware of the older man's prestige and power, but this awareness does not influence his own views, except possibly to the extent that the wide acclaim given to these views initially made him wish to look into them. This may be called a *rationality orientation*.

Secondly, the young man may not only be aware of the senior scholar's prestige and power, but his views may be influenced by a hope that some conformity to the authority's views will increase his own prestige and power. Operationally, this type of influence is indicated to the extent that

[126] Sarnoff and Katz, "The Motivational Bases of Attitude Change," *Journal of Abnormal and Social Psychology*, XLIX, No. 1 (1954), 115–24. For a revised version of the same paper, see Sarnoff, Katz, and McClintock, "Attitude-Change Procedures and Motivating Patterns," in Katz, Cartwright, Eldersveld, and Lee (eds.), *Public Opinion and Propaganda: A Book of Readings*, 305–12. A more recent study within the same theoretical framework is reported in Katz, Sarnoff, and McClintock, "Ego-Defense and Attitude Change," *Human Relations*, IX, No. 1 (1956), 27–45.

the younger man in his critical writings consistently applies laxer canons of criticism to the views of this authority than he does when discussing the views of other senior and junior scholars. This tendency may be termed the *manipulative orientation*.

Finally, there is the young man whose ego defense is too insecure to permit him to be wholly concerned either with "discovering the truth" or with advancing his career. His first concern is with reducing his personal anxieties, or his anxieties as a social scientist. The result is a strong emotional involvement with some authority in his field. This man becomes his mentor, and he identifies with his hero in a self-sacrificing manner. His life's ambition is to advance the reputation of this authority and his views; his gratifications as a scientist are all vicarious. This type of motivation for scientific views typifies the *authoritarian orientation*.

In real life, all three types of motivation tend to intermingle, in this field as in all others. One type may dominate, and more so in one field than in others. It is perhaps reasonable to expect a higher proportion of rationality orientation among scientists than in various other realms of life where the rationality attitude or "scientific method" is not equally highly valued. Another way of saying the same thing is that authoritarianism in the life of a scientist is more likely to be expressed in his family life, for example, than in his scientific work, where standards of rationality are much more clear and tend to be applied without mercy by critical colleagues.

By now it should be clear what is meant when I say that authoritarianism means a defensive predisposition to conform. An observable tendency to conform is a necessary but not a sufficient criterion. The manipulative conformity is the outcome of a social need to "get ahead," which may or may not in turn be derived from deficiencies in ego-defense. In fact, "ego-offense" is perhaps more characteristic of the manipulator than ego-defense in most cases. Authoritarianism is present only to the extent that (1) deficiencies in ego control are present and (2) they amount to a defensive predisposition for conforming to standards and commands supported by authorities.[127]

The relationship between psychological freedom and authoritarianism is not a simple matter of logical opposites. I believe that an increase in authoritarianism amounts to a reduction in psychological freedom, but several assumptions of empirical theory are necessary to reach this conclusion. And the converse is not always true: a reduction in psychological freedom does not necessarily correspond to an increase in authoritarianism.

Psychological freedom is the more general concept of the two. It refers to a smooth interaction and harmony between basic needs and overt behavior. The previous discussion in this chapter has tried to summarize and further develop a theory about the main factors influencing the growth of psychological freedom or the thwarting of this growth. Let me now try to outline the theory that authoritarianism is one typical outcome of deficiencies in psychological freedom.

---

[127] I shall also speak of an inverse authoritarianism as characteristic of people who instead develop a compulsion to nonconformity. The antiauthoritarian syndrome is discussed below in "Antiauthoritarianism and the Defensive Rebel," pp. 206–17.

I have observed that the psychological freedom of the newborn child is very high: he has no difficulties giving a loud overt expression to his motives. As long as he is attended to and emotionally assured of continued motherly love and tenderness, his basic security and his psychological freedom will persist almost unimpaired. Sooner or later, however, the child experiences the fact of life that love is not constant and unconditional, not even the love of his mother and father. This is the point at which anxiety is bound to come into his life or to become substantially intensified.

Limited amounts of anxiety are necessary ingredients in human life from then on, because interpersonal relationships are both very important for human needs and to some extent unpredictable, at least when they fall short of all-pervasive love. Also, we have seen that anxiety has the essential function of providing incentives for individual development. The "anxiety gradient" is man's most important teacher.

But the teacher may be too severe. Anxiety that cannot be faced gives rise to neurosis. By repression and other escape mechanisms, the self excludes the anxiety-provoking insights and to this extent becomes crippled or distorted. Communication between consciousness and the structure of needs becomes impaired to the same extent. Neurotic behavior aims at keeping the anxiety in check and does not contribute to the satisfaction of the repressed needs, which are still needs.[128] Anxiety that cannot be faced means, in other words, an impairment of psychological freedom.

There can be no doubt that the crucial social relationships of the average child are the relationships to his parents. For this reason, if there are some anxieties he cannot face, they are likely to emanate from these very special relationships. And more, they are likely to emanate from the basic source of strain in all parent-child relationships: the divergence between love and authority. Parents have the double role of being the source of love and tenderness and the source of the restraints and sanctions employed in trying to direct the socialization process. Some tentative evidence points to the validity of the following set of hypotheses about the genesis and growth of authoritarianism.

There are innumerable occasions in all family situations in which hostile impulses against the parents are likely to arise in the child. These impulses are always a source of some anxiety, since the child also loves his parents, or at least is dependent on their continual love and support. The child is more likely to be able to face and cope with these anxieties, other things being equal, if the parents are ready and able to tolerate overt expressions of this hostility against themselves. The child is more likely to be overwhelmed by these anxieties and repress his hostility if the parents have tended to punish and in this way banish all overt expression of hostility or insubordination against themselves.[129] *Authoritarianism tends to be the outcome of childhood situations in which the child has learned to repress most of his hostility against his immediate authorities—his parents.*

---

[128] It is possible that a partial reservation must be made for the mechanism of sublimation: exchanging a forbidden need satisfaction for a permitted, half-satisfactory substitute—for example, sport instead of sex.

[129] Insubordination, whatever else it may be, is a frequent way of expressing hostility. Defiance of an authority amounts to attacking it head-on.

These hypotheses are by implication also hypotheses about the maintenance of psychological freedom. Some preliminary evidence bearing on them will be reviewed later in this chapter.[130] But our evidence on psychological freedom is not limited to data on authoritarianism in this narrow sense. Other variables such as ethnocentrism, intolerance of ambiguity, or rigidity in problem-solving have been shown to correlate closely with authoritarianism—so closely that they are often considered part and parcel of an "authoritarian syndrome." There is also some tentative evidence on the existence of an antiauthoritarian syndrome of defensive tendencies. Furthermore, there are indications that both deprivation and indulgence in excess during childhood can lead to "fixations." All these defensive tendencies amount to deficiencies in psychological freedom.

The next two subsections have as their main task the stretching of the net, in assembling data on various important manifestations of defensiveness. Then follows a review of some data on and a resummary of my theory about how these various kinds of ego deficiency and defensiveness come about.

The Authoritarian Syndrome

"Syndrome," according to Webster, means "concurrence; a set of concurrent things," or specifically in medicine, "a group of signs and symptoms that occur together, and characterize a disease."[131] The "authoritarian syndrome" means a group of symptoms of authoritarianism[132] tending to cluster together, one of which is authoritarianism in the narrower sense, as has just been defined. Whenever I speak of "authoritarian tendencies," or of the "authoritarian personality," I shall refer to authoritarianism in the broad syndrome sense. "Authoritarianism" alone always refers to the narrower meaning, unless I specify otherwise.

One of the earliest descriptions of the authoritarian syndrome was given by Maslow: (1) a view of the world "as a sort of jungle in which man's hand is necessarily against every other man's . . . and in which human beings are conceived of as primarily selfish or evil or stupid"; (2) "the tendency to regard most or all other human beings as challenging rivals who are either superior (and therefore to be feared, resented, bootlicked, and admired); or inferior (and therefore to be scorned, humiliated, and dominated)"; (3) a tendency "to regard the 'superior' or stronger person

---

[130] In the subsection "Some Research on the Genesis of Defensive Syndromes," pp. 217–28.

[131] "The syndrome has a certain conceptual life of its own, laws and rules by which it functions and changes and which may for convenience be considered apart from the movements of any particular characteristic which is part of the syndrome. . . . A syndrome, whether it be security feeling, self-esteem, with which we have already dealt, emotionality, or activity, is a general flavor which can be detected or savored in practically everything that the person does, feels, or thinks. . . . For the philosophically minded psychologist we may say that the notion of the syndrome and the technique of syndrome analysis arises from a dissatisfaction with the concept of causality and also represents an attempt to combine synthetic and analytic methodologies, so that both wholes and specificities may be dealt with without doing violence to either." Maslow, "The Dynamics of Psychological Security-Insecurity," *Character and Personality,* X (1941–42), 331–32.

[132] I am not implying that authoritarianism in the broader syndrome sense is a disease; this is a question of preferences on how to define "disease."

as superior in everything," and vice versa for the perceivedly inferior person; (4) "a strong drive for power, status, external prestige"; (5) "hatred and hostility against *some* group or other, whichever happens to be most convenient"; (6) a tendency to judge people by external signs of status or strength; (7) a tendency to have "but one scale of values by which to measure all people and all achievements"; (8) a tendency to identify kindness with weakness, cruelty with strength; (9) a tendency to use people as mere instruments; (10) a tendency toward both sadism and masochism, toward both cruelty and bootlicking, as each situation may demand or admit. These are only the most important among the attributes he lists.[133]

So far, even the mere existence of authoritarian syndromes in certain personality types had in large part been a matter of conjecture. Freudian and Frommian theory provided the most important hypothetical premises, and the only quasiempirical support for the conclusions was found in the clinical experience of some psychoanalysts.

The Authoritarian Personality reports on the first major attempt to demonstrate the presence and characteristics of an authoritarian syndrome in existing personality types. In many ways the California study marks a new plateau in the growth of social psychology, both theoretically and researchwise. Theoretically, first, because this study was eminently successful in demonstrating the existence of authoritarian syndromes. Its success is underlined by hundreds of follow-up studies. Secondly, it gave some preliminary although somewhat shaky evidence for the Freudian assumption that childhood backgrounds are crucially important in the determination of adult personality types. Researchwise, the California study marks a new epoch in combining for the first time the techniques of clinical interviews and projective tests with the technique of survey questionnaires administered to sizable numbers of people. The California study certainly did not perfect this combination of techniques, but it initiated them and thus opened new avenues toward richer supplies of data and toward greater validation prospects.

No general evaluation of the California study is called for here. My interest in it is for present purposes limited to a search for two kinds of data: data bearing on the existence of authoritarian and antiauthoritarian syndromes and data bearing on their genesis. The first class of data will be considered in this and the next subsection, and the second class in the following subsection. Needless to say, I shall try to take advantage of competent critical reviews of *The Authoritarian Personality*[134] in evaluating both classes of data. I shall also discuss various data from later studies. But it must be emphasized that I have space for only the briefest kind of a sum-

---

[133] "The Authoritarian Character Structure," *Journal of Social Psychology,* XVIII (1943), 401–11. See also Maslow: "Self-Actualizing People: A Study of Psychological Health," *Personality Symposium,* VII (1949), 11–34. Maslow expresses his indebtedness to Fromm in the context from which I am quoting.

[134] The best informed and most valuable criticisms have appeared in Christie and Jahoda (eds.), *Studies in the Scope and Method of "The Authoritarian Personality."* See especially the contributions of Hyman and Sheatsley and of Christie. See also Luchins, "Personality and Prejudice: A Critique," *Journal of Social Psychology,* XXXII, (1950), 79–94.

mary of the most important research findings in this field, and it will be an impressionistic rather than a systematic summary.

The influence of Fromm's and Maslow's descriptions of the authoritarian character is evident in the make-up of the California F scale, composed of items designed to measure just the kind of attitudes the former writers had attributed to the authoritarian personality or character.[135] In its final shape, the F scale was considered capable of giving measurements on these nine variables within the authoritarian syndrome: (a) *Conventionalism:* rigid adherence to conventional, middle-class values (4 items); (b) *Authoritarian Submission:* submissive, uncritical attitude toward idealized moral authorities of the ingroup (7 items); (c) *Authoritarian Aggression:* tendency to be on the lookout for, and to condemn, reject, and punish people who violate conventional values (8 items); (d) *Antiintraception:* opposition to the subjective, the imaginative, the tender-minded (4 items); (e) *Superstition and Stereotypy:* the belief in mystical determinants of the individual's fate, and the disposition to think in rigid categories (6 items); (f) *Power and "Toughness":* preoccupation with the dominance-submission, strong-weak, leader-follower dimension; identification with power figures; overemphasis on the conventionalized attributes of the ego; exaggerated assertion of strength and toughness (7 items); (g) *Destructiveness and Cynicism:* generalized hostility, vilification of the human (2 items); (h) *Projectivity:* the disposition to believe that wild and dangerous things go on in the world, and the projection outward of unconscious emotional impulses (5 items); (i) *Sex:* exaggerated concern with sexual "goings-on" (3 items).[136]

These categories do not correspond wholly to Maslow's. The chief difference in emphasis appears to be that Maslow stresses "jungle-philosophy" as the central theme, while the California study stresses a hierarchical structuring of the world. Both themes express the same personality tendency, however, as applied to differently perceived social situations. In a society or realm of society perceived as static and well organized, the authoritarian personality will be concerned with power stratification. When he does not see any stable power structure, he will perceive a free-for-all fight to establish one. In other words, the difference in emphasis boils down to a difference, to some extent externally determined, between preoccupations with a static or a dynamic power structure. For the populations of Americans studied in the California project, the society in which they lived may have seemed fairly well stratified with respect to power.

[135] Debts are expressed not only to Fromm and Maslow, but also to Erikson, Chisholm, and Reich. See *The Authoritarian Personality,* p. 231. The scale is called "F scale" because it was believed that it measured "potential fascism." The broader term "authoritarianism" was preferred in the title. Each scale item took the form of a statement in a questionnaire (briefest example: "Familiarity breeds contempt"), and the respondents were asked to indicate their attitude to each statement by marking it with one of six symbols ranging from "strong support, agreement" ($+3$) to "strong opposition, disagreement" (-3).

[136] *Ibid.,* pp. 255–57, cf. 245, 253, 260, and 846. Some items occur in more than one subscale, and several versions of the F scale were used in the California study, with total number of items varying between 30 and 38.

The only clear-cut difference between the F scale conception of authoritarianism and Maslow's is that the F scale deliberately excludes reference to ethnic prejudice. This was done because a separate measure of *ethnocentrism* was desired; I shall come back to the California E scale shortly. When I in the present study talk about authoritarianism in the syndrome sense I include ethnocentrism, unless I say otherwise.

It would lead much too far afield to consider the evidence on all the nine variables in the F scale, to say nothing of all the additional variables that Maslow and a number of later theorists and experimenters have attributed to the authoritarian syndrome. My inquiry in this subsection will be confined to, first, a consideration of evidence from the California study and a couple of later studies pertaining to the reliability and validity of the F scale. This first problem is to demonstrate the existence of an authoritarian syndrome, not to draw a map of its specific components.[137] Secondly, I shall consider evidence on the relatedness between high scores on the F scale and ethnocentrism. This is the problem of demonstrating that the authoritarian syndrome includes a proneness to racial prejudice. Finally, I shall consider evidence on another set of components in the authoritarian syndrome, which has been named "intolerance of ambiguity."[138]

For my immediate purposes, the most important result of the California study is that the reality of the authoritarian syndrome was demonstrated. It was shown (a) that individuals who scored "high" on some F scale items tended to score "high" on most other items as well and (b) that all the different population samples used tended to exhibit a roughly parallel dispersion along the continuum from high to low scores on the F scale. In other words, it was found that the F scale has psychological unity and that it can be used as an instrument to differentiate between "highs" or "authoritarian personalities" and "lows" or "nonauthoritarian personalities."

Complete cross-correlations between scores on all F scale items were worked out only for one population in the California study. This group consisted of 517 women students in an elementary psychology class at the University of California in Berkeley. On the average, the scores on single items intercorrelated positively with each other above the one percent level of significance. And when the scores on each item were correlated with the scores on the remainder of the scale, every one of them correlated significantly at considerably above the one percent level.[139]

Many criticisms have been leveled at the authors of the California study for the lack of caution in interpreting some of the findings, in view of the fact that no representative population sample was used and in view of

---

[137] The map implied in the F scale is, of course, an artifact. It may be assumed that authoritarian syndromes can be found also with other scales introducing slightly different variables. Much further research is needed before we can identify and rank all components of an authoritarian syndrome characteristic of given persons or groups in the order of the relative importance (and most meaningful delimitation) of each component.

[138] Frenkel-Brunswik, "Intolerance of Ambiguity as an Emotional and Perceptual Variable," *Journal of Personality*, XVIII (1949), 108–43.

[139] *The Authoritarian Personality*, pp. 261–62.

various other methodological shortcomings as well.[140] One of these other shortcomings has to do with the intercorrelations between F scale scores and the scores of the same population groups on other attitude scales, notably the E scale (Ethnocentrism)[141] and the PEC scale (Politico-economic Conservatism).[142]

In the first place, it was sometimes overlooked that the formulation of scale items is a quite arbitrary process, so that it has no real meaning whatsoever to observe that a group or an individual scores higher on one of these scales than on another.[143] Secondly, and more important, the authors committed a mistake in believing they could combine two purposes in their development of the F scale: build an instrument for the indirect measurement of prejudice and at the same time measure the relationship between ethnocentrism and the authoritarian syndrome. The F scale was developed in stages by exclusion of the items that correlated least well with the E scale, until the correlations between the two scales reached a level of .77. This procedure certainly served the purpose of developing an indirect measure of anti-Semitism, useful in situations where this issue is a ticklish one, but to the same extent it is no longer permissible to treat this subsequent intercorrelation as a finding.[144]

Nevertheless, much significance remains in the fact that it was possible to find plausible indices of anti-Semitism, anti-Negroism and other kinds of ethnocentrism, which in the various populations studied consistently tended to correlate highly with the F scale measure of authoritarian tendencies. For all the methodological imperfections in the California study, it demonstrated for the first time by means of survey techniques the presence of very general personality tendencies, with a scope wide enough to include reliable variation patterns both inside and outside of the range of the F scale.[145]

One crucially important aspect of the California study must be left out of account here: the attempt to validate by independent measures the personality syndromes revealed by the questionnaire data. For the first time

---

[140] See especially Hyman and Sheatsley, in Christie and Jahoda (eds.), *Studies in the Scope and Method of "The Authoritarian Personality."* The majority of around 2,000 respondents were middle-class residents of the San Francisco Bay area and members of some organization, through which they were contacted.

[141] "A primary characteristic of ethnocentric ideology is the generality of outgroup rejection." See *The Authoritarian Personality*, pp. 147 and ff., especially p. 150.

[142] The California findings on politico-economic conservatism appear less convincing than many other findings, chiefly because of similarities in content between the F scale and the PEC scale. See Hyman and Sheatsley in Christie and Jahoda (eds.), *Studies in the Scope and Method of "The Authoritarian Personality,"* pp. 73–74. Also, radicalism-conservatism is more of a surface variable than are ethnocentrism and authoritarianism and therefore less relevant to our psychological theory. Also for reasons of space limitations, there will be no discussion of evidence on politico-economic conservatism in this chapter.

[143] One example: "Once again the group means on PEC are significantly higher than those on E . . . , suggesting that the level of conservatism is higher than the level of ethnocentrism." *The Authoritarian Personality*, pp. 164–65.

[144] *Ibid.*, pp. 222 ff.; and Hyman and Sheatsley, in Christie and Jahoda (eds.), *Studies in the Scope and Method of "The Anthoritarian Personality,"* pp. 74 ff.

[145] *The Authoritarian Personality*, especially pp. 262–69.

in behavioral research, an attempt was made to combine survey techniques with an extensive use of clinical interviews as well as projective techniques.

This was a pioneering venture, and methodological perfection was not to be expected. Indeed, quite strong and sometimes well-founded methodological criticisms have created considerable doubt about the validity of the findings from this part of the study.[146] Nevertheless, let me list these tentative findings from the clinical interview data: Authoritarian personalities, as compared to nonauthoritarians, tend to exhibit (1) more severe *repressions,* or more restricted selves; (2) more *cognitive prejudice,* or a stronger tendency to project their own aggression and other undesirable traits onto outgroups; (3) more of a tendency toward *conventional conformity* and toward rejection of nonconformist tendencies both in themselves and in other people; (4) *power-orientation,* or a preoccupation with problems of power; and (5) a general *intolerance of ambiguities* in both cognitive and emotional realms.[147]

It would not seem bold to assume that by now it has been definitely established that authoritarianism, which is one important type of deficiency in psychological freedom, tends to occur as part of a whole syndrome that characterizes an authoritarian *and* ethnocentric personality. It remains to be considered whether corroboration has been found also for the somewhat more tenuous California findings culled from clinical interviews and projective data that relate intolerance of ambiguity to the authoritarian syndrome. The significance of this inquiry to the problem in this chapter will be more apparent if I now reintroduce some explicit reference to the theory of psychological freedom.

It has been suggested that authoritarianism is one likely outcome of a childhood situation in which impulses of hostility against parents have given rise to great anxiety and have been repressed. What the child has "learned" is the necessity for uncritical submissiveness toward authority figures. But he has also "learned" some other things, it would seem to follow from the same premises, and these following conclusions would seem to make tentative sense out of a number of findings from the California study and related, more recent studies.

In the first place, as we have seen already, the child has learned the importance of finding nondangerous objects for whatever hostility impulses he is unable to repress. At first it may be the boys in the next street. Later the Jews, the Negroes, or the communists will do. Or, as among the Navaho Indians, the supposed witches may serve as the scapegoats. The relationship between authoritarianism and ethnocentrism or prejudice, which has been discussed already, makes sense from this point of view. With a high degree of psychological freedom, an individual is able to face the existence of hostile impulses in his own self, and he either keeps them under

---

[146] See especially the papers by Hyman and Sheatsley and by Christie, in Christie and Jahoda (eds.), *Studies in the Scope and Method of "The Authoritarian Personality."*

[147] *The Authoritarian Personality,* chaps. IX–XV.

conscious control or he expresses aggression against those who in his rational judgment have earned his hostility.

Secondly, and this is the hypothesis before us, the authoritarian person has acquired the mental habit of strict categorizing, both emotionally and cognitively. A rigidly defended ego must impute rigidity to the external world of facts and values. Both ambiguity and flexibility and even complexity are threatening and therefore to be denied or shunned.

Thirdly, the authoritarian individual is likely to conform and demand conformity to convention whenever possible. This is one way to avoid ambiguous situations, as we shall see.

Fourthly and finally, so far as this book is concerned, the authoritarian person is likely to suffer from ambivalence in his attitude toward himself, and he may be expected to try to overcome his deficient self-esteem by building a cognitively glorified self-image. Anxiety about one's own worth may plausibly give rise to this type of "argument" to the effect that one's self is worthy of esteem.

Let us now first consider the factor of intolerance of *emotional* ambiguity. What the authoritarian personality cannot face in interpersonal relationships is emotional ambivalence or even complexity. His cognitive insight must be adjusted, and if necessary distorted, to make his social surroundings seem suitable objects for his love, hate, or indifference. The authoritarian person must glorify his parents, since they must seem to justify his complete love and no hostility at all. And the same goes for other people he loves, and for his movement if he is a member of one, and for his country to the extent that he is a nationalist. For the same reason he can see no good intentions and never a good act or an excusing circumstance in the behavior of, say, the Jews, the Negroes, or the communists or whoever constitute his main outgroup.

In a series of studies of prejudice in children Else Frenkel-Brunswik has been collecting evidence on the possible connection between ethnocentrism (with condemnation of outgroups) and glorification of parents. In one of her preliminary reports she states:

While unprejudiced children are more apt to see positive as well as negative features in their parents and can accept feelings of love and hate towards the same persons without too much anxiety or conflict, ethnocentric children frequently seem compelled to dramatize the image of the parents by seeing them once, and openly, as altogether good, and then, and mostly covertly, as altogether bad. These latter children split the positive from the negative sides of their feelings and attitudes rather than become aware of their coexistence. This pattern of denial of ambivalence constitutes a break in the integration of personality.[148]

[148] "Further Contributions by a Contributor to 'The Authoritarian Personality,'" in Christie and Jahoda, (eds.), *Studies in the Scope and Method of "The Authoritarian Personality,"* p. 240. Negative feelings of prejudiced children toward their parents are revealed by projective techniques: "Many of the children in this group who display only glorification and admiration for their parents in direct questioning omit the parents from the list of people they would choose as companions on a desert island. Or in their responses to parental figures on the Thematic Apperception Test, they tend to stress only the coercive and punitive aspects of parents." *Ibid.*

Intolerance of *cognitive* ambiguity has in several neat experiments been shown to correlate with ethnocentrism. It is possible to distinguish between two aspects of this need for strict cognitive categorizing: the fondness for clear-cut stereotypes, and the tendency to hold on to stereotypes as well as other concepts and insights irrespective of pertinent new experience. Both stereotyping and persevering behavior are necessary for all of us. What typifies the authoritarians or ethnocentrics, as various experiments indicate, are unusually high degrees of oversimplification in stereotyping and of rigidity in perseveration.

A "stereotype," as Krech and Crutchfield point out, may be either a sociological or a psychological concept: "(1) It may refer to a tendency for a given belief to be widespread in a society . . . [or] (2) the concept may refer to a tendency for a belief to be oversimplified in content and unresponsive to the objective facts."[149] Let me choose the psychological concept, but for the moment leave out its dynamic dimension, and define a stereotype as an oversimplified factual belief. Frequently the term is limited to oversimplified beliefs about different nations or other kinds of population groups, but this is a purely practical limitation with no independent significance in psychological theory. Highly stereotyped perceptions of individuals would seem to be psychologically equivalent to correspondingly oversimplified notions about larger groups.

Jones reports on a study in which 80 high scorers and 80 low scorers on the F scale, all Navy recruits, were asked to describe their impressions of a platoon leader (in another regiment) on the basis of listening to excerpts from an interview recording. The following conclusion is pertinent to our immediate problem: "In the perception and judgment of others, authoritarians seem to be more insensitive than nonauthoritarians to the characteristics of others. This is true even when the attribute of personal power or forcefulness, to which authoritarians are allegedly sensitive, is experimentally varied."[150]

A different kind of confirmation of the hypothesis that authoritarianism is related to a need for cognitive oversimplification is furnished by Frank Barron, who has found that authoritarians tend to have a general preference for simplicity in their art appreciation, while nonauthoritarians tend to have a taste for complexity.[151] This makes it plausible to consider extreme stereotyping tendencies just one aspect of a pervasive need for simplicity in one's perceptual and cognitive categories. This in turn may be considered one general approach toward facilitating the defense of an insecure ego.

Convincing tests of the personality-relatedness of extreme over-all tendencies to stereotype are more likely to appear with reference to such factors as personal impression-formation or artistic taste than with reference to national or group stereotypes. In most communities there are institutional

---

[149] Krech and Crutchfield, *Social Psychology,* p. 171.

[150] Jones, "Authoritarianism as a Determinant of First-Impression Formation," *Journal of Personality,* XXIII, No. 1 (1954), 126.

[151] "Complexity-Simplicity as a Personality Dimension," *Journal of Abnormal and Social Psychology,* XLVIII, No. 2 (1953), 163–72.

pressures relating to group stereotypes, and it is usually not easy to tell to what extent extreme stereotypers have developed primarily because their personalities require simplicity or primarily because they have been especially sensitive to, or exposed to, group norms pertaining to stereotypes.

An interesting illustration of this difficulty is given by B. Terry Prothro, who found that anti-Negro prejudice among 383 Louisiana adults was frequent also among subjects who were low on general ethnocentrism. Anti-Semitism, on the other hand, was highly correlated with general ethnocentrism.[152] It is an inescapable conclusion that many people have anti-Negro prejudice induced by social pressures rather than personality propensities. The additional and somewhat more subtle point that belongs here is this: Correlations between anti-Semitism and general ethnocentrism, while they seem to confirm the importance of personality factors predisposing toward anti-Semitism, tell us nothing about possible relationships between ethnocentrism and needs for stereotypes. Many communities and families tend to induce stereotypes of varying extremity. It appears most plausible to believe that anti-Semites may be prone to hold extreme stereotypes about Jews because of their hostility much more than because of a need for cognitive simplicity. This is still largely a matter of conjecture. What data like those of Jones and of Barron seem to indicate is that a need for cognitive simplicity is likely to be one additional factor in the total explanation of the stereotypes of ethnocentric individuals.

Let us now consider the dynamic side of the general tendency to be intolerant of cognitive ambiguity. Rigid perseveration in stereotypes and in beliefs and other habits has been shown to correlate with ethnocentrism and can therefore be assumed to relate inversely to psychological freedom.

The most convincing series of experiments leading to this conclusion has been reported by Milton Rokeach. He selected students who were either high or low on ethnocentrism scores and presented them with a number of simple problems. First came a series of ten arithmetical problems, in which the first five could be solved by the same mental operation. The last five problems, on the other hand, were solvable by the same method but could also be solved in a much simpler way. It turned out that the 35 non-ethnocentric students were almost as rigid as the 35 ethnocentrics in solving problem no. 6, but the former caught on to the simpler method much more quickly, and by problem no. 10 more than twice as many in the former group as compared to the latter group had switched to the simpler method. "The highs solved an average of 2.23 problems [out of five] in a rigid manner as against an average of 1.37 problems solved rigidly by the lows." Similar results were obtained in an experiment on direction-giving problems on a simple map of a few blocks in an imaginary city.[153]

---

[152] "Ethnocentrism and Anti-Negro Attitudes in the Deep South," *Journal of Abnormal and Social Psychology*, XLVIII, No. 1 (1952), 105–8.

[153] "Generalized Mental Rigidity as a Factor in Ethnocentrism," *Journal of Abnormal and Social Psychology*, XLIII, No. 3 (1948), 264 and 259–78. Rokeach has also hypothesized about and studied additional aspects of intolerance of cognitive ambiguity, notably "concreteness" in thinking and "narrow-mindedness" in cognitive outlook. These problems come close to the

Another experiment is reported by Jack Block and Jeanne Block, who studied norm formation in judgments of the autokinetic phenomenon. Watching a small and rather dim source of light in a dark room, each subject was asked to indicate by pushing a button when the light started to move (or seemed to do so, due to the autokinetic illusion). Five seconds later the light would go off, and the subject would estimate in inches the distance between himself and the light (on a scratch pad in the dark). This procedure was repeated a hundred times for each subject, who used on the average 45 minutes on the whole experiment. It was found that ethnocentric subjects tended to establish a norm, in this case a persistent distance estimate, considerably more rapidly than did the nonethnocentrics.[154] This might perhaps also be seen as a study of stereotyping, but the main point is that the subjects tended to stick to their norm over time, and the ethnocentrics needed an anchor sooner than did the nonethnocentrics.

Else Frenkel-Brunswik reports on an experiment on children in which the "stereotype" was given at the outset, but its adequacy in describing what the children were seeing was gradually removed. A picture of a dog was shown,

followed by a number of pictures representing transitional stages leading finally to the picture of a cat. At every stage the subjects were asked to identify the object on the given card. In spite of the fact that the cards were not too well drawn for the purpose, distinct trends became evident. The prejudiced group tended to hold on longer to the first object and to respond more slowly to the changing stimuli. There was greater reluctance to give up the original object about which one had felt relatively certain and a tendency not to see what did not harmonize with the first set as well as a shying away from transitional solutions.[155]

Another line of experiments suggest that rigidity in problem-solving tends to vary with amounts of frustration in the problem-solving situation. Richard Christie has provided data confirming this hypothesis both in college students and in grade school children. His procedure with the students was first to administer a number of somewhat complex arithmetical problems that could all be solved by the same method. Next followed a Rokeach-

---

problem of stereotyping, but must be left out of the present account. See *ibid.*, and further Rokeach, "A Method for Studying Individual Differences in 'Narrow-Mindedness,'" and "'Narrow-Mindedness' and Personality," both in *Journal of Personality*, XX, No. 2 (1951), 219–33 and 234–51; and "Prejudice, Concreteness of Thinking, and Reification in Thinking," *Journal of Abnormal and Social Psychology*, XLVI, No. 1 (1951), 83–91. More recent studies are reported by Rokeach and Eglash, "A Scale for Measuring Intellectual Conviction," *Journal of Social Psychology*, XLIV (1956), 135–41; by Rokeach and Fruchter, "A Factorial Study of Dogmatism and Related Concepts," *Journal of Abnormal and Social Psychology*, LIII, No. 3 (1956), 356–60; and in two reports by Rokeach, in which research findings and theoretical problems are given equal attention: "Political and Religious Dogmatism: An Alternative to the Authoritarian Personality," *Psychological Monographs*, LXX, No. 18 (No. 425, 1956), 1–43, and "On the Unity of Thought and Belief," *Journal of Personality*, XXV, No. 2 (1956), 224–50.

154 "An Investigation of the Relationship Between Intolerance of Ambiguity and Ethnocentrism," *Journal of Personality*, XIX, No. 3 (1951), 303–11.

155 "Intolerance of Ambiguity as an Emotional and Perceptual Variable," *Journal of Personality*, XVIII (1949), 128.

type test problem, solvable by the same method but also by a much simpler approach. The minority who switched were excluded from the crucial experiment. In the majority, it was assumed that a "set" had been established. Afterwards, an experimental group was given a problem that was unsolvable, while a control group was given a solvable problem. Finally, an additional problem, different in type from the earlier ones, was given to both groups. It turned out that the experimental group, which by now presumably was frustrated by their fruitless efforts on the unsolvable problem, averaged more than twice the time that the nonfrustrated group spent on solving the last problem.[156]

Data such as these[157] appear to support the contention that authoritarianism, or let me say the authoritarian-ethnocentric syndrome, is only *one* kind of deficiency in psychological freedom. Another and a more general type of deficiency is attributable to *frustration*. This concept may for my purposes be defined as the blocking of one or more of the individual's goals, or the impact on him of a situation in which some pressing need remains unfulfilled.[158] It has been demonstrated also in rat experiments that severe frustration reduces the capacity for translating pressing needs into need-reducing behavior.[159] The important theoretical conclusion that follows from these various observations is, I believe, that *authoritarianism may be considered one chronic source of frustration*, which in life situations may or may not be augmented by situationally induced frustration.

A neat confirmation of the interconnection between characterological and situational types of frustration has been provided by Shirley Adler, one of Christie's students. On the basis of Maslow's Security-Insecurity Test,[160] 54 insecure and 54 secure New York University undergraduates were selected for the experiment. One half of each group was alternately put in a task-oriented and in an ego-oriented situation for arithmetical tests. Task-orientation here means that the subjects are given the impression that the experimenter is interested in how the problems can be solved rather than in judging each individual's performance. In the ego-oriented situation the test is called an intelligence test in which each subject's performance will be compared to that of all the others. The assumption is that this type of ego-orientation for most subjects will be more likely to provoke anxiety and frustration during the test.[161] The measure of rigidity was the time used to solve a different kind of problem after a habit had been established in a series of six inherently similar problems. It turned out that the

---

[156] *The Effects of Frustration Upon Rigidity in Problem Solution*, pp. 296–97. The experiment on grade-school children was similar in most respects, and the results came out in the same direction.

[157] See also below, pp. 206–28.

[158] See Murphy, *Personality*, pp. 305 ff. Cf. below, pp. 301–3.

[159] See Maier, *Frustration: The Study of Behavior without a Goal*.

[160] Maslow, Hirsh, Stein, and Honigmann, "A Clinically Derived Test for Measuring Psychological Security-Insecurity," *Journal of General Psychology*, XXXIII (1945), 21–41.

[161] The goal is presumably to better on the problems than most others, or to avoid doing worse. This goal is blocked temporarily both by complexities in the problems and by the absence of knowledge about how the others are doing.

insecure group in the ego-involved situation averaged high rigidity scores, but so did the secure group in the task-oriented situation. Both the task-oriented insecures and the ego-oriented secures did considerably better on the test problem. It is concluded that "too high a level of motivation resulted in fixed and rigid behavior, while too little motivation made for an expenditure of least effort. Intermediate levels of motivation provided optimal conditions for problem-solving."[162]

The measure of rigidity in Adler's study leaves something to be desired, since it also is taken to indicate lack of motivation. However, since two kinds of motivational factors are manipulated as independent variables and thus accounted for, this is not a serious objection.[163] The value of this study, it seems to me, is in the confirmation it provides for the functional theory of anxiety expounded above, following Kierkegaard and Sullivan. Anxiety, or frustration,[164] furnishes an essential stimulus for human growth and learning, unless and until the amount of anxiety or frustration exceeds the individual's ability to cope with it. Relatively secure individuals have a higher "threshold" for situationally induced anxiety compared to relatively insecure individuals. Authoritarians have a lower frustration threshold compared to individuals who are psychologically free; in extreme cases, the latter have no repressed anxieties whose defenses can be exploded in anxiety-provoking situations.

Intolerance of ambiguity is a more general syndrome than authoritarianism, even in the F scale sense. There are some reasons to believe that also antiauthoritarians tend to be high on intolerance of ambiguity, as we shall see in the next subsection. Furthermore, it is also a more basic syndrome in the sense that it seems more immediately connected with the ego-defense mechanism of repression.[165] Repression distorts the external world as well as the self in terms of acceptable categories; the underlying anxiety demands strictness and rigidity in these categories. Authoritarianism and anti-authoritarianism are types of interpersonal orientation facilitating social intercourse and a semblance of self-esteem for individuals who are low in psychological freedom and who are therefore fearful of ambivalence and ambiguity in their emotional and perceptual-cognitive worlds.

Realistically speaking, the world is full of uncertainties, contradictions, ambiguities, and it takes a superhuman amount of psychological freedom to face all the confusing facts of life. We all have to distort, simplify, and categorize—but some more than others. The more we are able to face ourselves, the more chaos can we tolerate in the social world around us.

---

[162] Adler, *The Effects of Ego-Involvement on Rigidity in Thinking.*

[163] In fact, it is less of an objection in this case than in the experiments by Rokeach and Christie referred to above.

[164] "Frustration" is a wider concept than "anxiety." Anxiety is always frustrating, but not all frustrations provoke anxiety.

[165] A related, if somewhat more limited and tentatively formulated point, is made by Else Frenkel-Brunswik: "It may well turn out upon further evidence that intolerance of perceptual ambiguity is related to a broader psychological disturbance of which prejudice—itself often a deviation from the prevalent code, especially in school—is but another manifestation." "Intolerance of Ambiguity as an Emotional and Perceptual Variable," *Journal of Personality,* XVIII (1949), 128.

Antiauthoritarianism and the Defensive Rebel

Let me define antiauthoritarianism as *a defensive predisposition to oppose uncritically standards and commands supported by authorities.* The antiauthoritarian syndrome, correspondingly, is a group of attitudes tending to correlate highly with antiauthoritarianism. And the antiauthoritarian personality is a type of person characterized by this attitude syndrome.

Research data available on the antiauthoritarian syndrome are as scant as the data on the authoritarian syndrome are plentiful. In fact, it can hardly be said that it has been conclusively demonstrated that an antiauthoritarian personality type exists. Yet, there are strong theoretical grounds and some empirical indications to this effect. In other words, it appears to be the most fruitful course, both theoretically and researchwise, to assume that the extreme antiauthoritarian exists as a rigid, ego-defensive personality type, not just as a conformist in extremist milieus or a severe but rational social critic.[166]

It seems a useful point of departure in a theory of psychological freedom to hypothesize that severe childhood anxiety in child-parent relationships may be solved in at least two analytically distinct ways: The child represses his hostility toward the parents (or the more authority-invested of the two) and becomes "good"; or he represses his dependency needs and becomes "bad."[167] The "good" child, meaning the child who is always obedient at the cost of developing or maintaining his own capacity for spontaneous expression, is likely to develop an authoritarian personality. The "bad" child, who tends to disobey and be consistently hostile to parents and perceived parent substitutes, is likely to develop an antiauthoritarian personality. Elements of both syndromes are probably present in all of us, to the extent that we in our distant past have submitted to more parental authority than we could integrate in the self, or we have been given and been able to accept less parental love than was needed to build our own self-esteem. But most of us have more of the one syndrome than the other, and the higher our psychological freedom, the less we have of either of the two syndromes.

The authoritarian personality is deficient in psychological freedom because he represses awareness of conflict with authority figures and of hostility toward them. He channels all his aggression toward outgroups and lives in a simplified world of black and white, unable to face the ambiguities and other anxiety-provoking aspects of a more realistic conception of himself and the world around him.

The antiauthoritarian personality is deficient in psychological freedom in the following ways. He represses awareness of his own weakness and dependency needs. He sees all authorities as bad and wicked, and all weak people as exploited and persecuted. He, too, is prone to black-white thinking. He, too, is unable to tolerate the awareness of a complex, ambiguity-ridden world and unable to see the complexity of human motivations in himself and others.

---

[166] See above, pp. 191–92 and note 126 for discussion of and reference to Sarnoff's and Katz's three types of motivations for attitudes.

[167] See above, pp. 183–85.

A tentative distinction should be made between two types of ego-defensive rebels. Up to this point I have been talking of antiauthoritarians, or persons who are neurotically hostile toward all authorities. But it may be assumed that there are also authoritarian rebels, persons who have neurotic hostility toward all ingroup authorities only but who are consistently submissive to all demands of certain outgroup authorities with whom they identify. It is a reasonable assumption that some, though by no means all, Western communists, for example, may exhibit the latter type of deficiency in psychological freedom.[168]

It will be convenient to consider the limited research data available on both attitude syndromes in this subsection, without differentiating sharply between the two contexts. The distinction has not always been clearly made in these researches. Also, they tend to bear on both syndromes simultaneously, whether or not this is anticipated or even observed by the writers in question.

Else Frenkel-Brunswik, in her summary of interview results in *The Authoritarian Personality*, notes that "there is a distinct sub-type among extreme low scorers in whom liberal ideology becomes a cliché that may include an undue glorification of the underdog, and who at the same time shows signs of rigidity in his personality makeup."[169] Adorno, in a more speculative chapter, suggests, perhaps for the first time, that there may be authoritarian rebels as well as rigid antiauthoritarians. Among high scorers, he finds a type characterized by an ambivalent hatred of all authorities, coupled with an underlying desire to capitulate and make common cause with them. He concedes, however, that it may be impossible to distinguish between the authoritarian rebel and the antiauthoritarian personality, at least on a purely psychological level.[170] Among low scorers, Adorno finds the "rigid" type and the "protesting" type, both of which may be considered rebels.[171] In fact, all the "low scoring syndromes," including the "genuine liberal," might have been considered antiauthoritarians of one sort or another, had I not chosen to include the criterion of defensiveness in the definition of this term. But neither Adorno's chapter nor any other chapter in the same volume provides any conclusive systematic evidence for the psychological unity of an antiauthoritarian or a low-scoring, ego-defensive syndrome. In fact, these authors repeatedly state that their low scorers tended to exhibit more variety in types than did the high scorers.[172] Their main concern, anyway, was to study the potentially fascist or authoritarian personality.

Daniel J. Levinson, one of the authors of the California study, later

[168] Edward Shils appears to take it for granted that all of them do. See "Authoritarianism: 'Right' and 'Left,'" in Christie and Jahoda (eds.), *Studies in the Scope and Method of "The Authoritarian Personality,"* pp. 24–29; and also below, pp. 209–10.

[169] *The Authoritarian Personality*, p. 481.

[170] *Ibid.*, pp. 762–63.

[171] *Ibid.*, pp. 771–78.

[172] *Ibid.*, for example, p. 771: "The low scorers are as a whole less 'typed' than the high scorers." Or p. 964: "The low scorers were found to exhibit a wide variety of clinical pictures and complaints."

collaborated with Lawrence A. Dombrose in a study trying to differentiate between more extreme and less extreme low scorers. From an initial non-representative sample of 100 college students, college administrators, and social workers, 40 subjects were found who scored below a certain limit on the California E scale. All subjects had also been scored on a new scale on ideological militancy-pacifism (called the IMP scale), where high scores indicate pacifism and low scores militancy. Significant intercorrelations ($r = .74$) were found between scores on the E scale and the IMP scale in the group of 40 nonethnocentrics. Dombrose and Levinson conclude that "those who *strongly* reject ethnocentrism tend toward militancy in their programs for the propagation and realization of democratic values, whereas those who *moderately* reject ethnocentrism tend toward pacifistic programs."[173] A correlation of .67 was found between the IMP scale and the F scale, indicating differences in broader personality characteristics between more moderate and more extreme liberals.

The authors are aware, however, that these findings do not prove that the more extreme liberals are defensive antiauthoritarians; nor do they prove that the "pacifists" are less ego-defensive than the "militants"; perhaps, indeed, all it proves is that "pacifists" tend to be men of a peaceful disposition.

Clinical studies would be required to bring out the inner dynamics which makes it so difficult for the "pacifistic" democrat to oppose with intensity the authoritarian ideas represented in the E and F scales. . . . The consistent intensity of response on the part of the militant lows to the E, IMP, and F scales raises similar questions for further research. What personality variables determine the intensity of their opposition to authoritarianism and the militancy of their efforts to realize democratic values? To what extent does this intensity reflect dogmatism, to what extent a mature ability to see issues clearly and take a decisive stand?[174]

Milton Rokeach, who has pursued the problem of *dogmatism* as a personality variable, has found (in his student sample and according to his scale) that dogmatism correlates much more highly with authoritarianism than it does with either ethnocentrism or with political conservatism. He concludes that there probably exists a dogmatic personality syndrome and that there is a dogmatism on the left as well as on the right.[175] But he has not demonstrated the existence of an antiauthoritarian syndrome in the sense hypothesized in the present subsection.

It seems to me that Irving A. Taylor has come the closest to demonstrating experimentally a tendency to rigidity, or high perceptual closure, among antiauthoritarians. In a population of 253 Houston, Texas, university students, both the F scale and an ethnic social distance scale were

[173] "Ideological 'Militancy' and 'Pacifism' in Democratic Individuals," *Journal of Social Psychology*, XXXII (1950), p. 112; cf. pp. 101–13. Note that "pacifism" rather unconventionally is used as synonymous with moderation, or "tender-mindedness" (see below, pp. 210–11).

[174] *Ibid.*, pp. 111–12.

[175] "Dogmatism and Opinionation on the Left and on the Right," *American Psychologist*, VII (1952), 310–11. (Abstract); "Political and Religious Dogmatism: An Alternative to the Authoritarian Personality," in *Psychological Monographs*, LXX, No. 18 (No. 425, 1956), 1–43; and "On the Unity of Thought and Belief," in *Journal of Personality*, XXV, No. 2 (1956), 224–50.

administered, as well as a couple of copying-by-pencil perceptual closure tests.[176] The most interesting result came out of a comparison of the groups that were consistently high, medium, or low on both the F scale and the social distance scale. These groups may for my purposes be hypothesized to be composed of predominantly, or in part, authoritarians, nonauthoritarians and antiauthoritarians respectively. This is what he found:

Comparison of perceptual closure means for the categories of the social attitude samples revealed a significant curvilinear relationship for the consistent sample only. . . . There was the finding that extremes were similar with respect to perceptual closure. This was interpreted as supporting the contention that extreme liberals and extreme conservatives are basically similar with regard to personality structure as manifested through perception.[177]

What they tend to have in common, apparently, is a high generalized intolerance of cognitive and emotional ambiguity.

Let me now consider some of the main researches bearing on the "authoritarian rebel." Much of the effort in this field has been devoted to attempts to demonstrate the assumed psychopathology of communists or to attempt to understand and to know how to counteract the appeals of communism.

It is superficially quite plausible to argue from the basis of political similarities, as Edward Shils does, that communists ought to be considered "authoritarians of the left."[178] But his sharp criticisms of *The Authoritarian Personality* for failing to take this position explicitly are hardly well placed, for these main reasons: (1) The California study started out as a study of anti-Semitism and gradually broadened its scope to include potential fascism and the authoritarian syndrome; (2) Although the field work was done at a time when communism caused no great concern for most Americans, the California study did produce the first, if extremely limited and tentative, information on both the rigid low scorer and the rebel high scorer.

Apart from the dubious pertinency of Shils's main criticisms, it seems to me that his argument suffers from a recurrent defect of confusing inductive conclusions from psychological data with deductive inference from political data. He states, for example:

The Bolshevik rule that when temporary tactical collaboration with other groups is necessary, the greatest pains must be taken to retain the complete identity of the Party and to avoid any trend of collaboration which at any point might approximate a genuine fusion provides evidence that the "intolerance of ambiguity" in the definition of situations is certainly not a monopoly of the authoritarianism of the Right.[179]

---

[176] In this kind of test, the subjects are asked to reproduce "just as they áre seen" a couple of simple drawings containing gaps or breaks, as well as a design containing several figures. The relative tendencies to fill in the gaps, both in the drawings and in the design, are taken to indicate relative tendencies to perceptual closure.

[177] *Perceptual Closure and Extreme Social Attitudes,* pp. 92–93.

[178] "Authoritarianism: 'Right' and 'Left,' " in Christie and Jahoda (eds.), *Studies in the Scope and Method of "The Authoritarian Personality,"* especially pp. 30–42.

[179] *Ibid.,* p. 42.

The fact that this political approach is thought expedient in communist party tactics does not prove that party members personalitywise are intolerant of ambiguities in general. At most, it suggests as a promising hypothesis, as yet unproven, that many people join the party primarily in search of certainties that are badly needed in their ego-defensive systems. Some people may perhaps prefer political certainties without scoring very high on intolerance of ambiguity. Some people may also possibly become communists for reasons of rationality based on information available to them, or for reasons of conformity to small group pressures, or to the norms imputed to admired individuals, living or dead. Let me now consider the principal evidence that can be marshaled toward solving this controversial problem.

Two important empirical studies in this area have been made in recent years, one under the direction of H. J. Eysenck in England and the other under Gabriel A. Almond in the United States. The Eysenck project, to be considered first, is the more ambitious one in terms of theory. Its aim appears to be the derivation of general laws for the psychology of political behavior; the study of communists is only incidental to the theoretical purpose. The study directed by Almond, on the other hand, has the main practical purpose of studying the appeals of communism, among Americans, British, Frenchmen, and Italians.

In *The Psychology of Politics* Eysenck presents considerable amounts of data in an effort to prove that two factors only "appear sufficient to account for the great majority of observed relationships between social attitudes" in democratic countries. "One of these factors is the well-known Radicalism-Conservatism continuum (R-factor). The other, which is quite independent of the first, was called Tough-minded versus Tender-minded (T-factor) in memory of a similar distinction made by William James in the philosophical field."[180] Eysenck notes that this last distinction has much in common with Koestler's distinction between the yogi and the commissar. As a preliminary approximation, Eysenck suggests that "the tender-minded set of opinions appears to be dominated by ethical, moralistic, superego, altruistic values, while the tough-minded set of opinions is dominated by realistic, worldly, egoistic values."[181]

This T-factor has a certain common sense plausibility, but the absence of any even moderately specific definitions of the two terms is not reassuring about the theoretical usefulness of the distinction. It is true that Eysenck defines these concepts operationally in terms of the scales he is using to measure this dimension, if it is a dimension; his technique is a factorial analysis. But even a brief glance at the scale items held indicative of tough-vs. tender-mindedness raises serious doubts as to the correspondence of these statements to conventional uses of the two terms.[182] And even if one

---

[180] *The Psychology of Politics*, p. 266. See also Eysenck, "Primary Social Attitudes as Related to Social Class and Political Party," *British Journal of Sociology*, II, No. 3 (1951), 198–209, especially p. 207.

[181] *Psychology of Politics*, p. 132.

[182] Examples of statements which, if accepted, are held by Eysenck and his collaborators to indicate tough-mindedness: "People suffering from incurable diseases should have the choice

could seriously consider the T-dimension plausibly established by Eysenck, his most important conclusion, as Richard Christie convincingly has demonstrated, is based on misinterpretation of his own data. Eysenck claims that "Fascists were found to be a tough-minded Conservative group, Communists a tough-minded Radical group. Conservatives and Socialists were found to be Conservative and Radical respectively on the R-factor and intermediate with respect to the T-factor."[183] Computing from Eysenck's own figure No. 26, Christie finds that the communists actually tend to score roughly half as tough-minded as the fascists do, if the mean of Eysenck's "neutral" group is taken as the base.[184]

Of particular interest in the present context is Eysenck's statement that the California F scale is a measure of authoritarianism and not just potential fascism, since he claims to have found "Communists to make almost as high scores on this scale as Fascists."[185] A few pages later he states that "the F scale is essentially a measure of tough-mindedness rather than of Fascism" and claims as proof for this contention a series of scores obtained by his collaborator, Thelma Coulter: in an unspecified sample of soldiers, 83 noncommunists-nonfascists averaged a score of 75 on the F scale, compared to an average of 94 for 43 male communists and of 159 for 43 male fascists.[186] It seems clear to me that Christie's interpretation of these scores is the more plausible one:

The obvious fact here is that communists *do not* ". . . make almost as high scores on this scale as Fascists . . ." since the difference between communist and fascist scores is an extremely large 65 points whereas the communists differ from the "neutral" group by only 19 points. Once again, Eysenck arbitrarily lumps communists and fascists together in an attempt to indicate their similarity.[187]

And in a more recent study of various English and American populations, Rokeach reports that among 137 English college students, of whom 13 were communists, the latter actually scored *lower* than all other groups (conservatives, liberals, Attlee socialists, and Bevan socialists) on the F scale.[188]

---

of being put painlessly to death"; "A white lie is often a good thing." Examples of statements held to indicate tender-mindedness: "The universe was created by God"; "Birth control, except when recommended by a doctor, should be made illegal." *Ibid.*, pp. 277–79. These statements, in fairness, are among the least plausible ones, in my judgment.

[183] *Ibid.*, p. 266.

[184] *Ibid.*, p. 141, and Christie, "Eysenck's Treatment of the Personality of Communists," *Psychological Bulletin*, LIII, No. 6 (1956), 411–30; see especially pp. 419 and 425–30. A briefer and more limited but no less damaging inquiry which arrived at a similar conclusion is reported by Rokeach and Hanley, "Eysenck's Tender-Mindedness Dimension: A Critique," *Psychological Bulletin*, LIII, No. 2 (1956), 169–76. Both these critical papers are in the same journal immediately followed by replies from Eysenck and rejoinders from his critics. Christie's rejoinder contains a further elaboration on the point referred to in the text; cf. "Some Abuses of Psychology," *Psychological Bulletin*, LIII, No. 6 (1956), 439–51.

[185] *Psychology of Politics*, p. 149.

[186] *Ibid.*, pp. 152–53.

[187] "Eysenck's Treatment of the Personality of Communists," *Psychological Bulletin*, LIII, No. 6 (1956), 425.

[188] "Political and Religious Dogmatism: An Alternative to the Authoritarian Personality," *Psychological Monographs*, LXX, No. 18 (No. 425, 1956), 34. On Rokeach's opinionation and dogmatism scales, on the other hand, the communists in the same group score higher than all the other factions.

The only plausible quantitative data on motivation patterns of communists in several Western countries have been provided by Gabriel A. Almond and his collaborators. Almond recently reported on an intensive interview study of 211 ex-communists, consisting of roughly equal numbers of American, British, French, and Italian former communists.[189] Granting the unrepresentativeness of the sample, the usefulness of this report for my purposes is further limited by the lack of exactitude in psychological descriptions, perhaps a necessity in view of the limited resources available for tackling exceedingly complex problems.

Almond found three main types of neurotic susceptibility to communism: hostility, isolation, and self-rejection. Even if we must take these data with a grain of salt, it is interesting to note that American and British communists in his sample tend to have a much higher incidence of all three types of neurotic susceptibility, as compared to their French and Italian comrades. Also, middle-class respondents report a much higher incidence of neurotic predispositions than those from the working class. Finally, and this will be discussed in a later context, former high-echelon communists report far fewer instances of neurotic motivations to join, as compared to low-echelon and rank-and-file ex-communists.[190] Almond reports that "the feeling most commonly manifested among respondents was resentment, antagonism, rebelliousness, and hatred. In the majority of the cases the resentment appeared to be situationally induced and in conformity with community patterns. But in a substantial number of cases[191] it appeared to be a pattern of chronic and unconscious hostility resulting from family and childhood experiences."[192] It would seem, although it is by no means certain, that most of *these* neurotically inclined communists would be rigid low scorers, rather than authoritarians.

Both "isolation" and "self-rejection" are factors closely connected with deficiencies in self-esteem.[193] Almond points out that loneliness can be situational, or it can be neurotically self-imposed by a type of person "who rejects and withdraws from others because of some deep distrust of men, some fear of being improperly used and hurt."[194] Self-rejection, again, may involve feelings of weakness or unworthiness, or both. "The neurotic adult whose damaging experience occurred in early childhood may carry with him permanently the consequences of such mistreatment in the form of feelings of inadequacy and inferiority, confusions of identity and of role,

---

[189] *The Appeals of Communism.* The author and his collaborators realized that ex-communists cannot provide a sample representative of present-day communists, but they tried to reduce this bias by excluding from their study all ex-communists who had discussed their experiences as party members publicly after their defection, and took various other precautions as well. On the whole, the data appear fairly plausible and are cautiously interpreted. Certainly, they are more informative than no data at all.

[190] *Ibid.*, Chap. 10. For further reference to this last finding, see below, pp. 309–10.

[191] One third of the American and British respondents, one fourth of the Italians, and one fifth of the French. *Ibid.*, p. 261.

[192] *Ibid.*

[193] So is hostility, but in a different way. Neurotic aggressiveness indicates self-hatred covered up by repression of dependency needs and self-assertiveness. Neurotic self-rejection and feelings of isolation indicate conscious or preconscious deficiencies in self-esteem; remedies are sought in self-sacrificing identifications.

[194] *Ibid.*, p. 272.

feelings of unworthiness and of sinfulness. Regardless of his objective situation, he is constantly under pressure to defend himself against the defects which he feels inside himself."[195] This last sentence is strongly reminiscent of the most important theme in Hoffer's *The True Believer*.

If defensively hostile communists are likely to be antiauthoritarians, it would seem equally plausible to hypothesize that those who suffer from lack of self-esteem are likely to be authoritarians in most cases, since they are likely to try to compensate by self-sacrificing identifications with persons perceived as strong or worthy of admiration.

However, there are also indications in Almond's data to the effect that perhaps majorities of communists, and especially among Frenchmen and Italians, fail to exhibit either authoritarian or antiauthoritarian defensiveness. Only among the American respondents did a majority of 58 percent report motives for joining the party that are classified as neurotic. The percentages among the British, French, and Italian respondents, respectively, were 48, 25, and 31, and the average for all respondents was 41 percent.[196]

Another category of data bearing on this problem can be extracted from the tabulations on the political attitudes of ex-communists after their defection from the party. One would expect from authoritarians as well as antiauthoritarians a kind of Budenzlike conversion to some opposite extreme. But at the time of the interviews only 6 percent of the respondents reported conversion to religion, 2 percent were extreme rightists, and 6 percent extreme but noncommunist leftists. By far the largest group, 41 percent, reported views of the moderate left, followed by the politically indifferent and those who had become trade unionists only (13 percent and 12 percent).[197] It is hardly likely that these people even in their period of communist affiliation were authoritarians or antiauthoritarians in my psychological sense, and certainly not if we build on the Freudian basic assumption that neurotic mechanisms and behavior will tend to persist, as a general rule, unless or until therapy or some extremely fortunate and far-reaching interpersonal events intervene.

Herbert E. Krugman, one of Almond's principal collaborators, has investigated 35 case studies of present and former communists undergoing psychoanalysis; these cases were supplied to him by 22 leading American analysts. He reports that "some degree of homosexuality is the most frequently mentioned conflict against which these communist patients are defending themselves," and that "*when the analysts were asked about the functions of communism in the lives of their patients, they were most likely to say something about the way in which communism helped the patient to express either hostility or submissiveness* without feelings of guilt. These

[195] *Ibid.*, p. 280.
[196] *Ibid.*, p. 243. Other categories of motives, tabulated for all respondents, were: ideological interests, 91 percent; self-oriented interests, 47 percent; group-related interests, 39 percent. There are multiple responses, of course. Perhaps it should be stated again that the validity of these data is highly questionable; even the categories themselves invite serious doubts as to their meaningfulness. Yet, it may also be said once again that these are the only available quantitative data in this field.
[197] *Ibid.*, pp. 357 ff.

two functions were noted in 10 and 8 cases, respectively, whereas no other function of communism received more than four mentions."[198]

There is neither space nor any great use in this context for considering the complexities of these cases, as, for example, the different tendencies in men and women patients in developing and solving their homosexual problems. Krugman's observations appear to support the impression gained already that deficiencies in psychological freedom among communists can be connected with authoritarianism in some cases and with antiauthoritarianism in other cases. It seems again a plausible assumption that the anti-authoritarians are conspicuous among those who seek a superego platform for the expression of hostility, while the authoritarians are prominent among those who seek an excuse for extreme submissive behavior.

For essentially the same reasons that American radicals, being fewer and socially less rewarded, are likely to include a higher proportion of defensives than American conservatives and liberals, it is plausible to expect a relatively high incidence of defensive syndromes among American communists today. In addition, there is the authoritarian attraction of Soviet power, a mighty ally that no other radical movement can match. Again, there are the tremendous social and legal pressures against communists at the present time, which may attract masochists more powerfully than other movements and which conceivably also may make masochists out of once relatively healthy individuals.[199]

When all this has been said, however, it remains to be underlined that beyond Almond's limited and uncertain data we have no evidence on what proportion of communists in any given country are defensives or psychologically free; neither do we know what proportions of the defensives are authoritarians and what proportions are antiauthoritarians.[200]

Another line of research toward isolating a different type of "rebel" personality has been attempted by Howard V. Perlmutter and Arthur J. Brodbeck. These writers have been interested in the xenophile, or the ethnocentric in reverse. Just as there is defensiveness among both extremes on the authoritarianism variable, one might expect to find the same phenomenon also at the lower negative end of the ethnocentricism scale. What might be difficult to predict, starting from the present theoretical scheme, would be the relative prevalence of authoritarian and antiauthoritarian tendencies among persons with strong outgroup–ingroup preferences.

Perlmutter, in a paper on the xenophilic personality, fails to differentiate between the authoritarian and the anti-authoritarian syndrome. He hypothesizes, and quite plausibly, that there are basic similarities between the authoritarian and the xenophile, but he reduces this hypothesis without hesitation to the following prediction: "Individuals scoring higher on Xenophilia should score significantly higher on Authoritarianism than

---

[198] "The Role of Hostility in the Appeal of Communism in the United States," *Psychiatry,* XVI, No. 3 (1953), p. 256 and pp. 253–61.

[199] See below, pp. 233–35.

[200] There probably are also other species of defensives, among communists and non-communists alike. See above, pp. 192–94, and below, pp. 223–26.

individuals scoring low on Xenophilia."[201] An equally plausible prediction, it seems to me, would expect the xenophiles to score significantly lower on authoritarianism. And perhaps a *more* plausible prediction, which Perlmutter apparently did not check on, would state that xenophiles probably tend to exhibit more extreme scores on authoritarianism, both high and low, compared to nonxenophiles who are also nonethnocentrics.

It must be said that Perlmutter found confirmation for the prediction he did test. By implication, the first of my suggested alternative predictions was disconfirmed; the second one was not tested. The subjects in Perlmutter's experiment, 140 female and 130 male students at Boston University, were given questionnaires including many F scale items as well as ten items designed to constitute a xenophilia scale. These items "emphasized preferences for foreign objects, persons, institutions over their domestic counterparts." It was found in both the male and the female student groups that "High Xenophiles" scored significantly higher on authoritarianism, as compared to "Low Xenophiles."

These findings are hard to evaluate, partly also because the findings refer to means of the distributions of each group, and it seems probable that there have been few defensive xenophiles among the respondents. Considerable numbers of relatively extreme xenophiles would have to be studied before one could hope to describe reliably one or more defensive xenophilic syndromes.

In another experiment bordering on the same problem, Perlmutter found correlations between what he misleadingly calls "low self-esteem" and a desire to live abroad for a year (with all expenses paid). Taken at face value, this finding would support the theory that xenophiles tend to be defensives, since deficiencies in self-esteem are a primary source of repression. The trouble is that Perlmutter really found the opposite of what he thought he found. People who report *no* undesirable traits in their self-image are likely to have low self-esteem, as I have suggested,[202] not high self-esteem, as he assumes. And people who attribute five or more undesirable traits to themselves are likely to have a high rather than a low self-esteem, or else they would scarcely have the courage to see themselves in such a critical light. As I read Perlmutter's data, I conclude that respondents with high self-esteem and a critical self-image were less defensive, more outgoing, and more interested in exploring the world, as compared to respondents with low self-esteem and an uncritical self-image, who were hunting for security rather than adventure.[203] But this interpretation makes the "foreign-minded" *less* defensive than the "domestic-minded" respondents and implies that the present data have no bearing on either the authori-

---

[201] "Some Characteristics of the Xenophilic Personality." In the conclusion the author states that he has postulated a "Xenophilic Anti-Authoritarian syndrome."

[202] See above, pp. 175–76. Cf. also Frenkel-Brunswik, "Social Research and the Problem of Values: A Reply," *Journal of Abnormal and Social Psychology*, XLIX, No. 3 (1954), 467.

[203] "Relations between the Self-Image, the Image of the Foreigner, and the Desire to Live Abroad," *Journal of Psychology*, XXXVIII (1954), 131–37. Another finding which stands up better, but is less relevant to my discussion, is that among four main European countries, the respondent's choice for a year abroad appears to coincide with similarity between self-image and the image of the inhabitants in the preferred country.

tarian or the antiauthoritarian xenophile. Indeed, a desire among young students to live abroad for a year, with all expenses paid, can hardly be considered a symptom of neurotic tendencies, even in a somewhat chauvinistic era.

A more sophisticated approach toward understanding the dynamics of the xenophile was taken in an experiment by Brodbeck and Perlmutter, in which a 26-item scale for self-dislike was applied. These items are presumably better indicators of a person's real attitudes toward himself than are self-image check lists, because in this case the respondent is asked more concrete questions about what he usually does, not general questions about who or how good he is. But, as the authors are aware, this approach is still far from fool-proof against repressive distortions.[204] In this survey 141 female and 132 male Boston University students were given the self-dislike scale along with F scale items and the Perlmutter xenophilia scale. Among the male respondents, Brodbeck and Perlmutter found significant positive correlations between xenophilia and self-dislike. Among the female respondents, on the other hand, no significant correlations were found, only slight tendencies in the same direction.[205] The authors speculate that women perhaps are more prone to repression of guilt and thus would be less likely to report correctly on feelings of self-dislike. Here is certainly an intriguing field for further research, in which persistent sex differences may well give us unique opportunities for empirical study of complex oedipal processes.

A clearer demonstration of the dynamics by which low self-esteem may create[206] hostility against ingroups is presented by Irving Sarnoff in his study of anti-Semitism among Jews. Utilizing several projective techniques as well, he used as his main tool a 44-item Jewish anti-Semitism scale. These are his principal findings: the Highs (on the JAS scale) exhibited a greater incidence of negative attitudes toward their parents and toward themselves. The lows had a higher incidence of positive attitudes (measured independently of the negative attitudes) both toward themselves and toward their parents.[207]

By logical necessity, xenophilia and ethnocentrism are opposite characteristics. One cannot at the same time tend to reject all outgroups in favor of the ingroup and reject the ingroup in favor of one or more outgroups. Empirically, as Brodbeck and Perlmutter suggest, the relationship is more complex, however, for it is not always obvious who should be considered the outgroup and who the ingroup. A second generation German-Ameri-

---

[204] One indication that the instrument worked is the finding of consistently increasing self-dislike among low, intermediate, and high (partial F scale) authoritarians, though significantly only for the male respondents. If repression interfered strongly one would expect higher authoritarians to get lower scores on self-dislike. This did not happen in either the male or the female group.

[205] Brodbeck and Perlmutter, "Self-Dislike as a Determinant of Marked Ingroup-Outgroup Preferences," *Journal of Psychology*, XXXVIII (1954), 271–80.

[206] I say *may* create, for the causality is, of course, not demonstrated or easily demonstrable. Underlying factors may determine both tendencies.

[207] "Identification with the Aggressor," *Journal of Personality*, XX, No. 2 (1951), pp. 199–218.

can who prefers things German over things American should probably not be considered a xenophile; the question would be more uncertain if he likes French institutions still better. "Xenophilia or ethnocentrism must be defined with respect to sociological properties of the primary socializer."[208] But if the crucial criterion is a sociological one, then one should not expect marked differences in personality dynamics between xenophiles and ethnocentrics. One man's ingroup may psychologically be another man's outgroup, even if they belong to the same community and the same ethnic and religious group. The psychologically important variable is not the choice of ingroup, but the tendency to differentiate sharply between ingroup and outgroup.

More extreme tendencies of this kind are evidence of intolerance of ambiguity, which in turn may be considered part of a broader syndrome of defensive tendencies. Depending on the person's tendency to submit to or to challenge authorities, he may be called an authoritarian or an antiauthoritarian personality. It appears probable that xenophiles as well as ethnocentrics in more extreme cases will tend to be extreme also in either authoritarianism or in antiauthoritarianism. It may perhaps be speculated that ethnocentrics may tend to cluster more at the authoritarian end, and real xenophiles more at the antiauthoritarian end of this continuum. More research is needed, however, before even this modest type of relationship can be considered established.

From the point of view of psychological freedom, all these four personality characteristics are equally symptoms of defensiveness, or deficiencies in psychological freedom. I shall now inquire whether we have any evidence bearing on the general problem of the origin and development of such deficiencies.

Some Research on the Genesis of Defensive Syndromes

Authoritarianism and antiauthoritarianism are not the only types of deficiencies in psychological freedom, as I have suggested. Even if we consider both syndromes simultaneously, and note the important elements they have in common—above all, a high intolerance of emotional, perceptual, and cognitive ambiguity—it cannot be inferred that all defensive behavior shares this characteristic. But it so happens that most empirical data on patterns of defensiveness in adult personalities are derived from studies of the authoritarian syndrome or some of its components (occasionally components characteristic also of the antiauthoritarian syndrome).

Reliable data on the genesis of defensive syndromes are far from plentiful. I shall first review some data, more or less tenuous, bearing directly on the development of authoritarian personalities. Afterwards I shall discuss some implications for my theory of psychological freedom of a somewhat wider range of data bearing on child training practices, culture, and personality.

Some attention to the childhood backgrounds of extreme ethnocentrics

[208] Brodbeck and Perlmutter, "Self-Dislike as a Determinant of Marked Ingroup-Outgroup Preferences," *Journal of Psychology*, XXXVIII (1954), 272.

and extreme nonethnocentrics was given in the California study. The clinical interviews, in particular, sought to elicit information in this area, but also the questionnaires and the projective techniques yielded some data that were given significance as clues to childhood experience. The importance attributed by the authors to this line of inquiry is indicated in the concluding chapter of the California study, in which the following is announced as the "most crucial result" of the inquiry, in their opinion:

Thus a basically hierarchical, authoritarian, exploitive parent-child relationship is apt to carry over into a power-oriented, exploitively dependent attitude toward one's sex partner and one's God and may well culminate in a political philosophy and social outlook which has no room for anything but a desperate clinging to what appears to be strong and a disdainful rejection of whatever is relegated to the bottom.[209]

The theory of psychological freedom outlined in this chapter leads me to expect that this conclusion is likely to be valid and true, but the California study has not convincingly confirmed it. My theory is very much indebted to the theory underlying the California study, and the correspondence between my expectations and theirs is by no means a matter of pure coincidence only. But it must be said that independent validation of this particular and, indeed, crucial conclusion is missing in the California study.

The chief difficulty is in the factual unreliability of the information given by the interviewees about their childhood backgrounds. The authors are perfectly aware of this shortcoming: "It is difficult to say how much the image of the parent corresponds to reality and how much it is a subjective conception."[210] Now, for some purposes, such as the study of the authoritarian syndrome, this difficulty is not important. But when we are concerned with the problem of the genesis of a personality syndrome, this is a crucial difficulty. Hyman and Sheatsley remark, with a fair amount of documentation, that the authors tend to "oscillate between the view that these reports (on childhood backgrounds) have only a *psychological reality* in conveying the subject's personality, and the view that they have *objective reality* as an accurate description of the subject's actual family life."[211]

What is called for is an approach that includes independent validity checks on this kind of data. Some work in this direction has been attempted, particularly by Else Frenkel-Brunswik in the United States and by Eskil Bjorklund and Joachim Israel in Sweden. The evidence is still scant, as we shall see in a moment, but it may be remarked at the outset that even a scant amount of this latter kind of evidence justifies some optimism about the prospects for validation of the arsenals of as yet tenuous data on genesis problems in *The Authoritarian Personality*.

Investigations of adult personalities, as in the California study, always afford very limited possibilities of validating data on childhood back-

---

[209] *The Authoritarian Personality*, p. 971.

[210] *Ibid.*, p. 358.

[211] Hyman and Sheatsley, in Christie and Jahoda (eds.), *Studies in the Scope and Method of "The Authoritarian Personality,"* p. 99.

grounds by interviews with parents. Many respondents will have lost their parents, and others will have parents in poor health. Important selective factors such as the relative physical health of different personality types may interfere to cast doubts on the results of interview data to be obtained from parents available for interviews. Then, the childhood days of most respondents are far removed, and the memory of parents is subject to much distortion in this sensitive area.

Else Frenkel-Brunswik has sought to get around this difficulty in a series of studies of prejudice in children. She was able to distinguish between ethnocentric and nonethnocentric syndromes in children, much in the same manner as high scorers and low scorers were differentiated and studied in the California study. Although she has not yet published any specified quantitative data on the subject, she has on at least two occasions reported significant relationships between parental attitudes to children and the children's proneness to racial prejudice. In one paper she reports:

As may be seen from the interviews with the parents, the liberal child, in contrast to the ethnocentric child, is more likely to be treated as an equal and to be given the opportunity to express feelings of rebellion or disagreement. . . . Interviews with parents of ethnocentric children show an exaggerated social status-concern. . . . The parents of the ethnocentric child are often socially marginal. The less they can accept their marginality, the more urgent becomes the wish to belong to the privileged groups. . . . With this narrow and steep path in mind such parents are likely to be intolerant of any manifestation on the part of the children which seems to deter from, or oppose, the goal decided upon.[212]

It is unfortunate that the study of parental behavior was a somewhat neglected side-concern in this report and that the limited data are presented in extensive theoretical wrappings only and not in neat and naked tabulations. A few somewhat more explicit data are reported on in a more recent paper, however, in which Else Frenkel-Brunswik and Joan Havel discuss some results from a study of 81 children and of the mothers or both parents of 43 of them. Positive correlations, though statistically inconclusive due to the small numbers, were found between the prejudice of parents and of their children toward each of five different minority groups.[213] However, as the authors note, they do not know to what extent this correlation, if it is valid, is an outcome of direct influence on the attitudes in question and to what extent the influence is indirect, "via a more general formation of character." No evidence, in other words, is contributed in this paper toward explaining the genesis of defensive syndromes.

In another context Frenkel-Brunswik reports, again without giving any numbers, on data she has collected on the socioeconomic history of the families of extremely ethnocentric and of nonethnocentric children:

One of the chief purposes of obtaining this material was to see whether or not the feeling of marginality which is so important to ethnocentrism is determined by sudden changes in the socio-economic status of the families. The assumption in

212 "A Study of Prejudice in Children," *Human Relations*, I, No. 3 (1948), 302.

213 "Prejudice in the Interviews of Children: I. Attitudes Toward Minority Groups," *Journal of Genetic Psychology*, LXXXII (1953), 131 and 91–136.

collecting such data was that loss of status might undermine an individual's social security and that gain in stature might lead to all kinds of attempts to maintain the gain. This hypothesis was only partially confirmed; families with a long history of privileged socio-economic status seemed to be on the whole less ethnocentric than families with unstable histories; but instability of status, *per se,* went almost as often with tolerance as it did with ethnocentrism.[214]

Another attempt toward tracing the impact of parental behavior on child development was made in a Swedish study by Bjorklund and Israel.[215] Here again, unfortunately, this was only a side-concern. The main concern of these investigators was to inquire how widespread authoritarian patterns of child-rearing are in Sweden and to determine the principal personality and social structure determinants of "high" versus "low" authoritarianism of parents in relation to their children.[216] In only one chapter do they attempt to trace the impact on the child of relatively authoritarian versus relatively nonauthoritarian parents. However, only 24 children could be studied, and they differed in sex, in age (from 7 to 12 years old), and in having or not having siblings, older or younger. A number of psychological tests were employed, including a few straight interview questions, but the sample studied was so small and so heterogeneous that there were no results of any substance. But some interesting tendencies were found, and perhaps the most useful result of this part of the investigation was to show the feasibility of studying the impact of types of upbringing on children by administering psychological tests to them. It is to be hoped that resources will be found for further studies along these lines on a larger scale and for follow-up studies on the same children later on.

The guiding hypothesis in this part of the Swedish study—that "if the parents have an authoritarian ideology of upbringing, this gives rise to more frustrations [for the child] than if they had a nonauthoritarian ideology"[217]—must at the present time be judged incomplete. In a more recent American study—conducted by W. H. Sewell, P. H. Mussen, and C. W. Harris—of relationships among specific child training practices, in which the technique of factor analysis was used, it was found that parents who are permissive in not punishing children for misbehavior also tend to participate in little activity with the child and to treat him casually.[218] It is at the very least a possibility that neglect of the child may involve worse frustrations and also lead to greater ego-deficiencies in the child than more punitive, authoritarian ways of upbringing. One of the main difficulties in this area of inquiry is the likelihood that many tendencies with conflicting po-

214 "Interaction of Psychological and Sociological Factors in Political Behavior," *American Political Science Review,* XLVI, No. 1 (1952), 59. Also see below, pp. 229–32.

215 *The Authoritarian Ideology of Upbringing.*

216 Authoritarian upbringing, according to Bjorklund and Israel, may be defined as "social relations between adults and children that are characterized by clearly defined roles of dominance and submission." Nonauthoritarian upbringing, correspondingly, is expressed in parent-child relations determined by well-defined roles of equality. *Ibid.,* p. 13.

217 *Ibid.,* p. 227; cf. pp. 23–24.

218 "Relationships among Child Training Practices," *American Sociological Review,* XX, No. 2 (1955), 137–48.

tential effects on the child are combined in the same parent's behavior as a parent.[219]

Although there must be hundreds of studies bearing on one aspect or another of interrelationships between infancy or childhood experience and later personality development,[220] my inquiry must be limited to brief references to research bearing on three questions. (1) What do we know about the relative importance of infancy, childhood, and later experience in the growth of psychological freedom? (2) What do we know about the effects of love and authority, or in general of indulgence and deprivation, in the first years, on the later development or maintenance of psychological freedom? (3) What do we know about the growth of self-esteem and its relationship to psychological freedom?

Harold Orlansky advances a number of reasons for assuming that important influences on personality formation occur after infancy. He cites ethnological data from cultures in which extremely indulgent care of infants is practiced, but where the average adult nevertheless seems to be insecure, selfish, suspicious.[221] His main conclusion is that "the neonate and young infant is an immature animal organism culturally 'neuter' and psychologically uncommitted (to the extent that its constitution has not committed it), which can only slowly and with much parental effort and the gradual maturation of its faculties, be socialized."[222]

W. Dennis has come the closest, so far as I know, to confirming by experiment on human infants that the first six months are rather unimportant in character development. He raised twin girls from birth till they were seven months old in extreme isolation, separated from each other and not spoken to or played with in any way during the experimental period. He claims that they "yielded during most of the first year a record of development not distinguishable from comparison records of infants in normal environments."[223] However, the experiment does not furnish any

---

[219] There are psychologists who argue that we still know virtually nothing about how children should be brought up in order to achieve maximum mental health; we are inclined to believe that this is to overstate our ignorance, wide as it is. D. O. Hebb, for example, gives vent to his skepticism in rather strong words: "For all we know, a lot of spanking, or unsympathetic parents, may only help to prepare the child for the trials of maturity. It cannot be assumed that what produces emotional disturbances in the infant is bad—nor that it is good: the long-term effects may be the same as the short-term, unrelated, or opposed." *The Organization of Behavior: A Neuropsychological Theory.*

The Institute of Child Welfare in Berkeley, California, has over the past three decades collected longitudinal data on many individuals from early childhood on. When these data are analyzed, we may well gain fairly definite knowledge about much that is now subject to speculation concerning the relationship between the child's upbringing and his personality as an adult.

[220] For a recent survey, cf. Child, "Socialization," in Lindzey (ed.), *Handbook of Social Psychology*, II, 655–92.

[221] "Infant Care and Personality," *Psychological Bulletin*, XLVI, No. 1 (1949), 34. He also cites the fact that boys and girls tend to be treated in exactly the same way as infants but differentially as children, and concludes that later personality differences "must be attributed to biological factors and the differential cultural conditioning of post-infant years." But he leaves open the difficult question of how much each of these two factors may outweigh the other one in importance.

[222] *Ibid.*, p. 41.

[223] "Infant Development under Conditions of Restricted Practice and a Minimum Social Stimulation," *Journal of Genetic Psychology*, LII (1938), 149–58.

conclusive proof of its hypothesis. For all we know for sure, the twin girls may yet reveal, on the psychoanalyst's couch, that these first six months were not as unimportant as the experimenter assumed.

It must be admitted that there is no conclusive experimental evidence on the relative importance of infancy and childhood in personality formation. Clinical evidence on this problem is not to be trusted, for the same reason that the data of *The Authoritarian Personality* on this problem have been largely discounted: It is impossible to furnish reliable checks on the exact extent to which the patient's reconstruction of the distant past is distorted, under the impact of urgent needs that have brought him to the psychiatrist in the first place.

As to the relative weight of childhood and adult experience, there is no choice but to rest on common sense to a large extent. Personalities can undergo deep changes even in advanced years, as, for example, during psychoanalysis or after religious conversions. Again, such experience as war service can brutalize once humane individuals. and a good love relationship can apparently bring out all kinds of humane instincts in a once hardened misanthrope. When all this is said, however, observation shows that many childhood characteristics apparently remain embedded in all personalities and that patterns of individual predispositions strongly influence reactions to later experience.[224]

Let me now turn to the second of my three problems: What do we know about the effects of love and authority in the first years for the later development or maintenance of psychological freedom?

It has been assumed earlier that as infants we start out with a high degree of spontaneity but that our capacity for free expression is progressively reduced as interpersonal anxieties enter our lives. If anxieties cannot be faced, neurotic repressions occur, and intrapersonal communications are not only strained but to some extent blocked.

The most important anxieties of infancy and early childhood presumably arise in the relationship to the parents, in which an initially unmixed indulgence gradually becomes mixed with deprivations of various sorts. Typically, though far from always, the parents are at first the source of love and tenderness only, but they gradually begin to inflict punishments of various kinds as they take on the role of authorities charged with directing the socialization process. Deprivations may perhaps be said to be administered from the very start, in so far as mothers fail to feed their babies on demand. In any case, the refusal of the mother's breast and later the toilet training are typically the first occasions of recurring frustrations and anxieties in the infant and the young child.

Child psychologists charged with advising parents have at different

---

[224] Jan Smedslund argues cogently that all human learning proceeds on the basis of what the individual has learned previously, and he criticizes many learning theorists and experimenters for neglecting this cumulative aspect of human learning. He suggests that the difficulties in curing many neuroses stem from their origin at the very basis of the individual's learning experience, from his very first interpersonal relationships. *A Critical Evaluation of the Current Status of Learning Theory.*

times advanced a variety of recommendations on breast feeding vs. bottle feeding, the proper time and procedures for weaning, toilet training, and other kinds of disciplining of the child. The variety of advice from recognized authorities suggests that there is as yet no very firm basis of knowledge in this field. Orlansky, after discussing a number of more or less relevant experiments, concludes:

It can be conceded that social scientists have failed to produce a definitive answer to the question of the relation between infant disciplines and character development, because of a general lack of historical and cultural sophistication, the difficulty of establishing the validity of the personality measurements employed, and the difficulty of isolating single factors for study. It is hard to see how the last obstacle, in particular, can be overcome.[225]

Orlansky surely overstates the difficulties, however, especially when he continues: "Social phenomena can not readily be subjected to the type of crucial experiment which enables the scientist to support or discredit an hypothesis." This is true as far as it goes, but misleading, since it states that an ideal is impossible and by implication rejects the possibility of approximating the ideal. As we shall see in a moment, it is possible to design experiments that give partial and tentative confirmation to a theory without isolating each single factor at a time. It is by the cumulative effects of such efforts that empirical theory-building is guided, in child psychology as in other fields.

Psychoanalytic theory, it must be admitted, has succeeded in gaining wide and deep influence largely in the absence of even indirect experimental evidence. The last decade, however, has seen great strides in the testing of psychoanalytic theories. Work on the authoritarian personality has been cited above at some length. In this context it would seem appropriate to consider a recently opened field of inquiry that focuses on the concept of *fixation*.

Otto Fenichel describes the process of fixation as follows:

In mental development the progress to a higher level never takes place completely; instead characteristics of the earlier level persist alongside of or behind the new level to some extent. Disturbances of development may occur not only in the form of a total arresting of development but also in the form of retaining more characteristics of earlier stages than is normal.[226]

Fixations may have a variety of determinants; these two, he suggests, may be among the most important:

1. The consequence of experiencing excessive satisfactions at a given level is that this level is renounced only with reluctance; if, later, misfortunes occur, there is always a yearning for the satisfaction formerly enjoyed.
2. A similar effect is wrought by excessive *frustrations* at a given level. One gets the impression that at developmental levels that do not afford enough satisfaction, the organism refuses to go further, demanding the withheld satisfactions. If the frustration has led to repression, the drives in question are thus cut off from

225 "Infant Care and Personality," *Psychological Bulletin*, XLVI, No. 1 (1949), 38.
226 *The Psychoanalytic Theory of Neurosis*, p. 65.

the rest of the personality; they do not participate in further maturation and send up their disturbing derivatives from the unconscious into the conscious.[227]

The most sophisticated statement of a psychoanalytic theory of fixation, so far as I can judge, is found in Erik Erikson's *Childhood and Society,* in which the cultural dimension of the problem also is well integrated. In the course of his discussion, Erikson suggests that premature toilet training and premature disciplining in general perhaps can have serious repercussions for the individual's capacity to exert free choice in his later life. "Much political apathy may have its origin in a general feeling that, after all, matters of apparent choice have been fixed in advance—a state of affairs which becomes fact, indeed, if influential parts of the electorate acquiesce in it because they have learned to view the world as a place where grown-ups talk of choice, but 'fix' things so as to avoid overt friction."[228] This may be called a theory of general fixation on passivity as against effort. It does not easily lend itself to empirical confirmation, however, at least not at the present time.

Fixations are perhaps at first limitations on autonomy or potential freedom rather than on actual psychological freedom. They interfere with maturation, or the growth of new motives, without necessarily blocking the expression of the already existing motives. However, as the child grows up, more pronounced fixations[229] are likely to put him out of step with his social surroundings and their expectations about him, and he is likely to repress his fixation motives in order to allay anxieties about being different or queer.

It is possible to theorize that the repression of dependency needs characterizing the antiauthoritarian personality is the outcome of a dependency fixation in most cases. And the authoritarian syndrome may in part be the outcome of repressed fixations on aggression against prematurely or inconsistently disciplining parents. However, it must be admitted that I am now swimming in deep waters. The only categorical statement I wish to make about the connection between fixations and the two defensive syndromes is that they are all either expressions of or likely sources of deficiencies in psychological freedom.

John M. Whiting and Irvin L. Child have tried to provide an empirical check on Fenichel's two hypotheses, cited above, by utilizing ethnological data from seventy-five nonliterate societies. They set out to seek correlations between indulgences and deprivations in childhood care, on the one hand, and tendencies toward fixations[230] in the average adult personalities, or institutionalized cultural and behavior fixations, on the other hand, in

---

[227] *Ibid.*

[228] *Childhood and Society,* p. 270. The word "fix" refers of course to the behavior of grownups, as interpreted by the child. It has no immediate connection with the word "fixation," which refers to a deep-going psychological process in the child.

[229] And more specific ones than the passivity fixation suggested by the observation quoted from Erikson.

[230] "The essence of the notion of fixation, as we understand it then, is the idea that events occurring in childhood with respect to a particular system of behavior, e.g., oral or sexual behavior, may bring about a continued importance or prepotence of that system of behavior, in comparison with the importance it would have had in the absence of those events." *Child Training and Personality: A Cross-Cultural Study,* p. 130.

significant numbers of these societies. More specifically, they differentiated between five types of indulgences/deprivations as well as fixation indications: oral, anal, genital, dependency, and aggression.[231] They report some tentative confirmatory evidence on the relationship between *infancy* deprivation and fixation, and between *later childhood* overindulgence and fixation, though with somewhat more conviction in the former than in the latter case. Also, they found more support for Fenichel's two hypotheses with respect to fixations on oral, dependency, and aggression needs and much less bearing on anal and genital needs.[232]

This is surely a fruitful avenue for future research. Another advantage of using ethnological data is the possibility of drawing inferences about social structure determinants of neurosis patterns, though there are serious pitfalls to be avoided in this approach.[233]

At the present stage of knowledge on the effects of parental love and parental authority on the child's psychological freedom, relying on psychoanalytic theory and noncrucial research data, the most plausible position would seem to be somewhat as follows:

1. Parental love and tenderness are crucial prerequisites for the development of infants and children into adults without great loss of psychological freedom.[234] The child is likely to be able to cope with anxiety only to the extent that he is emotionally assured of unconditional love and support. Deprivations in this crucial aspect of his first social relationship are likely to lead not only to fixations but to repression and neuroses—and more so the earlier they come.

2. Parental discipline can preserve the child's psychological freedom through a successful socialization process only to the extent that (a) it does not reduce the child's assurance of unmitigated love and tenderness, apart from the frustrating moments of punishment, and (b) it does not put demands on the child before he is mature enough to be able to understand and heed them.[235]

Perhaps both conclusions can be seen in terms of the anxiety theory discussed earlier in this chapter. Undiluted love and tenderness allay the anxieties of the infant and the young child. At the earliest age there is no ego control capable of coping with the hazards of life. As a capacity for ego control develops, parental discipline provides, if the child is fortunate, anxieties of the right amounts (the amounts he can cope with) and of the right kinds (directing his learning processes toward culturally and socially

---

[231] "It might of course be argued that dependent and aggressive behavior are already embraced in the Freudian account of fixation, the former under the rubric of oral dependence and the latter under the rubrics of oral and anal sadism. We prefer, however, to assume that dependence and aggression may more usefully be treated as separate systems of behavior." *Ibid.*, p. 133.

[232] *Ibid.*, especially pp. 315–17.

[233] Cf. below, pp. 228–32.

[234] Much research evidencing the advantage of maternal over institutional care is reviewed in Bowlby, *Maternal Care and Mental Health*.

[235] Mowrer describes five important functions of parental discipline while emphasizing that "only those parents who love their children deeply can discipline them properly" (meaning "effectively" in terms of constructive results). "Discipline and Mental Health," *Learning Theory and Personality Dynamics*, pp. 465–70. For an impressive discussion of eight stages in individual maturation, see Erikson, *Childhood and Society*, pp. 219–34.

desirable behavior). One of the findings of Whiting and Child appears to be better explained in terms of anxiety theory than in most other terms: Fixations resulting from overindulgence suggest that need-gratification to the extent of a *total* removal of anxiety makes it difficult to integrate this need functionally with the other components in the total need structure. Anxiety at times is the oppressor, but is at all other times the teacher, whose complete absence in any important realm of life results in fixations. Fixations in turn tend to give rise to anxieties about pathological symptoms instead of anxieties about gratification of real needs.

The final part of my discussion in this section concerns the problem of self-esteem, its determinants and its relationship to psychological freedom.

An individual's self-esteem has been defined as the cathexis of the self, or the love of the self.[236] It was suggested, in the same context, that a high self-esteem probably makes it possible to maintain a critical self-image. Also, it makes it possible to identify with other people in a self-expanding manner, while for the person with low self-esteem his tendency will be to invest his self almost completely in his most important identifications. Low self-esteem is symptomatic of deficiencies in ego control, leading to identification as a defense mechanism, in search of a new and more worthwhile self-substitute or "identity."

It has been suggested in the first chapter that some of the current trends in psychology and anthropology point toward increasing recognition of a number of universal human needs, not only biological but also social needs. A motivating assumption[237] of the present book is that all human beings *potentially* want freedom of choice—that is, to the extent that they are psychologically free. A far more modest assumption, which in our lifetime may well be conclusively confirmed, is the following: *All human beings desire self-esteem, in so far as self-esteem is or seems to be obtainable for them.*

Eric Hoffer, to whom I feel much indebted in this problem area, may on superficial reading seem to take a somewhat different view:

We acquire a sense of worth either by realizing our talents, or by keeping busy, or by identifying ourselves with something apart from us—be it a cause, a leader, a group, possessions and the like. Of the three, the path of self-realization is the most difficult. It is taken only when other avenues to a sense of worth are more or less blocked. Men of talent have to be encouraged and goaded to engage in creative work.[238]

Hoffer distinguishes between self-esteem and *pride*, which he calls "the explosive substitute for self-esteem":

Pride is a sense of worth derived from something that is not organically part of us, while self-esteem derives from the potentialities and achievements of the self. We are proud when we identify ourselves with an imaginary self, a leader,

236 See above, p. 175.

237 I am not saying *underlying,* for the rationale of the present study does not rest on the validity of this assumption.

238 *The Passionate State of Mind,* p. 19.

a holy cause, a collective body or possessions. There is fear and intolerance in pride; it is sensitive and uncompromising. The less promise and potency in the self, the more imperative is the need for pride. The core of pride is self-rejection. It is true that when pride releases energies and serves as a spur to achievement, it can lead to a reconciliation with the self and the attainment of genuine self-esteem.[239]

It is true, as Hoffer suggests in the former of the two passages, that men easily drift into the pursuit of pride-promoting identifications and neglect the development of their independent selves.[240] It often seems easier to try to avoid the anxieties of individual existence, involving lonely choice, than to face them, but it is much more satisfying in the long run to face the anxieties and make use of these incentives toward the development of an acceptable self. As it turns out, this is the only way toward ultimately *reducing* the anxieties of human existence. The sense of worth achieved by the pride of self-sacrificing identifications is only a pseudosubstitute for self-esteem. It is a defensive orientation, imbued with "fear and intolerance," since its props are external, essentially outside the individual's control. Only genuine self-esteem can in the long run render the external world nonfrightening.

Else Frenkel-Brunswik observes that ethnocentrism is more incipient and flexible in "high" children as compared to "high" adults: even the ethnocentric child tends to seek "more primary satisfaction of his psychological needs," and "the ethnocentric child is more accessible to experience and reality than the ethnocentric adult who has rigidly structured his world according to his interests and desires."[241] This observation supports my contention that all children have a high degree of psychological freedom, unless or until they meet anxieties and fears with which they cannot cope. The developmental problem of psychological freedom is therefore, strictly speaking, more of a conservation problem than it is an achievement problem.

And yet, the psychological freedom of the mature person is, of course, a more complex phenomenon than that of the child, since the adult's needs and capabilities are more complex. His sympathies and self-expanding identifications are wider, and his ability to promote the needs of his wide self by means of rationality and "judiciousness"[242] is likely to be greater, to the extent that he is free from ego-defensive preoccupations.

I adopted, in Chapter 3, the value position that psychological freedom

---

[239] *Ibid.*, pp. 18, 23.

[240] "Keeping busy," incidentally, may be one way of "realizing our talents," but it may also be an avenue of flight from the consciousness of self, depending on the degree to which the work is considered as a means toward goals of our own.

[241] "A Study of Prejudice in Children," *Human Relations*, I, No. 3 (1948), 304–5. The last words are perhaps not happily chosen; "his ego-defensive needs" are presumably more important in this context than his initial and more spontaneous interests and desires.

[242] Erikson uses this term as an antonym for "prejudice, an outlook characterized by prejudged values and dogmatic divisions": "Judiciousness in its widest sense is a frame of mind which is tolerant of differences, cautious and methodological in evaluation, just in judgment, circumspect in action, and—in spite of all this apparent relativism—capable of faith and indignation." *Childhood and Society*, p. 371.

is desirable to an unlimited extent, from the individual's point of view—that there are no significant incompatibilities between psychological freedom and other freedom values. From the point of view of social interaction, on the other hand, it is clear that the outward expression of the individual's basic motives is not always appropriate; it may reduce his own social freedom or the social freedom of other individuals.[243] In other words, a high level of psychological freedom may conceivably contribute toward conflicts between freedom *demands* in social interaction. On the whole, however, as the following chapters will bring out, it is the low rather than the high levels of psychological freedom that tend to lead to or aggravate conflicts between demands for social freedom.[244] To the extent that ego-defensiveness is overcome and the "know thyself" ideal approached, there are reasons to believe that people to a greater extent will tend to behave spontaneously in a manner not destructive of the important interests of their neighbors, unless they are misinformed through no fault of their own.[245]

It must be granted, then, that the ideal of a maximum psychological freedom, when placed in a social context, does not require or even allow a completely unrestrained outward expression in action of all the individual's basic needs or motives. But a complete *awareness* in the individual of all his important motives remains an unqualified normative ideal, so far as my value position is concerned."[246]

SOCIAL STRUCTURE AND PSYCHOLOGICAL FREEDOM

The problem of how social structure variables affect the psychological freedom of individuals is difficult, and significant data bearing on it are scant.

This problem is very different, of course, from the problem of how *attitudes* are affected by social structure factors. Even the problem of tracing social determinants of ethnocentric or fascist orientations is a wider problem than the one at hand. I am in this context not concerned with the determinants of intolerant attitudes, important as this problem is in the study of social freedom.[247] The dependent variable here is *defensiveness*—my shorthand term for deficiencies in psychological freedom—as manifested in attitudes and behavior. Ethnocentrism, like intolerance, may but need not be defensive. Authoritarianism, on the other hand, has been de-

---

[243] See above, p. 88.

[244] See below, pp. 297–312.

[245] I tend to agree with Rousseau's words that "the people is never corrupted, but it is often deceived, and on such occasions only does it seem to will what is bad." "The Social Contract," in *The Social Contract and Discourses*, p. 26.

"I do not believe that the good is only a 'reaction formation' against the bad, that man's creative impulses are simply ways of dealing with and taming his destructive ones, that love is an outward negation of hate. . . . I am willing to go further than this and assert that the constructive and cohesive forces, both in the individual and in society will spontaneously find their way if certain limiting and constricting ones are removed, more especially fear and anxiety." Carl Binger, quoted with approval in Henry V. Dicks, "In Search of our Proper Ethics," *British Journal of Medical Psychology*, XXIII (1950), 8. Cf. above, pp. 88 and 171.

[246] The only possible qualification is that *sublimation* at times may, though only temporarily, serve the individual's over-all needs. But *repression* never solves any problems.

[247] See below, pp. 303–7.

fined as a defensive predisposition to conform uncritically to standards and commands supported by authorities,[248] and is thus always a manifestation of defensiveness, to be distinguished from nondefensive obedience to authorities. Antiauthoritarianism is another manifestation of defensiveness, as we have seen, and fixation may (but need not) be a third.[249]

It is by no means a matter of course that social structure variables have an impact on the psychological freedom of individuals. It is possible to take the extreme position that all deep-going personality tendencies, including enduring defensive predispositions, are entirely determined biologically and/or during infancy. Freud and some of his successors have come closer than most other psychologists to holding such a view, but none of them, so far as I know, actually came very close to it. For one thing, psychoanalysts have always recognized the potentialities of therapy and analysis in curing many kinds of neuroses, and the significance of the social relationships of patients for the chances of successful cures. Neo-Freudians like Fromm and Horney, and above all Harry Stack Sullivan, have emphasized the importance of the present social situation of the patient, in diagnosis as well as in therapy, more strongly than some of the more orthodox Freudians, but this is a matter of new emphasis rather than new insight.

If it is granted, then, that social factors do influence the growth and reduction of neuroses, also after infancy, it may be said that each society can place its own impact on the level of psychological freedom in two ways. First, social structure factors probably have an indirect impact, by influencing the attitudes of adults who are parents. Both the more basic and the more superficial aspects of this impact may have their effect on their ways of bringing up children. Secondly, social structure factors probably have a direct impact on adult individuals, strong enough to be capable of affecting not only attitudes but trends in neuroses and levels of psychological freedom.

The present state of knowledge is woefully inadequate on both these problems, crucial though they are to the whole field of mental health and public policy. I shall briefly discuss the problem of the indirect impact via parental influence first and then the problem of the direct impact of institutions on the individual's capacity for free expression.

The problem of parental influence has been touched on already in two contexts. Reference has been made to Else Frenkel-Brunswik's tentative report of a higher incidence of ethnocentrism in families with socioeconomically unstable histories compared to other families with a record of continually privileged circumstances. Also, I have discussed some recent data on the relative incidence of various types of fixations in a number of different cultures.[250]

A good deal of work has been done in surveying differences in child-rearing practices in different socioeconomic classes and also between the

---

[248] See above, p. 190.
[249] See above, pp. 206 and 223–26.
[250] See above, pp. 219–20 and 223–26.

"castes" of Negroes and whites in the United States.[251] Considerable differences have been found along class lines as well as caste lines, in some respects confirming the widespread belief that lower-class parents tend to be more permissive than middle-class parents and Negroes in either class more permissive than whites.

Yet the significance of such findings for my problem has yet to be demonstrated. One can speculate, of course, that a greater degree of permissiveness tends to produce less frustrating childhood situations, with less severe anxieties and consequently a smaller incidence of repressions and enduring neuroses in the developing personalities. Yet, the previously mentioned finding of Sewell, Mussen, and Harris should recommend much caution in such speculation. They found a tendency of intercorrelation between permissiveness and a casual treatment of children, with a low participation of parents in the activities of their children. For all we know, these last factors may more than outweigh the lower incidence of strict discipline in predisposing children toward enduring neuroses.[252]

Economic or political insecurity, or prestige group marginality, may well make parents tense and anxious and may make them pay less attention to their children, be less loving and permissive, or pass on many of their anxieties to their children. On the other hand, a frustrating social situation may equally well turn the attention of many parents much more strongly to their own families, as havens where they find peace and recognition and unconditional love. Socioeconomic marginality may, in other words, make for more gratifying or less gratifying home surroundings for the child, or there may be no substantial effect in either direction. So far we know virtually nothing about the indirect impact of social class and caste circumstances, via patterns of child-rearing, on the child's enduring capacity for free expression.

With respect to the comparative study of cultures, in tracing the impact of child-rearing practices on the incidence of low psychological freedom, the situation is substantially the same, except for the promising new type of data provided by Whiting and Child.

In several well-known studies Margaret Mead has demonstrated correspondence between disciplinarian upbringing and aggressive "authoritarian" adults in some cultures and permissive, tender child-rearing and also nonaggressive, easy-going adults in other cultures.[253] The trouble with this kind of data is that nothing is known about what is cause and what is effect. As Hebb has suggested, Mead's data might be interpreted as showing only the obvious: "In one tribe the adults are easy-going, and so the children

---

[251] For example, Davis and Havighurst, "Social Class and Color Differences in Child Rearing," *American Sociological Review*, XI (1946), 698–710; Ericson, "Social Status and Child-Rearing Practices," in Newcomb and Hartley (eds.), *Readings in Social Psychology*, pp. 494–501; and Maccoby, Gibbs, *et al.*, "Methods of Child-Rearing in Two Social Classes," in Martin and Stendler (eds.), *Readings in Child Development*, pp. 380–96. Cf. also Havighurst and Davis, "A Comparison of the Chicago and Harvard Studies of Social Class Differences in Child Rearing," *American Sociological Review*, XX, No. 4 (1955), 438–42. The most recent study is by Sears, Maccoby, Levin, and collaborators, *Patterns of Child Rearing* (1957).

[252] See above, pp. 220–21.

[253] Cf. especially, *Sex and Temperament in Three Primitive Societies.*

are treated well; in another the adults are aggressive, and the children are treated harshly."[254]

It is also known that patterns of child-rearing tend to vary from one nation to another in the modern world, and many attempts have been made to develop explanations of "national character" on this basis. One of the least convincing examples of such endeavors is Geoffrey Gorer's theory that the swaddling of Russian infants tends to make adult Russians passive and hostile.[255] Arild Haaland in a recent study adopts a skeptical attitude to the many theories advanced to explain the growth of German Nazism as a consequence of an authoritarian family structure in Germany.[256]

A recent critical survey of the literature on national character suggests that one weakness in many studies is a tendency to fall for the obvious temptation of trying to explain a great deal on the basis of very few variables. In the first place, even the concept of national character, or "modal personality," is suspect in theorizing until there is some empirical confirmation of the expected regularities. Secondly, although it may be a convenient research strategy to focus attention on the socialization of the child,[257] this does not make it fruitful to try to develop theories of national character development in heavy reliance on child-rearing patterns as the main independent variable.[258]

Even a fully satisfactory study of child-rearing practices in relation to developing differentials in national character would not necessarily bear on the present problem, however. Such a study would enlighten us on determinants of psychological freedom only if the "character" or modal personality of one nation definitely is more free or less neurotic (repressed) than that of another. I doubt whether there is any good reason for expecting clear national differences of this nature, at least within nations in a similar stage of technological development.

If we extend our horizon to the comparative study of aboriginal cultures, however, ascertainable differences of this nature may well be expected. Indeed, such differences were reported on in the study of Whiting and Child. They reported a number of convincing correlations between certain institutionalized deprivations of the child and tendencies in the same cultures to develop the related negative fixations, and a number of less con-

[254] *The Organization of Behavior,* pp. 265–66, note. See also Klineberg, *Social Psychology,* p. 434.

[255] Gorer and Rickman, *The People of Great Russia.* Cf. Goldman, "Psychiatric Interpretation of Russian History: A Reply to Geoffrey Gorer," *American Slavic and East European Review,* IX (1950), 151–61.

[256] Haaland, *Nazismen i Tyskland: En analyse av dens forutsetninger* (Nazism in Germany: An Analysis of Its Determinants), pp. 170–94.

[257] Mead, "The Study of National Character," in Lerner and Lasswell (eds.), *The Policy Sciences: Recent Developments in Scope and Method,* p. 74.

[258] Cf. Inkeles and Levinson, "National Character: The Study of Modal Personality and Sociocultural Systems," in Lindzey (ed.), *Handbook of Social Psychology,* II, 977–1020, especially p. 999. See also Inkeles, "Some Sociological Observations on Culture and Personality Studies," in Kluckhohn and Murray, with the collaboration of Schneider (eds.), *Personality, in Nature, Society, and Culture,* pp. 577–92. Other methodological shortcomings in various comparative studies of child-rearing and personality in different nations and different cultures are cited in Orlansky, "Infant Care and Personality," *Psychological Bulletin,* XLVI, No. 1 (1949), p. 27.

vincing correlations between institutionalized overindulgences of the child and tendencies toward positive fixations.[259]

Here is a frontier of research, it seems to me, which is likely to give way in the foreseeable future—and we can hope to learn much more than we now know about social and cultural determinants of individual repression in each society's modal or average personalities.

This is not exclusively a question of child-rearing practices, of course. The direct impact of social structure determinants on adult personalities may be fully as important, in many cultures, as the indirect impact through the family in creating or preventing deficiencies in psychological freedom. It is convenient to discuss this problem of the direct impact from two opposite angles: What do we know about social situational factors that tend to break down mental health and psychological freedom? Secondly, what do we know about social influences tending to bolster psychological freedom— for example, by promoting a high self-esteem in the individual?

Writers such as Erich Fromm, A. H. Maslow, Karen Horney, Lawrence K. Frank, and Robert Lindner have in various writings posed the problem of "the sane society," or the society with institutions maximally instrumental to the satisfaction of the basic needs of individuals. I have discussed this problem briefly in an effort to evaluate the desirability of therapy toward social adjustment from a psychological freedom point of view.[260] Important as this literature is from a philosophical and a political point of view, it is not sufficiently empirically based to carry much information on the present problem. It is still largely a matter of conjecture and sweeping interpretations just how different types of stable social institutions tend to affect the incidence and types of neuroses of the individuals in each type of society. This is an area in which more research is feasible and very much needed. It should be possible, for example, to compare types and occurrences of neuroses over time within professions differing in competitive pressures, as a beginning toward understanding the psychological impact of a competitive society.[261] Also, the ratio between levels of aspiration and actual achievement or achievement probabilities surely is a source of frustration and perhaps neuroses, and more so in some classes or countries than in others. Here again there would seem to be much room for fruitful basic research. Differences in economic and social security, again, may be very great even within the same communities, but not much has been done by way of systematic inquiries into the impact of these differences on mental functioning.

---

[259] See above, pp. 224–26.

[260] Cf. above, pp. 182 and 186–88. Cf. also Maslow, "Human Motivation in Relation to Social Theory," in Shore (ed.), *Twentieth Century Mental Hygiene: New Directions in Mental Health*, and Horney, *The Neurotic Personality of Our Time*.

[261] As another beginning, cf. Billig, Gillin, and Davidson, "Aspects of Personality and Culture in a Guatemalan Community: Ethnological Rorschach Approaches," *Journal of Personality*, XVI (1947–48), 153–87 and 326–68. The authors give as their impression that the social organization of the Indians on the whole provides more security for the individual than that of the Ladinos, for three main reasons: There is less competitiveness and emphasis on gaining wealth; there is a more pervading and stable family system; and religious patterns and attitudes pervade almost all aspects of the Indian culture. *Ibid.*, pp. 157–58.

There are, so far as I know, two kinds of data available on social structure variables tending to disrupt personality integration. Both refer to institutions in flux or in drastic change, not to stable institutions. The first kind of data bears on the effects of anomie, the second on psychological effects of crisis situations such as war.

Durkheim's study of *Suicide* is still an unsurpassed empirical study of psychological consequences of anomie. His findings have been discussed in a previous context, and the concept of anomie has been dealt with in several contexts. Suffice it to repeat here that anomic breakdowns represent a real threat to the individual's security and also to his psychological freedom. Increasing psychological freedom serves to enable individuals to tolerate more anomie or more freedom, and, conversely, sudden rises in institutional confusion or anomie may lead to serious neuroses in individuals who had not developed sufficient psychological freedom to be able to live with poorly structured outlooks and situations. Rising suicide rates occur and surely also rising rates of despair and neuroses that do not culminate in suicide. These lesser but still serious effects of anomie can be inferred from the increases in suicide but have not yet been satisfactorily demonstrated independently.[262] Here, again, is an area where research of importance to basic theory is much needed. The more we learn about people's ability to live with anomie, the more assurance we have that the struggle for expanding freedom on all levels can be carried forward without sociologically or psychologically necessary set-backs.[263]

It has been suggested that perhaps the most general determinant of defensiveness, or deficiencies in psychological freedom, is the element of *frustration,* meaning the blocking of individual goals or attempts at need-satisfaction. Authoritarianism is considered one chronic source of frustration, derived from the failure of personality integration and the resulting unawareness of and failure to satisfy some of the basic needs. Other examples of chronic frustrations interfering with psychological freedom are antiauthoritarianism and perhaps many fixations. An experiment has been referred to, in which it was indicated that characterological chronic frustration can be augmented by the frustration of situational stress.[264]

Anomie can be termed a chronic situational source of frustration to individuals who have insufficient inner freedom for coping with it. Although anomie does not block any specific goals for the individual, it may block the satisfaction individuals seek in relating themselves to others in the pursuit of stable, common goals. This need is probably present in all individuals, but it is more urgent and all-pervasive in individuals whose conscious selves fail to communicate effectively with their own basic needs and wishes. The desirable way of preventing anomic suffering, then, from a

[262] Durkheim's data are referred to above on pp. 78–79; the concept and the phenomenon of anomie are discussed on pp. 77–83, 102, 113–14, 119–21, 124–25, and 274–80.

[263] I have concluded that the average man's degree of psychological freedom can never be too high from the point of view of security against anomie. But it can be too low, within a society offering a substantial degree of social and potential freedom. Cf. above, pp. 87–88 and 113–14.

[264] See above, pp. 204–5.

freedom-oriented point of view, is to do whatever is possible to permit children to grow up with their psychological freedom unimpaired, so that they can live with conscious goal values firmly anchored in their basic need structures.

Much research has been done with respect to certain more acute and specific situational sources of frustration and their effect on personality integration. The objective of most of this research has been to find out something about factors affecting adjustment to life in the armed forces, especially in wartime. The practical problem from the military and the governmental point of view is, of course, the procurement of effective soldiers. The rejection or later screening out of "psychoneurotics" is instrumental to this goal, since these people on the whole make unreliable soldiers and, moreover, easily become more seriously mentally ill under the strains of military life. Apart from the personal tragedies, these developments cause tremendous expense for the government concerned.[265]

To what extent is an effective screening possible at the time of recruitment? This is a practical question bearing directly on the present theoretical problem: To what extent are psychoneurotic breakdowns in the military forces the result of personality predispositions, and to what extent are they the outcome of situational traumas and stresses? That both sources of frustration tend to interact, in varying proportions, seems fairly well established by now. Roy R. Grinker and John P. Spiegel conclude:

Examination of those men who fail to readapt to life in our democratic social structure shows, with considerable consistency, that they were predisposed in a characteristic way to the irreversible change which overtook them under the stress of combat. By predisposition is meant not a pre-existing neurotic illness nor a familial trait, but a weak spot within the personality, a concealed Achilles' heel, which rendered the individual sensitive to the forces which act upon him in combat.[266]

J. G. Sheps and F. E. Coburn reached a similar conclusion, after studying a sample of 100 "normal" Canadian soldiers who were wounded and hospitalized; 27 of them reported nervous difficulties in army life and were judged likely to develop battle neurosis if placed in the front line again. However, these authors found no differences between these 27 and the other 73 soldiers on the variety of psychiatric and psychological tests employed. "This would appear to indicate that, having removed by screening the men obviously predisposed to neurotic reaction, little prediction can be made about the remainder. Whether these succumb to the mental hazards of combat appears to depend on whether the stress they are exposed to happens to strike the chink in their particular armor."[267]

---

[265] It has been estimated that neuropsychological casualties are sixteen times more likely to be permanent than all other illnesses. In 1942 over half of the patients in American Veterans Administration hospitals were psychoneurotic cases. For reference, see Christie, Walkley *et al., An Exploratory Study of Factors Affecting Transition to Army Life,* p. 3.

[266] *Men under Stress,* p. 455.

[267] "Psychiatric Study of One Hundred Battle Veterans," *War Medicine,* VIII (1945), 235–37. Quoted in Christie, Walkley *et al., An Exploratory Study Affecting Transition to Army Life,* p. 4.

In support of this conclusion, Richard Christie, Albert T. Walkley, and their collaborators refer to studies indicating that the British psychoneurotic cases coming out of Dunkirk in 1940 tended to be different from the breakdowns occurring at the Normandy beachhead in 1944. Psychoses produced by the trench warfare in the First World War tended to differ from both these types of psychoses of the Second World War. Christie, Walkley, and their collaborators find that "the most plausible conclusion appears to be that different sorts of soldiers become psychiatric casualties in the three situations."[268]

It would lead too far, of course, to enter into a more detailed discussion of the different types of traumatic situations, in or out of military life, that are likely to affect the different types of personalities in a catastrophic manner. The point I have wished to support is that situational circumstances can indeed, if they are sufficiently trying or strategic in hitting individual weaknesses, impair a previously normal state of mental health and psychological freedom. In the words of Grinker and Spiegel, pleading for public understanding for the neurotic symptoms of many returning veterans, "These men have had their birthright of independence exchanged for psychological and physical symptoms, inferiority feelings or socially unadapted behavior."[269] The best parental care in the world is no guarantee that a person will maintain a healthy ego through the traumas of military experience.

It is evident that stress situations outside of military life can have equally serious effects on individual personalities. The experience of imprisonment can certainly be mentally unbearable for some people. The death of a loved one can lead to severe neurosis or death. The modern trend in psychiatry, perhaps most effectively spearheaded by the late Harry Stack Sullivan, acknowledges these conclusions as a matter of course. Not only may traumatic experiences have a profound impact on mental health, but the lesser differences between better and worse interpersonal relations may for many people tip the scale toward health or disorder.

The last question before us is this: What do we know about social circumstances that tend toward bolstering psychological freedom?

A large part of the answer has been implied in the immediately preceding discussion. If many types of situation bring about mental disorders in various personalities, it follows that it is conducive to mental health to prevent or reduce the impact of such events. Peace is clearly more conducive to mental health than is war for most persons. The absence of frustrating circumstances and anxieties beyond what the individual can cope with is clearly conducive to psychological freedom. As A. H. Maslow put it in a recent talk, "the good things of life are in themselves the ultimate therapy."[270]

The relationship between the material standard of living and mental

268 *Ibid.*, p. 4.
269 *Men under Stress*, p. 449.
270 Briefly reported on in the *New York Times*, March 15, 1955.

health is not necessarily, of course, a one-to-one correspondence. The United States, with the world's highest consumption of goods, has very serious problems of mental illness.[271] And the Scandinavian countries have traditionally some of the highest living standards and some of the highest suicide rates in Europe.[272] Although it has by no means been conclusively demonstrated, these effects possibly are the outcome of a level of anomie too high for many individuals in these countries to cope with

It must be granted that prosperity in an individualistic, competitive society may weaken the average person's sense of purpose in life, if he does not have purposes firmly anchored in his own basic needs. On the other hand, if we assume a given level of social solidarity, or (in negative terms) of anomie, it may be conjectured that increasing standards of material living, at least up to a certain point, should bolster the average level of psychological freedom. I draw this conclusion from the assumption that the most general source of deficiencies in psychological freedom is in amounts of frustration and anxiety beyond what the individual can cope with and integrate. Clearly, moderately increasing standards of material living reduce the worries and frustrations of the average man, provided he can predict and rely on such a prospect. Paraphrasing Maslow's words, just cited, the security of access to regularly increasing supplies of the good things in life is for most men the ultimate therapy and the ultimate prophylactic.

However, with respect to some of these good things, we are on less certain grounds. Spiritual and intellectual development, as Kierkegaard has brought home so forcefully, may indeed be more conducive to neurosis than to mental health: doubts are created, and some kinds of doubt are difficult to live with for most persons. So much to suggest a good deal of caution in theorizing about the impact of "intellectual living standards" on psychological freedom; I shall not try to disentangle this difficult problem in the present study.

Perhaps the most fruitful avenue toward strengthening psychological freedom by social and political means leads through devising better techniques for enhancing the self-esteem of the average individual. The importance of a high self-esteem for psychological freedom has been brought out already.[273] The problem I am posing here is that of shaping institutions so that they tend to encourage expressions of mutual esteem between interacting individuals and to discourage attitudes and expressions of contempt toward individuals on account of stereotypes about role or group attri-

[271] "At the present rate, one of every twelve children born each year will need to go to a mental hospital sometime in his life; over one-half of all of our hospital beds are occupied by mental patients," according to Howard A. Rusk, writing in the *New York Times*, October 31, 1954.

[272] It may be mentioned in passing that Svend Ranulf claims that there is statistical evidence for a positive correlation between degree of intellectual freedom and the rate of suicides in a given community. One principal exception is provided by the Jews: "The fact of belonging to a persecuted or obnoxious minority has the effect of creating among this minority a solidarity which is not weakened by the development of the intellect." *The Jealousy of the Gods and Criminal Law at Athens: A Contribution to the Sociology of Moral Indignation,* II, 292–93.

[273] See above, pp. 76–79.

butes.[274] This is one field in which the schools in many countries have done good work, but the attitudes learned in the school will tend to wither unless they correspond to institutional realities in later life.

Propagation of esteem and respect for other persons as individuals never does any harm, I believe. But in order to do much good it is necessary (1) that the level of psychological freedom be high enough to reduce the need for scapegoats and (2) that the most important institutional rewards and punishments in daily life be in harmony with the same precepts. I believe that the second factor reinforces the first. To the extent that institutions encourage expressions of mutual respect in social interaction, the level of self-esteem will be enhanced, in most individuals. The individual's self has been defined as the sum of reflected appraisals. It is true that unfavorable appraisals by others do not affect us much if our self-esteem has been strongly established. But many favorable appraisals by others are required to establish a sturdy self-esteem in someone who did not acquire it as a child.

One of the most challenging research and policy problems of our time, it seems to me, is how to institutionalize patterns of mutual respect that are conducive to the growth of self-esteem in all people. Lasswell has called this ideal the commonwealth of mutual deference.[275] Adam Curle has discussed the same question as the problem of the right "social spacing."[276] More recently, J. Bronowski has discussed the same topic in these vivid terms:

The city clerk and the razor gang, the tax collector and Azeff the great *agent provocateur,* the girl on the beach and Murder, incorporated—their inarticulate mouths all utter one cry. And their cry is one with the wish of the church-warden and the toff and the squire's lady. They want a place in the world. They want to be among friends. And they want to stand and be recognized. They want someone in their street to nudge his wife and say, "There goes that Mr. X who is doing so well." It does not seem too much to ask of society. But the hour is late; the distance from the center of our society to the doss house and the sandy edges of factory towns grows appalling. We have to divide the distance, and to find at each step some unit of respect, some recognition of place for those who live there. Society is not a pyramid but a body, and the cells must be neighborly. . . . We have failed . . . in finding how to give recognition to what is everywhere individual. We must mend this to survive.[277]

[274] The problem is emphatically not one of encouraging pretended esteem toward individuals whose personal behavior is thought reprehensible. Rather, it is to encourage an initial assumption that people deserve politeness, and to discourage contempt for an individual *because* he happens to be a janitor, a professor, a banker, a Methodist, a Negro, or a Swede.

[275] For instance, in *The Analysis of Political Behavior: An Empirical Approach,* pp. 2, 36.

[276] "The Sociological Background to Incentives," *Occupational Psychology,* XXII (1948), 26. See also Curle, "Incentives to Work: An Anthropological Appraisal," *Human Relations,* II, No. 1 (1949), 41–47.

[277] *The Face of Violence,* p. 59. Cf. Arendt: "What proved so attractive (in the 'activism' of totalitarian movements) was that terrorism had become a kind of philosophy through which to express frustration, resentment, and blind hatred, a kind of political expressionism which used bombs to express itself . . . and was absolutely willing to pay the price of life for having succeeded in forcing the recognition of one's existence on the normal strata of society." *The Origins of Totalitarianism,* p. 324.

It would seem that the fields of industrial sociology and psychology so far have provided most of the research data available of relevance to this important problem of social structure-determinants of self-esteem.[278] Also, and this has been closer to the specific concern of industrial research, data have been provided on the effects of self-esteem stimulation on such factors as worker productivity, loyalties, and economic demands.

Outside the industrial setting, however, there is a wide and virgin field, it seems to me, in which important work can be done to design and test social innovations conducive to the increase of self-esteem among good numbers of people. The ramifications of the problem extend over the whole area of social institutions, but especially crucial areas perhaps are the more obvious authority-subordination relationships. Bureaucracy, public relations, and propaganda are general functional categories of fields in which there is room for research on factors bearing on the self-esteem both at the giving and the receiving end. Among specific institutions that could both develop and use such research may be mentioned police and military organizations, national and especially local governments, political parties, and, of course, companies and unions.

There may also be something to learn from data on social structure and self-esteem in different nations and in different cultures. What difference, for instance, does it make that Americans tend to be strictly individualistic in their desires for achievement, while Russians apparently more often take pride in group achievements instead? Is individualism or collectivism in the small community more conducive to supplying opportunities to gain a sufficiency of self-esteem for everyone? Certain aboriginal cultures may conceivably have done better than our own in this particular respect. Thus, an anthropologist gives us the following impression of what the Apache Indians had achieved:

I think that we shall have to abandon the use of the word "medicine-man" or acknowledge that the Apaches are a nation of medicine-men. I have worked among three Apache tribes, and I have found scarcely a person of middle age who is not the custodian of some ceremony and the recipient of some supernatural power. Each individual plays his part in the great economy of ritual. One has the songs which must be sung when the war shield and spear are made. Another can raise a dust storm and save his people from detection by the enemy. Another can cure the loathsome sores that attack the face when "snake sickness" is contracted. Each has his feeling of importance. Each is buoyed up by the knowledge that "he who speaks to him" will guide, advise, and protect him.[279]

This is one way of providing for self-esteem all around. Maybe there are other ways that could be institutionalized in the communities of our own culture.

When all this has been said, we must not lose sight of the probability that childhood circumstances are of basic importance in determining self-esteem. This theory has been developed in earlier sections and some data

---

[278] For a recent survey, see Haire, "Industrial Social Psychology," in Lindzey (ed.), *Handbook of Social Psychology*, II, 1104–23.

[279] Opler, "The Concept of Supernatural Power among the Chiricahua and Mescalero Apaches," *American Anthropologist*, XXXVII (1935), 70.

have been referred to in the preceding section, and so it need not be reiterated here. Suffice it to say that a secure ego control, providing a stable modus vivendi between impulses and conscience, is likely to be conducive to a stable and positive self-esteem. If this fundament for a positive self-esteem has been built during childhood, adverse appraisals of others that may occur later in life are much less damaging than they would be in the absence of such a basis. If no substantial positive self-esteem has been developed in the home, it will take a lot of social recognition and affection and praise to build it later in life.[280]

We are still far away from the stage of behavioral science where we can hope to test the relative importance of child-rearing practices and social structure demands and opportunities in determining self-esteem development in large as well as in small numbers of people. In the meantime we can only proceed on the assumption that research should be done on both kinds of variables, and, if possible and plausible, the findings should be adapted toward increasing promotion of self-esteem and psychological freedom.

---

[280] Hoffer suggests that achievements prodded by anxieties over one's worth may lay the basis for a genuine self-esteem. I am not denying this, only implying that even great achievements must be recognized and praised by at least a few important others to have this effect. Only in rare cases may it be sufficient to have the conviction that the achievement will be praised some day, or would have been by someone who is now dead or for other reasons not present. Cf. above, pp. 226–27.

5

Determinants of Social Freedom

𝒥he term "function" has been used in several contexts already, but it has never been properly introduced because it has not been very much needed before now. My references to "function" or "functional analysis" have been limited, except for a section in Chapter 4, to statements to the effect that I believe social facts have functions. This has remained a postulate without elaboration.[1] The definitions of the freedom values in Chapter 3 aimed at conceptual clarification and surface descriptions, and discussion of the developmental or dynamic problems was postponed. The dynamics of psychological freedom were discussed in Chapter 4, in which a section was given to the exposition of a "functional theory of anxiety." This was a theory about the utility of anxiety as a general phenomenon in the individual's life and growth. Apart from this section, the term was not used prominently in that chapter, for the discussion was primarily psychological and in psychological theory there is a wealth of other dynamic concepts to choose from; "need," "motive," "identification," "ego-defense," and many other concepts refer to processes, not static phenomena. Following Alexander, I also have defined "ego," "id," "superego," and "ego ideal" as personality *functions* rather than structural components.

Dynamic psychological analysis is, first of all, the study of the motivational processes in the individual's personality (though almost always in social interaction, directly or indirectly). Those psychologists who are specialists in such processes as perception or learning neglect the motivational aspect of these phenomena only at their peril. Dynamic social analysis, on the other hand, proceeds on a different level, which Louis Schneider has termed the *synergic* level. This term refers to the conjoint effects of motivated actions looked at from the point of view of an observer interested in motivation and its effects, not primarily for an individual but for a social system.[2]

---

[1] Cf. above, especially pp. 73, 165 and 191.

[2] Schneider, "Some Psychiatric Views on 'Freedom' and the Theory of Social Systems," *Psychiatry*, XII (1949), 251–64. Cf. Schneider, "Functional Analysis and the Problem of Order," in Ogle, Schneider, and Wiley, *Power, Order, and the Economy: A Preface to the Social Sciences*, pp. 94–100.

Robert Merton suggests that the *distinctive* intellectual contributions of the sociologist are found primarily in the study of "unanticipated consequences."[3] Throughout this discussion I shall by *sociological analysis* understand analysis proceeding on the synergic level, studying social effects accumulated as unanticipated effects of individual acts in pursuit of individual goals and of individual expressive behavior.[4]

Sociological theory is not as well equipped as is psychology with dynamic terms—terms that are essentially functional enough to make "function" itself nearly superfluous. Social phenomena have, on the whole, the advantage of being more easily ascertainable as facts, compared to the psychological phenomena of the unconscious. Yet this may be more of an apparent than a real advantage. It is possible that a Freud of sociology has yet to come: a man who will discover new ways of grappling with the more basic problems of institutional change. Perhaps the advances in the behavioral sciences will become spectacular following the invention some day of bold new conceptions of general functional components in institutional pressures. The best we can do today in the study of social interaction, or the study of behavior on the "synergic level," is to make the most of the concept of "function." Functional analysis is in the social sciences the closest approximation to what motivational analysis is in psychology.

The first great proponent of functional analysis as an approach to empirical social science was Emile Durkheim. His approach was improved, applied in field studies, and given wide currency by social anthropologists such as Bronislaw Malinowski and A. R. Radcliffe-Brown. More recently, sociologists have taken the lead toward its further sophistication. Robert Merton and Talcott Parsons have contributed the most, it would seem, and this chapter and the next will borrow extensively from their writings.

A *function*, for the purposes of this book, means an effect of behavior tending to increase the probability that this kind of behavior will continue or recur. Merton uses a similar concept: "*Functions* are those observed consequences which make for the adaptation or adjustment of a given system."[5]

The opposite of a function has been called a *dysfunction* by Merton, who defines dysfunctions as "those observed consequences which lessen the adaptation or adjustment of the system."[6] A dysfunction, I conclude, is an effect of behavior tending to decrease the probability that this kind of behavior will continue or recur.

As Merton also points out, there may be *nonfunctional* consequences

[3] *Social Theory and Social Structure: Toward the Codification of Theory and Research*, pp. 66.

[4] Expressive behavior as contrasted to coping behavior is behavior with no time perspective, or no goal beyond the expression itself. Cf. Maslow, "The Expressive Component of Behavior," in Brand (ed.), *The Study of Personality: A Book of Readings*, pp. 362–76, and below, p. 313.

[5] *Social Theory and Social Structure*, p. 50; and Aubert, *Om straffens sosiale funksjon (On the Social Function of Punishment)*, pp. 2–3. My formulation follows Aubert's variation on Merton's concept.

[6] Merton, *Social Theory and Social Structure*, p. 51.

of behavior, too—effects that neither increase nor decrease the prospects of more of the same kind.

Note that the same behavior pattern may be functional and dysfunctional for different groups or individuals in the same society. In such cases one must specify for whom an institution is functional and for whom it is dysfunctional—*i.e.,* one must estimate the relative strength and scope of the pressures likely to support and of the pressures likely to oppose that behavior pattern. From this objective point of view a pattern is functional for society as a whole within a given span of time if it is more effectively supported than it is opposed, and it is dysfunctional in the opposite event. One must be careful, however, to specify the time perspective. If a long-term perspective is chosen, one must take into account the social process as a whole and allow for instabilities and tendencies toward change. For example, local gangsters may for brief periods make law enforcement dysfunctional if the police forces are weak; yet this state of affairs is likely over a period of time to stimulate new pressures toward strengthening the forces on the side of the law. In democratic societies, and indeed in all societies, law-enforcing institutions are always functional if considered over the long run.

A given kind of behavior can be functional and dysfunctional in different respects for the same person or group, psychologically as well as sociologically. A marriage, for example, may have some consequences encouraging and others discouraging its continuation, and, moreover, the same aspects or episodes may be ambivalently received by each person. They are functional on one level of motivation and dysfunctional on another level.

Strictly speaking, we can rarely be sure about the exact range of functional and dysfunctional tendencies of given kinds of behavior. All we can demonstrate, by the test of whether an institution continues or not, is what Merton calls *the net balance of functional (or dysfunctional) consequences.* If an institution exists, all that the functional analyst can and should assert offhand is that up to the present moment there is a net balance of functional over dysfunctional consequences of the institution. It has so far proved to be (primarily) functional, for groups large enough or strong enough to preserve it.

Questions about future functionalism can be approached on the basis of theory and research. They become more complex the more specific we wish to be about functional and dysfunctional components. Similarly, specific questions about the component functions and dysfunctions in the past may be just as complex, but they cannot be avoided if one wishes a dynamic or developmental understanding of the institution in question.

The main task in this chapter is to attempt a rough functional analysis of the chief determinants of social freedom, or more specifically freedom from coercion. One important group of determinants consists of certain basic features that apparently are found in all human societies, or at any rate in all large and complex societies. Another group of determinants is psychological: to what extent are relatively enduring and general personality factors affecting the role of coercion in society? A third group is the sum of political institutions characteristic of modern democracy. I shall be concerned primarily with the most general social determinants of social freedom, though I shall also consider some general political determinants, as well as—in the last section—some psychological determinants.[7]

The policy problem, given the value position of this book, can be stated as a problem of making the freedom-reducing pressures and institutions dysfunctional for ever larger groups over time, and of making functional those that tend to expand the general amount of freedom from coercion. With respect to psychological factors, it is a problem of encouraging freedom-allowing tendencies and of discouraging or neutralizing freedom-denying tendencies. An inquiry with parallel policy implications pertaining to potential freedom will be attempted in Chapter 6.

Let us consider what are the basic philosophical implications, if any, of adopting the functionalist approach to social analysis. Dorothy Gregg and Elgin Williams argue that "Nothing follows from functionalist (and economic) principles with more cogent urgency than the doctrine of 'cultural relativism.' On this view, cultural systems, stemming as they do from inborn individual wants and basic needs, are each uniquely expressive of the group or people involved. It follows that there are no universal standards of value or morals."[8]

It is true that functional analysis and, indeed, any sober-minded study of many cultures must arrive at the *fact* of cultural relativism—that institutions, including ethical standards, show considerable variation from one culture to another. Yet it is quite unwarranted to conclude from this simple observation that there cannot be any universal standards of value or morals.

In the first place, the variety of forms may have elements in common—cultural universals underlying the diversity. I suggested in an earlier context that the study of such universals may provide data toward a science of universal human values, which will also indicate universal factors in human need-satisfaction.[9]

Secondly, even in areas in which no universal consensus on values is found, it is fully compatible with a relativist acknowledgment of this situation to argue that some cultural norms and forms are superior to others, in making superior contributions to human welfare. "To say that certain aspects of Naziism were morally wrong—is not parochial arrogance. It is—or can be—an assertion based both upon cross-cultural evidence as to

---

[7] A fourth group of determinants, beyond the scope of this book, are the specific institutions of one particular country or community. Studies in this area are very much needed, and a number have been forthcoming in recent years—for example, the Rockefeller-supported series of volumes in the Cornell Studies in Civil Liberty, and the various inquiries sponsored by the Fund for the Republic. References to such factors in this book are for purposes of illustration only; my task is limited to a more general analysis. For examples of this kind of literature, see Gellhorn, *Security, Loyalty, and Science* (in the Cornell series), and his more recent study, *Individual Freedom and Governmental Restraints*. John Cogley's *Report on Blacklisting* is among the studies sponsored by the Fund for the Republic.

[8] Gregg and Williams, "The Dismal Science of Functionalism," *American Anthropologist*, L, No. 4 (1948), 604–5.

[9] Cf. above, pp. 11–14.

the universalities of human needs, potentialities, and fulfillments and upon natural science knowledge with which the basic assumptions of any philosophy must be congruent."[10] I would add that assertions of this kind can be made without any empirical foundation at all. Functional analysis and cognitive cultural relativism are perfectly compatible with a strong belief in and even an absolute commitment to definite standards of value or morality. The banner of cultural relativism has been used to challenge efforts such as those of the United Nations to make certain human rights recognized and vindicated in all cultures.[11] Yet this is certainly not a necessary consequence of *empirical* relativism or of the functional analytical approach to the study of cultures.

Functional analysis can, as Merton has shown, imply either a conservative or a radical bias. It can also, he suggests, be liberated from either one— that is, if it is possible to define a middle position (of this I am not at all sure). Merton takes issue on the one side with Gunnar Myrdal, who has claimed that "a description of social institutions in terms of their functions must lead to a conservative teleology,"[12] and on the other side with Richard LaPiere, who has asserted that functional analysis must "affront all those who believe that specific sociopsychological structures have inherent values."[13] On his own part Merton says: "To the extent that functional analysis focuses wholly on functional consequences, it leans toward an ultra-conservative ideology; to the extent that it focuses wholly on dysfunctional consequences, it leans toward an ultra-radical utopia. 'In its essence,' it is neither one nor the other."[14]

There is much more than this to the political implications of functional analysis, as Merton's discussion makes clear. One's degree of readiness to search for and accept *functional equivalents* of existing institutions is probably closely related to one's general position on the conservatism-radicalism continuum. A closely related question is the problem of *functional prerequisites* of social order: the conservative will tend to see a larger number of the existing institutions anchored in functional necessities, while the radical will consider a smaller number of them necessary. I shall postpone the consideration of these concepts until my discussion of the general social determinants of social freedom.[15] Another pair of concepts should be defined right away, however. In Merton's words, "*Manifest functions* are those objective consequences contributing to the adjustment or adaptation of the system which are intended and recognized by participants in the system; *Latent functions,* correlatively, being those which are neither intended nor recognized."[16]

[10] Kroeber and Kluckhohn, with the assistance of Untereiner, *Culture: A Critical Review of Concepts and Definitions,* p. 178.

[11] Cf. "Statement on Human Rights" by the Executive Board, *American Anthropological Association,* June 24, 1947, quoted below, pp. 376–77.

[12] *An American Dilemma,* p. 1056.

[13] *Collective Behavior,* p. 56.

[14] *Social Theory and Social Structure,* pp. 38–42.

[15] Cf. below, pp. 265 ff., especially 273–74.

[16] Merton, *Social Theory and Social Structure,* p. 51. Consequences that are recognized only after an act but were not intended or expected should be considered latent functions. If the act recurs, even regrettable consequences are manifest functions in so far as they are anticipated.

This distinction, again, favors neither the radical nor the conservative in its legitimate implications. It simply serves to remind the scientific observer of the fact that there is more to social institutions than meets the eye of the participants. Awareness of the probability of latent functions complicates the problem of institutional change, but it also complicates the problem of how to foster the endurance of given institutions in changing times and situations. It is always a complex problem to inquire which functions of an institution, whether manifest or latent, are crucial to its preservation. More important and equally complex is the rational problem of deciding what institutions are crucial in serving a desirable function, whether manifest or latent.

The crucial criterion of the latent function is that it is not recognized by the participants in the institutional system. If it exists without being recognized, it presumably goes without saying that it is not intended, at least not by the present participants. One of the tasks of the behavioral scientist is to recognize latent functions of institutions. If he imparts his discoveries to the participants, he may or may not succeed in making manifest certain functions that were previously latent. His success in this respect presumably depends on whether the participants under observation share with the scientist the conviction that these functions are valuable and significant to their own interest as participants in the social system.

Dysfunctions are presumably never manifest, except if they are perceived as inseparable from constructive functions that outweigh them. Behavior patterns that were recognized as wholly dysfunctional by and for the participants would presumably change at once. Latent dysfunctions can persist, but here again the behavioral scientist may succeed in making them manifest. In this case, he is likely to carry influence in instituting behavior change, if the dysfunctions are found to be of consequence for and by those who behave, without being compensated by positive functions of greater consequence.

Having decided that functional analysis does not necessarily carry any specific policy implications, let me consider somewhat further its philosophical and general theory-building implications. My commitment to functional analysis rests on premises that have much in common with Hume's position on the origin of moral conventions.[17] I am here concerned with analyzing institutions in terms of existence and prospects, not value or validity, but the underlying assumption of functional analysis is essentially the same. I assume that an institution and perhaps any social fact exists and endures only in so far as it has a function in serving someone's or some group's need, conscious or unconscious, and serves it "better" than alternate if (subjectively) equally accessible behavior patterns. In other words, the "fittest" social facts survive.

Considering the plausibility of this assumption, and its apparent usefulness as a source of clues for explanations about "how things got that way," it is at first rather surprising that so much controversy has raged among social anthropologists about the merit of functional analysis. The

[17] See above, p. 33.

point at issue seems, however, to have been more a question of the possibility of such an approach than of its desirability. The main reason for the opposition of "historicists" against "functionalists" was, it would seem, a profound distrust among the former of attempts at theory-building in cultural anthropology. This attitude is in turn to be explained by the fact that historicism began as a sobering and most fruitful reaction against the grandiose evolutionary theories of nineteenth-century anthropologists. The more recent controversy has to a large extent, it appears, been a matter of asserting or denying the feasibility of a systematic theory of cultural growth and behavior.[18]

If you once accept the possibility of explaining the dynamics of social and cultural behavior systematically over time—at least to the point where you consider efforts in this direction worth investing—then it would seem that you cannot get around the position of functional analysis or some equivalent. You cannot without inconsistency deny the utility of this approach, even if it may not exclude other, supplementary approaches. You can dispense with it only if your task is a purely descriptive one. The "whys" of society and culture are functionally interrelated, if they are related at all.

The historian's task is essentially a descriptive one, to the extent that he is not a sociologist, a psychologist, or a philosopher of history. His "explanations" may be almost pure descriptions of sequences, in which motivational processes are dealt with as constants, or at any rate are referred to in oversimplified, static categories, such as "benevolence," "cautiousness," "anger," "patriotism." As Radcliffe-Brown and others have pointed out, this sort of historical "explanation" may coexist in peace with a functional explanation, which proceeds on a different level:

One "explanation" of a social system will be its history, where we know it—the detailed account of how it came to be what it is and where it is. Another "explanation" of the same system is obtained by showing (as the functionalist attempts to do) that it is a special exemplification of laws of social physiology or social functioning. The two kinds of explanation do not conflict, but supplement one another.[19]

With respect to dialectical materialism, again, there is no necessary conflict with functional analysis. The philosophy of materialism involves many additional assumptions, however. One of them can be stated as asserting that man's ideas are shaped by the material circumstances of himself and his class, so that certain drastic improvements in these circumstances have the function of liberating the minds of those who cease to be exploited. The Marxists view the capitalist system as dysfunctional in its later stages, as tending toward its own destruction. The dialectical processes in historical development, again, could well be analyzed in functional terms, if stripped of metaphysical (nonconfirmable) assumptions. No Marxist has to my

---

[18] For a convenient if sketchy summary of the most important aspects of the controversy, see Gillin, *The Ways of Men: An Introduction to Anthropology*, chap. 28.

[19] "On the Concept of Function in Social Science," *Structure and Function in Primitive Society: Essays and Addresses*, p. 186.

knowledge tried to do this, but Merton has demonstrated that it can be done.[20]

Lasswell and McDougal have followed the classical economists in formulating an assumption essentially equivalent with functionalism as a general "postulate of maximization": "The alternative selected by the individual or group is the one expected to leave the chooser in the best net value position."[21] My only objection to this kind of formulation is that it unintentionally gives excessively narrow rationality-oriented connotations. The authors, unlike the classical economists, understand the maximization postulate as involving the whole organism, with unconscious processes and goals as well as conscious considerations, and they conceive of the self as expanding by the process of identification. And yet, the term and the definition cited give associations about that mythical rational specimen, the "economic man," or his twin brother, the political man as conceived by James Mill and others. These kinds of associations are avoided if we use the terminology of functional analysis.

The philosophical flexibility allowed by the approach of functional analysis may be exemplified by referring to Clyde Kluckhohn's study of *Navaho Witchcraft*, in which the postulate of functionalism has also been very clearly stated:

No cultural forms survive unless they constitute responses which are adjustive or adaptive, in some sense, for the members of the society or for the society considered as a perduring unit. "Adaptive" is a purely descriptive term referring to the fact that certain types of behavior result in survival (for the individual or for society as a whole). "Adjustive" refers to those responses which bring about an adjustment of the individual, which remove the motivation stimulating the individual. Thus, suicide is adjustive but not adaptive.[22]

By philosophical flexibility in this context I mean the lack of commitment to definite metaphysical or value assumptions. Kluckhohn's approach permitted him to do what no historicist or Marxist could have done: to examine an institution such as witchcraft, so easily dismissed as *merely* superstitious and pathological, in order to try to explain its existence or endurance in terms of a general theory of behavior, without either condemning or defending it.

Freedom from coercion, in its various manifestations, is on the social level an institutional complex to which my support is committed. In this chapter, however, I am not concerned with advocating or promoting the extension of social freedom. My present task is to formulate hypotheses on the extent to which various kinds of social institutions, psychological factors, and political institutions bear on the growth or decline of individual freedom from coercion, in general and for the marginal, least privileged men. This is in principle a complex of empirical problems to be approached by means of a philosophically noncommitted functional analy-

[20] *Social Theory and Social Structure*, pp. 39–41.

[21] *Law, Science and Policy*, working paper, Part II, p. 19.

[22] *Navaho Witchcraft*, p. 46. In the first sentence in the quoted passage "the members of the society" should be interpreted to mean "one or more members of the society."

sis. My conclusions must be as useful to foes as to friends of freedom of expression, not because I wish to be fair to both sides but because my conclusions will not stand up empirically if my value position has been allowed to interfere with the process of functional analysis.

CONCEPTS OF "POWER"

"Power" ("influence") refers to an individual's degree of control over his security. More specifically, *the "power" of an individual refers to the probable difference his own effort will make in his access to or advancement of values (including access to more power) in desired amounts and kinds.*[23] This was my preliminary definition of this important concept. In the same context in the introductory chapter I suggested that it may be useful to distinguish between the feeling and the fact of having power. I also asserted that one man's power may but need not imply restrictions on the social freedom of other men.

A second occasion for discussing some uses of a power concept was found in Chapter 3, in the section given to the definition of "social freedom." Without getting down to theoretical fundamentals, I suggested a few terms to indicate different types of power exercise and power role. It would seem useful, I anticipated, to distinguish between *independent* and *dependent* power and between the roles of power *subject,* power *agent,* and power *object.* Depending on the nature of the motives of power exercise, I recommended a distinction between *purposive* and *institutional* power. With respect to the means of power, the following rough typology was proposed: *physical force,* actual or threatened; *other value deprivations (or indulgences),* or threats (promises) of such; *fraud*; and *persuasion.*[24]

These terms all refer to "power" in an objective sense. In a third context, however, the term has been reintroduced with a somewhat different slant, which includes attention to psychological consequences of the *feeling* of having power. In Chapter 4, a section was headed "The Infant's Quest for Security and Power." Most of the terms listed in the previous paragraph have no immediate relevance for the kind of "power" the infant strives for. The following pages will include some elaboration on these statements.

Patrick Mullahy, Harry Stack Sullivan's student, was quoted in Chapter 4 on the following psychological definitions of the term: "Power refers to any activity where there is accomplishment, satisfaction of needs, mutual attainment of goals not distorted by unfortunate—that is, thwarting—experience. . . . To gain satisfactions and, particularly, security, is to have power in interpersonal relations."[25] Keeping in mind Sullivan's peculiar

[23] See above, pp. 19–20. "Power" and "influence" are in this book synonymous terms. I believe this is the most confusion-proof way of relating the two terms to one another, given the wide overlap in their usage, in scientific journals as well as in everyday language. This alternative of relating both terms to the same concept is suggested in Simon, "Notes on the Observation and Measurement of Political Power," *Journal of Politics,* XV, No. 4 (1953), 500–516.

[24] Cf. above, pp. 91–94.

[25] Cf. above, pp. 163–64, and Mullahy in Sullivan, *Conceptions oof Modern Psychiatry,* pp. 243–44.

usage of "security,"[26] I conclude from these passages that power in interpersonal relations in his sense is equivalent with basic security as defined in this study: the relative absence of anxiety.

In another passage quoted in the same context, Mullahy attributes to Sullivan a conception of power referring to "the expansive biological striving of the infant and states characterized by the feeling of ability, applying, in a very wide sense, to all kinds of human activity."[27] This is power in the sense of *power motive*. Sullivan's own example of early manifestations of the power motive is the infant's reaching out for the full moon, a manifestation that is invariably frustrated and is superseded by more successful avenues, such as the use of crying.[28]

The power motive is still not very different conceptually from the sense of self-confidence associated with basic subjective security. It is to be distinguished sharply from the narrower concept of *power drive*, however; Mullahy does not explicitly define this term, but gives an account of the genesis of this phenomenon. I shall discuss the merit of this hypothesis below; his formulation is quoted here because it is the closest approximation in Mullahy's paper toward an implicit definition of the term:

A "power drive" develops as a compensation when there is a deep, gnawing, inner sense of powerlessness, because of early frustration of the expanding, developing latent potentialities of the organism.[29]

"Power drive," I infer, can designate a defensively exaggerated and rigidified power motive.

It is possible to employ at least two psychological concepts of power, parallel to my two concepts of subjective security. I have considered Sullivan's and Mullahy's use of the term in a sense approximating my concept of basic subjective security or low anxiety. Another not implausible way to define power would be in a sense approximating "absence of fear": "Power" could mean a sense of confidence (a) that there are no external dangers of consequence ahead or (b) that the individual is able to cope with whatever dangers he perceives or anticipates. Or one might include reference to positive plans of action, so that power becomes a sense of confidence in a person's control over the circumstances on which the success of his plans depends.

To prevent unnecessary confusion, I shall in this and the following two chapters studiously avoid the implicit use of "power" in either of these two psychological meanings. When referring to the individual's control of fear or anxiety I shall prefer terms such as "self-confidence," "self-esteem," or "sense of power." In the latter expression, and in expressions such as "power motive" and "power drive," I consider the psychological reference sufficiently explicit to bar misinterpretations. The same goes for "perceived

26 Cf. above, p. 162.

27 Cf. above, pp. 163–64, and Mullahy in Sullivan, *Conceptions of Modern Psychiatry*, p. 242.

28 *Ibid.*, p. 14. Crying does not bring the moon to the infant but may furnish him with agreeable substitutes or distractions.

29 Cf. Mullahy in Sullivan, *Conceptions of Modern Psychiatry*, p. 242. See my discussion below, "Some Psychological Determinants," especially pp. 297–301.

power," meaning the individual's perceived or imagined control over his perceived security.

In all other kinds of contexts, "power" shall refer to the individual's actual or probable control over his objective security.

It is time now to advance toward a more adequate concept of power, as compared to the preliminary definition that has had to serve so far. Let us consider a few of the clearest and most explicit definitions available in the literature:

The Power *of a Man,* (to take it universally,) is his present means to obtain some future apparent Good.[30]

Power . . . means security for the conformity between the will of one man and the acts of other men.[31]

"Power" [*Macht*] is the probability that one actor within a social relationship will be in a position to carry out his own will despite resistance, regardless of the basis on which this probability rests.[32]

Power may be defined as the production of intended effects.[33]

Power is participation in the making of decisions. G has power over H with respect to the values K if G participates in the making of decisions affecting the K-policies of H. . . . A decision is a policy involving severe sanctions (deprivations). . . . Policy is a projected program of goal values and practices.[34]

The exercise of influence consists in affecting policies of others than the self.[35]

Power . . . is present to the extent to which one person controls by sanction the decisions and actions of another.[36]

Social power is: (1) the potentiality (2) for inducing forces (3) in other persons (4) toward acting or changing in a given direction.[37]

Common to most of these definitions is the idea that power has to do with decision-making and with affecting the decisions of others. But they differ in their assumptions about the motives on which decisions are based. Max Weber asserts explicitly that power consists in overcoming resistance, while at the other end Ronald Lippitt and his associates conceive of (social) power as the process of inducing motives of certain kinds in the power object. The rest of the definitions are not explicit on this point; most of them make the acts or the outcome of decisions of others the crucial issue, regardless of underlying motivations. Only the definitions of Thomas Hobbes and Bertrand Russell focus entirely on the impersonal effects of power; an ambitious artist's ability to paint a good picture is Russell's first example of "forms of power."[38]

The question of the significance of the motives underlying decisions may be split in two: Lippitt and his associates may differ from Weber in

---

[30] Hobbes, *Leviathan,* p. 43.
[31] James Mill, "Government," in Burtt (ed.), *English Philosophers,* p. 56.
[32] Weber, *The Theory of Social and Economic Organization,* p. 152.
[33] Russell, *Power: A New Social Analysis,* p. 35.
[34] Lasswell and Kaplan, *Power and Society,* pp. 75, 74, 71.
[35] *Ibid.,* p. 71.
[36] Easton, *The Political System,* p. 144.
[37] Lippitt, Polansky, and Rosen, "The Dynamics of Power: A Field Study of Social Influence in Groups of Children," *Human Relations,* V, No. 1 (1952), 39.
[38] *Power,* p. 35.

assumptions both about the origin of and about the type of motive behind the decisions at issue.

In the first place, is it an essential criterion of power that the decision effectuated would not have come about without the use of power? Antoine de Saint-Exupéry in his fairy tale *The Little Prince* describes the occupant of a small planet who fancies himself the mightiest of all kings, since he commands the whole universe—for example, he commands the sun to rise every morning and to set every night, and the sun never fails to comply. What this little king enjoyed, if my terminology is applied, was security, not power, in his relationship to the sun and the universe.

The second issue is the type of motive on which compliance is based. As an illustration one may choose a story, no doubt invented in Denmark, about Tsar Peter the Great visiting Copenhagen and being taken to the top of the famous Round Tower by the Danish king. To impress his host with his power, the tsar orders one of his men to jump off the tower to a certain death and is obeyed instantly. The Danish king replies that he considers his own power greater than the tsar's because he can do what the tsar cannot do: sleep safely with his head in the lap of any one among his subjects. Assuming that the story were true and the king's proud boast were justified, who would be the more powerful monarch? Weber's definition would make only the tsar powerful, if applied to the assumed evidence of this story only. The definition quoted from Lippitt and his associates, on the other hand, would probably make only the king a man of power.

For my part, I wish to be quite explicit in considering both kinds of monarchical prerogatives, if successfully exercised, as irrefutable evidence of power. The difference between the two kinds of power exercise, as exemplified in ideal type in my example, is the difference between "coercive" and "manipulative" power. This difference corresponds closely, as we shall see, to the distinction between social and potential freedom.[39] Although the topics of manipulative power and potential freedom belong in the next chapter, let me for a moment employ my pseudohistorical example for a comparison between coercive and manipulative power: Whom should we consider more "powerful" within his country, the tsar or the king?

It seems to me that the king should be declared the winner of this contest, for these reasons. (1) Being in control of the affections of his subjects (as the story assumes), he would be able to count on more than their automatic obedience; he could expect them to exert themselves whenever he so required, because they *identified* with him. (2) There was a greater harmony between the values of monarch and subjects in Denmark than in Russia; consequently, the Danish king had a greater incentive potential for voluntary obedience at his disposal.[40]

[39] Carl J. Friedrich makes the related observation that power can be generated either by consent or by constraint, or by both in combination. *Constitutional Government and Democracy: Theory and Practice in Europe and America*, pp 22–24.

[40] Cf. Merriam: "Power is not strongest when it uses violence, but weakest. It is strongest when it employs the instruments of substitution and counter attraction, of allurement, of participation rather than of exclusion, of education rather than of annihilation. Rape is not an evidence of irresistible power in politics or in sex." *Political Power: Its Composition and Incidence*, p. 180. Cf. also below, pp. 317–18.

I have made a not wholly warranted assumption, however, in asserting that the safety of the Danish king among his subjects shows that they identify with him. If such a safety existed, the reason may instead have been that they had *internalized* various moral or legal norms, including the norm that thou shalt not kill, whether majesties or lesser men. Let me now turn to a more systematic statement of what has been learned about types of power processes.

For purposes of studying opinion change, Herbert C. Kelman has proposed a useful analytical scheme of three processes of social influence on opinion formation; he acknowledges that in actual fact they tend to intermingle, in varying proportions:

Compliance refers to the case where a person adopts an opinion which another person wants him to adopt, without actually believing it; identification refers to the case where a person accepts publicly and privately an opinion which another person holds, by taking over this person's role without any actual concern for the content of the opinion; and internalization refers to the case where a person accepts the content of an opinion which was originally introduced to him by another person, and integrates it with his own values.[41]

Let me broaden these definitions beyond the scope of opinion change and adapt them to the needs of my theory. *Compliance* refers to obedience or conformity without a conviction that this behavior is desirable in itself. *Identification* has in personality terms been defined as taking place to the extent that the individual comes to consider the general needs of other persons his own, or more important than his own.[42] In social process terms, identification refers to a readiness to obey or conform motivated by the perceived needs of specific other persons, which have become the individual's own needs or have become more important than the needs he perceives as his own. *Internalization*, finally, means a readiness to conform to norms that have become integrated in the individual's self or in his cognitive outlook.

This last term is not a happy one, as Kelman acknowledges, because its usual meaning in psychological literature is a narrower one; internalization as a rule means inclusion in the superego or ego.[43] What Kelman emphasizes is the *content-orientation* in the third process of influence. The person who is influenced, or the power object, is conforming by way of a relatively rational acceptance of the content of the influence.

The empirical value of Kelman's distinction hinges on whether a diagnosis in his terms helps us to predict under what circumstances opinions or other behaviors imparted by influence processes will tend to persist. He suggests, and quite plausibly—though it is not yet convincingly confirmed by experiment—the following probability rules: Opinions motivated by mere compliance will persist only as long as the influencer or his sanctions are in operation. Opinions motivated by identification will persist regard-

[41] "Opinion Change through Social Influence: A Discussion of Three Processes."
[42] See above, pp. 174–78.
[43] Cf. above, pp. 88–89 and note 85.

less of whether the object of identification is around, so long as the latter is salient in the mind of the influencee. Internalized opinions, finally, will persist independently of the presence or expected presence of the influencer and are independent of the saliency of the original process of influence. Depending on the degree of integration in the individual's cognitive outlook or personality, all the way from a superficial acceptance to incorporation in the ego, or internalization in the strictest sense, this sort of a new opinion can be challenged with ease or difficulty by rational argument.[44]

To the extent that these probability rules hold in processes of influencing opinions, it is fair to assume that the same tendencies will be discernible in all power processes. Forced obedience is likely to wither when the show of force ceases, whereas obedience motivated by identification with the power subject will induce conformity to his rules as long as he is remembered affectionately and saliently. An internalized conformity to the influencer's norms may (but need not) be persisted in indefinitely, even after the power subject, say a teacher, is long forgotten.

It was on the basis of this insight, essentially, that empiricists such as Locke, Godwin, and John Stuart Mill declared that benevolent despotism is worse than the more malicious varieties, since it tends to enslave the minds as well as the bodies.[45] Tocqueville lamented the state and prospects of freedom in the American democracy for the same reason; to him, a democratic majority could and probably would, if unrestrained, be more tyrannical than an autocratic despot.[46] Rousseau, again, was even more explicit when he expressed the opposite value position in his advice to the legitimate government (the agent of the general will) that it should not confine itself to demanding mere obedience: "It is much better to make [men] what there is need that they should be."[47]

The exercise of power does not necessarily reduce social freedom; it does not necessarily produce perceived external restraints. Whether exercise of power always reduces someone's freedom in *some* sense is a complex question that does not need an answer here. I shall get somewhat closer toward an answer to that question in the next chapter, for it will depend most of all on the delimitations I choose to specify for the concept of potential freedom. A discussion of processes of power exerted by inducing identification or internalization belongs in the next chapter, too, as they are among the determinants of potential freedom.

In the present context my focus on the power concept is limited to the power to induce compliance, in Kelman's sense. Exercise of this kind of influence always reduces someone's social freedom.

Are there also other determinants of social freedom, which are inde-

[44] This last probability rule depends also, and perhaps even more crucially, on another variable that may be partly independent of the degree of internalization—namely, on the function of the opinion for the individual. Cf. above, pp. 191–92.

[45] Cf. Locke, *Two Treatises on Civil Government*, p. 202; Godwin, *Political Justice*, I, 238; J. S. Mill, "Representative Government," in *Utilitarianism*, pp. 278, 289.

[46] *Democracy in America*, I, 273, and above, p. 96.

[47] "A Discourse on Political Economy," in *The Social Contract and Discourses*, p. 297; and above, pp. 62 and 95.

pendent of the exercise of power by individuals? What about the "power of institutions"? As we shall see in the next section, all external social restraints on the individual, including institutional restraints, are effective only in so far as they are implemented by individuals exercising power. My analysis will make it clear that all enduring patterns of social interaction have institutional aspects and that institutions are nothing more than the readiness of individuals to exert power under certain conditions.[48]

Before attempting a final formulation of my power concept, let me approach it from still another angle. What suggestions have been made in the literature about ways toward measurement of power?

First of all, it should be pointed out, as Herbert A. Simon does, that measurements of power are not necessarily to be expressed in cardinal numbers. It is out of the question to try to match in the realm of power Plato's dubious feat of proving that a king lives 729 times more pleasantly than the tyrant does.[49] The alternatives are ordinal numbers, expressed by "greater than" or the like, and vectors, when complex phenomena consisting of several variables are to be compared. In the latter case, only a partial ordering, or an ordering of specified variables, is possible.[50]

Simon, whose discussion of power relies heavily on the work of Lasswell and Kaplan, defines power as these authors define influence. To Simon, as to this writer, these two terms are synonymous. "The exercise of influence (influence process) consists in affecting policies of others than the self."[51] Simon calls it "an asymmetrical relation between influencer and influencee" but stresses the fact that power never becomes completely a one-way phenomenon; power relationships may alternately be viewed as two opposite asymmetrical relations. Simon is aware that the measurement problem becomes increasingly complex as we take into account an increasing number of variables in the social system. Only within the limits of very specific assumptions can we say, he suggests as an example, that the power of the American President "can be measured by the number of bills he vetoes where the veto is not overridden."[52]

Another difficulty is in the fact that some kinds of statements about power have effects on the realities of power. If the populace of Argentina once estimated the power of Peron to be dictatorial, this very estimate served to increase Peron's actual power at the time. Valid statements and predictions on political power may be possible, Simon concludes, provided we can distinguish between the role of the outside scientific observer, whose statements are not taken very seriously by citizens and rulers, and on the other hand the role of the citizen, whose perceptions of power immediately influence the actual state of power. The clues for the scientific observer are

[48] Cf. below, pp. 258–59 and 262–64.

[49] *The Republic*, p. 354.

[50] Cf. Simon, "Notes on the Observation and Measurement of Political Power," *Journal of Politics*, XV, No. 4 (1953), pp. 512–15.

[51] *Ibid.*, p. 503, and Lasswell and Kaplan, *Power and Society*, p. 71. Cf. above, p. 248.

[52] Simon, "Notes on the Observation and Measurement of Political Power," *Journal of Politics*, XV, No. 4 (1953), pp. 504–6. Cf. below, p. 256.

these: "Observations of the distribution of values and of attitudes regarding legitimacy constitute two significant kinds of indirect evidence about the distribution of power. A third, of critical significance, are the expectations of the participants in the power situation."[53]

Simon is not explicit about ways to apply these criteria in research, but it seems to me that he has come as close to an empirically fruitful statement of the problem as is possible at the present stage. These criteria seem to lend themselves to further specification toward application in research. Studies of the distribution of one type of value at a time can be done easily in the case of wealth; with more difficulty with reference to affection, enlightenment, and well-being; and with the greatest difficulty in the case of power, which involves all or several of other values as well. Studies of the distribution of attitudes toward legitimacy can make an important contribution, however, toward remedying the difficulties involved in direct studies of power distribution, as legitimacy attitudes are important determinants of power. An even better remedy is a study of factual expectations with respect to power exercise. It may be difficult to decide to what extent such expectations are determinants of and to what extent they are determined by the underlying facts of power. But it can be assumed that they are good indices, in times of relative stability at least, of the realities of power distribution, and they can be studied quantitatively.

Lasswell and Kaplan, whose work provides the basis for Simon's discussion, suggest that the problem of measurement be approached by breaking the "amount" of power down into three components:

The weight of power is the degree of participation in the making of decisions; its scope consists of the values whose shaping and enjoyment are controlled; the domain of power consists of the persons over whom power is exercised.[54]

The weight of power can in principle be measured; in fact, many studies of small groups have sought to refine the techniques for and propose generalizations about determinants of the relative weight of power in these special settings.[55] The scope, consisting of the range of values being controlled, is hard to measure, since values tend to be incommensurable. It is more feasible, starting out from Simon's formulation, to approximate measurements of the distribution of certain specified values (money would be an example, whether acceptable to him or not). The domain, finally, can but should not be measured until and unless the value criteria are limited and specified. Even then a counting of noses in the power domain would for the study of freedom be useless unless some measure is included of the relative importance of each value in question for each individual.

Perhaps the question of the usefulness of the Lasswell-Kaplan power concept has been discussed in a frame of reference too broad to do it justice. If I find Simon's version more useful as a tool in the general study of

---

[53] *Ibid.*, pp. 511–12, 515–16.
[54] *Power and Society*, p. 77.
[55] Some hypotheses are summarized in Festinger, "Informal Social Communication," in Festinger *et al.*, *Theory and Experiment in Social Communication*, pp. 3–18.

freedom, the former approach may still be well suited for the study of more specific freedom problems. Lasswell and McDougal are on a later occasion discussing the clarification of "shared power" as one of the goals for democratic policy. They are not rigorously adhering to the Lasswell-Kaplan definition, but some of their new descriptive criteria in the same vein appear promising in terms of both theoretical significance and measurement possibilities:

Power is shared when the political myth favors the pattern of general participation in the making of decisions. . . . Power is shared when in fact as well as in myth there is general participation in decision-making. . . . Power is shared when the balancing process maintains a strong presumption against the use of power in great concentrations, whether in the form of regimentation, territorial or functional centralization, or of militarization.[56]

These are questions eminently suited for research, and their bearing on the problem of social freedom is rather obvious.

Another approach toward the measurement of power was proposed almost twenty years ago by Herbert Goldhamer and Edward A. Shils: "The amount of power exercised by an individual may be measured . . . by the ratio of his successful power acts to all of his attempted power acts."[57] This specification would, however, leave Saint-Exupéry's little king, who commands the sun to rise and to set, mightier than all earthly despots.

A more valuable criterion is suggested later in the same paper, after the introduction of a vaguely indicated distinction between manipulative and coercive power. As between coercive power-holders, the authors suggest, "power varies directly with the severity of the sanctions that the power-holder can impose."[58] The underlying psychological assumption seems a plausible one: My chances of making other persons with no love for me or sense of obligation toward me go out of their way, that is, beyond reasonable institutional expectations, to promote my interests or values, would seem to depend in large measure on what I in turn can do for them, or against them. Yet, what I *can* do may be less crucial than the perceptions these persons get about what I *will* do, with what probability, under what circumstances. Among men of power who rely mainly on coercion—if there are any—the ruthless and resolute are apt to have more power than the more humane and inhibited, if their control over sanctions is equal.

Quite a different approach toward the evaluation of amounts of power has been taken by Floyd Hunter, who is distinguished as being the first, so far as I know, to attempt an empirical study of the power structure within a fairly large city. His procedure was a simple sociometric one. A list of 175 names was compiled on the basis of suggestions from various sources

---

[56] *Law, Science and Policy*, working paper, Part III, pp. 3–5. The other four out of seven propositions seem to me less immediately reducible to operational terms, without, at any rate, some further auxiliary definitions or theoretical clarification.

[57] "Types of Power and Status," *American Journal of Sociology*, XLV, No. 2 (1939), 176. This is only one of several alternative ways these authors suggest for the measurement of power.

[58] *Ibid.*, p. 178.

among residents of the city. Other residents were used as "judges" to name the most powerful ten names among those on the list. On the basis of cumulative ratings of the judges. Hunter selected 40 names and proceeded to describe the power behavior of these people, focused on certain issues of interest to them. It must be said, however, that this study, *Community Power Structure: A Study of Decision Makers,* admirable as it is as a journalistic survey, lacks the analytical rigor of terms and hypotheses that could have given it significance for political theory. But this sort of approach may prove valuable in the future, if better instruments and more precise hypotheses are employed.

Another purely descriptive study of power is Robert A. Gordon's *Business Leadership in a Large Corporation.* Gordon studied not a city, but the two hundred largest corporations in the United States. His conceptual scheme is much superior to Hunter's, and he reveals various trends of great interest to the study of corporate behavior. Gordon does not address himself, however, to the general problem of the measurement of power.[59]

I know of no other approaches toward power measurement comparable in sophistication to those of Goldhamer and Shils, Lasswell and Kaplan, and Herbert Simon. Most studies of power as a general problem have been more concerned with describing its various manifestations than with developing conceptual tools for further research. A second purpose has frequently been to take a moral position against the use of certain kinds of power.[60]

In conclusion I shall now try to improve on my preliminary definition of power and, at the same time, define the crucial subconcepts of coercive power and manipulative power.

Let me advance step by step. *"Power"* may first of all refer to an individual's capacity to affect the behavior of other individuals and groups; *"exercise of power"* may refer to the process of affecting other people's actual or potential behavior. *"Behavior"* I shall understand in the broadest sense: it may refer only to locomotive or verbal behavior at the one extreme and at the other extreme include also motivational, cathectic, affective, and cognitive behavior. Behavior may also, of course, affect motives without ever affecting overt behavior, but this is a limiting case that shall not be of concern here. For practical purposes, power over other men's motives is equivalent with power over their potential overt behavior as well.

This is a different point of departure from my preliminary formulation, restated in the first paragraph of this section.[61] A person's degree of control over his security may at first seem possibly independent of his control over other people's behavior. Yet, personal "control over security" is

---

[59] See also Brady, *Business as a System of Power.* Brady's study is a scholarly exposé of propensities of large corporations toward cartel building and of their readiness in the past to support fascism if their power is threatened by democratic forces.

[60] See Merriam, *Political Power,* Chap. 5, "The Shame of Power"; and Russell, *Power,* Chap. 17, "The Ethics of Power."

[61] See above, p. 248.

different from "security"; it refers to the probable difference a person's own effort will make in his continued access to values. To the extent that security is perfect, in the sense that the individual is assured access to all values he desires, and is assured success for all goals he wishes to promote, power is superfluous. In the psychological "power drive" sense of power, it is also true that the quest for power begins where the sense of security ends, for the infant and for the adult.[62]

On the level of social analysis, which concerns me here, the exercise or even the potential of power can have a function for the individual, then, only to the extent that his security is incomplete. Needless to say, in actual life this is invariably the case, even for the firmly entrenched dictator—in fact, more so in his case than in the case of a man with few wants and few personal or public ambitions.

The reason for stating these trivialities is that they help us find the way to a combination of the two approaches just stated (or restated, in one case) toward a satisfactory definition of power. If the end of power invariably is access to or advancement of values, "power" differs from "security" in that power also involves the ability to produce effects on other people's behavior. The probable difference a man's effort will make for his access to or effective promotion of values depends first and foremost on his capacity to direct other people's behavior. There are, of course, other factors, too, such as the bounty of virgin nature, or the availability of nonsocial values such as sunshine and scenery or of man-made wealth. Except for isolated hermits, however, even access to sunshine and scenery may depend on social relationships, too, and access to man-made wealth is invariably socially regulated.

Excluding both the isolated hermits and the all-pervasive valued objects (such as air and water) from my concern, I conclude, as a general rule, that for practical purposes the individual's future access to and advancement of values depends on (a) his *security,* or the degree of assurance that his access to values will continue or expand, and, to the extent that this trend is *not* assured; (b) his *power* to direct human behavior towards remedying the uncertainty or unfavorable trend.

Let this be the final power concept in the present study: *"Power" ("influence") is an individual's capacity for attaining or advancing values by way of affecting with his own behavior the behavior of others. "Exercise of power (influence)" is the process of attaining or advancing values by affecting the behavior of others.*

Let us note that power is always exercised by individuals. The "power of an organization" is the aggregate (sum, product, or some other mathematical function) of the power of its board, members, and supporters.[63] The "power of an institution" is the aggregate of the power of those who

---

[62] Cf. above, pp. 163–64 and 166.

[63] Stanley Schachter defines the "internal power of the group" as "the magnitude of change the group can induce on its members." The pressures on each member are in large part determined by group factors, but they are exerted in each case by other members. Cf. Schachter, "Deviation, Rejection, and Communication," in Cartwright and Zander (eds.); *Group Dynamics: Research and Theory,* p. 224. Cf. also Festinger, Schachter, and Back, *Social Pressures in Informal Groups: A Study of Human Factors in Housing,* pp. 165–66.

employ sanctions on its behalf, whether institutionally (automatically) or deliberately, or in other ways induce motives toward conformity. The "power of public opinion" is equivalent to the power of an aggregate of institutions plus an aggregate of the independent power of policy makers, opinion leaders, and men in general. In each case, the exercise of power is by individuals, one or more at a time, even if in turn the power behavior of individuals in large part is determined by their social roles and the inter-constellations of these. Thus men of great power can exercise it with very little effort on their own part, as a rule.

"*Coercive power*" is an individual's capacity for attaining or advancing values by achieving compliant behavior in other individuals as a result of actual or anticipated sanctions, provided compliance for these others means abandoning strongly motivated alternate intentions. Sanctions strong enough to achieve this result are "coercive sanctions"; their effect depends both on motivational predispositions in the power object and on the situation in which he finds himself.

"*Manipulative power*" is an individual's capacity for attaining or advancing values by inducing motives in other individuals toward conformity with his wishes, in the absence of or independently of coercive sanctions. Characteristic motive patterns are identification with favorable symbols or individuals, or internalization, in the very broadest sense of attitudes and beliefs, ranging from superficial acceptance by rational persuasion to the growth of profound conviction by a combination of overpowering influences, rational and nonrational.

Both coercive and manipulative power are by my definition (potentially) effective in affecting behavior. If attempts are ineffective, I wish to speak of attempted power exertion, or attempted coercion or manipulation, respectively.

Power exertion is not necessarily intended.[64] A power subject may in some situations wish to step out of his power role but may find himself affecting behavior and advancing values, nevertheless, and he may at times unwittingly act as the power agent of others. Many foolish autocrats have unwittingly diverted the loyalties of their subjects to potential rebel leaders; to this extent they have unintentionally behaved as power agents of the latter.

The classification of effective power exertion into coercion and manipulation is not logically exhaustive. Power exertion is functional only in the absence of certainty that potential power objects will conform anyway. Correspondingly, coercion is functional only in the presence of strong motivations in the relevant individuals not to conform. In the absence of such a trend rather mild sanctions may be sufficient to bring about conformity, and I have chosen to adhere to convention in not terming these mild sanctions coercive.

With this addition, however, I believe the classification is exhaustive: effective power exertion consists either in (a) noncoercive but effective perceived external pressures, (b) coercion, or (c) manipulation.

[64] Cf. above, p. 91. See also p. 22, on political behavior.

With the noncoercive perceived external pressures I shall not be concerned at all from here on; these pressures do not bring about important restrictions on freedom. Freedom from coercion is the topic of the remainder of this chapter, and freedom from manipulation is the topic of Chapter 6.

SOME GENERAL SOCIAL DETERMINANTS

Institutions, Roles, and the Social System

Any group[65] of interacting individuals can be studied as a social system, whether small or large, organized or not. George C. Homans, following the general orientation of Talcott Parsons, states in his definition that the social system consists of "the activities, interactions, and sentiments of the group member, together with the mutual relations of these elements with another during the time is group is active."[66] According to Parsons and his associates, "the social system is, to be sure, made up of the relationships of individuals, but it is a system which is organized around the problems inherent in or arising from social interaction of a plurality of individual actors."[67] The social system, one may conclude, is a system of interpersonal behavior. Personality variables of participating individuals are elements in the social system *in so far* as they bear on the interaction with other individuals.

In calling a group or society a *system* one implies an important assumption: that the behaviors constituting the system are *functionally interrelated*. It should be stressed that this is a pragmatically necessary assumption that may or may not have validity within a metaphysical system of beliefs. There may well be some elements of interpersonal behavior, maybe more in some individuals than in others, that are completely unrelated to preceding as well as to following interpersonal events. It must remain my working hypothesis, however, that this is the exception rather than the rule. Discoveries of functional interrelationships provide the only data on which a dynamic social theory can be based.[68]

What are the basic elements of a social system? That pioneer in functional analysis, Emile Durkheim, in his early work proposed the following definition of a *social fact*:

A social fact is every way of acting, fixed or not, capable of exercising on the individual an external constraint; or again, every way of acting which is general throughout a given society, while at the same time existing in its own right independent of its individual manifestations.[69]

---

[65] "Group" is a more inclusive term than "society." It refers to any number of interacting individuals, from two upwards to the whole of humanity, if we confine our attention to human groups.

[66] *The Human Group*, p. 87.

[67] "Some Fundamental Categories of the Theory of Action: A General Statement," in Parsons and Shils (eds.), *Toward a General Theory of Action*, p. 7. For more specific definitions of "social system" as well as "personality system" and "cultural system," see *ibid.*, pp. 54–55, and a number of additional contexts in this volume and in Parsons, *The Social System*.

[68] Cf. above, p. 246. See above, p. 23, for a related, more general discussion of a pragmatically necessary bias in favor of "determinism," or a belief in causation in the most general sense of this word.

[69] *Rules of Sociological Method*, p. 13.

Let us disregard the somewhat ambiguous last clause of the sentence and observe that there are at least two elements in Durkheim's "social fact": an element of actual or potential external restraint on the individual and an element of generality throughout the group. At times he uses "institution" as a synonym: "One can . . . designate as 'institutions' all the beliefs and all the modes of conduct instituted by the collectivity."[70]

As Talcott Parsons has emphasized, Durkheim gradually outgrew his conception of institutions as primarily external constraints on the individual. He came to see that the threat of sanctions normally plays a minor part in producing conformity to institutions. More important is the moral authority of institutions: they become internalized as part of the individual's "given" situation, as he sees it, or as part of "his" value orientation, affecting his goals or his norms. Man is not an independent, narrowly rationalistic individual pursuing his "interest" with sanction probabilities (rewards and punishments) as his only guide. Man is a social being, relating himself to others by identification and internalization. He acquires moral obligations—if indeed he is not to some extent socially tuned from his very birth.[71]

The pattern of institutions thus becomes "a constitutive element in the individual's own concrete personality. . . . He is not placed in a social environment so much as he participates in a common social life."[72] But man is still an individual, too, and his social behavior must be studied in terms of its functions both for his own personality integration and for the integration of the social system. Man can play his part in maintaining the social system only if he in the process can maintain his own balance as an organism and a personality.

With the latter subject I have dealt extensively in the preceding chapter, in which I inquired into the determinants of man's maintenance of a maximal integration and expression of his basic personality predispositions. My principal frame of reference in this chapter and the next is the social system, not the individual personality. I wish to inquire into institutional determinants of the degrees of coercion and manipulation of men. In so far as institutions operate primarily through sanctions, in accordance with Durkheim's earlier view, this discussion belongs in the present chapter. In so far as they operate through inducing moral convictions, or other motives uninfluenced by the immediate sanctions, the functions of institutions are properly discussed under the topic of potential freedom, in the next chapter.

In his earlier work, Parsons has developed a "voluntaristic theory of action" as an alternative and in part a synthesis of the categories of human behavior employed, sometimes implicitly, by such writers as Emile Durkheim, Vilfredo Pareto, and Max Weber. The basic element in Parsons' early theory is an abstraction named a *unit act*. This concept refers to a

[70] *Ibid.*, p. lvi (from the author's preface to the second edition). In the same context Durkheim defines sociology as the science of the genesis and functioning of institutions.
[71] This last point is discussed above, p. 171. The substance of the paragraph draws on Parsons, *The Structure of Social Action*, especially pp. 378–408 and 463.
[72] *Ibid.*, p. 399.

constellation of (1) an actor, (2) a goal, (3) a situation (conditions and means), and (4) a normative orientation of the actor, bearing on his choice of means.[73]

More recently, in developing further the social system frame of reference, Parsons has found the concept of *social role* more useful than "unit act" as an elementary unit of analysis:

A social system is a system of the actions of individuals, the principal units of which are roles and constellations of roles.[74]

The institution should be considered to be a higher order unit of social structure than the role, and indeed it is made up of a plurality of interdependent role-patterns or components of them.[75]

Systems of patterned expectations, seen in the perspective of their place in a total social system and sufficiently thoroughly established in action to be taken for granted as legitimate, are conveniently called "institutions."[76]

It is more congenial to me to consider *every sanctioned behavior expectation persisting through time* as an *institution,* and this usage appears to have considerable following in the literature, even if it must be admitted that the term has been used in a variety of ways. S. F. Nadel, who reviews a number of definitions, settles for a formulation akin to mine, though minus the sanction requirement: "By institution, then, we shall mean a standardized mode of social behavior or, since social behavior means co-activity, a *standardized* mode of co-activity."[77]

Nadel does indicate in the same context that he considers it superfluous to state explicitly that institutions always carry at least a minimum of sanctions, such as social approval or disapproval at the very least—as he puts it, "institutions are norms."[78] They regulate expectancies, and people tend to have a stake in the stability of their expectancies of each other's behavior. Nadel objects quite properly to other definitions in which the sanction requirement is too specific to apply to all types of what he would call institutions. And yet it seems to me that he assumes too much when he in effect asserts that all "standardized modes of co-activity" are sanctioned. It is at

---

[73] *Structure of Social Action,* pp. 44–45.

[74] Parsons and Shils in *Toward a General Theory of Action,* p. 197. Cf. Parsons: *The Social System,* p. 8, note 4. "Social *role,*" Parsons and associates define, "is that organized sector of an actor's orientation which constitutes and defines his participation in an interactive process." *Toward a General Theory of Action,* p. 23. Cf. below, p. 264, for my definition of "role."

[75] *The Social System,* p. 39.

[76] *Essays in Sociological Theory, Pure and Applied,* p. 35.

[77] *The Foundations of Social Anthropology,* p. 108. The most frequent point at issue between diverging definitions is irrelevant to the question whether my definition (or Nadel's) is preferable to that of Parsons; the question on which writers have differed the most is whether "institution" should be defined more abstractly in terms of behavior or more concretely in terms of organizations. Cf. *ibid.,* pp. 107–11.

[78] Nadel offers no explicit definition of "norm." The following sentence in the text presumably paraphrases what he intends to say with these three words.

My usage of "norm" differs from Nadel's. It parallels the meaning of "institution," except that "norm" is on a higher level of abstraction, in the system of culture, not the social system. Regardless of actual behavior prospects, *a "norm" is an expectancy or a desire about behavior, whether the individual's own or that of other people.* Institutions always imply and indeed "realize" norms, but many norms are not institutionalized. Cf. above, p. 14, note 28.

the very least a possibility that certain customs in social interaction can be strictly neutral. This is not much more than a quibble, for it must be admitted that *neutral customs,* or customs that are not *institutionalized,* that is, armed with the teeth of sanctions, however feeble, must be exceedingly rare: "What has been spoken of as 'neutral custom' can be known as wholly neutral only if departure from it proves not to be a debit entry in a man's career and does not carry that flavor of mild misdemeanor which shows itself in gossip, covert or overt ridicule, or in provision of good taunting material to build up the adversary's case in a dispute; in a word, if in truth nothing is done about it."[79]

A *sanction* is any type of restraint on individual behavior that is viewed as an inducement toward or away from a certain kind of behavior.[80] In E. Adamson Hoebel's words:

The positive sanctions step up all the way from the lollipop, the smile, the pat on the back, applause, to honorific positions, bonuses, medals and citations, to posthumous enshrinement. The negative sanctions range from the curled lip, the raised eyebrow, the word of scorn and ridicule, the rap on the knuckle, and refusal to invite back to dinner; through economic deprivation, physical hurt, prolonged social ostracism, through imprisonment or exile to the ultimate in social ostracism—execution.[81]

Sanctions function most effectively in support of institutions when they are anticipated well in advance, so that their potential force can influence motives and behavior in a relaxed rather than in a crisis fashion. Institutional sanctions can by definition be anticipated, though perhaps usually not with full accuracy. Homans makes the point that "virtual" or hypothetical behavior changes are projected, in everyday life, much more frequently than actual behavior changes are carried out. Consciously or unconsciously, we keep asking ourselves how the other person would react to a variety of behavior alternatives on our part, before we act. It is through these kinds of projections, Homans says, that "intelligence takes part in control."[82] Carl Friedrich makes essentially the same point, as applied to politics, in his discussion of "the rule of anticipated reactions": "The influence of public opinion or of Parliament upon the conduct of governmental affairs is as devoid of ascertainable manifestations as the influence of a courtesan upon her royal master. Why should this be so? Because the person or group which is being influenced *anticipates the reactions* of him or those who exercise the influence."[83]

[79] Llewellyn and Hoebel, *The Cheyenne Way: Conflict and Case Law in Primitive Jurisprudence,* p. 25.

[80] Cf. above, p. 89.

[81] *The Law of Primitive Man: A Study in Comparative Legal Dynamics,* p. 15.

[82] *The Human Group,* p. 292.

[83] Friedrich claims that to his knowledge the "rule of anticipated reactions" had not been previously stated in exact form. He speculates further that the operation of this rule more frequently leads to inaction than to action, at least in democracies. Cf. Friedrich, *Constitutional Government and Democracy: Theory and Practice in Europe and America* (1941 edition), pp. 589–91 and note 17. This passage is from the last chapter in the 1941 edition, entitled "A Sketch of the Scope and Method of Political Science." This chapter is deleted from the 1950 edition. Cf. also Simon, *Administrative Behavior: A Study of Decision-Making Processes in Administration Organization,* pp. 129–30.

Note that sanctions are not necessarily tied to institutional behavior, even if institutional behavior is always sanctioned. The purposive exercise of power, as the alternative to institutional power behavior, may also carry sanctions with it, and always does in the case of coercion or attempted coercion. Manipulative power, on the other hand, does not necessarily carry any sanctions.[84]

Now let me return to the concept of role, in the theory of Parsons the principal unit in the analysis of social systems. A *role,* I should define, *is an institution,* or a sanctioned behavior expectation persisting through time, *focused on a given individual or category of individuals and specified with respect to what behaviors are expected of him (them) under what circumstances.*[85] There is no substantive difference between this concept and Ralph Linton's widely quoted definition: "A status . . . is simply a collection of rights and duties. . . . A role represents the dynamic aspect of status. When [the individual] puts the rights and duties which constitute the status into effect, he is performing a role."[86]

All social interaction is in varying degrees regulated or influenced by institutions, and all institutions include role expectations, specified with respect to individuals and/or circumstances, as well as types of sanction. Now, if it were possible to regulate all social behavior, including motivations, completely by institutional pressures, we should have the ideal type of a society entirely without potential freedom, but, paradoxically, with a maximal social freedom, since institutions are no longer external restraints if they once have become internalized so that they govern motives as well as overt behavior. If, on the other hand, the external behavior patterns could become completely enforced throughout a given society, while motivations otherwise were left free, we should have a society with a minimum of social freedom, while the potential freedom could be wide. The third extreme, if we can conceive of a complete absence of regulation, would amount to the complete absence of a social system, or of an integrated society.

The problem of social as well as potential freedom hinges in large measure on the range of social life within which institutions are necessary, how specific institutions must be (or what leeway they can allow) in the various realms of life, and how strictly they must be sanctioned. A society that relies heavily on elaborate and strictly enforced institutional sanctions is an oppressive one, whether its political constitution is democratic or autocratic. A society that has a minimum of regulations and a minimum of enforcement is likely to be an anomic society. The problem of social freedom may be phrased as the problem of reducing the scope and amount of coercive sanctions as much as is possible without giving rise to more serious anomic strains than the social system and most individual personalities can bear.

---

[84] Cf. below, p. 319.

[85] The expectations can be more specific or more diffuse, and may or may not be specified with respect to which other persons are involved. These and other "pattern variables" are discussed in Parsons and Shils (eds.), *Toward a General Theory of Action,* pp. 76–91.

[86] *The Study of Man,* pp. 113–14. This definition is quoted with approval in Homans, *The Human Group,* p. 11. Homans himself writes, in the same vein, "a norm that states the expected relationship of a person in a certain position to others he comes into contact with is often called the *role* of this person." *Ibid.,* p. 124.

Basic Functional Prerequisites of Social Systems:
Institutions, Laws, Political Authority

There are at least two lines of approach toward formulating plausible hypotheses about what minimum conditions are essential for the continuation of any and all social systems. I am interested in uncovering such essentials of social interaction as embody external and possibly coercive restraints on the participating individuals.

One approach, which is congenial to social anthropologists, is the search for cultural universals. If certain value orientations or institutions or prohibitions can be found in operation in all cultures and societies that we know, it is not far-fetched to hypothesize that these phenomena serve some common function that is essential to the existence of any society of human beings. In the words of A. L. Kroeber and Clyde Kluckhohn: "The mere existence of universals after so many millennia of culture history and in such diverse environments suggests that they correspond to something extremely deep in man's nature and/or are necessary conditions for social life."[87]

Kroeber and Kluckhohn give the following examples of cultural universals, among others: Indiscriminate lying, stealing, or violence within the ingroup is nowhere tolerated. The incest tabu has "essential universality." Human suffering is never valued positively as an end in itself. The fact of death is everywhere ceremonialized. "All cultures define as abnormal individuals who are permanently inaccessible to communication or who fail to maintain some degree of control over their impulse life."[88]

The second approach has the advantage of focusing on the functional prerequisites of the social system as something apart from universal personality and biological needs. It emphasizes analytical theorizing instead of empirical generalization. It starts out with an analysis of the needs of simple social systems and gradually develops a more complex theory, which can be tested in its particulars by generalizations from anthropological data. This is the approach I shall take in the following pages; a later subsection will consider some data in the spirit of the first approach.

Perhaps the most general kind of prerequisite of all social systems is the existence of *institutions,* to insure some measure of reciprocity or, to descend to a still more general level of analysis, to insure some measure of stability and predictability in social interaction.

Only a hermit can theoretically exist without social institutions to guide his choice among alternatives of behavior. A Robinson Crusoe could *perhaps* live as an entirely rational man, guided only by efficiency norms toward maximizing his subsistence and reserves. But as soon as a Friday enters the picture, a social relationship emerges. And both become vitally interested in seeing a pattern of behavior regularity developed. Friday's behavior is part of Crusoe's situation, and the more of it Crusoe is able to predict, the better able he is to utilize all aspects of his situation to pro-

[87] *Culture: A Critical Review of Concepts and Definitions,* p. 178. The relevance of cultural universals for value theory has been discussed above, pp. 12–13.
[88] *Ibid.,* p. 177.

mote his ends. And Friday, of course, has an interest in Crusoe's behavior. They need rudiments of a language, for one thing, and other mutually accepted signs referring to wishes and intentions that reoccur with some regularity.

In less amiable master-slave relationships institutions serve the same basic functions. Suppose that two men living in isolation had settled the question of their status relative to one another by sheer force and that the physically stronger man keeps the weaker one working for him as a slave. This is as elementary an embryo of a society as is possible, consisting of one social relationship and patterned independently of the culture or institutions of any larger group. In so far as this relationship lasts, certain rules for the behavior of both men are given by the situation itself as soon as it becomes stabilized. These norms are different for each of the two roles. For the slave, the master's will is the law, up to a certain limit. The master on his side will recognize some limits beyond which he had better not push his demands on the slave, lest he become desperate and react in some unpredictable way. The action on both sides as just described is assumed to be entirely rational in intent, but even in this embryo of a society emerging institutional patterns are evident. Elements of institutions or roles are essential aspects of all human relationships; they provide mutually stable and predictable factors in both the situational and the normative orientations within which social interaction is carried out.[89]

The larger the number of people and the more complicated the web of social relationships constituting a social system, the more essential is the need for predictability of human behavior. The average city dweller deals in his everyday life with large numbers of people, most of whose functions are specifically though not always explicitly defined and are carried out in an extremely regular way. We are very dependent on these regularity patterns. To mention just one example, think of the confusion in a skyscraper city if the elevator men go on strike. Strikes and lockouts are powerful weapons just because they upset institutionalized expectations and force a lot of people to appraise their situations and their goals all over again.

Now, if every human being acted completely rationally, one might ask, would that not bring forth equally stable behavior patterns? If every member of society could be expected to pursue his goals as efficiently as possible, would it not then be easy for everyone to predict and adjust to the anticipated action of one's neighbor? Jeremy Bentham and the utilitarians came close to this view. It is mistaken in several respects, however. It is theoretically conceivable that one ultimate goal could dominate a

---

[89] Herskovits makes in effect the same point when he describes in similar terms the general functions of sanctions (defined above, p. 89, cf. 263): "They are the underlying forces that give an inner logic to the behavior of a people, which, in patterned expression, make possible that prediction of behavior" which is all-important for social integration. *Man and His Works: The Science of Cultural Anthropology,* p. 222. In my terminology, sanctions are necessary aspects of institutions; Herskovits on the same page defines "sanctions" somewhat loosely in terms which may be interpreted as nearly equivalent with my "institutions": They are "the underlying drives, motivations, 'unconscious systems of meanings' that govern the reactions of a people."

personality to the extent that most of his immediate goals and means were predetermined and thus his concrete behavior to a large extent made predictable.[90] But even if all personalities were structured in this streamlined fashion, and even if their dominant ultimate goals, moreover, were identical, their behavior would not be uniform, for the simple reason that each person acts in a partly unique situation. As every chess player knows, it takes strong intellectual effort to predict in detail rational action from the point of view of even a single other individual. In life as in chess, moreover, there is always the probability that our neighbor will make some mistakes, however clearly his pursuits are defined to himself and others. We are all subject to ignorance and error, and so the rational action of each of us becomes even less predictable from the other fellow's point of view, if indeed not from our own, too.

Let us conclude, then, that *the existence of institutions,* no matter for the moment what kinds, *is the most general prerequisite of an enduring social system.* "Society is possible only on the basis of order," and "order" means a pattern of institutions governing the bulk of social interaction.[91]

One attempt to draw up an explicit list of prerequisites for enduring institutional patterns, or enduring social systems, has been made by David F. Aberle and his associates. Prior to listing a number of prerequisites, these authors state four conditions that would terminate the existence of a society: the biological extinction or dispersion of the members; apathy, or cessation of individual motivation, in the members; the war of all against all; or the inclusion of one society into another.[92]

The functional prerequisites of a society, according to Aberle and his associates, are the following: provision for adequate relationship to the environment and for sexual recruitment; role differentiation and role assignments; communication; shared cognitive orientations; a shared, articulated set of goals; the normative regulation of means; the regulation of affective expression; socialization; and the effective control of disruptive forms of behavior.[93] The first category would seem to lend itself better to inclusion among the conditions for terminating a social system. All the categories that follow, however, state various aspects of the general necessity of institutions, specified by deductions from Parsons' theory of action.

If social systems require a large measure of institutionalized behavior, it may at first seem plausible to conclude that they require institutionalization of the various aspects of behavior as well. In modern psychology the interdependency of the various aspects of behavior has become recognized to the extent that some authors come close to abandoning entirely the conventional distinctions between perceptions, attitudes, and emotions, at least for many purposes, and prefer to talk about unified "dynamic

[90] This is theoretically, but not practically, conceivable. Cf. above, p. 9.

[91] Hoebel, *The Law of Primitive Man,* p. 12.

[92] Aberle, Cohen, Davis, Levy, and Sutton: "The Functional Prerequisites of a Society," *Ethics,* LX, No. 2 (1950), 103–4. This fourth condition is not a condition for enduring social interaction; a pattern of interaction can exist within a number of social systems at the same time, and it is not necessarily a calamity for the participants in an interaction pattern if one or more of their social systems cease to exist. Cf. below, p. 275.

[93] *Ibid.,* pp. 104–11.

systems."[94] A similar orientation focusing on institutional behavior would make one expect as a matter of course that institutions regulating, for example, cognitive orientation would also regulate expectations as to goal orientation and affective expression.

At this point it is easy to commit a logical fallacy, however. Granted that institutions are essential for social interaction, and granted that institutions regulate many aspects of motivational and overt behavior, it by no means follows that institutional regulation of these various aspects of behavior are equally essential for interaction. All we can deduce logically is that at least one aspect of behavior must be institutionally regulated.

Aberle and his associates do not commit this fallacy. Their approach is an inductive one, and they discuss each hypothesis in their list on its own merits. I shall not endorse or dispute their hypotheses in this context. The present discussion of functional prerequisites proceeds in very general terms to prepare the ground for the problems of deviation and anomie. Perhaps Aberle and his associates prove too much. Let me postpone this kind of inquiry until the next subsection.

There may be other typologies of prerequisites that are general and yet bear more immediately on the problem of coercion in social systems. Perhaps anthropologists who focus on legal developments can be of greater use in illuminating the more basic sociological limitations on the possibilities for maximizing social freedom.

E. A. Hoebel in his most recent book suggests that not just institutions in general but also *legal* institutions perform "certain functions essential to the maintenance of all but the very most simple societies."[95] A social norm is legal, according to his definition, "if its neglect or infraction is regularly met, in threat or in fact, by the application of physical force by an individual or group possessing the socially recognized privilege of so acting."[96]

This definition of "law" strikes me as a happy one. It makes the crucial criterion the social recognition or institutionalized expectation of coercion by persons specified as to status and role, applied as sanctions against the deviators. In our culture, in which the cruder forms of physical violence are monopolized by the state, it would seem that the crucial problem in studying the conditions for maximizing freedom from coercion is the problem of defining the minimum prerequisites for society in the way of legally sanctioned coercion. Extralegal physical coercion is on the whole effectively discouraged by the agencies of the Law. There are exceptions, but there are no difficult theoretical controversies to disentangle in this connection. The overwhelming consensus is in favor of applying the best knowledge toward approximating a state of affairs in which "crime does not pay," and physical coercion exerted over adult individuals by unauthorized per-

---

[94] Cf. especially Krech, "Notes toward a Psychological Theory," *Journal of Personality,* XVIII, No. 1 (1949), 66–87.

[95] *The Law of Primitive Man,* p. 275.

[96] *Ibid.,* p. 28.

sons is in almost all cases consensually considered and dealt with as criminal behavior.

According to Hoebel, there are at least four general and essential functions served by legal institutions: (1) to define permitted and forbidden activities, in order to maintain social integration; (2) to allocate authority over physical coercion, in order to prevent or reduce intragroup feuding; (3) to dispose of trouble cases, in order to prevent continual feuding; and (4) "to redefine relations between individuals and groups as the conditions of life change . . . to maintain adaptability."[97] The first of these functions is common to all institutions with sufficiently strong sanctions. The last three, on the other hand, are peculiar to legal institutions, and there are good grounds for believing that these are essential functions, or prerequisites in the strictest sense, at least in all societies that are large enough to consist of more than one primary or face-to-face group.

I have suggested that the existence of institutions is the first prerequisite of a social system. Now let me combine the second and third functions of laws in Hoebel's list, and propose the following general prerequisite of all social systems beyond the primary group level: *The effective existence of laws, or institutions that in fact regulate the permissible and generally approved exercise of physical coercion, is a prerequisite of all enduring social systems larger than primary groups.*[98]

The nonexistence of laws and legal authority would mean the absence of criteria and means for settling specific conflicts and feuds between individuals, and there would be no effective brake on a drift toward multiplying feuds and, indeed, toward a state of "the war of all against all." Aberle and his associates, following Hobbes, listed such a state as one of the conditions terminating the existence of society.[99]

Yet there is more to legal institutions than a mere allocation of authority over the exercise of physical coercion. Nobody is authorized to exercise completely arbitrary coercion; not even a dictator can get away with this in the long run. A certain regularity is required. Legal coercion, in whatever amounts, if any, must be institutionalized. This requirement may be read into the prerequisite just formulated ("regulate"). It is also a nearly obvious conclusion from the first prerequisite—the existence of institutions: if patterns of regularity are required in all enduring social interaction, they must *a fortiori* be required if social interaction is to endure after the intervention of physical coercion.

The fourth and last item on Hoebel's list of functions of the law is the redefinition of relations between individuals and groups as the conditions of life change, or the maintenance of adaptability. This is the function, not of laws as institutions, but of law in the making, or the institutions

---

[97] *Ibid.,* pp. 275 ff.

[98] "Physical coercion" refers to actual physical violence as well as coercion by threats of physical violence or other interference with physical integrity, such as confinement to jail. Charles H. Cooley defined "primary groups" as those groups which are "characterized by intimate face-to-face association and cooperation." *Social Organization,* p. 23.

[99] See above, p. 267.

that decide how laws are made. It is not so much a legal as it is a *political* prerequisite of a society, as we shall see.

Karl N. Llewellyn and E. A. Hoebel have on an earlier occasion stressed a most important characteristic of legal institutions, a characteristic that may but need not place its impact on nonlegal customs and institutions. This is the presence of elements of rationality, at least in the sense of conscious decision-making: "Other institutions can grow by mere drift. . . . But with the legal, the recurrent impact of conscious thought is inescapable, though the range of the conscious thinking may remain narrow, step by step. For in any conflict situation—and conflict situations present the legal problem, par excellence—drive elicits challenge. And challenge forces conscious shaping of issues, conscious moves to persuade or to prevail by other means."[100]

The content of laws is not spurious. The same authors suggest two content prerequisites for enduring legal norms: They must on the whole be "somewhat understandable" to the population as a whole, and they must on the whole be generally believed to serve the common good.[101]

The system of legal norms is everywhere shaped by at least two main influences: by the settlement of cases (or "trouble-cases" in Llewellyn's terminology); and by the more general norm-making of political authorities. Both types of decision-making are essentially political, in the sense that they decide, whether in a specific case or as a general policy, "who gets what, when, how." Politics is, as Easton has suggested, "the authoritative allocation of values as it is influenced by the distribution and use of power."[102]

Political decision-making, as opposed to pure institutional behavior, involves adaptation to changing circumstances, notably changing patterns of power distribution. If this adaptive function were not a constant element in the social process, institutional behavior patterns would continue unchanged until the discrepancies between norms and effective power constellations would reach the breaking point of political and social disorganization. But it is not enough that intelligence is applied to serve this adaptive function; there must be some authoritative way of creating conformity to some of these decisions of a political nature. What is needed is a certain minimum of *political authority*.

This prerequisite cannot be equated with a need for a centralized political regime. In the first place, the existence of a powerful and legitimate political regime is no assurance that the adaptive function of political authority is being served. The history of our civilization is replete with examples of political regimes that came to violent endings because they had relied wholly on the assumed sanctity of traditions, instead of doing something intelligent about mental and material trends affecting their effective power positions.

Secondly and more important, enduring political regimes are not necessary for the endurance of political authority. All that is required is some-

---

[100] *The Cheyenne Way*, p. 278.
[101] "The tolerances here are huge, but they have limits." *Ibid.*, p. 288.
[102] *The Political System*, p. 146. Cf. above, p. 20.

thing broader or more elementary: authoritative political institutions. The British, American, and Scandinavian constitutions are examples of authoritative sets of rules for political development. Without requiring a specifically defined authoritative political elite, these basic institutions perform the essential function of political authority. Among all the more or less rational recommendations toward revising laws and creating new legislation, these constitutional laws or customs make it clear which of the recommendations are to be invested with legal status. Political authority exists to the extent that a certain governing group or a certain political process is generally recognized as the only legitimate source of new laws and legally binding institutions.[103]

The chief function of authority in general, with special reference to public administration, has been said to be the achievement of "a very great flexibility in the division of the work of making decisions."[104] The chief function of political authority is, as we have seen, the achievement of some flexibility in the legal institutions, without paying the price of confusion and anomie.

"Authority" has often been equated with "power."[105] Merton has in one context defined authority as the power of a given status or role: "Authority, the power of control which derives from an acknowledged status, inheres in the office and not in the particular person who performs the official role."[106] Authority does not *derive* from an acknowledged status, as I wish to conceptualize it; it *is* a generally acknowledged directive. Or, more strictly speaking, *authority (authoritativeness) is the quality by virtue of which directives are obeyed independently of external sanctions.*[107]

It follows from this definition that authority is never illegitimate in an objective sense. If a claim to authority is widely considered illegitimate, it is no longer valid: it does not in fact establish or refer to actual authority. Yet "legitimacy" can also be used in relation to moral standards or norms that "ought to" be authoritative on one ground or another. In this book the latter term is used in the same objective, descriptive sense as "authority." It is, however, considered a synonym and will therefore not be discussed separately. But Max Weber's three "pure types of legitimate authority" may be worth considering for a moment.

Weber says that there may be three types of grounds on the basis of which legitimate authority can be claimed: rational, traditional, and

---

[103] This political process is likely to be a very complex one in a complex society. The American, British, and Scandinavian political processes, for example, assign important roles in the making of laws not only to the legislators but also to the courts, the governments, and the voters.

[104] Simon, Smithburg, and Thompson, *Public Administration,* p. 185.

[105] Roberto Michels, for example, has proposed this definition: "Authority is the capacity, innate or acquired, for exercising ascendancy over a group." "Authority," in *Encyclopedia of the Social Sciences,* Vol. II.

[106] *Social Theory and Social Structure,* p. 195.

[107] Cf. Barnard: "Authority is the character of a communication (order) in a formal organization by virtue of which it is accepted by a contributor to or 'member' of the organization as governing the action he contributes." *The Functions of the Executive,* p. 163.

I am leaving open the question of the reference of the "quality" in my definition; it may be the quality of a social relationship, a social role, of a personality, of a social structure, of a social situation, etc.

charismatic. He calls the corresponding types of authority legal, traditional, and charismatic. In the first case, obedience is given to an institutional order; the leader is vested with authority because and in so far as he serves institutionally defined objectives. In the case of traditional authority, obedience is given to the person who has inherited or been given the authority role, without conditions. Charismatic authority, finally, is created by the widely attributed "sanctity, heroism or exemplary character of an individual person, and of the normative patterns or order revealed or ordained by him."[108]

It would seem that the authority of democratic government comes the closest to the legal type of authority; the authority of the pope comes closer to the traditional type; and both Lenin's and Hitler's authority approximated the charismatic type. Weber's typology is a "pure" one, however; none of his types fits completely with any actual type, but each can be approximated. The point that belongs in this context is that political authority can serve its basic social functions without being democratic. It can but need not consist entirely in an impersonal institutionalized process, which may or may not be democratic.

A social system does not require a highly organized political regime, then. All that is necessary is that the essential function of political authority be carried out. In aboriginal societies political authority tends to be of a traditional type, and it may function within a minimum of social organization. An example of a relatively informal but effective way of revising a legal norm is given by Llewellyn and Hoebel. The Cheyenne Indians, who had a minimum of formal political organization, were used to a system of extensive mutual borrowing. After the introduction of horses in their tribes, individuals frequently borrowed each other's horses, and this frequently led to trouble cases, since the Indians became very dependent on their horses. But on one occasion a "court" of four chiefs, engaged in settling such a case, declared: "Now we shall make a new rule. There shall be no more borrowing of horses without asking. If any man takes another's goods without asking, we will go over and get them back for him. More than that, if the taker tries to keep them, we will give him a whipping."[109]

The third prerequisite of any enduring social system larger than the primary group may now be formulated as follows: *The existence of political authority, meaning some generally recognized power or procedure for changing or creating legal norms, is a prerequisite of all complex social systems.* "Generally recognized" means that most participants in the social system in fact consider that they must or ought to obey the revised laws in the same way as before they were revised.

I have now stated three basic functional prerequisites that I believe are crucial for the endurance of any social system larger and more complex than primary groups. There must be institutions, legal institutions, and political

[108] *The Theory of Social and Economic Organization*, p. 328.
[109] *The Cheyenne Way*, p. 128. Cf. Hoebel, *The Law of Primitive Man*, p. 24.

authority. The first of these three prerequisites apply to all social systems without exception.

Rather than continue this inquiry in an effort to identify further prerequisites,[110] I shall in a moment change the focus of my inquiry. Instead of considering further the general prerequisites of interaction from the point of view of the endurance of the social system, I shall now consider these same prerequisites more specifically as they affect the interacting individual. To what extent, if any, must he suffer coercion by virtue of his mere membership in any social system?

Before leaving the concept of functional prerequisites, however, let me briefly mention the complementary concept of "functional equivalent." In his theoretical framework for functional analysis Merton introduces also the concept of functional alternative, equivalent, or substitute. This concept "focuses attention on the *range of possible variation* in the items which can, in the case under examination, subserve a functional requirement. It unfreezes the identity of the existent and the inevitable."[111] Given a certain social function generally perceived as necessary, the conservative will tend to consider the institution serving it a functional prerequisite, while the radical will be prone to thinking of functional equivalents that are more to his liking in other respects. If a particular institution is called a functional prerequisite, this denies by implication the possibility of functional equivalents.

On the general level of analysis in the preceding pages it is hardly possible to think of functional equivalents of such high level abstractions as institutions, laws, and political authority. These are consequently functional prerequisites in the strict sense.

With respect to particular institutions, laws, or types of political authority, on the other hand, I believe in a general assumption against their status as prerequisites. As a working hypothesis, at least, I would always assume that the functions that one institution serves might also be served approximately as well by another. For example, we have seen that democratic authority may be functionally equivalent, *from a general social system point of view*, with other kinds of authority.

Yet, the specific nature of a true functional equivalent is not easy to determine. A sophisticated social theory and a wealth of experience or data are required to explore fully the manifest and latent functions of a given institution and, even more, to predict the manifest and latent functions of a possible substitute.[112] A detailed knowledge of private and public goal

---

[110] Talcott Parsons points out that there are cultural prerequisites also, such as language and a minimum accumulation of empirical knowledge. Legal institutions, it may be added, certainly presuppose or imply cultural development of norm systems. Parsons also distinguishes between "universal imperatives, the conditions that must be met by any social system of a stable and durable character, and second, the imperatives of compatibility, those that limit the range of coexistence of structural elements in the same society." *The Social System*, pp. 26–36 and pp. 167 ff. On further social prerequisites, see also Aberle *et al.*, "The Functional Prerequisites of a Society," *Ethics*, Vol. LX, No. 2 (1950).

[111] *Social Theory and Social Structure*, p. 52.

[112] For an interesting application of functional analysis, based on data from two differently organized Israeli settlements, see Schwartz, "Functional Alternatives to Inequality," *American Sociological Review*, XX, No. 4 (1955), 424–30.

values is a condition for appraising the relative importance of the various manifest and latent functions.

Institutional change is frequently a necessity for meeting new situations, and approximate equivalents for valuable functions must in such cases be searched for on the basis of far from perfect knowledge. The behavioral scientist presumably has great potentialities in public service as a predictor of the hypothetical functions, manifest and latent, of contemplated institutional change. These potentialities exceed his present achievements and exceed even more the actual use that is being made of the knowledge and techniques available at the present time.

Deviation, Coercive Punishment, and Anomie

If I have found that institutions, laws, and political authority are functional prerequisites of all social systems of even a modest complexity, I have also said that social sanctions are essential. And social sanctions always involve potential punishment. Even apparently "positive sanctions," which function to encourage conformity by prospects of reward, are as a rule "negative" at the same time: the possible absence of reward is in most cases psychologically equivalent to possible punishment. There are no known societies without the functional equivalents of crime and punishment. Even more, there are in fact no known social systems, not excluding small face-to-face groups, without pressures punishing deviators.

Institutions imply sanctions, but not necessarily, from the argument developed so far, *coercive* sanctions. "Coercion," as I use this term, refers to (a) actual physical violence or (b) the application of sanctions strong enough to make the individual abandon his own strong and enduring wishes.[113]

It may be said categorically that actual physical violence is not a functional prerequisite of all social systems, not even of all complex social systems. For example, many university or college communities could be cited as examples of fairly complex social systems that have endured over considerable time in the absence of appreciable physical violence, at least among adults. I do not know of any whole country or even city that has been able to do entirely without violence for any length of time, but it is not impractical to envisage and to seek to promote approximations of such a state of affairs. This objective is, indeed, the most crucial component in my goal of freedom maximization, since I consider coercion the supreme political evil and physical violence of serious proportions the worst kind of coercion.[114]

It seems to me that there are two apparent alternatives to coercion in the maintenance of social institutions, and both alternatives can be approximated by political means. One approach is to try to adjust institutional patterns toward closer harmony with individual inclinations, if the latter are widely shared and widely compatible. The other is to try to manipulate individual inclinations toward closer harmony with institutional patterns.

[113] Cf. above, p. 93.
[114] See above, pp. 93–94.

Both alternatives have clear empirical limitations, however. Keeping modern large-scale democracies in mind, it must be observed that there are wide individual differences in inclinations and values, and it is therefore in many contexts impossible to engineer institutional developments toward greater harmony with all individual interests. It is quite possible, however, to find areas of near-universal consensus—for example, with respect to certain political institutions. Secret ballots and majority rule are today rather universally accepted by citizens of democracies, and these institutions are on the whole enforceable with a minimum of coercion. Rules of military conscription, on the other hand, require a lot of coercion in their application, and it is probable that only a minority would become soldiers of their own volition, at least in peace time.

Democratic political leadership can be viewed as the art of manipulating both institutions and men at the same time; it is not a question of one or the other. Given a lack of sufficient consensus to provide a basis for generally acceptable institutions, or given certain institutional requirements that, regardless of acceptance, are deemed essential for the interest of the social system, the question the democratic government is likely to ask itself is this: To what extent can we achieve the necessary amount of collaboration by (a) propaganda or information efforts and by (b) attempts to adjust our policies to the demands of the discontented?

There are empirical limitations on the feasibility of noncoercive manipulation of men as well as institutions, however. A totalitarian government in full control of all the mass media of communication is perhaps able to produce a very high degree of voluntary conformity to its decrees and to the institutions it encourages, but only at the price of severe coercion against even modest expression of deviation. A democratic government, on the other hand, is almost invariably challenged by opposition forces whenever its policies depart from principles on which there is already a wide agreement.

The question still remains: What are the minimum amounts of coercion requirements common to all complex, imperfect societies? Let me choose another formulation, which in effect is somewhat narrower: *What are the minimum general coercion requirements to keep anomie within tolerable limits in social interaction?* The advantage of the latter phrasing is that I avoid making the endurance of any and all social systems my main concern. A pattern of social interaction is itself a social system, and it may exist within a substantial number of other social systems, such as a friendship group, a profession, a community, a nation, and so on. I am now concerned with inquiring into the minimum coercion requirements in social interaction, and I do not care if larger systems unessential to the interaction in question fall by the wayside. To prevent intolerable anomie it may, for all I wish to assert at this point, be sufficient that one social system larger than or identical with the pattern of face-to-face interaction endures as a system.

It is important to keep in mind in this context that I have chosen the human rights approach instead of Bentham's majoritarianism as a means of weighing priorities among value demands. The problem of determining the minimum of coercion essential to the endurance of a social system does not present itself to me, consequently, as the problem of determining the minimum number or percentage of citizens or group members who must suffer coercion in the interest of the whole. Rather, it is the problem of determining what are the worst kinds of coercion that one or more individuals must endure. My human rights approach affirms that the execution or torture of even one individual, even a supposedly depraved individual, is a worse violation of freedom in a society than is the mere imprisonment of a thousand individuals.

A beginning has been made in asserting that substantial physical violence is the worst kind of coercion. An extremely wide consensus is probably possible on this value judgment, as a general principle. And it is probable that infliction of severe physical violence on marginal individuals could in fact be considerably reduced, and perhaps eventually be completely done away with, in democratic communities and societies. To the extent that this possibility can be demonstrated, I believe that there are possibilities for a wide agreement also on the judgment that this objective should have top priority in a free society.[115]

Beyond this point, however, we are on shaky ground. The consensus possibilities seem much slimmer with respect to comparative judgments about degrees of coercion short of physical violence. What is worse for the average man, to risk jail for six months or to risk losing his livelihood? Only a very few general remarks can be made around this topic, and they should be based on a brief reconsideration of the problem of anomie.

Anomie implies *confusion* with respect to goals or norms, or both. Absence of goals is hardly conceivable among individuals with biological and social needs, but paralyzing conflicts between goals may occur and such a degree of elasticity that the goals lose all substance and provide no criteria for judging achievements.[116] Absence of institutional norms is conceivable and is, indeed, approximated in certain life situations in which cold and hard rationality rules supremely.

There is no conclusive evidence that I know of to suggest that institutionalized, that is, generally accepted and sanctioned, goals are essential to assure meaningful social interaction. A society can give its citizens full freedom, one may assume, in their choice of public goals. It is true that

---

[115] This supposed possibility of agreement is in many societies still only a future prospect, even as a general principle. Many American and some European states still maintain capital punishment, and in many cases without much controversy at the present time. Cf. above, p. 137. Lately, however, the issue has become important in Britain, where a bill asking for the abolishment of capital punishment achieved a majority in the House of Commons, only to be defeated in the House of Lords, thus creating something approximating a constitutional crisis; an uneasy truce was established in 1957 with a partial reform bill. Arthur Koestler's *Reflections on Hanging* apparently exerted much influence in this controversy. On the American scene, cf. Sellin (ed.), *Murder and the Penalty of Death* (1952), Weihofen, *The Urge to Punish* (1956), and Playfair and Sington, *The Offenders. The Case Against Legal Vengeance* (1957). However, a standard text such as Bishop and Hendel's *Basic Issues of American Democracy* contains no reference to this issue.

[116] This is the principal cause Durkheim ascribes for the rising numbers of suicides in times of financial boom.

many writers, as diverse in general orientation as Hobbes, Burke, and Laski, have argued that there is a need for a common agreement on fundamentals to make a democratic system work.[117] Others, however, have argued, in my opinion more persuasively, that an agreement on basic goal values is not only unnecessary but may be dangerous to the freedom of inquiry and belief. I agree with Carl J. Friedrich, who concludes that "what binds a free people together is not an agreement upon fundamentals, but a common way of acting in spite of disagreement on fundamentals."[118]

Friedrich argues in support of his conclusion that the American democracy has endured in spite of, or perhaps because of, enormous differences in the past in fundamental value orientations—religious, cultural, and economic. It takes much less to confirm my own proposition in this context, which is a much more modest one, that wide disagreements and confusions about public or group goals need not be a bar to enduring social interaction. The danger of anomie can never, so far as I know, in itself justify coercion against individuals because they deviate on fundamental goal values.[119]

With respect to behavior norms the situation is a different one, as Friedrich also indicates in the passage just cited. We are now back again with the most fundamental prerequisite for any social system, simple or complex: a minimum system of institutions, implying a general agreement to conform to certain norms, is necessary in any enduring interaction between men. And a second prerequisite for more complex systems, it was found, is the maintenance of *legal* institutions, meaning institutions regulating the legitimate use of physical coercion.

Durkheim was the first sociologist who advanced a convincing theory of punishment as a means of reducing anomie. He challenged the old idea that punishment primarily serves to reduce the risk that the delinquent will break the law again or to persuade potential delinquents to take heed. Durkheim's great discovery was in effect that punishment of crimes serves to bolster the *morale* of the great majority. Punishment of criminals demonstrates to everybody's satisfaction that there are "valid" principles of right and wrong; there are norms for conduct that one may follow in safety and good conscience. The true function of punishment, says Durkheim, "is to maintain social cohesion, while maintaining all its vitality in the common conscience. . . . That is why we are right in saying that the criminal must suffer in proportion to his crime . . . punishment is above all designed to act upon upright people, for, since it serves to heal the wounds made upon collective sentiments, it can fill this role only where these sentiments exist, and commensurately with their vivacity."[120]

---

[117] Aberle *et al.* state, but without much supporting argument: "Without an articulated set of goals the society would invite extinction, apathy, or the war of all against all." "The Functional Prerequisites of a Society," *Ethics*, LX, No. 2 (1950), 108.

[118] *The New Belief in the Common Man*, p. 181. Cf. Riesman, *Individualism Reconsidered*, p. 36.

[119] Coercion against this kind of nonconformist may conceivably be justified on the basis of other types of danger—for example, in times of war. Cf. above, pp. 117–18.

[120] *Division of Labor*, pp. 108–9. See also Mead, "The Psychology of Punitive Justice," *American Journal of Sociology*, XXIII (1918), 577–602, and Aubert, *Om straffens sosiale funksjon*, Chap. 11.

All that Durkheim really says in these passages—and so far I agree with him—is that punishment in fact serves this morale-building function. He does not exclude the possibility of functional equivalents of coercive punishment. With respect to the possible necessity of coercion, these passages actually assert less than I did in stating that laws are a functional prerequisite of any society—laws being defined as institutions that regulate the permissible and generally approved exercise of physical coercion. Durkheim says that punishment has a constructive sociological function beyond the mere protection against the recurrence of delinquent acts; I am saying that it is essential that a society have rules for regulating the legitimate use of coercive punishment and (other) physical violence. Durkheim does not and neither do I state that coercive punishment is a functional prerequisite of all social systems. On my part I am merely saying that coercive punishment, in so far as it exists, to a substantial degree must become authorized or "licensed" by institutional order if this order is to endure.

It is possible, I believe, to approach a state of affairs in which shared institutions can be preserved without *social* coercion, including political coercion. The coercion of certain impersonal circumstances, such as illness, accidents, and death, can never be avoided. But it is possible, under conditions that are ideal in every respect, to envisage a psychological freedom and self-esteem so highly and generally developed that humanitarian benevolence invariably prevails over envious aggression—and a system of social and political institutions so eminently reasonable and solidly rationalized from a humanitarian point of view that conformity is achieved without the use of coercion over adult and mentally sane citizens.

For a long time, however, this goal is bound to remain in the distance. Realization of it will be approached, I believe, if it becomes widely accepted (1) that this goal is not a sociological impossibility and (2) that it is supremely worth striving for approximations of it. In the meantime, however, we must acknowledge that aggressive impulses of serious consequence do persist, that the self-esteem of many individuals remains severely deficient, and that a tough competitiveness between individuals is encouraged in many countries. As long as these conditions are with us, coercive sanctions certainly remain a functional prerequisite as applied to behavior norms. More strictly speaking, they are what Parsons would call imperatives of this particular type of empirical system.[121] In this kind of society much authorized coercion sanctioning behavior norms appears necessary to prevent more and worse kinds of unauthorized coercion.

The determination of the minimum amounts of coercion required to preserve a particular social system, or valuable aspects of it, is in principle an empirical problem. The search for functional equivalents of punishment is always going on in an enlightened society, and with increasingly sophisticated behavioral sciences more and more significant small-scale experiments can be expected to improve our knowledge. For example, certain prisons in the Scandinavian countries and elsewhere have been made "open," thus relying on more cooperation with and less severe coercion of

[121] *The Social System,* pp. 484 and 167. Cf. above p. 273, note 110.

the prisoner. There is also a tendency, notably in regard to juvenile delinquents, to substitute psychological treatment for punishment. Vilhelm Aubert discusses the possibilities of carrying this trend further and poses the problem whether psychological treatment can become a functional equivalent for punishment, taking into consideration manifest as well as latent functions of punishment. With respect to the latent functions of punishment, with which Durkheim was concerned, Aubert concludes that the legal machinery for determining "guilt" or "blame" is more important for the public's morale than the actual inflicting of punishment on the criminal. And the morale of the victim of the crime may be bolstered to some degree by the public characterization of the delinquent as a sick person instead of a bad person; one who must be subjected to treatment.[122]

It must be emphasized at this point that psychological treatment is not *necessarily* less coercive than punishment. In his utopian novel *One*, David Karp describes life in a totalitarian, democratic welfare state, in which all punishment has been abolished, while at the same time an intensive system of thought control is in operation. The undercover agents of the Department of Internal Examination have no qualms about reporting on heretical remarks of their neighbors, since heretics are never punished.

No one was punished—not for anything. People whose thinking was antisocial, heretical, were adjusted—by therapy, psychoanalysis, instruction, and understanding. In time the roots of their heresy, their antisocial thinking were torn up, exposed to the light, and withered. That was the concept of the State—no man was outside the fold of mankind. Wrong doing stemmed from wrong concepts. . . . Sin no longer existed—merely error.[123]

As it turned out, however, a lot of coercion was needed to make some heretics undergo treatment, and more and worse coercion followed if the treatment was unsuccessful in stamping out the heretic's individuality. But it was not called punishment.

In our society, in which the objectives of the psychological treatment of delinquents would be much more modest, we may assume, it is possible to envisage a much reduced role of coercion in the rehabilitation of these people. Also, it is possible to envisage a reduced incidence of crime, to the extent that personalities do not become warped and unfree in their formative years, and to the extent that social institutions become better tuned to fulfilling basic human needs.

The problem of anomie must be studied within the framework of particular societies, then, to decide the minimum amounts and kinds of coercion required to assure enduring social organization. Both psychological and political factors are important determinants of the tolerance of levels of anomie in various social systems. The functional prerequisites of institutions, laws, and political authority do carry some amounts of coercion in their wake in all societies that we know, but with vast differences from one society to another. I have stated my belief that there is no basic minimum

[122] *Om straffens sosiale funksjon*, pp. 220–27.
[123] *One*, pp. 22–23.

of coercion requirements common to all social systems. I hypothesize instead that levels of psychological freedom and cultural (political-economic-ideological) developments in each society are the main determinants of the coercion requirements that may or may not (in each society) be essential to stave off anomic disorganization.

Some Data on the Generality of Laws, Authority, Institutions, and Sanctions

In the two preceding subsections I have tried to develop and substantiate a few hypotheses on functional prerequisites of social systems and about sociological limitations on social freedom that can be attributed to these prerequisites. At least two kinds of empirical data can be brought to bear on these speculations.

One kind of confirmation of the theory of functional prerequisites, and of the generality of the three types of prerequisites suggested, can be supplied if we find that the most primitively organized communities in the world have institutions and the beginnings of laws and political authority. I shall refer briefly to a very few data from a couple of primitive communities.

A second kind of data bearing more specifically on the universality of the sanction aspect of institutions has been provided in experiments on small groups within our own culture. A few data of this nature are referred to toward the end of this subsection.

My hypotheses on the general *sociological* coercion requirements in social interaction can be summarized as follows: Institutions are a prerequisite of any interaction system. Laws and political authority are necessary at least in all systems exceeding the primary group in size and complexity. Coercive pressures to create overt adherence to institutionalized goals are not sociologically necessary—not essential to prevent anomie and social disintegration in every conceivable society. A minimum of coercion to guarantee a measure of obedience to institutions, laws, and political authority may be necessary in all imperfect societies but, if so, probably on psychological and political rather than on sociological grounds.

The Siriono of Eastern Bolivia form some of the most primitively organized communities in existence. They live in seminomadic small bands, in so far as they have not become acculturated, and live by hunting and food-gathering. There is normally no contact between each band. A few years ago Allan R. Holmberg spent some time with the Siriono, in part under aboriginal conditions with a band of sixty to eighty members. Almost all the energies of these people are consumed in the search for food, and there is almost no social solidarity beyond the immediate family. There are only the most embryonic beginnings of a cultural development, beyond a common language and a few very primitive tools and techniques.

Were it not for the fact that the band supplies sex and marital partners, the Siriono might well have lived in scattered independent families, Holmberg concludes.[124] Yet this is an essential function of the band, and the band exists, and its existence is based on or expressed in a number of primitive institutions, including legal institutions. The status of men depends primarily on their ability as hunters, and the status of women on their food-gathering and child-bearing abilities but most of all on the status of their husbands. High status of men is accompanied by access to more sex partners or spouses and by a positive ratio of insulting others over being insulted by others.[125]

The legal system is a simple one; legal norms are few and elastic but not entirely absent. There is an embryonic principle of reciprocity in food-sharing and wife-sharing and a grudgingly acknowledged right to demand favors in return for favors given. Holmberg heard about only two cases of murder, both apparently unpremeditated. "In both instances the murderers were banished (or left) the band for a considerable time, but they returned later and resumed normal life." Incest and rape are rare and are believed to be punished by supernatural sanctions, causing sickness or death. Excessive adultery of a married woman may provoke her husband to throw her out, and she becomes subjected to public ridicule. Holmberg concludes: "Generally speaking, it would seem that the maintenance of law and order rests largely on the principle of reciprocity (however forced), the fear of supernatural sanctions and retaliation, and the desire for public approval."[126]

Political authority is virtually nonexistent in these small bands. A nominal chief heads each band, but the exercise of his theoretical power "depends almost entirely upon his personal qualities as a leader. . . . There is no obligation to obey the orders of a chief, no punishment for nonfulfillment."[127] Political authority has been called a prerequisite of any social system beyond the primary group. The Siriono bands are primitive primary groups, and the virtual absence of political authority may help explain why they never developed more complex levels of social organizations and culture.

E. A. Hoebel in his recent book has a chapter on an almost equally primitively organized type of community in the far North—the Eskimos. Like the Siriono, they live on a small margin, if any, of safety from starvation. They, too, live in mobile primary group communities, with rarely more than one hundred persons in each. "An ordinary Eskimo local group is made up of more or less than a dozen somewhat interrelated families."[128]

The Eskimos have a more advanced technology than the Siriono; their harsher climatic conditions certainly pose a more urgent challenge on mental resourcefulness. Eskimo law is somewhat further developed, and there is the beginning of political authority as well. Eskimo culture maintains a large number of tabus, and the sense of sin is highly developed.

---

[124] *Nomads of the Long Bow: The Siriono of Eastern Bolivia*, p. 98.
[125] *Ibid.*, pp. 58–59.
[126] *Ibid.*, pp. 60–61.
[127] *Ibid.*, p. 59.
[128] *The Law of Primitive Man*, pp. 67 ff.

Many sins are considered a menace to the whole community and thus acquire legal consequences. For example, there is a basic tabu against eating game from the sea and game from the land at the same time, and it is believed that both kinds of animals will shun the territory if this tabu is broken. There is in effect a "law" against breaking this tabu, and severe sanctions may be ordered by the "shaman."[129]

Murder is not necessarily an effective violation of Eskimo law. But repeated murders by the same person make him a public enemy, subject to execution by an agent of the community. The agent may be the headman or an *ad hoc* agent charged with this particular duty. Even the headman does not act by virtue of his own authority, however, but receives his power from the consensus of the community.[130] But the office of the headman, although not a formal office, is a beginning toward political authority. A man is considered headman only to the extent that others accept his judgments. Headmen are good hunters, "who by their extended acquaintance with the traditions, customs, and rites connected with the festivals, as well as being possessed of an unusual degree of common sense, are deferred to and act as chief advisors of the community."[131] In other words, headmen must know and conform to institutions and laws, but they must, in addition, be sound and rational decision-makers. "Such are the germs of political authority among the rude societies of mankind."[132]

The vast majority of human cultures in existence today or until recently have more highly developed systems of political authority than we find among the Eskimos. Reference has been made to informal authority processes among the Cheyenne Indians.[133] Among African cultures, the Nuer of Sudan, we are told, "have no government, and their state might be described as an ordered anarchy. Likewise they lack law, if we understand by this term judgments delivered by an independent and impartial authority which has, also, power to enforce its decisions."[134] In my sense of the term, though, derived from Hoebel's, the Nuer certainly have laws or institutions that in fact regulate the permissible and generally approved use of violence. For example: "Blood-feuds are a tribal institution, for they can only occur where a breach of law is recognized since they are the way in which reparation is obtained. Fear of incurring a blood-feud is, in fact, the most important legal sanction within a tribe and the main guarantee of an individual's life and property."[135] Political authority, again, while strictly limited is not totally absent among the Nuer.[136]

---

[129] *Ibid.*, p. 73.

[130] *Ibid.*, pp. 88–90.

[131] Quoted, in *ibid.*, p. 82, from Nelson, *The Eskimo about Bering Strait.*

[132] Hoebel, *The Law of Primitive Man,* p. 82.

[133] See above, p. 272.

[134] Evans-Pritchard, *The Nuer: A Description of the Modes of Livelihood and Political Institutions of a Nilotic People,* pp. 5–6; see also pp. 150–91.

[135] *Ibid.*, p. 150.

[136] "Leopard-skin chiefs and prophets are the only ritual specialists who, in our opinion, have any political importance." For example: "Feuds are settled through the leopard-skin chief and he plays a minor role in the settlement of disputes other than homicide. . . . On the whole we may say that Nuer chiefs are sacred persons, but that their sacredness gives them no general authority outside specific social situations." *Ibid.*, pp. 5–6 and 172–73.

Hoebel in *The Law of Primitive Man* discusses five systems of "primitive law-ways," starting with relatively simple Eskimo law and ending with relatively complex Ashanti law. There is no need for present purposes, however, to cite further instances of legal institutions in apparently lawless aboriginal cultures. I have not *proved* that political authority exists in all cultures except the very most primitive ones, such as the Siriono, but I have marshaled some evidence in support of the theory that laws and authority are functional prerequisites of all social systems of greater complexity than primary groups.

Let me now turn to another source of data with some bearing on the generality of institutions and sanctions: experiments on small groups within our own culture. These miniature social systems cannot tell us much about laws and political authority, which have been postulated as prerequisites for larger systems only. But they can illuminate the emergence of institutions and sanctions as immediate factual consequences of simple social interaction brought about by the establishment of small, task-oriented groups.

An important experiment elucidating the general relationship between deviation and sanctions in small groups has been reported on by Stanley Schachter.[137] The experiment was conducted in a series of thirty-two meetings, each staged as the first meeting of a club and each, of course, involving different subjects. All the subjects were male college students; each club had from five to seven members (the subjects of the experiment) and three paid participants who were perceived by the subjects as fellow club members. Schachter himself acted as the leader of each club.

In order to manipulate the variables of *group cohesiveness* as well as the *relevance* of the experimental discussion topic to group purposes, four types of clubs were set up, each eight times. Cohesiveness, meaning "the total field of forces acting on members to remain in the group," was high in two types of clubs, the case-study and the movie clubs. The first one was purportedly set up to advise lawyers and social workers on the treatment of delinquents, and the second to see movies and advise on programming for a local theater. All subjects in these clubs had indicated high interest in participating. The low-cohesiveness groups were the editorial clubs and the radio clubs. The first kind was supposed to submit requested editorial advice to a new national magazine, the second was supposed to advise a local radio station on programming. In these two groups all subjects had indicated little interest and a preference for joining one of the former kinds.

The experimental discussion topic was how to deal with a specific "real" case of a juvenile delinquent. This same case was brought up for discussion in all thirty-two opening meetings, although it was relevant to the objectives of the case-study and editorial clubs only, not to the movie and radio clubs. Thus, there were four combinations of the two important group variables:

---

[137] "Deviation, Rejection, and Communication," *Journal of Abnormal and Social Psychology*, XLVI (1951), 190–207. Reprinted in Cartwright and Zander (eds.), *Group Dynamics*, pp. 223–48. My references are to the latter source.

1. High cohesiveness-relevant issue (Hi Co Rel): Case-study Club
2. Low cohesiveness-relevant issue (Lo Co Rel): Editorial Club
3. High cohesiveness-irrelevant issue (Hi Co Irrel): Movie Club
4. Low cohesiveness-irrelevant issue (Lo Co Irrel): Radio Club

Each club member, after preliminary introductions, read a short version, sympathetically written, of a juvenile delinquent's story. Immediately afterwards, each subject indicated what he felt should be done with the boy, on a seven-point scale from "all-love" to "all-punishment." Then the three paid participants gave their prearranged opinions: the "deviate" was in favor of the extreme punitive solution, the "mode" took the middle position among those indicated by the subjects, while the "slider" started as an extreme deviate but gradually in the course of the discussion came around to the modal opinion. So much for a brief sketch of the incentives operating (1) on maintaining this particular social system and (2) maintaining attention to this particular decision-making goal.

The attitudes of the subjects toward the deviate after the 45 minutes of discussion were compared to the attitudes toward the mode (the paid participant with the modal position) and toward the slider.

One measure of these attitudes was a sociometric ranking. Each member of the club was at the end of the meeting asked to rank everyone else in the order of his desirability as a club member. These relationships were found: The variables of cohesiveness and relevance have apparently no effect on group evaluation of those who at the outset (the mode) or gradually (the slider) conform to group norms. The deviate gets a significantly lower rating in all groups, however, and he is rejected more strongly in high than in low cohesive groups. No evidence was found in this test in support of a hypothesis that relevance of the discussion issue to group goals would affect the degree of rejection.[138]

The second measure of the attitudes of subjects toward the deviate was brought out in a series of nominations for three different committees purporting to be necessary to carry on the club's work. "With instructions emphasing competence for the job, the members of each club nominated people for membership on the Executive, Steering, and Correspondence Committees. Rejection is coordinated to assignment to the least attractive committee. The Executive was the most attractive committee and the Correspondence the least attractive."[139] In all groups except the Lo Co Irrel, the deviate was nominated significantly more often than chance for the Correspondence Committee and less often than chance for the Executive Committee. In this situation, in which the instructions had stressed the competence considerations, the relevance of the discussion issue to the group goals affected the degree of rejection significantly, the rejection being stronger in the high-relevance groups. The cohesiveness-variable did not significantly affect the outcome of this test, however.

The experiment as a whole would seem to lend support to the following hypotheses about role behavior and sanctions in small, task-oriented groups:

[138] *Ibid.*, p. 235.
[139] *Ibid.*, p. 236.

"Persons in the mode and slider roles will be rejected less (if at all) than will persons in the deviate role." The severity of the rejection of deviates is likely to be affected by at least two variables in interaction relationships: "With cohesiveness held constant, rejection will be greater in relevant groups than in irrelevant groups. . . . With relevance held constant, rejection will be greater in high cohesive than in low cohesive groups."[140]

Could it be that these experimental data are the outcome of cultural factors peculiar to American society, or even peculiar to the subculture of male college students in the American Middle West? With only relatively slight variations, the experimental procedures of Schachter's study have been repeated in seven European countries, as a part of the first study by the recently established Organization for Comparative Social Research.[141] This time, the subjects were schoolboys in their early teens, and the experimental session purported to be the first meeting of a boys' aviation club. This time instead of three paid participants there was only one, the deviate. Again, while the deviate in the American experiment did not actually present obstacles to any immediate goals of the groups, in the European experiment his disagreement actually meant loss of valuable time, from the point of view of the subjects.

There were again two principal independent variables. First, the valence, or the desirability, of the goals for which the groups were competing: "Valence is manipulated by varying the attractiveness of the goals." The second variable was high vs. low *probability of reaching the goal*. The relevance of the experimental discussion to group goals, which was manipulated in the American experiment, was this time a constant; the relevance was consistently very high.

To achieve high valence, one half of the clubs were told that it was not certain that this particular club would continue, since the number of aviation-interested boys had been greater than anticipated. And they were told that the chances that each club could continue depended on which club built the better model airplanes from one of five available kits. The continuance of the club was presumably a very important goal for each subject. The low valence goal, given the other half of the clubs, was the prospect of tickets to a showing of a documentary film on cargo planes, which again was supposed to depend on which clubs built the better planes. The probability variable, again, was manipulated by giving half of the high valence and half of the low valence clubs the impression that most clubs could continue, or obtain the movie tickets, and giving the rest of the clubs the impression that only a few could be chosen.

Among the five model plane kits, one was definitely less attractive to the boys than the four others. The paid participant was instructed to choose this particular kit and thus for a time prevent a consensus and apparently waste a certain amount of time which the group could have used in going ahead with building from one of the more desirable kits.

There were two measures of rejection of the deviate, both administered

[140] *Ibid.*, p. 247.
[141] Schachter *et al.*, "Cross-Cultural Experiments on Threat and Rejection," *Human Relations*, VII, No. 4 (1954), 403–40.

immediately after the discussion in which his deviation was expressed. First, a sociometric social preference scale: each subject was asked to rate everyone else in the club on a five-point scale ranging from a strong desire to work with him to a strong desire not to work with him. Secondly, a sociometric role preference scale: each subject was asked to vote for a president of the club—and in the process to rank all the boys according to their suitability or competence for the presidency. Let me quote from the authors' conclusions: "Rejection appears to be a virtually universal reaction to a deviate. In all countries and in all societies the deviate is considered relatively undesirable on both sociometric and role preference measures."[142]

Clearly, the group dynamics approach to the study of some of the most general sociological determinants of limitations on social freedom carries great promise. Conclusions from the two experiments referred to here have been supported and additional materials of relevance have been provided in various other experiments. The number of studies being done in communication and decision-making processes appears to be increasing steadily and promise increasingly accurate information on the general determinants of individual freedom in task-oriented groups.[143]

The data I have referred to make no distinction between coercive and noncoercive sanctions. Clearly, a sociological tendency in groups to prefer collaboration with and leadership by norm-sharers does not necessarily bear on the deviating individual's freedom from coercion. But one may assume, other things being equal, that group situations producing pronounced rejection tendencies coerce the deviate more often than those producing only mild rejection tendencies. Since the fact and degree of coercion depend in part on the motivations of the object of sanctions, these experiments could not produce any immediate data: the deviates were in all cases paid participants. It is much harder to devise group experiments in which both the "majority" and the "minority" will behave spontaneously. Yet it is probable both that new experimental techniques will be devised to meet this problem and that increasingly useful techniques will be developed in the study of majority and minority behavior in the decision-making processes pertaining to real-life tasks.[144]

The Extension of Rationality: Formal Organizations and Social Freedom

Bertrand Russell, in the Preface to one of his books, asserts that there were two main causes of social and political change in the nineteenth century: "The belief in FREEDOM which was common to Liberals and Radicals,

---

[142] *Ibid.*, p. 437.

[143] Various other studies are included in Cartwright and Zander (eds.), *Group Dynamics.* Others are found in a volume edited by Hare, Borgatta, and Bales, *Small Groups: Studies in Social Interaction.* Also, an entire issue of the *American Sociological Review* (Vol. XIX, No. 6 [December, 1954]) is devoted to reports on small groups research.

[144] Asch has conducted various experiments in which the majority were stooges and the minority of one was the naïve subject. More recently, Crutchfield has devised a new technique that seems to make the use of stooges superfluous in certain kinds of approximate equivalents to small group experiments. Cf. below, pp. 360–65.

and the necessity for ORGANIZATION which arose through industrial and scientific technique."[145] My approach asserts that the dilemma of social freedom versus social organization is a perpetual one, making for continual strains and change in any society. All individuals want both privacy and community, and all want leisure and work and certainly many products of labor. No society has found a balance between freedom and organization suitable to all its citizens. Quite possibly, such a balance cannot be found because the same individuals may at the same time wish for incompatible amounts of privacy and community.

Community implies institutional limitations on freedom, we have seen. A complex society also brings with it laws to regulate the proper use of coercion and political authority to press for deliberate objectives. *Organizations* within a society institute a further extension of authoritative and deliberate power exertion. "Formal organization," says Philip Selznick, "is the structural expression of rational action."[146] He quotes with approval Chester Barnard's definition which I, too, find more useful than any other that I have seen: "The most useful concept for the analysis of the experience of cooperative systems is embodied in the definition of a formal organization as a system of consciously coordinated activities or forces of two or more persons."[147]

There are elements of rationality in laws and political authority, we have seen. In the establishment of formal organization, rationality is the primary incentive. And in achieving the continuance of established organizations, while informal institutional pressures in fact may be equally or more important, considerations of rationality make up the official justification.

The rapid growth of formal organizations, both in number and size, is one of the pronounced characteristics of our time, and this development surely has a profound impact on the status and prospects of individual freedom. But there is no simple antithesis between freedom and organization, as might appear on the surface. Organizational power does impose restraints on the individual, whether coercive or manipulative or other, but the accomplishments of organizational activity have in many ways served to expand the individual's freedom. For example, the workingman's freedom from coercive pressures has in our culture demonstrably been expanded in many ways through the efforts of trade unions.

Another facet of the "organizational revolution" is that it tends to substitute cooperation in formal organizations around deliberate interests or ideas for the traditional cooperation patterns in informal groups such as the family, kinship system, or small community. This means a greater specificity and fragmentation in social interaction. A greater proportion of relationships becomes specifically defined in relation to deliberate purposes

---

[145] *Freedom and Organization, 1814–1914*, p. 8.

[146] Cf. "Foundations of a Theory of Organization," *American Sociological Review*, XIII (1948), 25.

[147] Barnard, *The Function of the Executive*, p. 73. Cf. Simon, Smithburg, and Thompson, *Public Administration*, p. 5: "Thus, by *formal organization* we mean a planned system of cooperative effort in which each participant has a recognized role to play and duties or tasks to perform."

and devoid of a deeper affective meaning.[148] The individual splits his activities among more social relationships the more he becomes "organized" for a variety of purposes.

The growth of organizations makes many individuals feel rootless because they acquire a multiplicity of organizational roles and cannot always keep straight which of them express their own "real" personalities and because family, community, and traditional ways of doing things fade into the background. On the other hand, the many kinds of organizations in urban communities also provide many individuals with new roots because chances improve with the greater number of choices of organizational activity that some of them have purposes fully tuned to the individual's own values.

The organizational segmentation of social interaction also tends to create anonymity among men. In small rural communities everybody knows everybody; this may result in a sense of belongingness but also in a denial of privacy. In large cities the average individual may have less chances for an equally strong sense of belongingness, but he also has greater freedom from the often extremely coercive pressures of small community norms and opinions. Increasing urbanization means increasing division of labor and an increasing number of formal organizations. In the city the individual may find an alternate, close-knit community, or an organizational equivalent in satisfying his community needs. To the extent that he has psychological freedom and can tolerate some chaos, he can interact in many social systems during the same period—formally organized as well as informal social systems.

A distinction must be made between voluntary and involuntary membership in formal organizations, for the two kinds of belonging have, of course, different consequences for social freedom. This difference is a matter of degree. Even citizenship in a state is not completely compulsory. Most states permit emigration, and those that fail to do so cannot prevent some citizens from escaping as refugees. Even though for many citizens "membership" in a state is virtually not a matter of choice, citizenship need not be considered a coercive restraint on individual freedom because the individual may be happy with his citizen status or he may take it for granted, even if he lives under a dictatorship.

In our culture membership in certain other kinds of organizations as well is probably experienced as coerced or coercive. In certain trade unions, for example, demands may be made both on the pocketbooks and on the political expression of the members as a condition for continued membership in good standing. And the livelihood of the individual and his family may virtually depend on his conformity to the demands of union "bosses." While the trade unions on the whole have achieved tremendous increases in the freedom of workers from the coercion of the employers and from the vicissitudes of the business cycle, some of them have tended to institute a

---

[148] The "pattern variables" developed by Parsons and associates would be useful in an analysis of this aspect of the organizational revolution. I must limit this discussion, however, to a brief statement of some of the problems this development raises for social freedom.

new kind of servitude. In certain "racketeering unions," indeed, the coercion of crooked union leaders has been fully as severe as that of the old-time worst type of exploiting employer.

Other organizations, such as churches in various small communities, may also demand participation even of unwilling individuals. Church membership and church-going may be coercive in the sense of being an unwanted restraint that must be accepted by those who need social prestige or customers for their trades. For the greater number, however, particularly in cities, church-going surely is voluntary and most certainly not coercive.

At the permissive extreme on the continuum between voluntary and involuntary memberships in organizations we have such phenomena as hobby clubs, debating societies, promotional outfits for special ideas such as Esperanto or nudism—organizations that only rarely involve coercive restraints on their members. People may, of course, for reasons of ego defense become so dependent on some of these organizations that they would take a lot of pushing around rather than quit. Given a certain minimum of psychological freedom, however, these memberships tend to be entirely voluntary, and normally there is no coercion of members by such organizations.

One may conclude that formal organizations do not necessarily institute coercion of their members, and that coercion consequently is not a general sociological necessity in organizational behavior any more than it is in institutional behavior. On the other hand, an element of voluntarism or consent is probably necessary even in the most coercive organizations. Kenneth Boulding writes that there are three general bases for organizational cooperation: identification with the purpose of the organization; rewards of membership; or coercion, defined as fear of the consequences of not serving it. But he adds: "There must always be some small element of identification with the purposes of the organization if *effective* cooperation of an individual is to be obtained. Even the slave and the conscript must in some sense be willing to be enslaved or conscripted, and there is some threshold of unwillingness below which no amount of coercive power can force individuals to contribute."[149]

If organizations do not necessarily establish coercive power for their leaders over their members, it still remains to be asked if certain types of member behavior are more likely than other types to provoke punitive or even coercive organizational sanctions. I shall not discuss in this connection the general dynamics of institutions and sanctions. Organizations create institutions of their own, certainly for their members and at times for outsiders, too. Deviations from institutional expectations and from other types of consensus provoke sanctions in all social systems, including, as we have seen, primitive aboriginal communities as well as small experimental groups in our culture.

In Selznick's discussion of "derived imperatives" for organizations, much of his analysis applies also to social interaction beyond formal organ-

[149] *The Organizational Revolution,* pp. xxxi–xxxii.

izations, but he emphasizes throughout the elements of rationality and explicitness that are characteristic of organizational behavior. Institutional behavior is often automatic or merely habitual; organizational behavior may become automatic but is invariably instituted at first on rational grounds. Moreover, as Selznick stresses, organizations are likely to encourage continued attention to rational problem-solving, at least on the part of their leaders. Leaders, at least, have a stake in the preservation of their organizations, and the exigencies of their role encourage them to address themselves rationally toward solving the problems bearing on the status and prospects of their organizations.

Perhaps the most general source of tension and paradox in the analysis of organizational behavior, says Selznick, is "the recalcitrance of the tools of action."[150] Since an organization generally is instituted for the conscious coordination of behavior, its members become in a sense tools for its officials or leaders. But individuals, even strongly committed organization members, invariably have goals of their own. These goals may overlap with but can never be wholly identical with organizational goals or the goals of organization policy-makers. This makes for a certain "recalcitrance," which prevents organizations, including states, from achieving complete totalitarian power.

If a given degree of coercion potential is assumed in an organization, what can be said in general about types of membership behavior that are likely to result in actual coercion? Deviating behavior, obviously, but deviating with respect to what types of norms? Selznick suggests five types of behavior that are particularly likely to provoke determined organizational countermeasures.[151]

First is behavior affecting the organization's external security. An example of this is threats of members to "expose" malpractices to nonmembers. Renegades who talk publicly are considered the worst enemies of organizations, and tendencies in that direction among those who are still members are likely to be given much attention by leaders.

Second is behavior affecting the internal stability of lines of authority in the organization. Deviation that is unintentional is one thing; deviation that presents a deliberate challenge to organizational authority is much more likely to produce punitive countermeasures. This is one reason why intellectuals tend to suffer the most under totalitarian regimes: they are more likely than most other kinds of people to be deliberate and systematic and "ideological" in their expression of opposition, however guarded this expression may be.

Third is behavior affecting the stability of informal power relations within an organization. There is always an informal power structure that more or less overlaps with the formal one but that is more effective. Consequently, behavior tending to "upset" these working relationships, even if

---

[150] *TVA and the Grass Roots: A Study in the Sociology of Formal Organization*, pp. 252–53.

[151] "Foundations of the Theory of Organization," *American Sociological Review*, XIII (1948), 20–30.

the reformer carries the formal rules of the organization in his hand, is likely to be punished by those in actual power.

Fourth, a sense of continuity in policy or in legitimate ways to formulate policy is encouraged in every organization. Frequently shifting policy recommendations, or challenges to the legitimacy of formally or informally operating procedures for policy-making, are likely to provoke sanctions, even if they come from people high up in the organization—or, indeed, especially if they come from recognized leaders, whose words carry influence.

The fifth and final category on Selznick's admittedly incomplete list is behavior endangering the "homogeneity of meaning with respect to the meaning and role of the organization."[152] "The minimization of disaffection requires a unity derived from a common understanding of what the character of the organization is meant to be. When this homogeneity breaks down, as in situations of internal conflict over basic issues, the continued existence of the organization is endangered." I have in the preceding subsection indicated that conformity with respect to goals is not a general prerequisite of social systems. In an organization, however, such a conformity is more crucial, since its goals provide the asserted justification for its existence. Lip service to its goals, at least, is wanted, or as a basic minimum no challenge to its basic goals. People may join a political party for purely social reasons, but they will no longer be welcome if they insist on challenging its basic policy outlook. Such a challenge, as well as talk about the futility or even harmfulness of an organization, is, if coming from a member, likely to provoke the exercise of whatever sanctions the organizational leadership controls.

These kinds of deviation, then, are likely to lead to rationally organized sanctions in organizations that have power. One may conclude that the degree of coerciveness of organizations over their members depends on at least these variables: (a) the degree of involuntariness of the membership status; (b) the power of the organization, or the sanctions available to its actual leaders (this variable is likely to correlate highly with the former one); (c) the degree to which organizational goals deviate from important individual goals, thus tending to provoke deviating individual behavior; and (d) the extent to which individual deviation is perceived as a threat to the imperatives of organizational continuity.

The growth of organizations is a consequence of the rising number of problems facing individuals and groups in an increasingly complex society. In turn, organizations create new problems and further complexities, necessitating further organization, in a reciprocal, self-generating process. The larger and more complex the society, the greater is not only the number of problems, but also the number of problems that can be grappled with effectively only by large-scale organizational effort, involving many people.

[152] *Ibid.*, p. 30. What Selznick lists are not, strictly speaking, types of behavior likely to be sanctioned, but "derived imperatives" for the maintenance of the organizations. I am making the short-step inference that behavior perceived as threatening each of these imperatives is particularly likely to provoke the exercise of whatever sanctions organizational leaders have access to.

Public goals, or values held by individuals as citizens, that is, values oriented to conceptions of the public interest, can be the objectives of both private and governmental organizations. Private goals, on the other hand, or goals held by individuals promoting their personal value positions, are legitimately the objectives of private organizations only. Governmental organizations are not supposed to promote private goals, except in the sense that they afford most private activities protection in promoting the public values of justice, law and order, and human rights.

Our time has witnessed an increasing scope of governmental organization and activity. This again is a reflection of the increasing complexity of modern societies and the increasing magnitude of many of the problems that confront modern man. Governmental agencies have on the whole greater resources and can apply more forceful measures to assure cooperation and conformity. This does not mean, as most of the English empiricists and the Manchester liberals assumed, that increased governmental activity necessarily means more exercise of coercion. Many governmental activities are instituted to reduce the amount of coercive pressures on the individual. A governmental enforcement of principles of fair play in business competition, for example, is likely to increase the social freedom of most businessmen. If it coerces a few, this coercion is perhaps less severe than the coercion suffered earlier by larger numbers.

An "Iron Law of Oligarchy"?

"Among all the constant facts that can be found in all political organisms," wrote Gaetano Mosca sixty years ago,

one is so obvious that it is apparent to the most casual eye. In all societies . . . two classes of people appear—a class that rules and a class that is ruled. The first class, always the less numerous, performs all political functions, monopolizes power and enjoys the advantages that power brings, whereas the second, the more numerous class, is directed and controlled by the first, in a manner that is now more or less legal, now more or less arbitrary and violent, and supplies the first, in appearance at least, with the instrumentalities that are essential to the vitality of the political organism. . . . [Moreover] the larger the political community, the smaller will the proportion of the governing minority to the governed be, and the more difficult will it be for the majority to organize for reaction against the minority.[153]

Robert Michels has demonstrated that this tendency toward concentration of power holds not only in the state, but also in certain other political organizations. In fact, he demonstrated strong tendencies toward oligarchy in the parties on the left and concluded that the other parties would show the same tendencies, if not much more of the same:

The study of the oligarchical manifestations in party life is most valuable and most decisive in its results when undertaken in relation to the revolutionary parties, for the reason that these parties, in respect of origin and programme, represent the negation of any such tendency, and have actually come into existence out of opposition thereto. Thus the appearance of oligarchical phenomena

---

153 *The Ruling Class,* trans. by Kahn, ed. by Livingston, pp. 50, 53.

in the very bosom of the revolutionary parties is a conclusive proof of the existence of imminent oligarchical tendencies in every kind of human organization which strives for the attainment of definite ends.[154]

Michels concluded that there is an "iron law of oligarchy":

the majority of human beings, in a condition of eternal tutelage, are predestined by tragic necessity to submit to the dominion of a small minority, and must be content to constitute the pedestal of an oligarchy. . . . Oligarchy is, as it were, a preordained form of the common life of great social aggregates.[155]

Pareto makes the same kind of observations. Almost everywhere one finds a "governing class of relatively few individuals that keeps itself in power partly by force and partly by the consent of the subject class, which is much more populous. . . . The governing class is not a homogeneous body. It too has a government—a smaller, choicer class (or else a leader, or a committee) that effectively exercises control."[156]

Unlike Pareto, however, Michels was concerned with determining the sociological limitations within which it is possible to realize democratic ideals. He was a democrat by preference, even if he wanted to be realistic about it. He implies, I infer, that he would approve of the present chapter's inquiry when he asserts that "it would be erroneous to conclude that we should renounce all endeavours to ascertain the limits which may be imposed upon the powers exercised over the individual by oligarchies (state, dominant class, party, etc.)."[157] This is the problem of social freedom that is before us.

"The principal cause of oligarchy in the democratic parties," Michels asserts, "is to be found in the technical indispensability of leadership."[158] He nevertheless affirms his faith in democracy, in the sense of a government by the people: "It would be an error to abandon the desperate enterprise of endeavouring to discover a social order which will render possible the complete realization of the idea of popular sovereignty."[159] It is hard to conceive of a complex society, however, in which leadership can be done away with. Indeed, after coming to the almost equivalent conclusion that political authority is a functional prerequisite of any complex social system, I find it difficult to share this belief in "government by the people" in a strict sense as an ideal toward which it makes sense to strive.

It seems to me that Joseph A. Schumpeter is more realistic than Michels in his application of the same empirical insights toward a reformulation of the democratic creed. The role of "the people" in a democratic society is not to govern, or even to lay down the general decisions on most political issues, says Schumpeter. The electorate's role is "to produce a government, or

---

[154] *Political Parties: A Sociological Study of the Oligarchical Tendencies of Modern Democracy*, p. 11.
[155] *Ibid.*, p. 390.
[156] *The Mind and Society*, IV, 1569, 1575.
[157] *Political Parties*, pp. 404–5.
[158] *Ibid.*, p. 40(.
[159] *Ibid.*, p. 405.

else an intermediate body which in turn will produce a national executive or government. And we define: the democratic method is that institutional arrangement for arriving at political decisions in which individuals acquire the power to decide by means of a competitive struggle for the people's vote."[160]

The chief virtue of this conception of democracy, it seems to me, is in its clean break with past illusions of the kind that Mosca, Pareto, and Michels have attacked. For Schumpeter, furthermore, democracy is a means to something else, not an end in itself. For him, it is a means toward arriving at political decisions that are at once authoritative and subject to a majority's consent, at least on issues important enough to loom large in election campaigns. For me, also, democracy is a means toward something— toward building a society with maximal human rights, or with a maximum of freedom for all individuals, especially freedom from coercion.

Schumpeter affirms, in other words, a faith in "democracy" in a sense that takes cognizance of the fact that, as Michels saw, leadership is indispensable in a state as in any other organization. He also goes much further than Michels does in elaborating how and why the prerequisites of political authority in fact make a mockery out of popular sovereignty as portrayed in many classic as well as current conceptions of democracy. In the first place, a complex society creates complex political problems, and politicians tend to become specialists in many ways; and a minority of specialists is not easily controlled effectively by a majority of nonspecialists, even among a highly intelligent and responsible citizenship. Furthermore, in our time, if the majority of the populace feels strongly on certain issues, chances are that effective manipulators have been at work. "The will of the people is the product and not the motive power of the political process."[161]

Perhaps Schumpeter overstates his case, or underestimates the extent to which a democratic public opinion can be a motive power in the political process. There are certain basic issues on which even highly organized and centralized propaganda campaigns may fail to sway or convert a spontaneous public opinion. For example, I believe that in the last few years a strong and largely autonomous public desire for a more conciliatory foreign policy has had its independent effects in Western Europe and probably also in the United States and the Soviet Union. Schumpeter fails to allow sufficiently, I believe, for the influence a public opinion may exert by means other than political elections. David Truman's theory of potential groups would seem a useful corrective: Men of power, if they are realistic, are likely to be continually aware of various limits on their authority as well as their power, beyond which they can go only at the peril of provoking nonconformity as well as the formation of alignments aiming at challenging their power.[162]

---

[160] *Capitalism, Socialism, and Democracy*, p. 269. J. S. Mill was thinking along similar lines when he wrote: "Men, as well as women, do not need political rights in order that they may govern, but in order that they may not be misgoverned." *Representative Government*, p. 391.

[161] *Ibid.*, p. 263, and pp. 250–64. I shall return to this problem; cf. below, especially pp. 331–34.

[162] Cf. above, pp. 138–39.

One may also question the absolute terms with which Michels asserts that leadership or oligarchy is an organizational necessity. His study of revolutionary socialist parties is actually a less crucial inquiry than he thought it was: in spite of their humanitarian goal values, such parties are probably more likely to be oligarchical than are more moderate or status-quo parties, for the simple reason that they are revolutionary. The more ambitious the goals of an organization, and the stronger the challenge facing it, the more it presumably will tend to take on the structure of an army, with strong leadership and discipline.

Instead of his assumption, I would pose the following hypothesis. The more rational effort an organization invests in challenging an accepted institution, or in defending a widely challenged institution, the more oligarchical it will tend to become. The less effort that is needed to promote the policies of a given organization, to turn the hypothesis around, the more genuine internal democracy and membership influence can it afford. Institutions and rationality are complementary means of social coordination; the stronger a set of values is protected institutionally, the less deliberate authority and discipline does it take to defend or promote them.[163] Contrary to Michels' basic assumption, both the parties on the extreme left and on the extreme right tend to be more oligarchically organized than the center parties. Social democratic parties, for example, can afford a greater amount of dissent and membership influence partly because the communist parties— for good reasons—tend to bear the brunt of the hostility of the conservative forces.

My conclusion is that there is no general iron law of oligarchy operating as a characteristic of all social systems, or even of all political organizations. True, political authority is needed, but the minimum prerequisite is an authoritative constitutional process for decision-making. It is possible to conceive of organizations operating in a fully democratic manner, in the sense that the leaders continually can be effectively challenged by genuine membership preferences. Indeed, certain existing organizations with moderate goals and a secure position are in fact operating with a very high degree of internal democracy. The International Typographical Union in the United States, we are told, "has a fully developed two-party system. . . . Freedom of speech and expression is not only permitted but made effective by the guarantee of space in the official journal for dissent and criticism of the leadership. . . . There are provisions for initiative and referendum." It is surely not by chance that this union is supposed to have the most complete job control in the world and that it has enjoyed on the whole peaceful though far from subservient relations with employers.[164]

It is possible to envisage a utopian ideal, toward which approximations are sociologically feasible, of a society in which all important organizations,

[163] Cf. below, the introduction to Chapter 6, especially pp. 315–16.
[164] Fisher and McConnell, "Internal Conflict and Labor-Union Solidarity," in Kornhauser, Dubin, and Ross (eds.), *Industrial Conflict,* pp. 132–52. For a more recent and also a much more detailed study, see Lipset, Trow, and Coleman, *Union Democracy: The Internal Politics of the International Typographical Union* (1956).

including the state itself, operates on principles analogous to those of the International Typographical Union. Approximations can be hoped for, I believe, to the extent that (a) a wide range of effective human rights has been vindicated, so that the stakes even of the least privileged are not extreme, which also presumably means that extremist policies would not have a wide appeal; (b) there is a consensus on certain basic democratic and humanitarian values, including some minimum shared criteria for what constitutes further progress, or a joint sense of a basic direction; and (c) a high level of security has been reached, not only against anomie, but also against more specific external dangers such as war.

In the meantime we have a highly imperfect world and also highly imperfect democracies. In this situation I believe it is unfortunate to operate with conceptions of democracy that may give large numbers of people the illusion of powers that they do not have. Indeed, this can stimulate a smugness that reduces effective public participation to a level much below what could otherwise be attainable. I prefer a more realistic conception, also because this follows from my general principle affirming the desirability of increasing potential freedom even at the expense of immediate losses in social freedom or freedom from coercion.[165]

And Schumpeter's definition, meanwhile, puts the emphasis where it belongs: the essential element in the democratic process is the power of majorities to decide between alternative policies, by way of institutionalized competition for the people's favor. The basic issues must be placed effectively before a public that is enlightened by spokesmen for policy alternatives, who must enjoy free speech to perform this function. To the extent that controversy on political issues is institutionally guaranteed, in other words, and majorities have a veto on basic issues and top leadership, to that extent we have the institutional prerequisites for the growth of political freedom and human rights. Conceived in this manner, democracy is in varying degrees a reality in the West, and can to this extent be a process in the service of expanding freedom. There are deficiencies in all existing democracies. From a freedom-oriented point of view, and utilizing the insight embodied in Schumpeter's persuasive definition, the first points on democracy's agenda should be to perfect the protection of free controversy on political issues and to increase the electorate's opportunity to choose between real alternatives, on the most important political issues at each time.

The attainable limits of social freedom depend in part on the sociological prerequisites and propensities discussed in this section. They also depend, of course, on the more specific constellation of institutions characteristic of a given society.

There is another type of variable that is as general as the sociological factors I have been discussing and that bears equally on the general dynamics of social freedom. I refer to the psychological variables. Even if I have found that there appears to be no sociological necessity for coercion

[165] Cf. above, p. 106.

in every social system, there may still for all we know be psychological propensities in man that necessitate coerciveness in every human society.

Hypotheses on a Possible "Power Drive"

There are two broad classes of social factors serving to limit freedom, we have seen—the pressures emanating from institutions and those instigated by individual power subjects. Power agents can act on behalf of institutions or on behalf of power subjects, and they usually combine the two functions.

The power of institutions limits potential freedom more often than social freedom, for enduring institutions are usually internalized, so that their restraints are not perceived as such. But to the more autonomous individuals who no longer accept the institutionalized patterns as necessarily right, and also to the more rebellious individuals who have a taste for nonconformity, institutions can be fully as coercive as the arbitrary commands of a power subject.

The power of individuals, deliberately exerted for their own purposes, or exerted in appeasement of their own neurotic or healthy needs, affects the social freedom of others more often than their potential freedom, for the exertion of noninstitutional power invariably produces changes in institutionalized expectancies. The restraints they impose are normally new with each power act and cannot therefore be internalized. However, if the power objects *identify* with the power subject or power agent, the restraints may not be perceived as such and are therefore not coercive. In this chapter I am only concerned with coercive power; the problem of manipulative power will be dealt with in the next one.

Assuming now that the most important class of restraints on social freedom is instituted by power subjects, directly or through power agents, it becomes important to ascertain what some of the main types of motivations for exerting power are.[166] Is the wish to exert power something inherent equally in every human personality, so that his actual power exercise depends primarily on his social or political situation? Do different personalities differ greatly in this propensity? If there are differences, what are the main psychological factors tending to produce a strong or a weak desire for power?

Bertrand Russell, like many nonpsychologists, has been inclined to emphasize the social more than the personality circumstances:

When a moderate degree of comfort is assured, both individuals and communities will pursue power rather than wealth; they may seek wealth as a means to power, or they may forgo an increase in wealth in order to secure an increase of power. ... In the course of this book I shall be concerned to prove that the fundamental

---

[166] Power agents may act also on behalf of institutions as their deliberate guardians; cf. below, p. 319. My inquiry bears on the types of motivation for this kind of power behavior also.

concept in social science is Power, in the same sense in which Energy is the fundamental concept in Physics.

But he, too, grants that the love of power "is very unevenly distributed, and is limited by various other motives, such as love of ease, love of pleasure, and sometimes love of approval."[167]

Other writers have emphasized psychological circumstances affecting degrees of desire for power, as I, too, shall do in the present section. And I am emphasizing such factors as independent variables, not as constants. Whether or not great power tends to corrupt all power subjects is not a concern in this context. But by implication at least I am trying to locate psychological factors influencing degrees of the individual's "corruption," or intolerance, or tendency to coerce others, or desire for getting a chance to coerce others.

Harry Stack Sullivan and Harold Lasswell have both been interested in this problem, and a couple of their hypotheses were quoted without comment in the chapter on psychological freedom.[168] It is time now for an attempt to consider the probable validity of these propositions, which will now be cited more fully.

"A 'power drive,' in the narrow sense, results from the thwarting of the expansive biological striving and the feeling of the lack of ability," says Patrick Mullahy, in his attempt to outline a systematic statement of Sullivan's theory.

In other words, a "power drive" is learned, resulting from the early frustration of the need to be, and to feel, capable, to have ability, to have power. A "power drive" develops as a compensation when there is a deep, gnawing, inner sense of powerlessness, because of early frustration of the expanding, developing latent potentialities of the organism. Later acculturation and experience may, and frequently does, add to the early frustration and sense of powerlessness. A person who has a feeling of ability and power does not need to gain, and will not seek, dominance or power *over* some one. A person who manifests a "power drive" does seek to dominate others.[169]

Note the two uses of the term "power": a "power motive" is equivalent to a need to develop and use one's abilities, or in general a need for expressing one's individuality. This sort of power is wholly an intrapersonal phenomenon, in the sense that it does not necessarily, and perhaps not usually, aim at domination over others. It is a concept closely related to psychological freedom, or capacity for self-expression, and it is no great distortion to consider them as identical concepts, for my purposes at least.

The "power drive," or the need to dominate, is the kind of power that immediately raises the problem of the social freedom of those who are the actual or intended targets. The problem of their potential freedom may also

---

[167] *Power*, p. 12.
[168] See above, p. 164. Karen Horney takes the same position as Sullivan and Lasswell, though in the context of a more popular and cursory discussion. Also, she points out that we owe much to Alfred Adler for these insights. Cf. *The Neurotic Personality of Our Time*, Chap. 10.
[169] Mullahy, in Sullivan, *Conceptions of Modern Psychiatry*, p. 243.

arise, if manipulative means are used, or if the power objects identify with the dominant person to the extent that they are not aware of any coerciveness. This problem must be left out in this context, however, except as a reservation in my hypothesis, which is otherwise an application of Sullivan-Mullahy's:

Levels of social freedom in a society tend to be higher, the higher the levels of psychological freedom of those who exert power. Levels of social freedom tend to be lower, the lower the levels of psychological freedom of power subjects and power agents, except in so far as power is exerted by manipulative instead of coercive means.

Harold Lasswell has formulated hypotheses to essentially the same effect:

Our key hypothesis about the power seeker is that he pursues power as a means of compensation against deprivation. *Power is expected to overcome low estimates of the self,* by changing either the traits of the self or the environment in which it functions. . . . Our hypothesis about the power-accentuating type is that power is resorted to when it is expected to contribute more than any alternative value to overcoming or obviating deprivations of the self.[170]

The only weakness in this compressed formulation, in my judgment, is in the lumping together of "changing either the traits of the self or the environment in which it functions." For present purposes it is essential to distinguish between an inner "power" to adjust and the exercise of external power to make other persons adjust their behavior to one's compensatory needs.[171]

In later contexts Lasswell and his collaborators have discussed the problem of the *political personality*. He is conceptualized as a close relative, at least, of the personality dominated by a "power drive" in Sullivan-Mullahy's sense: "The *political man* (homo politicus) is one who demands the maximization of his power in relation to all his values, who expects power to determine power, and who identifies with others as a means of exchanging power position and potential."[172] In a forthcoming volume Lasswell and McDougal describe the "political man" as a "power centered person" and quite properly warn against confusing a politically active man with a political personality in this sense.

The political man in their description is one who (1) acquires perspectives that make him (a) emphasize the demand for power, (b) expect power to exert a decisive influence on value outcomes, and (c) justify power in terms of common values; he also (2) acquires skills sufficient for at least a minimum degree of effective political participation.[173] The main differences between this type of man and the man with a power drive ap-

---

[170] *Power and Personality,* pp. 39, 40.

[171] A third possibility within the reference of Lasswell's formulation is the power to make use of things, or impersonal resources, without necessarily in this case, either, limiting anybody else's freedom or power.

[172] Lasswell and Kaplan, *Power and Society,* p. 78.

[173] Lasswell and McDougal, *Law, Society and Policy,* working paper, Part II, Chap. 4.

pears to be, first, that his arena of power-seeking is specified as political and, secondly, that there is no hypothesis implied in this definition of the political man about how he became that way. It is a weakness in much of Sullivan's writing that many of his important concepts imply empirical assumptions, even if these often are both profoundly plausible and at times quite original. Moreover, in theorizing on the emergence of the political man Lasswell and McDougal are in accord with Sullivan's position:

A general proposition is that *the accent on power rather than some other value in the social process has come because limitations upon access to other values have been overcome by the use of power.* In the broadest sense, therefore, power is a defense. Individuals turn to it in the hope of overcoming low estimates of the self when appraised in terms of any or all values. When non-power values fail to remove deficiencies, hope is focussed upon power. . . . Political personalities come into being by the use of power as a defense against threatened or actual loss of values.[174]

And in one statement the authors are quite specific in referring to certain types of childhood circumstances as an influence probably pushing in the direction of power accentuation:

When we try to account for the component of the self on whose behalf power is sought (and especially the primary ego), one general proposition appears to be that extreme egocentric fixation reflects an environment that provides meager emotional support during early years.[175]

It has been suggested in Chapter 4 that most parent-child relationships are more or less strained by the parental authority-function, which at times overshadows the child's sense of being loved unconditionally and induces hostility in him. If there is not much love to start with, this hostility is, of course, magnified. But in any event this hostility is likely to induce guilt feelings and lead to repression, especially if parents react severely against the show of hostility. Two patterns of repression are particularly significant: the child may repress primarily his hostility and develop submissive, authoritarian attitudes; or he may repress primarily his dependency needs and develop aggressive, antiauthoritarian attitudes. Most children, of course, combine elements of both, in so far as they learn to repress, and all the attitudes that are the outcome of repression are more or less ambivalent, containing latent tendencies in opposite directions.

The man with a strong power drive, in Sullivan's sense, or Lasswell's political man, is perhaps as a rule, one may conclude, someone who as a child tended to repress primarily his dependency needs. The man who is an extreme admirer of strength is perhaps more often one who instead tended to repress his hostility against parents. But reality is much more complex than this double hypothesis would indicate. In the first place, the man who admires strength may for this reason be an ideal strong man's lieutenant, and in this way exert much power himself and develop a strong taste for power exertion through his identification with his chief. And the man with a strong power drive may experience severe disappointments on his road toward political or economic power and be forced to abandon his ambi-

[174] *Ibid.*
[175] *Ibid.*

tion; if so, he will presumably try to enjoy a sense of power vicariously, by identifying with some strong power figure. Also because of the ambivalence of most ego-defensive attitudes, the power drive and the "submission drive" are closely related and may interchange as the social circumstances dictate.

My general conclusion, then, is that both types of repression in infancy and childhood may influence the growth of a power drive. Or, to reverse the focus: *The better the child has been enabled to preserve his psychological freedom, the less likely is the adult to develop a taste for exerting power over other people.*

The preservation of a high psychological freedom may depend on other circumstances as well as upbringing, we have seen. All these circumstances, consequently, may influence the possible genesis of a power drive as well.

Hypotheses on Frustration and Aggression

It has been suggested in Chapter 4 that *frustration* is a more general determinant of deficiencies in psychological freedom than is authoritarianism or antiauthoritarianism. These defensive syndromes may be considered sources of two more specific kinds of chronic frustration. I have defined frustration, in conformity with much usage, as the blocking of one or more of the individual's goals or the impact on him of a situation in which some pressing need remains unfulfilled.[176] It is not a very exact definition, but it will do for the present very cursory survey of contemporary knowledge and opinion. Note that the blocking of any goal is frustrating, though to a lesser degree the less strongly the goal was desired. But an unfulfilled need is frustrating only if it is a continually activated or pressing need, not if it is or was a sublimated or a genuinely extinguished need. The thesis that a power drive is a probable result of various kinds of repression-producing experience, notably in childhood, can perhaps be seen as one more specific derivation from a more general thesis: that frustration tends to produce aggression. In its "classical" formulation, the frustration-aggression thesis was formulated by a group of Yale psychologists on the eve of the last world war.[177] They argued that frustration normally leads to aggression, unless a way is found around the blocking of the goal or some satisfactory substitute goal is achieved. They also argued that aggression always is due to frustration of some sort.

Both propositions are difficult to confirm or disconfirm in any exact sense, since both frustration and aggression are matters of degree, and there are so far no operationally defined lower limits to the applicability of these terms. In consequence, it is always possible to discover possible sources of previous frustration to "explain" aggression, and it is always possible to detect or assume latent aggression, at least, toward the self or others, in a person who has suffered some frustration.

Nevertheless, these propositions are useful general working hypotheses,

[176] See above, p. 204.

[177] Dollard, Doob, Miller, Mowrer, and Sears, *Frustration and Aggression.* These authors define frustration as "*that condition which exists when a goal-response suffers interference.* Aggression is independently defined as *an act whose goal-response is injury to an organism* (or *organism-surrogate*)." *Ibid.,* p. 11. Cf. also the reservations taken by the authors in Miller *et al.,* "The Frustration-Aggression Hypothesis," *Psychological Review,* XLVIII (1941), 337–42, and Sears, "Non-aggressive Reactions to Frustration," *ibid.,* pp. 343–46.

and they have stimulated much research, in which their derivations and applications in socially and politically important contexts have been examined. I shall limit this discussion to a brief mention of one of the neatest of these studies. At a boy's camp in New England, Neal E. Miller and R. Bugelski administered a test of attitudes toward the Mexicans and the Japanese, in a situation in which they were able to study the impact of a totally unrelated frustrating experience on these attitudes. The boys were requested to sacrifice several hours of their leisure time to answer a large number of uninteresting questions, mostly too difficult for them also, and this "examination" lasted so long that they missed the weekly "Bank Night" at the local movie theater. Half of the boys were given the attitude test on the Mexicans before the ordeal and the test on the Japanese afterwards, and the order was reversed for the other half of the boys. As expected, the attitudes toward both outgroups were more unfavorable in the responses given after the hours of frustration than in those given before.[178]

It may be concluded from this and other experiments that intolerance toward racial, religious or political outgroups, whatever their main determinants, may be reinforced by many kinds of frustrations in everyday life. The reverse relationship is also plausible—that effective social policies aiming at increasing the contentment of the citizenry may as a by-product also serve to increase the harmony between or reduce the intensity of conflicts between various minority groups.

The most dubious of the propositions advanced by the Yale group is the most specific one: "The expression of any act of aggression is a catharsis that reduces the instigation to all other acts of aggression."[179] The implication of such a view is that aggression should be encouraged, almost, in those we want to help—for example, our children. The analogy is a simple mechanical one: aggressiveness is accumulated by frustrations like water in a reservoir, which must be tapped some time or the dam will break. A more dynamic analogy would compare bursts of aggression to short-circuits in a complex electrical system. It would take the view that aggression can be controlled, or, in the analogy, that undesired high voltages can be transformed and channeled into useful energies, or at least that dangerous fires can be prevented if short-circuits do appear.

From the point of view of learning theory, the latter analogy seems the more plausible one. For responses to various types of frustration are presumably subject to the learning process, in the sense that those responses tend to be repeated that tend to produce the best balance of need-satisfactions under each set of circumstances. Even if a burst of aggression offers relief, it may also produce damage of one kind or another, or it may produce guilt. It is always a possibility in child-rearing, for example, that children may learn to express some of their aggressive impulses indirectly

---

[178] Referred to in Dollard *et al., Frustration and Aggression,* pp. 43–44. Cf. N. E. Miller and R. Bugelski, "Minor Studies of Aggression. II: The Influence of Frustrations Imposed by the In-Group on Attitudes Expressed toward Out-Groups," *Journal of Psychologoy,* XXV (1948), 437–52.

[179] Dollard *et al., Frustration and Aggression,* p. 53.

in activities that are not perceived by others as aggressive and be effectively rewarded for mastering this type of response to frustrations.

The main propositions of the Yale group are largely accepted today, though not without many criticisms and modifications. Perhaps S. Stansfeld Sargent's criticism expresses the most widely shared objection—that the Yale group has tended toward a "description of behavior chiefly in terms of stimuli and overt responses, to the neglect of intervening organismic factors."[180] And among the latter, Sargent includes depth variables such as anxiety-producing remnants of past experience.

Theodore Newcomb, whose textbook in social psychology utilizes constructively the insights of a variety of schools of psychology, takes the view that frustration is likely to lead to aggression chiefly depending on whether and to what extent the frustrating event is perceived as a threat.[181] The goal-oriented person, as long as he can maintain this orientation, will see every manageable frustration as a challenge to his resourcefulness and endurance. If an unmanageable frustration merely blocks a nonessential goal, he will find a substitute goal. But if the goal in question is considered essential, or the frustration in other ways is viewed as a threat to himself, and a threat that he does not know how to overcome, aggression is likely to result. When the rational faculties give up, aggression takes over.

But we are all aggressive some of the time. None of us can be goal-oriented all the time and master every obstacle blocking our path. None of us is without anxiety, and anxiety always implies a threat-orientation so far as it goes. But we differ greatly in our reactions to specific types of frustrations, for our goals differ and our anxieties differ. These complexities in human nature greatly magnify the problem of predicting and controlling aggression. For the purposes of planning for freedom, all we can conclude from the frustration-aggression hypothesis is that the more social satisfaction and economic security a society offers the average man, the better the hope that he will live in peace with his neighbors; the less aggression, the less coercion; and the less severe frustration, on the whole, the less aggression.

Even the best living standards may produce gloomy frustrated lives and much aggression, however, if there is more *anomie* than most people, given their levels of psychological freedom, are able to cope with. Deficiencies in psychological freedom remain the most basic source of frustration, and also the source least accessible to political remedies. Let me now make a brief excursion into this general problem area.

Defensive Syndromes, Conformity, and Intolerance

The need for stereotypes has been discussed briefly in the previous chapter and will be discussed again in the next.[182] This need raises problems of psychological and of potential freedom. An abnormal inclination to stereotype may divorce overt consciousness from basic motives; it always

---

[180] "Reaction to Frustration—A Critique and Hypothesis," *Psychological Review*, LV (1948), 108–14.

[181] *Social Psychology*, pp. 353 and 352–60.

[182] See above, pp. 201–2, and below, pp. 355–57.

impedes insight and restrains the individual's vision in coping with the external world.

Variations in the need for stereotypes also raise problems of social freedom, however, although not in the individuals themselves. Even an extreme dependence on grossly stereotyped notions is not perceived as an imposition of external restraints. That this state of affairs eventually is going to lead the individual into frustrations and restraints, because reality refuses to conform to his simple map, is another matter, which I must leave out of the present discussion.

The important problem of social freedom to be discussed here arises from the fact that a strong dependence on stereotyping implies or is related to a general threat-orientation and tendencies toward intolerance in interpersonal relations. The individual who fears cognitive disorder and ambiguity may not experience coercive restraints on that account, but he will be inclined to impose coercive restraints on others, if they are perceived as threatening to his system of order. Or he may support political coercion against minorities who for the sake of good order in his map of the universe must be considered "bad" in one way or another.

Stereotypes are images that tend to become systematized in dogmatic beliefs or ideologies; the problem of dogmatism is the same problem. And phrased in the language of dynamic psychology, and seen as a psychological problem, the issue before us is the impact of the individual's intolerance of ambiguity on his readiness to act coercively or support intolerant acts.[183]

All human beings experience some intolerance of ambiguity. We all yearn for at least a few certainties in life, and we want to *know*, perhaps especially in cases where we despair of being able to inquire fully. Dogmatism "is so natural to man that it is not likely to be a preserve of the past," says Leo Strauss, and he defines dogmatism, following Lessing, as the inclination "to identify the goal of our thinking with the point at which we became tired of thinking."[184] "The demand for a final proof springs less from hope than from fears," says Charles L. Stevenson. "When the basic nature of a subject is poorly understood, one must conceal his insecurity, from himself as much as from others, by consoling pretenses."[185] This depends of course also on the importance of a given problem for the individual, whether personally or professionally. A scientist, I believe, is likely to be dogmatic and intolerant according to the ratio between his belief that he is expected to master a given problem and his conviction or repressed suspicion that he does not really master it at all. Mothershead's hypothesis is probably sound: "Indeed, I suspect that there may be a positive correlation between the emotional intensity with which a controversial belief is defended and the absence of reflective thought about that belief by him who thus defends it."[186]

[183] Cf. above, pp. 199–205.

[184] Quoted from Lessing's letter to Mendelssohn of January 9, 1771, in Strauss, *Natural Rights and History,* p. 22.

[185] *Ethics and Language,* p. 336.

[186] "Some Reflections on the Meanings of Freedom," *Journal of Philosophy,* XLIX (1952), 671.

Controversies between scientists are not likely to raise serious problems of social freedom. But it is easy to see that the same psychological dynamisms are likely to operate in the political struggle—and there frequently with far more serious consequences. John Morley has stated this point well in his famous essay, when he says that "those who are least really sure about their opinions, are often most unwilling to trust to persuasion to bring them converts, and most disposed to grasp the rude implements of coercion, whether legal or merely social."[187]

Both authoritarian and antiauthoritarian personalities are basically afraid of ambiguities within their psychological fields. They have repressed from consciousness some of their basic needs, which remain active in the unconsciousness and are only precariously kept out of awareness. Protection against threatening insights is furnished by a rigid categorizing in the cognitive and attitudinal fields, with strict distinctions between black and white, good and bad, superior and inferior, ingroup and outgroup, etc. Since the extremely defensive individual cannot consult his own basic needs, or all of them, he must have his answers to the recurring problems of life systematized and ready-made. *Any influence that brings disorder into his system provokes intense anxiety.* Any possible insight that may have this effect is a threat and subject to strenuous repression efforts.

My discussion of the authoritarian syndrome in Chapter 4 has brought out one important aspect of this relationship between a general intolerance of ambiguity and a tendency toward a sharp dichotomy between ingroup and outgroup: it was found that there is in general a high intercorrelation between authoritarianism and ethnocentrism.

Perhaps it should be emphasized again that there is no sharp dichotomy between defensive and nondefensive personalities. All of us suffer from some deficiencies in psychological freedom, and none of us, except perhaps some extreme psychotics, is entirely without awareness of any of his basic needs. But the degree to which we suffer from defensive syndromes is probably one important influence on the degree to which we feel threatened by certain types of behavior or people, or become intolerant of certain outgroups and nonconformists.

Dogmatic, intolerant attitudes do not always produce overtly aggressive behavior. A. D. Lindsay refers to one example in which the aggression is projected into the future and into the next world when he quotes a Protestant's plea many years ago: "Why should we object to co-operating with Catholics in this world, we know what will happen to them in the next."[188] But this sensible limitation on overt aggressiveness is rare, probably due to the fact that aggression tends to enter only the fields or situations from which goal-orientation and rationality have left. A contributing circumstance is in the sanction requirement of every enduring institution: deviation is normally a threat against established conventions and attitudes, and their own dynamics encourage aggression against deviators, as we have

---

[187] *On Compromise*, p. 121.
[188] *Toleration and Democracy*, p. 7.

seen. Those who are personality-predisposed to aggression, or those whose personal security systems depend on the sanctity of a certain institution, may, of course, be expected to react *more* aggressively against deviators than others. But *some* aggression is expected of all "right-thinking citizens" when important mores are violated.[189]

Among defensive syndromes I have in the previous chapter mostly confined my attention to authoritarianism and antiauthoritarianism. Both personality types are likely to share a fundamental tendency toward intolerance of cognitive and emotional ambiguity, I have found, and some research data to this effect have been reviewed. However, the authoritarians and the antiauthoritarians are likely to differ much in their impact on the state of social freedom in their society. The fact that both are basically intolerant may make each type equally prone to impose coercive restraints in their immediate circle of dependents. But in the society at large it is likely that authoritarian personalities will tend to encourage restrictions on social freedom, while antiauthoritarians on the contrary will tend to encourage less rather than more coerciveness.

Authoritarians tend to develop submissive attitudes and authoritarian loyalties, and thus they serve to strengthen the hands of the men of political or economic power. Their predisposition to intolerance makes them jealous guardians of conformity to authority commands and to conventions. Those who challenge the authorities are at the same time challenging important props in the security systems of authoritarian personalities and are consequently likely to be subjected to whatever means of aggression each authoritarian conformist has at his disposal.

Antiauthoritarians, on the other hand, are because of their defensive rebelliousness destined to bear the brunt of the struggle against the dictates of authorities and authority-invested conventions. They may in turn be intolerant and aggressive against those who conform, but the antiauthoritarians seem to be invariably a small minority, and are therefore not in a position to exert much coercive control. Their struggle has almost always been against coercion, especially large-scale political coercion, and in favor of the social freedom of the individual. Their influence has helped create societies in which nondefensive people are permitted to choose relatively freely in deference to their own individual convictions whether or not to conform to each institution, or to each command of the political authorities.

This is not to say that societies in the interest of freedom expansion ought to do whatever can be done to produce antiauthoritarian personalities. For defensive syndromes—apart from dooming the individuals in question to chronic frustration—always produce, as we have seen, ambivalence and a closeness of opposites in their overt expressions. The anti-

[189] I believe Svend Ranulf is overstating his case, therefore, when he concludes that "the disinterested tendency to inflict punishment is a distinctive characteristic of the lower middle class, that is, of a social class living under conditions which force its members to an extraordinarily high degree of self-restraint and subject them to much frustration of natural desires." That such factors tend to increase and intensify the use of this socially approved outlet for aggression, is beyond doubt. *Moral Indignation and Middle Class Psychology*, p. 198.

authoritarian may at times easily turn into an authoritarian—either an authoritarian rebel, an authoritarian conformist, or an intolerant man of power, as the circumstances may dictate.

In consequence, one may conclude from these considerations that the best hope for social freedom is in the encouragement of psychological freedom by all possible means or in the education of a population in which as few individuals as possible have defensive needs either to conform or to rebel. Some limited insights into how social circumstances may affect psychological freedom have been reviewed in the last section of Chapter 4.

Authoritarianism and Positions of Power

"Where powers beyond the capacity of human nature are intrusted, vices the disgrace of human nature will be engendered." This statement of Godwin's[190] has a tautological ring, but it expresses the nonpsychologist's stress on situational variables as determinants of coercive power behavior. It assumes that power corrupts the power subject to a degree depending chiefly on the amount of power exerted.

My position is that the corruption, brutality, or coerciveness of the power holder depends probably even more on his personality predispositions. Intolerance of ambiguity in everyday life makes for intolerance of "ambiguous people." It implies also a general habit of rigid dichotomizing, or black-white thinking, along with fear and hatred of the black, or "bad," people. Authoritarians also tend to be submissive and thus as followers tend to strengthen the hands of leaders. What if they themselves become leaders? And what are the chances in modern societies for the achievement of positions of economic or political power by authoritarians?

These are the two questions before us. The first one I shall pass quickly over, for it appears evident that those who are intolerant and aggressive as followers will be no less intolerant and aggressive as leaders. Indeed, the position of leadership will tend to increase their intolerance and aggressiveness, for the fears and anxiety of previously insecure people will probably be much increased if they become powerful and can lean on nobody else for protection. Defensive submissiveness is dynamically speaking close to its opposite, defensive domination. This type of leader, then, is likely to try to compensate for and repress his frustrating anxiety by being "tough"— or aggressive and intolerant—in his dealings with those subjected to his power.

It may safely be asserted, then, that the prospects for social freedom are brighter in a society, the higher the levels of psychological freedom among those who exert power, especially among those who exert much power.

Now the second question: Which type is more likely to achieve positions of power, the relatively free personality or the more defensive one?

Superficially it seems plausible to argue that a strong power drive— which has been diagnosed as a defense mechanism—is likely to increase the individual's chances for reaching positions of power. This view is taken

[190] *Political Justice*, I, 251.

by Bertrand Russell, for example, who argues that "those who most desire power are, broadly speaking, those most likely to acquire it. It follows that, in a social system in which power is open to all, the posts which confer power will, as a rule, be occupied by men who differ from the average in being exceptionally power-loving."[191] Those who are exceptionally power-loving are presumably the same as those who have a power drive in Sullivan's sense or are power-centered personalities in Lasswell's and McDougal's sense. But Lasswell and McDougal are on more solid ground psychologically, I believe, when they observe that defensiveness sets a limit to the adaptability of the individual to political participation. Speaking of the power-centered authoritarian personalities, they argue: "Not the top spots, but a circumscribed, prescribed and secure chair in the bureaucracy is the type of role to which they are well adapted. With the re-enforcement of the administrative setting, they are able to keep their destructive impulses from discharging too disruptively in immediate personal relations. The hazards of running for office, or of promoting new projects, put a tremendous strain on the compulsive character."[192]

For example, the same authors suggest, if we consider the careers of the greatest American Presidents, they hardly fit our conception of the power-centered personality. The following general hypothesis is formulated: *"The leaders of large scale modern politics where comparatively free institutions exist are oriented toward power as a coordinate or secondary value with other values, such as respect (popularity), rectitude (reputation as servants of the public good), and wealth (a livelihood)."*[193]

On different grounds, Lasswell and McDougal advance essentially the same hypothesis concerning the recruitment of the top leadership in dictatorships: *It is improbable that the top leaders of an established totalitarian regime in an industrial society are recruited from "authoritarian personalities."* Their argument here is that people with strong internal conflicts have poorer survival chances in an atmosphere of terror and anxiety; better off are those "who have relatively few internal conflicts and are comparatively free to make realistic appraisals of the environment."[194]

Conclusions of a similar sort are drawn by Fillmore H. Sanford after reporting on a field study of authoritarianism in the attitudes of nonleaders toward leaders and leadership. But he introduces a distinction between pressures "from above" and "from below" in the recruitment of leadership. Authoritarians will rarely be selected as leaders, he suggests, where followers have a free choice, but they may well be appointed by those higher up, where *they* have a free choice.[195]

It is true that authoritarians are submissive to their leaders or chiefs and may ingratiate themselves with some of them in this way, but most persons

191 *Power,* p. 14.

192 Lasswell and McDougal, *Law, Science and Policy,* working paper, Part II, Chap. 4.

193 *Ibid.*

194 *Ibid.*

195 *Authoritarianism and Leadership: A Study of the Follower's Orientation to Authority,* especially pp. 181–82.

with authority, unless they are authoritarian personalities themselves, will tend to have more confidence in the less submissive, or at any rate the less defensively submissive, subordinates. Moreover, in our democratic age most jobs involving people are performed more easily by leaders who get along well with their followers, and this is well known also at the peaks of the various power pyramids. This much, at least, has been established by industrial psychologists and sociologists. Consequently, even if Sanford's distinction between pressures from above and pressures from below may perhaps have some validity, its importance is open to doubt when we consider that even the selection from above for leadership positions will tend to prefer relatively nonauthoritarian personalities, who are more likely to get along well with their subordinates or followers.

There is not sufficient evidence from research to claim that the cited hypotheses on authoritarianism and positions of power are firmly established. But some data with an indirect bearing on the problem before us are available, and they tend to confirm the hypotheses.

Lasswell and McDougal refer to a pioneer study by John B. McConaughy and associates, who obtained the collaboration of 18 out of the 170 members of the legislature in South Carolina for a series of psychological tests. Their scores were compared to scores obtained with samples of the general (white) population in the state. These political leaders were found to be "less neurotic, more self-sufficient, and decidedly more extroverted; but they were only slightly more dominant." If these 18 solons are slightly more dominant in their behavior or attitudes than most people, this is explained more plausibly by the requirements of their profession than by assumptions attributing to them a neurotic power drive.[196]

One finding from Gabriel A. Almond's study of the appeals of communism comes the closest, at the present time, to confirming the probable validity of the thesis that defensive authoritarians tend to be left out of the top power positions in democratic as well as in many nondemocratic power structures. If Lasswell's and McDougal's speculations about persons chosen for leadership are valid in relatively authoritarian organizations, they are more likely to hold in relatively democratic ones. Let me further assume that communist parties tend to be relatively authoritarian organizations.[197]

On these assumptions it is highly significant that the former communists in Almond's sample had been less neurotic in their attitudes toward communism, the higher up in the party's power hierarchies they had been placed. Very roughly twice as many former rank-and-file communists had

[196] Lasswell-McDougal's warning against confusing the politically active man with the personality-predisposed "political man" should be kept in mind. McConaughy's study is briefly referred to in Lasswell and McDougal, *Law, Science and Policy*, working paper, Part II, Chap. 4.

[197] An "authoritarian organization" means an organization with centralized power and authority; no inferences should be drawn from the use of this term about types of objectives or personnel. Note that the logic of my argument in the text is similar to that of Michels, except that I am making the opposite assumption about the communist parties, compared to his assumption about the social democratic parties, which he believed could be expected to have the least authoritarian type of organization of all political parties. Cf. above, especially pp. 292–93.

joined the party to satisfy neurotic needs, it was found, compared to the proportion of former high-echelon communists about whom the same was true, in the judgment of Almond and his collaborators.[198]

If it is true that communist parties tend to select relatively unneurotic and consequently nonauthoritarian personalities for the most important leadership positions, then it appears probable that other political parties with more effective rank-and-file influence exhibit the same tendency to a considerably greater extent.

It is unfortunate that there is so little research bearing convincingly on the problem before us: the extent to which various societies and organizations are likely to place authoritarian personalities in positions of power. For the immediately following problem is a highly significant one for the state and prospects of social freedom: On what kinds of factors do the trends in these selection processes primarily depend?

For the average man's degree of freedom from coercion, the proportion of authoritarian personalities in his society is much less significant than the proportion of power effectively exerted by authoritarians. As Riesman has observed in a different context: "A character type may be in a minority but nevertheless become dominant by virtue of its strategic location, or its appeal as a model for others."[199] In the first place, authoritarians in power are likely to be less humanitarian than others and to tend to coerce more people in worse ways. Secondly, if power is accompanied by prestige, authoritarians in power are likely to have their attitudes and values imitated by many, so that the amounts of coerciveness also on these grounds are likely to increase.[200]

The clearest, most conspicuous, and most tragic modern example of a whole country being ruled primarily by a defensive personality was Germany under Hitler. No country is ever ruled by one man only, but Hitler has probably come as close to enjoying supreme political power as anyone has in recent years. He may or may not have been a psychotic, but that he was at least severely neurotic is generally agreed. Arild Haaland in a recent review of much of the literature concludes cautiously that all we can be sure about is that "Hitler expressed a will to power and a lack of sensitivity far beyond what is usually considered desirable or normal."[201] I conclude that he was severely deficient in psychological freedom and that he compensated by developing a defensive power drive. I also conclude that Germany after the defeat and the depression provided one setting in which it was possible for a defensive to achieve dictatorial power.

When *The Authoritarian Personality* was published, it was at once pointed to as a politically important work, providing insights on essential

---

[198] *The Appeals oof Communism*, pp. 254–56. Cf. above, pp. 212–13, for other references to this study, along with some critical comments on the nature of the data.

[199] "Some Observations on the Study of American Character," *Psychiatry*, XV, No. 3 (1952), 333 and 338.

[200] I am not saying that more of the followers will become authoritarian personalities in the same way, for adult personalities are not subject to fundamental change by the process of imitation. But it is conceivable that the growth of punitive attitudes could have consequences in child-rearing practices, with the result that there might be more authoritarian personalities in the next generation.

[201] *Nazismen i Tyskland*, p. 554.

psychological influences toward democracy or toward fascism.[202] It is true that this volume, and the many subsequent studies it has influenced, have taught us much about tendencies toward potential fascism and other kinds of authoritarianism in ordinary people and their important bearing on a would-be dictator's chances to get ahead. The problem of reducing incentives toward authoritarian submissiveness, or increasing psychological freedom, is now widely recognized as a vital long-range educational policy problem for every democratic society.

What is not so widely recognized is the necessity of studying authoritarianism in its relationship to various types of incentives in the political process. This is an area in which much thought and research is needed. Oliver Garceau a few years ago called attention to the importance of "developing an understanding of leader (behavior) in situation and episode."[203] What is urgently needed, I believe, is a focusing of research on the types of incentives toward or away from politically aggressive and coercive behavior—a research that combines the use of dynamic psychological categories with more attention than hitherto to political (structure and process) determinants of the total incentive situations, for various types of personalities in various types of political situations.

To help us learn how to increase the levels of psychological freedom is only one of the contributions behavioral science can give to the prevention of fascism and related dictatorial systems. Another thing we must learn is how to give those who have neurotic power drives harmless outlets for their ambitions and how to make sure that much power is not given to people with strongly authoritarian syndromes. With more insights into the complex interplay between political incentives and personality types, it will become increasingly feasible to develop constitutions and laws with built-in mechanisms to restrain or prevent neurotically rooted political coercion.

The main conclusion to be drawn from my inquiry into the problem of psychological determinants of social freedom is a very simple one: *The more psychological freedom, the more social freedom* in a society, other things being equal. The main qualification to this simple thesis is that the proportion of psychologically reasonably free persons in the population as a whole is less important than their relative weight in political and other power processes.

Since there are no inherent limitations on the degree of psychological freedom attainable by individuals under optimal circumstances, I conclude that there is no permanent *psychological* necessity for coercion in social relationships or in political societies. I have found in the previous section

---

[202] Cf. Flowerman, "Portrait of the Authoritarian Man," *New York Times Magazine,* April 23, 1950: "Findings of recent scientific investigations reveal that the real menace to democracy is not the brutal dictator but the anonymous man-in-the-crowd on whose support the dictator depends for power. . . . It requires authoritarian ["authoritative" in the article is clearly a misprint] personalities to take hold of authoritarian ideas; it takes authoritarian personalities—thousands and even millions of them—to build an authoritarian state."

[203] "Research in the Political Process," *American Political Science Review,* XLV, No. 1 (1951), 78.

that coercion is not a sociological prerequisite for all social systems either. But given the present levels of psychological freedom, and our far from ideal practices in social and political organization, there is no prospect that coercion of man by man can be abolished for a long time to come.

As an ultimate goal for political development, however, the abolishment of coercion is a realistic ideal on both psychological and sociological grounds, so far as our knowledge extends today. In this sense a faith in man's and society's perfectibility appears justified. It is certainly recommendable as a working hypothesis, at least, in the behavioral sciences as well as in politics.

6

Determinants of Potential Freedom

RATIONALITY AND INSTITUTIONS

In the study of personality a distinction is frequently made between expressive behavior and purposive or coping behavior. Maslow's description of the two behavior types involves, it seems to me, a number of unproven and at times questionable empirical assumptions.[1] For my purposes, the analytical distinction can be stated in very simple terms: Coping behavior is behavior in pursuit of objectives not instantly achieved, or, if instantly achieved, objectives sought for their usefulness in terms of further objectives. It is behavior motivated over time. Expressive behavior, on the other hand, is behavior that is either unmotivated or is motivated only by a need for the kind of activity in question.[2] Expressive behavior is behavior without any achievement motive for the individual, that is, without any value or function external to the value or function of the activity itself.[3]

In sociological analysis, which proceeds on the synergic or aggregate level of social interaction, another distinction can be made that has much in common with the one just referred to. This is the distinction between rational and institutional behavior.

Rationality as an ideal type of behavior implies a double effort on the part of the individual: (1) to define his aims clearly and consistently at each time and (2) to employ the best available knowledge to discover the most efficient way to promote the given or chosen aims. For present purposes a broad interpretation of this definition (demanding only a bare minimum of effort on the part of the individual) is required; one that is broad enough to be contrasted with the broad category of institutional behavior. This distinction may be phrased in terms somewhat analogous to the distinction between coping and expressive behavior.

---

[1] "The Expressive Component of Behavior," in Brand (ed.), *The Study of Personality: A Book of Readings*, pp. 362–76, especially p. 364. Cf. Brand in *ibid.*, p. 15. I prefer Maslow's term "coping behavior" over the more widely used but looser term "purposive behavior," because "coping behavior" more clearly refers to a personality, not a social-system frame of reference.

[2] Maslow questions the generally accepted notion that all behavior is motivated. I wish to avoid committing myself on this issue, which is tied up with the question of how "motivation" ought to be defined. *Ibid.*, p. 363.

[3] For purposes of systematic psychological theory, a third type of behavior should be added: defensive behavior, which is behavior in pursuit of a special type of objective—namely, the reduction of anxiety or the defense of an insecure ego.

Rational behavior is behavior guided by perceived efficiency norms directed toward given or chosen goals, conscious or unconscious. It is motivated over time by objectives separable from the activity itself.

Institutional behavior is behavior conforming to institutional expectations, with no motivations beyond the habit or conscious inclination to conform to or "do right" in terms of such expectations.

To make the classification exhaustive, two more categories should be included on this level of analysis. *Anti-institutional behavior* is behavior with no motivation beyond the habit or conscious inclination toward nonconformity or "doing right" in challenging conventional expectations. *Non-institutional and nonrational behavior,* finally, is behavior neither conforming to institutions nor motivated by purposes over time. Purely expressive behavior belongs in this category.[4]

The categories of principal interest in the study of manipulative power and potential freedom[5] are "rational" and "institutional" behavior. Before I attempt to apply these categories in a theory, I wish to stress again that they are purely analytical constructs. No concrete sequence of behavior is completely rational or completely institutional. The most rational scientist, at one extreme, is guided also in his work by institutional standards of conscientiousness, integrity, language, etc. The most faithful true believer, at the other extreme, is in much of his behavior guided by rational considerations about how to communicate well, how to make a living, how to strengthen his ingroup and their institutions. It is evident, nevertheless, that the proportions of rational versus institutional behavior can vary greatly from one individual to another, from one sequence of behavior to another, and from one pattern of social interaction to another. These differences are found in actual behavior patterns as well as in institutional role expectancies.

I have listed three fundamental prerequisites of any enduring social system (larger than the primary group): social institutions, laws, and political authority.[6] Let me now reformulate this conclusion by seizing on the crucial function of political authority in the social system: the making of rational decisions that will be heeded, regardless of deviation (within limits) from institutional expectations.[7] Institutional conformity does not always require political authority or even decision-making; conformity to rational public policies requires both. An enduring social system needs, if I may now reformulate my earlier conclusion, (1) institutions, (2) rationality,

---

[4] To achieve a logically exhaustive classification, two further categories would have to be added: antirational behavior and both-institutional-and-rational behavior. The latter category is plainly useless for purposes of analyzing rational vs. institutional behavior. And antirational behavior is an empirical absurdity, I believe, even in the limiting case of extreme masochists. Behavior that appears antirational in terms of manifest purposes invariably will be found to be rational, in the present broad sense of rational, in terms of some latent, perhaps unconscious, purpose.

[5] "Potential freedom" has been defined as "the relative absence of unperceived external restraints on individual behavior." See above, p. 95.

[6] Cf. above, pp. 265–72.

[7] It has been suggested that political authority may be manifested in nothing more concrete than an authoritative political process. See above, pp. 270–72.

and (3) legal institutions that define and enforce respect for some proper minimum categories of institutional norms and rational decision-making.

The most general function of institutions in the social system is to promote its stability. The most general function of rationality is to promote all desired values other than stability.[8] Legal institutions serve to maintain some balance between institutional stability and rational adaptability.

The balance in the social system between rationality and institutions has a more obvious counterpart in the personality system: institutional behavior is governed by habits, including habitual perceptions of right and wrong, while rational behavior is governed by deliberate efforts to promote given or chosen purposes. A person shifts his attention to promote rationally whatever purposes preoccupy him at one time and another. Wherever his attention is not, he falls back on more or less automatic habits of conformity (or nonconformity) to institutional expectations. An individual requires institutions because (a) he needs habits, for his attention cannot be everywhere at the same time, and (b) the bulk of his habits must be tailored to the needs of social interaction, since individuals interact in one way or another all the time. Only generally shared institutions can provide mutual tailoring of habits. An individual also requires rationality, however, since he has individual organismic and probably also social needs to take care of, beyond the common core of needs that institutions may serve for many people simultaneously.

An individual's potential freedom, or the relative absence of unperceived external restraints on his behavior, is necessarily limited by all institutions that he unwittingly internalizes or takes for granted. It follows that a "complete" potential freedom is an absurdity and that the problem of maximizing potential freedom requires some specification as to the types of restraints that should be minimized. This problem will be discussed in the next section. For the present, let us consider somewhat further, in the most general terms, how the distinction between rational and institutional behavior may elucidate some aspects of the problem of potential freedom.

Imagine two extreme types of political system: one a system in which all independent power is concentrated in one hand and another in which a maximum of equality in power-sharing is practiced.

The extreme or *ideal type of democracy* in Lasswell's conception as "shared power" is somewhat difficult to visualize, partly because neither Lasswell nor anyone else to my knowledge has tried to relate the problem of the degree of power-sharing to the rationality-institutions dimension in social organization. If a society is highly and meticulously institutionalized, to the point where there is little independent scope for power exercise, a high degree of democracy in this sense is possible. This state of affairs, which may be called institutional democracy, seems to have been approximated among the Fox Indians of the Central Algonkians in the Great Lakes area. Walter B. Miller, after describing the organization of Fox society in the almost complete absence of "vertical authority," suggests that the utility

---

[8] This is, of course, an indirect way of promoting fundamental stability, too, if we assume that surface changes to accommodate needs and objectives create a more contented populace.

of "authority" in cross-cultural analysis is increased if it is interpreted to include "horizontal authority" as well.[9]

If, on the other hand, the degree of institutionalization is low, as in a society tending toward anomie, it can presumably be preserved as a social system only by way of a highly hierarchical power structure. An anomic democracy is difficult to conceive of as an ideal type. Anomie and power-sharing cannot both, I believe, be carried very far in the same society. The less conformity to institutional patterns, the more rational authority is required to insure social cooperation in the promotion of public values. This authority may have a more or a less tenuous majoritarian base, but it has to be strong enough to overcome anomic disintegration.[10]

The extreme or *ideal type of autocracy* in the sense of monopolized power is achieved in a society in which all individuals except the ruler behave either institutionally or submissively to a maximal degree. Here again, however, the degree of institutionalization, and especially the degree of entrenchment of the traditions, must be considered. In the tradition-bound autocracy, on the one side, the rational ruler must define as part of the given situation a whole range of institutions that he cannot change. In the flexible autocracy, on the other hand, the ruler has the power to revise institutions and to institute new ones.

Flexible autocracies can be approximated from a variety of directions. One approximation is the totalitarian state, in which the ruling group tries to revise a wide range of institutions to promote its policies and in which individual privacy is continually invaded by organized efforts to promote support or at least the resemblance of support for flexible government policies. No totalitarian government, however powerful, is the master of all institutions, however; churches and many other institutions have proved able to hold their own in a number of endurance tests.

An autocracy striving to alter institutions is not necessarily an enemy of freedom of expression. On the contrary, it may strive to promote institutional change in order to increase individual freedom, for institutions can be just as oppressive of social and potential freedom as the most ruthless exercise of deliberate power. When, for example, modern anthropologists promote institutional changes in aboriginal societies, this or some related purpose is frequently in mind.[11]

[9] "No course of action was agreed on by the council unless all members were in accord with the final decision. . . . The whole decision-making mechanism was characterized by extreme reluctance to permit decisions as to action to be concluded by any group smaller than the participating group itself." Miller, "Two Concepts of Authority," *American Anthropologist*, LVII, No. 2 (1955), 284–85 and 271–89.

[10] This argument is parallel to my previous argument on the relationship between "power" and "security"; power is important only to the extent that there is insufficient security for the attainment of goals. Likewise, political authority is required for keeping a social system going only to the extent that institutions are not sufficiently all-pervasive and "binding" to achieve the same purpose. In a complex society institutions must always to some extent be supplemented by political authority, just as few individuals are in a position to have all their value demands satisfied without active exercise of power. Cf. above, p. 258.

[11] The Vicos hacienda experiment in Peru, administered by Allan R. Holmberg for Cornell University, is the most promising present enterprise in this field. It is a situation in which a high concentration of power is employed in an effort to build up the prerequisites in the local Indian population for an eventual wide sharing of power. Cf. O'Hara, "Science and the Indian," *Natural History*, LXII (1953), 268–75 and 282–83, and Collier and Collier, "Experiment in Applied Anthropology," *Scientific American*, CXCVI (1957) 37–45.

For the degree of potential freedom in a society, the distinction between democracy and autocracy is less important than the distinction between institutional and rational power exercise. In a moderately anomic democracy (an ideal type could not be conceptualized in this case), as in a flexible autocracy, a good proportion of the political power exercised is noninstitutional. The leaders are relatively free in their choice of political objectives as well as in their choice of means for insuring the cooperation of followers. This is on the double assumption that the leaders as well as the followers are relatively autonomous of traditional institutions.

In a tradition-bound democracy with a high degree of power-sharing, as also in a highly tradition-bound autocracy, there is a narrow scope for political leadership. Political developments are largely predetermined by the dynamics of institutional interrelationships.

The social freedom of the average individual would in theory be very high in the extreme type of a highly institutionalized and tradition-bound society, whether it were a democracy or a dictatorship, for he would be taking the restraints on his freedom for granted. In real-life societies, at least in our contemporary civilization, the entrenchment of institutions in individual personalities is rarely that deep-going and universal, however. As a consequence, the difference between democracy and dictatorship tends to be very important from the point of view of social freedom. No complex society can do entirely without political authority to supplement institutions, and the exercise of this authority, or of power in its support, is likely to be much more ruthless in a nondemocratic country, in which opposition more easily becomes treason or subversion.

For the potential freedom of the individual, on the other hand, the difference between high and low degrees of institutionalization is more important than the difference between democracy and dictatorship. Individual autonomy is severely limited in a strongly tradition-bound society, whether the limited sphere of political authority is or is not exercised from a democratic basis. In an anomic democracy, and also in a flexible dictatorship, the individual tends to be relatively free in this sense, provided, of course, that the dictatorship's control over communication has not already succeeded in establishing new institutions in the minds as well as in the overt behavior of the populace. Oppression affects potential freedom only to the extent that it is no longer perceived as oppression.

I argued in an earlier context that coercive power is in a sense weaker than manipulative power.[12] Coercive power can bring about compliance, but this compliance ceases if and when the power is no longer effective, and the compliance is limited to the heeding of specific commands. Manipulative power, on the other hand, can induce conformity to a wide range of norms by the processes of identification and internalization. Identification can insure conformity as long as the power subject or the symbols representing him remain salient in the minds of the power objects. Internalization can insure conformity throughout the lives of the individuals affected. Moreover, both identification and internalization, unlike coerced compli-

[12] See above, pp. 251 and 252–53.

ance, tend to produce a "responsible" kind of conformity. The voluntary conformist differs from the involuntary one in that he is motivated and flexible enough to add elements of rationality or efficiency in promoting the norms or purposes for which he has been recruited.

"Rape," as Merriam has observed, "is not an evidence of irresistible power in politics or in sex."[13] A man's power over a woman won by love or seduction obviously is enormously greater than the power won by unmitigated rape. An essentially equally striking contrast can be drawn between the power of an autocrat who has won the affection of his subjects and the power of an autocrat who is hated. This is why no modern dictatorial regime spares any effort in trying to influence public opinion in its favor. The more all-embracing such efforts are, the closer we get toward a totalitarian society, in which, if one considers the extreme ideal type, all opinions of every subject are shaped by the political regime. This extreme of a totalitarian system, which can never be very closely approximated in real life, would be immensely strong, in the sense that no coercion would be needed to maintain it.

In relatively democratic countries the advantage of manipulation over coercion as a general technique of power is in some respects greater. In addition to the considerations just advanced, which are as valid for democratic leaders as for dictatorial rulers, comes the more immediate, institutionally channeled dependence of democratic leaders on their followers and voters. A democratic system provides for regular elections; if these are honest, a democratic regime can be voted out of office. Moreover, it is sure to be voted out of office if it tries to remedy deficiencies in manipulation of public opinion with large-scale coercion against its opponents. Once public opinion has come to consider a certain minority subversive or traitorous, political coercion can in a democracy supplement manipulation, but it can never replace manipulation. In one respect, then, democratic leaders have even stronger reasons for perfecting the techniques of political manipulation than have the rulers in a nondemocratic system. They do not, at least not to nearly the same extent as the latter, have recourse to coercion as a substitute for effective manipulation.

In at least two other respects, however, manipulative techniques of maximal efficiency are more urgent for a dictatorial regime than for a democratic one. First, political defeat is on the whole less of a calamity for a democratic regime. In a democracy defeated political leaders more often both keep their heads and can hope for an early comeback. Second, the policy objectives perhaps, and almost certainly the means of their implementation, are more likely to be in harmony with institutionalized political expectations in a democracy than in a dictatorship. This means that smaller amounts of manipulation are required to keep public opinion in line. The greater the discrepancies between governmental policy trends and the genuine demand trends in public opinion, the greater efforts are required to keep a government in power, other things being equal.

13 *Political Power*, p. 180.

Coercive power behavior always carries sanctions, unlike institutional power behavior. It is necessary to step carefully, however, in explaining this proposition. The first part of it is true by definition; the second part may at first seem contrary to common sense.

Institutional behavior is behavior directed by internalized norms. The extreme type of institutional behavior is the behavior of Fromm's "automaton conformist," which is something different from the behavior of the appointed or self-appointed guardian of institutions. The automaton conformist is not necessarily concerned with exercising negative sanctions against nonconformists; his reaction may instead be one of bewilderment and withdrawal. Or again, he may exercise sanctions, which—intentional or unintentional on his part—may be experienced as coercive by the nonconformist or would-be nonconformist.

The guardian of institutions, on the other hand, behaves rationally as well as institutionally. The rational component of his behavior in this role is likely to have a coercive intent, and also a coercive effect, if his power is greater than that of the nonconformist. The institutional component of his behavior is likely to be of little scope if he has made a program of promoting conformity. This component consists in personal habits without coercive intent, but if they are frustrated, the rational and punitive conformity-demanding behavior may be triggered off.

The influence of the automaton conformists may be just as oppressive of potential freedom as the influence of the zealous guardians of tradition. And the influence of the radical innovators may *become* just as oppressive as that of the traditionalists, if they by charisma or propaganda monopoly succeed in having a new set of institutions internalized in the population.

I have indicated that there is no such thing as a complete potential freedom, either in real life or as a goal value or ideal that can make sense conceptually. It is necessary to distinguish between types of institutional pressures. I have made a basic distinction between specially supported and nonspecially supported institutions—or between manipulation in the interest of other people at the expense of the interest of the object of manipulation and manipulation in his own interest or in his interest as part of the common interest of all. This led to the following formulation of a more limited sense in which I advocate the desirability of a maximal degree of potential freedom: *I wish to see maximized the ability and potential incentive of every man to resist manipulation, whether institutional or deliberate, in so far as the manipulation serves other interests at the expense of his own.*[14]

Let us now consider the thorny problem of how to develop criteria for distinguishing between manipulation at the expense of and manipulation not at the expense of the power object. This task presents us with a double problem, as we shall see, of distinguishing between specially and nonspecially supported institutions and between exploitative and nonexploitative rational exercise of manipulative power. "Special interests" may be served by institutional as well as by rational behavior.

[14] See above, p. 97.

"SPECIAL INTERESTS" AND MANIPULATIVE POWER

One trouble with the concept of freedom from manipulation, we have seen, is that "manipulation" is a very wide concept. There is probably no social interaction going on that does not include elements of manipulation. Most communication, if not all, includes conscious or unconscious attempts at regulating the supply of information in the interest of encouraging or discouraging certain types of behavior.[15] Even the most detached reports on scientific experiments, for example, are not entirely free from elements of manipulation, in the sense that both findings and words are usually selected with some audience in mind and with the intention of trying to give that audience a coherent and correct impression. Minimally, we all want to communicate so that we are understood.[16] In most cases, however, we also want to communicate so that others will regard us with favor and treat us with some respect or affection, or courtesy at the very least. A maximal freedom from manipulation in this broad sense is probably a nonsense-concept and is certainly not a plausible goal value.

Nor would it be an improvement instead if I suggested that freedom from manipulative *power* should be maximized. Manipulative power means an individual's capacity for attaining or advancing values by inducing motives in other individuals toward conformity with his wishes, in the absence of or independently of coercive sanctions.[17] I certainly would not consider it a worthwhile goal formulation to hope for a maximum freedom from this kind of power, which is broadly enough conceived to include the mutual influence exerted in the best of marriages or friendships, in collaboration toward joint tasks, and indeed in probably all social interaction. Some criterion for distinguishing desirable kinds of manipulation from undesirable kinds is clearly a necessity if the maximization of potential freedom is to remain an intelligible and a worthwhile political goal.

My value position on this issue has just been restated as follows: I wish to see maximized resistance capacities against *special interest manipulation,* while recognizing that much manipulation is "nonspecially supported"—that is, in the individual's own interest or in the common interest including his own.[18] I do not include in this goal conception a reduction in the amounts of attempted special interest manipulation. I believe that the cross-pressures of manipulative communications, whether specially or nonspecially supported, in general are useful stimulants in individual learning processes. It is the ability and the incentive of the individual to resist special interest manipulation that I wish to see maximized.[19]

---

[15] See above, pp. 98–99. Purely expressive behavior could be an exception, but it is not generally considered as a kind of "communication."

[16] This is the limiting case. It may be argued that a selection of information with only these purposes in mind—of giving the most relevant facts to encourage realistic behavior—should be considered a case of entirely nonmanipulative communication. Yet, the tendencies referred to in the following sentence in the text are likely to emerge even in such a situation, and they are definitely manipulative in my broad sense of the word.

[17] See above, p. 259.

[18] See above, p. 319.

[19] It should probably be considered valuable to be able to resist many nonspecially supported manipulative pressures, too; but I have to shy away from the difficult task of suggesting general criteria for deciding under what circumstances this ability and incentive would be desirable.

A "special interest group" is not necessarily suspect from a freedom-oriented or democratic point of view. Indeed, a pluralist society presupposes a large number of groups looking out for their own interests first, though preferably also taking the interest of the public into account. It would seem that an ideal type of a monolithic totalitarianism would be the only system entirely without special interest manipulation, and real-life approximations to this pure type of a political system presumably would tend to transform the government or the privileged party hierarchy into a superspecial interest group, even if it may also have the public interest at heart.

Such considerations make our problem a more complex one than the problem of "sinister interest" of Bentham and his followers: "Interest," Bentham defined, "when acting in such a direction and with such effect as to give birth to falsehood, may be termed sinister interest."[20] The distinction between truth and falsehood, or between perceived truth and perceived falsehood, is unfortunately not as simple as Bentham tended to assume, neither in logical nor in psychological terms. Elements of manipulation exist in most if not all social interactions, and the line between elements of manipulation and elements of deliberate fraud is difficult to draw.

In attempting to distinguish special interest group manipulation from other kinds of manipulation I have no moral issues to settle. What I am looking for are criteria for detached inferences about the degree of overlap between the interest that the manipulative power is intended to serve and the presumed interest of the power objects or the community as a whole.

These criteria cannot refer to the degree of consent successfully induced. Walter E. Sandelius has argued that "the lowest level of state power is that which requires continuous application of force, as in the power of a conquering army. From this it rises through degrees of consent to a point at which consent becomes altogether active and preponderant.[21] On the very same page he condemns the Soviet system, which, he says, "is not founded on that philosophy of trust in the human spirit which promises to unite men." It apparently never occurs to him as a possibility that consent to the basic policies of the Soviet regime may be "altogether active and preponderant" among sizable majorities of Soviet citizens. I am not claiming that this is certainly the case, but I am inclined to believe that it is and I am almost certain that this is the state of affairs in China today.[22] However that may be, the point I wish to make is simply this: even the greatest enthusiasm for a political regime is not a guarantee that a full freedom of expression, or a "good society," exists. If support for the regime is manufactured by way of a monopoly of control over the media of mass communication, supplemented by severe coercion against oppositional elements, then I would not wish to speak approvingly of a "high level" of state power.

The degrees of intensity and universality of induced consent may be the

20 Cf. "The Rationale of Judicial Evidence," *Works*, VII, 385; cf. *ibid.*, pp. 530–31, and III, 600–601 and 621–22.

21 "Reason and Political Power," *American Political Science Review*, XLV (1951), 713.

22 Cf., for example, the thoughtful reports of Martin, "China in Uniform," *New Statesman and Nation*, May 7, May 14, and May 21, 1955, and also Cameron, *Mandarin Red*, and Gale, *No Flies in China*. "I fancy," says Gale, "that a far higher proportion of Chinese agree with the policies of the Chinese Government than of English with the policies of any particular English Government." *Ibid.*, p. 188.

outcome of at least two important factors: the correspondence between public policies and genuine public wishes, and the effectiveness of mass manipulation. These two factors probably tend to intercorrelate, to a limited extent, since manipulation would tend to be more effective the fewer genuine grudges there are to overcome. If a political regime relies heavily on a highly organized propaganda monopoly, however, and ruthlessly suppresses all political dissent, one must conclude that no amount of evidence of public support to the regime can prove that the people's genuine interests are not being exploited in the interest of the ruling few. This is not necessarily the case because it depends on the circumstances and the caliber of the leaders. But when a dictatorship becomes entrenched, it would take a rare combination of human qualities to prevent some of the men of power from taking special interest advantage of their great power. I am not saying with Lord Acton that power always corrupts or that absolute power always corrupts absolutely. I am saying, however, that a political system resting on the enthusiastic support of a deliberately misinformed public poses great temptations for the men of power.[23] Manipulative power, I have suggested, tends to be more effective than coercive power in serving the purposes of the powerful.[24] The totalitarian dictator in modern times is therefore likely to be far more powerful than those old-time despots who relied mainly on terror in bolstering their power.

The difference between private and public goals in the focus of manipulative efforts is another distinction of no great help in establishing criteria for special interest manipulation. It goes without saying that both the carrot and the stick are used in promoting private goals favoring special interests. It is important to step carefully on this issue, though. The leaders of a special interest group are human beings with complex value orientations, and by no means all their values are likely to reflect the objectives promoted by the organization or group that they normally represent. For example, a number of "enlightened" employers, small and large, have at one time or another favored public policies that would limit their own freedom of action or profit opportunities as employers. Many persons, even leaders in special interest groups, are quite capable of placing a higher importance on their citizen responsibilities, as they see them, especially in times of crises.

In social analysis, however, one has to deal with general and preponderant tendencies more than with exceptional men. And it is safe to say that most persons with a heavy private stake in public policy issues will tend to be influenced by this private interest[25] in their political activity on related issues—at least most of the time.

Without prejudging the motives of individuals, then, it is always per-

---

[23] At times these opportunities can be limited by a type of power structure at the top that encourages some dissension or mutual suspicion, so that the powerful few tend to police each other.

[24] Cf. above, pp. 251–53.

[25] This private interest is not necessarily a matter of money. It may be a matter of personal power or prestige within an organization or a community, or a matter of gaining affection and respect, or of bolstering one's self-esteem by exhibiting courage, skill, or power, etc.

tinent to the problem of potential freedom to inquire into the incentive situation within which each representative of a special interest group is acting, in so far as it can be ascertained. If considerable wealth is at stake, for example, then the public in general ought to have access to this information, which may not be crucial but ought to be one element in the total evaluation of the recommendations put forward in the name of the group or by people who are intimately associated with it. Or, to speak in factual instead of in value terms, the level of potential freedom in a society is likely to be higher, the greater the extent to which the public is informed about all the ascertainable interests of the various organizations and groups that participate in recommending and shaping public policies.

One difficulty is that all interests, even all strong interests, are not easily ascertainable. But most of them are, and particularly the really "heavy stakes" in terms of wealth and power. This general problem of "pinning down" private interests and motivations in public affairs is one problem area in which progress in the behavioral sciences promises a steady improvement in methods and in extension of insights. This progress will be in the service, it is hoped, not of moral recrimination, but of increasing the public's resistance to special interest manipulation.

It does not follow that every public policy that brings to light pertinent facts about parties and pressure groups is a policy serving to promote potential freedom. This depends in part on the criteria for selecting the information intended for the public. A law requiring publicity for all election campaign expenditures of all parties and candidates clearly increases the supply of information relevant to certain public issues of concern to the voters. On the other hand, a law requiring publicity of this sort only for certain parties would, in all probability, serve to reduce rather than increase potential freedom. While the supply of information in a quantitative sense would be increased, it would because of its selection bias tend to become misleading information, to some extent.

This argument can be used, for example, against a proposal advanced some years ago by Morris L. Ernst, a prominent American lawyer and civil libertarian, to the effect that there ought to be full publicity about finances, membership rolls, and so forth of the American Communist party. He urged that the marketplace of ideas "is no longer free when competitors may enter it anonymously and fight democracy while they hide under the cloaks of democracy."[26] Superficially, such an arrangement would seem to make for a better informed choice of attitudes toward communism in America. Actually, unless all political groups were subjected to the same rules *and their data were given similar publicity,* all that would be accomplished would be an increase in the current deficiencies in potential freedom on the issue of communism in the United States. The Communist party would receive an additional official stamp of being a group of men whose activities and ideas

[26] Cf. *New York Herald Tribune,* December 9, 1947. On the following day the same paper reported the opposing view of Arthur Garfield Hays, another prominent and in my view a more consistent civil libertarian.

a priori must be shunned without critical thought about the possible merits of what they are trying to do or say at one time or another.[27]

Public disclosures of facts selected to throw new oil on the fire of current prejudices never serves the expansion of potential freedom. I am not, of course, implying that even a strongly anticommunist attitude is a prejudice, or an irrational and undesirable attitude. But I am implying that many types of current anticommunist attitudes are irrational and undesirable from a freedom-oriented point of view—for example, attitudes depicting every communist as an intentional traitor and adherent of force and violence in current politics, who should be barred from employment even in nonsensitive jobs, from public housing projects, from leaving the country, or should even be put in jail.[28]

It goes without saying, on the other hand, that a fanatical communist, like every fanatic, carries his own kind of blinders in restriction of his potential freedom. If it is unjustifiable on the basis of all available information to consider every communist a fool or a knave, it is no more justified to prejudge every strong anticommunist, or even every fascist, anti-Semite or Negro-hater as a thug or a crook in somebody's pay.

We all need stereotypes and oversimplifications in order to orient ourselves economically and sensibly in a bewilderingly complex world.[29] What the ideal of potential freedom emphasizes is the desirability of our not becoming slaves of our stereotypes—especially not of those that are promoted by special interest groups. Widespread stereotypes tending toward the total condemnation of all individuals with certain unpopular ideas or engaging in certain unpopular political activities are invariably supported by special interest groups, regardless of what other factors (including their inherent degree of plausibility) may combine to give them a wide acceptance.[30]

---

[27] Politically more important is the argument that in the present climate of opinion such a law would automatically increase coercive pressures against individual communists. The *Daily Worker* on December 10, 1947, editorially reported on a talk by Eugene Dennis, general secretary of the Communist party, in which he made the following argument—and it is not an easy one to disprove: "Dennis urged that Congress enact a resolution pledging that no Communist or other progressive shall lose either his civil liberties or his right to work in Government or private employment because of political belief or activity. 'I pledge,' Dennis told the slanderers of the Party, 'that on that day that Congress adopts such a resolution, every single member of my Party will be more than happy and willing to declare publicly his Communist affiliation of which he is so proud.' "

[28] Some data from Stouffer's recent volume are instructive: 51 percent of a cross-section of the American people would put all admitted communists in jail, and 77 percent would revoke their citizenship. Being asked about the nature of the communist threat as they saw it, however, only about 8 percent referred to the danger of sabotage and only 8 percent mentioned espionage, while about 28 percent referred more or less directly to the danger of conversion to communist ideas. *Communism, Conformity, and Civil Liberties*, pp. 43–44 and 157 ff.

Sidney Hook's well-known argument to the effect that membership in the Communist Party constitutes *prima facie* evidence of unfitness to teach is in my judgment an example of a prejudiced argument. To him, every Communist teacher who remains in the party must be presumed to accept its discipline without compromise. Since Hook for good reasons does not approve of the collection of evidence in the classroom, it would be very hard for anyone condemned under his sweeping rule to show that he is a teacher of integrity. Surely there must be a sizable proportion of Communist intellectuals who have doubts and reservations about various party practices long before they decide on the irrevocable step of leaving the party. Cf. *Heresy, Yes—Conspiracy, No*, especially pp. 181–93.

[29] Cf. below, pp. 355–56.

[30] Stereotypes tending to condemn all the popular and conventional ideas, on the other hand, may reflect neurotic antiauthoritarian orientations; they are less likely to become widespread, however, and are less likely to be supported by strong interest groups.

I have not tried to define a "special interest" very strictly. I wish to avoid a definition of certain groups as once and for all special interest groups, for even such people as publicly registered "lobbyists" are not always exerting special interest manipulation even in their lobbying activities. Some of them may at times, perhaps exceptionally, work for policies without reference to, or even detrimental to, their own private interests or those of their organizations. In times of national crisis, notably, even "organization men" frequently are capable of taking a broader view of the national interest. And it may be said that, on the other hand, many individuals without relevant group affiliations are busily and effectively pursuing their own special interests in their political activities.

The closest I have come toward a definition of special interest manipulation is to call it manipulation in favor of certain interests at the expense of the interests of those who are being manipulated. And I have said that this approach implies an objective concept of "interest." Let me now reconsider the five criteria I have suggested for ascertaining the individual's objective interest:[31]

The last of the five criteria asserts that it is in a man's interest to gain access to all important information available that bears on alternatives of behavior, including value choice, that are or can become open to him. This, however, is the basic criterion for deciding whether or not manipulation is going on, regardless of whether this otherwise is or is not in the individual's own interest or in the common interest.

The other four criteria are more helpful toward identifying special interest manipulation. It is in a man's interest, I assume, (1) to achieve a maximum mental health and psychological freedom; (2) to develop his talents and potentialities toward maturity and achievement; (3) to gain an adequate access to valued things and events according to freely expressed preferences and (4) to have some assurance that circumstances will continue to favor his freedom, growth, and value position. Manipulation that interferes with one of these four interests without demonstrably serving one or more of them is likely to be special interest manipulation. It is assumed, therefore, that all manipulation goes on in somebody's interest—if not in the interest of the power object, then in somebody else's. If it is in the public interest, then it is in some sense in the interest of the one being influenced, too.[32]

One difficulty is that this objective usage of "interest" leaves factors of perception and intention out of account. What if the manipulator intends to bless the object of his communications with some hopelessly unrealistic panacea, and what if a truly constructive policy is being propagated to someone who is stubbornly refusing to see the light? These are not in-

---

[31] Cf. above, p. 97.

[32] This is a very different point, of course, from Rousseau's argument that men can be forced to be free. (Cf. above, pp. 52, 56 and 104–105.) *Coercion* of individuals may be justifiable in the public interest; but the interest of individuals in not being coerced generally can be assumed to outweigh, from their point of view, their own stake in whatever public interest may be served by coercing them. If *manipulation* is clearly in the public interest, on the other hand, there is likely to be more of an even balance between the individual's share in the public interest and his interest in a maximal potential freedom. It interferes with one interest while serving another.

stances of special interest manipulation. Consequently, I am not in this book asserting that it is good to increase the resistance of all individuals to this kind of manipulative power nor am I implying that the maximization of such resistance would be bad or value-neutral. I am trying to limit the scope of this investigation to what I believe I can handle—in this context, the problem of tracing the determinants of resistance to special interest manipulation in an objective sense. To the extent that people become resistant to propaganda favoring special interests, however, it is a fair assumption that their ability to judge also other kinds of propaganda on their merits will tend to grow. I would tentatively believe that, on the whole, such a development is desirable, although I do not wish to explore this problem in this book.

Every society needs institutions to endure, as we have seen. Institutions, or the norms, values, and symbols associated with them, form the core of a society's *culture*. "Culture is an abstract description of *trends toward* uniformity in the words, acts, and artifacts of human groups."[33] The existence of institutions and culture as such is surely in the common interest, unless Rousseau was right when in his second *Discourse* he argued that society itself was instituted by the rich among the prehistorical savages, in order to induce the poor to accept perpetual inequality as the legitimate state of affairs.[34] Whatever its origin, society is surely here to stay, and so are institutions and cultures, and I am sure this in the public interest if there is such a thing as a public interest. The choice among possible contents and directions of cultural developments, on the other hand, is a matter on which men may differ, and in which special interests may have private stakes.

Even such a fundamentally entrenched cultural orientation as that of nationalism in the modern world is clearly not unaffected by the manipulative power of special interest groups. William Godwin considered patriotism, or the love of one's country, as "another of those specious illusions which have been invented by imposters in order to render the multitude the blind instruments of their crooked designs."[35] More balanced views can in our days be founded on research into the actual psychological and socio-economic functions of nationalist attitudes.

Religious institutions, again, satisfy basic needs of many persons, perhaps of majorities in our culture. That does not mean that particular types of religious institutions cannot also satisfy important economic interests of special interest groups. "To the Conservative," wrote Horace Greeley nearly a century ago, "Religion would seem often a part of the subordinate machinery of Police, having for its main object the instilling of proper humility into the abject, of contentment into the breasts of the down-trodden, and of enduing with a sacred reverence for Property those who have no personal reason to think well of the sharp distinction of Mine and Thine."[36] The classic studies of Max Weber and R. H. Tawney give ample evidence of the

[33] Kroeber and Kluckhohn, *Culture. A Critical Review of Concepts and Definitions*, p. 182.
[34] *The Social Contract and Discourses*, p. 250; cf. above, pp. 50–51.
[35] Godwin, *Political Justice*, II, 43.
[36] *Recollections of a Busy Life*, pp. 524–25.

significance of Protestant religion for the promotion of private economic enterprise.[37]

The point I wish to make is this: even if we assume that an individual needs religion, the type of religion he has come to accept may severely limit his potential freedom, because these particular dogmas and institutions may oppress his individuality in order to enhance the status of priests or protect the safety of property privileges. Again, even if we assume that the endurance of a society or a state demands some measure of nationalist identification, the type of nationalist beliefs people acquire may also serve, for example, to suppress basically tolerant attitudes in favor of fears and suspicions providing incentives toward high armament budgets, which in turn furnish prosperity in many quarters of a private enterprise economy.

These possibilities point to perhaps the most basic difficulty in conceptualizing "freedom from special interest manipulation," which is the limited sense in which the maximization of potential freedom is always valuable, according to my position. How can we separate those aspects of basic institutions that serve mainly special interests from those serving the public interest, or the interests of those who conform? There is no quick and easy answer that I know of. All I can suggest in general terms is that increasingly sophisticated behavioral theory and research techniques will increase our ability to distinguish between *genuine* and *manufactured* human needs, wishes, and desires. And there are several avenues of promise in this direction.

First, there is the avenue of psychological theorizing and research associated perhaps especially with the names of Fromm and Maslow. "There are at least five sets of goals, which may be called basic needs," writes Maslow.

These are briefly physiological, safety, love, esteem, and self-actualization. . . . These basic goals are related to each other, being arranged in a hierarchy of prepotency. This means that the most prepotent goal will monopolize consciousness and will tend of itself to organize the recruitment of the various capacities of the organism. The less prepotent needs are minimized, even forgotten or denied. But when a need is fairly well satisfied, the next prepotent ("higher") need emerges, in turn to dominate the conscious life and to serve as the center of organization of behavior, since gratified needs are not active motivators.[38]

This kind of theorizing is subject to empirical consolidation or questioning over time. It is too abstract to lend itself to some crucial experiment, but the weight of accumulating inferential evidence will fortify it or weaken it.

[37] Ascetic Protestantism "broke the bonds on the impulse of acquisition in that it not only legalized it, but (in the sense discussed) looked upon it as directly willed by God." Weber, *The Protestant Ethic and the Spirit of Capitalism*, p. 171. Cf. Tawney, *Religion and the Rise of Capitalism: A Historical Study*.

[38] Maslow, "A Theory of Human Motivation," in Harriman (ed.), *Twentieth Century Psychology*, p. 46. Cf. above, pp. 11–12. I have been implying some hierarchy of human needs in my assumption about objective human interests; cf. above, pp. 97 and 325. W. I. Thomas proposed the following general classification of four "human wishes": the desire for new experience, for security, for response, and for recognition. *The Unadjusted Girl*, p. 4. Lynd lists nine universal human "cravings" in *Knowledge for What? The Place of Social Science in American Culture*, pp. 193–97. Fromm, in *The Sane Society*, lists five human needs stemming from universal conditions of man's existence.

Institutions serving these needs are to this extent not the instruments of special interest groups at the expense of the interests of most of those who conform to them.

Another avenue is the search for cultural universals among human needs and techniques for satisfying them. Social anthropologists have provided data toward building up a conception of a *consensus gentium*—a conception of "the nature of the raw human nature—*i.e.,* that human nature which all cultures mold and channel but never entirely remake."[39] Institutions which are virtually universal in human societies are to this extent above suspicion of being mere instruments for special interest groups.

A third avenue is to analyze the origin of institutional patterns, if they are of sufficiently recent origin. If much promotional activity has preceded a particular institution, chances are that it does not correspond to a genuine need in the population. But there are two reservations to be made on this point. First, new institutions may serve old and genuine needs in new ways; the introduction of the potato in Europe, for example, was surely a service to the general interest, even if it took a lot of persuasion and coercion in many places to get it accepted. Secondly, once manufactured needs may conceivably become genuine, in the sense that their satisfaction enduringly enhances human happiness or freedom and would continue to do so in the absence of any continued special interest manipulation. The need for an automobile, for example, tends to become a genuine need in this sense for those who have once become used to having one. The need for a new automobile every second year, which many Americans may feel quite strongly, has surely not become a genuine need, on the other hand: in the absence of advertising and snob appeal, most car owners presumably would be glad to keep their cars as long as they are in good condition or until substantially better cars are brought on the market. The approach on this avenue of investigation, to sum up, is to study the incentive situations of those who brought about the emergence of a new institution but also to consider the extent to which the institution tends to endure independently of continued promotional activities.

I have anticipated, in my automobile example, a fourth avenue toward identifying institutions serving manufactured needs in the special interest of certain groups. This is the approach of analyzing the incentive situations of those who are currently most active in supporting a given institution. If organizations of American industries urge a "tough" foreign policy for the United States, the sincerity of their spokesmen need not be doubted, but it would be wise to consider their advice on the background of their interest in continued prosperity, which may be seen as in part dependent on an amount of governmental purchasing that is likely only in a tense world. On the other hand, if people with only a consumer's stake in the American economy urge a large aid program to economically underdeveloped areas, it is more likely that their incentives are derived wholly from their view of the general interest of the nation or of humanity.

It goes without saying that advocates of the general interest may be in

---

[39] Kroeber and Kluckhohn, *Culture. A Critical Review of Concepts and Definitions,* p. 178; cf. above, pp. 12–13. Cf. also Lynd, *Knowledge for What?,* p. 189, on the same point.

error as often as the advocates of special interests—in fact, probably *more* often, since most people tend to keep better informed about their special interests than about the general interest. A general interest is less directly and obviously relevant to one's immediate welfare, and it is also much more complex and difficult to be well-informed about.

A fifth avenue of research in the service of an expanding potential freedom would focus, not on the type of needs served by an institution or on the type of incentive situation in which the influencer acts, but on the personality make-up of the influencers. Men of power are not easily accessible to really thoroughgoing psychological study, as on the psychoanalyst's couch. But even without their cooperation there are numerous clues in their behavior that, if assembled and interpreted, can furnish materials toward a realistic assessment of their levels of psychological freedom. This kind of data may for political reasons and at times perhaps for humanitarian reasons not be readily disseminated. Also, such data may easily be misused in furnishing materials for excessive arguments *ad hominem* in political controversy. What people say should be weighed on its own merits, regardless of who they are. Yet in a total evaluation of a political situation, information about deficiencies in psychological freedom in important quarters should not be left entirely out of consideration. If a powerful politician hates other nations because of a defensive need for scapegoats, the ability and incentive of most citizens to refuse to believe everything he says about these other nations would be improved by general access to this information.

One might perhaps question whether manipulation for ego-defense purposes should be called special interest manipulation and thus fall within the scope of my inquiry concerning potential freedom. It is granted that this is indeed a special case of "interest"—a kind of "interest" that arises from deficiencies in psychological freedom and essentially consists in keeping anxiety at bay without facing the basic causes of anxiety. This is emphatically an individual special interest, not the special interest of a group. From the power object's point of view it makes no great difference, however, whether the information and propaganda he is exposed to serve special neurotic individual needs or special group interests. If it induces motives in him to act against his own interests, then his potential freedom is being reduced by special interest manipulation. Assuming, for example, that the average American citizen had a stake of his own in winning the Second World War and that his newspaper kept persuading him, and with some success, that President Roosevelt deliberately had brought the country into the "wrong war"—whether this newspaper's publisher had a purely neurotic hatred against "that man," or whether he had a financial stake in a show of such a hatred, would in itself make no great difference for those he kept influencing or, indeed, for society as a whole.

Manipulative power is always exercised by individuals, because "power," as I have defined it, is exercised by individuals. But this exercise of power need not be deliberate, and it need not be autonomous. We may exercise power as agents of other individuals or as agents of institutions. The "power of an institution" has been defined as the aggregate of the power of those who employ sanctions on its behalf or who in other ways induce motives toward conformity.[40]

I disregard in this chapter the kinds of power that are exercised by way of sanctions, except as these are taken for granted and are internalized. For example, if a boy does not contradict his father because he fears some kind of punishment as a result, then we have an example of coercive power, or at least power by way of external restraints, which limits social freedom. Manipulative power, which limits potential freedom, is exercised in a slightly different situation, in which the boy does not contradict his father simply because he would consider it the wrong thing to do; in this situation he would consider that he deserved punishment if he had done the wrong thing.

Limiting this discussion to manipulative power, I shall argue that individuals with special interests may exercise such power either directly or indirectly, and, if indirectly, either rationally or by way of institutions. These are analytical conceptions, of course; usually all three elements are involved in any situation or process in which manipulative power is exerted.

The direct exercise of manipulative power takes place to the extent that a power subject is in a position to influence other people's motives, independently of sanctions, by way of direct communication; and I consider advertising in the mass media of communication as a "direct" exercise of influence in this context. Indeed advertising, whether commercial or political, is the typical example of a direct exercise of manipulative power in favor of special interests. This kind of power behavior is always rational; it is always behavior guided by perceived efficiency norms directed toward given or chosen goals, whether conscious or unconscious.[41]

The effectiveness of manipulative power is likely to be affected by the extent to which the manipulator is in a position to exercise authority or to utilize authority for his purposes. A president or a king is clearly in a stronger position to induce motives of a given kind, on the whole, compared to an average politician, not only because he gets better publicity for his views, but also because it makes a difference to more people that these are *his* views. To take another example, if a producer of a "health food" can utilize in his advertising campaign the authority of medical doctors who endorse his product, presumably he is in a position to persuade more people —except, perhaps, if medical doctors have been found willing to sponsor so many products that their authority in such contexts has declined very much.

The indirect exercise of manipulative power favoring special interests can be either rational or institutional, or, what in practice is more common, it can be both. Rational indirect manipulation consists in utilizing existing institutions for special purposes or in utilizing power agents. For example, the institution of Christmas gift-giving presumably would persist even without any rational pressure from merchants and their organizations, but it is obvious that the average person's conception of what is proper behavior

---

[40] See above, pp. 258–59.

[41] Cf. above, pp. 313–14. This does not preclude the possibility that the goal in a sense may be an "irrational" one, such as the goal of bolstering a deficient ego; this is also a kind of "special interest," as we have seen (above, p. 329).

at Christmas time is in part shaped by deliberate efforts on the part of mercantile interests. Mother's Day gift-giving is an institution that largely has been manufactured by such interests, and indications are that a corresponding Father's Day gift-giving is in the process of becoming institutionalized at the present time. A less innocuous example of rational indirect manipulation *not* utilizing existing institutions is the use of fraudulent information in a political campaign. It is widely believed that United States Senator Millard Tydings of Maryland was defeated in his bid for reelection in 1950 in large part because of a widely circulated doctored photograph falsely showing him side by side with Earl Browder, the former chairman of the American Communist party.[42]

Alternatively, the indirect exercise of manipulative power favoring special interests can be purely institutional, in principle at least. Racial segregation and discrimination is in various parts of the world an institutional pattern that is strongly promoted by rational interests, such as the employer interest in cheap labor and in dissension between groups of workers. In many communities, on the other hand, segregation may be taken completely for granted by everyone on both sides of the color line. This would be an example of a purely institutional kind of indirect special interest manipulation. Nobody deliberately lifts a finger to maintain the pattern, because nobody would think of challenging it. But the social analyst may conclude that this kind of institution clearly operates in the special interest of a minority at the expense of a majority's interest.

This is a limiting case perhaps. As I have pointed out, most special interest manipulation tends to utilize both institutions and rational promotion, directly and indirectly. From the point of view of potential freedom, each kind of special interest manipulation poses undesirable restraints, regardless of whether sanctions are utilized or not.[43]

The most acute problem of potential freedom in our time undoubtedly arises out of the highly developed modern propaganda and advertising techniques. For the first time in history, it appears technically possible for one man, if he has sufficient wealth or political power, to control significant parts of the thought and motivations of millions of men. It has become possible, to an unheard-of extent, "to buy popular consent not by deeds—fair or foul—but by the unscrupulous manipulation of people's innermost desires, for purposes not their own."[44] David Riesman has said that the way to get ahead in America nowadays is no longer to invent a better mousetrap, but to put the old mousetrap in a new wrapping.[45] In the same way, it may be feared that the way to get ahead in national politics to an increasing extent is to invent new slogans to wrap around old and discredited policies.

This development is due not only to the growth of the mass media of

[42] "McCarthy: A Documented Record," *The Progressive*, XVIII, No. 4 (1954), 66.

[43] Only sanctions that have come to be taken for granted as "right" and "just" bear on potential freedom, I have said. Sanctions amounting to external restraints bear on social freedom.

[44] Pinner, *Political Values: An Exploratory Investigation*, p. 5.

[45] *Individualism Reconsidered*, p. 104.

communication, but it follows also from the increasing levels of urbaniza-tion with the consequent weakening of the bonds of traditional institutions. These are interdependent processes, of course. The city dweller is more exposed to mass media manipulation than is the farmer, on the whole, who is likely to be more tradition-bound.[46] To the extent that the urban person is exposed to conflicting propaganda, he may become more critical and sophisticated; but to the extent that all propaganda runs the same way, he may become a more ready tool for the powers that be.

Those who control the main media of communication—if they agree among themselves—are not limited to the dissemination of all the argu-ments supporting the particular policies they desire and to the suppression or distortion of opposing arguments. What is more potent in many modern democracies, they also can create the illusion that their own ideas on im-portant issues are very widely held.[47]

In the past, from the dawn of civilization up to recent times, the prin-cipal limitations on potential freedom tended to be traditional and institu-tional. It is true, as we have seen, that Plato believed in lying for the good of the public and that Roman men of power and later the Vatican utilized religion as a means of social control. But they relied on firmly embedded institutional patterns, which at most could be subjected to very slow and gradual changes. And in most aboriginal communities, custom is king to an even greater extent—and this kind of a king can be extremely oppressive of individual human potentialities. In our modern civilization, however, I believe that the deliberate and direct kinds of manipulation pose the greater menace to potential freedom.

Mass manipulation is not necessarily an evil. I have suggested that uni-versal indoctrination in support of very general humanitarian goal values may be valued positively, provided there is no coercion involved, of even a single individual. I have also suggested that the fomenting of discontent among even happily oppressed peoples, by way of making them aware that they are oppressed, should be valued positively even though their new awareness creates a situation of coercion where there was none before. I have previously cited with approval an experiment in which social scientists have taken on the responsibility of manipulating the behavior of a com-munity of Peruvian Indians toward greater social and potential freedom, away from a system of traditional subjection.[48]

The potentialities in our culture for effective special interest manipula-tion are probably even greater, however, than the potentialities for manipu-lation in the general interest. While the latter should not always be valued positively, my position entails a consistently negative evaluation of *effective* special interest manipulation. In pluralist democracies, different sources of manipulative power may cancel each other out, leaving many individuals

---

[46] "The State agricultural extension agent (in hierarchical Japan) can act with about as little authoritarianism in improving old methods of agriculture as his counterpart can in Idaho." Benedict, *The Chrysanthemum and the Sword*, pp. 86–87.

[47] Cf. Barker, *Reflections on Government*, p. 110.

[48] Cf. above, p. 316, note 11.

better educated and more autonomous in the process. Yet, as we shall see, there is a distinct tendency for possessors or controllers of great wealth to develop common views and to be in a position to promote their interests with far greater success because of their control of wealth.[49]

In totalitarian countries, on the other hand, the rulers have a wider scope than even the wealthiest American capitalists in getting the desired motives induced into masses of people. When there is no effective opposition, in Hannah Arendt's words, the rulers can afford an "extreme contempt for facts as such, for in their opinion fact depends entirely on the power of man who can fabricate it."[50] Modern dictatorships, like modern democracies, tend to be relatively flexible, not tradition-bound. Institutional manipulation, at least in politics, appears everywhere on the wane, relatively speaking, and deliberate manipulation seems to be increasing everywhere in our modern civilization. Ever fewer aspects of politics escape deliberate policy efforts.

The problem of autonomy for modern man remains in part a problem of achieving the ability and incentive to question the usefulness and value of conformity to inherited institutions. An even more and increasingly important part of the problem, however, is the achievement of similarly detached and independently critical attitudes toward rational suggestions about how he ought to behave, including authoritative suggestions. I have in this section tried to point out various directions for research that can provide data and insights essential for increasing the general readiness to resist special interest manipulation.

It goes without saying, however, that our aim cannot be a total elimination of subservience to special interest manipulation. It is no great evil, for example, if advertising influences people to buy one kind of soap rather than another. "What I call my beliefs are wholly mine," says John L. Mothershead, Jr., "only if I have earned them by inquiry into their truth and other value."[51] But we can never hope to, nor should we want to, make all our beliefs our own in this strict sense. It is the important parts of our beliefs, the parts that bear on our welfare and vital freedoms, or those of other people, which should be rescued from the influence of special interest manipulation. What we believe about the merits of different kinds of soap, for example, is on the whole much less important to ourselves and our society than what we believe about the merits of different political parties or different social institutions and policies.[52]

In my desire to see autonomy from special interest manipulation extended, my value position parallels the one adopted with respect to extending human rights with special reference to coercion: the special interest manipulation of more important beliefs should be resisted with a greater

---

[49] Cf. below, pp. 348–51.

[50] *Origin of Totalitarianism*, p. 340.

[51] "Some Reflections on the Meanings of Freedom," *Journal of Philosophy*, XLIX, No. 21 (1952), 670.

[52] Becker makes essentially the same point in his *Freedom and Responsibility in the American Way of Life*, p. 42. See also Packard, *The Hidden Persuaders*.

urgency than the manipulation of beliefs bearing less heavily on the individual's and his society's welfare.[53]

On the whole, consequently, the problem of political special interest manipulation is a more serious one than the commercial variety. It is likely to be a particularly serious problem in dictatorships, unless the rulers are exceptionally enlightened and devoted to the general welfare. It is an increasingly serious problem in democracies, too, perhaps especially in big and wealthy democracies, in which the stakes of the "political game" as well as the resources for campaign and pressure investments may be tremendously large.

SOME GENERAL SOCIAL DETERMINANTS

General Functional Prerequisites: Their Bearing on the
Freedom from Special Interest Manipulation

Much of what has been said in the previous chapter about functional prerequisites of social systems bears equally on social and potential freedom. The problem of social as well as potential freedom hinges in large measure, I have suggested, on the range of institutions that are sociologically necessary in the various realms of life. What degree of conformity do they require, and how severely must they be sanctioned?[54] It was found that social institutions, laws, and political authority are functional prerequisites of all social systems more complex than primary groups. Let me briefly recapitulate the significance of these conclusions with special reference to potential freedom.

An institution is a sanctioned behavior expectation persisting through time within a social system. The existence of institutions provides the basis for communication and cooperation among men. In so far as conformity is achieved by mechanisms other than inducing a fear of sanctions, institutions operate as limitations on potential, not social, freedom. Limitations on potential freedom are often necessary and need not be undesirable, according to my value position. The only institutions I wish to characterize *in general* as undesirable, in varying degrees, are those that effectively encourage conformity in the interest of persons other than those who conform, at the expense of the conformers. Although some amount of institutions and sanctions are sociologically necessary, I have in the previous chapter concluded that there is no general sociological necessity for coercion, so far as I know. The corresponding question in this section is whether some amount of manipulation of people in the interest of others or of the whole society *at their expense* is sociologically necessary.

A second prerequisite for the endurance of complex social systems is the existence of laws or institutions that regulate the permissible and generally approved exercise of physical coercion. Again, I have not said that coercion is necessary, but only that, to the extent that physical coercion occurs, there

---

[53] The parallel with the human rights approach breaks down only at one point, it seems: a "worse" manipulation of the political beliefs of a few is not necessarily a worse calamity than the "lesser" manipulation of the beliefs of a great many, if we can expect that the few will be outvoted by the many.

[54] Cf. above, especially pp. 264 and 274–80.

must be some recognized way of distinguishing between legitimate and illegitimate coercion, at least in principle and in the last resort. This pre-requisite implies the necessity of one kind of limitation on potential free-dom: among citizens in general, there must be a general readiness to up-hold the laws and to disapprove of crime. Clearly, there is no sociological necessity for a wide approval for any specific law, but there must be some minimum consensus on criteria for determining what is the law and on the general principle that most laws should be obeyed whether one approves of their contents or not. All laws in our culture, and perhaps in all cultures, purport to be in the general interest, or at least not clearly contrary to the general interest, and one may tentatively suggest that no necessity for special interest manipulation can be derived from the sociological necessity of laws. But, if so, the same problem comes back in disguise when we try, as we must, to determine some criteria for grounds on which specific laws may be disobeyed, without endangering the social fabric as a whole.

A third and last prerequisite of complex social systems, according to my inquiry in Chapter 5, is the existence of political authority, or some generally recognized power or procedure for changing or creating "valid" legal norms. This is once again a prerequisite that not necessarily implies coer-cion, even if no known political government so far as I know has been able to get along entirely without coercion. All that is minimally required is some authoritative process for political decision-making, and it is not in-conceivable that societies may come to exist in which all citizens will accept their systems of political authority as just and conformity-deserving. This presupposes a consensus that is hardly possible without some indoctrina-tion—at least of children—in the acculturation process. Now, does the con-tinuation of political authority necessitate some minimum of special in-terest manipulation in the interest of leaders or elites at the expense of followers or "masses"? This, too, is a problem to be considered in this section.

Is a minimum of special interest manipulation a sociological necessity, in the sense that the stability of the essential structure of institutions may depend on this kind of mechanism? The answer might superficially seem negative, on the following grounds. Institutions are necessary for the con-tinuation of social interaction. Every individual has a stake in this con-tinuation. Therefore, it follows logically that no manipulation in favor of essential institutions can be at the expense of his interest.

No concrete institution, however, is likely to be a prerequisite for the endurance of social systems; there are presumably functional equivalents. What is needed are institutions in general, not any specific institutions. But conformity pressures and conformity inducements are always related to specific institutions. And it may be that the sociological minimum of an institutional structure by necessity includes at least a few institutions in favor of special interests at the expense of those of the conformers in general. For one thing, it may be that no society can endure without vertical social class divisions, which institutionalize the division of labor by assigning more desirable work to some strata and less desirable work to others. There may be some truth in the *Communist Manifesto* proclamation that the history of all hitherto existing society is the history of class struggles; and it may be that this is a sociological necessity, so that every social system, including communism, must maintain some institutions in the special interest of some ruling class in order to endure.

There is no conclusive evidence to this effect, however. Indeed, I have found reasons to doubt the general validity even of Michels's "iron law of oligarchy."[55] One can envisage organizations and whole societies enduring without exploitation by the leadership. Consequently, my answer to the question before us is a cautious negative: the general prerequisite of institutions and sanctions does not necessarily entail, so far as I know, the necessity also of some minimum of special interest manipulation.

Legal institutions purport to be in the general interest. It follows from the immediately preceding discussion of institutions in general that there is no clear necessity that certain laws *must* involve special interest manipulation if a society is to endure. Admittedly many laws in every existing society that I know are instituted in the interest of some group at the expense of others, and yet all citizens are with varying degrees of effectiveness indoctrinated to the effect that all laws are to be obeyed.

However, the general principle of obedience to the law must be assumed to operate in the general interest. If workers are indoctrinated with respect for the rights of employers, and vice versa, this does not necessarily entail special interest manipulation, although it may do just that, in effect, if the rights—or privileges, properly speaking—of one group far exceed those of the other. There is no sociological prerequisite apparent from these considerations. Conceivably, an enlightened society may be offering a sufficiently "fair deal" to everyone, so that obedience to laws in general can operate in everybody's interest, or at least not against some particular group's interest, when considered in toto.

However, while recognizing the prerequisite of a minimum of laws, it may be asked what this general requirement of social systems involves for the individual. The prerequisite of legal institutions involves a need for obedience to the laws to a certain extent, and the extent may vary from one social system to another. I have suggested in an earlier chapter that not all laws should necessarily be obeyed, according to my value position. I consider constitutions and laws primarily as instruments of an expanding freedom, and if a new law cuts down on important freedoms such as the freedom of speech, then I should recommend nonviolent disobedience to such a law. No legislature should be authorized to pass laws that cut down an accumulated inheritance of freedoms, except in the interest of protecting it against imminent and serious dangers, and on the assurance that the cuts will be restored again after the briefest possible interval.[56]

This kind of disobedience to laws is assumed to be in the general interest, and propaganda for this kind of disobedience, consequently, does not amount to special interest manipulation. Gandhi's campaign for disobedi-

[55] Cf. above, pp. 295–96.
[56] Cf. above, pp. 144–46.

ence to the British law forbidding the gathering of salt from the ocean clearly was not a special interest campaign, while the British campaign for obedience to this law was.

On the whole, to sum up, a complex social system does require a certain minimum of laws and obedience to laws. Campaigns for disobedience of particular laws may or may not entail special interest manipulation, and the same is true about campaigns for obedience to specific laws of a controversial nature. All in all, there is probably no general requirement for special interest manipulation to be read into the prerequisite of legal institutions in enduring social systems.

Political authority, like institutions and laws, is in the general interest in the sense of being a functional prerequisite for the endurance of complex social systems. It, too, involves manipulation of attitudes, since authority exists only in so far as it is recognized as legitimate or "authoritative." Can we conceive of governments that attempt to manipulate attitudes *only* in the general interest, as they see it?

A minimum of special interest manipulation is an unavoidable consequence of the political authority-requirement of complex social systems, I believe. Institutions and laws can theoretically operate entirely in the general interest. Political authority may approximate this ideal, but not reach it, not even theoretically. The political authority-requirement does not necessitate enduring concentrations of power in a few hands, but it does minimally designate certain people to make certain kinds of decisions at a given time. Even if these people are devoted to all their fellow men, it is inconceivable that they would not wish to promote a favorable appreciation of their own leadership, or at the very least seek to protect themselves against unjustified recrimination. This is the theoretical minimum of special interest manipulation, it would seem, in the exercise of political authority.

The Marxists, and also such sociologists of knowledge as Karl Mannheim, have tended to go further than this, and they argue that all leadership tends to be partial to the special interests of those who lead. Mannheim only excludes the classless, free-floating intelligentsia, while Marxists often exclude communist regimes, which are supposed to abolish all class divisions and all exploitation of man by man.[57]

The class struggle, according to the view of many Marxists, does not always amount to violent conflict. If the ruling class succeeds in imbuing the rest of society with its values and norms, a violent class struggle may be a potentiality rather than an openly perceived and acknowledged state of affairs. As a present-day Soviet author puts it:

The difficulty of the class struggle of the proletariat against the bourgeoisie is precisely that the exploiting classes do not retain their rule by violence alone— by means of open, physical suppression with the help of the state. The obsolescent exploiting classes strive to suppress the masses spiritually, to poison the minds of the toiling masses with the venom of their reactionary ideology.[58]

[57] Cf., for example, the *Communist Manifesto,* and Mannheim, *Ideology and Utopia,* especially pp. 136–46.
[58] Konstantinov, *The Role of Advanced Ideas in the Development of Society,* pp. 66–67.

It may be that every ruling class, not excluding that in the Soviet Union, must imbue "the toiling masses" with a spirit of deference and gratitude to the authorities. Indeed, those who classify certain ideas as "poison" are likely to be more strongly concerned than others with the manipulation of men toward acceptance of "true" ideas. And the more manipulation from above becomes institutionalized, the more must we expect of opportunities for special interest slants.

On this ground, one should expect totalitarian authorities to tend toward more manipulation *and* more special interest manipulation than democratic authorities, to the extent that the latter are more tolerant. On the other hand, democratic authorities have an interest of their own in the effective manipulation of voters, and a particular stake in the special interest in maintaining their own power through the test of the ballot. All in all, however, since the stakes of power are likely to be less extreme in democratic systems, and for a couple of additional reasons, I have earlier in this chapter concluded that dictatorships tend to utilize more effective means of manipulation than do democratic regimes.[59] Monopolies in manipulation media certainly give more opportunities also for manipulation in the special interest of those in control.

No political authority can do entirely without special interest manipulation. Approximations toward this elusive ideal are more feasible, I conclude, (a) the more genuine dedication to the public interest there is in the political leadership, (b) the more the ultimate authority rests in an institutionalized democratic process that gives opponents of the regime a hearing and a chance to take over, and (c) the less of a tendency there is among rulers and opposition groups to consider ideas they do not like as dangerous "poison."

Determinants of Types of National Loyalty Demands

So far as [society] controls us, consistently with our nature as moral persons, it controls us from within, and not with the force of an external presence; it controls us as freely accepted and genuinely appropriated thought, which is part of our own personality. And as we must freely accept if we are ourselves to be free, so we may also be bound, in hours of crisis and ultimate decision, to reject it freely for just the same reason.[60]

This statement by Ernest Barker strikes me as a cogent expression of the basic problem of national loyalty, its nature and its proper limitations. If society controls us from within, we are to that extent not "free" in the sense of potential freedom, however. It may be eminently in our interest to be "controlled from within" by the institutions of a good society, nevertheless; a complete potential freedom would mean a complete isolation, if indeed it is not a nonsense-term.[61]

To the extent that society controls us from within, we are automatically loyal to this society. But we may be loyal also as autonomous persons—as

[59] Cf. above, p. 318.
[60] Barker, *Reflections on Government*, pp. 17–18.
[61] Cf. above, pp. 96–97 and 320.

persons who are capable and informed enough to choose whether to conform or not to conform. Since my concern in this chapter is with freedom from special interest manipulation, the problem of national loyalty as a whole does not fall within my purview. Loyalty to a good society is not in general an undesirable limitation on potential freedom. What I wish to consider are loyalty requirements beyond the loyalty that grows by itself among congenial institutions and policies. It is here I expect to find special interest manipulation purporting to be in the general interest.

Before the rise of popular democracy and general suffrage there was not much concern with the political attitudes of the average man. You had to be a "somebody" to participate in politics and to make it matter whether your thoughts were loyal or seditious. In our time, and more so the more fear of war there is, virtually every citizen's loyalty to the nation is considered important by those responsible for the nation's security. We have just seen that national loyalty may be quite automatic, in the sense that we come to take these norms for granted, but that it also may be the deliberate outcome of a more or less autonomous choice. Another distinction suggested is between a humanistic and an authoritarian type of loyalty.[62] Let me now consider how these two distinctions relate to each other, and how each of the four types of loyalty affects the individual's susceptibility to special interest manipulation in the name of the national interest.

Automatic loyalty and automatic conformity are necessary, in many realms of life, for the individual and for the society. We need habits that we can take for granted, just as social interaction requires institutions, including institutionalized ways of bringing about institutional change. Yet, the orientation toward our nation is important enough in our lives to deserve a share of our attention and deliberate thought. From a government's point of view, an unquestioning and ill-informed loyalty may appear preferable to a questioning, well-informed, and perhaps somewhat conditional loyalty. But this will particularly be the case, I submit, if the men in the government have special interests to promote, over and beyond the national interest, or even at its expense, or else they are very strongly convinced that their policies are the only correct ones and are urgently necessary.

For society, an automatic readiness to conform and even to cheer closes off all intelligent contributions toward policy formation from the mass of conformists and flag-wavers. This is indeed the democratic counterpart to the old pattern that must have toppled many a monarch from his throne: the pattern of surrounding him with flatterers and yes-men who were incapable of applying any brakes to dangerous policies. For the individual, an automatic national loyalty deprives him of autonomy over really important aspects of his own life. He becomes clay in the hands of the policymaker, who is in a position to exploit him freely, if he wishes, for his own purposes. A pattern of automatic and unconditional national loyalty does not necessarily mean that more than a bare minimum of special interest manipulation is going on—the minimum that follows with all political

[62] See above, pp. 110–11.

authority—but it surely does leave the field wide open for political exploitation. It also bars the growth of the individual to the stature he potentially is capable of achieving. "When the personal consciousness emerges from the merely tribal consciousness," says Ludwig Lewisohn, "—there is the birth of liberty." Without autonomous individuals, he adds, society is "as stagnant as a rotting pool."[63]

The distinction between automatic and autonomous loyalty has much in common with the distinction between authoritarian and humanistic loyalty. The one distinction focuses on the effect of loyalty—unconditional or conditional conformity—; the other on the psychological basis of loyalty—whether it is motivated by submissiveness to authorities or fidelity to personal insights and values. An authoritarian loyalty, I have said, is a loyalty that has been imposed on the individual from without. Although it has become internalized, an authoritarian loyalty has not become harmoniously integrated with the individual's basic motives. A humanistic loyalty, on the other hand, is an identification expressive of basic motives in the individual, whether or not it originally has been imposed from without. A humanistic loyalty is an indication of psychological freedom, while an authoritarian loyalty involves elements of defensiveness, in my sense of the term.

Two points of caution may be in order at this point. In the first place, an authoritarian loyalty may be apparent rather than real. People may catch on to the fact that obedience and conformity is expected of them, and, especially if they are manipulatively oriented, they may see their own best interest advanced by behaving as though they have an authoritarian loyalty. A genuine loyalty presupposes a genuine identification, and a real authoritarian loyalty presumably involves a low self-esteem and a self-sacrificing type of identification with some authorities.

The second cautionary point is that the present context easily lends itself to confusing psychological freedom with potential freedom. Let me point out again that all nonautonomous loyalties involve limitations on potential freedom, whether undesirable or not, for potential freedom means the relative absence of nonperceived external restraints, and loyalties that are taken for granted involve norms that limit the potential freedom of choice. Yet some such loyalties may and others may not be compatible with a maximal level of psychological freedom, which means harmony between basic needs and overt consciousness and expression.

An automatic loyalty, while it is unconditional, is not necessarily an authoritarian loyalty. A readiness to accept every new directive from a certain distant authority is unlikely to produce behavior expressive of basic individual motives, it is true, since the latter presumably have some stability, or at least a dynamics of their own. But an automatic loyalty to the nation is quite compatible with the absence of an automatic loyalty to the nation's government and its policies. One may take for granted an obligation to serve the national interest without always taking the government's word for what the national interest is at each time. An automatic loyalty to gen-

---

[63] *Up Stream. An Autobiography,* p. 197; cf. pp. 158–60.

eral principles or values is compatible with a maximal level of *psychological* freedom, I believe, while an automatic loyalty to specific policies or to the policies of specific people hardly is explicable in terms other than authoritarian submissiveness, except, perhaps, in some cases of close personal friends.

An autonomous loyalty is the outcome of deliberate choice and is therefore compatible with a maximal potential freedom. This kind of loyalty tends to be of the humanistic rather than the authoritarian type. It tends to indicate a high level of psychological freedom as well, for the ability to make decisions in detachment from institutionalized norms presumably in most cases presupposes a corresponding capacity to make decisions in detachment from ego-defense needs.[64] On the whole, one may conclude that loyalties expressive of psychological freedom—that is, humanistic as against authoritarian loyalties—tend to widen the scope of autonomy and potential freedom as well, without ever, even approximately, eliminating the sphere within which people and norms command our automatic loyalties.

Given these propensities, what are some of the factors determining the strength and the types of loyalty demands emanating from institutions, laws, and political authorities, in any complex social system?

Let me concentrate on the demands emanating from political authorities, which represent one crucial focus of rational exercise of power in the social system. The impact of institutions and laws has been implicit in the immediately preceding discussion. Let me also make it explicit why in this subsection I am discussing *national* loyalty requirements instead of loyalty requirements in general. The demand for national loyalty appears in our present-day Western civilization much more strongly sanctioned and all-pervasive than any other loyalty demand. Therefore it has more bearing on freedom problems than other loyalty demands have.

It may be said right away that there are no institutional or rational pressures demanding autonomous as against automatic loyalty patterns. Even if a rather special social fact such as the argument of this book could be considered a "rational pressure," it would be a contradiction in terms to say that it would be a pressure toward more autonomous identifications. By definition, people cannot be induced to identify autonomously. All that can be done is to liberate individuals from pressures toward automatic loyalties and to give them the information that makes informed individual choice possible. The choice itself, if it is to be autonomous, can come only from inside the individual.

The type of national loyalty that governments ought to encourage, if they are interested in the promotion of long-term national security, is, as I

[64] Yet this it not always the case. For example, a person may have been exposed to the "debunking" of a particular institution and be in a position to decide autonomously whether to conform to it or not, even if he in general for ego defense reasons has a strong need to obey or disobey given authorities, in other contexts of special importance for him. On the other hand, a psychologically free person with a humanistic national loyalty may be exposed to manipulation that limits his autonomy in many contexts and imbues him with automatic loyalties to certain national policies.

stated before, a humanistic national loyalty. Humanistic loyalties tend to be more stable and dependable, and they tend to encourage the free flow of critical intelligence contributing toward wise policy-making. The type of national loyalty that most governments do encourage, however, is the authoritarian variety, even in democratic countries. For one thing, governments tend to have certain definite policies, and they are interested in promoting loyalty to their own leadership and policies, not just national loyalty in general. They want loyal supporters much more than they want patriots with open minds in search of the best leaders and policies. And it is always convenient in the short run to have authoritarian subjects who accept the word from above without asking questions.

This tendency is, as a first hypothesis, likely to be much more pronounced in totalitarian than in democratic countries, because the latter are committed to the belief that men are fallible and that political leaders and policies ought to be criticized and even replaced from time to time. Totalitarian regimes, therefore, depend more heavily on large-scale manipulation than democratic regimes tend to do, as we have observed already.

Secondly, the tendency toward encouraging authoritarian loyalties is likely to be more pronounced in large than in small democracies, on the whole. A huge population makes it seem more urgent to reduce the diversity of views and behaviors; there are limits to how many variables political leaders and bureaucrats can handle in their own minds. We all require some simplicity in our categories, and these people are no exceptions.[65] But it must be added that federalism and decentralization presumably can offset this particular incentive toward encouraging authoritarian instead of humanistic loyalties.

A third general hypothesis is that governments of states that are extremely insecure, that is, concerned with the threat of war, are likely to be more concerned with inducing authoritarian loyalties than are other governments. Paradoxically, the strongest powers are apt to be most insecure in this sense, since the size of armaments presumably correlates with the sense of danger. When tensions abate, pressures toward conformity and toward punishing suspected nonconformists tend to abate also.[66]

A fourth hypothesis that may be advanced is closely related to both the first and the third. The more strongly an enduring conflict has tended to affect the perception of the motivations, symbols, and ideas of the opposite sides, so that the dichotomy takes on the moral simplicity of good versus evil or truth versus falsehood, the more urgently needed will an authoritarian indoctrination appear to be, from the point of view of those who

[65] "In our new society there is a growing dislike of original, creative men. The manipulated do not understand them; the manipulators fear them. The tidy committee men regard them with horror, knowing that no pigeonholes can be found for them." Priestley, *Thoughts in the Wilderness,* p. 127. All except one of the essays in this book have appeared in the *New Statesman and Nation* during the last few years. They offer some of the most perceptive comments I have seen on the increasingly serious modern problem of mass manipulation.

[66] Cf. for one example among many, Oakes, "The Security Issue: A Changing Atmosphere," *New York Times Magazine,* August 14, 1955. A major reason for the improvement in tolerance, the author states, "is the at least superficial improvement in the international situation."

control the media of manipulation. If you consider certain ideas as dangerous poison, you want to make sure that nobody, if possible, gets exposed to
them or is allowed to examine them on their merits. Ideologists are, unlike
philosophers, concerned with the action-oriented conclusions that men
reach; they are less interested in whether they arrive at these conclusions
by their own lights or by indoctrination from outside. By the same token,
ideologists in a conflict situation tend to be even more concerned with
making men ready for unconditional support of certain policies. And for
this objective, an effective authoritarian indoctrination is the only dependable road, if there is any dependable road.[67]

It would certainly be possible to expand on these four hypotheses and to
submit additional ones, but I must move on and, first of all, make explicit
the relationship of these hypotheses to the problem of freedom from special
interest manipulation.

There is no logically necessary connection between authoritarian loyalty
patterns and special interest manipulation. All political authority involves
some minimum elements of special interest manipulation, I have suggested,
but these elements are not by logical necessity any larger, say, in a totalitarian
country than in a democratic country. Conceivably, each type of regime
may be completely devoted to the public welfare, as each group of leaders
perceives it.

Yet, it may be said as a general rule that the more authoritarian the national loyalties of most people in a given country become, the greater are
the opportunities for special interest manipulation. In sociological analysis
we are concerned with generalizations, not with saintlike exceptions, and
it may safely be generalized that special interest manipulation will tend to
increase with increased opportunities.

It is the amount of successful, not the amount of attempted, special interest manipulation that always constitutes undesirable limitations on potential freedom, according to my value position. Stated in these terms, my
generalization becomes even more plausible in terms of the preceding
analysis, it would seem. The more authoritarian a citizenry has become in
its national loyalty orientations, the more susceptible it will be to effective
special interest manipulation carried out under the shelter of patriotic slogans.

A pattern of humanistic loyalties, on the other hand, considerably narrows down the opportunities for effective special interest manipulation. In
fact, it would impose quite a strain on any government, since the loyalty to
its policies would depend mostly on the contents of these policies. Patriotic
slogans would be ineffective as a substitute for policies genuinely beneficial
to and protective of the public interest as the public perceives it.

A social and political system entirely without authoritarian loyalties is
a distant utopia, though I am not aware of any sociological necessities ruling
it out as a realistic future goal. In the meantime, one may assume, the level

[67] In recent years, certain intensive indoctrination campaigns aimed at prisoners or other
captive audiences, in stress situations, have given rise to bitter political controversy. These
campaigns have been called "reeducation" by those who approved, in each case, and "brainwashing" by those who disapproved.

of potential freedom, or freedom from special interest manipulation, is affected negatively by the amount of effective pressures in favor of authoritarian loyalty demands. It is affected positively by the relative absence of, or ineffectiveness of, such pressures.[68]

Some Additional Types of Incentives Affecting Potential Freedom

Many other social and cultural variables bear, of course, on the levels of potential freedom in a given society. I cannot undertake to survey them all or even to refer to all the more important ones. This area of investigation is sufficiently uncharted and unstructured to allow for wide disagreements in judgment on what factors are more important than others. The concept of potential freedom is itself a far-from-finished tool, which can be sharpened only by further use and will be affected by the contexts in which it is applied.

Before leaving the topic of social determinants of potential freedom, however, it may be instructive to make brief inquiries into one or two areas of loyalty demands besides the demand for national loyalty. I shall direct a few remarks to the subjects of religious attitudes and of attitudes toward "free enterprise" in economic matters, both in relation to special interest manipulation. On the latter topic, I shall especially be concerned with the issue of free enterprise as treated in contemporary newspapers. After that, I shall try to outline a few propositions on factors that may tend to counteract the means actually being employed for the management of men's minds for special interest purposes.

In his discussion of disagreements in belief versus disagreements in attitude, Charles L. Stevenson states an important aspect of the problem of potential freedom: "But the serious question concerns not what people now want; for in this connection people want, and have always wanted, what they cannot clearly articulate, and perhaps want an absurdity. The serious question concerns what people *would* want if they thought more clearly."[69]

This book does not proceed on the rationalist assumption that people ideally should strive only for attainable objectives and go about attaining them as effectively as possible. But I have adopted this value position: I favor doing whatever can be done toward maximizing the possibility for the individual to perceive adequately and pursue effectively his own interest, without being swayed by special interest manipulation.

A traditional religion plainly cannot be debunked as just an opiate for the people. This phenomenon is too universal to allow for its explanation in simple manipulative terms. Many great religious leaders and inspirators have certainly been great and genuine "do-gooders"—a word that ought not to evoke derogatory associations. Many have been "saints" in the sense that serving the welfare and salvation of their people or all of humanity has been virtually their only type of motive.

---

[68] Although it is not relevant in this context, it should be mentioned that national loyalty demands may also seriously affect social freedom, as coercive measures may be substituted when manipulation does not suffice.

[69] *Ethics and Language*, p. 31.

When religions become organized into churches, however, it is plain that these organizations develop interests of their own, and it is also evident that they are in an enviable objective position to bolster these interests by way of special interest manipulation. This is not to suggest that churchmen are likely to be deliberate manipulators, more than or even as much as people with authority in other and more pronounced interest organizations. But I do suggest that churchmen have an incentive to bolster attitudes favoring the interests of their church as an organization, its clergy, and indirectly also those who contribute the most to the support of the clergy. This last aspect of the incentive situation of many clergies has in the past helped to make many of the Christian churches align themselves strongly with economically privileged classes against the underdogs, though in our days this is much less common.

Probably for the best of motives, churchmen have tended to encourage ignorance and incomplete information on a variety of topics. One obvious topic is the question of the existence of God. So far as the influence of almost any Christian church reaches, expressions of doubt and controversy on this issue are discouraged.[70] On the contrary, the impression is encouraged that people cannot live well, or lead good lives, without faith in God. Or else, people are encouraged to take it for granted that societies cannot endure without a shared faith in a personal God.[71]

I do not wish to imply in this context that I reject this last proposition. All I wish to affirm here is that it is not obviously true and that it is possible and desirable to make inquiries into all propositions postulating freedom-restricting functional prerequisites of social systems. Manipulation that induces unrealistic beliefs to the effect that certain behavioral postulates cannot be challenged empirically should probably always be considered special interest manipulation. Proponents who are wholly convinced of the strength of their own insights would presumably wish to see them challenged and debated—especially, of course, if they share John Stuart Mill's insight that only the necessity of defending a belief can keep it vigorous and alive.[72]

A special area in which most Christian churches, and above all the Roman Catholic church, deliberately has fostered ignorance among people in general is birth control. From the point of view of this book, withholding birth control information is a most undesirable limitation on freedom, even when it evokes no protests from opposition groups. The right to

---

[70] It is interesting that a report from a recent debate on this issue over British radio was given a box on the front page of the *New York Times*, January 20, 1955. It is also noteworthy that this brief report gave nearly three times as much space to the views of the believer as to those of the unbeliever (5½ to 2 inches). One would have thought the latter's views to have the higher news-value to an American newspaper audience.

[71] Sometimes good church people make extravagantly specific claims of this nature. Witness, for example, the following rhetorical query: "Can anyone tell me where we are going to get young fellows to become surveyors, Englishmen, Scotsmen and Irishmen, unless our common life is based on religion?" Cited in the "This England" column of the *New Statesman and Nation,* January 29, 1955.

[72] "Unless it is suffered to be, and actually is, vigorously and earnestly contested, it will, by most of those who receive it, be held in a manner of a prejudice, with little comprehension or feeling of its rational grounds." "On Liberty," in *Utilitarianism, Liberty, and Representative Government,* p. 148; and above, p. 45.

choose whether and when to have children is in my view one of the fundamental human rights, which in principle can and should be extended to
all human beings. So fundamental is this right for the individual's welfare
that I should not hesitate to advocate disobedience to statutes that would
prohibit the dissemination of this sort of enlightenment.[73]

However one may feel about the practicality of this conclusion, though,
it may be objected that the fostering of ignorance on methods of birth control is not necessarily an example of special interest manipulation, since the
clergy or the church derives no obvious gains from this doctrine. It may
also conceivably be in the interest of most people to come to see sex life as
good and satisfying only as a means to the growth of a family.

On the first point, any principle that is effectively induced by authority
without supporting evidence is likely to enhance the status and power of
that authority. On the second point, it is plain that many if not most persons
do want an active sex life even if they for many good reasons want no
children or a planned number of them. These two grounds are sufficient,
I believe, to make this a clear example of an institutionalized special interest
manipulation. An additional ground is the disregard of Catholic authorities for humanity's common interest in finding a way to prevent over-
population of our planet by means other than illness and war.[74]

Not only do organizations tend to develop interests of their own. Within
organizations, leaderships and staffs tend to develop their own interests
vis-à-vis their memberships.[75] Referring primarily to business corporations,
Robert A. Brady has stated: "In many cases, perhaps making the rule rather
than the exception, career men run associations, and much association activity seems a by-product of expansion of pointless tasks and 'services,'
bureaucratically overstaffed and incompetently run by functionaries whose
main efforts are devoted to proving to a gullible membership that the completely or primarily useless is of overwhelming importance."[76]

Philip Selznick has discussed the same problem in more general and
less sarcastic terms as a general problem in bureaucracy: "The use of in-
termediaries creates a tendency toward a *bifurcation of interest* between the
initiator of the action and the agent employed. . . . In order to be secure
in his position, the bureaucrat must strive to make himself as independent
as possible from the ranks . . . [he] must seek a personal base *within* the
group itself: some mechanism . . . which can be used to maintain his organizational fences."[77] It may be argued that *control of relevant information*—the manipulator's crucial weapon always—is invariably more complete in the hands of organizational leaders than in the hands of members

[73] Cf. above, pp. 145–46.

[74] Catholic governments of countries belonging to the World Health Organization have
strongly opposed even fact-finding studies of population problems in the present world. Leaders in communist countries, incidentally, have in the past tended to display a similar negative
attitude toward serious studies of population problems. More recently, however, there are
signs of a salutary change of orientation on this issue in some communist-governed countries,
above all in China.

[75] Cf. above, pp. 292–93.

[76] *Business as a System of Power*, pp. 311–12, note 29.

[77] "An Approach to a Theory of Bureaucracy," *American Sociological Review*, VIII, No. 1
(1943), 50–52.

or outsiders, at least in the long run. This creates an enduring incentive toward special interest manipulation from above. A number of organizations purport to have every bit of information about organization matters available to the public or to their memberships, but it would be super-human to live up to such a pretension all the time, even with the best of intentions. Even clergies are not superhuman, and in the past they have been tempted to suppress scandals, even in many cases where honesty and justice clearly would have dictated a different course.

In all interest organizations the same kinds of manipulation from the leadership down should be taken for granted as one of the facts of life. This assumption implies no cynicism with respect to human motivations, but a belief that even the best of motives are the outcome of the individual's orientation to his total incentive situation. A determined intention to avoid the manipulation of motives of subordinates or outsiders in their own interest may greatly reduce the elements of special interest manipulation in certain organizations, but they can never be entirely abolished.

The ideology of "free enterprise" or "private enterprise" is a more rational orientation than a religious belief, at least in the sense that it is held and advocated as a means to promoting the good society (or more limited interests) in this world only. To many individuals, it is true, this ideology may be equivalent to a religion in more ways than one. Challenging it, for example, may not be permitted, in some quarters—neither the attitude itself nor the super- or substructure of beliefs about what free enterprise accomplishes in the modern world.

There is strictly speaking no such being as "the American businessman." When speaking of American businessmen's values and ideologies, I refer to the attitudes and beliefs that appear instrumental in the kinds of incentive situations in which most of them find themselves.[78] I assume that there are common elements in the various contexts in which these people act, some of which are: (1) the desire to make a profit; (2) the belief that businessmen exert a legitimate function and deserve reasonable amounts of profits; and (3) the belief that the state should not interfere with the businessman's freedom to make profits—that is, beyond what may be necessary to protect him against unfair competition or hardships caused by foreign competition or depression times or, maybe, technological change. Thurman Arnold has described in *The Folklore of Capitalism* how the large corporations as "juridical persons" have come to profit from encouraging attitudes toward them analogous to attitudes toward real persons. The attempts of the New Deal to impose controls on the large corporations were fought in the name of "liberty" much as if the basic liberties of individuals had been under attack.

I am not concerned here with the merits of "free enterprise" or the

---

[78] I speak of *American* businessmen rather than businessmen in general only in order to simplify the discussion. Much of what is said may be applicable to all businessmen, but I wish to avoid considering such factors as the varying degrees of cartellization or state control or political commitments of businessmen in the various national economies. The importance of businessmen and business values in American society has been emphasized and described, for example, by Harold J. Laski in *The American Democracy,* especially Chap. 5, and by C. Wright Mills in *The Power Elite.*

merits of economic planning. I only wish to state parenthetically that the prefix "free" does not mean that human freedom *necessarily* is fuller under free enterprise than under public planning. The question of what combination of private enterprise and public planning would allow the maximum vindication of human rights is an empirical one that has by no means been settled.[79] This question has, unfortunately, been subjected to discussions marked by narrow partisan prejudice more often than by detached, open-minded inquiry.[80]

My concern is instead with free enterprise ideology as an instrument of effective manipulation in the special interest of businessmen, particularly on the American scene. Even if all the empirical assumptions of free enterprise advocates were true and even if all their value positions were acceptable to the investigator, my inquiry of special interest manipulation could proceed in much the same way, since my task is to analyze the general problem and not to discuss the merits of particular influence processes. And I am not launching an exhaustive inquiry into the whole dynamics of this particular kind of influence process. I only wish to refer to one or two of its aspects as examples of types of incentives toward reducing the potential freedom of modern man. I shall be particularly interested in the role of mass media such as the press in this context.[81]

The English utilitarians tended to take it for granted that "truth" will win out if given an equal chance with "falsehood."[82] But the premise of equal care and skill on behalf of opposing ideas is no more realistic today, on the whole and on important political matters, than the premise of a free market, as postulated by utilitarian economists and Manchester liberals. James Mill warned governments that "to attach advantage to the delivering of one set of opinions, disadvantage to the delivering of another, is to make a choice."[83] In modern democracies, and perhaps most acutely in the United States, the denial of a fair hearing for unorthodox political ideas is not so much a problem of rewards and punishments that the government may apply by rational policies. Rather, it is a problem of incentives that are institutionalized in a social structure dominated by men of wealth, or their views and values.

Few would claim, for example, that controversies on the merits of free enterprise versus public planning in American public forums today can

[79] Strictly speaking, this is an empirical question only if it has been agreed what the priorities should be in a hierarchy of human rights.

[80] For a notable exception, see Kelsen, "Democracy and Socialism," *Conference on Jurisprudence and Politics*, No. 15 (1954), pp. 63–87.

[81] It would be tempting to speculate on the various reasons for the much stronger hold that free enterprise ideology apparently has on nonbusinessmen in the United States than in virtually any other country. Part of the answer is clearly in the unmatched living standards of the United States, to which a high freedom of business enterprise no doubt has contributed. But another part of the explanation is probably in the fact that the mass media of communication became effective instruments for denouncing political socialism before socialism had become an effective political force. The United States is today probably the only democratic country in which there are no mass media controlled by principled opponents of private enterprise and no mass organizations on the left that are able and willing to champion a political alternative to the present development.

[82] See quotations from James Mill's "Liberty of the Press," on pp. 43–45.

[83] "Liberty of the Press," p. 278, and above, p. 44.

easily proceed on the basis of equal skill on both sides and equal rewards on both sides. Well-educated young people almost invariably find the greater rewards in the service of private enterprise. Even if they enter government service, they will soon find that a belief in a free economy is more compatible with a good career than is a belief in a socialist or controlled economy. Only those who choose the academic profession, on the whole, have the opportunity to combine a successful career with the maintenance of socialist views.

Note that this is not so much a problem of social freedom as it is a problem of potential freedom. For every young man who deliberately departs from his political convictions in order to promote his career, there must be fifty who imperceptibly to themselves adjust their beliefs to make them more compatible with the expectations of other people who have power over their career prospects. As Harold J. Laski puts it: "We check our impulses at their birth lest they involve us in departures from the norm."[84] We are much happier if we can persuade ourselves either that our beliefs and attitudes have not changed or that they have changed for "good" and impeccable reasons; and most of us tend to be successful in this way of dealing with ourselves.

We are no longer coerced or externally restrained when we have come to believe in the ideas we are professing to share. But it may be asked: If it is in our interest to hold these ideas, can our conformity be described as the outcome of special interest manipulation? Is this manipulation in favor of business interests at the expense of our own interest, if our conversion in fact advances our career prospects?

A successful career is undoubtedly in the interest of every person who desires it and may be in the interest of others, too. But it is also in our interest that the rewards in a career should be due primarily to the merits of our performance. To be sure, it is in our interest to have good luck, but in a basic sense it is *not* in our interest to be rewarded for adjustments that tend to disrupt our psychological freedom. For example, if we start out with a faith in brotherhood and solidarity among men, then presumably, if we are psychologically free (and young people are apt to have more psychological freedom than older people), this faith corresponds to fundamental value commitments and identifications in harmony with our basic needs. If external circumstances such as an authoritative ideology make us abandon once spontaneously chosen identifications and value commitments, chances are that our new identifications and commitments are less in harmony with some of our basic motives. Either we are aware of this and feel pressured, and our social freedom is reduced. Or we repress this insight and feel free, and our psychological freedom is reduced.

In the latter instance, our potential freedom also is reduced, even if it is not entirely clear that this is a case of special interest manipulation, as this term has been defined. We have been induced to alter our views in deference to the interests of others, at the expense of a maximal fidelity to our spontaneous value orientation. We may be rewarded in terms of more

---

[84] *The Danger of Obedience and Other Essays*, p. 6.

money and prestige and consequently more social freedom in some respects. Nevertheless, I consider this an undesirable interference with the individual's potential freedom—his freedom to develop a maximal autonomy vis-à-vis institutional and rational pressures primarily in the interest of other persons or groups.

The impact of pressures favoring freedom of economic enterprise should be studied not only in its individual but also in its social ramifications. John Stuart Mill, who struggled valiantly to keep the *London and Westminster Review* in operation during the 1830s commented after its demise: "I do not believe that any devices would have made a radical and democratic review defray its expenses."[85] The high quality of this review cannot be disputed, and yet it had to go, for the simple reason that a capitalist society does in fact attach advantage to the expression of some views and disadvantage to the expression of others. This poses a general problem for democratic government, which Barker has stated as follows: "Democracy is a process of discussion. Discussion requires publicity—full and fair publicity—for every point of view. That requirement is not satisfied so long as the power of wealth controls the means of publicity. The wealth-owning class can at present acquire a predominant weight in the process of discussion, not in the strength of what it has to say . . . but in the strength of its purse."[86]

With special reference to the contemporary American press, Robert M. Hutchins has said: "Of course we have a one-party press in this country, and we shall have one as long as the press is big business, and as long as people with money continue to feel safer on the Republican side."[87] Whether or not America has a one-party press, it is clear that the press disseminates only one opinion concerning the desirability of freedom of business enterprise and, above all, concerning the desirability of freedom from restrictions on newspaper publishers. A. D. Lindsay once remarked that "the moving speeches we make about the supremacy of law in the world would not sound so well if we had to say the supremacy of lawyers."[88] Similarly, the moving pleas for safeguarding the freedom of the press would sound less urgent if instead it was made a plea for the complete freedom of news publishers to make their editors publish and repress according to the dictates of their own (the publishers') business and political interests. "Just as big business," says Riesman, "has been able to marshal for the defense of 'property' against governmental interference most of our small farmers and businessmen who fear for their kind of eighteenth-century property, so the press and radio lords have been able to marshal for the defense of their kind of 'freedom' most of our intellectuals who fear for their kind of Voltairean freedom."[89]

M. Alderton Pink, an English friendly critic of democracy, asserts that

---

85 *Autobiography*, p. 207.
86 *Reflections on Government*, pp. 109–10.
87 *Freedom, Education, and the Fund*, p. 61.
88 *The Modern Democratic State*, p. 113.
89 "Civil Liberties in a Period of Transition," in Friedrich and Mason (eds.), *Public Policy*, III (1942), 74–75.

the press of his country is not free in any real sense, for "the working journalist never for a moment thinks that he is free to express his own views on any public question." He says we must decide "whether it is better for the restrictions to be imposed by private and often anti-social agencies or by the community itself." He concludes by stating as his own conviction that it is better "to risk a State dictatorship of opinion in order to avoid a much less desirable business dictatorship"; he recommends a British Press Corporation analogous to the British Broadcasting Corporation, as a lesser evil.[90]

A recent American Commission on the Freedom of the Press reached a more cautious set of conclusions: "If modern society requires great agencies of communication, if these concentrations become so powerful that they are a threat to democracy, if democracy cannot solve the problem simply by breaking them up—then those agencies must control themselves or be controlled by government. If they are controlled by the government, we lose our chief safeguard against totalitarianism—and at the same time take a long step toward it."[91] Even these moderate conclusions were on the whole received with hostility by American newspapers. As Hutchins said on the same occasion from which I have already quoted him, in an address to the American Society of Newspaper Editors: "You are the only uncriticized institution in the country. You will not criticize one another, and any suggestion that anybody else might do so sets you to muttering about the First Amendment."[92]

I do not wish to leave the impression that I consider the American press primarily as one huge instrument for the manipulation of attitudes toward support of free enterprise, or free enterprise in newspaper publishing. The integrity and quality of many American newspapers are in some respcts among the highest in the world. For one thing, there are few countries in which candidates of the main parties, or even of unpopular splinter parties, can count on as fair reports of their speeches in newspapers of opposite colors as American politicians on the whole are in a position to. The solid professional education and improving prestige and status of working journalists in America, and the increasing strength of organizations such as the American Newspaper Guild, may increasingly curtail the power of newspaper publishers to manipulate reader attitudes at will.[93]

"You may believe, as I do," says J. B. Priestley, "that if the citizens of Great Powers were more sharply militant, less like sheep, then States would

---

[90] *A Realist Looks at Democracy*, pp. 151, 155, 156.

[91] *A Free and Responsible Press*, by the Commission on Freedom of the Press (1947), p. 5 and pp. 90–96. Compare the more specific recommendations for the British press in the *Report of the Royal Commission on the Press 1947–49*, pp. 155–79. The late Louis Wirth observed in his Presidential Address to the American Sociological Society in December 1947: "If it is consensus that makes an aggregate of men into a society, and if consensus is increasingly at the mercy of the functioning of the mass communication agencies as it is in a democratic world, then the control over these instrumentalities becomes one of the principal sources of political, economic and social power. The harnessing of this power is an infinitely more complex and vital problem than any previous challenge that the human race has had to meet." *American Sociological Review*, XIII, No. 1 (1948), 12.

[92] *Freedom, Education, and the Fund*, p. 59.

[93] Readers who are *effectively* manipulated are of course without incentive to apply sanctions of their own by switching to other newspapers (in cities which have more than one).

soon be less like wolves."[94] This is in my opinion a superb statement of the most important political problem of potential freedom and special interest manipulation. I am on the whole in this book concerned with the problem of freedom maximization for the individual for his own sake and for its own sake, regardless of whether freedom is instrumental to advancing other values, such as an improved democratic process. But security against war is a most important time dimension of most freedom values. And one of the most dangerous aspects of present-day efficiency in mass manipulation techniques is, I agree with Priestley, the weakening of effective democratic brakes on policies launched by cynical or fanatical or ill-informed men of power.

This remains a serious problem even if it can be convincingly argued that effective special interest manipulation frequently can augment the happiness of those who are influenced. This is perhaps often the case— when, for instance, flattery is being employed.[95] The mass media in democratic countries on the whole have a vested interest in flattering their readers. To quote Priestley again: "To succeed in mass communications you must flatter the customer and never disturb him. And that, of course, is what is happening, on a gigantic scale in America, and on an increasing scale here and elsewhere. . . . Everything must be made smooth and easy. No effort must be required. History must be falsified, science distorted, religion sentimentalized, human relations hopelessly over-simplified, so that nobody is challenged, disturbed, asked to reflect or feel deeply."[96]

In turn this creates a kind of a "vested interest" in the public, too, not to be bothered by demands of effort on their part as consumers of mass media. In Dwight MacDonald's words, "The masses, debauched by several generations of this sort of thing, in turn come to demand trivial and comfortable cultural products. Which came first, the chicken or the egg, the mass demand or its satisfaction (and further stimulation) is a question as academic as unanswerable. The engine is reciprocating and shows no signs of running down."[97]

What happens to the individual who dislikes and rebels against the cheap, superficial, and often misinforming contents of many of the mass media? Nothing at all; he lives in a free country, in which people are not coerced or pushed around without apparent necessity. Speaking of Great Britain, Plamenatz says that "the present danger in this country is not so much that those who have unpopular and valuable opinions will be ill-treated as that no one will take any notice of them. . . . From the enormous variety of opinions . . . we take refuge in the narrow circles of our intel-

---

[94] *Thoughts in the Wilderness,* pp. 15–16.

[95] Floyd Hunter says in *Community Power Structure,* pp. 180–81: "The nearest the writer came to hearing a man say he practiced guile was in a statement made by one of the power leaders when he said, 'The way to manipulate men is to flatter them. The little fellow earning around $5,000 a year likes to feel that he is in on things. We do bring him in on certain projects like the Community Chest drive. He gets publicity, and he is flattered. The next time you ask him to do something he will fall all over himself to make good.' "

[96] *Thoughts in the Wilderness,* p. 10. Priestley adds: "Fifty years ago there was little of this mass catering. Even a popular newspaper was rather better than its average reader, who was expected to make some effort." *Ibid.,* p. 11.

[97] "A Theory of Mass Culture," *Diogenes,* No. 3 (1953), pp. 16–17.

lectual friends, among whom a few familiar ideas and prejudices circulate."[98]

Emphasizing the political side to the mass manipulation problem, Riesman wrote some years ago that vested interests in our time have come to rely less and less on repressive measures alone to keep "dangerous thoughts" from creating obstacles to the pursuit of their interests. Being in control of the mass media and other power centers, men of power much prefer to create by behind-the-scenes manipulation, a *climate of opinion* favorable to their own purposes.[99] Totalitarian governments, of course, have been in a position to become the masters of such techniques.

What are some of the factors that conceivably may work to, and be used to, offset these apparent trends toward more and more effective management of men by manipulative means?

Local autonomy, or decentralization in as many areas as is practicable, is one way toward diminishing somewhat the huge inequality in manipulative power in modern mass societies. Decentralization can be brought about geographically or in other ways. For example, a chain of newspapers can be somewhat decentralized by giving each local editor full responsibility for his own paper or, conceivably also, by giving full autonomy to, say, the business editors, literary editors, political editors, and columnists used by the chain as a whole.

Another social structure variable affecting potential freedom is the degree of vertical mobility in a society, and notably the degree to which it is possible for individuals to make great gains or losses in wealth and power by competing successfully with others. If the stakes are great, people come to feel justified in using ruthless means. The cruder kinds of coercion are barred by our legal institutions, but there are few laws that prevent even the most ruthless manipulation, beyond outright fraud in money matters. Social institutions affording a modicum of security without the temptations of tremendous gains in wealth and power are probably conducive to live-and-let-live attitudes, at least more so than institutions tending toward making "one man's death the other man's bread," as a Norwegian proverb has it.

Third, the amounts of anomie certainly must have some bearing on the levels of potential freedom. But here it is necessary to distinguish between rational and institutional infringements on individual autonomy. A low level of anomie means a high level of regulations that have become traditional. These institutions may well operate in the special interest of rulers or ruling classes and may be thoroughly oppressive of individual development and expression. Slaves of customs may be as unfree as the slaves of dictators. But a high level of anomie, while it makes a high level of potential freedom possible, also may release a different set of forces to subvert this freedom. A highly anomic society, as Merton has pointed out, may tend to develop ruthlessness in the choice of means, as common norms of

---

[98] *The English Utilitarians,* p. 132.

[99] "Civil Liberties in a Period of Transition," in Friedrich and Mason (eds.), *Public Policy,* III, 71.

propriety and decency become weaker. This trend may open the way toward maximal use of the most effective manipulation techniques for rational purposes.

My tentative conclusion is, nevertheless, that a relatively high level of anomie—though, of course, below the level where it leads to social disorganization—is vastly preferable to a low level, from a potential freedom point of view. It is not so much the amount of manipulation effort that I wish to see reduced as the individual's ability and incentive to resist manipulation that I wish to see increased. This ability is nil in a society with minimum anomie and optimum fatalism. It can be high in a highly anomic society, even if modern manipulation techniques are used. Provided, only, that it is a pluralist society, with competing power centers.

The fourth proposition, then, is that a pluralist society, in which many important issues are controversial, and manipulation efforts come from all sides, leaves a wider scope for potential freedom than a "monist" or ultimately a totalitarian society. The more controversy going on around important issues in a given society, the more fertile is the soil for a high level of potential freedom, permitting individuals a truly free and well-informed choice on how to run their own lives.

The crucial aspect of pluralism, for this purpose, is its impact on the educational process. It is important that individuals acquire skeptically inquiring minds while they are in their formative years and are in the process of articulating their basic value commitments, if they believe they have any. Yet, it must be added that these effects of a vigorously free educational process are likely to wither later in life, unless society as a whole is at least moderately hospitable to controversy and experiments on important social and political issues.[100]

Levels of potential freedom, including freedom from special interest manipulation, are determined by the attitudes of individuals toward one another and toward ideas and issues. These attitudes are in part determined by factors in the social and political structure of the society in which they live. I have tried to discuss some of these factors, and have formulated a few tentative propositions. But attitudes reflect not only social but also psychological realities. Again, I am plunging into an area in which data bearing immediately on my problem are sparse; but let me again resort to speculation to try to fill in the gaps, this time on the problem of psychological determinants of levels of potential freedom.

SOME PSYCHOLOGICAL DETERMINANTS

A complete potential freedom is an impossibility in sociological as well as in psychological terms. I have suggested that a complete potential freedom is as hard to conceptualize as a goal of maximizing everybody's power over everybody else.[101] And for the individual personality, it may now be added, a complete potential freedom would mean not only a complete absence of community with others and of culture; it would also mean non-

100 Cf. above, pp. 98–99.
101 See above, pp. 96–97.

functioning of whatever kind of a "mind" there would be left. It is a non-sense-term.

The Need for Stereotypes

"For the most part we do not first see, and then define, we define first and then see. In the great blooming, buzzing confusion of the outer world we pick out what our culture has already defined for us, and we tend to perceive that which we have picked out in the form stereotyped for us in our culture."[102] In his famous discussion of stereotypes many years ago, Walter Lippman also quoted John Dewey's explanation: "The problem of the acquisition of meanings by things, or (stated in another way) of forming habits of simple apprehension, is thus the problem of introducing (1) *definiteness* and *distinction* and (2) *consistency* or *stability* of meaning into what is otherwise vague and wavering."[103]

Our minds cannot function without some order. Our perceptions of the external world are of no service to us unless and until we can attach some meaning to them, in terms of previously established categories. Since no set of categories can be complete enough to give "boxes" for all the infinite variety of concrete experience, our perceptions must be simplified—they must be stereotyped.[104] We must *abstract* aspects of our sensory experience, which give us the basis for classifying them according to their significance for our own needs and interests.

This habit of stereotyping and abstraction is one of the most important products of the learning process of every individual. And it is a shared learning process; the particular stereotypes and abstractions the individual acquires are not selected at random by him. Of the great and perhaps infinite number of concepts and possible principles of order, each society has institutionalized the selection of limited numbers, which are ordinarily the only ones effectively available to the growing child—unless he creates new concepts.[105] These limited numbers of concepts and stereotypes in each society constitute an important aspect of its culture. "In every culture," says Lawrence K. Frank, "the individual is of necessity 'cribbed, cabinned, and confined' within the limitations of what his culture tells him to see, to believe, to do, and to feel."[106]

No individual's outlook is entirely shaped by his culture, however; not even the most rigidly institutionalized aboriginal community can suppress individual differences in attitudes and beliefs completely. But there are

[102] Lippmann, *Public Opinion*, p. 61.

[103] *Ibid.*, p. 60.

[104] By a stereotype I understand an oversimplified factual belief—oversimplified in the sense that it distorts a more complex reality. Cf. above, p. 201.

[105] John Dewey points out how limited is the individual's opportunity to create his own concepts: "Fond parents and relatives frequently pick up a few of the child's spontaneous modes of speech and for a time at least they are portions of the speech of the group. But the ratio which such words bear to the total vocabulary in use gives us a fair measure of the part played by purely individual habit in forming customs in comparison with the part played by custom in forming individual habits. Few persons have either the energy or the wealth to build private roads to travel upon." *Human Nature and Conduct*, p. 59.

[106] Quoted by Blake, Ramsey, and Moran in Blake and Ramsey (eds.), *Perception: An Approach to Personality*, p. 15.

great differences in the degree of individuality encouraged in a highly developed individualistic and anomic culture, on the one side, and a rigidly structured, traditionalistic culture, on the other side. Also, and this is the problem confronting us in this context, in each culture there is considerable difference in the degree to which individuals assert their individuality at the expense of conformity, even if one assumed that the exposure to conformity pressures is equal. In other words, psychological factors also affect the degree to which the individual achieves his potential individuality; not only the social pressures and incentives to which he is exposed. The need to stereotype is one of the factors influenced by the individual's personality; others will be discussed in subsequent subsections.

It is true that the need to stereotype, or maintain oversimplified categories for our perceptions and cognitions, is common to all human beings. At the same time, however, it is also clear that some individuals experience this need more strongly and tend to carry their stereotyping much further than others do. Individuals in the same culture differ greatly in their general ability to tolerate uncertainties, ambiguities, or even chaos in realms of life of importance to them.

It has been suggested in Chapter 4 that a general tendency toward intolerance of ambiguities is an important aspect of deficiencies in psychological freedom. Various evidence has been cited, to the effect that the authoritarian attitude syndrome tends to include a general intolerance of ambiguities, both emotional and cognitive. The same tendency has been found as an integral part of the antiauthoritarian attitude syndrome. Not only is there a tendency toward maintaining *more* unrealistic stereotypes and categories in people with these attitude syndromes; there is also a tendency in such people to apply their stereotypes more indiscriminately and more persistently in spite of conflicting evidence. Authoritarians, and antiauthoritarians, tend to persevere in their unrealistic factual beliefs, thus exhibiting more rigidity than other individuals.[107]

I have also suggested that this aspect of psychological defensiveness, in my broad sense of the term, is likely to be the outcome of repression or the inability to cope with anxiety. In this way, ego-defensiveness gives the individual a stake in a number of stereotypes. They give him a sense of order and a sense of protection, inside his defense system, against the menace of "dangerous" new insights. There is no use in repeating here the propositions in Chapter 4 on the dynamics of repression. For present purposes, it may be stated in one sentence that all the childhood and social structure influences aiding the developing individual in maintaining his initial psychological freedom will also tend to make him less extensively and intensively dependent on rigid categorizing of his life's experience and thus promote his potential freedom.

In order to maximize an individual's capacity and incentive to develop and live by his own individuality, with maximum perceptiveness and understanding of the full variety of experience that life has to offer, it is above

---

[107] See above, pp. 200–205, and 208–9.

all necessary to provide the preconditions for a maximal psychological freedom. The alternative is a greater degree of confinement behind the partial blinders of stereotypes, which may give a sense of protection for the anxiety-ridden but also limit their vision.

Perceptions of the Self and Potential Freedom

Not only the external world is perceived and cognated in more or less stereotyped terms, but the same is true about the individual's picture of his self. The self-image develops out of social interaction by means of language and other cultural symbols. It has been suggested that the level of self-esteem, or the love of the self, tends to affect the cognitive self-image in at least two ways. In the first place, a high self-esteem tends to equip the individual with the courage to perceive himself relatively realistically, while a low self-esteem tends to produce cognitive compensations by way of a failure to perceive important weaknesses in the self, and a tendency to exaggerate its virtues. In other words, low self-esteem tends to produce a more stereotyped and a more glorified self-image.[108]

Secondly, the level of self-esteem affects also the more basic constitution of the self: it tends to determine the nature of the individual's identifications, which may produce a wider or a more narrow self. I have distinguished between two types of identification: Self-expansive identification takes place to the extent that the individual comes to consider the general needs of other persons *his own*; his self is expanded by the process of identification. Self-sacrificing identification, on the other hand, takes place to the extent that the individual comes to consider the general needs of others more important than those he sees as his own; this kind of an identification process produces not only a maligned but also a narrow self. A low self-esteem tends to produce a narrow self; a high self-esteem a wide self, in this manner.[109]

A high level of self-esteem tends to indicate a high level of psychological freedom.[110] It may be concluded that a wide self, as well as a cognitively realistic self-image, also are indications of a high psychological freedom. But what is the significance of these considerations for potential freedom?

"Unperceived external restraints on individual behavior"—my synonym for limitations on potential freedom—are restraints only if they interfere with the individual's actual or potential behavior. Manipulative power is exercised when motives are induced toward conformity with the wishes of the manipulator, in the absence of or independently of coercive sanctions. While effective coercion produces compliance, effective manipulation produces either identification or internalization. Identification narrows or broadens the self; internalization affects its value commitments and cognitive outlook and the self-image.

Effective manipulation always reduces the individual's potential freedom, as certainly as coercion reduces his social freedom. But depending on the personality of the one being influenced, the same types of manipulation

---

[108] Cf. above, pp. 175, 200, and 215.
[109] Cf. above, pp. 176–78.
[110] See above, pp. 178–79.

may vary greatly in freedom-reducing effects. This is true of both special interest and nonspecial interest manipulation. The latter is not necessarily undesirable, even if its effects should reduce potential freedom considerably.

Personalities who maintain a high psychological freedom through their socialization process tend to internalize only such norms as can be and are integrated with their biologically rooted individual motives. This statement in a sense places the cart before the horse: more accurately speaking, children who are induced to internalize only those norms that can be integrated with their biological needs and with each other tend to maintain a relatively high level of psychological freedom—and along with it a positive self-esteem, a realistic self-image, and self-expanding identifications.

The structure of the self-image and the interpersonal delimitation of the self are probably among the important determinants of the individual's susceptibility to manipulation. But the relationship is likely to be complex, and it may be advisable to interject a word on the conceptual relationship between potential freedom and the structure of the self.

The individual's "behavior," as it is affected by nonperceived external restraints, refers to his identification and internalization behavior as much as to his overt behavior. But these former behaviors, in structuring and expanding the self, are in a sense prerequisites to a meaningful statement of the problem of potential freedom. Individual autonomy would be a meaningless concept unless there is already a structured self. Yet, at any specific point of time, the further structuring of the self, by way of new identifications and internalizations, amounts to limitations on the individual's potential freedom, whether unavoidable or not and undesirable or not.

This is another side to the fact that a complete potential freedom is a nonsense-concept: every personality must be structured, and every ego structure, every self, is the outcome of nonperceived external restraints. These may have been imposed by culture and institutions or by rational manipulation, whether during the child's socialization or later on. The problem of maximizing the individual's potential freedom should be limited by one specification, I have suggested: it is the freedom from special interest manipulation I wish to see reduced. Let me now add another, alternative delimitation of the problem: given an individual with internalized norms and identifications, at a specific point of time, the problem of potential freedom can be stated as the problem of making all his important decisions from then on as autonomous as possible.

This problem is not a very meaningful one, however, in so far as the individual has self-sacrificing identifications. If he seeks his sense of worth entirely in persons or causes outside himself, an increased autonomy from various norms and institutions does not contribute to his potential freedom in any real sense, since he carries built-in mechanisms toward dependency. The most that "debunking" of particular institutions can do for an extreme self-sacrificer is to make his self-negating identifications more total, by making him less inhibited by conventions.

The problem of maximizing potential freedom is not very meaningful if we assume as given a highly stereotyped, glorified self-image. This is invariably a protection against low self-esteem or against the awareness of other threatening circumstances. If data and insights are brought across for the purpose of fostering autonomous choice about whether to conform to specific institutional or authority demands, all that the individual can gain is a readjustment of his ego-defense system. His behavior cannot, given my present assumptions, become autonomous in any full sense, since it is dictated by his neurotic needs.

Returning to the empirical problem of potential freedom in relation to the self, I now drop the assumption that a certain type of self is given as a constant. Instead, let me consider the type of self an independent or intervening variable in order to suggest one or two hypotheses on its impact on potential freedom levels.

First, take the narrow self of an individual seeking his security and satisfactions vicariously through self-sacrificing identifications. The outlook for his potential freedom can be improved only to the extent that an improved self-esteem can loosen his symbiotic dependence. A pattern of self-expanding identifications, on the other hand, implies a personal self-sufficiency or emotional solvency that makes for a psychological capacity to gain a high degree of potential freedom.

Secondly, take the stereotyped, glorified self-image of an individual basically preoccupied with ego-defense. His outlook for autonomous choice on how to relate himself to conventions can be improved in any real sense only to the extent that he learns to cope with some of his anxieties by tolerating some of the painful insights about himself. An ego-defensive threat-orientation makes a genuine independence impossible so far as it goes. A realistic self-image, or one that includes good as well as bad aspects of importance in the total picture, indicates a level of anxiety sufficiently low to allow a good amount of genuine independence in important matters.

A general summary of these propositions can be stated as follows: the problem of increasing potential freedom becomes a meaningful one only if we assume that a minimum level of psychological freedom *is or can be* attained by the individual. If this is granted, then it may be proposed that the higher the level of psychological freedom becomes, other things being equal, the better is the outlook for increasing the level of potential freedom.

Differences in Independence of Judgment

"In a rough sense," suggests Robert Dahl, "the essence of all competitive politics is bribery of the electorate by politicians."[111] I am afraid this view is too optimistic. For bribery is a two-way process, in which one favor invariably is given in return for another. In politics I fear that manipulation or even conscious fraud frequently takes the place of bribery: the electorate is given only the appearance of favors instead of actual favors.

The degree to which manipulation or fraud can be substituted for a real service of public needs depends, of course, also on the electorate's enlightenment. But now I must be more specific: it depends on the relationship

[111] *A Preface to Democratic Theory*, p. 68.

between its general enlightenment, independence of judgment, and access to full understanding of the issues involved. If it were possible to construct scales for each of these variables and to score an electorate or its most effective spokesmen on each scale, this could be said: the higher the scores on either scale, the better the outlook for effective resistance to political special interest manipulation. Of these three variables, only independence of judgment is primarily a psychological concept, to be discussed in this section.

Independence of judgment is probably a personality trait not limited to specific fields such as the political.[112] A man who is easily persuaded in matters political is probably easily persuaded also in other contexts. But two reservations are necessary. The individual's independence of judgment should be weighed only within his important psychological fields; it is no proof of a susceptibility to dependency if a man easily is persuaded on an issue that he considers utterly unimportant. Secondly, independence of judgment must be studied in relation to given amounts of information, if possible. If A is more easily persuaded than B on an issue X, on which A is more poorly informed than B is, one cannot conclude that A has less independence of judgment, psychologically considered. For all we know, the reverse may be true, on issues where A's information is equal to B's.

One appealing feature of the by now classical experiments of Solomon Asch is precisely that he investigated differences in independence of judgment in situations in which the individuals compared had exactly the same "knowledge" or information. And the issue of controversy was an artifact of the experiment, so that it was not related to the different motivational predispositions and preferences of the subjects. Asch's measurements were in these important respects as "pure" as humanly possible. If there are fundamental personality differences in independence of judgment, his procedures were well adapted to bringing them out.

The "issues" in those experiments consisted of a series of twelve simple perceptual judgments. For example, one vertical line on a piece of cardboard at the left is given as a standard. On another piece of cardboard placed beside it are three vertical lines, one of which is as long as the standard. The subjects are asked to state which of the three it is. Each group consists of seven to nine subjects, all of whom except one are the experimenter's "stooges" or previously informed subjects, who act under secret instructions from the experimenter. Their task is to establish a norm against which the one innocent subject's independence of judgment is tested. Each member of the group is called on to report which line on the card at the right is as long as the standard line. Each of the stooges has been told to give specific wrong answers to seven of the twelve ques-

---

112 "Probably there is no single general factor of persuasibility, in the sense that every individual can be assigned a single score which will represent his degree of susceptibility to any and all situations where changes in attitudes or opinions are elicited. On the other hand, the opposite assumption of complete specificity seems to be unwarranted. . . . There is reason to expect that some more or less general factors of persuasibility will eventually be isolated, on the basis of which accurate predictions can be made as to how different individuals will respond to various series of discrete communications on different topics." Janis, "Personality Correlates of Susceptibility to Persuasion," *Journal of Personality*, XXII, No. 4 (1954), 506.

tions. The one innocent subject is every time called on to give his answer last, after the establishment of an apparent consensus. The lengths of the three lines at the right vary sufficiently to make it easy and obvious to tell the right answer—except for the powerful norm created by the strong appearance that everyone else unanimously expresses a different judgment.[113]

Considerable individual differences were found. Reporting on a series of thirty-one experiments on college students, giving the responses of thirty-one minorities of one, Asch found that six of them gave only correct answers, and thus proved entirely independent of the group norm. Another seven subjects yielded only once. There were ten who yielded two or three times, while the remaining eight yielded four or more times out of the seven times they were subjected to a majority norm giving the wrong answer.

In later experiments Asch increased the contradiction between the majority norm and the individual's perception by increasing the difference between the stimuli. "There was an increase in the proportion of those who were entirely independent. But for the others the conflict was all the more severe."[114]

Asch also varied the strength of the norm. In one series of tests, he reduced the number of paid participants to one person. As a result, most experimental subjects reported only correct answers, but "we were able to observe the germs of the reactions that under more forceful pressure appeared in clear form. None of the subjects disregarded the reports of her partner and few failed to be relieved by the final disclosure."[115] In another series of tests, one "ally" was introduced: one member of the cooperating group, seated in the third position (and answering third), was instructed to give correct answers. This time the majority effect was "markedly weakened" but not abolished.

In the present context I am not concerned with social structure determinants of independence versus yielding, beyond reporting that group experiments such as these have brought out marked individual differences. I am interested in the psychological mechanisms leading to independence or yielding. I also want to explore some personality correlates of these mechanisms.

On the first question the Asch experiments contributed important information. Immediately after each experiment, the naïve subject was interviewed by the experimenter, who wanted to explore in some detail his perceptions of and reaction to the dilemma in which he had found himself.[116]

Among those who gave independent answers, there were those who did

---

[113] Asch, *Social Psychology*, Chap. 16, especially pp. 451–57. The experimenter always explained the nature of the experiment to the "naïve" subject after each test, and it is reported that "nearly all subjects expressed interest and most were glad of the opportunity to have experienced a striking social situation from which they felt they had learned a lesson." *Ibid.*, p. 456.

[114] *Ibid.*, p. 476.

[115] "As the experiment progressed, contagious, and in some instances, uncontrolled, laughter swept the group. . . . Little did these persons realize how they would have acted and looked if they were stripped of the group support of which they were hardly aware." *Ibid.*, pp. 476–81.

[116] *Ibid.*, pp. 465–73.

so with confidence and those who did so under considerable doubt. But even those who were confident in trusting their own senses frequently were very much disturbed by the apparent discrepancy between their own senses and those of all the others. The nonconfident independent subjects, on the other hand, were willing to admit that their own judgments were wrong—in this sense they could be considered yielders—but reported them anyway.

Among the yielders, there were three principal types. First, those who yielded due to *distortion of perception*: they "saw" the same as they thought the majority saw, in all or in some of the judgment tests. Secondly, there were those who yielded because of *distortion of judgment*: they decided to disregard or doubt their perceptions, in their belief that a unanimous majority probably was right. Third, there were those who yielded due to *distortion of action*: they trusted their own perceptions, but they suppressed their own better judgments in order to conform to the majority norm because they did not want to appear different.

This last group of yielders is uninteresting from the point of view of potential freedom. They are yielding to perceived external restraints; they are not, unlike the two other groups, induced to change perceptions or attitudes as a consequence of manipulation. The last group of yielders act much as if they had been coerced, even if the issue in which they yielded was not sufficiently important to them to justify a description of the pressure as coercive.[117]

Those who yielded on perception or judgment did perhaps in most cases initially perceive the majority consensus as an external restraint, but they were quick to accept it as a basis for their own perceptions or judgments. From then on, only their potential freedom was reduced.

Among the independents, only the confident ones kept their potential freedom unimpaired through the experiments. Those who gave the correct answers in the belief that they were wrong were to this extent no longer free in the sense of potential freedom. They had been manipulated into disbelieving the veracity of the clear reports of their own immediate sense-experience—even if they acted on these reports nevertheless.

Asch gives scarce information on the personality backgrounds of his subjects.[118] But Frank Barron, one of his collaborators, later reported on various personality tests given to subjects who had yielded or had shown independence of judgment during Asch-type experiments.

In Barron's experiments there were twelve critical trials instead of seven. For his comparative purposes "yielders" were those who yielded eight or more times and "independents" those who never yielded. About 25 percent of his college student subjects were yielders, and another 25

---

[117] Cf. above, p. 93.

[118] It appears a drawback in his experiments that he sometimes used male and sometimes female subjects, and sometimes both together, without allowing for the possibility of sexual differences. Crutchfield more recently has found less independence among female students than male students in his own experiments. Cf. Crutchfield, "Conformity and Character," *American Psychologist,* X (1955), 196, and "Personal and Situational Factors in Conformity to Group Pressures," a paper read at the Fifteenth International Congress of Psychologists in Brussels (1957).

percent were independents. The most significant finding for my purposes was in support of the hypothesis that the yielders would exhibit more general intolerance of ambiguity than the independents, or, in Barron's words, "that Independents would be more likely than Yielders to be able to deal comfortably with complex, apparently contradictory phenomena."[119]

This supportive evidence was furnished by the administration of a Figure Preference test. Barron had in previous experiments demonstrated that authoritarians tend to prefer simplicity in art, unlike nonauthoritarians who tend to prefer some complexity.[120] This difference is likely to be due to different levels in general tolerance of ambiguity. He found in the present experiment that the yielders were significantly more likely than the independents to prefer the simple figures.

A variety of other tests was given at the same time, and many different tentative conclusions are reported. Let me mention only one more of these: "Independents tend to be in communication with their own inner life and feelings, and are introceptive rather than extraceptive. They have empathy."[121] In other words, those who are high in psychological freedom—or are aware of their own basic experience and needs—tend to have more propensity for independence of judgment than those who are low in psychological freedom. The latter, in the absence of a strong internal anchoring of fundamental attitudes and beliefs will presumably be more dependent on external cues. They cannot develop the same degree of autonomy.

It has been suggested in the previous subsection that a high psychological freedom increases the chances for a high potential freedom.[122] This is not yet a confirmed empirical finding; it is only a hypothesis, even if it is a very plausible hypothesis on theoretical grounds. Barron's data certainly do not detract from its plausibility, to say the very least.

The best supporting evidence to date has been supplied by Richard S. Crutchfield, in a series of recent experiments, and his research technique is likely to furnish conclusive evidence on our hypothesis within the foreseeable future. Briefly described, Crutchfield has invented an apparatus that makes it possible to perform Asch-type experiments without the use of stooges; every subject participating is naïve about the purpose of the experiment. Five subjects at a time are seated next to each other in cubicles, are exposed to the same problems presented on slides, and each is asked to indicate his own answer by turning the appropriate switch on a panel in his cubicle. He is in most cases receiving "information" automatically about how the others are answering before he is called on to give his own answer, by the appearance of small numbers on his panel. But the wiring is so arranged that it is the experimenter, seated behind the subjects, who is sending the "information," which in all the test trials is distorted in order

---

[119] "Some Personality Correlates of Independence of Judgment," *Journal of Personality*, XXI, No. 3 (1953), 291 and 287–97.

[120] Cf. "Complexity-Simplicity as a Personality Dimension," *Journal of Abnormal and Social Psychology*, XLVIII, No. 2 (1953), 163–72; and above, p. 201.

[121] "Some Personality Correlates of Independence of Judgment," *Journal of Personality*, XXI (1953), 296.

[122] Cf. above, p. 359.

to give the Asch-type test of independence of judgment.[123] Perhaps the principal advantage of this innovation in technique is in the fact that the experimenter does not need any "conspirators" and can test several subjects at the same time.[124] This opens the way for testing carefully sampled populations in the future.

Crutchfield's preliminary data derive mainly from a study of fifty male participants in a three-day assessment program at the Institute of Personality Assessment and Research at the University of California in Berkeley. Their average age was 34 years; most of them but not all had had some college training. Forty other participants were used as control subjects, who gave their judgments without being exposed to "information" about the answers delivered by the others. "The distribution of judgments of these control subjects on each slide was subsequently used as a baseline for evaluating the amount of group pressure influence on the experimental subjects."[125]

The proportions of yielders and independents were rather similar to those obtained by Asch in comparable experiments. But the fact that Crutchfield's subjects were subjected to a large number of other tests under the assessment program provided a previously unmatched opportunity for discovering personality correlates of independence of judgment.

The over-all result is a striking demonstration that the yielders, or "conformers" as Crutchfield calls them, tend to be high scorers on most of the measures relating to characteristics of the authoritarian syndrome.[126] For example, F scale scores correlated .39 with conformity; the conformers tended to have relatively nonpermissive attitudes toward children; they tended to have less self-insight, less ability to tolerate ambiguity, more idealization of parents, more racial prejudice, and a greater emphasis on external and socially approved values.

The significance of this type of experiment for understanding political conformity pressures is brought out very strikingly in Crutchfield's report. For his technique was adapted as well to questions about political attitudes as to purely perceptual tests. Let me quote from his report:

Here are two salient examples (of conformity tendencies pertaining to social issues). An expression of agreement or disagreement was called for on the following statement: "Free speech being a privilege rather than a right, it is proper for a society to suspend free speech whenever it feels itself threatened." Among control subjects, only 19 per cent express agreement. But among the experimental subjects when confronted with a unanimous group consensus agreeing with the statement, 58 per cent express agreement.

Another item was phrased as follows: "Which one of the following do you feel is the most important problem facing our country today?" And these five alternatives were offered: Economic recession. Educational facilities. Subversive activities. Mental health. Crime and corruption.

---

[123] "Conformity and Character," *American Psychologist*, X (1955), 191–98.

[124] Crutchfield followed the example of Asch in that he always interviewed the subjects after each experimental session and always informed them fully about the nature and purpose of the deception.

[125] "Conformity and Character," *American Psychologist*, X (1955), 192.

[126] Cf. above, Chap. 4, pp. 194–205.

Among control subjects, only 12 per cent chose "Subversive activities" as the most important. But when exposed to a spurious group consensus which unanimously selected "Subversive activities" as the most important, 48 per cent of the experimental subjects expressed this same choice.

I think that no one would wish to deny that here we have evidence of the operation of powerful conformity influences in the expression of opinion on matters of critical social controversy.[127]

There are many empirical studies of resistance to propaganda available in the literature, but most of them are trying to bring out the general psychological and social mechanisms involved in mass communication, or the mechanisms bearing on different types of propaganda content. A few studies, however, have tried to bring out and explain some general personality differences in susceptibility to persuasion. Some of Crutchfield's data are in this category, and I shall briefly refer to one other study in this field, by Irving L. Janis.[128]

In this study seventy-eight male college students were exposed to and had to memorize the main points in three exhortatory magazine article-type communications. The first one argued that two out of three movie theaters would go out of business within the next three years as a result of television. The second argued that in two years the meat supply available for each person would be reduced to one half of the present level. The third communication predicted a completely effective cure against common colds within the next year.

All of the subjects had four weeks earlier participated in a "survey" that had also included requests for opinions on these three questions. After being exposed to the experimental propaganda, they were interviewed about their beliefs on these issues once more. On each item about two thirds now lowered their estimates, that is, changed in the direction of the propaganda assertions.[129] Thirty-two of the 78 were classified as "high" on *persuasibility*, having been influenced on all three issues, and 25 as "low," having been influenced on only one or none at all of the issues.

Clinical reports were available on 16 of the 78 subjects, since these had sought counseling on various personal problems. Hypotheses were developed from these clinical data and later tested by a personality inventory given to the whole group.

The most interesting aspect of this study, in my judgment, is in its indications that low persuasibility may be just as "neurotic" as high persuasibility, depending on the circumstances. The principal hypotheses, for which support was found, are these two: "(a) Persons with low self-esteem tend to be more readily influenced than others. (b) Persons with acute symptoms of neurotic anxiety tend to be more resistant than others."[130]

---

[127] "Conformity and Character," *American Psychologist*, X (1955), 197.

[128] "Personality Correlates of Susceptibility to Persuasion," *Journal of Personality*, XXII, No. 4 (1954), 504–18.

[129] There was also a control group that was interviewed simultaneously, before and after the experiment, but without being exposed to the propaganda.

[130] *Ibid.*, p. 518.

The first of these fits in readily with my previous discussion, but the second one might at first seem to contradict it. However, neurotic anxiety is likely to be combined with intolerance of ambiguity—or a flight into rigid cognitive categories. This is likely to increase the resistance to many types of communication, but this resistance hinges less on their contents than on the perception of the degree of authority of the communicator, in all probability.

The principal weakness in the study reported by Janis is precisely that we do not know the articulate and inarticulate perceptions or guesses each subject may have entertained as to who was arguing in each case and on what authority. But the study contributes a valuable and much needed stress on the point that conformity or nonconformity in itself is a less important issue in theory and practice than the types of processes resulting in the persistence or change of attitudes. High levels of potential freedom are indicated, not so much by nonpersuasibility and nonyielding, as by the ability to operate autonomous, need-integrated criteria for deciding when to be and when not to be influenced.

The autonomous persons, in Riesman's definition, are "those who on the whole are capable of conforming to the behavioral norms of their society . . . but are free to choose whether to conform or not."[131] In another context the same author says: "The nonconformity which I admire may be defined as a map of the world made from where the given individual sits, not from where somebody else sits—an individualized map but not a crazy one, since it has some basis in reality, including social reality."[132]

Speaking of the defensive conformists, Else Frenkel-Brunswik argues that "the absence of a genuine incorporation of the values of society accounts for the rigidity of the conformity."[133] Another possible outcome of this nonintegration of social values, as she has pointed out elsewhere, is an equally rigid nonconformity.

To achieve a high degree of individual autonomy, then, it is first of all necessary to achieve a good integration between overt behavior or consciousness and the structure of basic individual needs. If a high level of psychological freedom once has been achieved, then the individual's potential freedom is realized to the extent that his needs and behavior are related realistically to the resources and opportunities open to *him* in the external world, and to the extent that he can and will resist manipulative interference with his realistic vision. The realism of his perceptions depends on his amount of reliable information also, of course.

There is no such thing as a complete potential freedom, we have seen. I have also argued that a minimum of manipulation in favor of humanitarianism, human rights, and *general* freedom values is desirable from a total freedom maximization point of view. And I have found that the social system requirement of political authority carries a necessary minimum of special interest manipulation in its wake.

---

[131] *The Lonely Crowd*, p. 278; cf. above, p. 97.
[132] "Marginality, Conformity, and Insight," *Phylon*, XIV, No. 3 (1953), 243.
[133] *Psychoanalysis and the Unity of Science*, p. 300.

Within these limits, then, it is possible and also desirable to raise the levels of potential freedom by political means. In so far as psychological freedom can be increased, this will improve the outlook for potential freedom as well. But effective political measures toward increasing potential freedom are more probable in matters of social organization, such as improved education, encouragement of political controversy, more freedom for unpopular minorities to present their views, and other factors referred to in previous sections of this chapter.[134]

[134] Fénelon's ironic admonition is still worth remembering: "Render your subjects prosperous, and they will speedily refuse to labour; they will become stubborn, proud, unsubmissive to the yoke, and ripe for revolt. It is impotence and misery that alone will render them supple, and prevent them from rebelling against the dictates of authority." Quoted in Godwin, *Political Justice*, I, 210–11.

CONCLUSION

———

7

Policies toward Freedom

Jn the original version of his essay on the liberty of the press, Hume concluded that "this liberty is attended with so few inconveniences, that it may be claimed as the common right of mankind, and ought to be indulged them almost in every government." This statement expresses an important aspect of my approach, too. Hume had ridiculed Locke's notion of "social contract" as a basis for human rights, but in passages such as this one it is apparent that he saw, as I see, the need for some functional equivalent freed of metaphysical presuppositions.[1] If a certain type of freedom is desired by some, my argument runs, and it can be extended to all who may want it without creating conflicts between them, or conflicts with other, more important freedom-demands (not just "conveniences"), then this type of freedom should *ipso facto* be considered a human right. No majority and no government should have any authority to interfere with freedoms that on this criterion can be considered human rights.

This philosophy of human rights can be considered analogous in certain respects to the philosophy of natural law. I assume that there are certain principles of justice that are potentially acceptable to all mankind. They correspond to objective requirements pertaining to certain universal human needs and can therefore be claimed as valid, potentially at least, in all cultures that permit and encourage an expanding individual freedom.

I am assuming only the most general categories of needs. In fact, it suffices for my argument to assume only one universal need—for self-expression. But I would wish to add also the need for growth: the need for expression of the potential self, or of what the individual is capable of becoming.

On this double assumption, the universal desirability of a maximal freedom for all individuals is a clear conclusion. Psychological freedom makes the individual capable of knowing and expressing what is in him; it realizes to this extent the two objectives of "know thyself" and "be thyself." Social freedom, especially freedom from coercion, gives the individual the opportunity to express himself in accordance with his inclinations, in so far as they are compatible with the essential needs of others. Potential

---

[1] Cf. Hume, *Theory of Politics,* edited by F. Watkins, pp. 132, 193–214.

freedom, especially resistance against special interest manipulation, rescues the individual from becoming the willingly exploited tool of the interests of others, and it permits him both to be concerned with the development of his own needs according to their own dynamics and with acquiring the knowledge that facilitates their optimal satisfaction.

Let me further assume that a maximal freedom is considered equally desirable for all men and women; that each human life is equally deserving of maximal opportunities for developing all its potentialities, in so far as these are not self-defeating or defeating the potentialities of others.

Here is precisely where the most difficult empirical problem arises: how do we determine the criteria for compatibilities between various freedom values for the same individual and between various freedom demands of different individuals? And in cases of conflict, how is it possible to lay down priority criteria that are potentially acceptable to all?

I cannot solve this problem, but I suggest that the most promising avenue toward a never fully attainable solution is opened up by the political and legal instrumentality of human rights. Even the most basic human rights are not natural rights in any traditional sense, for they presuppose either a government able and willing to enforce them or a demand of enforcement directed at some political authority.[2] But it is possible that they can *become* natural rights in a different sense, to the extent that the behavioral sciences can demonstrate that each right corresponds to a universal human need—a need actually or potentially rooted in all human beings everywhere.

Yet, even if and when this happens, it still is less misleading to speak of human rights rather than natural rights. A huge sum of long-term achievements in civilization and culture has developed human nature to the point at which human beings can sense a need for—to cite one example—freedom of speech. In the extreme state of nature, there are few needs beyond biological essentials common to all men. At an extremely high level of cultural development, on the other hand, one may assume that all or most men, regardless of their particular strain of culture, will experience an actual need for free speech, if not also more specialized needs such as artistic experience.[3] Throughout this argument, I presuppose the probable validity of some such theory as Maslow's, on the hierarchy of human motives. New and "higher" motives are born only as more basic and essential motives receive satisfaction, and the individual comes to take their satisfaction for granted.[4]

There is at least one more respect in which my conception of human right departs from the traditional notions of natural right. Needs that in fact can be realized for all individuals *within a given society* should provide the basis for establishing the corresponding array of human rights within that society. Human rights are freedoms that are demanded by some and are of such a nature that they can be extended to all individuals within a

[2] Cf. Friedrich, *Constitutional Government and Democracy,* p. 160.

[3] Cf. above, pp. 11–12 and especially 327.

[4] Egon Fridell, I believe, has said that in his dreams every person is a Shakespeare. We may all have creative intellectual and artistic powers deeply embedded in our nature, which may become needs for expression in a society capable of satisfying our more pressing needs.

given society without curtailing comparable or more basic freedoms in the same or in any other society. Some cultures may stress some needs or enforce some human rights at the expense of other possibilities, while other cultures may reverse these priorities between conflicting freedom demands.

The problem of determining priorities between human rights is perhaps the thorniest of all the problems raised by my approach toward a theory of the free society. What should the majority's role be in this decision-making process? We remember Solomon's advice to the father who wanted to divide his lands justly between his two sons: let the older son divide the lands in two halves, and let the younger one choose his half. Let the majority of citizens, I suggest, choose which freedoms or rights are of the more basic importance for human well-being and establish a set of general priorities—guided by the information of social scientists, but yet autonomously according to the prevailing and enduring attitudes. But let the minority of responsible rulers see to it that the more basic rights are granted under the law to all citizens without exception before conflicting and less basic rights or privileges are granted to anyone.

This is in a broad sense a statement affirming the desirability of constitutional governments for the establishment and expansion of human rights everywhere. Constitutions are, according to my position, primarily instruments for the growth of human freedom by the gradual expansion of human rights. To the extent that a constitution serves this function, it should be imbued with sanctity. To the extent that it obstructs it, or fails to protect past accomplishments in human rights, it should be disobeyed. Democratic constitutions have on the whole been favorable to the growth of effective human rights. Perhaps the reverse is also true, that the growth of freedom has been favorable to the preservation of democratic constitutions.[5]

There are several basic advantages to a constitution, particularly a constitution that enjoys the protection of an *enlightened* judicial review, in the struggle for protecting and expanding human rights. First, there is the power of a constitution, backed up by an alert court, to prevent popular majorities from abolishing the human rights of unpopular minorities.

Second, there is the establishment of a permanent presumption favoring established rights if there are conflicts with new freedom demands. The drawback to this presumption is that it also tends to favor established privileges against human rights demands. But among rights, the loss in freedom by curtailing established ones generally outweighs the gains won by instituting new ones, unless the new rights are consensually considered more essential. In such cases the heavy machinery of constitutional amendments is available, and heavy it ought to be for these purposes.

Third, constitutions are important symbols, capable of vesting the rights of the humblest minority with great national significance. Constitutions

---

[5] "To assume that this country has remained 'democratic' because of its Constitution seems to me to reverse the relation; it is much more plausible to suppose that the Constitution has remained because our society is essentially 'democratic.'" Dahl, *A Preface to Democratic Theory*, p. 143.

alone are capable of making minority human rights—rights desired only by minorities, though open to all who wish to claim them—permanently strong enough to prevail against majority preferences.

Fourth, constitutions provide procedural stability for the political struggle. They furnish the rules of the game for the democratic or pluralist political process. They offer a set of enduring criteria for the making of decisions when powerful groups are in conflict. The various sources of economic, professional, and cultural influence operate as an extraconstitutional system of checks and balances, but the constitution provides the procedures for checking and balancing.

Needless to say, the constitution proper is surrounded with a mass of social institutions and psychological incentives, which might in theory prevail even if the constitution one day were abolished. But in the last resort it is the constitution itself, in so far as people with power are loyal to it, that enjoys the protection of legal sanctions. Indirectly, however, these sanctions support also political practices that are not themselves matters of law.

This view of the significance of democratic constitutions is essentially utilitarian. I favor a constitution purely as an instrumentality in securing a maximization of freedom for all individuals. I have claimed that this objective is more susceptible to specification than the orthodox utilitarian objective of the greatest happiness for the greatest number. I have argued that freedom from coercion is the supreme good and that therefore freedom from coercion should be the first priority objective. As a second priority consideration, however, freedom of political speech should take precedence over other freedoms, since it is instrumentally more crucial than other freedoms. And freedom of such political speech as in effect and intention is limited to the discussion of general principles should under no circumstances be curtailed.

An equally important advantage in specificity is gained by my rejection of the majoritarian felicity calculus in favor of a human right approach, which focuses on the freedom enjoyed by the marginal man. It is for the majority to decide on general priorities in the importance of conflicting freedom demands. Under a constitutional democratic system, this decision-making process is a crucial aspect of the continuing political struggle. It is for the political scientist, if and when he has the necessary resources of theory and research, to decide which freedom demands are universally attainable and thus should be considered human rights, except in so far as they conflict with more basic human rights. It is for the government and the courts, finally, to enforce the constitution and the laws by seeing to it that the established human rights are granted to all and to extend human rights according to preferred priorities within the limits of what is possible. The priority scheme should itself be in the constitution, to prevent frequent changes, but it should in principle be based ultimately on majority decisions—regardless of whether the majority enjoys a level of potential freedom sufficient to permit us to speak of a genuine majority choice.

Since I focus my attention on the marginal, least privileged man, it is much easier for me to measure trends in freedom than it would be for a

Benthamite to measure trends in the happiness of the greatest number. The case study method can give important data, given the present approach. And, since various kinds of marginal men are more likely than others to seek or become exposed to court decisions, it is possible to study cases quantitatively and thus arrive at tentative conclusions on trends.

When this has been said, it remains to be stressed that the difficulties in achieving reliable and valid quantitative techniques in this field remain very great. The hope for progress rests perhaps primarily on an improved body of political theory, which is capable of producing increasingly realistic research models.[6] The function of these models is to make explicit all the necessary assumptions bearing on an empirical inquiry, to guide the interpretation of data, and to make it possible to manipulate the various factors as constants or variables, as research circumstances and improving insights permit. This field of inquiry is in the foetus stage, but it is certainly capable of being born alive, given the research techniques developed in neighboring disciplines. Practical studies utilizing the felicity calculus are to the present writer more difficult to envisage.

By focusing on the freedom of the least free, we may one day be able to estimate differences in levels of freedom between different countries in a nonpartisan spirit and with the authority of science backing up our findings.

But there are two good reasons for not venturing into intercountry studies yet. First, we are not ready for them, either in terms of theory or in terms of research techniques. It is much more feasible to study trends in a given country or, even more, in a given community. Intercountry comparisons of this nature should not be tried before theories and techniques have been improved in a series of acceptable studies of trends over time within given countries.

Second, trend studies are really much more important for advancing the cause of freedom than are international comparisons. Different countries have different histories. When we consider what Russian society was like only fifty years ago, for example, it is no wonder that its standards of living and of freedom today in most respects that we consider important are inferior to those of the advanced Western countries. What I would find much more significant than comparative studies would be some data on trends in freedom, in Russia as well as in other countries. Intercountry comparative research studies, even if they were possible today, could easily have their meaning distorted and become part of the propaganda struggle of the Cold War. Used in this way, they would serve to hinder rather than

[6] Harold Lasswell in his Presidential Address to the American Political Science Association in 1956 has taken an optimistic view of the adequacy of available scientific resources for many practical purposes. He deplores the dearth of effective contributions so far by his profession toward national policy-making: "We have displayed no intellectual initiative in furnishing guidance to those who are in command of modern knowledge and its instrumentalities." However, the intellectual tools of political science are now advanced enough, he argues, to make important practical contributions feasible. For one thing, it is possible now on a scientific basis "to project a comprehensive image of the future for the purposes of indicating how our overriding goal values are likely to be affected if current policies continue." Cf. "The Political Science of Science," *American Political Science Review*, L, No. 4 (1956), 967, 978, and 961–79.

help the growth of freedom and human rights in the various countries—unless one takes the psychologically indefensible view that the West can aid human rights in the communist world by keeping international tensions high and scaring the men in Moscow and Peiping.

An example of this internationalist dilemma is furnished by the way the deliberations in the United Nations Commission on Human Rights have been carried on. Mutual recriminations between communists and anti-communists have been prevalent, rather than serious attempts at suggesting gradual improvements in a nonrecriminatory spirit. And press reports have tended to stress the rivalry even more, at the expense of cooperative attitudes.

In short, I for one should want to contribute to comparative research projects on the state of human rights in different countries only on one condition, assuming now that adequate theoretical models and techniques were at hand: I should want to be very sure that the data were intended primarily as a guide for improvements, in an internationalist spirit, and not as materials to prove how bad or inferior a given country or a given political system is.

"Human right" is strictly speaking a conception that knows of no national boundaries. And my position is that if a certain freedom is readily attainable all over the world, so far as natural resources and scientific knowledge are concerned, then it should be considered a universal human right. If in some countries economic or political privilege gets in the way, I consider this a violation of human rights. For a human right is born, I have argued, the moment it becomes clear that it is objectively attainable without prejudice to other rights, provided it is desired by some of those concerned.

Given the present division of the world into states, it is within each state that the practicality of human rights must be determined. Countries with different cultural and political heritages may differ today in their ability to guarantee various freedoms to all citizens, even given the best intentions on the part of the governments concerned. The struggle for freedom maximization must for practical reasons also be fought within each country in order to institute the desirable changes in national constitutions, laws, and practices.

But humanity is one, and he who cares for freedom and human rights cares for freedom and human rights everywhere. He will not only hold that suppression abroad is a potential threat against freedom at home, but also that suppression is evil wherever it occurs. There are anthropologists who have tended to carry their respect for other people's cultures to the point where they in theory would condone and wish to preserve even the harshest oppression of the individual provided this pattern is traditional. After the last war the position of "cultural relativism" was very widely supported among American anthropologists. The executive board of the American Anthropological Association in 1947 even submitted a letter to the United Nations Commission on Human Rights, in which it was urged that questions of rights can only be judged in the context of specific cultures.

Three principles were advanced, apparently with the authority of the Association to back them up:

[1] The individual realizes his personality through his culture, hence respect for individual differences entails a respect for cultural differences. [2] Respect for differences between cultures is validated by the scientific fact that no technique of qualitatively evaluating cultures has been discovered. [3] Standards and values are relative to the culture from which they derive so that any attempt to formulate postulates that grow out of the beliefs or moral codes of one culture must to that extent detract from the applicability of any Declaration of Human Rights to mankind as a whole.[7]

This is a strange set of conclusions, and I believe that few of the leading anthropologists today would wish to sign the same document. Some have taken issue strongly with the position of cultural relativism.[8] Granted that one should have respect for cultural differences, it by no means follows that cultures cannot be evaluated or that standards and values are relative to each culture. For free individuals, standards and values are ideally matters of individual choice. Every person's choice is influenced by his culture, but the great men of various cultures have exhibited so much similarity in values that one must assume that there are either universal human propensities or universal cultural elements, or more likely both. But even if this had not been the case, the standards each of us has should be absolute for each of us. So far from refraining from evaluating other cultures, all informed individuals should do as much evaluating as possible, to exert crosscultural influence favoring mutual understanding and improvements toward a crosscultural humanitarianism. It is preposterous to state that there is no technique for "qualitatively evaluating cultures." The techniques are legion, provided only that we make our values and thus our evaluation criteria explicit in each context and do not generalize in praise or condemnation from a narrow set of criteria.

What remains valid in the cited recommendations is the underlying conviction that the relationship between personality and culture is an extremely complex one and that outsiders should not tamper with other people's culture without being aware of the vast range of consequences that may ensue. Whole cultures have been destroyed in the past by the well-intended efforts of missionaries and others who wanted to help without knowing how. Even people with empiricist leanings in their own countries have often assumed that "primitive" cultures were simple and that "enlightened" legislation could be introduced by colonial government *fiat*. They have in such settings behaved like eighteenth-century rationalists and would have deserved a rebuke by Edmund Burke.

I conclude, then, that empirical problems of human rights extension must, indeed, be seen in their complex cultural settings. But my commitment to the raising of individual freedom levels everywhere recognizes neither national nor cultural boundaries.

---

[7] "Statement on Human Rights" by the Executive Board, American Anthropological Association, June 24, 1947, in *American Anthropologist*, XLIX, No. 4 (1947), 539–43.

[8] Cf. above, especially pp. 12–13 and 243–44; and also pp. 232, 235–38, and 328.

THE PROPER SCOPE AND LIMITS OF MAJORITY
INFLUENCE IN A FREE SOCIETY

The present problem can be viewed as in part a short-range and in part a long-range policy problem. Partly, it is the problem of what actual influence majorities, nonautonomous as their members largely are, should have on the policies of contemporary societies aspiring toward freedom. Partly, it is the problem of the long view: if societies become more genuinely free, and majorities achieve increased autonomy in political attitudes, how much majority influence would then be desirable?

I shall inquire into the long-range problem first, since it is closer to an ideal type formulation. Since this inquiry will have consequences for my discussion of the more practical contemporary problem, the latter can be discussed more briefly afterwards. But note that it is not, in a strict sense, an ideal type problem I am now about to consider, for I am concerned with attainable degrees of freedom and autonomy, not theoretically extreme degrees: How free can a society become, under optimal conditions,[9] and given powerful policy efforts toward the maximization of freedom for all during many years? This is a very general question, permitting only a very general answer, but that will do for present purposes.

Levels of psychological freedom can become very high, given optimal conditions also for the child in most families, even if repressions and defensiveness in my broad sense surely cannot be entirely abolished. Levels of social freedom, also, can be high, since it is sociologically possible to approach a society that can get along without coercion. Levels of potential freedom pose a more complex problem: they can be raised but not as much as the levels of psychological or social freedom. In the first place, the social system's requirement for a minimum of political authority necessitates some manipulation that invariably tends to include some special interest manipulation. The mere fact also of living in a society necessitates many other kinds of limitations on potential freedom, limitations that need not be considered undesirable in any way. (All value commitments limit our potential freedom, but they are not for that reason undesirable.)

How autonomous can a majority become, under optimal conditions? This question is the same as the question I have just tried to answer, about how much potential freedom it is possible to achieve. Let us assume that there is considerable resistance to special interest manipulation and that up to half of the desires of a large majority are genuinely autonomous, with only the remaining half induced by propaganda and promotion serving special or general interest. (This may be a much too optimistic assumption, even if such a measurement were possible.) In such a society the autonomous component of the will of the majority would be likely to be humanistically oriented and in favor of further advances in freedom. Even on this assumption, however, I should be in favor of considerable constitutional limitations on majority influence, on three principal grounds. In the first place, there are certain questions to which there are, or can be developed, right and wrong answers. Some of these that bear intimately on the ex-

---

[9] Such as peace in the world, absence of internal dissension on the desirability of freedom, high levels of mental health and education, etc.

tension of individual freedom ought in principle to be removed from decisions by majorities—even humanistic, tolerant majorities.

Second, there are many questions that require much information and work as a prerequisite to an intelligent answer. Some of these that bear intimately on the possibilities for consistent policy-making and policy coordination over time ought again to be handled by those who are competent. The number also of even simple questions decided by majorities should be limited, for many simple questions may require as much time and effort as a few complex ones.

Third, there are policy decisions that may or may not affect minority groups detrimentally without being of great concern to majorities. These should be subject to a veto by minorities who can prove that their human rights have been infringed on, or that they in other ways have been unjustly treated.

Brief elaborations are called for.

The human rights approach to the maximization of freedom distinguishes between rights and privileges: rights can be extended to all citizens, privileges by their nature to some only.[10] This very criterion of "right" makes it in part an empirical question whether a certain desired value is a right or not. To the extent that the resources of an advanced science of political behavior are available, it is in principle possible to state whether a given value can be given to all. I say *in part*, for there will frequently be detrimental consequences for other rights, and then the question of value priorities comes in.

To the extent, however, that certain freedoms have become generally recognized as more basic than others, it is for the political scientist to state whether they can become vindicated as human rights or not. If a positive conclusion is reached, on the basis of solid evidence, then a free society should be committed to extend this freedom (perhaps access to the best medical care or to planned parenthood information—to choose somewhat controversial examples) to all its citizens, regardless of majority opinion.

General priorities between freedoms must ultimately be decided by majorities, however, since these are questions of value.[11] Given my present optimistic assumptions, these majority decisions will be enlightened and humanistic. Decisions on the extent of privilege, or about degrees of tolerance for traditional privileges, must also in principle be under the majority's jurisdiction, since privileges tend to affect the majority's opportunities adversely, at least in some respects.

Now the second category of questions—those that require much information and work for intelligent answers and bear intimately on the possibilities for consistent policy-making.

Many theorists have implied, but few have asserted explicitly, that the ideal and ideally desirable democracy would have all political questions

[10] Cf. above, pp. 6–7.
[11] However, there ought to be a strong presumption against curtailing a once established human right; only a complete consensus on the superior importance of an alternate, conflicting right should make it yield.

settled by majority vote. Even Rousseau, who would in principle have the ideal "general will" settle all issues, did certainly not consider a majority vote an infallible criterion of this will. Today, most political scientists who have devoted any attention to the practical problems involved would agree with L. T. Hobhouse, who wrote almost fifty years ago that "the multiplication of elections is not good for the working of democracy."[12]

Speaking of the tendency in many American states toward placing a variety of issues on the ballot, combining elections with numerous referenda, Harold F. Gosnell, a contemporary political scientist, observes: "The jungle ballot in the United States is a product of the utilitarian theory which emphasizes the rational character of human behavior. . . . In the United States the elective principle has been carried to an absurd extreme. Psychologists and publicists have pointed out for many years that the voters are capable of exercising only the most general choices."[13] Gosnell speaks of a "fatigue curve" in the voter's interest in political issues.[14]

Even in the very free society I am postulating for the moment, I do not expect voters to be thoroughly rational and well-informed on all issues. I believe Gosnell's fatigue curve is a general psychological phenomenon, not a product of present-day democracies. I assume that the voter will be motivated to, and capable of exercising, many more choices than he can manage today, but not all equally well. I assume as a general rule for all imperfect societies that *the more issues the voters are asked to decide, the less thought and attention the average voter will give to each issue.*

I conclude that most policy questions, and above all the technical questions and the questions of detail, should be decided by those who govern, not by the majority, also in the society that I hope to see in the future. This for two reasons: the chances that the remaining questions will be subject to approximately genuine majority decisions will be increased; and, what is at least equally important, the government's opportunity to govern will also be increased. There will be better hope for consistency among government policies, so that the one does not defeat the purposes of the other. And there will be better hope for consistency over time also, so that a policy may endure and be tested by experience regardless of short-term changes in the moods of the electorate.

But what I insist on as essential is that the most basic issues must be decided by majority vote, except in so far as they affect the extension of once established human rights. And on the basic issues the voters must be offered real possibilities for choice.

The tenor of Lippmann's book *The Public Philosophy* appears to be that issues of foreign policy are too complex for the average man to understand and that the authority of the expert and the statesman should be much increased in this field. I agree that many specific problems of foreign policy —the less important ones—ought to be left to the government's discretion. But here is precisely an area in which the majority should be given much more real influence on the basic issues than it has today, for issues of peace

---

[12] *Liberalism*, p. 247.

[13] *Democracy: The Threshold of Freedom*, pp. 270–72.

[14] *Ibid.*, p. 275.

and war affect everybody's freedom fundamentally. And these basic issues can be simplified much more than most governments would like to admit.

The most basic political question, in a sense, is one that the average man can answer with more authority than anyone else: does he like the present state of affairs? Does he want the government and its policies to continue, or does he insist on a change? At intervals of a few years this question ought to be put before the voters, and they ought to have a real choice between alternative men and alternative policies, domestic as well as foreign.

The greater the number of issues placed before the people, the greater is the opportunity of manipulators to create the attitudes they want on the more important issues, with the greatest stakes for rulers as well as ruled. In my hypothetical free society, the tendencies will be the same, if the effects less extreme. Consequently, I favor a constitution under which genuine majority choice on the most basic issues is assured, at the expense of majority influence on less basic issues. The less basic issues should, also in the interest of more consistency in the fullfillment of the more basic mandates, be largely left to the goverment's discretion. M. Alderton Pink quotes with disapproval from an editorial in the *London Times* many years ago; I quote the same lines with approval, in line with the foregoing considerations: "The Parliamentary system has not only to express but to organize the national will, and above all to found a national policy on it. It has to relate government to opinion, but it has also to convert opinion into government. The end of representation is, after all, not representation but government itself."[15] To Pink, this conception indicates the failure of representative government; to me, such a system would indicate its triumph, if by "organizing the national will" is meant making articulate the basic needs or wishes of the majority and relating them to the basic political issues.

Thirdly, certain policy decisions may or may not affect minority groups detrimentally, without being of great concern for majorities.

Democratic government has been called a process of "steady appeasement of relatively small groups."[16]

The late William James is said to have observed that democracy is a system of government in which the government does something and waits to see who "hollers." Then it does something else in order to relieve the "hollering" as best it can and waits to see who "hollers" at the adjustment.[17]

Politics must in large measure proceed by trial and error—especially in view of the limited guidance political scientists have been able to provide up to now. But even with the best scientific resources government, like science itself, must try out new ideas and policies every so often, and it cannot be sure in advance that some people will not be hurt.

The point I wish to make here is that the majority should not, even in a much improved society, be the sovereign judge of whether a minority got hurt or not. The minority in question can give a more valid answer—though not, of course, an impartial one.

[15] *A Realist Looks at Democracy*, pp. 176–77.
[16] Dahl, *A Preface to Democratic Theory*, p. 146.
[17] Smith, *The Promise of American Politics*, pp. 199–200.

This is really an application of the first of my three principles for limiting the proper scope for majority rule. While the majority ultimately must approve some general scheme of priorities in human rights, it is not for the majority to pass on whether all should be entitled to the once established or generally preferred and enforceable human rights. It is for the legal and political experts to decide whether the minority that hollers is justified in hollering. Ideally, the criterion in this decision, whether it is taken ultimately by the courts or by the government, should not be the power of the minority groups in question, but only the question of whether human rights or equal justice under the law has been denied. Weak minorities need redress more urgently than strong minorities do. The decision on whether a grievance is justified is a judicial one, and is probably best handled by an independent judiciary.

So far I have assumed a much freer and more tolerant population than we have today. I have chosen to formulate my principal preferences on the scope of majority influence in the framework of these assumptions, which are the most optimistic I can imagine with respect to the possible competence, humanitarianism, and tolerance of a majority. Even under such circumstances, then, I favor three kinds of limitations on majority influence. Majorities should never be allowed to curtail more basic rights in the interest of less basic rights or privileges. Majorities should not decide less basic issues until they have become competent and motivated to make genuine decisions on more basic issues. Majorities should not have the authority to decide whether or not minority interests have been unjustly victimized.

In the present society, given contemporary patterns of mass manipulation, I am certainly not in favor of a greater scope for majority decisions than in the more ideal society I have had in mind till now. The question one must ask is whether there ought to be some further limitations on majority influence in the democratic societies existing today.

In the following discussion of current realities I prefer to talk of majority vote instead of majority influence, since the latter term has been used to designate *autonomous* or independent influence. And in discussing the role of majority vote, I shall refer to general elections as well as the majority vote in a national legislature, which is an instrumentality supposed to represent a majority vote in the electorate. Representative democracy is, of course, something very different from direct democracy, and great libraries have been written to explain and argue about the nature of this difference. I am making no assumptions in the following discussion to the effect that representatives really *represent* the electorate. I am making only two assumptions, both of which I believe are realistic. Both the representatives and their constituents are deficient in potential freedom, and thus frequently induced to work for purposes not truly their own (and also not truly those of their constituents, in the case of representatives). Secondly, there tend to be, under normal circumstances, roughly parallel trends in the moods and policy orientations in majorities of national assembly members and in majorities of articulate constituents. Minority views among constituents are frequently unrepresented, but majority opinions are usually heeded, in normal times, whatever their origins.

It would have been easy to argue that the institution of majority vote in the modern state should be almost entirely abolished, had there been any alternative more conducive to freedom than a democratic constitution. But the fact is that majoritarian institutions, while they do not by magic transform men into autonomous individuals, immune to special interest propaganda, nevertheless permit and sometimes encourage the expression of whatever autonomy has been achieved.[18] It is in itself no tragedy that people vote the way they are told, moreover, unless they are told to vote in a way that curtails or endangers established levels of freedom. Majoritarian democracy tends to permit more flexibility than oligarchy or autocracy, and it therefore offers the better chances for growth toward more autonomy in most people. Besides, there is less coercion in states with free elections, since voters tend to react against flagrant coerciveness in most cases. And the right to vote is likely to be one factor tending to enhance psychological freedom. The average man has a personal stake in the majoritarian conception of democracy: it is an aspect of his dignity as an individual that he believes he has as much power as his neighbor or anyone else when election time comes.[19]

Majoritarian institutions are not tampered with without some risk. I believe, nevertheless, that limitations such as those suggested above can and should be promoted, by democratic constitutional means. The concept of *human rights* granted equally to all has a strong appeal to majorities, much stronger than the concept of *minority rights* that in the past often was equivalent with property privileges. The idea of reserving only the more basic decisions for the public may be harder to get widely accepted, but this may change if most people become aware of the extent to which their neighbors are in fact being manipulated by special intersets.[20] Some voters may also consider the need for long-term policy planning a crucial consideration on this issue. The third proper limitation on majority rule in a free society—of not permitting majorities to be the judges of minority complaints—is to some extent practiced today in various democracies, especially in countries where the courts have the power of judicial review of legislation and governmental decisions.[21]

[18] E. M. Forster offers *two* cheers for democracy, "one because it permits variety and two because it permits criticism." *Two Cheers for Democracy*, p. 79. Apart from that, he has not much to say in its favor, but this is no mean accomplishment of our civilization, to the extent that it is being preserved in our democracies.

[19] Perhaps this is an exaggeration, since many people do not vote, or do not see their right to vote as important in these terms. But I believe this point of view is an inarticulate potential also in such people; it would become articulate in most of them if they should be denied the right to vote.

[20] In some countries, notably Switzerland, in which the many votes make citizenship quite a burden, my proposal might for that reason have some appeal. One of the principal reasons why many Swiss women are against female suffrage is precisely the amount of work that it takes to exercise the right to vote.

[21] But there are exceptions. For example, when these lines were written it was reported in the Oslo morning papers (October 26, 1955) that the Norwegian Secretary of Justice had resigned, since a majority in the Parliament had turned down his plan for paying damages that he believed the state owed to one unpopular minority: public officials who had been suspended or fired after the war for conduct during the war but who had never been found guilty of treason in the courts.

Further limitations are feasible and desirable in at least one direction, I believe. Cultural and educational matters should so far as possible be under the jurisdiction of those who have a strong concern for these questions. And the media of mass communication, since they have a strong impact on cultural and educational developments, ought to be subjected in one way or another to the modifying influence of educators and cultural elites.[22]

This is a controversial problem area, in which there are some temptations toward limiting oneself to vague generalities. However, these last pages of my study are frankly devoted to stating some of this writer's policy preferences, given the ideals and reality-conceptions expounded in previous chapters. At this point I shall yield to the opposite temptation, therefore, and be quite specific and controversial in my recommendations. They are not the only possible deductions from my general position, it should be stressed, and the following policy suggestions are only tentatively put forward, aiming at discussion rather than adoption.

I shall pass quickly over the question of educational curricula and problems of priorities in scientific research. Nobody would wish majority votes to decide which authors should be used in school texts, even if some misguided people in America and elsewhere have urged a majority veto against various objectionable authors. Again, nobody has suggested that majority votes should guide scientists in their research—except possibly the scientists studying public opinion.

It is true that state educational systems in principle are subject to some control by those who finance them, namely, the legislatures. But only the very basic policy issues such as criteria for admittance are the proper concern of the legislators. More specific issues in education are widely conceded to be the business of the specialists in education.

It is also true, and it was even more true in Thorstein Veblen's days,[23] that business interests in America often have interfered with the freedom to teach, by virtue of their power on innumerable boards of trustees, but also by virtue of the high prestige of businessmen in American communities. "In no other country," as Laski has observed, "is it so simply assumed that the opinions of a successful businessman are important."[24] It is a sad paradox that the ideas of specialists in making money are much more highly valued, on the whole, than the ideas of specialists in ideas. But American businessmen are gradually becoming better educated, it would seem, and are also developing more respect for the educators and their demands for autonomy. And through the great foundations, the fruits of much big business in America are distributed to promote education and scientific knowledge under the guidance of many of the best scientists and educa-

---

[22] "Cultural elite" may be a dangerous term to use. I am referring to professional intellectuals and creative artists, but also to all others who have strong interests and competence in these questions. Elites are dangerous only if they are closed to outsiders; a genuine cultural elite is always anxious to widen its circle.

[23] Cf. *The Higher Learning in America: A Memorandum on the Conduct of Universities by Business Men.*

[24] *The American Democracy*, p. 170.

tors. Thus, one important minority is gradually to a greater extent sharing its influence with another—the proper one. The influence of the majority of the electorate is not being substantially increased, which is fortunate.[25] Nobody has yet proposed that professors should be elected or research grants awarded by majority vote.

But in the media of mass communication there is much talk about the sovereignty of popular preferences. This kind of talk frequently serves as a cloak for special interests who are doing their utmost, intentionally or not, to keep these preferences at adolescent levels.[26] The principle of freedom of the press serves to buttress economic interests of publishers, we have seen;[27] and when trash is poured out on the market because people buy it, those same interests will have us believe that it would be undemocratic to oppose the mass production and distribution of what people want.

But the media of mass communication probably have an impact on most people's education and personality development equal to if not much stronger than that of the schools.[28] If this is the case, as I believe it is, then I reject the doctrine of consumer democracy in the area of mass communication. I wish, for one thing, to see the privileged freedom of publishers reduced in order to promote the potential and psychological freedom of the whole citizenship. I do not favor a ban on trash, except possibly in the field of children's reading, and on the more extreme sadism-, perversion-, and brutality-portraying literature *if it can be established reliably* that these materials, in fact, breed sadism, brutality, or perversion.[29] But I would recommend such measures as public subsidies to encourage publications maintaining high standards, whether in journalism or in fiction, and a nonconfiscatory but severe taxation of the worst publications. I believe there are groups of outstanding scientists and artists in all countries capable of judging the question of quality and of reaching unanimous verdicts on what

[25] The Reece Committee's investigation of the large foundations was one recent attempt to bring pressure to bear on behalf of the electorate. It may have had some limited effect toward discouraging boldness in the policies of some foundations, but on the whole this foray under democracy's banner appears to have been a propitious failure.

[26] A theory of the economic and political dynamics of this tendency is presented in C. Wright Mills, *The Power Elite,* Chap. 13: "The Mass Society," pp. 298–342. See especially p. 317: "The standard strategy of manipulation is to make it appear that the people, or at least a large group of them, 'really made the decision.' "

[27] See above, pp. 350–51.

[28] J. B. Priestley is a pessimist on this score: What guarantee do we have, that even the best schools "can successfully challenge the proprietors of the *Daily Scream,* the TV, radio and film experts, the advertising gang, the haters of the arts, the slow murderers of eager hopeful living. Who, so far, is winning all along the line?" He concludes: "Meanwhile, we spend more and more on Education, hoping rather desperately that somehow and sometime the values of the school will triumph over those of the streets outside the school. And this costs so much that we cannot afford to change and improve the towns that receive our boys and girls after they have left school. The environment they know in their later teens, probably their most formative years, is a dreary mess of cheap commercial values, in which any fire kindled in the classroom is likely to be soon damped down and smothered." *Thoughts in the Wilderness,* pp. 52–53.

[29] I doubt that there will ever be any evidence to suggest that there are any harmful effects of straight, merely lust-provoking pornography, on the other hand, and therefore I see no basis for censorship here, except *possibly* restrictions on sale to minors. Cf. Walter Gellhorn, "The Supreme Court on Obscenity," *Columbia University Forum,* I, No. 1 (1957), 38–40.

is really bad, without political or artistically sectarian or antisectarian prejudice.

In the communist countries the press has been given primarily an educational function, but it has also been put in a political straitjacket that would be intolerable in the West. But is there no third choice, as J. B. Priestley has asked, or must we either have the *Daily Screamer,* or the *Official Gazette?*[30] I believe institutions such as the British Broadcasting Corporation and its Scandinavian counterparts point toward a third alternative, and I believe there is some hope that developments of this kind are possible also in the newspaper business, though the time is probably not ripe yet. I do not hope for an eventual public newspaper monopoly, however. Instead I should like to see established local and national public press councils, with some limited powers toward creating incentives for increasing the standards and improving the taste and honesty in newspapers and magazines. These councils should not be elected by majority vote. They should be appointed, and ideally they should consist of three kinds of people: educators, journalists and other publicists, and consumers.[31]

This type of measure is suggested only because I believe that present levels of potential freedom are grossly inadequate to prevent successful special interest manipulation by the mass media, in favor of producing public demands for ever lower levels of taste and intelligence in newspapers and magazines. If majorities become autonomous enough to resist this trend, and to demand more quality in the publications they buy and support, then I should favor a return to the present almost complete absence of public attempts at regulation.

Even in a much freer society than ours, if I may summarize, I should favor three kinds of limitations on majority influence: Decisions about the extension of human rights should be automatically in favor of the individual, to the extent that general priorities are consensually established. Minor policy questions should be left to the government, to increase its ability to govern and to increase the prospect for effective majority choice on the main issues. Questions of equal justice under law and equity for complaining minorities should be settled, not by majorities, but by judicial procedures.

In our own society I favor these same limitations on majority rule and at least one more: In cultural and educational matters the greatest influence should be with the educators and cultural elites. In this area I include the media of mass communication. I favor reducing the privileged freedom of publishing for profit by instituting public incentive-creating agencies. But I am not in favor of significantly limiting the consumer's freedom to read what he wants.

---

[30] *Out of the People,* p. 123.

[31] Substantially the same proposals are advanced by Priestley. Cf. *ibid.,* pp. 123–24. Less specific and more moderate proposals have been made both by the American Commission on Freedom of the Press and by the British Royal Commission on the Press. Cf. *A Free and Responsible Press,* by the Commission on Freedom of the Press, esp. pp. 124–33; and the *Report of the Royal Commission on the Press 1947–1949,* esp. pp. 164–74.

THE LOYALTY OF FREE INDIVIDUALS

"If I had to choose between betraying my country and betraying my friend," says E. M. Forster, "I hope I should have the guts to betray my country. . . . Such a choice may scandalize the modern reader, and he may stretch out his patriotic hand to the telephone at once and ring up the police."[32] Chances are that the English reader will not, for the British are more tolerant of unorthodoxy than most others, even of supposedly dangerous unorthodoxy. And more important, the British authorities are less likely than most other governments to force such a choice on the individual, even in times of crisis.

It will be noted that Forster does not recommend the betrayal of one's country—whatever such a term may plausibly mean. He is not in favor of treason, any more than Locke, Hume, or Bentham were in favor of revolution. What they all affirm in much the same way is that there are limits on the legitimate authority of the state over the individual. There are limits beyond which the individual should not be obedient. Beyond these limits it is an imposture to demand obedience of the citizen, and it should be his right and perhaps his duty to himself and his personal value commitments to resist and to be "disloyal."

Socrates, Giordano Bruno, Martin Luther, Thomas More, Thoreau, Matteotti, Martin Niemöller, are all examples of men who came to a point at which they refused to obey. Many of them were crushed, but their names are paid homage today. They chose to "betray" the authorities rather than betraying other and more important commitments. By their courage, these men and countless others have made authorities hesitate more than they otherwise would before placing individuals before a choice of this nature. Those in the United States in our time who have refused to sign loyalty oaths have in a small way contributed to the same struggle for preserving and expanding the ultimate sovereignty that every society owes to the individual. The state, said Thoreau, "can have no pure right over my person and property but what I concede to it." Yet the state is likely to help itself, at various times and on different pretexts, unless there are enough citizens around who have the guts to be bad subjects.[33]

Not only guts, but also the consciousness of being an individual are prerequisites for the exercise of individual sovereignty. Also, I submit, these are criteria of a free society, analytically speaking. "When the personal consciousness emerges from the purely tribal consciousness—there is the birth of liberty."[34] A society is free, in the total sense of freedom, to the extent that its members have the capacity, opportunity, and incentive to develop the principles of their own individual consciousness and to be faithful to them above all other considerations, even if this at times should place them severely at odds with the state and with public opinion. This is to me the most plausible practical meaning of the widely accepted theory that the state should exist for the benefit of individuals rather than the other way

---

[32] *Two Cheers for Democracy*, p. 78.
[33] Cf. "Civil Disobedience," pp. 659 and 654, in *Walden and Other Writings*.
[34] Lewisohn, *Up Stream*, p. 196; cf. above, p. 340.

round. However this may be, my conclusion is that the supreme loyalty of the individual belongs to his own convictions regardless of their content.

Yet it is evident that no state can persist unless there are limits to the kinds of convictions that individuals are permitted to put into practice. Some individuals, for example, are convinced that their race or religion is superior to all others, and some may even be convinced that inferiors of one sort or another ought to be exterminated. I am not denying that these people, too, ought to be loyal to their convictions. But I am suggesting that the state must see to it that persons who wish to reduce the human rights of others must not succeed in this endeavor. They ought to be allowed to argue their case, but not to instigate or call for specific violent action.

The state, or the political authorities, should therefore to a limited extent and without the use of coercion seek to encourage certain attitudes and discourage others—but only attitudes that are necessary either (1) to insure tolerance for a variety of convictions or (2) to insure a conditional loyalty to the constitutional authorities.

The more tolerance for a variety of opinions a citizenship has developed, the more individuals can live according to their own lights without coming into conflicts with others. This depends of course in part on the contents of convictions—some are inherently antisocial and antagonistic to others. On the whole, however, I have come to the conclusion that persons who enjoy a good degree of psychological, social, and potential freedom will develop humanistic and tolerant convictions. And on the political problem of producing a maximal freedom, I have concluded that a constitutional process of gradually expanding human rights offers the best hope.

My first proposal favoring some limited manipulation of the citizenry by the political authorities may, therefore, be rephrased as follows: they should encourage attitudes of unconditional loyalty to the heritage of human rights, and a loyalty to the democratic constitution conditional *only* on its continuous service as a bulwark for human rights. Some individuals will resist this type of manipulation, and this is their right. But most reasonably healthy and free individuals will find it congenial to their own personality predispositions.

Second, I said, the state should encourage a conditional loyalty to the constitutional authorities. Every social system requires a minimum of political authority. But I have argued that I want something more than an enduring society—I want an enduringly and increasingly free society. Therefore, I ascribe to political authorities the additional task of serving the cause of freedom maximization.

This cause is not served, however, by the prevalence of unconditional loyalty to governments and their policies. Governments with *carte blanche* to govern are not likely to preserve and respect past gains in freedom. If a government knows that the people will support it unconditionally in a crisis, then a crisis is more likely to come. This holds for democracies as well as dictatorships, and it is perhaps the most dangerous single aspect of modern patriotism.

William Godwin gave a succinct expression to the doctrine of individual sovereignty in defiance of demands for unconditional national loyalty: "I have a paramount obligation to the cause of justice and to the benefit of the human race. If the nation undertake what is unjust, fidelity in that undertaking is a crime. If it undertake what is just, it is my duty to promote its success not because I am one of its citizens, but because such is the command of justice."[35] To the extent that the great and little nations develop citizens with this kind of *Zivilcourage,* they are not likely to undertake "what is unjust"; they are likely to be instruments of freedom, human rights, and peace. "A nation whose citizens are sensitive to the claims of conscience and are not afraid to follow them," says Michael Polanyi, "is a free nation."[36] This is true *provided* the individual's conscience is to some extent autonomous and not the product of special interest manipulation, and *provided* it is in harmony with the individual's basic needs.

In his book *The Loyalty of Free Men* Alan Barth is in harmony with the best parts of the American heritage when he declares that "the test of a free society is its tolerance of what is deplored or despised by a majority of its members." "The argument for such tolerance," he continues, "must be made on the ground that it is useful to the society."[37] Here I take a somewhat different view: my argument is that freedom itself is the ultimate value realizable by political means and that more basic freedoms are inherently more urgently desirable than less basic freedoms. Tolerance of unpopular minorities is more important than the convenience of the greater number, for these minorities are likely to be the least privileged in freedom, with the most basic freedoms at stake.

The prevalence of tolerance toward those who are considered disloyal is not only compatible with national loyalty; it is a prerequisite of a widespread genuine loyalty to the state, as contrasted with a manufactured semblance of loyalty. In Barth's words,

loyalty in a free society depends upon the toleration of disloyalty. The loyalty of free men must be freely given—which is to say, that those who give it must be genuinely free to withhold it. Nothing is more fundamental to freedom than that this choice be a real one. The premise on which every free society rests, the American society more explicitly than any other, is that only through such freedom can loyalty be evoked and counted on to endure.[38]

I have argued that governments ought to encourage humanistic rather than authoritarian loyalties, if their concern is with freedom or with security for their nation primarily and with their own convenience only secondarily. And I have argued that loyalty is something that may grow, given the proper conditions; only a misleading and unstable semblance of it can be produced by coercive means. The late Zechariah Chafee, Jr., one of the two or three foremost champions of American freedom in our time, has stated this insight more persuasively than I could:

Behind the dozens of sedition bills in Congress last session, behind teachers' oaths and compulsory flag salutes, is a desire to make our citizens loyal to their

[35] *Political Justice,* II, 109.
[36] *The Logic of Liberty: Reflections and Rejoinders,* p. 46.
[37] *The Loyalty of Free Men,* p. 230.
[38] *Ibid.,* p. 231.

government. Loyalty is a beautiful idea, but you cannot create it by compulsion and force. A government is at bottom the officials who carry it on: legislators and prosecutors, school superintendents and police. If it is composed of legislators who pass short-sighted sedition laws by overwhelming majorities, of narrow-minded school superintendents who oust thoughtful teachers of American history and eight-year-old children whose rooted religious convictions prevent them from sharing in a brief ceremony—a government of snoopers and spies and secret police—how can you expect love and loyalty? You make men love their government and their country by giving them the kind of government and the kind of country that inspire respect and love: a country that is free and unafraid, that lets the discontented talk in order to learn the causes for their discontent and end those causes, that refuses to impel men to spy on their neighbors, that protects its citizens vigorously from harmful acts while it leaves the remedies for objectionable ideas to counter-argument and time.[39]

My argument in this book is theoretical and general, and there is no sufficient basis for a conclusion in terms of very specific policy recommendations. What I advocate is above all a type of active humanitarian commitment—an attitude that places identification with the human race above national loyalty, and a type of respect and concern for human individuality that induces each of us to react with whatever strength we have against all serious violations of human rights, wherever they occur. And I urge a reaction proportionate to the injustice suffered, regardless of whether the victims are many or few, and regardless of whether they are considered virtuous or wicked. Moreover, no matter whether coercion or manipulation is involved, each of us should stand ready to defend the sovereignty of the individual—of any individual, and regardless of whether he claims his sovereignty or not. From the point of view of responsibility ethics, those who are satisfied with less than their proper sphere of human rights and autonomy are not only "sinned against" but also "sinning," since in effect they acquiesce in undercutting the rights and autonomy of their neighbors as well as their own.

Let us agree that man is never the proper means of any purposes other than those rooted—actually or potentially—in his own individuality. Man himself is the only end. As I understand this principle, it should mean that the maximization of every man's and woman's freedom—psychological, social, and potential—is the only proper first-priority aim for the joint human efforts that we call political.

[39] *Free Speech in the United States,* pp. 564–65.

Bibliography

Aberle, David F., A. K. Cohen, A. K. Davis, M. J. Levy, Jr., and F. X. Sutton. "The Functional Prerequisites of a Society," *Ethics*, LX, No. 2 (1950), 100–111.

Adler, Shirley. "The Effects of Ego-Involvement on Rigidity in Thinking." Unpublished Ph.D. dissertation, New York University, 1953.

Adorno, Theodor W., Else Frenkel-Brunswik, Daniel J. Levinson, and Nevitt Sanford. The Authoritarian Personality. New York: Harper, 1950.

Alexander, Franz. Fundamentals of Psychoanalysis. New York: W. W. Norton, 1948.

——— The Psychoanalysis of the Total Personality. New York: Coolidge Foundation, 1929.

Alexander, Franz, and Helen Ross. Dynamic Psychiatry. Chicago: University of Chicago Press, 1952.

Allport, Gordon W. Personality: A Psychological Interpretation. New York: Henry Holt, 1937.

Almond, Gabriel A. The Appeals of Communism. Princeton: Princeton University Press, 1954.

American Anthropological Association (Executive Board). "Statement on Human Rights," *American Anthropologist*, XLIX, No. 4 (1947), 539–43.

Anshen, Ruth Nanda, ed. Freedom: Its Meaning. New York: Harcourt, Brace, 1940.

Arendt, Hannah. The Origins of Totalitarianism. New York: Harcourt, Brace, 1951.

Aristotle. Politics. Translated by Benjamin Jowett. New York: Modern Library, 1943.

Arnold, Thurman W. The Folklore of Capitalism. Garden City, N.Y.: Blue Ribbon Books, 1937.

Asch, Solomon E. Social Psychology. New York: Prentice-Hall, 1952.

Aubert, Vilhelm. Om straffens sosiale funksjon (On the Social Function of Punishment). Oslo: Akademisk forlag, 1954.

Barker, Ernest. Reflections on Government. London: Oxford University Press, 1945.

Barnard, Chester. The Functions of the Executive. Cambridge: Harvard University Press, 1938.

Barron, Frank. "Complexity–Simplicity as a Personality Dimension," *Journal of Abnormal and Social Psychology*, XLVIII, No. 2 (1953), 163–72.

——— "Some Personality Correlates of Independence of Judgment," *Journal of Personality*, XXI, No. 3 (1953), 287–97.

Barth, Alan. The Loyalty of Free Men. New York: Viking Press, 1951.

Bay, Christian, Ingemund Gullvag, Harald Ofstad, and Herman Tennessen.

Nationalism: A Study of Identifications with People and Power. 3 vols. Oslo: Institute for Social Research, 1950–53 (mimeographed).

Becker, Carl L. Freedom and Responsibility in the American Way of Life. New York: Vintage Books, 1955. First published 1945.

Bendix, Reinhard. "Compliant Behavior and Individual Personality," *American Journal of Sociology*, LVIII, No. 3 (1952), 292–303.

Benedict, Ruth. The Chrysanthemum and the Sword: Patterns of Japanese Culture. Boston: Houghton Mifflin, 1946.

Bentham, Jeremy. Works. 10 vols. Edited by John Bowring. Edinburgh: William Tait, 1843.

Bentham, Jeremy, James Mill, and John Stuart Mill. Essays. Edited by Philip Wheelwright. New York: Doubleday, Doran, 1935.

Bentley, Arthur F. The Process of Government: A Study of Social Pressures. Chicago: University of Chicago Press, 1908.

Berelson, Bernard, Paul F. Lazarsfeld, and William N. McPhee. Voting: A Study of Opinion Formation in a Presidential Campaign. Chicago: University of Chicago Press, 1954.

Bidney, David. "The Concept of Value in Modern Anthropology," in A. L. Kroeber, ed., *Anthropology Today: An Encyclopedic Inventory*. Chicago: University of Chicago Press, 1953. Pp. 682–99.

Billig, Otto, John Gillin, and William Davidson. "Aspects of Personality and Culture in a Guatemalan Community: Ethnological and Rorschach Approaches," *Journal of Personality*, XVI, No. 3 (1948), 153–87, 326–68.

Binkley, Wilfred E., and Malcolm C. Moos. A Grammar of American Politics: The National Government. New York: Knopf, 1949.

Bishop, Hillman M., and Samuel Hendel, eds. Basic Issues of American Democracy. New York: Appleton-Century-Crofts, 1951.

Bjorklund, Eskil, and Joachim Israel. "The Authoritarian Ideology of Upbringing." Mimeographed. Uppsala: Sociologiska Institution, 1951.

Blake, Robert R., and Glenn V. Ramsey, eds. Perception: An Approach to Personality. New York: Ronald Press, 1951.

Block, Jack, and Jeanne Block. "An Investigation of the Relationship Between Intolerance of Ambiguity and Ethnocentrism," *Journal of Personality*, XIX, No. 3 (1951), 303–11.

Blum, Gerald S. Psychoanalytic Theories of Personality. New York: McGraw-Hill, 1953.

Borgatta, Edgar S. "Sidesteps toward a Non-Special Theory," *Psychological Review*, LXI, No. 5 (1954), 343–52.

Bosanquet, Bernard. Civilization of Christendom. London: Sonnenschein, 1893.

—— The Philosophical Theory of the State. London: Macmillan, 1920. First published 1899.

Boulding, Kenneth E. The Organizational Revolution. New York: Harper, 1953.

Bowlby, John. Maternal Care and Mental Health. Geneva: World Health Organization, 1952.

Bradley, Francis H. Ethical Studies (Selected Essays). New York: Liberal Arts Press, 1951.

Brady, Robert Alexander. Business as a System of Power. New York: Columbia University Press, 1943.

Brand, Howard, ed. The Study of Personality: A Book of Readings. New York: John Wiley, 1954.

Brodbeck, Arthur J., and Howard V. Perlmutter. "Self-Dislike as a Determinant of Marked Ingroup-Outgroup Preferences," *Journal of Psychology*, XXXVIII (1954), 271–80.

Bronfenbrenner, Urie. "Toward an Integrated Theory of Personality," in Robert R. Blake and Glenn V. Ramsey, eds., *Perception: An Approach to Personality*. New York: Ronald Press, 1951. Pp. 206–57.

Bronowski, J. The Face of Violence. New York: Braziller, 1955.

Bunzel, Bessie. "Suicide," *Encyclopedia of the Social Sciences*, XIV (1935), 455–59.

Burdick, Eugene, and Arthur J. Brodbeck, eds. American Voting Behavior. Glencoe, Illinois: The Free Press, 1958.

Burtt, Edwin A., ed. The English Philosophers from Bacon to Mill. New York: Modern Library, 1939.

Bury, John B. A History of Freedom of Thought. London: Home University Library, Williams & Norgate, n.d.

Cameron, James. Mandarin Red. New York: Rinehart, 1955.

Campbell, Angus, Gerald Gurin, and Warren E. Miller. "Political Issues and the Vote: November, 1952," *American Political Science Review*, XLVII, No. 2 (1953), 359–85.

Campbell, Angus, Gerald Gurin, and Warren E. Miller. The Voter Decides. Evanston, Illinois: Row, Peterson, 1954.

Campbell, Angus, and Robert L. Kahn. The People Elect a President. Ann Arbor, Michigan: Institute for Social Research, 1952.

Cantril, Hadley, ed. Tensions That Cause Wars. Urbana: University of Illinois Press, 1950.

Cartwright, Dorwin, and Alvin Zander, eds. Group Dynamics: Research and Theory. Evanston, Illinois: Row, Peterson, 1953.

Chafee, Zechariah, Jr. Free Speech in the United States. Cambridge: Harvard University Press, 1941.

Chisholm, George Brock. "The Psychiatry of Enduring Peace and Social Progress," *Psychiatry*, IX (1946), 3–20.

Christie, Richard. "The Effects of Frustration upon Rigidity in Problem Solution," *American Psychologist*, V (1950), 296–97.

——— "Eysenck's Treatment of the Personality of Communists," *Psychological Bulletin*, LIII, No. 6 (1956), 411–30.

Christie, Richard, and Marie Jahoda, eds. Studies in the Scope and Method of "The Authoritarian Personality." Glencoe, Ill.: The Free Press, 1954.

Christie, Richard, Albert T. Walkley, *et al*. An Exploratory Study of Factors Affecting Transition to Army Life. New York: Research Center for Human Relations, New York University, 1952.

Cogley, John. Report on Blacklisting. New York: Fund for the Republic, 1956.

Collier, John, and Mary Collier. "Experiment in Applied Anthropology," *Scientific American*, CXCVI (1957), 37–45.

Commission on Freedom of the Press. A General Report on Mass Communication: Newspapers, Radio, Motion Pictures, Magazines, and Books. Chicago: University of Chicago Press, 1947.

Cooley, Charles H. Social Organization. New York: Scribner, 1912.

Crutchfield, Richard S. "Conformity and Character," *American Psychologist,* X (1955), 191–98.

Curle, Adam. "Incentives to Work: An Anthropological Appraisal," *Human Relations,* II, No. 1 (1949), 41–47.

—— "The Sociological Background to Incentives," *Occupational Psychology,* XXII (1948), 21–28.

Dahl, Robert A. A Preface to Democratic Theory. Chicago: University of Chicago Press, 1956.

Dahl, Robert A., and Charles E. Lindblom. Politics, Economics, and Welfare. New York: Harper, 1953.

Davis, Allison, and R. J. Havighurst. "A Comparison of the Chicago and Harvard Studies of Social Class Differences in Child Rearing," *American Sociological Review,* XX, No. 4 (1955), 438–42.

Davis, Allison, and Robert J. Havighurst. "Social Class and Color Differences in Child Rearing," *American Sociological Review,* XI (1946), 698–710.

Dennis, Wayne. "Infant Development Under Conditions of Restricted Practice and a Minimum Social Stimulation," *Journal of Genetic Psychology,* LIII (1938), 149–58.

Dewey, John. Human Nature and Conduct: An Introduction to Social Psychology. New York: Modern Library, 1930. First published 1922.

—— "Theory of Valuation," in *International Encyclopedia of Unified Science,* Vol. II, No. 4. Chicago: University of Chicago Press, 1939.

Dollard, John, Leonard W. Doob, Neal E. Miller, O. H. Mowrer, and Robert R. Sears. Frustration and Aggression. New Haven: Yale University Press, 1939.

Dombrose, Lawrence A., and Daniel J. Levinson. "Ideological 'Militancy' and 'Pacifism' in Democratic Individuals," *Journal of Social Psychology,* XXXII (1950), 101–13.

Durkheim, Emile. The Division of Labor in Society. Translated by George Simpson. Glencoe, Illinois: The Free Press, 1933. First French edition, 1893.

—— Rules of Sociological Method. Translated by Sarah A. Solovay and John H. Müller; edited by George E. G. Catlin. Glencoe, Illinois: The Free Press, 1950. First French edition, 1895.

—— Suicide: A Study in Sociology. Translated by J. A. Spaulding and G. Simpson. Glencoe, Illinois: The Free Press, 1951. First French edition, 1897.

Easton, David. The Political System: An Inquiry into the State of Political Science. New York: Knopf, 1953.

Edwards, Ward. "The Theory of Decision Making," *Psychological Bulletin,* LI, No. 4 (1954), 380–417.

Eisenmann, Charles. "On the Matter and Method of the Political Sciences," in Contemporary Political Science: A Survey of Methods, Research and Teaching. Paris: UNESCO, 1950.

Engels, Friedrich. Anti-Dühring (Herr Eugen Dühring's Revolution in Science). London: Lawrence, 1935.

English, Horace B. A Student's Dictionary of Psychological Terms, 4th ed., in Gardner Murphy, *Personality: A Biosocial Approach to Origins and Structure.* New York: Harper, 1947.

Ericson, C. "Social Status and Child-Rearing Practices," in Theodore M. Newcomb and Eugene L. Hartley, eds., *Readings in Social Psychology.* New York: Henry Holt, 1947.

Erikson, Erik H. Childhood and Society. New York: Norton, 1950.

Evans-Pritchard, Edward E. The Nuer: A Description of the Modes of Livelihood and Political Institutions of a Nilotic People. Oxford: Clarendon Press, 1940.

Eysenck, Hans J. "Primary Social Attitudes as Related to Social Class and Political Party," *British Journal of Sociology,* II, No. 3 (1951), 198–209.

———— The Psychology of Politics. London: Routledge and Kegan Paul, 1954.

Feigl, Herbert, and May Brodbeck, eds. Readings in the Philosophy of Science. New York: Appleton-Century-Crofts, 1953.

Fenichel, Otto. The Psychoanalytic Theory of Neurosis. New York: Norton, 1945.

Festinger, Leon. "Informal Social Communication," in Leon Festinger, Kurt Back, Stanley Schachter, Harold H. Kelley, and John Thibaut, *Theory and Experiment in Social Communication.* Ann Arbor: University of Michigan Press, 1950.

Festinger, Leon, Kurt Back, Stanley Schachter, Harold H. Kelley, and John Thibaut. Theory and Experiment in Social Communication. Ann Arbor: University of Michigan Press, 1950.

Festinger, Leon, Stanley Schachter, and Kurt Back. Social Pressures in Informal Groups: A Study of Human Factors in Housing. New York: Harper, 1950.

Fisher, Lloyd H., and Grant McConnell. "Internal Conflict and Labor-Union Solidarity," in Arthur Kornhauser, Robert Dubin, and Arthur M. Ross, eds., *Industrial Conflict.* New York: McGraw-Hill, 1954.

Flowerman, Samuel H. "Portrait of the Authoritarian Man," *New York Times Magazine,* April 23, 1950.

Forster, Edward M. Two Cheers for Democracy. London: Arnold, 1954.

Frank, Lawrence K. Society as the Patient: Essays on Culture and Personality. New Brunswick: Rutgers University Press, 1950.

Frenkel-Brunswik, Else. "Further Contributions by a Contributor to 'The Authoritarian Personality,' " in Richard Christie and Marie Jahoda, eds., *Studies in the Scope and Method of "The Authoritarian Personality."* Glencoe, Illinois: The Free Press, 1954.

———— "Interaction of Psychological and Sociological Factors in Political Behavior," *American Political Science Review,* XLVI, No. 1 (1952), 44–65.

———— "Intolerance of Ambiguity as Emotional and Perceptual Variable," *Journal of Personality,* XVIII (1949), 108–43.

———— "Psychoanalysis and the Unity of Science," *Proceedings of the American Academy of Arts and Sciences,* LXXX (1954), No. 4.

———— "Social Research and the Problem of Values: A Reply," *Journal of Abnormal and Social Psychology,* XLIX, No. 3 (1954), 466–71.

———— "A Study of Prejudice in Children," *Human Relations,* I, No. 3 (1948), 295–306.

Frenkel-Brunswik, Else, and Joan Havel. "Prejudice in the Interviews of Children: I. Attitudes toward Minority Groups," *Journal of Genetic Psychology,* LXXXII (1953), 91–136.

Freud, Anna. The Ego and the Mechanisms of Defense. New York: International Universities Press, 1946, 1954.

Freud, Sigmund. Beyond the Pleasure Principle. London: International Psychoanalytical Press, 1922.

———— The Ego and the Id. London: Hogarth Press, 1927.

———— The Future of an Illusion. New York: Liveright, 1928.

———— A General Introduction to Psychoanalysis. Translated by Joan Riviere. New York: Perma Giants, 1949.

———— Group Psychology and the Analysis of the Ego. New York: Liveright, 1949.

———— New Introductory Lectures on Psychoanalysis. Translated by W. J. H. Sprott. London: Hogarth Press, 1933.

———— The Problem of Anxiety (Hemmung, Symptom und Angst). Translated by H. A. Bunker. New York: Norton, 1936.

Freund, Ludwig. "Power and the Democratic Process: A Definition of Politics," *Social Research,* XV (1948), 327–44.

Friedrich, Carl J. Constitutional Government and Democracy. Boston: Ginn, 1950.

———— The New Belief in the Common Man. Boston: Little, Brown, 1942.

Friedrich, Carl J., and Edward S. Mason, eds. Public Policy: A Yearbook of the Graduate School of Public Administration, Vol. III. Cambridge: Harvard University Press, 1942.

Fromm, Erich. Escape from Freedom. New York: Rinehart, 1941.

———— Man for Himself: An Inquiry into the Social Psychology of Ethics. New York: Rinehart, 1947.

———— "The Psychology of Normalcy," *Dissent,* I (1954), 39–43.

———— The Sane Society. New York: Rinehart, 1955.

———— "Sozialpsychologischer Teil" ("Theoretische Entwürfe über Autorität und Familie"), in Max Horkheimer, ed., *Studien über Autorität und Familie.* Paris: Felix Alcan, 1936.

Gale, George Stafford. No Flies in China. New York: Morrow, 1955.

Garceau, Oliver. "Research in the Political Process," *American Political Science Review,* XXXXV, No. 1 (1951), 69–85.

Gellhorn, Walter. Individual Freedom and Government Restraints. Baton Rouge: Louisiana State University Press, 1956.

———— Security, Loyalty, and Science. Ithaca, N.Y.: Cornell University Press, 1950.

———— The Supreme Court on Obscenity. *Columbia University Forum,* I, No. 1 (1957), 38–41.

Gillin, John. The Ways of Men: An Introduction to Anthropology. New York: Appleton-Century-Crofts, 1948.

Godwin, William. An Enquiry Concerning Political Justice and Its Influence on General Virtue and Happiness. 2 vols. Reissued by Raymond A. Preston. New York: Knopf, 1926. First published 1793.

———— An Enquiry Concerning Political Justice and Its Influence on General Virtue and Happiness. 2 vols. London: Robinson, 1796.

Goldhamer, Herbert, and Edward A. Shils. "Types of Power and Status," *American Journal of Sociology*, XXXXV, No. 2 (1939), 171–82.

Goldman, Irving. "Psychiatric Interpretation of Russian History: A Reply to Geoffrey Gorer," *American Slavic and East European Review*, IX (1950), 151–61.

Goldstein, Kurt. Human Nature in the Light of Psychopathology. Cambridge: Harvard University Press, 1951.

—— The Organism: A Holistic Approach to Biology Derived from Pathological Data in Man. New York: American Book Co., 1939.

Gordon, Robert A. *Business Leadership in a Large Corporation*. Washington, D.C.: The Brookings Institute, 1945.

Gorer, Geoffrey, and John Rickman. The People of Great Russia. London: Cresset Press, 1949.

Gosnell, Harold F. Democracy: The Threshold of Freedom. New York: Ronald Press, 1948.

Grazia, Alfred de. The Elements of Political Science. New York: Knopf, 1952.

Grazia, Sebastian de. The Political Community: A Study of Anomie. Chicago: University of Chicago Press, 1948.

Greeley, Horace. Recollections of a Busy Life. New York: J. B. Ford, 1868.

Green, Thomas Hill. Lectures on the Principles of Political Obligation. London: Longmans, Green, 1921.

—— Works, Vol. III: Miscellanies and Memoir. London: Longmans, Green, 1888.

Greenacre, Phyllis. "The Predisposition to Anxiety," *Psychoanalytical Quarterly*, X (1941), 66–94, 610–38.

Gregg, Dorothy, and Elgin Williams. "The Dismal Science of Functionalism," *American Anthropologist*, L, No. 4 (1948), 594–611.

Grinker, Roy R., and John P. Spiegel. Men Under Stress. Philadelphia: Blakiston, 1945.

Haaland, Arild. Nazismen i Tyskland: En analyse av dens forutsetninger (Nazism in Germany: An Analysis of Its Determinants). Bergen: John Grieg, 1955.

Haire, Mason. "Industrial Social Psychology," in Gardner Lindzey, ed., *Handbook of Social Psychology*. Vol. II. Cambridge, Mass.: Addison-Wesley, 1954.

Haldane, John B. S. "A Comparative Study of Freedom," in Ruth Nanda Anshen, ed., *Freedom: Its Meaning*. New York: Harcourt, Brace, 1940.

Halévy, Élie. The Growth of Philosophical Radicalism. Translated by Mary Morris. New York: Kelley, 1949.

Hallowell, A. Irving. "Culture, Personality and Society," in A. L. Kroeber, ed., *Anthropology Today: An Encyclopedic Inventory*. Chicago: University of Chicago Press, 1953. Pp. 597–620.

Hamilton, Alexander, John Jay, and James Madison. The Federalist: A Commentary on the Constitution of the United States. New York: Modern Library, 1937. First published 1787–88.

Hare, Paul, Edgar F. Borgatta, and Robert F. Bales. Small Groups: Studies in Social Interaction. New York: Knopf, 1955.

Harriman, Philip L., ed. Twentieth Century Psychology. New York: The Philosophical Library, 1946.

Hebb, Donald O. The Organization of Behavior: A Neuropsychological Theory. New York: John Wiley, 1949.

Hegel, Georg Wilhelm Friedrich. Reason in History: A General Introduction to the Philosophy of History. Translated by Robert S. Hartman. New York: Liberal Arts Press, 1953.

Herskovits, Melville J. Man and His Works: The Science of Cultural Anthropology. New York: Knopf, 1948.

Hilton, Rodney. Communism and Liberty. London: Lawrence & Wishart, 1950.

Hobbes, Thomas. English Works. Edited by Sir William Molesworth and John Bohn. London, 1841. First published in 1642.

———— Leviathan, or The Matter Forme and Power of a Commonwealth, Ecclesiasticall and Civil. London: Everyman's Library, 1914. First published in 1651.

———— Philosophical Elements of a True Citizen, in Vol. II of his *English Works,* edited by Sir William Molesworth and John Bohn. London, 1841. First published in 1642.

Hobhouse, L. T. Liberalism. London: Oxford University Press, 1944.

———— The Metaphysical Theory of the State. London: Allen & Unwin, 1918.

Hoch, Paul H., and Joseph Zubin, eds. Anxiety. New York: Grune and Stratton, 1950.

Hoebel, E. Adamson. The Law of Primitive Man: A Study in Comparative Legal Dynamics. Cambridge: Harvard University Press, 1954.

Hoffer, Eric. "The Awakening of Asia," *The Reporter,* Vol. X, No. 13 (1954).

———— The Passionate State of Mind and Other Aphorisms. New York: Harper, 1955.

———— The True Believer: Thoughts on the Nature of Mass Movements. New York: Harper, 1951.

Holmberg, Allan R. Nomads of the Long Bow: The Siriono of Eastern Bolivia. Washington, D.C.: Smithsonian Institution, 1950.

Homans, George C. The Human Group. New York: Harcourt, Brace, 1950.

Hook, Sidney. Heresy, Yes—Conspiracy, No. New York: John Day, 1953.

Horkheimer, Max, ed. Studien über Autorität und Familie: Forschungsberichte aus dem Institut für Sozialforschung. Paris: Alcan, 1936.

Horney, Karen. Neurosis and Human Growth: The Struggle Toward Self-Realization. New York: Norton, 1950.

———— The Neurotic Personality of Our Time. New York: Norton, 1937.

———— New Ways in Psychoanalysis. New York: Norton, 1939.

———— Our Inner Conflicts: A Constructive Theory of Neurosis. New York: Norton, 1945.

Hume, David. Theory of Politics. Edited by Frederick Watkins. London: Nelson, 1951.

———— A Treatise on Human Nature. 2 vols. London: Dent, 1911. First published in 1738.

Hunter, Floyd. Community Power Structure. Chapel Hill: University of North Carolina Press, 1953.

Hutchins, Robert M. Freedom, Education, and the Fund. New York: Meridian Books, 1956.

Hyman, Herbert H., and Paul B. Sheatsley. " 'The Authoritarian Personality'—

A Methodological Critique," in Richard Christie and Marie Jahoda, eds., *Studies in the Scope and Method of "The Authoritarian Personality."* Glencoe, Illinois: The Free Press, 1954.

Inkeles, Alex. "Some Sociological Observations on Culture and Personality Studies," in Clyde Kluckhohn and Henry A. Murray, eds., *Personality in Nature, Society, and Culture.* New York: Knopf, 1954. Pp. 577–92.

Inkeles, Alex, and Daniel J. Levinson. "National Character: The Study of Modal Personality and Sociocultural Systems," in Gardner Lindzey, ed., *Handbook of Social Psychology.* Cambridge, Mass.: Addison-Wesley, 1954. Vol. II, pp. 977–1020.

James, William. The Principles of Psychology. New York: Henry Holt, 1890.

Janis, Irving L. "Personality Correlates of Susceptibility to Persuasion," *Journal of Personality,* XXII, No. 4 (1954), 504–18.

Jones, Edward E. "Authoritarianism as a Determinant of First-Impression Formation," *Journal of Personality,* XXIII, No. 1 (1954), 107–27.

Karp, David. One. New York: Vanguard Press, 1953.

Katz, Daniel, Dorwin Cartwright, Samuel Eldersveld, and Alfred McClung Lee, eds. Public Opinion and Propaganda: A Book of Readings. New York: Dryden Press, 1954.

Katz, Daniel, Irving Sarnoff, and Charles McClintock. "Ego-Defense and Attitude Change," *Human Relations,* IX, No. 1 (1956), 27–45.

Kelsen, Hans. "Democracy and Socialism," *Conference on Jurisprudence and Politics,* No. 15 (1954), pp. 63–87.

Kerr, Clark. "What Became of the Independent Spirit?" *Fortune* (July 1953).

Kierkegaard, Sören. The Concept of Dread. Translated and annotated by Walter Lowrie. Princeton: Princeton University Press, 1950.

Klein, Alan F. Society—Democracy—and the Group. New York: William Morrow, 1953.

Klineberg, Otto. Social Psychology. New York: Henry Holt, 1940.

Kluckhohn, Clyde. "Culture and Behavior," in Gardner Lindzey, ed., *Handbook of Social Psychology,* Vol. II. Cambridge, Mass.: Addison-Wesley, 1954.

———— Navaho Witchcraft. Papers of the Peabody Museum, Vol. XXII, No. 2. Cambridge, Mass., 1944.

———— "Universal Categories of Culture," in A. L. Kroeber, ed., *Anthropology Today: An Encyclopedic Inventory.* Chicago: University of Chicago Press, 1953. Pp. 507–23.

———— "Values and Value-Orientations in the Theory of Action: An Exploration in Definition and Classification," in Talcott Parsons and Edward A. Shils, eds., *Toward a General Theory of Action.* Cambridge: Harvard University Press, 1953. Pp. 388–433.

Kluckhohn, Clyde, and Henry A. Murray, eds. Personality in Nature, Society, and Culture. New York: Knopf, 1954.

Kluckhohn, Florence R. "Dominant and Variant Value Orientation," Working Paper, 1955.

———— "Dominant and Substitute Profiles of Cultural Orientation," *Social Forces,* XXVIII (1950), 376–93.

Koestler, Arthur. Reflections on Hanging. London: Gollancz, 1956.

Konstantinov, F. The Role of Advanced Ideas in the Development of Society. Moscow: Foreign Languages Publishing House, 1954.

Kornhauser, Arthur, Robert Dubin, and Arthur M. Ross, eds. Industrial Conflict. New York: McGraw-Hill, 1954.

Krech, David. "Notes Toward a Psychological Theory," *Journal of Personality,* XVIII, No. 1 (1949), 66–87.

Krech, David, and Richard S. Crutchfield. Theory and Problems of Social Psychology. New York: McGraw-Hill, 1948.

Kroeber, Alfred L., ed. Anthropology Today: An Encyclopedic Inventory. Chicago: University of Chicago Press, 1953.

Kroeber, Alfred L., and Clyde Kluckhohn, with the assistance of Wayne Untereiner. Culture: A Critical Review of Concepts and Definitions. Papers of the Peabody Museum, Vol. XLVII, No. 1. Cambridge, Mass., 1952.

Krugman, Herbert E. "The Role of Hostility in the Appeal of Communism in the United States," *Psychiatry,* XVI, No. 3 (1953), 253–61.

LaPiere, Richard. Collective Behavior. New York: McGraw-Hill, 1938.

Laski, Harold J. The American Democracy: A Commentary and an Interpretation. New York: Viking Press, 1948.

———— Authority in the Modern State. 2d ed. New Haven: Yale University Press, 1919.

———— The Danger of Obedience and Other Essays. New York: Harper, 1930.

———— Grammar of Politics. London: Allen & Unwin, 1929.

———— Liberty in the Modern State. London: Penguin Books, 1938. First published 1930.

Lasswell, Harold D. The Analysis of Political Behavior: An Empirical Approach. New York: New York University Press, 1948.

———— National Security and Individual Freedom. New York: McGraw-Hill, 1950.

———— "The Political Science of Science," *American Political Science Review,* L, No. 4 (1956), 961–79.

———— Power and Personality. New York: Norton, 1948.

———— Psychopathology and Politics. Chicago: University of Chicago Press, 1930.

———— World Politics and Personal Insecurity. New York: Whittlesey House, McGraw-Hill, 1935.

Lasswell, Harold, and Abraham Kaplan. Power and Society: A Framework for Political Inquiry. New Haven: Yale University Press, 1950.

Lasswell, Harold D., and Myres S. McDougal. "Law, Science and Policy." Working Paper, 1954.

Lazarsfeld, Paul F., Bernard Berelson, and Hazel Gaudet. The People's Choice: How the Voter Makes up His Mind in a Presidential Campaign. New York: Columbia University Press, 1948.

Lenin, V. I. The State and Revolution. New York: International Publishers, 1932.

Lerner, Daniel, and Harold D. Lasswell, eds. The Policy Sciences: Recent Developments in Scope and Method. Stanford, California: Stanford University Press, 1951.

Lewisohn, Ludwig. Up Stream: An Autobiography. London: Grant Richards, 1923.

Lindner, Robert Mitchell. Prescription for Rebellion. New York: Rinehart, 1952.

Lindsay, Alexander D. The Modern Democratic State. New York: Oxford University Press, 1943.

—— Toleration and Democracy. London: Oxford University Press, 1942.

Lindzey, Gardner, ed. Handbook of Social Psychology. Vol. II. Cambridge, Mass.: Addison-Wesley, 1954.

Linton, Ralph. "The Problem of Universal Values," in Robert F. Spencer, ed., *Method and Perspective in Anthropology: Papers in Honor of Wilson D. Wallis.* Minneapolis, University of Minnesota Press, 1954. Pp. 145–68.

—— The Study of Man. New York: Appleton-Century, 1936.

Lippitt, Ronald, Norman Polansky, and Sidney Rosen. "The Dynamics of Power: A Field Study of Social Influence in Groups of Children," *Human Relations,* V, No. 1 (1952), 37–64.

Lippmann, Walter. Liberty and the News. New York: Harcourt, Brace and Howe, 1920.

—— Preface to Morals. New York: Macmillan, 1929.

—— Public Opinion (1922). New York: Penguin Books, 1946.

Lipset, Seymour Martin, Martin A. Trow, and James S. Coleman. Union Democracy: The Internal Politics of the International Typographical Union. Glencoe, Illinois: The Free Press, 1956.

Llewellyn, Karl N., and E. Adamson Hoebel. The Cheyenne Way: Conflict and Case Law in Primitive Jurisprudence. Norman: University of Oklahoma Press, 1941.

Locke, John. Essay Concerning Human Understanding. Abridged and edited by Raymond Wilburn. London: Everyman's Library, 1947. First published in 1690.

—— Two Treatises of Civil Government. London: Everyman's Library, 1924. First published in 1690.

—— Works. 9 vols. London: Rivington, 1824.

Luchins, Abraham S. "Personality and Prejudice: A Critique," *Journal of Social Psychology,* XXXII (1950), 79–94.

Lynd, Robert S. Knowledge for What? The Place of Social Science in American Culture. Princeton: Princeton University Press, 1946.

Maccoby, Eleanor, Patricia K. Gibbs, *et al.* "Methods of Child-Rearing in Two Social Classes," in William E. Martin and Celia Burns Stendler, eds., *Readings in Child Development.* New York: Harcourt, Brace, 1954.

MacDonald, Dwight. "A Theory of Mass Culture," *Diogenes,* No. 3 (1953), pp. 1–17.

McDougall, William. An Introduction to Social Psychology. Boston: John W. Luce, 1918.

Machiavelli, Niccolo. The Prince and The Discourses. New York: Modern Library, 1940.

MacIver, Robert M. "Maladjustment," in *Encyclopedia of the Social Sciences,* Vol. X. New York: Macmillan, 1930.

MacIver, Robert M., and Charles H. Page. Society: An Introductory Analysis. New York: Rinehart, 1949.

Maier, Norman R. F. Frustration: The Study of Behavior Without a Goal. New York: McGraw-Hill, 1949.

Mannheim, Karl. Ideology and Utopia. New York, Harcourt, Brace, 1946.

Martin, William E., and Celia Burns Stendler, eds. Readings in Child Development. New York: Harcourt, Brace, 1954.

Marx, Karl, and Friedrich Engels. Manifesto of the Communist Party. New York: International Publishers, 1948. First published in German in 1848.

Maslow, Abraham H. "The Authoritarian Character Structure," *Journal of Social Psychology,* XVIII (1943), 401–11.

——— "The Dynamics of Psychological Security–Insecurity," *Character and Personality,* X (1942), 331–44.

——— "The Expressive Component of Behavior," in Howard Brand, ed., *The Study of Personality: A Book of Readings.* New York: John Wiley, 1954.

——— "Human Motivation in Relation to Social Theory," in M. J. Shore, ed., *Twentieth Century Mental Hygiene: New Directions in Mental Health.* New York: Social Science Publishers, 1950.

——— Motivation and Personality. New York: Harper, 1954.

——— "Self-Actualizing People: A Study of Psychological Health," *Personality Symposium,* VII (1949), 11–34.

——— "A Theory of Human Motivation," in Philip L. Harriman, ed., *Twentieth Century Psychology.* New York: The Philosophical Library, 1946. Pp. 22–48.

Maslow, Abraham H., Elisa Hirst, Marcella Stein, and Irma Honigmann. "A Clinically Derived Test for Measuring Psychological Security–Insecurity," *Journal of General Psychology,* XXXIII (1945), 21–41.

May, Rollo. Man's Search for Himself. New York: Norton, 1953.

——— The Meaning of Anxiety. New York: Ronald Press, 1950.

Mead, George H. "The Psychology of Punitive Justice," *American Journal of Sociology,* XXIII (1918), 577–602.

Mead, Margaret. Sex and Temperament in Three Primitive Societies. New York: Mentor Books, 1952.

——— "The Study of National Character," in Daniel Lerner and Harold D. Lasswell, eds., *The Policy Sciences: Recent Developments in Scope and Method.* Stanford, California: Stanford University Press, 1951.

Mead, Margaret, ed. Cooperation and Competition among Primitive Peoples. New York: McGraw-Hill, 1937.

Meiklejohn, Alexander. Free Speech and Its Relation to Self-Government. New York: Harper, 1948.

Merriam, Charles E. Political Power: Its Composition and Incidence. New York, London: Whittlesey House, McGraw-Hill, 1934.

Merton, Robert K. Social Theory and Social Structure: Toward the Codification of Theory and Research. Glencoe, Illinois: The Free Press, 1949.

Michels, Robert. "Authority," in *Encyclopedia of the Social Sciences,* Vol. II. New York: Macmillan, 1930.

——— Political Parties: A Sociological Study of the Oligarchical Tendencies of Modern Democracy. Translated by Eden and Cedar Paul. Glencoe, Illinois: The Free Press, 1949.

Mill, James. Analysis of the Phenomena of the Human Mind. Edited with additional notes by John Stuart Mill. London: Longmans, Green, Reader, and Dyer, 1869.

——— "Government," in Edwin A. Burtt, ed., *The English Philosophers from Bacon to Mill.* New York: Modern Library, 1939.

———— "Liberty of the Press," in Philip Wheelwright, ed., *Essays on Government, Jurisprudence, Liberty of the Press, and Law of Nations.* Garden City, N.Y.: Doubleday, Doran, 1935.

Mill, John Stuart. Autobiography. London: Longmans, Green, 1874.

———— Principles of Political Economy. 2 vols. New York: Appleton, 1864.

———— Representative Government. New York: Everyman's Library, 1951.

———— System of Logic, Ratiocinative and Inductive. 10th ed. Vol. II. London: Longmans, Green, 1879.

———— Utilitarianism, Liberty, and Representative Government. New York: Everyman's Library, 1951.

Miller, Neal E., and R. Bugelski. "Minor Studies of Aggression. II: The Influence of Frustrations Imposed by the In-Group on Attitudes Expressed toward Out-Groups," *Journal of Psychology*, XXV (1948), 437–52.

Miller, Neal E., *et al.* "The Frustration–Aggression Hypothesis," *Psychological Review*, XXXXVIII (1941), 337–42.

Miller, Walter B. "Two Concepts of Authority," *American Anthropologist*, LVII, No. 2 (1955), 271–89.

Mills, C. Wright. The Power Elite. New York: Oxford University Press, 1956.

Milton, John. Areopagitica and Other Prose Works. London: Everyman's Library, 1927.

Montesquieu, Charles Louis de Secondat, baron de. The Spirit of the Laws. Translated by Thomas Nugent. 2 vols. New York: Colonial Press, 1899.

Morley, John Morley, Viscount. On Compromise. London, New York: Macmillan, 1901.

Mosca, Gaetano. The Ruling Class. Translated by Hannah D. Kahn. Edited by Arthur Livingston. New York: McGraw-Hill, 1939. First published in Italian in 1895.

Mothershead, John L., Jr. "Some Reflections on the Meanings of Freedom," *Journal of Philosophy*, XXXXIX, No. 21 (1952), 667–72.

Mowrer, O. Hobart. Learning Theory and Personality Dynamics: Selected Papers. New York: Ronald Press, 1950.

———— Psychotherapy: Theory and Research. New York: Ronald Press, 1953.

Mullahy, Patrick. "A Theory of Interpersonal Relations and the Evolution of Personality," in Harry Stack Sullivan, *Conceptions of Modern Psychiatry.* New York: Norton, 1953. Pp. 239–94.

Murphy, Gardner. Personality: A Biosocial Approach to Origins and Structure. New York: Harper, 1947.

Murray, Henry A. Explorations in Personality. New York: Oxford University Press, 1938.

Myrdal, Gunnar. An American Dilemma: The Negro Problem and Modern Democracy. New York: Harper, 1944.

Nadel, Siegfried F. The Foundations of Social Anthropology. Glencoe, Illinois: The Free Press, 1953.

Naess, Arne, Jens A. Christophersen, and Kjell Kvalo. Democracy, Ideology, and Objectivity: Studies in the Semantics and Cognitive Analysis of Ideological Controversy. Oslo: Oslo University Press, 1956.

Nelson, Edward W. The Eskimo about Bering Strait. Washington: U.S. Government Printing Office, 1900.

Newcomb, Theodore. Social Psychology. New York: Dryden Press, 1950.

Newcomb, Theodore M., and Eugene L. Hartley, eds. Readings in Social Psychology. New York: Henry Holt, 1947.

Niemeyer, Gerhart. Law Without Force: The Function of Politics in International Law. Princeton: Princeton University Press, 1941.

Ofstad, Harald. An Inquiry into the Freedom of Decision: An Analytical Approach to a Classical Problem. 4 vols. Oslo: Institute for Social Research, 1954–55. Mimeographed. Forthcoming at the Oslo University Press.

Ogle, Marbury B., Louis Schneider, and Jay W. Wiley. Power, Order, and the Economy: A Preface to the Sciences. New York: Harper, 1954.

O'Hara, Hazel. "Science and the Indian," *Natural History*, LXII (1953), 268–75.

Opler, Morris E. "The Concept of Supernatural Power Among the Chiricahua and Mescalero Apaches," *American Anthropologist*, XXXVII (1935), 65–70.

Orlansky, Harold. "Infant Care and Personality," *Psychological Bulletin*, XLVI, No. 1 (1949), 1–48.

Packard, Vance. The Hidden Persuaders. New York: McKay, 1957.

Pareto, Vilfredo. The Mind and Society. Edited by Arthur Livingston. New York: Harcourt, Brace, 1935. First published in Italian as *Trattato di sociologia generale* in 1916.

Parsons, Talcott. Essays in Sociological Theory, Pure and Applied. Glencoe, Illinois: The Free Press, 1949.

——— The Social System. Glencoe, Illinois: The Free Press, 1951.

——— The Structure of Social Action. Glencoe, Illinois: The Free Press, 1949. First published in 1937.

Parsons, Talcott, and Edward A. Shils, eds. Toward a General Theory of Action. Cambridge: Harvard University Press, 1953.

Pennock, J. Roland. Liberal Democracy: Its Merits and Prospects. New York: Rinehart, 1950.

Perlmutter, Howard V. "Relations between the Self-Image, the Image of the Foreigner, and the Desire to Live Abroad," *Journal of Psychology*, XXVIII (1954), 131–37.

——— "Some Characteristics of the Xenophilic Personality." Unpublished paper. Cambridge: Massachusetts Institute of Technology, 1954.

Perry, Ralph Barton. Realms of Value: A Critique of Human Civilization. Cambridge: Harvard University Press, 1954.

Pink, M. Alderton. A Realist Looks at Democracy. New York: Stoke, 1930.

Pinner, Frank A. "Political Values: An Exploratory Investigation." Ph.D. dissertation, University of California (Berkeley), 1954.

Plamenatz, John P. Consent, Freedom and Political Obligation. London: Oxford University Press, 1938.

——— Mill's Utilitarianism, reprinted with a study of The English Utilitarians. Oxford: Blackwell, 1949.

Plato. The Republic. Translated by Benjamin Jowett. New York: Modern Library, n.d.

Playfair, Giles, and Derrick Sington. The Offenders: The Case Against Legal Vengeance. New York: Simon and Schuster, 1957.

Polanyi, Michael. The Logic of Liberty: Reflections and Rejoinders. London: Routledge and Kegan Paul, 1951.

Priestley, John B. Out of the People. New York: Harper, 1941.

———— Thoughts in the Wilderness. New York: Harper, 1957.

Prothro, L. Terry. "Ethnocentrism and Anti-Negro Attitudes in the Deep South," *Journal of Abnormal and Social Psychology*, XLVIII, No. 1 (1952), 105–8.

Radcliffe-Brown, Alfred R. Structure and Function in Primitive Society: Essays and Addresses. Glencoe, Illinois: The Free Press, 1952.

Rado, Sandor. "Emergency Behavior," in Paul H. Hoch and Joseph Zubin, eds. *Anxiety*. New York: Grune and Stratton, 1950. Pp. 150–75.

Rank, Otto. The Trauma of Birth. New York: Harcourt, Brace, 1929.

———— Will Therapy and Truth and Reality. New York: Knopf, 1950.

Ranulf, Svend. The Jealousy of the Gods and Criminal Law at Athens: A Contribution to the Sociology of Moral Indignation. 2 vols. Copenhagen: Levin and Munksgaard, 1933.

———— Moral Indignation and Middle Class Psychology. Copenhagen: Munksgaard, 1938.

Riesman, David. "Civil Liberties in a Period of Transition," in Carl J. Friedrich and Edward S. Mason, eds., *Public Policy*, Vol. III. Cambridge: Harvard University Press, 1942. Pp. 74–75.

———— "Democracy and Defamation: Fair Game and Fair Comment," *Columbia Law Review*, XLII (1942), 1085–1123.

———— Individualism Reconsidered. Glencoe, Illinois: The Free Press, 1954.

———— "Marginality, Conformity, and Insight," *Phylon*, XIV, No. 3 (1953), 241–57.

———— "Some Observations on the Study of American Character," *Psychiatry*, XV, No. 3 (1952), 333–38.

Riesman, David, with Nathan Glazer and Reuel Denney. The Lonely Crowd: A Study of the Changing American Character. Abridged by the authors. New York: Doubleday Anchor Books, 1953.

Riezler, Kurt. "The Social Psychology of Fear," *American Journal of Sociology*, XLIX (1944), 489–98.

Rokeach, Milton. "Dogmatism and Opinionation on the Left and on the Right," *American Psychologist*, VII (1952), 310–11.

———— "Generalized Mental Rigidity as a Factor in Ethnocentrism," *Journal of Abnormal and Social Psychology*, XLIII, No. 3 (1948), 259–78.

———— "A Method for Studying Individual Differences in 'Narrow-Mindedness,'" *Journal of Personality*, XX, No. 2 (1951), 219–33.

———— "'Narrow-Mindedness' and Personality," *Journal of Personality*, XX, No. 2 (1951), 234–51.

———— "On the Unity of Thought and Belief," *Journal of Personality*, XXV, No. 2 (1956), 224–50.

———— "Political and Religious Dogmatism: An Alternative to the Authoritarian Personality," *Psychological Monographs*, LXX, No. 18 (1956), 1–43.

———— "Prejudice, Concreteness of Thinking, and Reification in Thinking," *Journal of Abnormal and Social Psychology*, XLVI, No. 1 (1951), 83–91.

Rokeach, Milton, and Albert Eglash. "A Scale for Measuring Intellectual Conviction," *Journal of Social Psychology*, XLIV (1956), 135–41.

Rokeach, Milton, and Benjamin Fruchter. "A Factorial Study of Dogmatism and Related Concepts," *Journal of Abnormal and Social Psychology*, LIII, No. 3 (1956), 356–60.

Rousseau, Jean Jacques. The Social Contract and Discourses. Translated by G. D. H. Cole. New York: Everyman's Library, 1950.

Royal Commission on the Press. Report of the Royal Commission on the Press, 1947–1949. London: His Majesty's Stationery Office, 1949.

Russell, Bertrand. "Freedom and Government," in Ruth Nanda Anshen, *Freedom: Its Meaning*. New York: Harcourt, Brace, 1940.

—— Freedom and Organization, 1814–1914. London: Allen & Unwin, 1949.

—— A History of Western Philosophy. New York: Simon and Schuster, 1945.

—— Power: A New Social Analysis. New York: Norton, 1938.

—— In Praise of Idleness and Other Essays. New York: Norton, 1935.

—— Which Way to Peace? London: Michael Joseph, 1936.

—— Why Men Fight: A Method of Abolishing the International Duel. New York: Century Co., 1920.

Sandelius, Walter E. "Reason and Political Power," *American Political Science Review*, XXXXV (1951), 703–15.

Sanford, Fillmore H. Authoritarianism and Leadership: A Study of the Follower's Orientation to Authority. Philadelphia: Institute for Research in Human Relations, 1950.

Sanford, Nevitt. "The Dynamics of Identification," *Psychological Review*, LXII, No. 2 (1955), 106–18.

Sargent, S. Stansfeld. "Reaction to Frustration—A Critique and Hypothesis," *Psychological Review*, LV (1948), 108–14.

Sarnoff, Irving. "Identification with the Aggressor," *Journal of Personality*, XX, No. 2 (1951), 199–218.

Sarnoff, Irving, and Daniel Katz. "The Motivational Bases of Attitude Change," *Journal of Abnormal and Social Psychology*, XLIX, No. 1 (1954), 115–24.

Sarnoff, Irving, Daniel Katz, and Charles McClintock. "Attitude-Change Procedures and Motivating Patterns," in Daniel Katz, Dorwin Cartwright, Samuel Eldersveld, and Alfred McClung Lee, eds., *Public Opinion and Propaganda: A Book of Readings*. New York: Dryden Press, 1954. Pp. 305–12.

Schachter, Stanley. "Deviation, Rejection, and Communication," in Dorwin Cartwright and Alvin Zander, eds., *Group Dynamics: Research and Theory*. Evanston, Illinois: Row, Peterson, 1953.

—— "Deviation, Rejection, and Communication," *Journal of Abnormal and Social Psychology*, XLVI (1951), 190–207.

Schachter, Stanley, *et al.* "Cross-Cultural Experiments on Threat and Rejection," *Human Relations*, VII, No. 4 (1954), 403–40.

Schmideberg, Melitta. "Anxiety States," *Psychoanalytic Review*, XXVII (1940), 439–49.

Schneider, John G. The Golden Kazoo. New York: Dell, 1956.

Schneider, Louis. "Functional Analysis and the Problem of Order," in Marbury B. Ogle, Louis Schneider, and Jay W. Wiley, *Power, Order, and the Economy: A Preface to the Sciences*. New York: Harper, 1954.

—— "Some Psychiatric Views on 'Freedom' and the Theory of Social Systems," *Psychiatry*, XII (1949), 251–64.

Schumpeter, Joseph A. Capitalism, Socialism, and Democracy. New York: Harper, 1952.

Schwartz, Richard D. "Functional Alternatives to Inequality," *American Sociological Review*, XX, No. 4 (1955), 424–30.

Sears, Robert R. "Non-Aggressive Reactions to Frustration," *Psychological Review*, XLVIII (1941), 343–46.

Sears, Robert R., Eleanor Maccoby, Harry Levin, and collaborators. Patterns of Child Rearing. Evanston, Illinois: Row, Peterson, 1957.

Sellin, Thorsten, ed. "Murder and the Penalty of Death," in *Annals of the American Academy of Political and Social Science*, Vol. 284 (1952).

Selznick, Philip. "An Approach to a Theory of Bureaucracy," *American Sociological Review*, VIII, No. 1 (1943), 50–52.

———— "Foundations of a Theory of Organization," *American Sociological Review*, XIII (1948), 20–30.

———— TVA and the Grass Roots: A Study in the Sociology of Formal Organization. Berkeley: University of California Press, 1943.

Sewell, W. H., P. H. Mussen, and C. W. Harris. "Relationships Among Child Training Practices," *American Sociological Review*, XX, No. 2 (1955), 137–48.

Sheps, J. G., and F. E. Coburn. "Psychiatric Study of One Hundred Battle Veterans," *War Medicine*, VIII (1945), 235–37.

Shils, Edward. "Authoritarianism: 'Right' and 'Left,' " in Richard Christie and Marie Jahoda, eds., *Studies in the Scope and Method of "The Authoritarian Personality."* Glencoe, Illinois: The Free Press, 1954.

Shore, M. J., ed. Twentieth Century Mental Hygiene: New Directions in Mental Health. New York: Social Science Publishers, 1950.

Simon, Herbert A. "Notes on the Observation and Measurement of Political Power," *Journal of Politics*, XV, No. 4 (1953), 500–516.

Simon, Herbert A., Donald W. Smithburg, and Victor A. Thompson. Public Administration. New York: Knopf, 1950.

Smedslund, Jan. A Critical Evaluation of the Current Status of Learning Theory. Oslo: Institute for Social Research, 1953.

Smith, Thomas V. The Promise of American Politics. Chicago: University of Chicago Press, 1936.

Spencer, Robert F., ed. Method and Perspective in Anthropology: Papers in Honor of Wilson D. Wallis. Minneapolis: University of Minnesota Press, 1954.

Stevenson, Charles L. Ethics and Language. New Haven: Yale University Press, 1944.

Stouffer, Samuel A. Communism, Conformity, and Civil Liberties: A Cross-section of the Nation Speaks Its Mind. Garden City, N.Y.: Doubleday, 1955.

Strauss, Leo. Natural Right and History. Chicago: University of Chicago Press, 1953.

Strecker, Edward A. Their Mothers' Sons. Philadelphia and New York: Lippincott, 1951.

Sullivan, Harry Stack. Conceptions of Modern Psychiatry. New York: Norton, 1953.

———— The Interpersonal Theory of Psychiatry. Edited by Helen Swick Perry and Mary Ladd Gawel. New York: Norton, 1953.

——— "Tensions Interpersonal and International: A Psychiatrist's View," in Hadley Cantril, ed., *Tensions That Cause Wars*. Urbana: University of Illinois Press, 1950.

Symonds, Percival M. The Dynamics of Human Adjustment. New York: Appleton-Century-Crofts, 1946.

Talmon, J. L. The Rise of Totalitarian Democracy. Boston: Beacon Press, 1952.

Tawney, Richard H. Religion and the Rise of Capitalism: A Historical Study. New York: Penguin Books, 1947.

Taylor, Irving A. "Perceptual Closure and Extreme Social Attitudes." Unpublished Ph.D. dissertation. New York: New York University, 1954.

Thomas, William I. The Unadjusted Girl. Boston: Little, Brown, 1923.

Thoreau, Henry David. "Civil Disobedience," in *Walden and Other Writings*. Boston: Houghton, Mifflin, 1882.

Tocqueville, Alexis de. Democracy in America. 2 vols. New York: Vintage Books, 1954. First published in French in 1835 (Vol. I) and 1840 (Vol. II).

Truman, David B. The Governmental Process: Political Interests and Public Opinion. New York: Knopf, 1951.

Tussman, Joseph. "Contempt of the Electorate." An unpublished paper. Berkeley, California, 1953.

Veblen, Thorstein. The Higher Learning in America: A Memorandum on the Conduct of Universities by Business Men. New York: Viking Press, 1935. First published 1918.

Weber, Max. The Protestant Ethic and the Spirit of Capitalism. Translated by Talcott Parsons. London: Allen & Unwin, 1930.

——— The Theory of Social and Economic Organization. Translated by A. M. Henderson and Talcott Parsons. New York: Oxford University Press, 1947.

Weihofen, Henry. The Urge to Punish. New York: Farrar, Straus and Cudahy, 1956.

Wheelwright, Philip, ed. Essays on Government, Jurisprudence, Liberty of the Press, and Law of Nations. Garden City, N.Y.: Doubleday, Doran, 1935.

Whiting, John W. M., and Irvin L. Child. Child Training and Personality: A Cross-Cultural Study. New Haven: Yale University Press, 1953.

Whyte, William H., Jr. The Organization Man. Garden City, N.Y.: Doubleday, 1957.

Wile, Ira S., and Rose Davis. "The Relation of Birth to Behavior," in Clyde Kluckhohn and Henry A. Murray, eds., *Personality in Nature, Society, and Culture*. London: Jonathan Cape, 1949. Pp. 297–314.

Wilson, Richard B. "Freedom of Speech and Public Opinion." Unpublished Ph.D. dissertation, University of California (Berkeley), 1952.

Wirth, Louis. Presidential Address to the American Sociological Society in December, 1947. *American Sociological Review*, XIII, No. 1 (1948), 1–15.

World Council of Churches. The Responsible Society: An Ecumenical Inquiry. Geneva and New York: Study Department of the World Council of Churches, 1949.

Zawadski, Bohan, and Paul Lazarsfeld. "The Psychological Consequences of Unemployment," *Journal of Social Psychology*, VI (1935), 224–51.

Index